Hammond's
WORLD TRAVELOG
Classics Edition

Hammond's WORLD TRAVELOG

Hammond's WORLD

TRAVELOG

by
THE EDITORIAL STAFF OF
C. S. HAMMOND & CO.

with
Full-color and Duo-tone Photographs
plus 81 Maps of the World's Major Cities

C. S. Hammond and Company

MAPLEWOOD, N. J.   NEW YORK, N. Y.

Contents

EUROPE
- INTRODUCTION ... 5
- TRAVEL MAP OF EUROPE ... 6-7
- CITY MAPS:
    - London ... 9
    - Birmingham ... 14
    - Liverpool ... 15
    - Glasgow ... 17
    - Edinburgh ... 18
    - Dublin ... 21
    - Belfast ... 22
    - Paris ... 26
    - Marseilles ... 32
    - Brussels ... 36
    - Luxembourg ... 38
    - Amsterdam ... 40
    - Frankfurt ... 45
    - Munich ... 47
    - Hamburg ... 49
    - Berlin ... 50
    - Copenhagen ... 53
    - Oslo ... 54
    - Stockholm ... 56
    - Helsinki ... 58
    - Bern ... 60
    - Geneva ... 61
    - Zurich ... 64
    - Vienna ... 67
    - Lisbon ... 70
    - Madrid ... 73
    - Barcelona ... 75
    - Rome ... 78
    - Milan ... 83
    - Athens ... 86

AFRICA
- INTRODUCTION ... 89
- TRAVEL MAP OF AFRICA ... 90-91
- CITY MAPS:
    - Casablanca ... 93
    - Algiers ... 95
    - Alexandria ... 98
    - Cairo ... 99
    - Johannesburg ... 105

ASIA
- INTRODUCTION ... 107
- TRAVEL MAP OF ASIA ... 108-109
- CITY MAPS:
    - Damascus ... 110
    - Beirut ... 111
    - Teheran ... 112
    - Baghdad ... 113
    - Jerusalem ... 116
    - Bombay ... 118
    - Calcutta ... 120
    - Karachi ... 121
    - Tokyo ... 126
    - Hong Kong ... 127
    - Singapore ... 128
    - Bangkok ... 129
    - Djakarta ... 130
    - Manila ... 132

THE PACIFIC
- INTRODUCTION ... 133
- TRAVEL MAP OF THE PACIFIC ... 134-135
- CITY MAPS:
    - Sydney ... 136
    - Melbourne ... 137
    - Auckland ... 139

SOUTH AMERICA
- INTRODUCTION ... 141
- TRAVEL MAP OF SOUTH AMERICA ... 142-143
- CITY MAPS:
    - Caracas ... 145
    - Bogota ... 147
    - Lima ... 150
    - Rio de Janeiro ... 153
    - Sao Paulo ... 155
    - La Paz ... 157
    - Montevideo ... 160
    - Santiago ... 162
    - Buenos Aires ... 165

NORTH AMERICA
- INTRODUCTION ... 167
- TRAVEL MAP OF NORTH AMERICA ... 168-169
- CITY MAPS:
    - Ottawa ... 170
    - Quebec ... 172
    - Montreal ... 173
    - Toronto ... 174
    - Vancouver ... 176
    - Mexico City ... 177
    - Havana ... 188

THE UNITED STATES
- INTRODUCTION ... 197
- TRAVEL MAP OF THE UNITED STATES ... 198-199
- CITY MAPS:
    - Los Angeles ... 201
    - San Francisco ... 204
    - Seattle ... 207
    - Denver ... 209
    - Chicago ... 225
    - New Orleans ... 231
    - San Antonio ... 234
    - Miami Beach ... 238
    - New York ... 240
    - Philadelphia ... 243
    - Washington, D.C. ... 244
    - Boston ... 246
    - Honolulu ... 253

INDEX ... 254-256

Copyright © MCMLVI, MCMLVIII, and MCMLX C. S. Hammond & Co., Maplewood, New Jersey.
This work contains certain material originally published in THE TWA VACATION GUIDE and WORLD ATLAS Copyright © MCMLVI C. S. Hammond and Co. and GREAT CITIES of the WORLD Copyright © MCMLVIII C. S. Hammond & Co.

PRINTED IN U.S.A.

EUROPE

A trip to Europe is the ultimate goal of most Americans today as in generations past. The advantage we have over our predecessors is that with modern jet flight and luxurious ocean liners, the traveling is a comparatively simple thing. How natural that Europe should hold this fascination, for it is to this continent that most of us trace our ancestry and background.

From its beginnings in the splendor of Greek and Roman civilization, Europe, the most densely populated continent, grew until now in the various countries 50 languages are spoken; and the people, famous for their energy, talent and resourcefulness, are responsible for leading the world culturally and industrially for more than 2,000 years.

Fine Swiss watches, French perfumes and wines, Danish silver, English woolens and china, Irish linen and Belgian lace are examples of the numerous commodities still treasured and sought after by the people of the United States, and they attest to the artistry and ingenious craftsmanship of the European.

Built in the fifth century B.C., the Acropolis with its Parthenon beckons the tourist to Athens, for it was here that democracy was born. In a lighter vein, Paris might be called the birthplace of gaiety and good times, since this French city, with its Montparnasse quarter on the left bank of the Seine River, is the artistic hub and fun center of the country.

The fabulous Louvre Museum, Arc de Triomphe and Notre Dame Cathedral in Paris, as well as Rome's Appian Way and Colosseum, Switzerland's incomparable Alpine region, the enchanting city of Vienna on the famed Blue Danube River, colorful Madrid with its bullfights, and "foggy London town"—proud of its historic Bridge, Tower, Buckingham Palace and Westminster Abbey—are but a few of the myriad and varied attractions awaiting those who travel through Europe, which is truly the Mother Continent of our modern civilization.

Notes and Itinerary

Great Britain and Ireland

ST. PAUL'S CATHEDRAL

LAND OF TRADITION

Great Britain is a land in which the past is always becoming the present, in which history is inescapably part of the picture of today, and thus it is that Great Britain has become a storehouse of treasures that are both the work of nature and work of man. Her people, like Americans, are a heterogeneous race, evolving from Britons, Angles, Saxons, Danes and Normans; each region has developed local characteristics so that you find "the canny Scot, the austere North countryman, the lively Cockney and the talkative Welshman." You will find that they are a conservative race, hesitant to accept changes, but you will also find them a warm-hearted race, anxious to extend visitors a warm and genuine welcome. Great Britain is small, at no time are you more than a hundred miles away from the sea, and her highways and railroads are unexcelled. You may reach any section without an unduly long journey and the varying wealth of beauty in the British scene unfolding on either side will constantly delight you — her cities, little thatched cottages, ancient ruins, magnificent castles all surrounded in scenic beauty.

THE EMERALD ISLE

The storied "Emerald Isle," comprising Northern Ireland and the Republic of Ireland, is famed throughout the world for its verdant beauty. For generations poets have sung of its green hills and rugged coasts. From the hills the mists roll down across the countryside, and with the clear cool air helps to give Ireland its special greenness — an Emerald Isle indeed! Here you may meet on any country road the old jaunting carts in use today as they have been for centuries, see the ivied ruins of ancient castles and picturesque cottages along the wayside. Ireland presents its many scenic charms, as beautiful today as it has been through the centuries. Here, too, you will find a warm-hearted people proud of their land and happy to welcome the visitor.

FOOD AND DRINK

No trip to Britain is complete without a visit to a pub, short for public house. Pubs are many and various, defying classification. There are, however, two kinds to look for — the really ancient and the traditional "gin palace" with its monumental brass rails and fittings and its wealth of decorated glass in doors, windows and mirrors. You may drink mild or bitter beer, or you may prefer a glass of half and half; there is a great variety of beers and ales. Be sure to sample what was probably the beer that Shakespeare drank. This comes from a small brewery at Stratford-on-Avon and is called Flower's Bitter; it is very strong. Irish whisky and Scotch, of course are popular, though not as high proof as sold in the U. S. Gin, too, is popular and the dark, strong Guinness stout.

Outside the large cities, which of course have their share of restaurants with a continental cuisine, the fare is comparatively plain, not being embellished with spicy sauces or exotic ingredients. Here one gets his game, venison,

No. 10 DOWNING STREET   British Information Services

BUCKINGHAM PALACE   British Information Services

fowl and seafood *au naturel,* and it will prove a delightful change. Try roast beef and Yorkshire pudding. Ireland is famous for delicious prawns, lobsters, oysters and smoked salmon, and also for the unique Gaelic coffee. This beguiling potion consists of sugar, coffee, Irish whisky and thick cream. Tea is an institution which may consist of a complete supper, simple bread and butter, hot scones or crumpets, or a variety of biscuits (cookies).

SPORTS

The British of all classes are enthusiastic about sports. They love to shoot, to participate in games, to ride horses and bet on horse races and to fish. The great spectator sports are football (soccer and rugby) in the autumn and winter, cricket in the spring and summer and both flat-racing and steeplechasing. Hunting in England is restricted to fox-hunting on horseback. Not so in Scotland, where bird and game are excellent. Good fishing, especially for salmon, is found throughout Great Britain. Tennis is played all over and golf and water sports facilities are unexcelled.

The Irish also love sports of all kinds and here, too, you will find the best in hunting, fishing, golf and water sports. Trout fishing is particularly good, beginning in May when the trout and fisherman both go mad; the trout mesmerized by the May-Fly, the fisherman, by the trout. Hurling is Ireland's baseball and is a thrilling game to watch. Gaelic football and handball are typical Irish games. Flat racing and steeplechasing are almost equally popular in Ireland, and are equally exciting.

LONDON. Dr. Samuel Johnson, the 18th-century lexicographer, once wrote "when a man is tired of London, he is tired of life; for there is in London all that life can afford." Though the city, let it be admitted, does not contain all that Dr. Johnson's broad statement claims for it, London can provide such a wealth of interest, so many beautiful, ancient, historic, impressive and curious sights, so many diversions, occupations, entertainments and pursuits, that to live in London might almost be considered a profession. The character of London, like that of any other great city, does not reveal itself at first glance but requires at least a short acquaintanceship before it can be appreciated. With increased knowledge there will grow a deep affection for its jumble of past and present, practical and obsolete, beautiful and commonplace, majestic and homely, that together make up the London of today. This pulsing heart of the British Empire, so vast it comprises a country within itself, probably possesses the largest metropolitan area of any city in the world. With a history going back to Roman times, its people and its institutions have shaped the world's destinies for a thousand years. The oldest part of London, the tiny mile-square nucleus around which the sprawling metropolis grew, is known as the "City of London" or just simply "The City." Today the "City's" government which is endowed with greater powers than the surrounding twenty-eight boroughs, retains many features of the past. Its Lord Mayor, elected by the various trade guilds, takes office each year on November ninth, in a ritual whose pomp and pageantry dates back to medieval times. Just outside the original walled city, known in the days of the Romans as Londinium, are found a number of London's most notable landmarks. Here the Tower of London stands almost unaltered since it was built for William the Conqueror in 1078. Though this ancient

BIG BEN   British Information Services

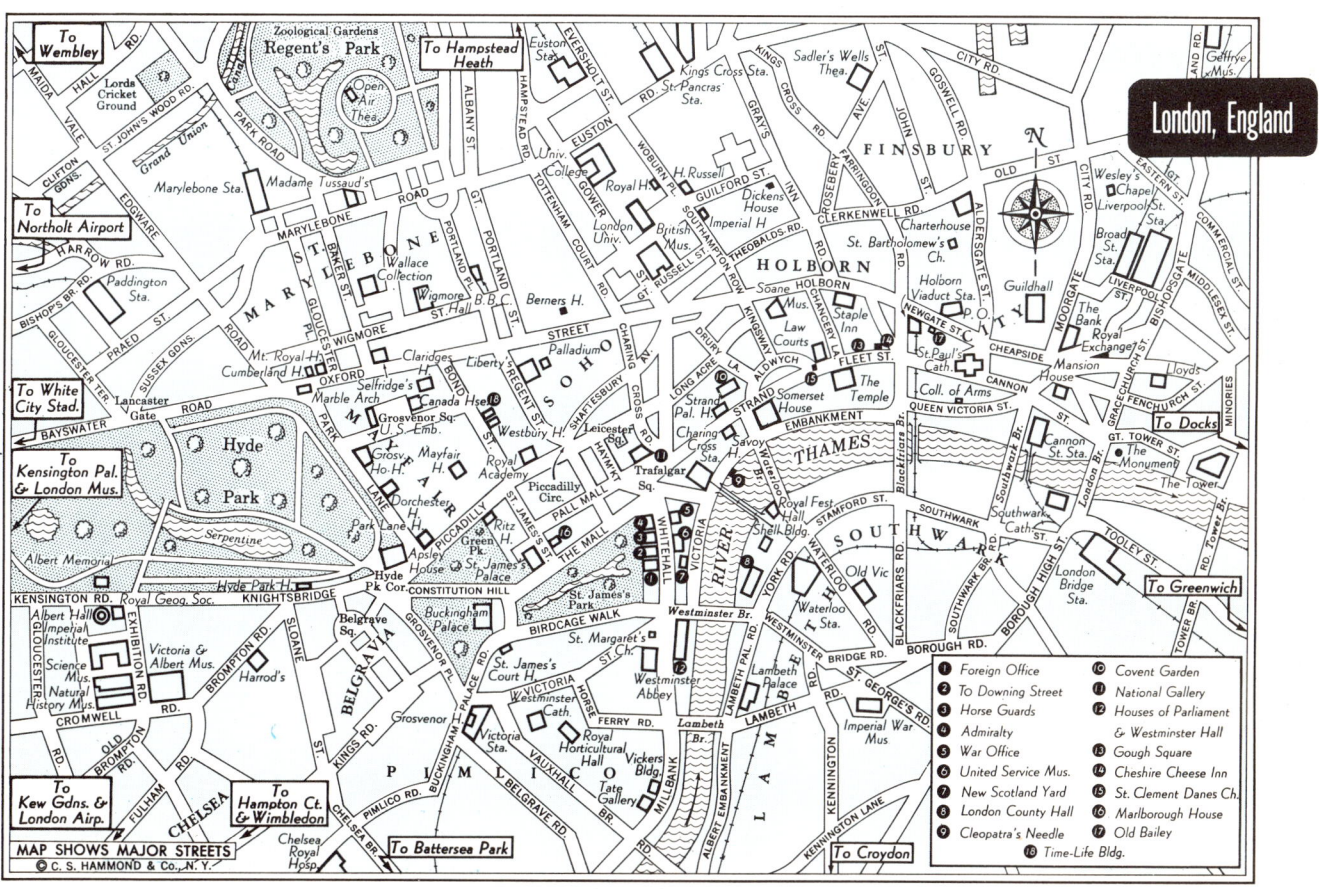

Norman castle has not seen the whole of London's long history, it has indeed seen most of it. Through the years, it has served as both a palace and a prison, though it is better known as the latter. A square granite paved plot known as Tower Green marks the site of the scaffold where such notables as Anne Boleyn, Catherine Howard and the pathetic and talented Lady Jane Grey were beheaded. The Tower of London is still guarded by the famous "Beefeaters" wearing the traditional scarlet, black and gold garb of a by-gone era. Adjoining Traitor's Gate, through which prisoners were usually brought to the Tower keep, is Wakefield Tower where the fabulous crown jewels of England are kept. This dazzling and historic collection includes the First Star of Africa, a 530 carat gem, the world's largest diamond. The biggest of several stones cut from the Cullinan diamond, it is mounted in the head of the Royal Scepter. Also on display is the Imperial State Crown containing some 3,000 diamonds and 300 pearls. Within a short distance of the Tower is Ludgate Hill, crowned by St. Paul's Cathedral. A magnificent building, the work of England's greatest architect, Sir Christopher Wren, it remained obscured to modern generations until the surrounding buildings had been reduced to a pile of rubble in the London Blitz. Also in the vicinity of the Tower are Tower Bridge and London Bridge, both spanning the Thames River. From the vantage point of London Bridge, the loiterer may view the busy scene of ships unloading in the Pool, a part of the Port of London which extends along the Thames for nearly seventy miles. Near the northern end of the bridge is the seething maelstrom of the City's business district where the Bank of England and the Royal Exchange with its golden grasshopper perched on top, look at each other across a vortex of purposeful traffic. But even at the conjunction of the city's busiest streets—Throgmorton Street, Threadneedle Street, Lombard Street and Cornhill with their temples of finance—romance and the old world are not far distant. The most historic building in the West End section is Westminster Abbey, which contains more historical treasures than any other building in Britain. Built in the year 800, it was originally used as a royal mausoleum and until the reign of George II only the kings of England were buried here. Outside the Abbey, a short distance from its north door, is a stone slab on which is engraved *T II*. This Roman boundary mark is over a thousand years older than the oldest stone in the Abbey. Across the roadway from the Abbey is the Palace of Westminster, the official name for the Houses of Parliament. When Parliament is sitting, a flag flies from Victoria Tower by day; by night a light burns in the clock tower from which the deep-throated bell—"Big Ben"—tolls each passing hour. Running due north from the Houses of Parliament, in a straight line to Trafalgar Square, is the broad thoroughfare known as Whitehall; and here flourishes the machinery of government—the Home Office, the Treasury, the War Office, the Admiralty and other governmental offices each housed in its own majestic and rather pompous palace. From Trafalgar Square the avenued Mall leads to Buckingham Palace. First used as a royal residence by Queen Victoria, it is the London home of Queen Elizabeth. Today on occasions of national rejoicing, Londoners gather in thousands in front of the palace gates to give vociferous vent to their happiness, their affection, their loyalty, and their hope that their Queen will appear on the balcony of the palace. Nearby, St. James' Palace is a mellow red brick Tudor building which is the official residence of the court. Englishmen have an aptitude for forming clubs, but nowhere do they cluster in such profusion as in St. James Street. They form, as it were, a link between the cold formalities of official

TRAFALGAR SQUARE British Information Services

TOWER BRIDGE · British Information Services

WESTMINSTER ABBEY
British Information Services

Whitehall and the garish distractions of irrepressible Piccadilly. All London is summed up in Piccadilly and to walk along it is almost to become a Londoner. Piccadilly contains everything — shops, hotels, restaurants, art galleries, clubs, private houses—and into it lead the main arteries of shopping—Regent Street, Haymarket, Bond Street, Albemarle Street, Dover Street and Knightsbridge. At one end is Piccadilly Circus where Eros presides and flower girls sell their scented wares, where traffic rushes around the fountain only because it is not allowed to rush over it. At the other end of Piccadilly is Hyde Park where ducks swim about on the Serpentine and where Londoners can lie on their backs in the grass and gaze up at the trees and the clouds beyond. And through the length of Piccadilly are Londoners going about their daily business, their daily pleasures and their daily lives.

INTERESTING PLACES AROUND LONDON

Within easy reach of London are a number of places of historic and other interest. Within 25 miles is **WINDSOR CASTLE**, an incredibly vast castle which has been the chief residence of British sovereigns for 850 years. It was to this fairy-tale castle, overlooking the Thames, that Shakespeare was summoned by Queen Elizabeth who requested of him a play with more about Falstaff. "Merry Wives of Windsor" was the resulting play. Here in **St. George's Chapel**, an outstanding example of Perpendicular architecture, repose the bodies of many English kings, including that of Charles I. The castle contains valuable paintings and furniture. Of particular interest are the **Albert Memorial Chapel** and the **Horse Shoe Cloisters** . . . . On the opposite bank of the Thames is the ancient and famous **Eton College**, founded in 1440 by Henry VI and containing a magnificent group of buildings known as School Yard. . . . Near here is **STOKE POGES** with the cemetery which was the scene of Gray's Elegy. . . . Downstream and near **EGHAM** is the island where King John put his seal to the Magna Carta in 1215. . . . Upstream from Windsor is **MAIDENHEAD** which affords punting on the Thames and, in the evening, dinner and dancing in the open air. . . . Situated on a particularly beautiful stretch of the Thames Valley is **HENLEY-ON-THAMES**, a quiet and attractive country town famous for its regattas. . . . Fifteen miles from London is **HAMPTON COURT PALACE** which was built by Cardinal Wolsey in 1515 and reluctantly handed over to Henry VIII ten years later. The old part is in excellent repair and the Palace contains most of the original **paintings of court favorites** by Sir Peter Lely. Many of the ceilings are by Verrio and much of the woodwork is by Grinling Gibbons. The **gardens** are beautiful and a visit to the Palace makes an ideal summer afternoon trip. Entrance is by the **Trophy Gate** leading to the fine **Great Gatehouse** (part of Wolsey's original building) and into the **Clock Court**, named after an astronomical clock constructed for Henry VIII. The **State Rooms** which were designed by Wren for William III, house many famous paintings, notably of the Italian school. The **Great Kitchen** contains interesting old cooking utensils and facilities. Some fine tapestries may be seen in the Great Hall. In the **William III Orangery** are the **Mantegna tempera paintings** of the Triumph of Julius Caesar. In the Gardens are the **Great Vine**, planted in 1768, the Maze and the famous **Chestnut Avenue**. . . . Not far from here is HAM HOUSE, built in 1610, formerly the property of the Duke of Lauderdale, a member of the famous "Cabal" Ministry. This house contains a unique collection of Stuart furniture. . . . At RICHMOND the view of the Thames from the top of Richmond Hill opposite the famous Roebuck Hotel is one of the finest in southern England. Here also is the historic **Sheen Palace**. . . . **SYON HOUSE** at Brentford is the historic home of the Dukes of Northumberland and is noted for its magnificent Adam interior, its State rooms, period furniture and paintings. . . . Across the Thames from Syon House are the lovely **Kew Gardens** which contain the famous botanical museum. . . . Also on the outskirts of London, is **KEN WOOD**, Hampstead, commanding a view of the city from the northern heights. A bequest of the late Lord Iveagh, this mansion is maintained as a typical country home of an eighteenth century gentleman.

THE SOUTHEAST OF ENGLAND

This section is the gateway to Great Britain and is rich in historical interest, romantic legends and quaint customs. It is also the playground of holiday-makers.

The county of **Kent** is a land of fragrant orchards, of hops and green grass, of moats and of ancient, red brick, timbered houses, a land where spring arrives gracefully and transforms the countryside into a land of great beauty. Observing the happy character of this land today, one can hardly realize what an apprehensive feeling must have dominated it during the days of 1940 when the hard-pressed British Expeditionary Forces returned to the towns of Ramsgate, Dover, Folkestone, etc. . . . **CANTERBURY** is the see of the Primate of All England and contains one of the loveliest and most ancient cathedrals in England. It was in this cathedral that Archbishop à Becket was murdered in 1170 on the steps to the altar. Here rests the body of the Black Prince, hero of the Battle of Poitiers, in his great effigy tomb. Fine examples of Roman mosaic pavements were discovered in the town during the clean-up of the bomb damage caused by reprisal raids during the last war. . . . Of the many inland places of interest in Kent, **TUNBRIDGE WELLS** is one of the most famous watering-places in England. Its chalybeate springs have been noted since 1606 and were known to Macaulay, Thackeray and Meredith. Of particular interest here is the **Pantiles**, a 17th century colonnaded row of shops. . . . Nearby are two of the most beautiful houses in England: **Penhurst Place**, the superb 14th century, ancestral home of Lord de L'Isle and Dudley; and **Knole**,

WHITTINGTON, GLOUCESTERSHIRE—A TYPICAL COUNTRY VILLAGE British Information Services

an ancient and famous house which covers five acres and is filled with treasures of every kind. Both are open to the public. . . . **ROCHESTER**, on the Medway River, is one of the historic routes from Dover to London and is dominated by its great **Norman castle**. The castle keep, with walls twelve feet thick, is a masterpiece of Norman military architecture. Rochester's Norman **Cathedral** possesses a particularly fine recessed doorway and beautiful carved woodwork. This place was beloved by Dickens and it was at nearby Gad's Hill where he spent his last years. . . . Along the Kentish coast are a procession of popular seaside resorts. **HERNE BAY**, with seven miles of sea-front and excellent facilities, is an ideal seaside center from which to explore Kent and Canterbury. . . . Below are MARGATE, popular since 1850 and BROADSTAIRS, a favorite of Dickens, which offers picturesque promenades, beautiful gardens, golf, tennis, cricket, bowls, concerts and dancing. . . . Nearby RAMSGATE specializes in sea fishing and yachting. . . . South is DEAL, scene of the landing of Julius Caesar in 55 B.C., an unrivaled center from which to enjoy a golfing holiday. Championship courses in the area are Sandwich, Deal, Cinque Ports and Walmer Castle. The ill-famed Goodwin Sands, marked by lightships and exposed at low tide, lie seven

THATCHED COTTAGE, SOMERSET British Travel Association

miles out to sea. . . . Below Deal is DOVER, a gay, charming town. Dover, chief of the ancient Cinque Ports, has always been in the front line of English history, and never was this more true than during the second World War. In the grounds of the formidable Dover Castle on the heights overlooking the town, is the oldest standing building in England, the Pharos or lighthouse which guided the Roman supply ships into the harbor. . . . A few miles away is FOLKESTONE, associated, as Dover is, with crossings to the Continent. It attracts many visitors with its racecourse, concerts and extensive gardens fronting the sea, from which one can see the coast of France on a clear day.

In Sussex, HASTINGS is famous as a holiday resort and as the place where in 1066 William the Conqueror, Duke of Normandy, defeated King Harold and made England his. The site of the battle is some seven miles inland, where the Battle Abbey now stands. The altar is said to stand on the spot where the Conqueror pitched his tent and ate his supper, with the English dead around him. . . . To the west is EASTBOURNE which lies at the foot of the lovely, rolling, turf-covered South Downs. Near this popular resort are several attractions, including the Long Man of Wilmington, a figure cut out by removing the turf from the face of the chalk downs and Beachy Head, a magnificent headland which drops a sheer 575 feet into the sea below. . . . Further along is SEAFORD, a charming little bathing and golfing resort and BRIGHTON, the "prince of seaside resorts," which provides every form of entertainment and distraction for the holiday-maker in a setting graced by the best in Regency architecture. George IV "created" Brighton as a resort and a constant reminder of him stands in the center of the town. It is his incredible pleasure Pavilion, an architectural extravaganza played on an Indo-Chino-Moorish theme. . . . In Hampshire County, PORTSMOUTH . . . . is England's largest navy yard and SOUTHSEA is a sunny and popular resort. Both give access to many fascinating sightseeing trips—Porchester Castle, Arundel Castle, Netley Abbey and Beaulieu Abbey and to the delightful Isle of Wight across the waters of the Solent. This is the big yachting center of England and is one of the most picturesque coastal islands.

THE SOUTHWEST COUNTRY

In Wiltshire is England's most important prehistoric monument, Stonehenge, the world-famous circle of vast neolithic stones standing on Salisbury Plain, where thousands of soldiers have found their military legs. . . . To the south is SALISBURY, with its magnificent cathedral. . . . Near the sea in Southampton is New Forest, a densely wooded, 93,000-acre tract which was formerly the royal hunting ground of William the Conqueror and is now the home of wild ponies. . . . EXETER is the county town of Devon and is picturesquely situated on the banks of the river Exe. Although severely damaged during the war, its chief glory, the cathedral, still stands. Adjoining it is the Old Close which contains some interesting old houses. In Rougemont Grounds may be seen the remains of the ancient city walls and of Rougemont Castle, erected by William the Conqueror. . . . At the mouth of the Exe is EXMOUTH, an attractive bathing resort with a good golf course and lovely gardens. . . . From Exmouth one may travel to Plymouth via the route through the open moorland of Dartmoor, a very scenic drive, or take the coastal road via the famous and equally beautiful resorts of TORQUAY and DARTMOUTH. . . . PLYMOUTH . . . . always near the heart of English history, is where Sir Francis Drake finished his game of bowls on the Hoe before setting sail to rout the Spanish Armada. Here is also where the Pilgrim Fathers set sail for the New World on the Mayflower in 1620. Being one of the chief seaports of the country, Plymouth was badly damaged during the last war, but with characteristic courage, her people have set to work to rebuild their pleasant, historic town. To sit on the Hoe and watch the diversity of shipping in the sound is a favorite summer pastime. . . . Across the river Tamar is the county of Cornwall, England's most westernmost toe. It is a land of legends, ancient history and of quaint customs; it is a land of cromlechs, dolmens and prehistoric circles. Remarkable among these landmarks obtruding from the past is the Trevethy Stone in the Looe Valley. There is an amazing similarity between Cornwall and Brittany on the west coast of France, a similarity which is extended to the astonishing resemblance between Mont St. Michel and St. Michael's Mount standing in Mounts Bay near PENZANCE. The latter is an excellent headquarters from which to explore the Lands End district and from here boats may be taken to the Scilly Islands. . . . The coasts of Cornwall are rugged and the scenery is bold and picturesque. Snug harbors and charming little seaside towns, where early spring brings bright flowers long before they bloom in any other part of England, provide everything needed for a happy, sunny vactionland. . . . Northeast of Cornwall, in Somerset, is BATH, the most celebrated of English spas. The Romans discovered the medicinal hot springs here in A.D. 44 and established an elaborate system of baths which today form the best preserved and most important Roman relics in Great Britain. During the eighteenth century it became a rendezvous of society who came to see not only the many visiting royalty, but also to see Beau Nash, the Master of Ceremonies. Bath is a planned city and its beauty is attributable to the ablest architects of the eighteenth century. It possesses a marked individuality which is at once recognized by the visitor who sees for the first time the architectural miracle of its crescents and classical buildings.

WALES

Although it has been 700 years since England and Wales became part of the same kingdom, the Welsh have managed to retain their own individuality and their own language.

In the south NEWPORT, although it is one of the main commercial ports, has an ancient history. Its castle, of which only a portion remains, dates from the close of the eleventh century. Three miles northeast of the town, at CAERLEON, are the remains of a Roman settlement that was the headquarters of the second Augustan Legion. The valley of the River Usk, which flows into the sea at Newport, vies with that of the Wye in the scenery which it has to offer. Close to its source the river flows past BRECON where a ruined castle and the ancient priory church of St. John, now a cathedral, may be seen. To the east are the Black Mountains, a tract of wild and open country. To the south are the Brecon Beacons, a country dear to the hearts of hikers. . . . Between Newport and

ROMAN BATHS, BATH British Information Services

Swansea are many places of interest and beauty. Caerphily Castle to the north of Cardiff is the largest and most remarkable of the castles Edward I built in Wales. **BRIDGEND** also has its ruined castle, and in its neighborhood are Ewenny Priory, Coychurch and Coyty. . . . SWANSEA stands at the entrance to the Gower Peninsula, an attractive stretch of wild and wooded country with a picturesque and irregular seacoast. . . . **KIDWELLY** and **CARMARTHEN**, each with its ruined castle, lie to the west. In the main street of Carmarthen is a carefully preserved oak tree upon which, according to local legend, the welfare of the town depends. . . . Inland and to the north the country becomes mountainous and more picturesque. On steep hills intersected by green, fertile valleys, narrowing as they ascend the heights, lakes and wooded slopes, heather and rock abound. The coastline is rugged and in many places precipitous. It is the haunt of all kinds of sea birds and of the gray seal. . . . One of the most popular seaside resorts in Wales is **ABERYSTWYTH**, where the visitor will find much to attract him. There are many sporting facilities, and, owing to its situation halfway up the coast of Wales, Aberystwyth makes an excellent headquarters from which to explore the countryside. . . . The visitor should not miss the beautiful **Elan Valley** in the neighboring county of Radnor. Here a chain of lakes, some natural and some caused by the flooding of the valleys, have made of the countryside a very picturesque Welsh Lake District. . . . Wales is noted for its fine castles. Most of these were built by Edward I (1272-1307) during his subjugation of the country. Harlech, close to Caernarvon and Conway at either end of the Menai Straits, which separate the Isle of Angelesey from the mainland, are among the best known. **CAERNARVON** is an excellent base from which to make excursions into the mountainous region known as Snowdonia. The ascent of **Snowdon**, the highest mountain in England and Wales, can be made by rail from Llanberis. At the summit is a hotel. . . . On the north coast of Wales are several seaside resorts which are much frequented by holiday-makers. **LLANDUDNO**, attractively situated in Orme's Bay, and **COLWYN BAY** are resorts where scenery, safe bathing and many entertainments may be found. **ABERGELE, RHYL** and **PRESTATYN** are other holiday resorts which have many attractions to offer the visitor. . . . Of inland holiday resorts **LLANGOLLEN**, on the river Dee, is famed for its salmon fishing.

THE MIDLANDS

England is always remembered by visitors for her lavish green countryside with its lovely trees, green grass and neat hedgerows; and nowhere is the countryside more typical than in the Midlands. Strangely enough, this is also the manufacturing center, with such industrial cities as Birmingham, Coventry and Wolverhampton.

BIRMINGHAM (Eng.) Birmingham, the great industrial giant of Warwick, England, boasts of being able to make anything from "a pin to a powerpress." This metropolis had indeed allied itself with industry as early as the 16th century. Surrounded as it is by districts rich in both coal and iron ore, Birmingham today ranks among such cities as Pittsburgh and its north American "godchild"—Birmingham, Alabama, as one of the greatest steel producing centers of the world. Included also among its major heavy industries are the manufacture of

ST. MARTIN'S, BIRMINGHAM British Information Services

14TH CENTURY BRIDGE OVER THE RIVER DEE, LLANGOLLEN British Information Services

munitions and the large-scale production of automobiles. Many of the copper and brass coins used by Britain and its colonies are minted in Birmingham. This city has often been an ardent crusader in reform movements both political and religious. It was in a suburb of Birmingham that James Watt and his partner Matthew Boulton founded their celebrated Soho metal works; other famous men whose names are associated with Birmingham are Joseph Priestley, John Baskerville and Joseph Chamberlain. Birmingham does not lack for cultural interests; it possesses a modern University, the outgrowth of several smaller institutions, its library probably contains the largest collection of Shakespearean books in the world and its museum houses one of the most important collections of paintings outside London.

THE COUNCIL HOUSE, BIRMINGHAM

Philip Gendreau

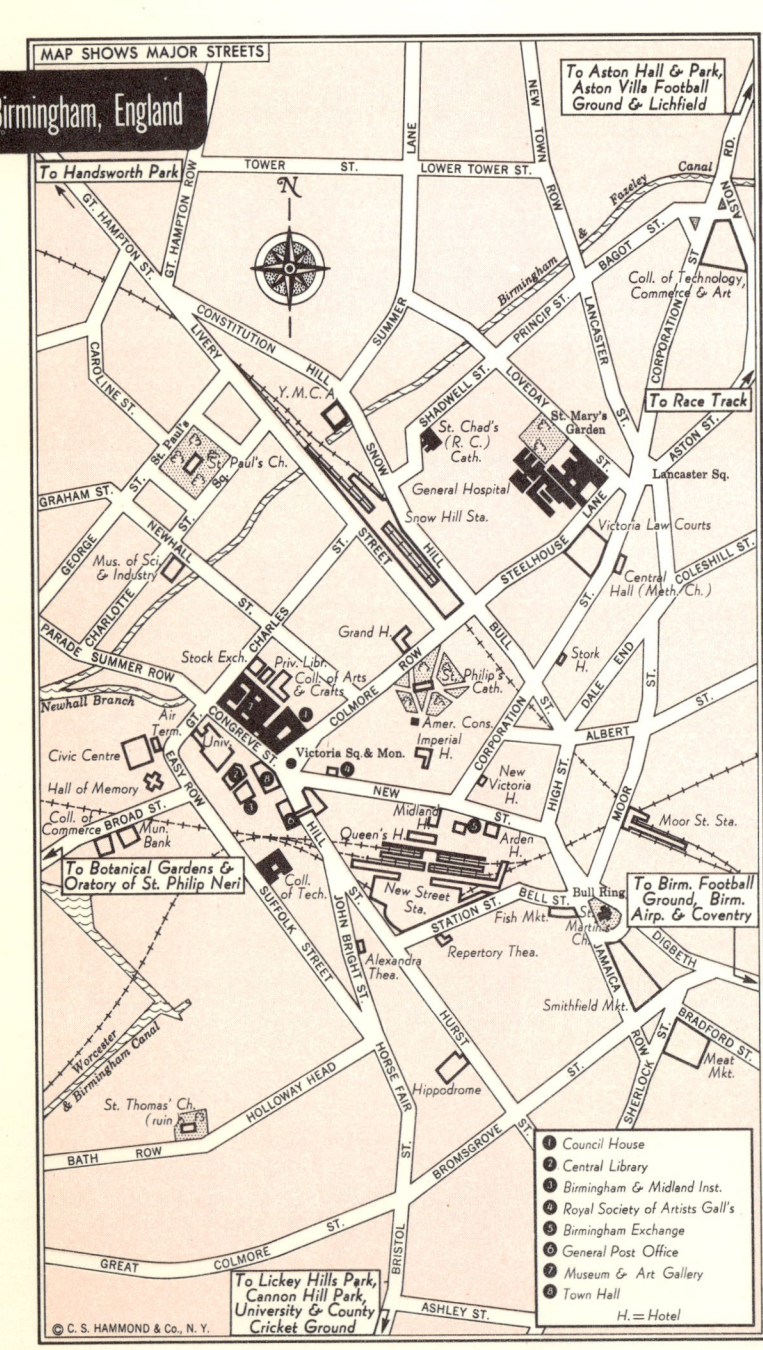

Northwest of Birmingham, in Staffordshire, **WOLVERHAMPTON** is a well-planned city that manages to retain a pleasant residential air, in spite of being a busy industrial center. . . . Nearby is **CANNOCK**, famous for its coal and **Cannock Chase**, a stretch of delightful moorland. . . . Also nearby is **LICHFIELD**, known for its red sandstone **cathedral** (one of the smallest, yet most graceful cathedrals in England) and its associations with the venerable Dr. Johnson. The lexicographer's birthplace is now a Johnson museum. . . . Southeast of Birmingham is **COVENTRY** . . . ., through which Lady Godiva is reputed to have ridden naked to save the townspeople from oppressive taxes levied by her husband. Today the city is the center of the automobile and cycle industry. . . . Southwest is romantic **WARWICK**, which contains some of the finest half-timbered architecture to be found in England and the magnificent **Warwick Castle** which stands four square and majestic on the banks of the river Avon. This is the greatest of British baronial castles and contains many well-known pictures and a fine collection of armor, including a helmet worn by Cromwell. . . . Adjoining Warwick is **LEAMINGTON** (the famous Royal Leamington Spa), a resort which makes an ideal center for exploring the neighboring countryside. . . . Nearby, at the northern extremity of the

ANNE HATHAWAY'S COTTAGE

British Information Services

14

lovely Cotswold Hills, and on the banks of the lazy-flowing Avon, is **STRATFORD-UPON-AVON**. This charming, historic town was the birthplace of Shakespeare and his home now houses the **Shakespeare Museum and Library**. **Holy Trinity Church** contains Shakespeare's tomb, on which is a doggerel inscription, attributed to the poet, threatening the would-be disturber of his bones. The **Shakespeare Memorial Theater**, in which the Shakespeare Festival takes place each year, is a modern building, built with funds subscribed in Britain and the United States. It is equipped with all the most up-to-date theatrical contrivances. Nearby is the charming flower-surrounded **cottage of Anne Hathaway**. . . . South of Stratford-upon-Avon lie the Cotswold Hills, generally known as the Cotswolds. Here all the buildings and roofs are made of the local honey-colored stone and the buildings represent the best of the graceful domestic Tudor architecture. The villages of **Burford, Bibury, Chipping Camden, Chipping Norton, Chipping Sodbury, Broadway and Moreton-in-Marsh**, to mention a few, are splendid examples of the Cotswold scene. . . . East of the Cotswolds, the ancient city of **OXFORD** is a happy combination of probably the most beautiful university city in the world and a thriving industrial town with one of Europe's largest automobile assembly plants. **High Street** or **The High** is an unforgettable sight with the beautiful Oxford college buildings lining either side. The colleges, twenty-one in all, are from 400 to 500 years old, and many have remarkably lovely gardens which sparkle like jewels in their somber setting of ancient lichen-covered walls. Of particular note is **Magdalen** with its beautifully proportioned tower and graceful bridge spanning the River Cherwell and its garden which has been tended almost since before history was written. . . . Nearby is **Woodstock** with **Blenheim Palace**, birthplace of Winston Churchill and home of the Duke of Marlborough, a major point of interest. . . . To the north is **BANBURY** of nursery rhyme fame, from which can be visited **Sulgrave Manor**, ancestral home of the Washington family, which houses the **Washington Museum** containing many relics of the first president of the United States.

LIVERPOOL. Liverpool is the chief port of Lancashire; indeed it is the second seaport of England and the fourth largest city of the United Kingdom. Although Liverpool is a manufacturing center with many different types of industries, its wealth and its commercial importance have always come from the sea. Its basins, docks and graving docks along the Mersey estuary cover an area of over six hundred acres and there are nearly forty miles of quays. Also included in its harbor facilities is a vast system of warehouses. These, as well as the docks and quays, are administered by the Liverpool Dock Board and all are public property. One of the outstanding features of the city is its magnificent cathedral which, when completed, will be the largest in England. It was designed by Sir Giles Gilbert Scott, whose winning design was accepted in 1904 when the architect was no more than twenty-one years old. The Walker Art Gallery contains one of the finest collections of paintings in the provinces. The University of Liverpool is renowned for its School of Tropical Medicine, which has made valuable contributions to the study of such diseases as yellow fever, malaria and sleeping sickness. Five miles from Liverpool is Aintree, the famous racecourse where, in March of each year, is run the Grand National Steeplechase over a track which presents bigger and stiffer hurdles than appear on any other racecourse in the world.

EAST ANGLIA

Between the Wash and the Estuary of the Thames is a country of fertile plains,

ST. GEORGE'S HALL, LIVERPOOL British Information Services

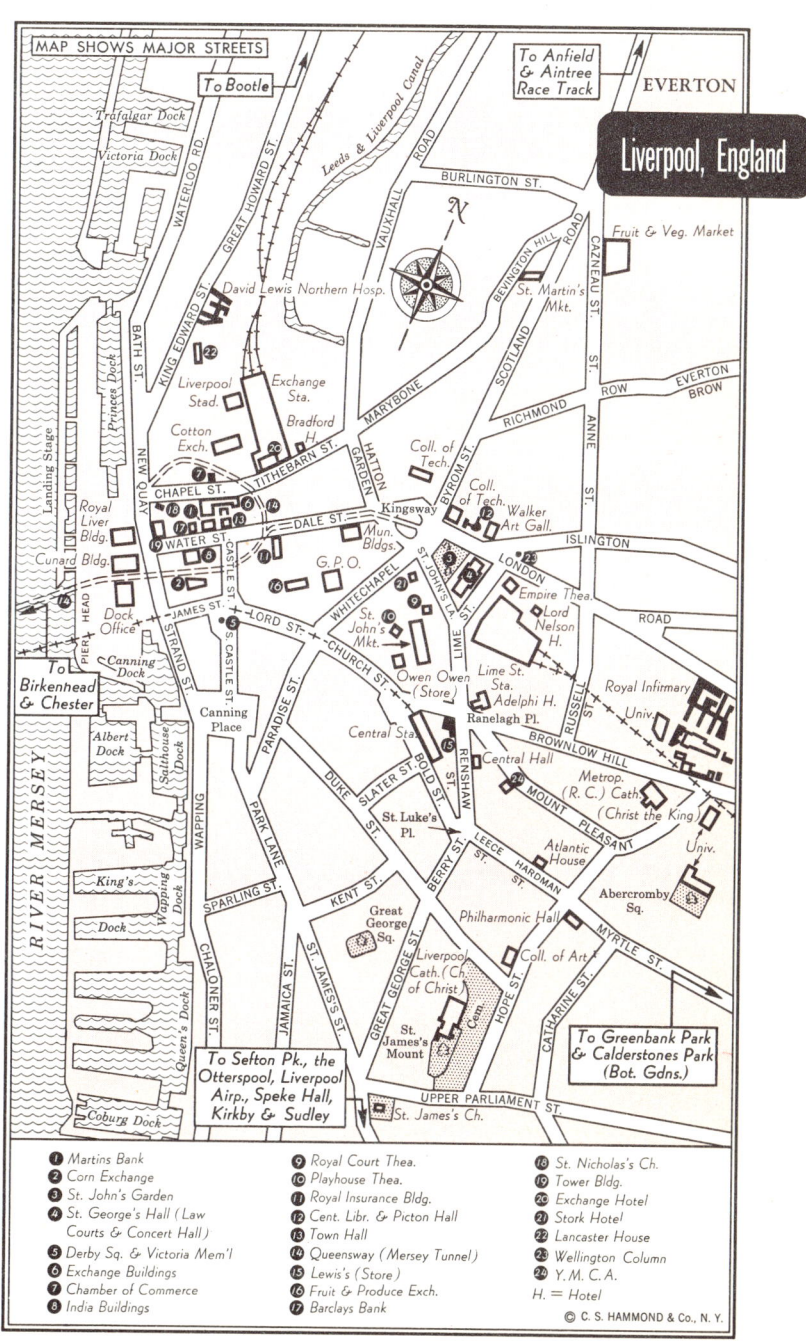

steeped in history and legend. This is East Anglia, originally a powerful Anglo-Saxon Kingdom and subsequently an Earldom of England. Today it is a rich grain and stock-raising region and has important fisheries.

CAMBRIDGE, as all the world knows, is where the scholastic youth of England, or at least such as have not gone to Oxford and other universities, is trained to face a competitive world. The colleges of Cambridge are an architectural feat whose glory is **King's College Chapel**, a superb Perpendicular building, perfect alike within and without. The visitor should make a point of seeing "The Backs," which are the backs of the colleges and their gardens running down to the river Cam. On a fine day in spring there is no lovelier scene. . . . Nearby **NEWMARKET** has been the center of flat-racing since the days of Charles II and you may see hundreds of horses being trained each day on Newmarket Heath. There are two race-courses in the town. . . . One of the great landmarks of this region is **Ely Cathedral**, in **ELY**, which takes its name rather unromantically from the eels which used to abound in the surrounding marshes. Its most notable feature is the graceful, Gothic central octagon which has been described as the most beautiful design in all Gothic architecture. . . . Fifty miles north of here is **NORWICH**, the beautiful county town of Norfolk. The two most notable features of Norwich are the **cathedral** and the **castle**. The **castle**, erected in the twelfth century, was refaced in 1840 and has now an undeniably modern appearance. After doing duty as the county prison for five centuries it now houses the **Norfolk museum**, which contains some fine examples of the Norfolk school of painting by Cotman and others. The **cathedral** is an impressive Norman building with a fine spire and beautiful flying buttresses. The **Norfolk Broads** may be explored from Norwich by boat. These delightful, flower-fringed, shallow lagoons and lakes are connected by streams and form a favorite

DOONE VALLEY, EXMOOR, DEVONSHIRE British Information Services

yachting and vacation center. . . . All along the coast of East Anglia are delightful seaside resorts with such famous names as Great Yarmouth, Gorleston, Cromer, Sheringham and Hunstanton. Hunstanton, in the north, is a convenient place from which to visit **Sandringham**, the country home of Her Majesty, The Queen, and the famous **Huntstanton** and **Hokkham Halls**.

THE NORTH OF ENGLAND

There is no part of England that offers so much contrast, such variety of scenery and interest, as the north of England. In the county of Yorkshire alone one may pass, within the distance of an afternoon's walk, from flat pastureland where cows stand hock-deep in good grazing to lonely moorland heights where the curlew's mournful cry echoes among the rocks. The north of England can claim even to have a language, or at least an accent of its own, one that is becoming more and more the standby of every aspirant to vaudeville renown, the accent of Yorkshire and Lancashire.

Yorkshire is divided into three Ridings, North, East and West. **YORK**, one of the most beautiful and historic towns in all England, is situated on the spot where the three Ridings meet. It contains so much to see that the visitor may just as well forget his timetable. An idea of the atmosphere of York may be gained from the fact that the curfew is still rung there and has been since William the Conqueror first ordered that fires should be covered at night as a precaution against accident. The best view of the massive and magnificent **Minster** is to be had from the **walls** which encircle the town. The **Minster** (England's largest medieval cathedral) was founded before history was written, and has existed in its present outward form since the year 1474, when a building program of 250 years was completed. Don't miss the many quaint sidestreets which, in many cases, possess the oddest of names and retain much of their medieval character. . . . Other places you will want to visit in Yorkshire include the cathedral town of **RIPON** with the famous ruins of **Fountains Abbey**, **HELMSLEY** which is an excellent center from which to see the **Yorkshire moors** and the superb Cistercian ruin of Rievaulx Abbey, **HARROGATE**, a beautiful spa with a 200-acre garden, **SCARBOROUGH**, the ultimate in seaside resorts and **WHITBY**, famous for its salmon, its Abbey, its picturesque streets and quaint houses and its amusement parks and other entertainments. . . . To the north is the county of **Durham** and the city of **DURHAM**, an architectural treasure. Durham's Norman **cathedral** and ancient castle, standing formidable on their great base of rock overlooking the river Wear are sights which should not be missed. Durham's university is one of the oldest in England. . . . Further north is Northumberland which possesses on the river Tyne one of the most famous ship-building districts in the world which cen-

THE LAKE DISTRICT British Information Services

ters around NEWCASTLE-on-Tyne. North of here is the rugged Border Country. A remarkable ancient monument is **Hadrian's Wall** which dates back two thousand years and runs across hill and dale from one side of England to the other, from Wallsend on the Tyne to Bowness on the Solway.... On the other side of England, across the Pennine Hills, is **CHESTER**, county town of Cheshire, with a medieval air thoroughly in keeping with its ancient history. The **Chester rows**, or galleries, fronting the first floors of the timbered Tudor buildings in the four main streets, are a famous feature of the town. The city walls form a complete circle and have survived intact to this day. In many parts of the town and around the cathedral are to be found delightful examples of what might be described as fairytale gingerbread architecture.... Passing northwards we come to the **LAKE DISTRICT**, the name given to a district of mountains and lakes in the counties of Westmoreland, Cumberland and Lancashire, although Cumberland has the largest portion of it. There are eleven lakes in all, of which the largest is **Windermere**. Though the highest peak in the district is no more than 3,000 feet high, the scenery is really impressive and has been the inspiration of many poets. Wordsworth lived at **Grasmere**; so did Coleridge. Shelley had a cottage at **Keswick**. There are many organized tours of the lakes, one of the finest being the drive from **Keswick** to **Buttermere**, past the lovely **valley of Borrowdale**, over the **Honiston pass** and back through Newlands. The rock-climbing in the Lake District can be a real challenge.

Scotland

Scotland is the land of romance. The rugged outlines of the highlands are the same today as they were 10,000 years ago. The red deer roam over the same hills. The salmon ascend the same rivers. The grouse fly over the same moors. Scotland has its own dress and its own music, and these, too, seem to have grown with and become part of the Scottish scene.

GLASGOW. Glasgow is a thriving commercial and industrial center in which almost every manufacture in Great Britain is represented. Scotland's most important seaport, the deepening through the years of its long river channel, allows ships from every port in the world to enter and clear its docks. Its colossal shipyards lining both sides of the River Clyde as far down as Greenock are world famous. Here, shipbuilders turn out every conceivable type of vessel from barges to battleships; many a huge Cunard liner has slid down the ways at Glasgow. Textiles too, hold a prominent place among the city's manufactures; it was at Glasgow that Turkey-red dyeing and chlorine bleaching were originated. Much of the famed Scotch whisky is blended and bottled at Glasgow's distilleries. In ap-

GLASGOW'S ART GALLERY — Philip Gendreau

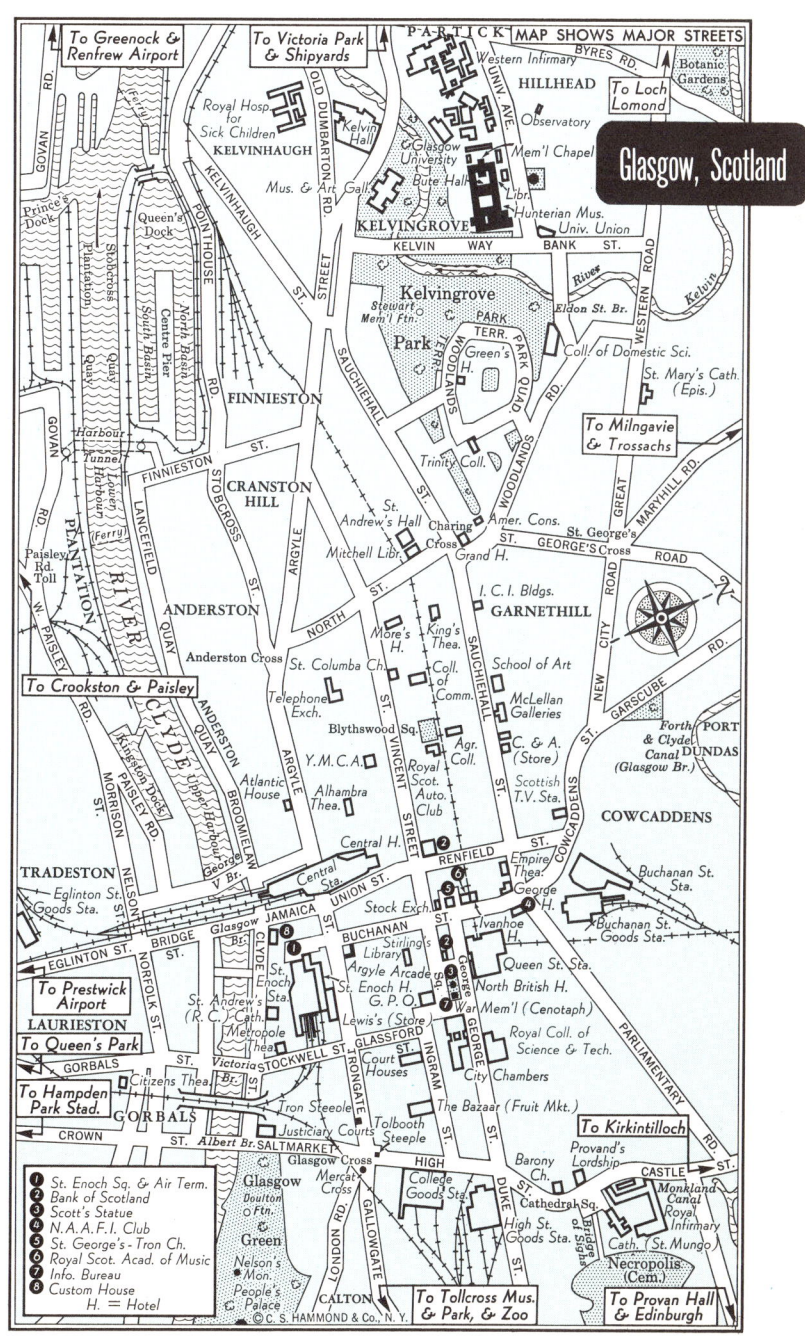

17

pearance a modern city, Glasgow has but few buildings of ancient vintage or of particular historic interest. Its oldest and most picturesque building is probably St. Mungo's Cathedral located in the northeastern section of the city. Built over the course of four centuries, it is a fine example of early English architecture and exquisite in its simplicity. Glasgow's famed university occupies a hill overlooking Kelvingrove Park and though founded in 1450, its Gothic buildings are of more recent construction. The university's renowned School of Engineering has established standards that are universally acknowledged. It was while working at Glasgow University that James Watt perfected the steam engine, an invention which helped make possible the modern steamship which has brought fame and prosperity to Glasgow.

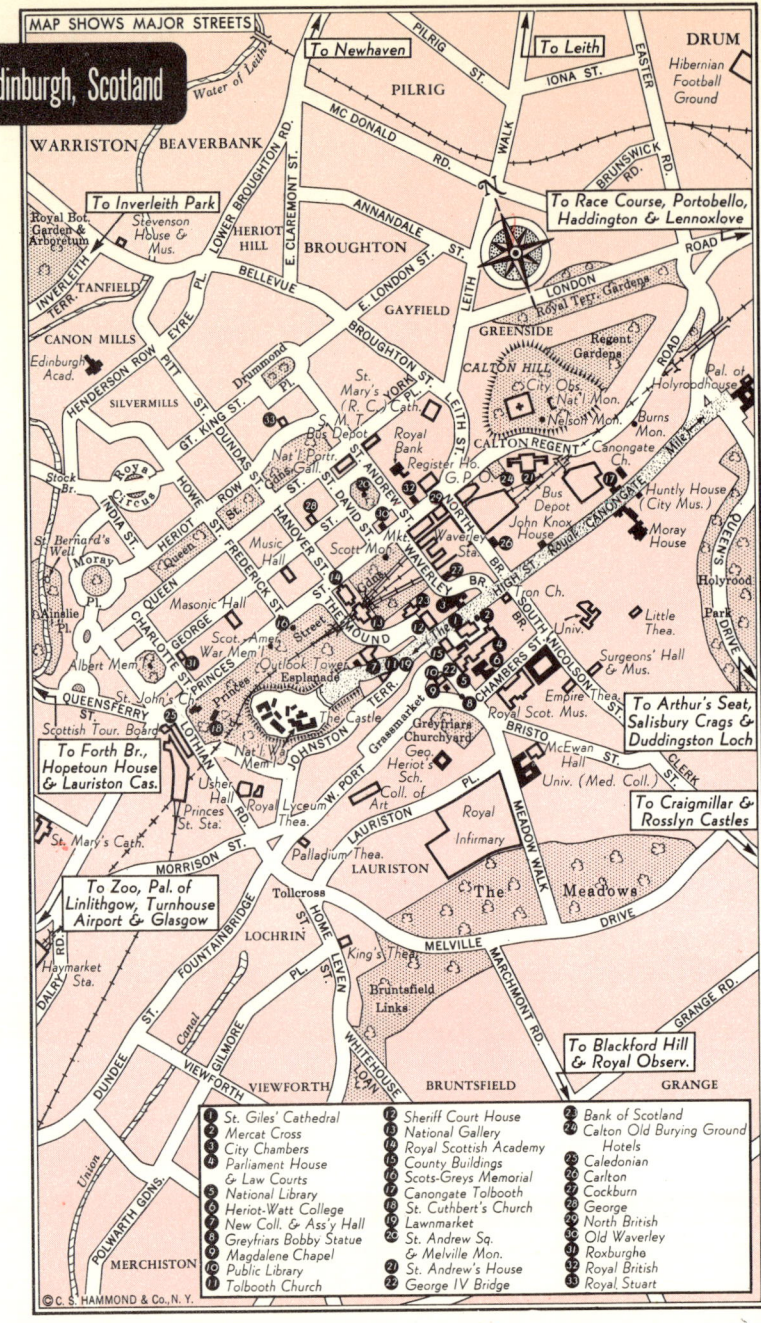

GEORGE SQUARE, GLASGOW British Information Services

THE UNIVERSITY OF GLASGOW British Travel Association

EDINBURGH — Edinburgh, Scotland's capital and guardian of its ancient history, spreads out upon a series of ridges near the southern banks of the Firth of Forth. South of Princes Street, which divides the old town from the new, Edinburgh's ancient 7th-century Castle looks down from its high, rocky seat on a city considered by many to be the fairest in Europe; a city whose wealth of classic architecture, whose abundance of buildings resembling Grecian temples has won for it the title of "Modern Athens." The Castle around which the city grew has long been famed for its historical associations with such names as Robert the Bruce, Mary Queen of Scots, and Charles Stuart. From it a steep and narrow road leads to the summit of Castle Rock where with the Palace buildings stands Scotland's impressive War Memorial honoring its men and women

ESPLANADE, EDINBURGH CASTLE British Information Services

SCOTT MONUMENT British Travel Association

who gave their lives in two World Wars. Here no detail of service has been forgotten, even mice and carrier pigeons are represented in the various panels and friezes which adorn this shrine. Running eastward, the Royal Mile connects Castle Rock with the Palace of Holyroodhouse which today serves as official residence of the Queen when she visits Edinburgh. Long a center of literature and learning, Edinburgh can count among her famous men: Sir Walter Scott, Lord Lister, Robert Louis Stevenson and Kenneth Grahame.

HOLYROODHOUSE British Information Services

South of Edinburgh is typical Border Country — hills and wooded slopes with compact little Border towns lying in sheltered valleys, through which run swift, impatient streams. This is the country so loved by Sir Walter Scott and you may visit the lovely home where he lived in **ABBOTSFORD**. The house and grounds contain many memorials of him and interesting relics collected by him.... Nearby are the abbey ruins of Melrose and Dryburgh. It was the monks at **Melrose Abbey** that, through their skillful manipulation of wool, paved the way for the growth of the important woolen industry in the Border Country. The heart of the Scottish hero, Robert Bruce, lies buried beneath the high altar of the abbey.... Nearby **Dryburgh Abbey** is the burial place of Scott. The abbey is a picturesque ruin charmingly situated in a loop of the River Tweed.... Up the valley of the Teviot is **HAWICK**, a modern town with a thriving woolen industry and an ancient history. The "Riding of the Marches," a custom observed each year here, celebrates the defeat of a body of English soldiers by the men of Hawick at Hornshole in 1514 after the Battle of Flodden. **Hermitage Castle** is one of the oldest standing baronial buildings in Scotland.... **PEEBLES** is an industrial center and also an attractive holiday resort which has many historical associations. The Tweed, on which it is located, and other neighboring rivers offer excellent fishing.... To the north, on the coast, is **DUNBAR** famous for its history and good golf. Dunbar saw the hurried embarkation of Edward II in 1314 after his defeat at Bannockburn; it also saw the elopement of Mary, Queen of Scots, with the unprincipled Bothwell. Today it is a popular holiday resort with a most unusual sea-water swimming pool in a delightful natural setting.... Nearby **NORTH BERWICK**, famous for golf, is another fashionable resort. **Bass Rock**, a precipitous pile that rises 350 feet from the sea, stands a mile off-shore and is a nesting colony for gannets.... In the southwest corner of the Lowlands lies Galloway, a county of high moorland and twisting valleys. This region is often neglected by the tourist and is well worth a visit. **DUMFRIES**, where Robert Burns is buried, is the gateway to this area and many delightful excursions may be made from here. **Lincluden Abbey, Caerlaverock Castle**, the charmingly named **Sweetheart Abbey** and **Argigland**, the birthplace of Paul Jones, who was gardener, pirate, admiral and founder of the American navy, are all within easy reach.... Westward, on the coast is the pleasant holiday resort of **GIRVAN** and **AYR**, famous as the center of the Burns country.... At **ALLOWAY**, on the outskirts of Ayr, is the cottage where the poet was born; in the center of the town is the **Auld Brig**, a Burns landmark which for five hundred years was the only bridge in the town; two and a half miles from Ayr is the **Brig o' Doon** which will be remembered in connection with Tam o' Shanter's wild ride on his mare, Meg. Close to the bridge is the **Burns Monument**, which takes the inappropriate form of a Grecian temple, in which are preserved the bibles exchanged between Burns and Highland Mary, Jean Armour's wedding ring, and many other Burns relics.... **PRESTWICK**, immediately north of Ayr, possesses one of the world's best international airports, is also a noted holiday resort.... It is a short journey north from Glasgow to **STIRLING**, the gateway to the highlands where the English and Scottish nobility journey for the grouse shooting which begins on August 12th and lasts until December 10th. Near Stirling is another impressive castle dating from the fourteenth century and now adapted to the requirements of a modern barracks.... At **BANNOCKBURN**, one mile away, the battle of that name was fought in the year 1314. The battle opened with single combat between the Scottish King Robert the Bruce, mounted on a shaggy pony and armed only with an axe, and the fully appointed English knight, Sir Henry de Bohin. The latter was split in half.... Go west from Stirling into the lovely **Trossach** country, the setting for the romantic episodes of "The Lady of the Lake" as well as for some of the dramatic scenes of "Rob Roy." Here a chain of lochs, set in the midst of imposing hills, runs from **Callander** in the east to the head of Loch Lomond in the west. Thence the road runs past **Loch Awe**, through the precipitous **Brander Pass** to **OBAN** on the coast, which is not only an excellent center from which to explore the western highlands, but also one from which to visit the islands — MULL, where wild goat are to be found; the tiny IONA where St. Columba landed with fifteen missionaries in the year 563 and founded a monastery (in the burial ground lies Duncan, victim of Macbeth); and the island of SKYE. This island, wild, lonely and still primitive, is dominated by the granite rocks of the giant Cuilins. The wet and misty climate produces weird atmospheric effects. Islanders will direct you to PORTREE, where Bonnie Prince Charlie took his leave of Flora Macdonald. . . . A short trip by steamer will take the visitor to the outer HEBRIDES where the islanders still speak Gaelic. He will find Lewis with its standing stones marking the graves of ancient warriors; Harris, home of Harris tweed; and North and South Uist. . . . From Skye the visitor may return by way of MALLAIG and take the road or railway past Loch Eil or Loch Eilt to FORT WILLIAM, which stands on the Caledonian Canal at the foot of Ben Nevis, the highest mountain in Great Britain. . . . Visit INVERNESS, the capital of the highlands where, in the third week of September, you may see the Northern Meeting of the clans who gather there for the highland games. Do not miss this event if you wish to see the full splendor of highland dress, the national sports and the music and dancing of Scotland at their best. . . . Northwest of Inverness are the wildest and loveliest parts of the highlands. Here is the home of the red deer, the haunt of the wild cat and the nests of the golden eagle. To walk through this lonely, unchanged country is an experience never to be forgotten. . . . Just east of Inverness is Culloden Moor where, in the battle of that name in 1746, the last hopes of the Jacobites for the return of the house of Stuart were finally crushed. . . . Loch Ness is one of the largest and deepest lochs in Scotland. Never more than a mile wide it is twenty-four miles long and in places 900 feet deep. The water has never been known to freeze. Throughout its length the loch offers on either hand changing scenery of hill and woodland typical of the beauty of the highlands. . . Between Inverness and Perth to the south are some of the greatest fishing grounds in Scotland. The road leads past the Cairngorm Mountains through the Grampians and runs beside the Spey, one of the greatest of all Scottish salmon rivers, through Kingussie, thence to Blair Atholl and Pitlochry on the Tummel, also famed for salmon, and finally to Dunkeld and Perth, between which are some of the most famous salmon pools of the river Tay. . . . An alternate route from Inverness to Perth, more interesting to the non-fisherman perhaps, follows the coast as far as ABERDEEN, a city built of granite. This is the chief city of northern Scotland and is also a pleasant resort with an excellent beach. . . . From here the road follows the valley of the Dee, another famous salmon river. Here, high up in the mountains, is Balmoral Castle, the Scottish home of the Queen; Invercauld House, where the head of the Farquharson clan lived, and Braemar Castle, a miniature Scottish castle perfect in every detail. At the nearby mountain resort of BRAEMAR is held the annual Royal Highland Games. . . . From Braemar the road winds upwards, past the Devil's Elbow, and then falls through Glen Shee and out to the coast and DUNDEE, of marmalade fame. This is the fourth largest Scottish city and is a prosperous manufacturing and ship-building center. . . . Near Dundee is Glamis Castle, parts of which date from the eleventh century. One of the finest and most picturesque of Scottish castles, it is the seat of the Queen Mother's family. . . . Below Dundee is PERTH, called the "Fair City." It is charmingly situated on the right bank of the Tay and is famed not only for its associations with Scott's novel "The Fair Maid of Perth," but also for the fine old church of St. John dating from 1126. . . . To those who are thinking of a golfing holiday, Scotland, which is the home of golf, has so many good courses to offer that it would be difficult to know where to start. Gleneagles, at Auchterarder, near Perth, and St. Andrews, the headquarters of golf, on the east coast of Fife, are courses which will be familiar, at least by name, to all players of the game. Other famous courses are North Berwick and Muirfield in the east; Turnberry, Prestwick and Troon in the west. There are many hundreds more and the visitor may be assured that wherever he happens to be in Scotland he will have a first-class course within reasonable distance.

BEN NEVIS — British Information Services

Ireland

DUBLIN. A salt wind blows into the heart of Dublin and the slopes of the Wicklow Hills seem to rise at the end of every street in the southern suburbs, while the Liffey flows down from the hinterland to a truly lovely harbor. The Irish capital, though, is renowned not alone for her exciting location but chiefly as a city of "character." Heart and soul of the fighting Emerald Isle, her turbulent, spirited history and particular flair for backing the losing side have lived up to the name given her by her Norse founders of *Dubh-linn,* "the black pool." In every age a city of vivid personalities, including such stellar literary lights as George Bernard Shaw and William Yeats, her activity has been begotten by a social life that has a strong element of adventure, even of peculiarity. Many of these brilliant men were scholars of the notable Trinity College, Dublin's ancient seat of learning. And greatest Dublin figure of them all was Jonathan Swift; one

FOUR COURTS, DUBLIN — Ireland Dept. of External Affairs

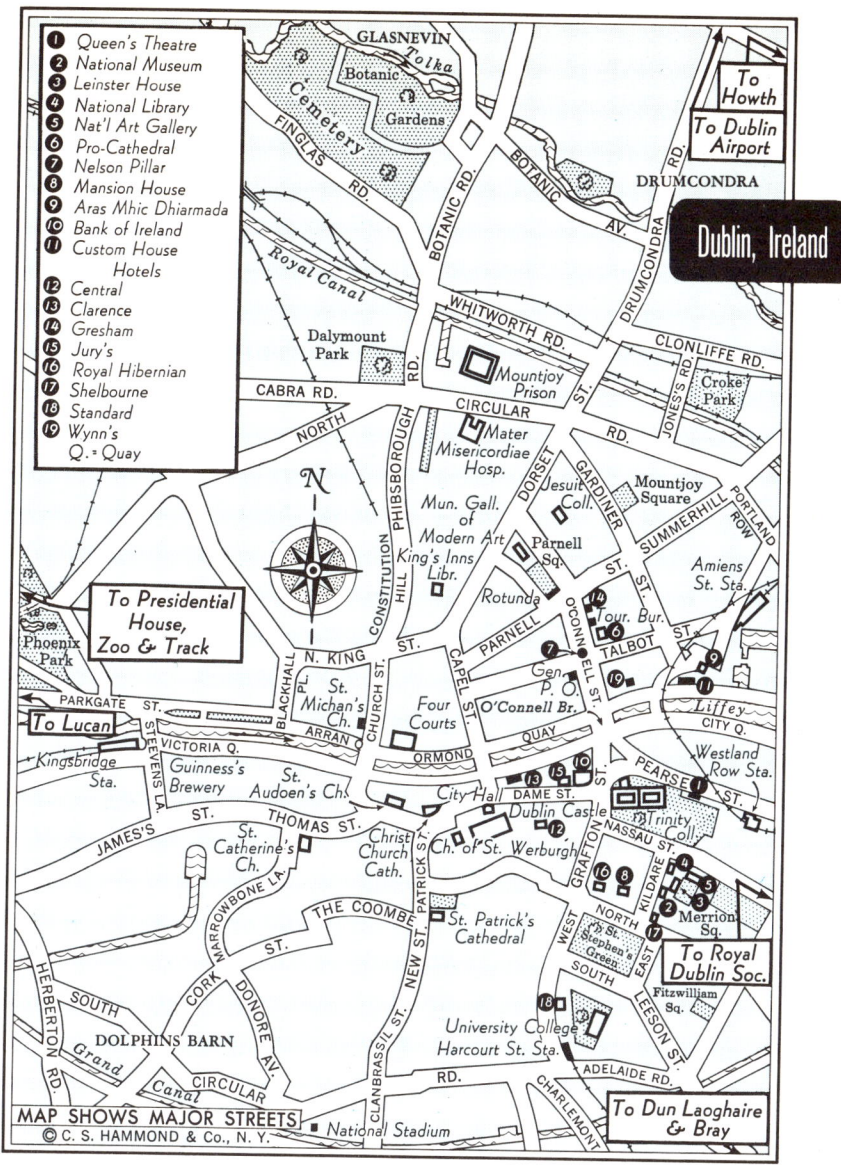

Dublin, Ireland

1. Queen's Theatre
2. National Museum
3. Leinster House
4. National Library
5. Nat'l Art Gallery
6. Pro-Cathedral
7. Nelson Pillar
8. Mansion House
9. Aras Mhic Dhiarmada
10. Bank of Ireland
11. Custom House

Hotels
12. Central
13. Clarence
14. Gresham
15. Jury's
16. Royal Hibernian
17. Shelbourne
18. Standard
19. Wynn's

Q. = Quay

MAP SHOWS MAJOR STREETS
© C. S. HAMMOND & Co., N.Y.

senses his somber and powerful personality ever imminent behind the life of the city. Gay, quick-witted, eccentric, famous, the Dubliner is embodied in a popular street ballad: "Oh, Dublin City, there is no doubtin',/Is the finest city upon the sea—/'Tis there you may see O'Connell spoutin',/And Lady Morgan making tea."

THE REST OF LEINSTER

Domed granite mountains, wooded valleys, deep glens, clear lakes and streams, moorland and bog and picturesque villages characterize the scene. All may be visited easily from Dublin. Just south of Dublin is the big yachting center of DUN LAOGHAIRE, BRAY, popular resort, and KILLINEY with its beautiful bay rivaling that of Naples. . . . An hour's drive south takes you through bold passes and glens of richly wooded beauty into the Wicklow Mountains, "The Garden of Ireland," with vast expanses of purple heath and golden furze. While here visit AVOCA, "The Meeting of the Waters," about which Thomas Moore created the poem, and GLENDALOUGH (Glen of two Lakes), a summer resort of great beauty. The "Seven Churches" here, primitive ecclesiastical stonework at least a thousand years old, are associated with St. Kevin and the beginnings of Christianity in Ireland. . . . See the picturesque old fishing town of WEXFORD with its narrow, winding streets. Each year Wexford stages a Festival of Music and Ballet which is exceptional. Nearby is the Norman Johnstown Castle. . . . KILKENNY is a city steeped in Ireland's history. From the nearby quarries it receives the title of "The Marble City." See the Cathedral of St. Canice, with its beautiful central tower and the Tholsel, or tollhouse, with its curious clock tower and front arcade. . . . Between Dublin and Kildare is the famous Curragh, where some of the best racing stock on earth is produced. . . . In the Royal County of Meath is TARA, site chosen by the High Kings of Ireland for their palaces. Here you can explore the beautiful Valley of the Boyne, famous as a battlesite and as a trout and salmon fishing region. . . . The counties of Westmeath and Longford abound in beautiful lakes and streams, including the Shannon in the center of Ireland. This area is dear to the hearts of sportsmen and sightseers alike. MULLINGAR, with its fine Cathedral, LONGFORD, a quaint market town, or ATHLONE on the Shannon make good headquarters from which to explore this beautiful country. . . . On the coast is the smallest county of Leinster, Louth. DUNDALK, its thriving industrial town, is convenient to a number of interesting spots: Carlingford Lough, renowned for its beauty; Blackrock, with good beaches; Greenore, excellent sea-fishing; Drogheda, an old and interesting seaport-industrial town on the Boyne, with St. Peter's Church, in which is the well preserved head of Ireland's martyr-saint, Blessed Oliver Plunket.

ULSTER

Ulster is a delightful combination of rugged mountains, intensively cultivated farms, great and small lakes and cities whose products are sold the world over.

BELFAST. Belfast, capital and largest city of Northern Ireland, is an industrial center whose large rope and linen factories have made its name almost synonymous with the fine Irish linen cloth and linen cord produced here. Its great shipyards, in operation since the late 18th century, have carried its fame to the corners of the earth. At the head of Belfast Lough, a small arm of the Irish Sea, the city is situated in surroundings of great natural beauty. The rugged glens of Antrim, the pretty farms of County Down and the vast blue expanse of Lough Neagh are close at hand. The focal point of the city is Donegall Square around which are found the Linen Hall Library and the City Hall. In front of City Hall stands a monument commemorating the

COUNTY ANTRIM British Information Services

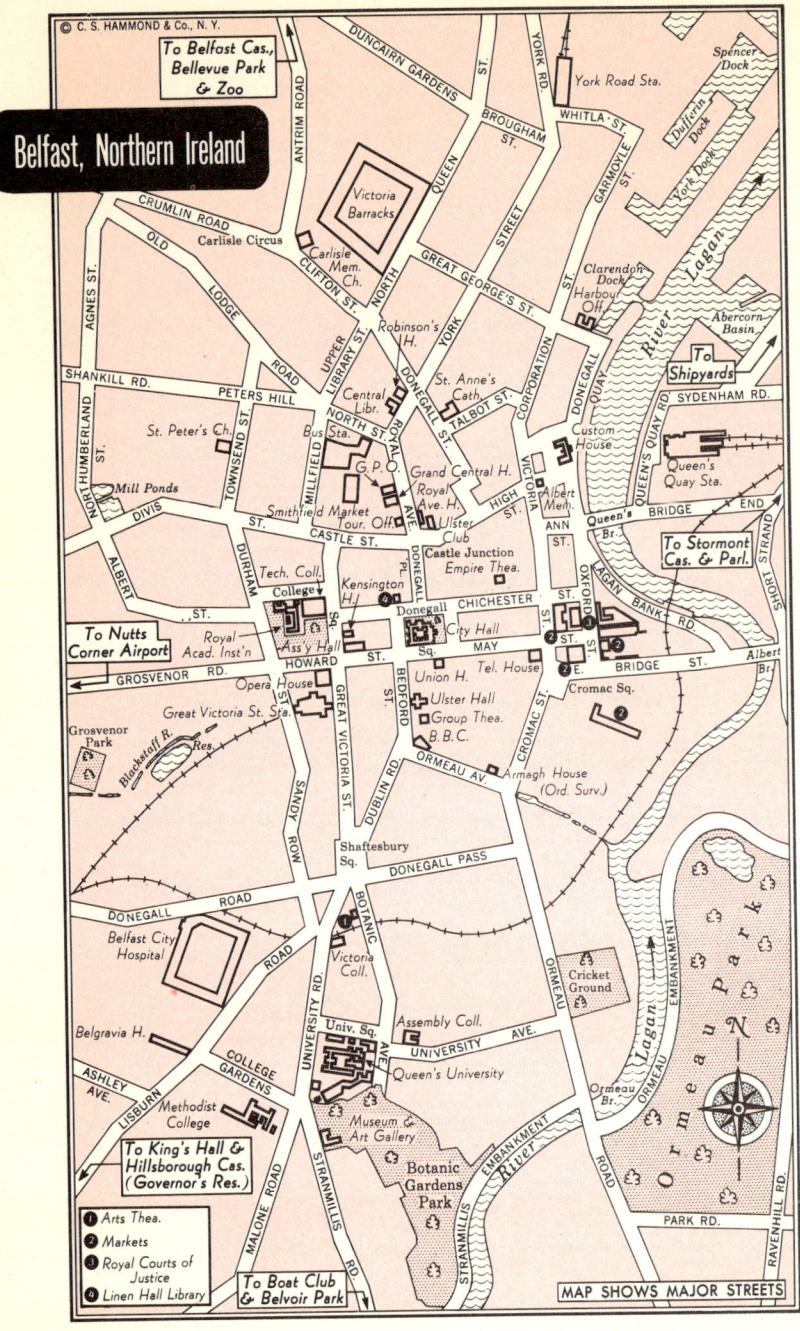

Stranraer; **BALLYCASTLE**, a resort with the fantastic Giant's Causeway and **PORTRUSH**, a golfing and seaside resort with fine beaches. Inland, see **ANTRIM**, with a **Round Tower** dating from the 10th century; **Lough Neigh**, largest lake in Ireland; **BALLYCLARE**, noted for good linens and **LISBURN**, in the valley of the Lagan, with the Maze Race Course.... County Down is rich agricultural country which combines low soft hills with the stark beauty of the **Mountains of Mourne** as they sweep down to the sea. Along the coast are the fine resorts **Bangor, Donaghadee** and **Warrenpoint** in the south, backed by the mountains.... Visit historic **DOWNPATRICK** and nearby **Inch Abbey** at the end of **Strangford Lough**. Visit **BANBRIDGE**, on the River Bann, famous in song and as a golfing and fishing center.... See **NEWCASTLE** at the foot of **Slieve Donard**, a sports center with a fine beach and easy access to the **Mournes** and **ARDGLASS**, famous for its herring.... County Armagh is a gentle county, noted for its apple orchards. Visit **ARMAGH**, the Ecclesiastical capital of Ireland, and its magnificent **Cathedral** on a hilltop overlooking the town.... **PORTADOWN** is a quiet town, where sports of all types are found in plenty and where you can buy good linen or pottery. The flower nurseries here are famous for their exquisite roses, including the newly perfected **blue rose**.... Derry is a county of many contrasts with much to attract tourists. Near good salmon and trout fishing, **LONDONDERRY** is an historical city where may be seen parts of the old city walls. Don't miss a visit to the Guildhall and to **Ship Quay Street**. See the **Cathedral** at the top of Gt. James' St.... Visit **COLERAINE**, famous for its linen and whiskey and **PORTSTEWART**, a resort noted for its safe beaches and coves.... Inland, **Tyrone County** is a mosaic of mountains, glen, river and lake, dominated by the Sperrin Mountains. **DUNGANNON**, once the stronghold of the O'Neill Clan and now a bustling center for the linen industry and a first-class base for sport, offers golf, fishing and horse-racing.... **OMAGH**, too, offers good fishing and golf and makes a convenient center for tour-

days which American soldiers, sailors and airmen spent in Northern Ireland prior to the invasion of North Africa and Europe. Royal Avenue and Donegall Place comprise the main shopping thoroughfares where the famous Belfast linens are sold. On the outskirts of Belfast are some of its finest buildings; Queens University, the Art Gallery and Museum in the beautiful botanical gardens and the Parliament buildings in Stormont Park. The people of Belfast are, for the most part, of Scottish and English descent and overwhelmingly Protestant in their religious faith; therefore, the city has long been a hub of opposition to Irish Home Rule.... From Belfast you can explore the Antrim coast and the famous and beautiful rugged **Glens of Antrim**. Coastal towns to visit include: **CARRICKFERGUS**, famous for its salt mines; **LARNE**, port for trips to

BELFAST HARBOR
British Information Services

GATHERING TURF, CONNEMARA Irish Travel Association

ing the beautiful valleys among the **Sperrin Mountains**. . . . Other attractive towns include **STRABANE, COOKSTOWN, POMEROY** and **BENBURB**, where the historic Battle of 1646 was fought and victory achieved by Owen Roe O'Neill. . . . **County Fermanagh** has some of the most wonderful lake scenery in Ireland. **ENNISKILLEN** is the link between **Upper and Lower Lough Erne** and has an interesting **Castle** and **Cathedral**. Near here is **Devenish Island** with one of the finest **round towers** in Ireland. . . . Visit **BELLEEK**, famous for its lovely, delicate china and pottery and **GARRISON** on the shores of Lough Melvin, famous for its "Sonaghan" and "Gillaroo" trout. . . . In the western part of the county are a number of interesting caves to explore. . . . **County Cavan** consists mainly of undulating pastoral land dotted with many mineral springs. Everywhere you will see cattle grazing and acre upon acre of potatoes. The town of **CAVAN**, with its interesting modern **cathedral**, is well-situated in the center of good hunting, shooting and fishing country. . . . Perhaps the most beautiful area of Cavan lies around **VIRGINIA**, with the lovely **Lake of Ramor** nearby, where you may swim, fish or boat. . . . **Monaghan** is a county of small hills, high hedges, twisting roads and a myriad of beautiful lakes. Here you will love the ancient market town of **MONAGHAN**, **CASTLEBLAYNEY**, another market town, with its famous **Hope Castle** and **CLONES**, famous for its **crochet lace** and **11th-century cross** in the market place. . . . **CARRICKMACROSS** is the home of the precious **Carrickmacross lace**. . . . The beauty of **County Donegal** is known the world over. Blue skies, high mountains, golden beaches, frowning cliffs give it an atmosphere all its own. An attractive holiday center is the seaside resort **BUNDORAN**, with its fine, sunny climate. . . . In the middle of **Lough Derg** is a tiny island where thousands of pilgrims go each year to St. Patrick's Purgatory to fast and do penitence. . . . The "wee" neat town of **DONEGAL** is scenically situated at the head of Donegal Bay. It boasts of the imposing ruins of **Donegal Castle**, the old stronghold of the O'Donnell Clan, **Donegal Abbey** and a striking modern **Church of the Four Masters**. . . . High on the banks of the River Erne, **BALLYSHANNON** is a popular seaside resort. . . . Southwestern Donegal is where the Donegal tweed industry centers and cottage industries and crafts abound. Two main centers are **KILCAR** and **ARDARA**. . . . North of **Dungloe** the fabulous country called **The Rosses** is as unspoiled now as a thousand years ago. Here is a combination of wild heather, strewn mountains peppered with unusual rocks, across which streams jump, struggle and gurgle the song of the Highlands of Donegal. And here flourishes the Gaelic tongue. . . . Near **MILFORD**, one of the best fishing areas, you can visit **Golan Loop** and **The Fairy Glen**. . . . The **Inishowen Peninsula**, between Loughs Swilly and Foyle contains a number of delightful holiday resorts. Along the coast are excellent, safe beaches. . . . To the south are the twin towns **BALLYBOFEY** and **STRANORLAR** astride the River Finn, both famous for salmon fishing par excellence.

CONNACHT

Connacht comprises a region of vast expanses of bogland, bare mountains, steep cliffs and beautiful lakes. In County Galway, you must see the ancient city of **GALWAY** on famed Galway Bay. Here you can see the **Spanish Arch** and **Spanish Parade**, Lynch's Castle, where you will learn the derivation of the word lynching, **Eyre Square** with its charming little **statue** of Padraic O'Conaire, one of Ireland's best-loved writers, marking the town's center, and the **Church of St. Nicholas**, where Columbus prayed before setting out for America. One of Ireland's great natural phenomena occur at the **Salmon Weir Bridge** where thousands of salmon pause on their journey to the vast stretches of Lough Corrib. If you are here in July, don't miss the **Galway Races**, a major social event. . . . From Galway steamers will take you to picturesque **Aran Islands**, locale of Flaherty's fascinating documentary film, "Man of Aran." . . . Island-dotted **Lough Corrib** affords the best trout fishing. . . . West of Galway is the fabulous wild, mountainous region, **Connemara**, dominated by the **"Twelve Pins,"** a stretch of land whose scenery changes with every shower and ray of sunshine. Northeast of this area is **Joyce's Country**, a paradise for hikers and climbers, famous for its picturesque mountain scenery. . . . Other places to visit in Galway are **Tuam**, with

DONEGAL FARMHOUSE Irish Travel Association

COBH, COUNTY CORK Irish Travel Association

its Cathedral and **Cross of Tuam**; **Ballinasloe**, famous for its October Horse and Cattle Fair and as a resort, and **Gort**, with its **leaning round tower** and queer **caves** with underground streams. . . . **County Mayo** is an area of small farms and more magnificent mountain and Atlantic scenery. . . . Connected to the mainland by a narrow bridge is the artist's haven and the nation's playground, **Achill Island** with its ocean air and its vast stretches of silvery strand lying between towering cliffs. Here nature is at its grandest; the seaward cliff face drops two thousand feet sheerly into ocean depths and though the strong winds blow, there is no bitterness in their blast. . . . On beautiful Clew Bay, the town of **WESTPORT** has a Continental air, its rows of lime trees lining the Mall by the river. . . . Nearby is **Croagh Patrick**, the lofty peak St. Patrick is said to have climbed that he might banish all snakes and venomous things from Ireland forever into the wide ocean. . . . **Sligo** is another beautiful sea-side county with a lake district that rivals Killarney. **SLIGO** is a busy and important market town and is a good center for exploring the Northwest of Ireland. . . . Nearby is **Lough Gill** with the small island of **Innisfree** mentioned by Yeats in his "The Lake Isle of Innisfree" and the **Caves of Kesh**. . . . **STRANDHILL** is a pleasant resort on the coast and, if you are a golfer, you should not miss the championship course at **ROSSES POINT**. . . . See Ballymote, with the remains of the Franciscan Friary and the castle built in 1300. . . . Two lakes set in great beauty are **Lough Gara**, and wind and rain-swept **Lough Talt** in the Ox Mountains, a good fishing lake. . . . County Leitrim has sent many of its sons and daughters to the U. S. It is a region of quiet and pleasant scenery, good hunting and fishing. Visit **CARRICK-ON-SHANNON**, a good center for hunting, shooting, tennis, fishing and other sports. . . . Lough Melvin is the native home of the "Gillaroo" and "Sonaghan" trout, both real "fightin' fish." . . . County Roscommon is an inland county which produces potatoes and has excellent cattle and sheep grazing land. In an abbey on an island in **Lough Key**, situated in scenic grandeur, is where were written the "Annals of Lough Cé" which now repose in the Trinity library in Dublin. . . . In ROSCOMMON see the Castle built in 1268 and the Cisterian Abbey built in 1257.

MUNSTER

Occupying the southwest of Ireland, Munster Province contains some of Ireland's greatest beauty spots. In the city of CORK, on the majestic River Lee, you will not want to miss **Shandon Church** with its famous bells, the modernistic church of **Christ the King**, the very beautiful **Franciscan Church**, famous for its murals, and the **Cork Public Museum**. . . . Six miles from Cork is **BLARNEY CASTLE**, where you may hang by the ankles and kiss the famous **Blarney Stone**. . . . On the coast are many attractive spots: **BALLYCOTTON**, famous for deep-sea angling; **CROSSHAVEN**, yachting, swimming and fishing center; **YOUGHAL**, with its fine beach and **COURTMACSHERRY**, with fine sea and river bathing and fishing. . . . Characteristic of West Cork, which couples some of the most beautiful scenery of Ireland with a glorious Atlantic coast line, is **Glengarriff**, with beauty beyond words. Here you find a mild climate, sub-tropical vegetation and the wonderful **Garnish Island**, featuring a delightful Italian garden. . . . County Kerry is probably the most beautiful part of Ireland. The towering hills, the wild Atlantic coast and the lush loveliness of Lakes of Killarney, make a visit to Kerry a "must." Make **KILLARNEY** with its lovely **Cathedral of St. Patrick**, your base for sightseeing and starting place for the fascinating "**Ring of Kerry**," an enchanting tour. You will see **PUCK FAIR**, where the Goat is crowned each August; **DERRYNANE**, birthplace of the Irish Liberator, Daniel O'Connell; **PARKNASILLA**, a beautiful resort, and **Windy Gap** which will give you one of the most spectacular views in Ireland. Visit **DINGLE** amidst rugged beauty and pre-historic ruins. Off-shore are the **Blasket Islands**. See **TRALEE**, capital of "The Kingdom," and **BALLYBUNION**, a popular resort with good golfing. . . . County Limerick and County Clare offer more typical Irish scenery with many lakes for good fishing and hunting and scattered ruins of old castles and abbeys. Here is famous **Shannon Airport**, where you can buy souvenirs, and the modern, bustling city of **LIMERICK**, with well-preserved Georgian buildings. See **King John's Castle**, the **Treaty Stone** and **St. Mary's Cathedral**. . . . From **ENNIS** you can tour the unique region of West Clare with the awesome **Cliffs of Moher**. . . . County Tipperary, famous in song, is rich, undulating, pastoral country. Visit **TIPPERARY** and **CASHEL**, famous for the prominent **Rock of Cashel**, where the Irish Kings were crowned.

ROCK OF CASHEL Irish Tourist Bureau

CLIFDEN, CONNEMARA Irish Travel Association

EUROPE

1. Courtyard of the Alhambra, famed Moorish palace, Granada, Spain
2. The majestic Acropolis, crowned by the Parthenon, rises above Athens, Greece
3. Rapallo, Italy, a fashionable seaside resort, popular with both Italians and foreigners
4. Rock of Gibraltar, mighty British stronghold, guards the entrance to the Mediterranean
5. A donkey pricks up a long ear as two Italian women exchange local gossip
6. Ancient stone windmills are still in use on the Balearic Islands, Spain

EUROPE

1. A woman leads her oxcart laden with sugar beets to market, Hesse, Germany
2. Man with an alpen horn, Lucerne, Switzerland
3. Canals thread their way through the heart of Amsterdam, capital of the Netherlands
4. The "Pferdeschwemme," a watering place for horses, Salzburg, Austria
5. The Bavarian Alps tower above Mittenwald, Germany, famed for the manufacture of violins

EUROPE

1. Basilica of St. Peter, world's largest cathedral, Vatican City, Rome, Italy
2. Göta Canal winds through 400 miles of scenic Swedish countryside
3. "The Little Mermaid" gazes across the harbor of Copenhagen, Denmark
4. Quaint picture-book towns nestle among the mountains of Switzerland
5. World's most northern city, Hammerfest, Norway is an important whaling port

EUROPE

1. The British Houses of Parliament tower above the River Thames, London, England
2. A crofter's cottage on the wild lonely and still-primative island of Skye, Scotland
3. The Arc de Triomphe symbol of national honor, stands in the Place de l'Etoile, Paris, France
4. "Beefeaters" in their colorful scarlet, black and gold uniforms guard the Tower of London, London, England
5. The graceful monument to Sir Walter Scott is a landmark of Edinburgh, Scotland

France

PARIS AND FRANCE

"La Belle France," a picturesque, exciting country of love for people of all ages has a unique appeal to the traveler. From lovely Paris, "City of Light," to Normandy and Brittany, land of Calvados and strawberries, to the quaint Basque country in the Pyrenees, to Strasbourg, of *pâté-de-foi-gras* fame, to the swank resorts of the Riviera, the people, customs, scenery — all are equally charming. Go to France to see Paris but don't forget to see as much as possible of the rest of France.

SMOOTH HIGHWAYS INTO THE PAST

While reveling in the enjoyment of her material pleasures, you will, as every visitor to this traditional land of liberty and fraternity, permanently enrich your own life with the heritage of Europe recorded in France's historic palaces, magnificent museums and Gothic cathedrals and storied past. Each region is easily accessible by smooth highways and national and local bus and rail service provide inexpensive travel. The people of each region still cherish their ancient customs and rituals and, especially on "fete" days, their colorful native dress. In Alsace, on the least provocation, gay processions march along the streets accompanied by shouts, bells, drums, bugles and flags flying high. In Normandy still can be seen processions of the "Charitons," dressed in their silver and gold embroidered costumes, escorted by bell-ringers and standard bearers. Women of Brittany still wear their charming lace caps and the men, their native suits. Everywhere past and present suffuse, making a delightful land and people.

DINE AND WINE WITH ABANDON

The art of preparing delectable dishes is instinctive with the French. Nowhere else in the world can be found the variety and mouth-watering goodness of their concoctions, from the "Cordon bleu" restaurants to the smallest of provincial inns. Good food deserves good wine and the wine of France is superb. To say nothing of her beautiful liqueurs. Let your "host" guide you in selecting typical local dishes and suggesting which wine to serve with each course, and by all means, forget diets and eat to your heart's content. Subtlety in the use of spices is the keynote of the French cuisine. However, the food is never spicy in the "hot" sense of the word, except for an occasional speciality. Chicken (*poulet, poularde*) and duck (*canard*) prepared in 1001 ways, according to the region, is always delicious. Shell fish specialities like *moules marinère* (mussels steeped in white wine), *crayfish bisque, crevettes* (shrimp) and, as a matter of fact, all fish dishes look and taste so good, even non-fish eaters find themselves savoring each morsel. Desserts in each region are intriguing. There seems an unending variety of little cakes, filled or not with some delicious cream, souffles, tarts, *crepes* (those delicious little pancakes flavored with different liqueurs), and fruit, fresh or preserved, served in any of the luscious flavored liqueurs. And with dessert comes the *fromage* (cheese) of which there is also an unending variety, a type to suit every taste. France is the home of such famous cheeses as Roquefort, Brie, Camembert and many others. One could go on forever, but let it suffice that you will heartily enjoy eating your way through France.

PANTHEON French Govt. Tourist Office

PARIS. Synonymous with gaiety, good food for gastronomes, gorgeous gowns, delectable wine, all the good things of life, is unrivaled, appealing Paris. The early morning mists on the Seine, the lazy-plying barges, the ever-patient fishermen, the spellbinding orators in the Chamber of Deputies, the gaunt, leafless trees along the quays in the fall, the flowering horse-chestnut trees in the spring, the breath-taking vistas from the bridges, the ageless, awe-inspiring beauty of the churches, the avid poets and painters, all this and much, much more is Paris. For centuries generation after generation of people from all over the world have gravitated to her narrow alleys and wide boulevards, for Paris "is not just a city, she is a world." To women, she is the undisputed center of high fashion, the acknowledged authority on what well-dressed beauties everywhere should wear. As style leader, the showings of top Paris dress designers draw all the editors, manufacturers and buyers of the fashion world, while their collections continually attract wealthy shoppers and less-wealthy window-shoppers. The noted Rue de la Paix is identical with Parisian elegance, an air every woman openly or secretly strives to exude. Not only the epitome of glamour, this fabulous capital has been a focal point of culture, too. In Paris, history, poetry and art sit on every doorstep, set the backdrop for everyday living, and great painters, musicians and writers have all been caught in the seductive web she weaves. The left bank of the Seine, lined by the famous open-air book stalls, is the intellectual and governmental section. Here is the Sorbonne, center of the University of Paris, perhaps the most influential and greatest school of liberal arts in Europe; the classical Church of Saint-Sulpice, with famous paintings by Delacroix, and noteworthy Saint-Germain-de-Pres, oldest church in Paris, dating from the eleventh century. The gallery of nearby Ecole des Beaux Arts, scene of the annual wild Art Students' Ball, displays works of Fragonard, David and Ingres. Radiating from the university is the Latin Quarter, second oldest and one

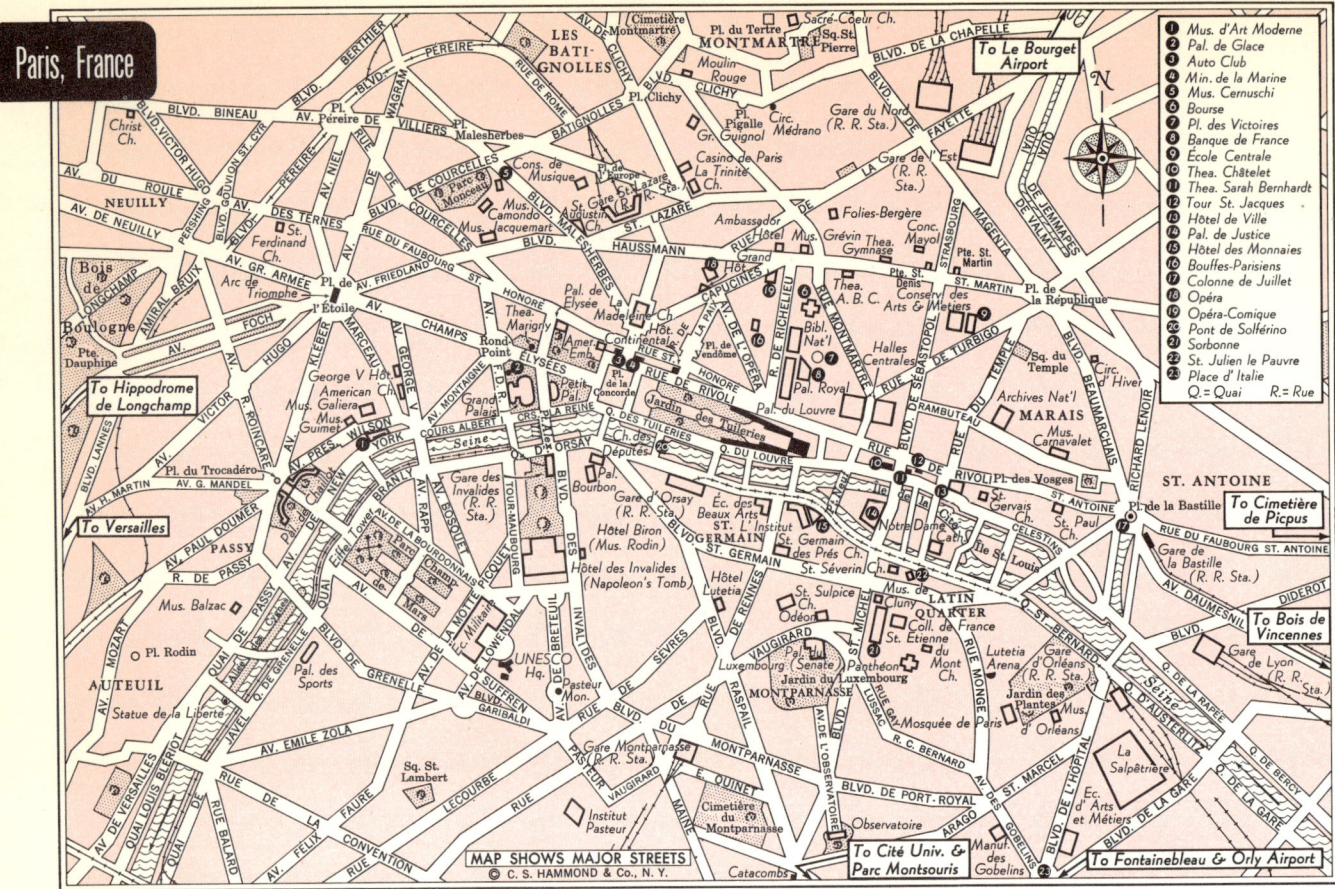

Paris, France

ILE DE LA CITE — Pan American World Airways

EIFFEL TOWER — TWA—Trans World Airlines

of the most picturesque sections in the city. For centuries these streets around Boulevard Saint-Michel have been the haunt of university students and teachers. Also in this area are the Cluny Museum, one of the fine medieval buildings still standing in Paris, housing a rare collection of medieval arts and crafts, and the Luxembourg Palace and Museum, surrounded by its beautiful gardens, housing contemporary painting and sculpture. The Quai d'Orsay is the center of government agencies, notably the foreign office, and the Chamber of Deputies sits in the Palais Bourbon. Although Frenchmen enjoy the luxury of disparaging their elected representatives and other parliaments sometimes are astonished at the

26

instability of French governments, attendance at a session of the Deputies is a most exciting experience, for the powerful, fiery oratory heard everyday in this hall is the most brilliant of any such gathering on earth. The right bank also contains a number of cultural attractions, including the Palais Royal, the Cardinal Richelieu palace where Louis XIV lived as a boy. In one wing is the Theatre Francais, or Comedie Francais, France's great national theater, which was founded by Louis. Avenue de l'Opera, leading from the palace to the Opera House, was the crowning achievement in the city planning of Baron Haussmann, Napoleon's prefect who inaugurated huge municipal improvements, concentrating particularly on the handsome wide boulevards and public garden parks, trademarks of modern Paris. Across from the Palais Royal is the enormous Bibliotheque Nationale, probably the best in the world, with especially fine collections in the Medals and Antiquities Room. Of course, no one ever forgets the glittering, clamorous Paris, the night life of Gay Paree. Here the streets are dark and menacing, figures hover in dimly lighted passageways and your imagination can easily recapture the atmosphere of stealth, brutality, robbery and murder in this, the heart of the former Paris underworld. Cabarets once frequented by notorious night birds are still found in the quarter, where apache and adagio dancers whirl in wild abandon — a dramatic contrast to the equally famous, smart night clubs with their atmosphere of discreet elegance. Most bewitching of all, however, is the Parisian himself. Shop girl, professor, sophisticated mannequin, artist or subway conductor, no matter what his profession, he is a special brand of exuberance, ironic gaiety and careless indifference — a unique combination of endless fascination. The ancient winding streets of Paris, the sidewalk cafes, the fine shops, the lovely public gardens and parks, the scintillating crowds unite to form a colorful mosaic of human warmth and culture.

IN THE ENVIRONS OF PARIS

VERSAILLES, nine miles southwest of Paris, is the vast, magnificent palace of Louis XIV surrounded by its park with probably the most beautiful gardens in the world. In the park are the **Grand and Petit Trianons**, pavilions built for the pleasures of Louis XIV, Madame Du Barry and later, Marie Antoinette. Visit the Museum, the fabulous **Hall of Mirrors** where the Peace Treaty was signed in World War I, the **Royal Suites** and Marie Antoinette's charming **hamlet**. The great **fountains** are turned on the first Sunday of each month from May to September. On the way to Versailles, don't miss a visit to the **porcelain factory** and museum at SEVRES. . . . RAMBOUILLET, thirty-five miles southwest of Paris, in the forest of Yveline, is the summer residence of the President of France. Francis I died here. The forest, intersected by valleys and lakes, is one of the loveliest of the Ile de France. . . . Still further is CHAR-

THE TUILERIES, PARIS

TRES, fifty miles southwest of Paris, with its famous **cathedral**, the finest Gothic cathedral in the world. Its statuary and stained-glass windows are superb.

Another great palace, FONTAINEBLEAU, sits in the heart of a vast forest twenty-five miles southeast of Paris. It dates to the 12th century and is full of memories of the court. Louis XIII was born here. Since Philippe-Auguste the kings of France have all added to it through the works of such great artists as da Vinci, Cellini and the noted gardener, Le Notre. A favorite residence of Napoleon, the striking interior decorations and Empire style furniture, the **throne room**, the **abdication room** all seem to be shrouded still with his personality. The **horse-hoof staircase** in the great courtyard was the scene of his farewell to the old guard in 1814. . . . Also deep in the forest of Fontainebleau is the village of BARBIZON which gave its name to the 19th century school of painting. Millet, Rousseau, Corot, Troyon and Dupré all lived here. Near here Millet painted his celebrated "Angelus."

Northwest of Paris is **ST.-GERMAIN-EN-LAYE**. The original chateau was built by Louis IX, but the rebuilding of Francis I has left only the **chapel** of the first building. Louis XIII lived here and Louis XIV was born here. In the palace is a wonderful museum of **Gallo-Roman antiquities**. The surrounding forest is a favorite holiday spot for Parisians. . . . On the way to St. Germain visit MALMAISON, residence of the Empress Josephine which houses a museum of Napoleonic mementoes.

SAINT DENIS, six miles northeast of Paris, is the burial place of the French Kings and is filled with **statuary and carving** representing the entire sweep of French history to the death of Louis XVIII. All that remains of the original abbey, built by Dagobert, Pepin and Charlemagne is the **crypt**. The **porch** and **two towers** date from the reconstruction of the Abbot Suger in the 12th century. The rest dates from the time of St. Louis, in the 13th century. . . . Twenty miles northeast of Paris, CHANTILLY is famous for the estate of the Constable de Montmorency which became the property of Prince de Condé in the 16th century. It contains a fine **park** designed by Le Notre and a **chateau** restored by the Duc d'Aumale in the 19th century. In the library is the famous medieval **illuminated manuscript**, the "Grandes Heures de Duc de Berry." This is the birthplace of the luscious *Creme Chantilly* or "whipped cream." . . . Further northeast is SENLIS with its 12th century **cathedral** and ruins of an old

HALL OF MIRRORS, VERSAILLES
French Govt. Tourist Office

Roman fortress and the Roman wall around the town. . . . Fifty miles northeast, in another great forest, the town of COMPIEGNE was the scene of the capture of Joan of Arc and where she was sold to the British for trial and burning as a witch. Here is an old Renaissance town-hall and a stately chateau built by Gabriel. It was here the Armistice was signed in 1918 and again when Hitler forced the French to sign in 1940.

At MEAUX, twenty-five miles east of Paris, is a beautiful 12th century cathedral. Its tower gives a good view of the field of the first Battle of the Marne in 1914. . . . Of particular interest to Americans is CHATEAU THIERRY, fifty miles east of Paris, which was the center of the battlefields of World War I. Near here is the American cemetery.

EASTERN FRANCE AND ALSACE

Picturesque little villages with peaked rooftops surmounted by the traditional stork nests nestle in deep valleys and thick forests. The scenery is eye-filling, the local inns are famous for their excellent food and Alsatian wines and the people are charming, friendly and colorfully costumed.

On the way to Nancy see VERDUN, dramatic symbol of World War I, and visit the forts and the Memorial. If possible, take a side trip to the fortified city of METZ which has many 13th to 15th century houses and the 13th century cathedral of St. Etienne. . . . On to NANCY . . . . city of King Stanislas. Visit the Town Hall, the Duke's Palace and, by all means, the Place Stanislas with its imposing wrought iron gates. . . . Near by more battlefields of World War I can be visited. . . . STRASBOURG . . . . beautiful, artistic capital city of Alsace, is interesting for its 11th century Gothic cathedral and its famous clock with moving figures, for the Church of St. Thomas where the Maréchal de Saxe is buried and the museum-palace of the Dukes of Rohan. The old districts have many quaint houses such as the Kammerzell, a beautiful 16th century Alsatian house, now an excellent restaurant.

The trip through the Vosges below Strasbourg is most delightful. . . . At COLMAR visit the Musée d'Unterlinden. . . . Continue through the 15th century village of OBERNAI to pictureque and historic hilltop of Ste. Odile, to the HOHWALD and the castle of Hoch Koenigsbourg which offers a panoramic view. . . . Near here are a number of quaint villages, including SELESTAT, RIBEAUVILLE and ORBEY, all famous for their vintage wines and good food. . . . GERARDMER, in the lake district, is famous for its cheese and as a resort. . . . Also in the Vosges is one of France's most beautiful spas, VITTEL. . . . Near here is the village of DOMREMY where Joan of Arc was born in 1412.

THE CHAMPAGNE COUNTRY

This is the country roughly limited by the triangle formed by Epernay on the south, Chalons-sur-Marne on the east and

ORANGERIE, VERSAILLES
French Govt. Tourist Office

Reims on the north, and from which, say the French, must come all the wine that bears this name.

In REIMS . . . . . . is the famous and magnificent 13th century Cathedral with its exquisite **rose window**, the **Fine Arts Museum** and the nearby **Fort de la Pompelle**. Spend an afternoon at one of the famous **champagne cellars**, Pommery for instance. . . . In EPERNAY it is worth while to see the **caves of Moet et Chandon**, a favorite place of Napoleon's. . . . Near Epernay, on the hill, is the lovely village of HAUTVILLIERS with its ancient **abbey**. Here tradition says, the happy monk Dom Perignon discovered in about 1700 the wonderful secret of bubbling champagne.

NORMANDY AND BRITTANY

This region compares favorably with any other in Europe for tourist appeal. The haunt of artists and writers, these provinces have a unique beauty. The people and the land have grown together in complete harmony. Quaint market towns, brightly colored regional costumes, rough hewn houses, colorful fishing ports, attractive farmsteads, green forests, rocky isles, sand beaches and the tang of salt air all combine to make a tourist paradise. Steeped in history, the region also boasts of many shrines, feudal castles, abbeys and medieval monuments and some of the most beautiful cathedrals in France. Incidentally, one can travel here for very little, especially in Brittany where hotels and pensions average from four to five dollars a day including food. And the food is always good.

First of the Norman cathedral towns is the capital, ROUEN · · · · · · · called by Victor Hugo "the hundred-spired town," but sadly damaged in World War II. See **the cathedral** with its remarkable tower or "lantern," the churches of St. Ouen and St. Maclou, the museums, the medieval **Hotel de Bourgheroulde**, the **Gros-Horloge** and the **market place** where Joan of Arc was burned. . . . West of Rouen on the coast are the fashionable resort towns of TROUVILLE and DEAUVILLE, either being an excellent place to week-end from Paris. But have a reservation; they're crowded in the summer months. . . . CAEN was the scene of the fierce battle in the summer of 1944 when the Allied Armies broke out of the beachhead. The grim walls of its abbeys epitomized the simplicity and severity of true Norman architecture. See the Church of St. Peter, the Abbey of St. Etienne, the Convent of the Trinity, and the Hotel d'Escoville. Local buses make trips to St. Laurent sur Mer, the U. S. Army cemetery on the bluffs overlooking **Omaha Beach**, to Vierville and Pte. du Hoe which was captured by means of rope ladders fired up the cliffs by rockets and to Utah Beach. . . . South of Caen, FALAISE is the castle town where William the Conqueror was born. . . . In BAYEUX see the superb 11th century, Norman Gothic **Cathedral of Notre Dame** and the famous 160-foot **tapestry** describing the conquest of England by William the Conqueror. The tapestry is on display in the old Episcopal Residence and is one of the most remarkable historical souvenirs extant. . . . To the southwest is ST.-LO, destroyed in June 1944, and COUTANCES with its fine **Cathedral**, one of the best examples of Norman architecture. Its **octagonal tower** or lantern is perhaps the finest of its kind in France. . . . At AVRANCHES you will get a wonderful view of **Mont Saint Michel**, one of the most inspiring monuments of all times. **Mont Saint Michel**, the great abbey on the rock in the sea, between Normandy and Brittany, is one of the great sights of the world. The huge rock, jutting 256 feet high out of the sea, is engirdled at the base with medieval turreted walls. Behind the walls the buildings of the village are scattered on three levels at the base of the rock. The lovely Gothic abbey crowns the very pinnacle, a gilded statue of St. Michael poised above

MONT ST. MICHEL

the entire structure. Visit the Abbey, the museums and be sure to take a walk around the **ramparts**. . . . On the northern coast of Brittany ST.-MALO is an interesting walled fishing port, from where Jacques Cartier sailed to discover the St. Lawrence. See the **castle of Anne of Brittany** and the **ramparts**. . . . Across the river Rance is DINARD, most popular resort of this "Emerald Coast." . . . Other towns in northern Brittany include the beautiful resorts of ST. LUNAIRE, ST. BRIAC and ST. CAST, ST. BRIEUC, the old fishing harbor of PAIMPOL, TREGUIER, birthplace of St. Yves, a small town with a medieval aspect and a cathedral which combines Gothic and Roman style, LANNION and MORLAIX.

Between Lannion and Brest is the most picturesque part of Brittany, dotted with massive granite churches with open belfries, quaint shrines and ancient monuments and customs that set the Bretons apart from the rest of France and reflect their Celtic origin and Druidical religious past. Remarkable are the religious ceremonies or Pardons (the French Tourist Bureau will give you the dates and places they occur).

From the seaport of BREST, almost completely devastated in World War II, you pass through PLOUGASTEL-DAOULAS, famous for its strawberries, on the way to QUIMPER, from where we get that charming ware decorated with figures and motifs of Breton design. Market day here is a most colorful sight. Visit the Cathedral. . . . Near by are the fishing harbors of CONCARNEAU, sardine fishing center. . . . To the east is QUIMPERLE, and the old fortress town of HENNEBONT with its interesting Breton museum. . . . At CARNAC are the famous prehistoric **dolmens** and **menhirs**, like Stonehenge in England. . . . AURAY is the shrine of Brittany and is famous for the **Pardon of Ste. Anne d'Auray** held every year on the 25th and 26th of July. . . . From the picturesque fishing port of QUIBERON, you can take a ferry to the beautiful island of Belle-Ile-en-Mer with its giant lighthouse. . . . VANNES has an excellent **museum** of Celtic and Roman antiquities, a 13th century cathedral and interesting medieval ramparts. From here trips may be taken by excursion boat to offshore islands, or by car or train to the old walled city of GUERANDE with its many towers and gates.... To the north of Vannes lies JOSSELIN, one of the most interesting castles in Brittany.... RENNES was the capital of the old duchy of Brittany in the middle ages and is still the intellectual capital of Brittany. It has many museums, a modern Cathedral, 17th century Palais de Justice and an impressive town hall in Louis XV style.... VITRE is another interesting castle town in the area.

THE LOIRE VALLEY

The district of the wonderful Chateaus of the Loire lies roughly between Orleans and Chinon, comprising the old provinces of Touraine and Anjou. Touraine, still called the "Garden of France," was the favorite playground of French Kings in the 15th and 16th centuries, and together with Anjou offers the tourist an unending variety of fabulous castles ranging in styles from medieval to refined Renaissance.

In ORLEANS, liberated by Joan of Arc in 1429, see the cathedral and the Statue to Joan in the center of the city. ... Nine miles from Blois is CHAMBORD, largest of the provincial castles and a favorite residence of Francis I, noted for its spiral staircase.... Nearby is CHEVERNY with its beautiful gardens, built by Louis XIII.... BLOIS is an interesting old city and its magnificent Renaissance castle overlooking the river recalls the pomp and pleasures of Francis I, and such ladies as Louise of Savoy, Diane de Poitiers, Catherine de Médicis and the girl who was later Mary, Queen of Scots. ... Between Blois and Tours are the castles of CHAUMONT and AMBOISE and VOUVRAY, famous for its sparkling wines.... TOURS is an attractive city connected with its suburbs by a lovely stone bridge across the Loire. See the Cathedral with its stained glass windows and fine facade, the 15th century square lined with gabled houses and the basilica where St. Martin is buried.... In the vicinity of Tours visit the castles of CHENONCEAUX, straddling the river Cher, AZAY-LE-RIDEAU, VILLANDRY, CHINON and LOCHES where cruel Louis XI tortured his victims and watched them swing from the trees of the orchard. Here he kept his unfortunate cardinal, La Balue, in a cage which permitted him neither to stand nor lie down. Above the torture chamber is the peep-hole where Louis watched the activities below.... In FONTEVRAULT see the tombs of the Plantagenets in the chapel of the famous abbey built in the 12th century.... SAUMUR is another castle town with also the well-known French cavalry school, well worth a visit.... ANGERS offers the Gothic Cathedral, the massive pentagon-shaped castle of King Rene and the world-known collection of tapestries of the Apocalypse.... Among the numerous other famous castles in the Loire Valley are LANGEAIS, LUYNES, PLESSIS-LES-TOURS, SULLY, USSÉ and VALENCAY.

VENDEE, VIENNE, THE CHARENTE

Below the Loire is a rich and pleasant countryside stretching down to the vineyards of Bordeaux. Although not as exciting tourist-wise as some other parts of France, the area is historically important and there are a number of interesting places to visit.

POITIERS was the site of the victory of the English under the Black Prince in the Hundred Years' War. The 13th century cathedral was built by Eleanor of Aquitaine and is a perfect example of Romanesque style. See the ancient Baptistry of St. Jean, the 11th century church of Ste. Radegonde and the two museums. ... Nearby is the site where Clovis defeated Alaric and his barbarian horde in 507 and where Charles Martel stopped the Saracen invasion in 732.... The historic seaport of LA ROCHELLE was the stronghold of the Huguenots. Its great watch tower and gate date from the 13th century. Of interest are its grim medieval towers, particularly the Tour St. Nicholas. ... COGNAC, along the lovely river Charente, and the neighboring town of JARNAC produce the great brandy of France. COGNAC is interesting as the birthplace of Francis I and for the chateaux-cum-warehouses of the famous manufacturers such as Hennessy, Martell and Otard, situated in the very castle of Francis I.... JARNAC, noted for Bisquit and Courvoisier, has a replica of the Louvre's Pavillon de Flore, now the main office of Courvoisier. Trips through the distilleries can be made.... ANGOULEME, home of Marguérite de Valois, sits on a high hill and is notable for the Byzantine touch of the architecture of its Cathedral of St. Pierre. BORDEAUX ...... in the heart of the world's finest wine growing district, is a city of fine restaurants. This busy port is an attractive city with a number of fine 18th

SPRINGTIME, NORMANDY

century buildings, a **Cathedral** and several important museums.... Villages near by notable for their wines are PESSAC for Graves; BLANQUEFORT and SOULAC for Médoc; BARSAC for Sauterne; and CADILLAC for St. Emilion.

BASQUE COUNTRY

Below the lake-dotted, thick, pine forests of Landes lies the country of the Basques. Here are found still preserved the picturesque customs, festivals, games and dances of a very ancient and interesting civilization.

Beautiful BIARRITZ, on the Basque coast, is one of the most elegant of the French bathing resorts with two casinos, night clubs and large hotels.... South of Biarritz are the beach resorts of GUETHARY, ST. JEAN DE LUZ and HENDAYE, on the border between France and Spain. From here you can cross the border to IRUN or SAN-SEBASTIAN.... Just north of Biarritz are the resorts of HOSSEGOR and CHIBERTA which is famous for its excellent golf course.... Next door to Biarritz is the cathedral city of BAYONNE with an historic old castle.... To really see the Basques, go inland to some of the villages and towns like USTERRITZ, MAULEON or ST.-JEAN-PIED-DE-PORT. Incidentally, there is wonderful fishing to be had near ST.-JEAN-PIED-DE-PORT, and also there are frequent exhibitions of the Basque national sport, **pelote**, a version of Jai Alai.

THE PYRENEES REGION

This is a land of bracing climate and cloudless skies, high valleys and lofty forest-clad mountains with snow and glaciers, forests and torrents, upland villages and castle-topped crags, watering-places and winter sports resorts.

PAU, in the heart of Gascony, is a major winter resort with its famous **terrace** affording a magnificent view of the mountains, its **castle** where Henry IV was born and its excellent **wine** and **pate de foi gras**. From this vicinity came a number of France's great warriors, including Jean de la Valette, d'Artagnan of the Three Musketeers and General Foch.... Miraculous LOURDES, where Bernadette saw Our Lady in 1858, attracts thousands of pilgrims each year who flock to the **basilica** erected above Bernadette's grotto.... Near by are resorts of CAUTERETS and GAVARNIE, and to the north, TARBES. This is the start of the most beautiful part of the Pyrenees.... The road to LUCHON crosses the Col d'Aspin, a pass 4500 feet in altitude, goes through BAREGES, well-known for its waters, past the impressive **Cirque de Gavarnie** (mule trips can be taken to the Cirque), via the **Tourmalet pass** (6600 ft.) and on down the valley to the "Queen of the Pyrenees," LUCHON. ... Near here are two other major resorts, BAGNERES DE BIGORRE and SUPER-BAGNERES, a summer-winter resort.... On to ST. GIRONS, LABOUICHE, known for its **underground river**, and the picturesque city of FOIX, over the Puymaurens Pass to LATOUR-DE-CAROL, a quaint little town and gateway to the romantic little principality of ANDORRA.... FONT-ROMEU, 6000 feet altitude, is the loveliest of summer resorts.... After the fortress of VILLEFRANCHE DE CONFLENT, built entirely of pink marble is PRADES, famous for its music festival where Pablo Casals was persuaded to play again.... After Prades is the entry to the LANGUEDOC, past the peak of Perthus. ... Below Perthus, on the coast, are the colorful fishing villages of BANYULS and COLLIOURE.... Northward are PERPIGNAN, with its turreted fortress and CARCASSONE, that masterpiece of medieval military architecture. The guides here are excellent and in the masonry you can trace the city's fascinating history from the time it was a Roman camp. Northwest is TOULOUSE .... capital of the Languedoc and rich in art treasures with its church of St. Sernin, the most beautiful Romanesque church in France, and a fine collection of sculpture in the Musée des Augustins. While in Toulouse, try some **cassoulet**, that famous local specialty made of lamb, pork, goose, onions, garlic and haricot beans, combined to make the most terrific thick stew you ever ate.... Northeast is ALBI, the "red city," scene of the bloody purging of the Albigesian heretics by Simon de Montfort. Blood is still suggested by the color of the construction stone of the whole city and of its extraordinary Cathedral of Ste.-Cecile. See the old quarters and monuments of mixed Roman and Gothic styles.

THE RHONE VALLEY

Provence has had a long and eventful history and one can still see in its cities founded by the Romans a number of the Old World's most impressive monuments. The terrain here is quite varied and the scenery delightful. Fertile valleys and plains dotted with vineyards, orchards, olive groves and gorgeous flowers, and, on the coast, the blue, blue sea and lush tropical foliage. Travel here is also a gastronomic delight. From here we get all those wonderful dishes *a la Provencal*, characterized by the zesty garlic and/or tomatoes. Provencales are intensely traditional and their folklore, exceptionally colorful and gay.

ORANGE boasts of its Roman theater and curious **Arch of Triumph**.... The richest, gayest, biggest city of the Valley, AVIGNON is where Pope Clement V came to set up his court in the time of the quarrels over the Papacy in the 14th century. The famous **Palace of the Popes**, the papal residence until Gregory XI returned to Rome in 1403, still stands with its great **towers** and arches. The famous bridge, **Pont d'Avignon** of the song, had

HARVEST, BORDEAUX WINE COUNTRY

French Govt. Tourist Office

originally 22 arches, of which only 3 remain.... The lords of the redoubtable **fortress of LES BAUX** were undisputed masters of Provence for years, and the medieval ruins are a tourist curiosity. Bauxite was first discovered here.... At the city of **ARLES**, with its relics of the Greek settlement five centuries before Christ, was found the famous Venus now in the Louvre. Visit the **Cloister of St. Trophime** and the two museums of art, pagan and Christian.... To the northwest lies the great monument to the Romans, **NIMES**, founded by Augustus. The most important relics are the great **Arena** where bullfights take place several times a year, the **Temple of Diana** which dates from before Christ, the **Maison Carée**, an Augustan temple, and the **Jardin de la Fontaine**. Near by is the **Pont du Gard**, a Roman acqueduct built in 19 B.C. . . . Southwest of Nimes is the winegrowing and University city of **MONTPELLIER** and near it some wonderful scenery, particularly the mountain village of **ST. GUILHELM-LE-DESERT**, favorite of painters. . . . **CAMARGUE**, the little island in the Rhone delta is a fascinating little world of its own. Local cowboys, called "guardians," herd cattle and small white horses in ranch-style. Their costumes and those of the women are most picturesque. **STE. MARIES DE LA MER**

NOTRE DAME DE LA GARDE *French Govt. Tourist Office*

is the chief center and is the shrine of the Gypsies. . . . Southeast of Avignon is **AIX-EN-PROVENCE**, capital of the scholarly king known as René the Good. **AIX** has an interesting **cathedral**, the **Cloister of St. Sauveur** and a museum of tapestries. Also near Avignon is **CHATEAU-NEUF-DU-PAPE**, famous for its fine red wines.

MARSEILLES. 2500-year-old Marseilles, France's oldest city, is a colorful, bustling port on the ageless Mediterranean. As an international sea station and long-time favorite with sailors, her whole atmosphere is permeated with the lusty flavor of the sea, giving her a definite charm and personality all her own, just as the seafarer's salty tang distinctly marks him from the landlubber. Even the accent and manner of speech of her inhabitants is unique. And since most of her trade is with the north coast of Africa, the eastern Mediterranean and the Far East, this teeming setting has an almost Oriental cast. Marseilles is noted for her world-famous bouillabaisse, that incomparable fish soup with an unusual flavor achieved here alone, because it is made with fish peculiar to this region. One of her most interesting buildings is

the curious stone church of St. Victor, with catacombs ranking among the earliest Christian evidences in Gaul. Most exciting of all, however, is the tiny island in the harbor containing the forbidding Chateau d'If, built as a castle in 1524 and later used as a state prison, made famous by the swashbuckling *Le Comte de Monte-Cristo,* by Alexandre Dumas, as the miserable dungeon from which the Count escaped.

AUVERGNE AND THE DORDOGNE

In the heart of the Massif Central, **AUVERGNE** is a country of volcanic origin. At the bottom of ancient craters lie translucent lakes surrounded by the dark-blue-green conifers, and everywhere the black lava points up the colorful villages and towns. To the south the turbulent

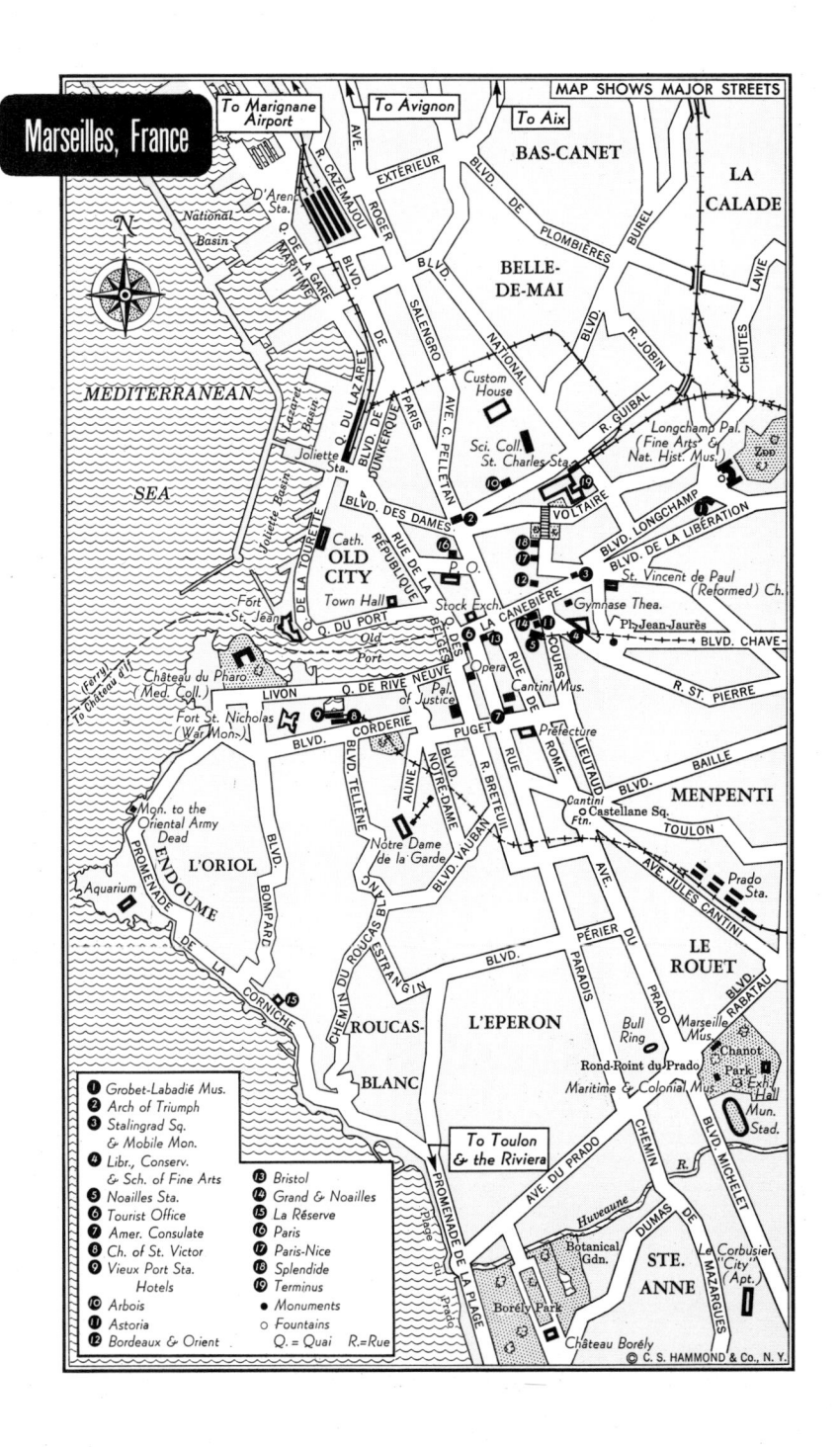

Tarn River winds through an impressive gorge. This region is known as the cradle of French architecture and on all sides are castles and magnificent churches with graceful outlines and primitive sculpture, among the best examples of Romanesque art.

LE PUY clusters around four great volcanic rocks. Long a pilgrimage center and an Episcopal see since the 6th century, the village boasts of a fine cathedral, old baptistry and a number of fine Romanesque and Gothic buildings. St. Michel, perched atop a needle rock, is one of the most photographed churches in Europe. . . . CLERMONT-FERRAND, capital of Auvergne, includes the medieval hill town of MONTFERRAND with a number of fine old houses. The Church of Notre Dame du Port is an enormous pile constructed of lava. . . . South of here, MONT-DORE at the foot of the Sancy Mountain is in the heart of the Massif Central and is well-known for its dead volcanoes and many thermal resorts. From here one can take excursions to the surrounding lakes.

Perhaps the most beautiful valley of the country, the DORDOGNE holds much to fascinate the traveler — the ever-present castles, ancient towns, the famous pre-historic caves built in rocks overhanging the river, hilltop villages, natural chasms and other natural phenomena, all of equal interest.

ROCAMADOUR is a tiny village, long a place of pilgrimage, perched atop sheer cliffs. . . . Not far from here is Padirac, a naturally formed deep chasm. . . . Near SARLAT, a pate de foi gras- and truffle-canning center were discovered the caves of Lascaux with extraordinary wall paintings suggesting Picasso. . . . PERIGUEUX, noted for rich art treasures and gastronomic delights, has the wonderful 12th century Cathedral of St. Front, perched high on a hill above the town and river, and an interesting museum of pre-historic relics. North of Périgueux is LIMOGES, capital of the Limousin and center of fine porcelain manufacture. Visits may be made to the large factories and there is a ceramics museum in the city. This was the birthplace of Renoir and the art gallery displays a number of his works. . . . Near here is the village of ORADOUR-SUR-GLANE, whose inhabitants were massacred by the Germans on June 10th, 1944. The French Government has made the village into a shrine, leaving everything as it was, including the piles of human cinders.

THE RIVIERA

No one needs to be told how beautiful is this "Cote d'Azur" with its white sand, blue sea and dazzling sunshine. An ideal vacation spot, the Mediterranean Coast offers everything from the charm of small villages to the excitement of large cities. Here is a gourmet's heaven and a water-sports fan's haven.

East of Toulon, the twisting coastal road runs along the rugged base of the Esterel Massif from ST. TROPEZ with its little white villas roofed with red tiles, through ST. MAXIME and ST. RAPHAEL to CANNES, the social capital, with its famous Promenade de la Croisette. . . . From Cannes the road leads to the chi-chi JUAN-LES-PINS and CAP D'ANTIBES. Along here gambling casinos, luxury hotels, smart bars, yachts, bikinis and underwater fishing are some of the delights to be expected. Hollywood's favorite Hotel du Cap or Eden Roc is perched on the top of a small peninsula and is noted for its small pool around which are sunned some very expensive bodies. In the old fortified town of ANTIBES is the Grimaldi Museum, to which Picasso has contributed greatly. . . . To the east is NICE · · · · · with its two casinos, big hotels, parks, shops and Promenade des Anglais, and also its old port, like an Italian town with narrow, twisting, climbing streets, noises and rich smells. Highlight of the Nice winter season (though the Riviera is now an all-year-round resort) is the famous Mardi-Gras festival, which leave the street cleaners face to face with staggering piles of flowers and confetti. . . . East of Nice the fabled Corniche Drive over the Turbie leads past VILLEFRANCHE, CAP FERRAT and BEAULIEU to MONTE CARLO in the romantic little principality of MONACO, with its own palace, courts, mint and police. Monaco exists on the gambling revenue of its gingerbread casino, but two of its principal interests are the splendid views from all parts of the massive rocks on which it is perched and the wonderful Oceanographic Museum. . . . Eastward is MENTON and its Bridge of St. Louis and SAN REMO on the Italian Riviera.

In the background of the Riviera is Upper Provence, a wild mountainous district of deep gorges in the foothills of the Alps with many hill towns of ancient stone that changes color with the light. Near Cannes is GRASSE, the perfume capital of France. . . . On the cliffs above the Cannes is VALLAURIS where Picasso has his atélier and where Rita Hayworth and Aly Khan were married. . . . In VENCE is the lovely chapel of St. Dominique decorated by Matisse. Between Cap Ferrat and Monaco is the fortified town of EZE, clinging to a sheer cliffside.

THE ALPS

The principal mountain region of France is that of the Alps, stretching from just above the Riviera through Savoy and Lake Geneva to the Jura. The Iserian Road across the French Alps is one of the most scenic and highest in Europe. Rivalling the world-famous peaks of Switzerland and Austria, these mountains have popular centers for climbing and skiing and many are only a couple of hours away from the Mediterranean. One can ski all day and, after a not-too-long drive, dine and dance at night in the snug warmth of the Riviera. Spas and watering places are among the most popular in France.

MENDING NETS, CANNES *TWA—Trans World Airlines*

33

ALPINE VILLAGE

Three of the principal spas are AIX-LES-BAINS, on beautiful Lake Bourget, ANNECY, with its long lake, and EVIAN on Lake Geneva. All have excellent facilities for sports and other recreation.

To list all ski resorts would be impossible in this limited space and the French Tourist Bureau can better tell you details concerning transportation, reservations, etc. Here we list only the major areas around which there are resorts with good facilities. In the **MONT BLANC REGION** are Mégève, Chamonix, Les Houches, St. Gervais; Les Contamines, Morzine and Las Clusaz.... In the **SAVOY REGION**, Val d'Isère, Courcheval, Les Allues and Valloire are popular centers. ... **DAUPHINE REGION** includes Alpe d'Huez and Villard-de-Lans.... The **HAUTES ALPES REGION**, Briançon, Serre Chevalier and Montgenevre.... In the **RIVIERA REGION**, Auron, Beuil and Valberg.... in the **PYRENEES REGION** are Font-Romeu and Barages.

LAND OF WINE

BURGUNDY. This ancient and historic province whose powerful dukes rivalled the kings of France, stretches roughly from LYON in the south to VEZELAY in the north and today is most notable for the delights of its vines and its kitchens. The noble wines include Chablis, Pouilly, Chambertin and Pommard.

At CLUNY is one of the most remarkable architectural and historic monuments of the region, the Abbey of Cluny, once the intellectual center of the Christian world.... In BEAUNE are the celebrated hospitals run by the monks. The most interesting is the Hotel Dieu, founded by Rollin in 1443, which preserves the aspects of the Middle Ages in its decor, uniforms and furnishings, its beds and utensils and its fascinating pharmacy. The Hotel Dieu is rich from its vineyards in Savigny, Meursault, Pommard and Volnay.... The charming town of VEZELAY, with its many medieval reminders, is celebrated as the resting-place of the bones of Mary Magdalene in the tremendous Romanesque Basilica of the Magdalene. ... In the village of ST.-PERE-SOUS-VEZELAY is a fine Gothic church.... Other cities and towns of interest in Burgundy include DIJON, interesting for its old Palace of the Dukes of Burgundy, its fine museum and other fine buildings, MACON, AUTUN and SAULIEU.... North of Vezelay lies the Cote d'Or and its great vineyards. In AUXERRE and in SENS are remarkable Gothic cathedrals, both of which are named St. Etienne. SENS is at the limits of the Ile de France, the "Chateau Country" adjacent to Paris.

DORDOGNE VALLEY

French Govt. Tourist Office

The Low Countries

PORTE DE HAL, BRUSSELS
Belgian National Tourist Office

GATEWAY TO EUROPE

The small constitutional monarchies of the Benelux countries — Belgium, Luxembourg and the Netherlands — provide opportunities for all kinds of holiday pleasure compressed into one vacation of sheer delight, for from the quaint to the cultural or the medieval to the modern is just a matter of minutes in these diminutive countries. Sturdy dykes, twirling windmills, colorful floral mosaics, quaint costumes, hoary traditions, strange customs, feudal castles, picturesque villages, peaceful parks, fragrant woods, lazy streams, busy canals, surging rivers, resurrected cities, thriving towns are there for the seeing. But most of all, they are famous for the magnificent museums and art galleries featuring their own great masters like Rembrandt, Vermeer, the Van Eycks and many others; their dramatic history— some of the fiercest fighting of World War II took place here — and glorious scenery, from Holland's renowned tulip land to the wild, rugged country of Luxembourg's Ardennes. Last but by no means least, these indomitable, hard-working peoples will welcome you with a heartfelt friendliness unsurpassed in any other part of the globe.

MANY TONGUES

The language of the Netherlands is, of course, Dutch, while the two national languages of Belgium are French and Flemish. The Grand Duchy of Luxembourg is a bilingual or even a trilingual country. Luxembourgish, a West Frankish idiom, is the everyday language spoken by all classes of the population, although German and, more particularly, French are the official languages. However, the people all over these three countries have a good knowledge of English.

FOOD SPECIALTIES

Everyone knows about the famous Dutch cheeses, and their fish dishes are almost equally well-known. Many of the world's best varieties of cheese are to be found throughout Belgium, too. However, the Belgian food specialties vary in different sections. The following meats and fish are featured: *carbonades flamandes* (braised beef, Flemish style) in all the Flemish towns; *fricadelles Bruxelloises* (small, thin braised steaks garnished with braised endives); *fritures d'anguilles et anguilles au vert* (fried eels, and eels, Belgian style, with shredded herbs, oil and vinegar) at Boitsfort near Brussels; *moules et frites* (mussels and French-fried potatoes) in the lowlands, but especially in Brussels, except in May and June; *poulets de Bruxelles* (chicken, Brussels style); *jambon d'Ardenne* (smoked ham); *waterzoeie de poisson et de poulet* (fish or chicken stews) at Antwerp and at Ghent; *tartines Flamandes au Jambon* (Flemish pastries with ham); *boudins* (sausages) at festivals and fairs and *lapin aux pruneaux* (rabbit with prunes) in Flanders. The famous Belgian tarts and pastries are Brussels wafers; siska wafers at Knokke; cheese tarts at Wavre, Mons and Brussels; rice tarts everywhere; rice and macaroon tarts at Liege, Verviers and vicinity and sugar tarts in the Walloon sections. Delicious Belgian cakes and biscuits, which may be exported, include: *noeuds de Bruges; kletskoppen de Bruges; boterletters* at Antwerp; almond breads; Greek breads; *bernardins; speculoos;* shortcake at Brussels and most other cities; *cramique* (a sweet brioche bread without raisins), also a Brussels specialty and mocha cakes at Ghent. Belgium is a large producer of standard beers, and there are some special varieties particularly identified with the country, in general of a heavy type and quite strong. Gastronomical specialties of Luxembourg include black pudding and sausages; mashed potatoes and horse-radish; smoked pork and broad beans; Ardennes ham, cooked and uncooked; jellied suckling pig; *gras-double*, Luxembourg fashion; sauerkraut and boiled potatoes; cooked cheese; *les pensées brouillées* (special pastries of the carnival season) and from April to September, trout and crawfish, Luxembourg fashion, and pike of the Sure, Moselle and Our. Brewing is a very old Luxembourg industry and the favorite drinks include Luxembourg beer, Luxembourg Moselle Wines, black currant wine of the Chateau de Beaufort and non-alcoholic grape juice.

Belgium

BRUSSELS . . . . or *Broeksele* (habitation near to the marsh), capital of Belgium, was originally founded in the seventh century. A halt for merchants became a *marche* (market), where the Grand Place now stands. This was the

35

cradle of Brussels. Although the incomparable Grand Place actually dates from the end of the seventeenth century, when it was reconstructed after the bombardment of 1695 by Louis XIV, most of the unique buildings grouped around it date from the fifteenth century. The **Hôtel de Ville** (Town Hall) is a beautiful example of Gothic architecture remarkable for its style, paintings and tapestries. Other buildings facing the famous square are the elaborate **Maison du Roi** (King's House), now housing the collections of the Communal Museum, and the **Maisons des Corporations** (Guild Houses) — reminders of the medieval craftsmen's guilds. The **Porte de Hal** (Hal Gate), with its collection of weapons and armor, is the last vestige of the old second town wall. At one end of the historic **Parc de Bruxelles** is the Louis XVI style **Palais de la Nation**, where Parliament sits. Across the park is the Louis XV style **Palais du Roi** (King's Palace) and on a third side the remarkable **Palais des Beaux Arts**, one of the finest concert halls in Europe. A few doors away are the **Musée d'Art Ancien**, showing paintings by such masters as Ingres, Delacroix, Van Eyck, Memling, Breughel the Elder and the Younger, Rubens, Teniers, Rembrandt and Vermeer van Delft, and sculpture including works by Rodin and Constantin Meunier; the **Musée d'Art Moderne**, containing canvases by Stevens, Rik Wauters, Courbet, Matisse and others, and the **Bibliothèque Royale**, with its beautiful collection of manuscripts. **Eglise Notre-Dame des Victoires**, south of these, is a masterpiece of later Gothic work. On its east side is the **Place du Petit Sablon**, surrounded by a splendid wrought-iron grill with varied designs. Forty-eight small columns each carry a statue by Dillens representing sixteenth-century trades. In the background are statues of the Counts of Egmont and Hornes, together with famous Belgians of the sixteenth century. Nearby is the **Musée Instrumental du Conservatoire Royal de Musique**, including more than 4,000 ancient and modern instruments. Across the Place Poelaert is the **Palais de Justice**, whose dome, fired by the Germans in 1944, has been reconstructed. In the northeastern part of the city is the **Colonne du Congrès** (Congress Column), commemorating Belgian independence, with the tomb of the Unknown Soldier, and **Collegiale des SS. Michel et Gudule**, the most important church in Brussels and one of the most beautiful Gothic cathedrals in Europe, representing several centuries work. With spendid stained-glass windows by Vernard van Orley, it contains a remarkable monument of the Duke of Merode and paintings by Rubens, Coxie, Van Orley and Nevez. Near the Grand Place is the popular **Manneken-Pis Fountain**, first mention of which is found in a document dating from 1452. Tours may be taken southwards to the green tide of the **Forêt de Soignes**, the most beautiful beech wood of Europe and the epic battlefield at the village of **Waterloo**; or northwestward to **Hekelgem**, where visitors to the

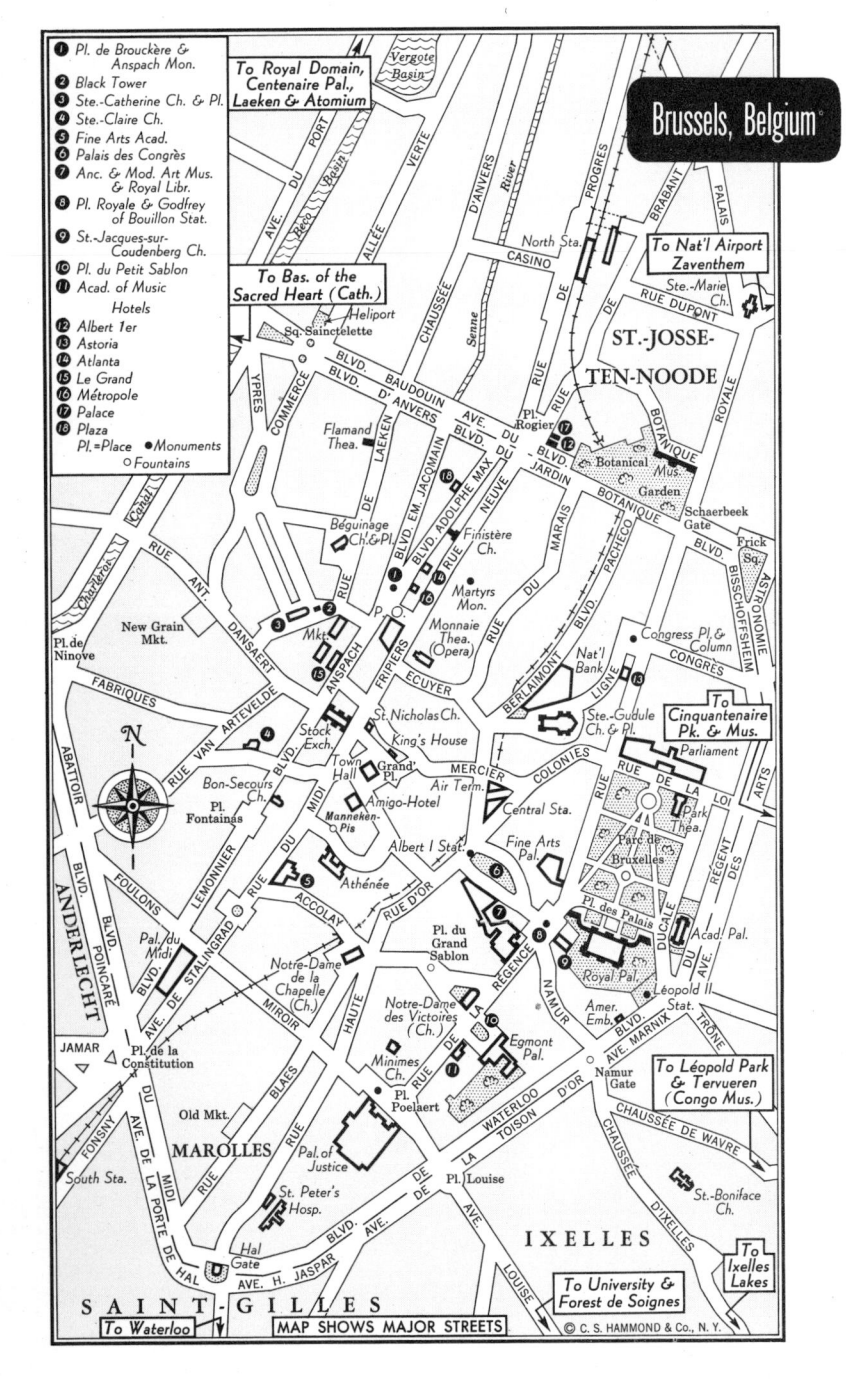

PALAIS DE LA NATION

CINQUANTENAIRE ARCADES
Belgian National Tourist Office

small cabarets may watch artists reproducing well-known pictures with vividly colored sand.... GHENT .... "city of flowers," is a textile production center and the second port in Belgium, connected to the North Sea by a first-rate ship canal twenty miles long. The "Vrijdagmarkt" (Friday Market) was the city forum of the Middle Ages. It was here that, on the occasion of their "Joyous Entry," Counts of Flanders took the oath to maintain the privileges of the city and the county. Near the market is the big wrought-iron gun belonging to the Burgundian period and popularly known as "Dulle Griet" (Mad Meg), which is seventeen feet long, weighs sixteen tons and "fired" stone balls weighing nearly 700-weight. Across the Leie (Lys) is one of the richest museums of Belgium, the Folklore Museum, containing a large collection commemorating the customs and traditions of the Flemish people. Nearby is the formidable Castle of the Counts, built in 1180 by Philip of Alsace, Count of Flanders and Vermandois. A striking reminder of feudal life, with its vast halls, underground rooms and collection of instruments of torture, this imposing fortress is one of the main centers of interest in the country. Grouped around St. Jorishof (St. George's Court) are the Middle Ages manorial residence, named Achtersikkel (literally: after-sickle) for its first owners, the Van der Sickelen, now the Royal Conservatoire of Music; the Belfry and 52-bell carillon, symbol of civic freedom, whose museum houses a collection of ancient bells; the Cloth Hall, built in 1425, meeting place of the Assizes, presided over by the *Halleheren* or gentlemen of the hall, for solving disputes connected with the wool and cloth trades; and the huge, quadrilaterally shaped, part-Gothic and part-Renaissance Town Hall, characterized by the various classical orders of the columns (Doric, Ionic and Corinthian) and the vastness of its rooms, each with its own history. A few doors east is St. Bavon Cathedral, comprising three distinct parts belonging to different periods. This cathedral contains magnificent pictures, among them the incomparable masterpiece of Jan and Hubert Van Eyck, the "Adoration of the Mystic Lamb" (1432). The Van Eyck brothers, who were born at Maeseyck, included their own portraits in the panel of the Just Judges. No church is so closely linked to the life and history of the city as St. Nicholas Church, with its famous oak choir stalls and its imprints of various ages and styles, although the oldest parts, in Romanesque, date from the beginning of the thirteenth century. Nearby on the Leie (Lys), are the Graslei (Quay of Herbs) Trade and Merchant Guild Houses, including the House of the Corporation of Free Boatmen, considered a masterpiece of the last period of Gothic style, and the "Spijker" (c. 1200), one of the finest specimens of Romanesque civic buildings. The Rabot, or small fortress, on the west side, a fine example of Middle Ages martial architecture, quite unaccountably escaped the destruction by which Charles V struck the entire defense system in 1540. The small Beguinage, a picturesque town within the city, is a vestige of religious life in the Middle Ages, where hundreds of beguines, or secular nuns, still wearing the ancient Flemish headdress, occupy quaint cottages or larger communal homes. The annual procession, marked by a carpet of natural flowers, on the 15th of August, Assumption Day, is well worth seeing.... Once a textile center and a great seaport, BRUGES, northwest of Ghent, is famed for its exquisite handmade lace, its network of placid canals, its steeply gabled old houses and its carillon in the town hall, where regular concerts are given by the carillonneurs. On the first Monday after May 2nd, the town holds the famous Procession of the Holy Blood, depicting the principal scenes from the Old and New Testaments. At the end of the procession comes the little decorated gold casket containing the drop of Holy Blood brought back from the Crusades by Thierry d'Alsace in 1150.... Belgium's sandy coastline is dotted with beach resorts. One of the best is KNOKKE ZOUTE, "the garden of the North Sea." Besides the two excellent courses at the Royal Zoute Golf Club and fifty tennis courts, visitors enjoy horseback riding in the pine woods and "land yachting" on the beach.... The great eighteenth-century painter, Peter Paul Rubens, who is buried in St. Jacques Church, dominates the artistic heritage of ANTWERP .... His canvases may be seen in the Royal Art Museum, the Plantin-Moretus Museum and Notre Dame Cathedral, and his home is open to visitors. Also, take an excursion on the Schelde, the Tamise, the Doel and the Albert Canal.... LIEGE .... a university, industrial and commercial center, is also a town of art and an old capital, containing many fine museums. Cesar Franck, sometimes called the founder of modern French instrumental composition, was born in Liege in 1822. Visitors will enjoy the trip south to Val St. Lambert, long a glass-blowing center, whose crystal works are housed in an ancient abbey.... So famous is the watering place at SPA, southeast of Liege, near the skiing area of Belgium, that the name "spa" has become a general term in the English language for a mineral-water resort.... The old tourist city of DINANT-SURMEUSE, city of the copper beaters, is dominated by a gaunt but attractive citadel. The hammered-copper craft has survived here since the thirteenth century, although the artisans now have to be supplied with copper from the Belgian Congo.... In the southeast corner of Belgium is the pretty town of BASTOGNE, focal point of the famous December, 1944, Battle of Ardennes. An unusual vast monument has been erected at the place called "Mardasson" in memory of the heroic resistance of the American soldiers during the offensive. Here also are the interesting Museum of the Ardennes Offensive and "La Cave," old headquarters of the American general, MacAuliffe.

Luxembourg

LUXEMBOURG, thousand-year-old capital of the Grand-Duchy, was, for many centuries, one of the most powerful fortresses in the world. Although dismantled, many remains have been preserved, particularly the ancient fortifications of the Citadel of St. Esprit, now transformed into charming parks with pleasant walks, especially picturesque around the lower town, including a network of underground passages and shelters or casemates hewn from the solid rock. The **Grand Ducal Palace**, residence of H. R. H. Grand Duchess Charlotte, was built in the sixteenth and eighteenth centuries, the older part in a remarkable Renaissance style. On the same square is the state's most outstanding church, the **Cathedral of Notre Dame**, with magnificent Renaissance sculptures (1613-1618) and a crypt containing the tomb of John the Blind, King of Bohemia and Count of Luxembourg. A few blocks southwest is the massive, stone-arched **Pont Adolphe**, one of the city's 65 bridges. The famous **Promenade de la Corniche**, unique in Europe, and the elegant **Spanish Turrets** are also of great interest. At the **military cemetery of Hamm**, 7,000 American soldiers of the rugged Third Army are buried, with their commander, General George S. Patton, Jr., among them. In the southwestern mining district, whose tall modern **furnaces** and **rolling mills** are open to visitors, is the neo-Gothic **church of Dudelange**, containing paintings by Dom. Lang, one of the greatest painters of the Grand-Duchy. **Esch-sur-Alzette**, district center, has a gorgeous **park** with a famous rose garden, noted for the extensive views over the three countries of France, Belgium and Luxembourg. At the frontier between Luxembourg and Lorraine are the modern, well-known thermal springs of **Mondorf-les-Bains**. The Moselle valley region in the east is an important vine-growing and wine-producing area, and the river provides fine fishing for ablet, bream, pike, redeye and perch. At any one of the pleasant little towns you may visit the noted wine cellars, like the **Caves St. Martin at Remich**. North of Luxembourg city are many small villages in idyllic settings, including **Junglinster**, well-known

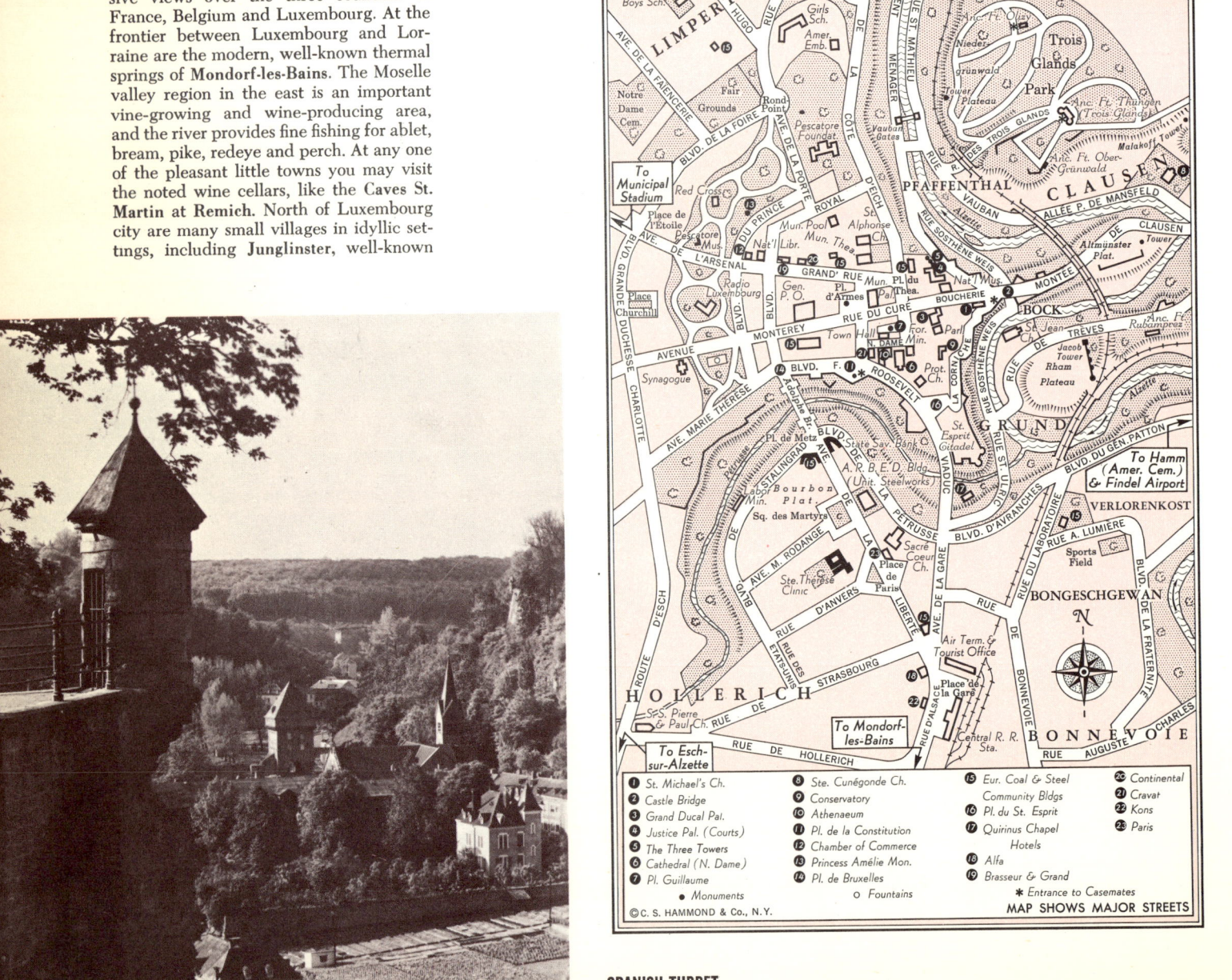

LUXEMBOURG CITY

Luxembourg National Tourist Office

SPANISH TURRET

Luxembourg National Tourist Office

for the tombstones of the knights of Linster and the romantic manor of the neighboring **bourglinster**; **Mersch**, surrounded by gentle hills covered with beech and firtree woods, whose church has a portal of real architectural curiosity; **Ansembourg**, having a magnificent feudal castle dating from the twelfth century, with a modern manor built in 1639, and **Tuntange**, with a church known for a Pieta of exceptional beauty.... ECHTERNACH, an important holiday center, is the northeastern gateway to the Miller's Dale. Its old patrician houses with their pointed gables, its narrow streets and alleys and its ancient ramparts have kept alive the atmosphere of a medieval town. The ancient Benedictine abbey, founded in the seventh century by St. Willibrord, consists of four wings, each 210 feet long, built round a large square central court, and includes a crypt dating from the Merovingian period (eighth century), with vaults adorned with frescoes painted about 1100. Equally famous is the fine park with its elegant Louis XV pavilion. Miller's Dale also includes **Berdorf**, in a region abounding in impressive and quaint sandstone cliff formations...
The uplands of the Ardennes in the north is another popular and picturesque holiday area, where the hunting is especially famous. Old, romantic VIANDEN was built in the ninth century on the banks of the Our, in scenery of wild grandeur. The formidable, thirteenth-century castle, one of the largest feudal fortresses of the continent, is a real architectural jewel unequalled on this side of the Rhine. During Victor Hugo's exile from France, this famous poet lived for a time in Vianden in a house now preserved as a museum. Old-world uses and customs are preserved in the Folklore Museum, featuring fine old furniture. The imposing ruins of **Bourscheid Castle**, an important medieval fortress between the Rhine and the Meuse, rise on a steep hill 450 feet above the spectacular valley of the Sur. West of Vianden, the small market town of **Esch-sur-Sure**, enshrined between steep crags and almost completely surrounded by the Sure, with its houses clustering 'round a rocky promontory, is dominated by the ruins of its massive castle and by the forbidding rocks which drop sheer into the river. The beautiful church in **Troisvierges**, in the extreme north, is well-known for its remarkable high altar.

The Netherlands

Resurrected ROTTERDAM .... is the second city of the Netherlands and one of the largest seaports in Western Europe. Much of the center was destroyed by bombing in 1940 but like the Phoenix, a fine new city is rapidly emerging from the ruins. The oldest section, **Delfshaven** (literally "port of Delft"), part of Rotterdam since 1389, is the place from which Pilgrim Fathers embarked for America on the *Speedwell* in 1620. Their departure is memorialized in the adjoining church, where their last service before embarkation was held. The two sections of the city on either side of the Maas are linked by the magnificent new **Maastunnel**, first Dutch river tunnel and a splendid example of engineering skill, with the land on the left bank forming the 750-acre **Waalhaven**, largest artificial basin in the world. At the center of the city are the gleaming new buildings, including the impressive Town Hall. Nearby are the statue of the famous philosopher and great scientist, Desiderius Erasmus, born in Rotterdam in 1469, and Ossip Zadkine's memorial statue, "Ruined City," expressing the sentiments felt on seeing the destruction. The Boymans Museum has rich collections of paintings, sculpture, drawings and prints. . . , Southeast at DORDRECHT, where many famous painters have lived, is the Grote Kerk (Great Church) with its massive, uncompleted, dark-rose tower and sixteenth-century choir stalls by Jan Terwen.... GOUDA, east of Rotterdam, is a busy market town whose name is a household word with cheese-lovers all over the world. Its Gothic-style, cathedral-like Town Hall is of extraordinary grace and its St. Janskerk has 31 wonderful stained-glass windows with 2,412 magnificent panels. The lovely Weighing-house by the cheese market is unusual. Go to Oudewater and be weighed on the medieval Witches Scales and after the traditional test, get the certificate proving you are not a sorcerer.... Between Rotterdam and The Hague is the lovely pottery city of DELFT, noted as the town of Vermeer. It still retains the atmosphere and character of a seventeeth-century town, because its spacious market square and quiet, tree-shaded canals are lined with picturesque old houses. "Het Prinsenhof" Municipal

REMBRANDT'S HOUSE Philip Gendreau

Museum, a former fifteenth-century monastery, was once the home of William the Silent, Prince of Orange, the Father of the Netherlands, and within its walls he was assassinated in 1584. His tomb, along with the rulers of the House of Orange, is in the Nieuwe Kerk..... GRAVENHAGE, or THE HAGUE, seat of the government, is renowned for the dignified charm of its Gothic and Renaissance architecture, its fine avenues and lovely parks and gardens. The name is derived from *Haghe* (hunting grounds) where *Graaf* (Count) Floris IV of Holland built a stronghold as early as 1229. This stronghold is the **Binnenhof** (Inner Court) with its majestic, gabled **Ridderzaal** (Hall of the Knights), built in 1280, Upper House (1652) and Lower House (1777) of the Dutch Parliament, some characterful gates and other government buildings. On the third Tuesday of September, the imposing and colorful opening of Parliament takes place, the only pomp and ceremony associated with the Dutch Royal House, when Queen Juliana and her retinue, accompanied by gala-dressed escort, rides in the Golden Coach pulled by eight ebony horses through the city. Adjoining the Binnenhof is "**Mauritshuis**" Art Gallery, a seventeenth-century palace, with its celebrated collection of old masters, including Rembrandt, Vermeer and Potter. The recently constructed **Peace Palace**, surrounded by a monumental iron fence and containing valuable gifts from many countries, is where the International Court of Justice sits. Scheveningen, seaside suburb of The Hague, combines the attractions of an old-world fishing village and a cosmopolitan holiday resort, largest and most fashionable in the country. A special magnet for music-lovers is the annual Holland Festival held from mid-June to mid-July, with outstanding organizations like the Hague Residentie Orchestra and the Netherlands Bach Society. . . . North of The Hague is LEIDEN, birthplace of

GRAND DUCAL PALACE Luxembourg National Tourist Office

Rembrandt. Its famous university was founded by William the Silent in 1574 as a reward for the heroism with which the townspeople had successfully resisted a prolonged siege by the Spanish invaders. Distinguished St. Peter's Church retains many memories of the Pilgrim Fathers. Visits can be made to the bulb fields extending northward, producing in the springtime a colorful symphony of incredible loveliness.... Among the most attractive towns is HAARLEM .... just west of Amsterdam, ancient residence of the Counts of Holland. Music lovers will be entranced by the 200-year-old baroque pipe organ, still one of the finest in the world, which was played by both Mozart and Handel, in the impressive Grote Kerk (Church of St. Bavo) overlooking the market place. The outstanding attraction, however, is the "Frans Hals" Art Gallery, containing an unrivaled collection of paintings by that great master. Near here, in Spaarndam, is the monument commemorating the legendary boy with his finger in the dyke, symbolizing the traditional courage of the Dutch in their ceaseless struggle against the sea.... Busy AMSTERDAM ..... capital of the

CANAL SCENE, AMSTERDAM

Netherlands National Tourist Office

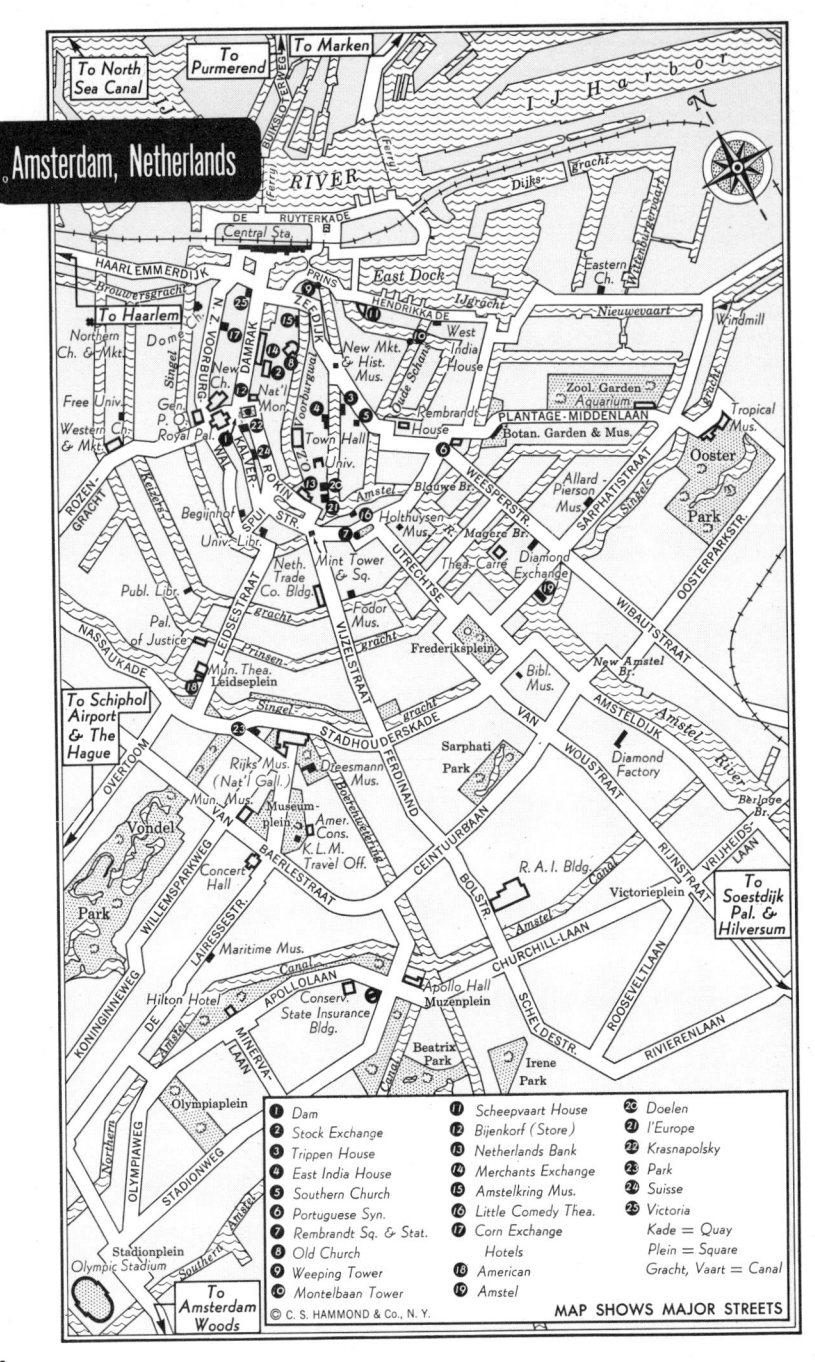

Netherlands, is a remarkable city whose growth can be traced in the concentric semicircles, like the rings of a tree trunk, of its main canals, along which stand proud patrician dwellings built by the merchant princes of the sixteenth and seventeenth centuries. The outer suburbs, on the other hand, are famous for their strikingly modernistic architecture and planning. A real cultural center, this city offers such magnificent displays as the world-famous collection of masterpieces of the Dutch school, including Rembrandt's renowned "Night Watch," at the "Rijksmuseum" (Netherlands National Gallery); "Rembrandthuis" Art Gallery, the artist's home from 1639 to 1658, and concerts by the celebrated Concertgebouw Orchestra. Heart of the capital is the greatly admired Royal Palace, originally built as the town hall. Don't miss the quaint fishing village of Volendam and the companion island of Marken, where the inhabitants still wear the colorful local costume; the flower auctions at Aalsmeer and the famous bastions at Naarden.... Off the coast at DEN HELDER, the naval base, is the Isle of Texel, a bird-lover's paradise, with one of the finest beaches in Europe. To the east is the impressive Afsluitdijk, the phenomenal 18-mile-long enclosing dam that cuts off the Zuyder Zee from the North Sea.... On the other side of IJsselmeer is Friesland, whose indomitable, independent inhabitants speak a language entirely their own, more similar to English than Dutch. The impressive, leaning Oldehove Tower has been LEEUWARDEN'S architectural landmark for four hundred years. The art treasures assembled in the Frisian Museum (antiquarian and historical) make it particularly noteworthy. Popta Slot, in Marssum, is a typical sixteenth-century Frisian castle. Some places of interest in the area are the Franeker Planetarium, constructed by a local wool comber in the latter part of the eighteenth century, and the former flourishing port of Hindeloopen, now known for its curious painted furniture.... The delightful region of woods and moorland surrounding ASSEN has some striking archeological landmarks known locally as "Hunnebedden" or "Giants' Beds," tumuli raised by the Germanic tribes who lived in this region over 4,000 years ago. In Drenthe Provincial Museum are many relics of these early inhabitants.... The unusual village of GIETHOORN, a little east of Noordoostpolder (North East Polder), is widely known as the "Venice of the North" because the streets are canals, with the old tree-shaded houses linked by high, narrow wooden bridges.... In the eastern part of Overijssel province, one of the oldest inhabited areas in Western Europe whose customs date from pre-Christian times, is ENSCHEDE. The **Town Hall** is admired for its modern design, while the **Twenthe Museum** possesses a choice collection of primitives. At nearby **Oldenzaal** is the striking, twelfth-century Church of St. Plechelmus.... Rural ZUTPHEN, with is ramparts and fortifications and winding streets, possesses many buildings surviving from the Middle Ages. Most important are the **Drogenaps Tower** and the **Grote Kerk,** with its collection of medieval books and manuscripts chained to the reading desks in the original manner. ... A favorite holiday ground is the region around HOOGE VELUWE NATIONAL PARK, whose chief attraction is the Kroller-Muller Art Gallery at Otterlo, containing the largest collection in the world — over two hundred — of works by Vincent Van Gogh.... In ARNHEM, on the park's southern edge, are a unique assemblage of old Dutch windmills, houses and other relics of Holland's rural culture, carefully re-erected at the **Netherlands Open-Air Folklore Museum.**... As is to be expected of a frontier stronghold existing since Roman times, NIJMEGEN .... city of Charlemagne, has many old buildings, despite the fact that it suffered considerable destruction during World War II. The oldest of these is the **Valkhof**, a ruined castle built by the Emperor Charlemagne in the eighth century.... The oldest fortified town in the Netherlands, MAASTRICHT, in the southernmost region, has endured no less than nineteen sieges in the course of its stormy history. **St. Petersberg**, originating from the limestone quarries worked here since Roman times, has 400 miles of underground caves and passages, with its unique art gallery painted on the white limestone walls and its mammoth pillared autograph book signed by the great and small of the past ten centuries. The U. S. Military Cemetery at **Margraten**, for American soldiers who died in World War II, contains almost 20,000 graves, all of which have been adopted by Dutch families in the vicinity who keep them covered with flowers.... HERTOGENBOSCH, also known as BOIS-LE-DUC, is famous for its truly great poem in stone, the **Cathedral of St. John,** built in the fifteenth century, a marvelous example of the purest flamboyant Gothic style.... The canals traversing the heart of UTRECHT .... situated right in the middle of Holland, are rather remarkable, with their wharves and cellars below the streets on either side. The fourteenth-century **Cathedral Tower**, a perfect specimen of medieval architecture, is the highest tower in Holland (332 feet), commanding a magnificent view extending as far as the IJsselmeer. In the surrounding countryside are numerous fine chateaux set in delightful woodlands, most notable being the **De Haar Castle** at Haarzuilens, with its thick walls, steep roofs and many pointed towers coming straight from the pages of a fairy tale.... MIDDELBURG, principal town on Walcheren, the southwest island which is rapidly recovering from the devastating floods of February, 1953, has a handsome **Town Hall**.

A TYPICAL CANTILEVER BRIDGE OVER CANAL Publishers' Photo Service

THE MUNTTOREN Philip Gendreau

41

Germany

ISARTOR GATE, MUNICH
German Tourist Information Office

CULTURE AND ROMANCE

Germany, the land of beauty and achievement, rich in the inspiration of an historic background and centuries of Western culture, and abounding in the hospitality which has been an outstanding characteristic of all Germanic peoples, from the very earliest times, is ideal for tourists. This country has always been celebrated for the cultivation of the fine arts, and especially in music and drama are the German people heirs to a great tradition. Of course, Germany's intellectual and educational life is world-famous, as are her valuable contributions to scientific research. You will enjoy seeing her many historic cities, famous health resorts and spas, the proud castles and tranquil villages — and, of course, the beautiful Rhine. For as Mark Twain said, Germany is a land of infinite variety, and without doubt, you too will find it so.

COFFEEHOUSES, BEER HALLS AND WINE CELLARS

The following are typical German specialities: *labskaus* (cured pork, mashed potatoes and, sometimes, herring, served with poached egg and pickled cucumber), a traditional sailors' dish popular throughout the coastal districts; *rundstück warm* (slice of bread or roll covered with slice of hot pork and gravy) and *pannfisch* (mixture of roast potatoes and fried fish), both Hamburg specialities; *braunkohl mit pinkel* (kale with cured pork chop, smoked bacon, smoked sausage and sausage with the addition of groats and served with roast potatoes), popular in Bremen and Oldenburg; chicken stew and roast goose, specialities of Bremen and Hamburg respectively, but known throughout the coastal region; eel soup, popular in Hamburg and other North German towns; *heidschnuckenbraten* (roast lamb), speciality of the Lüneburg heath; black rye bread and pumpernickel, Bremen and Oldenburg specialities, and all fish and shellfish, including oysters, lobsters and cockles. The Germans are renowned for their delicious pastries, especially butter cake and *bremer klaben* (rich Christmas cake with plenty of raisins and candied peel). Hearty eaters will also appreciate the pleasures of good drinking. The Germans are connoisseurs both of wines and beers. The country is mainly known for the light, dry white wines produced along the Rhine and Moselle valleys. The Rhine wines are the Rheingaus — generally conceded to excel any white wine produced anywhere — Rheinhessens and Palatinates. The Moselle wines have long had a reputation for healthfulness. The Roman poet Ausonius wrote more than 2,000 years ago that the Moselles were "balsam for the shattered nerves of modern man." Most famous of all the tasty German beers are the Bavarian beers. Hanover is the home of the *lütje lage* (a glass of beer and a glass of "corn brandy"), known in Hamburg under the name of *lütt un lütt*. Flensburg is associated with Jamaica rum which, with hot water and sugar, makes the grog popular everywhere in North

VINEYARDS ALONG THE RHINE
German Railroads Information Office

Germany. Popular specialities are also "tea punch" in North Friesland and "egg grog" in Helgoland, which, like the ordinary grog, is appreciated even on a hot summer day. Strong coffee is a favorite beverage all over Germany, while tea with candy (*kluntjes*) and cream is an East Frisian speciality.

COUNTRY OF THE RHINE

Through the heart of Europe flows the Rhine — the river that Walt Whitman called the most beautiful in the world and whose praise great men have sung in poetry and prose. The cradles of European culture north of the Alps stood along its shores, where great cathedrals in cities dating back to long before the Christian era, storied castles and romantic ruins speak eloquently of the glorious past. The vital artery of Europe, it is the classical route for travel. The cultural and economic center of the Lower Rhine where it flows into the Netherlands is **KLEVE**, scene of the Lohengrin saga. Picturesquely situated on an old Rhine island is **Kalkar**, a popular spot for artists, with the interesting **Church of St. Nicholas**, containing the world-famous art productions, like the wood-carved altars, of the Kalkar School. . . . **ESSEN** . . . . near where the Ruhr River flows into the Rhine, is the 1,100-year-old economic center of the Ruhr area, still a delightful scenic attraction. An ancient architectural monument, built in 796, is the **Essen-Werden Abbey Church**. . . . South of the Ruhr stretches the Bergische Land, with its black-and-white frame houses and its dikes damming up the water to form picturesque lakes. In the largest town of the Bergische Land, **WUPPERTAL** . . . . . is a unique suspension railway over the Wupper River. South of here is the health resort of **Wiehl**, in an area of dahlia cultivation. The **Wiehl Stalagmite and Stalactite Caves** are in the vicinity of **Homburg Castle**. The magnificent **Bergische Cathedral** in **Altenberg**, a treasure of Gothic architecture, nestles on the side of a hill near the well-known summer resort of **Odenthal**. There is a very unusual and interesting collection at the **Röntgen Museum**, the German radiography museum, in nearby **Remscheid**. . . . Back on the Rhine is **DUSSELDORF**, ... well-known center of art and fashion, the principal city of the Rhenish-Westphalian district, sometimes called the "Paris of Germany." The shops are among the best, especially those on the elegant **Königsallee**. The city also has one of the best **academies of art** and **art museums** in the country. The nearby silk town of **Krefeld** . . . . still boasts of the fascinating old moated castle of **Linn**. München-Gladbach, center of the German cloth industry, has important monuments of architecture, like the 1,000-year-old **Minster** and baroque **Town Hall**. Those who wish to re-live medieval times will find that time has in fact passed by **Zons**, the medieval frontier fortress and toll station of the archbishops of Cologne, between Düsseldorf and Cologne. The town **fortifications** are completely preserved, including the **Customs Tower**. . . . Center of the Rhineland is the cathedral city of **COL-**

RAESFELD CASTLE, WESTPHALIA German National Tourist Office

ROTHENBURG, BAVARIA German Tourist Information Office

PORTA NIGRA, TRIER

OGNE . . . . Founded in 38 B. C., it was the Colonia Agrippina of the Romans, and is now known as the city of fairs. The most famous landmark is, of course, **Cologne Cathedral,** whose renowned twin 515-foot spires were spared by the bombings of World War II. Taking hundreds of years to build — it was founded in 1248 and completed in 1880 — it is the result of many architects' plans. It is also noteworthy for its outstanding stained-glass paintings and sculptures of the Middle Ages, including Stephan Lochner's "The Three Magi," and valuable ecclesiastical vessels. Other outstanding churches are the **Church of the Apostles,** an important example of late Romanesque architecture, and **St. Maria im Capitol,** with its famous wooden doors. Cologne, naturally, is also famous for Eau de Cologne, called locally *Kölnisch Wasser,* which has been made here since the seventeenth century. . . . Between Cologne and Bonn is the garden city of BRUHL. It is worth a visit to see the rococo **Castle of Augustusburg,** the summer residence of elector Clemens August and now used for official functions by the West German government, with its famous staircase by Balthasar Neumann and rococo gardens. . . . Near the juncture of the frontiers of Germany, Belgium and the Netherlands, AACHEN . . . . is a well-known spa having the warmest springs in central Europe. During the Middle Ages, 32 kings and emperors were crowned in the massive **Imperial Cathedral,** which has the marble coronation throne of Charlemagne. The famous Imperial Hall is in the **Town Hall.** . . . Still further upstream is the old liberal university town of BONN . . . . booming capital of the Federal Republic, now crowded with civil servants and foreign embassy staffs. Two buildings, one modern, the other several centuries old, are of special interest: the new **Bundeshaus (Parliament House)** and the old house where Ludwig van Beethoven was born in 1770. The house and its furnishings have been restored in the manner of the years when the noted composer was alive. Music-lovers will be further interested to know that the **Old Cemetery** contains the graves of Robert and Clara Schumann, and that the city holds an annual **Beethoven Festival** in May. From Bonn there opens a fine panoramic view of the picturesque Siebengebirge (Seven Mountains), site of the Nibelungen legends, between the Sieg valley and Westerwald Hills, forming the northernmost wine-growing district of Europe. **Drachenfels (Dragon's Crag),** which boasts of more visitors than any other mountain in Europe, is the legendary home of the dragon that Siegfried slew, and the red wine made from grapes grown on its slopes is called Dragon's Blood. The famous medieval pottery town, Siegburg, is built around a high hill on which is located the **Michaelsberg,** an old Benedictine abbey founded in 1064. On the opposite bank of the river, where Bonn is, the Eifel Hills, Germany's largest red-wine belt, reach from the Lower Rhine to the Moselle. Great forests, dikes and the so-called "Maare" — somber lakes filling the craters of long-dead volcanoes — are characteristic of this rugged woodland district. Monschau, an idyllic eighteenth-century town in which life goes on unperturbed by modern changes, is a romantic frontier town of old half-timbered houses in the narrow valley of the Ruhr and at the foot of the mighty **castle** of the former Lords of Jülich and the Palatinate. Here are fine **mansions** of the clothmakers, one of which, the "Red House," is a museum. In the wintertime, this is a popular sleighing and skiing center. A little south of Bonn is historic **Remagen,** unforgettable for many American ex-GI's because this is the spot where the U. S. Ninth Armored Division found a bridge undestroyed in 1945 and swarmed across the natural barrier to the German heartland. The bridge which shortened the war is gone — it finally collapsed after thousands of U. S. soldiers had crossed it — but there are an old **Roman road** and a **Roman gate.** . . . KOBLENZ is a former Roman city situated where the Moselle flows into the Rhine. On the east bank is the mighty eleventh-century fortress of **Ehrenbreitstein,** a fortified place since it was a Roman camp. . . . Still further upstream, nestled between the heights of the Hunsrueck and the Taunus Hills, begins the most romantic stretch of the Rhine valley. Here is BOPPARD, the wine-growing town of old-world charm. High above the roofs rises the **Cathedral,** built in the twelfth and thirteenth centuries, with its vigorous and noble Romanic forms and a choir showing the transition to the new style. An idyllic **mountain railway** will take you over deep gorges to the heights of the Hunsrueck ranges, to the large and magnificent town forest. Above nearby St. Goar are the ruins of **Rheinfels Castle,** once one of the strongest fortresses along the river. On a rock on the right bank of the Rhine, in a cut where the river is at its narrowest point, is where the legendary blonde maiden — the **Lorelei** — sat and sang to lure the river boats to destruction. The **Pfalzgrafenstein,** a stone structure sitting in the middle of the river below Bacharach, was built by a local count in the fourteenth century as a toll gate, where he simply stretched a chain across the river and didn't let a boat through until the captain paid up. It has only one entrance, a door so high above the water that a visitor had to climb a ladder to get in. Friends of the Rhenish white wines will not fail to visit **Rüdesheim** where, legend says, Charlemagne brought the first grape vines. The medieval **Bromserburg Tower** has a wine museum telling the story of the long cultivation of the grape along the Rhine. Above the town is the **Niederwald Denkmal ("Watch on the Rhine"),** a monument erected by Chancellor Bismarck in 1871. . . . MAINZ, where Johann Gutenberg invented the printing press, is famed also for its wines and for its Mardi Gras festival, the Carnival. The **Gutenberg Museum** commemorates the invention of modern printing. In Winkel is the oldest stone house in Germany, built in 850. . . . West of Mainz, near the outlet of the Saar into the Moselle, is TRIER, a veritable open-air museum where all epochs are represented since the time of ancient Rome, when this was the largest city north of the Alps.

BAMBERG

... Across the river from Mainz, where the Main flows into the Rhine, is WIESBADEN . . . . . The Romans first discovered the health-giving quality of its mineral springs and it has been one of Europe's leading spas ever since.

FRANKFURT. "Were anyone to ask me if I could think of a place more befitting my birth, more suitable to my conception as a citizen and more agreeable to my poetic feelings, I could name no other town but Frankfurt am Main." Thus wrote Johann Wolfgang Goethe, Frankfurt's greatest son, in 1824. Today, Frankfurt continues to be a city full of life, buzzing with work, an economic center, an international meeting place and a stronghold of culture and science. The *Römer*, venerable City Hall of the late Middle Ages, flanks the famous market square in the Altstadt (old town). This building with its Kaisersaal and the Prince Electors Chamber was the scene of the German emperors' coronation banquets. Nearby is the red-sandstone St. Paul's Church, where the first German National Assembly was held in 1848-1849. The inner city is closely encircled by a garden belt, linking it with the residential sections, and throughout Frankfurt are well-kept gardens and parks with the smell of fresh grass and dainty blossoms in the air, while in the wide woods along the fringe of the city, good forest inns beckon for a leisurely afternoon's rest and conversation, accompanied by good strong coffee and excellent German pastries.

SCHAUSPIELHAUS

NEW AND OLD, FRANKFURT

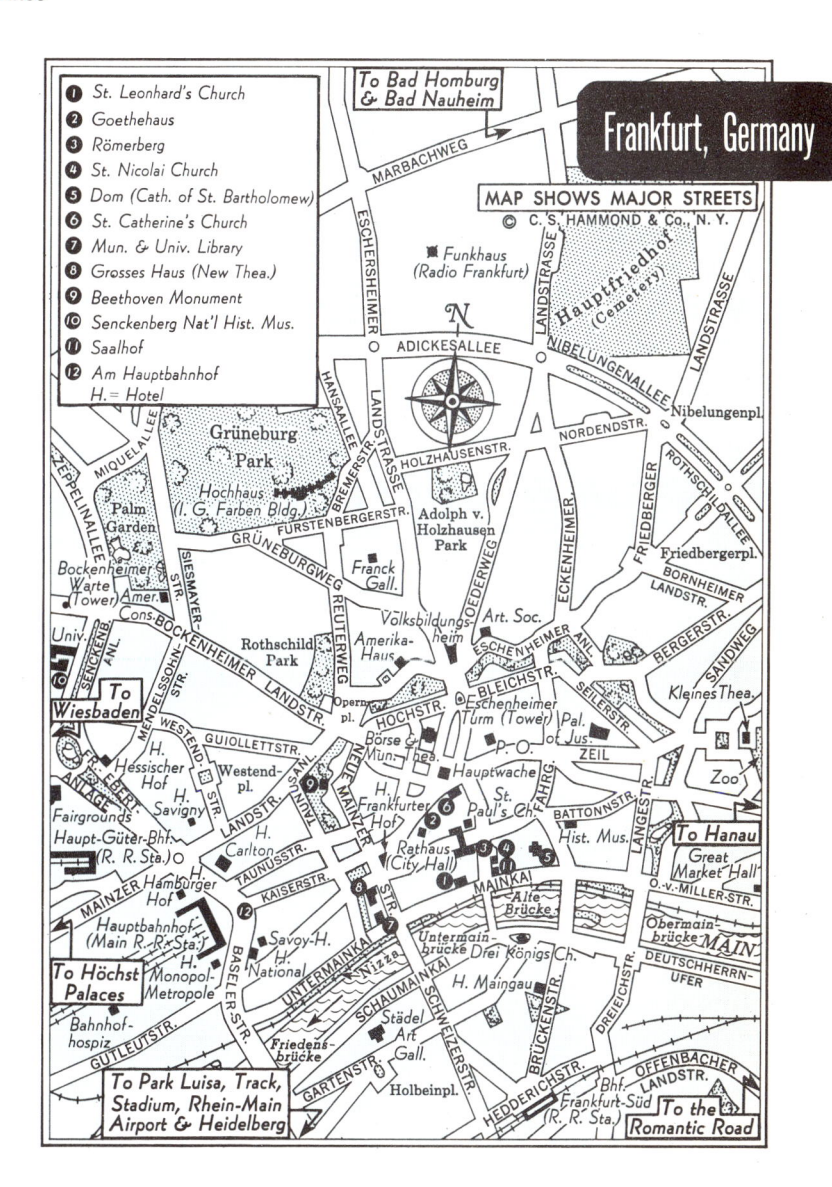

WASSERBURG, UPPER BAVARIA

German National Tourist Office

WORMS, with its ancient cathedral and impressive **Luther Memorial**, is a "must" in every Rhineland itinerary.... Upstream on the Neckar, which flows into the great river, is HEIDELBERG, ... Germany's oldest university town, with its historical stone **bridge** and the most spectacular **castle** in Germany. This magnificent castle was reduced to ruins in the wars of the 1600's, but the parts still standing span about 700 years. The courtyard forms the stage for the annual summer drama and music festival, while in the castle is a famous wine cask, the **Heidelberger Tun**, so big a stairway is required to get to the top. On the same hill above the castle is the **Königstuhl (King's Chair)**, which looks down on the beautiful Neckar valley from 2,000 feet up. Heidelberg University, Germany's oldest, was the setting for "The Student Prince" and some of the beer-and-wurst places portrayed in the operetta are still there, like the **Red Ox** and the **Goldener Hecht**, still serving students, as they have done for hundreds of years, in oak-panelled rooms covered with pictures and mementos of long-ago student life.

PICTURESQUE WOODS AND MOUNTAINS

The Black Forest, the woodcarving center, which runs along the east bank of the Rhine from Karlsruhe south to the Swiss border, isn't all forest anymore — there are a lot of cultivated fields — but it's one of the popular summer resort areas. BADEN-BADEN, with its matchless position in a lovely valley amid the forest and its unique walks — which may truly be said to be the most beautiful in the world — is the plushiest resort center in the area. The Romans used to bathe in its radioactive chloride hot springs, and kings, queens and the wealthy have been doing it ever since. There are horseback riding, golf (on Germany's best course), a season of horse racing, good music and the Casino.

THE BODENSEE

South of the Black Forest is a resort lake, Lake Constance, bordering Germany, Switzerland and Austria, a highly popular vacation area with the Germans and the warmest part of the country. CONSTANCE, on the lake, dates from the early days of pile settlements. A princely jewel of medieval beauty, it was an episcopal see for fifteen centuries and in 1415 was the seat of the famous council which sentenced John Huss to be burned at the stake. Points of interest include the **Merchants' Hall** by the lake, erected in 1380, containing the great Council Chamber where the conclave of cardinals met; the **Town Hall**, with its magnificent Renaissance Court, and many fine old **patrician** houses.

THE ROMANTIC WAY

In this region between the Main and the Alps, WURZBURG, known as the Rococo City, has the handsome, Renaissance-style residence of the former **Prince-Bishops**, a splendid example of the jubilant and joyous architecture of Balthasar Neumann. The vestibule in the middle of the building is a masterpiece of architecture and an admirable setting for the great **Mozart Festival** held here every June.... ROTHENBURG is a dream picture of medieval times as it rises high above the valley of the Tauber. The picturesque old streets and lanes, quaint towers, Gothic churches, Renaissance halls and well-preserved ramparts present a vivid picture of the old days of chivalry and knighthood. Every street, every house, even every stone of Rothenburg can tell its tale. Each year, in front of the **Town Hall**, one of the most exquisite in Germany, is performed the historical play entitled *"Der Meistertrunk."*... At the line of demarcation between the scenery of Franconia and that of Swabia, two landmarks adorn the Rieskessel with its waving fields of corn and austere-looking village churches: the "**Ipf**," a striking tablelike mountain and the "**Daniel**," a secular tower structure of St. George's Church in NORDLINGEN. Even to this day, the cry of the watchman can be heard at night echoing across the narrow streets and alleys from the top of the "Daniel." At the beginning of autumn the horse-loving peasants of the Ries meet here for the Scharlachrennen (Scarlet Race) on the Kaiserwiesen, which has become the finest venue for riding tournaments and contests in southern Germany.... AUGSBURG, ... the 2,000-year-old town between the Lech and Werlach Rivers, welcomes the visitor with an impressive picture of what was once the "German world-city of the Middle Ages." The **Maximilianstrasse**, with its fine Renaissance **fountains**, monumental **Town Hall** and the **Perlachturm**, is indeed regal in appearance. The **Rote Tor (Red Gate)** to the south of the town, with its walls, moats and bridge, provides the setting for Augsburg's famous open-air festival of drama and opera. From here the road that leads into the delightful scenery of the Allgäu mountains is the ancient Roman Via Claudia, the historical route from Germany to the south....

MADONNA, HEIDELBERG

German National Tourist Office

The Romanticists on the royal throne of Bavaria planned the castles of Neuschwanstein and Hohenschwangau, two of the finest castles in Germany, setting them on the summits of steep rocks in the mountainous district. With the storybook Neuschwanstein Castle, built from 1869-1886 in imitation of a medieval castle, King Ludwig II, patron and friend of Richard Wagner, intended to revive the world of Lohengrin and Tannhäuser.

THE BAVARIAN ALPS

MUNICH. Munich, the gateway to the Bavarian Alps, is a city with a great many historical associations—past and present—a city with an atmosphere completely unspoiled by bustling modernity. Lying midway between Strassbourg and Vienna, it is the most important town in southern Germany, also one of the largest European towns to be situated at so high an altitude. Founded in 1158, Munich was for centuries the capital of the independent kingdom of Bavaria, and in more recent times the birthplace of Nazidom. A heavy ring of munitions factories built by the Hitler regime made it an important target for allied bombings in World War II; however its protected location prevented much of the devastation suffered by other large German cities. After the Americans liberated Munich in 1945, the Temple of Honor, a memorial to the 16 Nazis killed in the "beerhall putsch," as well as other remnants of Nazi rule, were destroyed. Today, Munich has regained much of its former prominence as a cultural center of world fame. This is a city rich in museums, art collections and exhibitions, theaters and concert halls. Especially famous are the Munich Opera, the art treasures of the Old Pinakothek and the Deutsche Museum. Every year the inherent "joie de vivre" of Munich is expressed in three typical festivals—the Munich Carnival, the bock beer festival held each spring and "Oktoberfest" in the fall is one of Germany's gayest festivals. . . . **OBERAMMERGAU** is a woodcarving center nine out of ten years, but on the tenth year it is the home of the world's most famous pageant, the **Passion Play**. This ancient religious play was instituted in the year 1634 as a thank offering on the part of the pious little community for having been delivered from the plague then raging over Europe. . . . The jewel of the German Alps and a little market town of old-world character, **BERCHTESGADEN**, now a winter-and-summer resort for American military personnel in Germany, was Hitler's favorite hideout, but his Eagle's Nest has been destroyed. The skiing is very good — lifts are available — and nearby

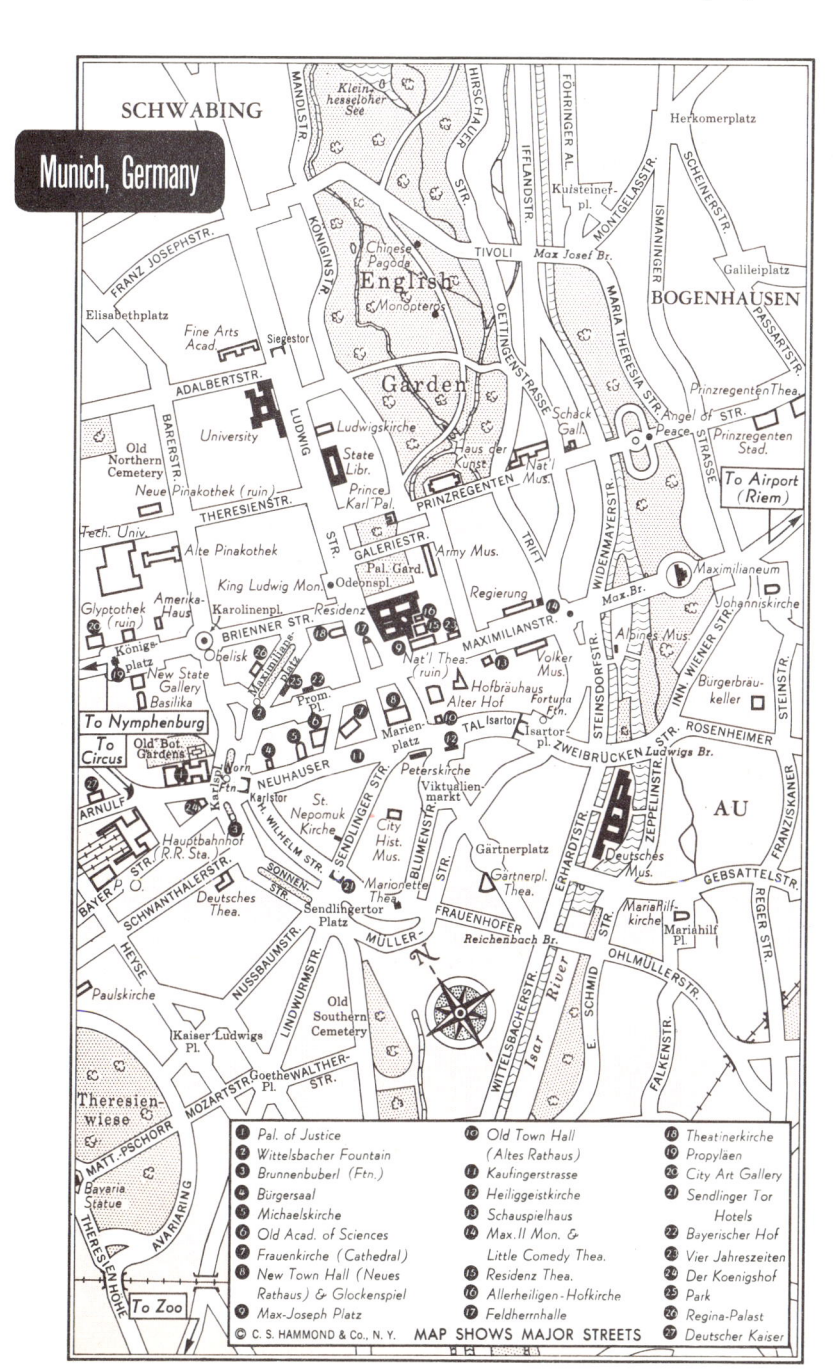

THE CITY OF MUNICH
German National Tourist Office

is the **Königssee**, one of the most beautiful of mountian lakes. . . . **GARMISCH-PARTENKIRCHEN** is the leading winter-sports center, as well as a health resort, with complete facilities. Mountain railways run to the top of the Zugspitze, highest mountain in Germany and the most celebrated peak in the Bavarian Alps. At the end of January comes the **International Winter Sports Week**. Another resort center is ancient **Mittenwald**, famous for violins.

OLD HANSEATIC TOWNS

The architecture of the North German Lowlands has quite a style of its own owing to the use of various types of brickwork for structural and decorative purposes. Another outstanding feature is the numerous half-timbered houses, many of them truly magnificent specimens. The life of

AMALIENBURG IN NYMPHENBURG PARK German National Tourist Office

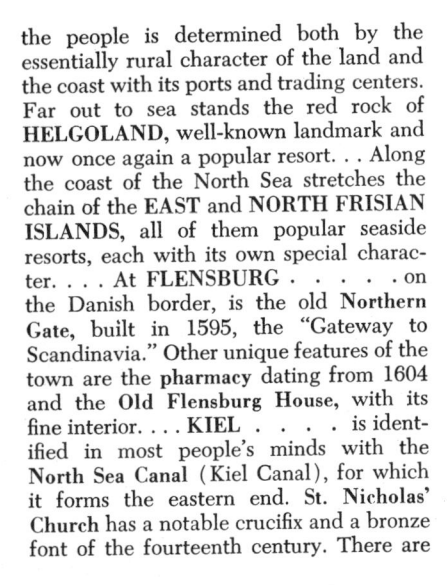

NYMPHENBURG German National Tourist Office

the people is determined both by the essentially rural character of the land and the coast with its ports and trading centers. Far out to sea stands the red rock of **HELGOLAND**, well-known landmark and now once again a popular resort... Along the coast of the North Sea stretches the chain of the **EAST** and **NORTH FRISIAN ISLANDS**, all of them popular seaside resorts, each with its own special character.... At **FLENSBURG** ..... on the Danish border, is the old **Northern Gate**, built in 1595, the "Gateway to Scandinavia." Other unique features of the town are the **pharmacy** dating from 1604 and the **Old Flensburg House**, with its fine interior.... **KIEL** .... is identified in most people's minds with the **North Sea Canal** (Kiel Canal), for which it forms the eastern end. St. Nicholas' Church has a notable crucifix and a bronze font of the fourteenth century. There are collections of works by Schleswig-Holstein painters dating from the seventeenth century in the **Hall of Art** and unusual items in the **Theatrical Museum**. There are many seaside resorts on the shores of the Baltic between Kiel and Lübeck, some very fashionable and others quiet and remote. ... The former Hanseatic town and presently flourishing port of **LUBECK** . . . . . . is generally regarded as the most beautiful town of northern Germany. In the Middle Ages, it was head of the League and its ancient buildings, lofty towers and old gabled houses furnish a vivid picture of its old prosperity when its proud burgesses held undisputed supremacy over the Baltic. The massive **Holsten Gate** at the entrance to the old quarters is a fifteenth-century medieval fortified gateway now housing a museum. Not far away is the splendid **St. Mary's Church**, one of the most admirable examples of low-German brick architecture and also one of the best specimens of early-Gothic in Germany. The combination of old and new in Lübeck extends into the arts where, for example, the fourteenth-century **St. Catherine's Church** has modern-style sculptures by Barlach, and **St. Anne's Museum** features arts and crafts going back to the thirteenth century, while **Behn House** exhibits modern paintings and sculptures. Lübeck's outer suburb of **Travemünde** is a popular seaside resort with a fine fishing harbor. The nearby town of **Eutin** is the birthplace of the illustrious Carl Maria von Weber, notable composer of "Freischütz," "Oberon" and other operas. One of the oldest edifices in Romanesque brick architecture is the beautifully situated **Cathedral**, founded in 1154, and the oldest North German church built of unhewn stone is **St. George's Church**, both in **Ratzeburg**, south of Lübeck.

WINTER, BAVARIAN ALPS German National Tourist Office

HAMBURG. The center of bustling Hamburg stands on former marsh islands in the angle between the Alster and Elbe Rivers and is honeycombed by a close network of alleys and narrow canals squeezed between the houses, with large brick office buildings standing on piles rammed deep into the ground or clinging firmly to the water's edge. An international rendezvous, renowned shipbuilding center and trading hub, she is Germany's largest seaport. Her life is determined by the unceasing ebb and flow which brings the cargo-heavy ships into the port and carries them out again, a characteristic shared by those other towns in the North German Lowlands whose amazing vitality and spirit were fused into the powerful Hanseatic League. Today Hamburg is still a Free and Hanse Town, one of the two in the German Confederation. Upon this independent tradition, a self-confident and orderly town has been developed by her hard-working, enterprising, self-reliant citizens. Especially revealing of this vital Hamburg spirit is the section known as "Twieten," where even the old streets are named for foreign countries, well-known trading firms or shipping companies.

. . . . Southeast of Hamburg is **LUNEBURG,** another former powerful Hanseatic town and now a spa and tourist center, situated in beautiful, lonely heath country. The town is predominantly late-Gothic in character, with old brick **patrician houses** of the fourteenth to sixteenth centuries. . . . In quiet, aristocratic **CELLE,**

FLENSBURG

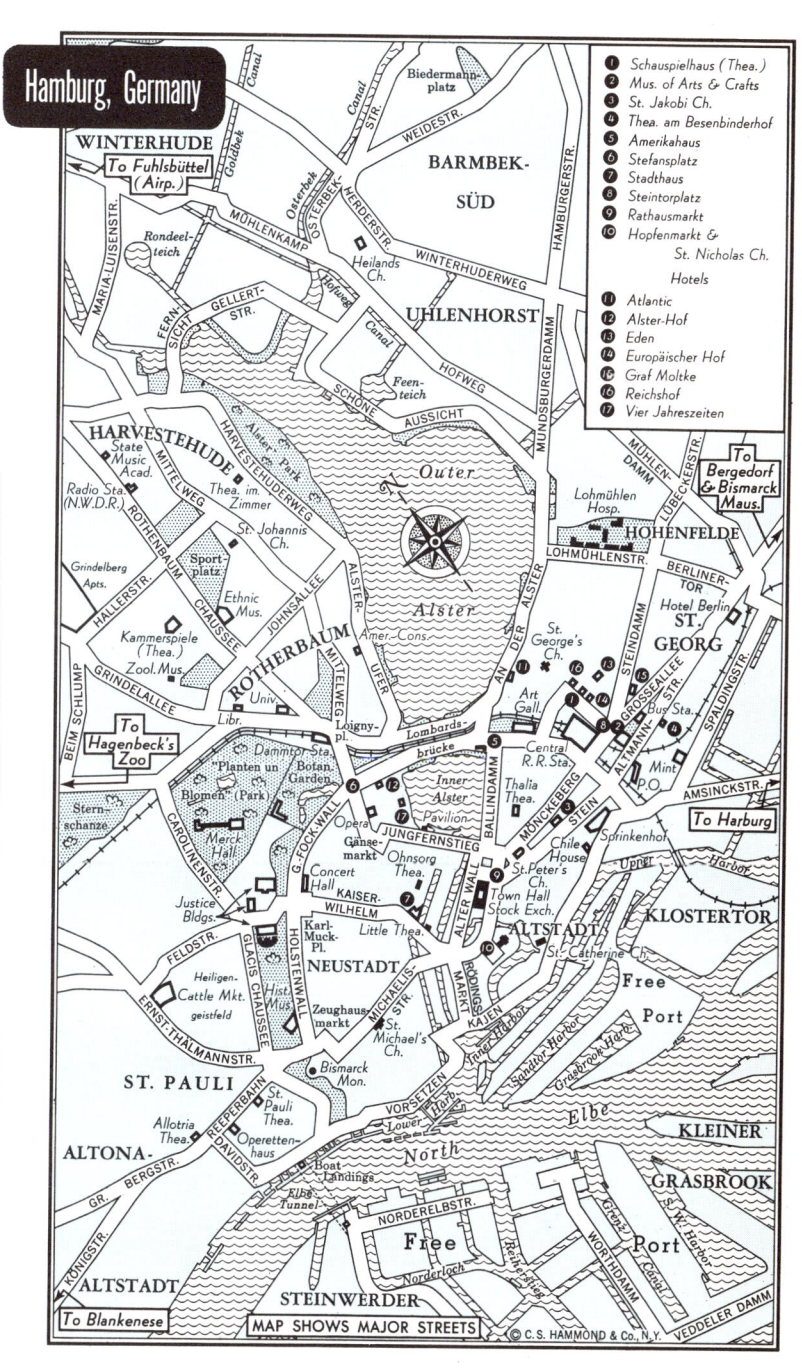

HAMBURG HARBOR

Hamburg, Germany

1. Schauspielhaus (Thea.)
2. Mus. of Arts & Crafts
3. St. Jakobi Ch.
4. Thea. am Besenbinderhof
5. Amerikahaus
6. Stefansplatz
7. Stadthaus
8. Steintorplatz
9. Rathausmarkt
10. Hopfenmarkt & St. Nicholas Ch.

Hotels
11. Atlantic
12. Alster-Hof
13. Eden
14. Europäischer Hof
15. Graf Moltke
16. Reichshof
17. Vier Jahreszeiten

49

southwest of Lüneburg, are old houses of the sixteenth and seventeenth centuries and the **Ducal Palace**, built by Italian architects in the seventeenth century, with a magnificent baroque interior, fine chapel and the oldest court theater. . . . Another free Hanse town is Germany's oldest port city, **BREMEN** . . . . In the historical records, it appears for the first time under the reign of Charlemagne. A leading member of the League, it became a free city in 1646 and in 1949 joined the German Federal Republic. In the center of the old **market place** is the **Roland Statue** (1404), landmark of the city, and flanking it are the noted Gothic **Town Hall**, built one year later, with a Renaissance façade and the oldest German "Ratskeller," and the Romanesque-Gothic **Cathedral** (1043), underneath which is the famous **Lead Cellar** containing several mummified bodies. The **Boettcherstrasse**, not far from the market place, has been reconstructed in the old Bremen style by leading artists and the ancient fortifications are now delightful **promenades**. A city noted for its monuments, Bremen's outstanding memorial is a sculptured group representing the "Bremen Street Musicians." The **Hall of Art** has a notable collection of 200,000 engravings.

BERLIN. In its long history, which began in the thirteenth century, Berlin has survived many vicissitudes. At present it is a divided city carved into two sectors, East Berlin and West Berlin. With their widely differing political and administrative policies, each contrasts sharply with

ENGLISH GARDEN, BERLIN

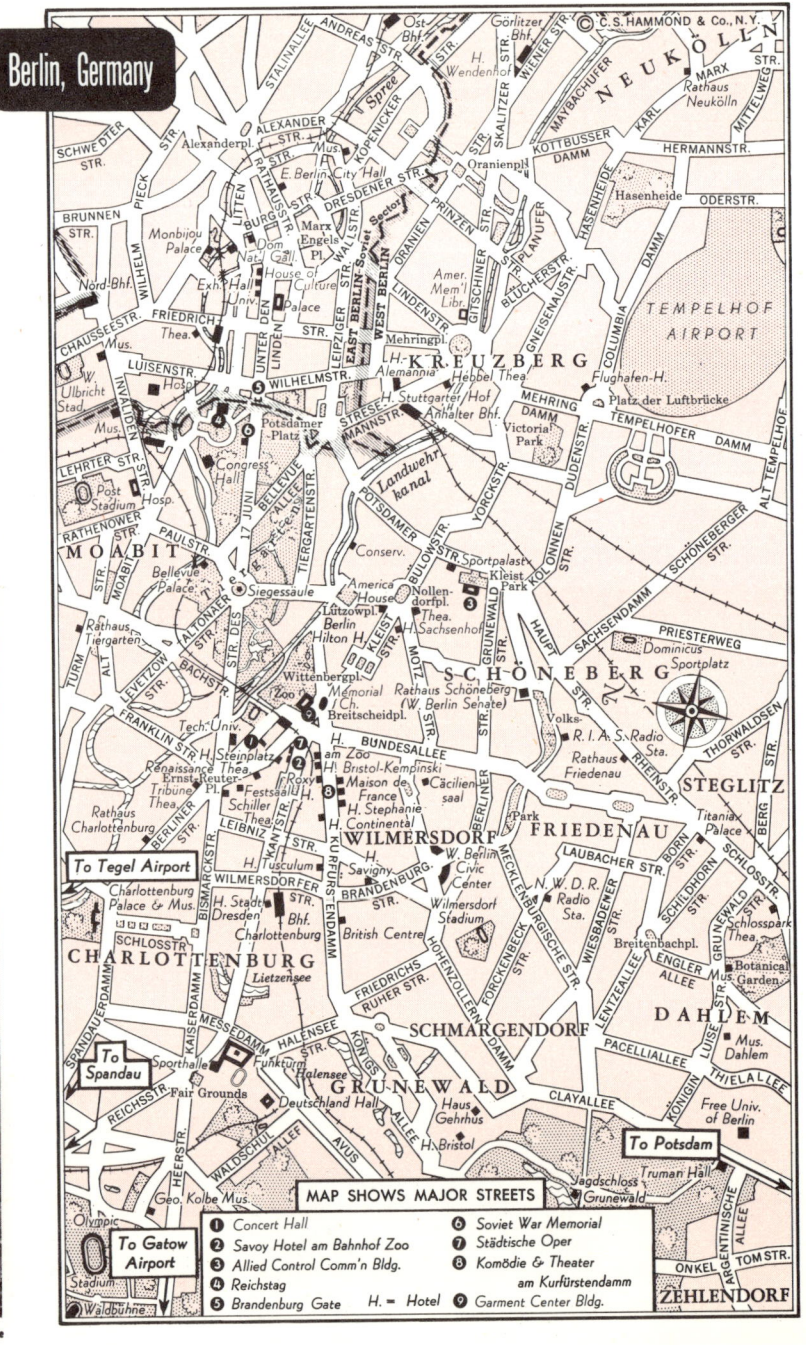

LUNEBURG

50

the other. There is much in communist-dominated East Berlin that is reminiscent of the Nazi regime; the fear, the drab despair remain, only the uniforms of the ever-present police have changed. On the other hand, West Berlin, isolated as it is in the Soviet Zone of Germany, has become a symbol of freedom and a refuge for those fleeing from communist oppression. More than a decade has passed since bombers and field artillery poured their terrible havoc on the Prussian splendor that was pre-war Berlin, yet even today the former capital of the German Empire still bears the deep scars of battle. With over one-fifth of the city destroyed at the close of World War II, many of its beloved landmarks are gone—the Kaiser Friedrich museum, the Hohenzollern palace, the famed bronze Quadriga statue that once so proudly surmounted Brandenburg Gate. Others, like the charred and gutted ruins of the Kaiser Wilhelm Memorial Church, stand as grim reminders of war's destruction. Yet despite her physical devastation, the industriousness of her people, their intellectual vitality and wit are in many ways responsible for Berlin maintaining her rightful place among the great metropolises of Europe and the world. In the Western sector much has been done to clear away the rubble, to rebuild and repair the damage. The beautiful Tiergarten which was totally destroyed has been restored to a semblance of its former old-world loveliness by gifts of trees from Great Britain and Japan. The zoological garden is again a major attraction. Modern buildings rise to fill some gaping emptiness; and with the aid of American dollars, Berlin has regained her industrial prowess. Factories are again turning out the electrical, fine mechanical and optical goods that German craftsmen have made world famous. Automobiles and heavy machinery roll from assembly lines and the printing and paper processing industries flourish. Along the Kurfürstendamm and Tauentzienstrasse, West Berlin's main thoroughfares, the many shops are well stocked and bustling with trade in contrast to the shops of East Berlin where only a few commodities are freely sold. Here too, the nightclubs, the restaurants and little sidewalk cafés, the theaters and cinemas are filled once more with the gay crowds and the laughter so long absent from Berlin. And from the New Town Hall in Schöneberg the deep voice of the 20,950-pound Liberty Bell rings out, for all to hear, its daily reminder of a newly-won freedom.

BERLIN'S FREE UNIVERSITY

THE HAVEL RIVER

Scandinavia

AMALIENBORG PALACE
Danish National Tourist Office

INIMITABLE HOSPITALITY

Although separate countries, each with its own special attractions, **Denmark, Norway, Sweden** and **Finland** make up a unit difficult for the traveler to separate. The indescribable beauty of lakes and woodland, ultra-modern architecture in ancient cities studded with historic monuments and reminders of bygone centuries, gently rolling plains ringed by massive mountains and fjords, and the high quality industrial products and wondrous handicrafts may be peculiar to one country only, yet a part of all four.

Of course, Scandinavia is a notable winter-sports area, where fine skiing is enjoyed even in the spring and summer in the arctic north. Perhaps not so well-known, though, is the fact that this whole area provides excellent fishing, marvelous swimming from extensive beaches of immaculate white sand and superb sailing.

American travelers will experience a particular kinship with these peoples, because of the very qualities which distinguish them from some other peoples of the world — the exquisite modern architecture, the high standard of living and the democratic social and political systems. So justly proud of their contributions to contemporary living, these Scandinavians also possess the one final attribute to make everyone's visit the truly unforgettable experience — their unmatched friendliness and hospitality.

GOOD FOOD

And lots of it — is another Scandinavian specialty. Although the traditional cold table or *smorgasbord* (*koldtbord* in Norwegian) is not as common since the war as it once was in Sweden, the big center table, groaning with good things, is still to be found, and in Norway it is still famous for its variety of dishes such as smoked salmon, fresh lobster and Norwegian shrimp. The other food feature common to most Scandinavian countries but extra-special in Denmark is the open-faced sandwich (*smorrebrod* in Danish, *smorbrod* in Norwegian), consisting of a thin slice of buttered bread, heaped with products from farm and sea in hundreds of combinations. Other taste delights in Denmark include the famed Danish pastry, tempting desserts, beer, akvavit and cherry liqueur, while in Norway, venison, ptarmigan in cream sauce, wild raspberries, cloudberries and brown trout are outstanding. As a matter of fact, in all these countries the fruits and berries are out of this world, and there is a variety of tasty sea food.

Denmark

COPENHAGEN. Developing from a 12th century fishing village, friendly and hospitable, Copenhagen has been considered the capital of Denmark since 1416. The city occupies a spot on the eastern shore of Zealand Island and is separated from Sweden by only a 20-mile stretch of water. Because of its fine sheltered harbor and its strategic location at the gateway to the Baltic, Copenhagen has for many years been considered one of the principal ports of Northern Europe. Also, as Copenhagen is a "free port" through which foreign goods can pass duty-free, it is an important trans-shipping center. A section known as Stroget is the heart of the city's business and commercial life. Here are found concentrated many of the city's office buildings, places of amusement, shops and colorful flower, fruit and vegetable stalls. The Langelinie (Long Line) is probably the most beautiful of Copenhagen's handsome boulevards. A favorite promenade, it sweeps along the edge of the Sound, affording a wonderful panorama of the city's harbor. Along this drive can be seen the famous statue of Hans Christian Andersen's "Little Mermaid." Immortalized in bronze, she gazes thoughtfully across the blue water. Amalienborg Square opens off the Langelinie. Here are found the four rococo mansions which comprise the Amalienborg Palace, residence of the Danish king. Once the homes of four noble families, the mansions were acquired for the king after a fire had destroyed the Christiansborg Palace in 1794. Today Christiansborg Palace, which five times in its long history has been demolished by fire or enemy attack, houses the Parliament (Rigsdag), the Supreme Court and the Royal Reception Rooms. The present Christiansborg Palace, restored 1907-1915, occupies a site where Bishop Absalon had built a palace in 1167. The crumbling ruins of the Bishop's palace may still be seen beneath the present one. The beautiful renaissance Rosenborg Castle is now a museum containing treasure of the Danish royal family, including the crown jewels and the royal regalia. In the heart of Copenhagen is the famed Tivoli, whose romantic gardens with their idyllic atmosphere, symphony orchestra, ballet, restaurants and scores of amusements and divertisements attract over four million guests during its summer season. Here a charming Pantomime Theater still preserves the commedia dell'arte. The Tivoli, created

TOWN HALL
Danish National Tourist Office

52

Copenhagen, Denmark

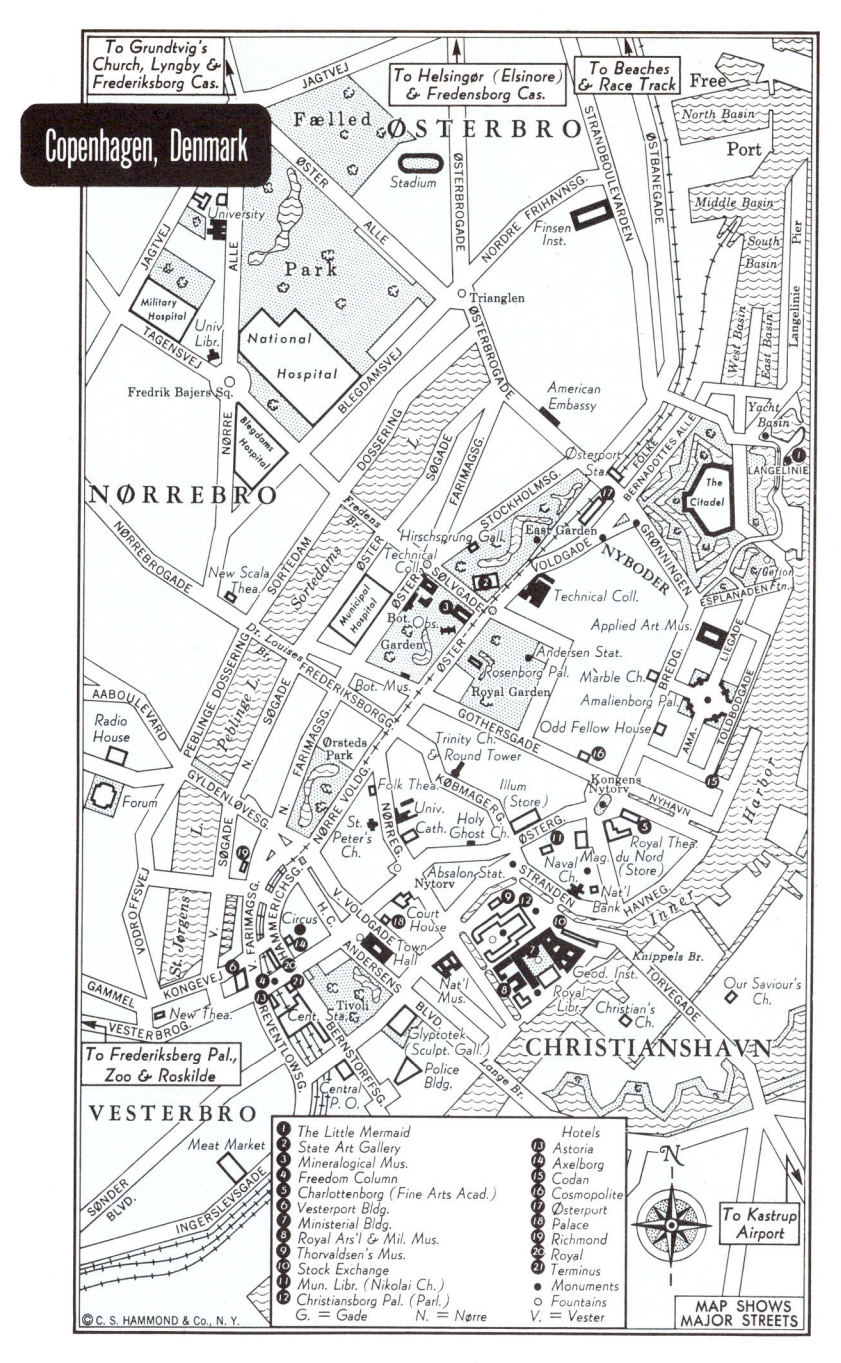

STOCK EXCHANGE BUILDING
Danish National Tourist Office

over a century ago by the genius showman Georg Carstensen, is truly the fairy garden of Denmark. Probably the most noted of Copenhagen's industries is the manufacture of the internationally renowned Copenhagen porcelain. Fired at exceedingly high temperatures, this lovely porcelain is distinguished for its subtle under-glaze colors of blue, brown, green and its exquisite glaze and translucency. West of the capital is **ROSKILDE**, the medieval capital, where the ancient, twin-spired **Cathedral**, founded in 1170, contains forty of Denmark's royal tombs. . . . At **RINGSTED** is St. Bendt (St. Benedict) **Abbey Church**, dating from the twelfth century, the finest Roman brick church in Scandinavia. . . . Near **SLAGELSE**, farther west, is the unique Viking stockade stronghold of **Trelleborg**, built in the year 1000, which in the wintertime garrisoned 1000 warriors. . . . Nearly all types of Danish scenery are to be seen on Funen Island, the "garden of Denmark," with its idyllic half-timbered country cottages and beautiful manor houses and castles. **ODENSE** . . . . third largest town in Denmark, is the native town of Hans Christian Andersen, beloved author of oft-told fairy tales, and his **birthplace** is now a museum. Beautiful St. Canute's Cathedral, an edifice of great effect, has a richly carved, brilliantly gilded altar piece and a remarkable pulpit. The **Old Funen Village** comprises seventeen old farm houses and dwellings collected from all parts of the island. . . . In east Jutland is the quaint, little town of **CHRISTIANSFELD** that still bears the stamp of the Moravians who settled here in 1773. The famous honey cake **bakery** still remains, and the **churchyard**, "God's acre," is extraordinary. . . . Across the moor is **RIBE**. Denmark's oldest medieval town, more than 1100 years old, noted for its narrow streets and incredibly low houses with storks nesting on the roofs. The impressive **Cathedral** was built about 1130. . . . Near **VEJLE**, on the east coast, is the **Jellinge Stone**, raised a thousand years ago, with inscription in runic letters, over King Gorm and his Queen Thyra. It contains the first graven image of Christ found in the North. . . . **SILKEBORG** is a comparatively modern town in the lake district, the fisherman's Eldorado, of Jutland. All through the summer months the **river steamers** maintain frequent service through the lakes, stopping at all points of interest. . . . Denmark's second largest city is **AARHUS** . . . . Here, in the splendid **Botanical Gardens**, an **old provincial town** has been revived picturing life in a Danish town right back to the sixteenth century, with ancient houses of historical value collected from the whole of Denmark. Historical plays are performed here, too. Every week organ concerts are held in **St. Clemens' Cathedral**, the longest church in Scandinavia. Visitors also like the strikingly modern **Town Hall** and **University of Aarhus** and the nine miles of bathing beaches encircling the town. . . . Across the Bay of Aarhus, on the peninsula of Mols, is the fairy-tale town of **EBELTOFT** with the smallest **town hall** in the world, and the watchman singing his songs every night. . . . **AALBORG** is the gay city of northern Jutland. At the town center is **Jens Bangs Stenhus**, Scandinavia's biggest and best-preserved private edifice from the Renaissance period, built by a wealthy seventeenth-century merchant, and Sct. Budolfi Kirke (St. Botolph's Church), with its unusual spire, rich furnishings and medieval mural paintings. Tours may be taken through the world-renowned Aalborg Akvavit (snaps) distilleries. A favorite with all is luxurious Kilden Restaurant.... From here one can visit the vacation spot of REBILD NATIONAL PARK, where an inspiring and picturesque observance of American Independence Day is held every year.... Moens Klint, on the east coast of the ISLAND OF MOEN is famed as a beauty spot because of the curiously formed white chalk cliffs rising steeply from the sea..... In the Baltic, southeast of Copenhagen, is the holiday island of BORNHOLM, a veritable bather's paradise with its long stretches of sandy beach and miles of sand dunes. Its historic round churches at one time served as fortresses.

Norway

OSLO. Since the time of the intrepid Vikings, life in fjord-bordered Norway has been influenced by the sea and Norsemen have been skillful and fearless seafarers. From the unbelievable voyages of Leif Eriksson to modern luxury cruises, these heroic sailors have recorded proud deeds of courage and daring on the earth's indomitable oceans. And Oslo, capital and coveted home port at the head of beautiful Oslo Fjord, is a city dominated by the water, containing many relics of their sailing tradition. Here, for instance, are three remarkable Viking ships, invoking exciting thoughts of that amazing early age. Here, too, is the *Fram*, which has been further south and north than any other ship in the world, since she was built for Nansen's polar expedition, was also used on Otto Sverdrup's expedition and, finally, by Roald Amundsen on his expedition to the South Pole in 1910. And more up-to-date, here is the renowned Kon Tiki balsa-log raft of Thor Heyerdahl. This love for the sea extends even into Oslo's sports life, for she has many excellent harbors for sailing and fishing craft and glorious beaches on her numerous lakes, rivers and the fjord.

FJORD JOURNEY

... Charming STAVANGER is in the "Fjord Country," an ideal holiday district. The twelfth-century cathedral, one of the most beautiful stone churches in Norway, has a pulpit with magnificent wood carvings. Venerable Kongsgaard School was used in the olden days as a residence for the king. Tours may be made of the Canning Industry School, only one of its kind in Scandinavia, and one of the large canning factories. A great tourist attraction is the steamer trip into the peculiar Lyse fjord, with Pulpit Rock, completely flat on top but rising 1,970 feet above the fjord.... During the years of Norway's greatness, BERGEN ..... also in the west-coast "Fjord Country," was virtually capital of the country for close on a century and a half (1164-1299) and at

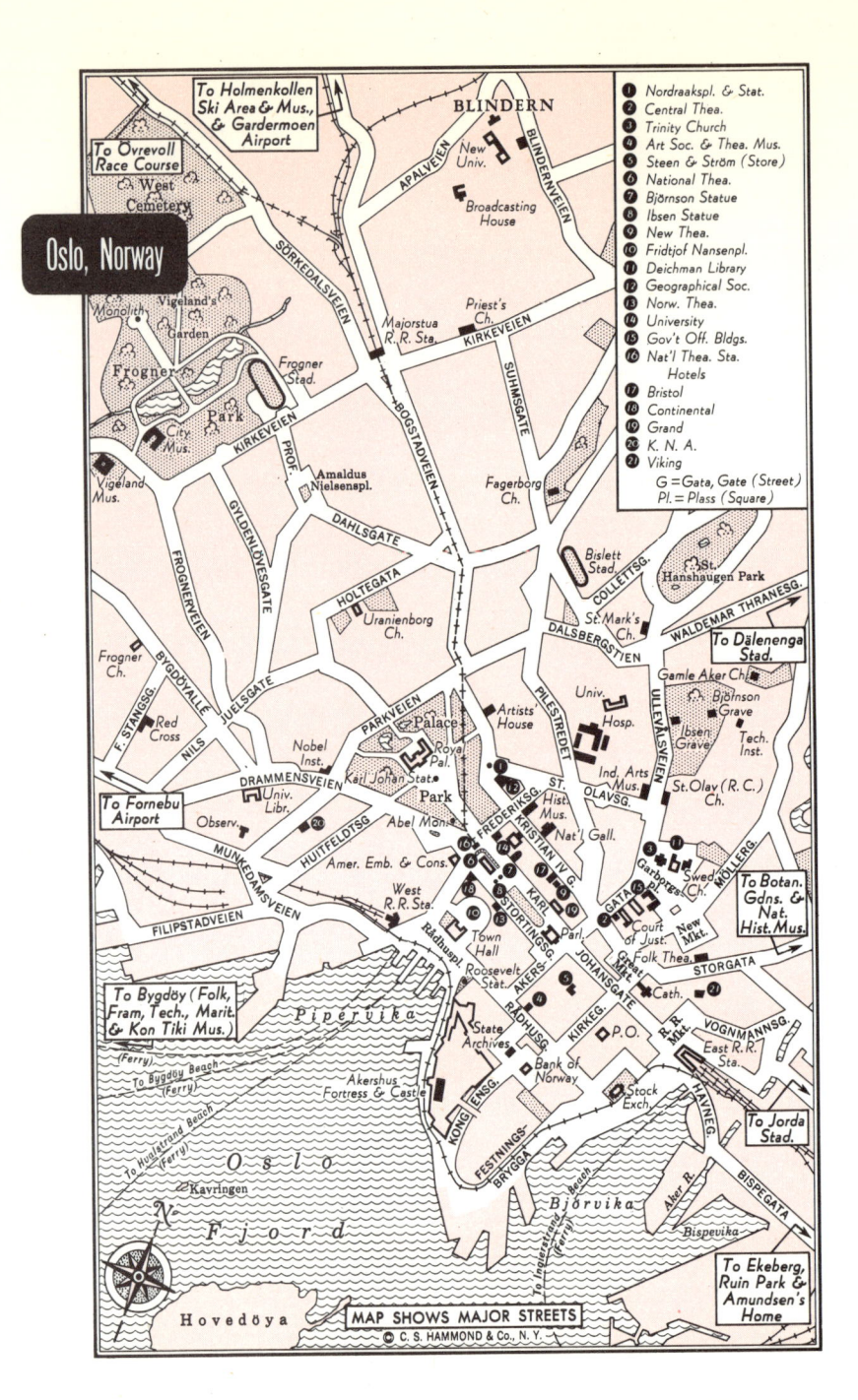

KON-TIKI MUSEUM

Austin C. Wehrwein

an early date became one of the important outposts of the Hanseatic League, vividly recalled by "Gamle Bergen" (Old Bergen), the Bryggen (Quays), Fantoft Stave Church and the Hanseatic Museum. The Bergen Festival, held in early June, includes intimate and orchestral concerts in Edvard Grieg's home, "Troldhaugen," and plays and folk pageants in the medieval castle of Bergenhus. The countryside is ideal for hiking and from the seven mountains surrounding the town there are magnificent views of the sea and land for miles around, especially from the top of Mount Floyen (1,040 feet). Not least of the town's attractions is the hustle and bustle of its picturesque streets, and the famous fish market as a focal point. As a matter of fact, the city has a well-merited reputation for its sea-food cuisine. Trips may be made via the Bergen Railway to famous ski and trout-fishing resorts like Al, Finse and Voss. . . . BALESTRAND is one of the leading holiday centers, situated on a promontory in the Sogne fjord. . . . GEIRANGER, one of the outstanding beauty spots of Norway, nestles at the head of the narrow Geiranger fjord with the graceful "Seven Sisters" and "Bridal Veil" waterfalls. . . . Bombed and entirely burned out in 1940, MOLDE, the "Town of Roses" on the Romsdal fjord, has been rebuilt, and is a center for fishing, swimming or mountain climbing. . . . Friendly little LILLEHAMMER, facing Lake Mjosa, is one of Norway's finest holiday resorts in the Gudbrandsdal valley north of Oslo, where national costume is still worn at work and play. The climate is particularly healthy and refreshing. . . . A favorite with visitors is TRONDHEIM, famous for its wide streets, but whose chief attraction is the magnificent Nidaros Cathedral, one of the proudest architectural treasures of the North. The kings of Norway are crowned in this cathedral. Close to this imposing Gothic edifice, which dates from the twelfth century, lies the 1,000-year-old Archbishop's palace. The old Governor's Residence (Stiftsgården), built in 1770, and now used as a Royal Palace, is Norway's largest timber building. . . . North Norway, consisting of the three counties of Nordland, Troms and Finmark, is situated almost entirely within the Arctic Circle. This is the home of those nomadic, reindeer-tending Lapps and the "Land of the Midnight Sun," where the traveler enjoys a profusion of blazing color and light such as no other scenery can offer. Perhaps the most outstanding holiday journey one can undertake is the wonderful twelve-day cruise by modern express steamer from Bergen or Trondheim along the entire coast past North Cape to Kirhenes and back. TROMSO, the "Capital of the Arctic," on an island, has a grand view of ice-covered mountains. Visitors may see in the sound the giant German battleship Tirpitz, sunk by the R. A. F. in 1944.

LOFOTEN FISHERIES

THE STAVE CHURCH

Sweden

On the west coast of Sweden, GOTHENBURG'S . . . . . . modern public buildings are outstanding examples of contemporary Swedish architecture, and the Art Gallery and Röhss Museum of Industrial Art contain exceptional collections. One of the most popular in Northern Europe, Liseberg Amusement Park has good restaurants, a music hall and theaters, in addition to the usual carnival attractions. Trädgårdsföreningen is perhaps the most beautiful of the many parks and the flowers in the Botanical Gardens are magnificent. Concert House, featuring an excellent symphony orchestra, is renowned for its particularly good acoustics. A favorite attraction is the three-day trip to Stockholm on the charming Göta Canal, through 400 miles of beautiful countryside. . . . To the north is the playground for those who love briny water and hot sun. Here are the finest sailing waters in Sweden and the annual international regattas at MARSTRAND are the festive climax of the yachting season. The cod fishing, too, is marvelous. . . . To the south is the popular west-coast resort of HALMSTAD, which prides itself on a famous fountain, "Europa and the Bull," by the contemporary sculptor Carl Milles. The beautiful medieval St. Nicolai Church, with its interesting sepulchral tablets, is noteworthy, while the Town Hall is an excellent example of modern architecture and construction. . . . BASTAD, an exclusive vacation center, is the site of major tennis and golf tournaments. . . . Located on the narrowest part of the sound between Sweden and Denmark, where some of the best tuna fishing in the world is to be found, HALSINGBORG . . . has had great importance for years. **Kärnan**, the central bastion in the medieval castle, the most remarkable relic of its kind in Scandinavia, still dominates the city scene,

TOWN HALL, STOCKHOLM

Swedish National Travel Office

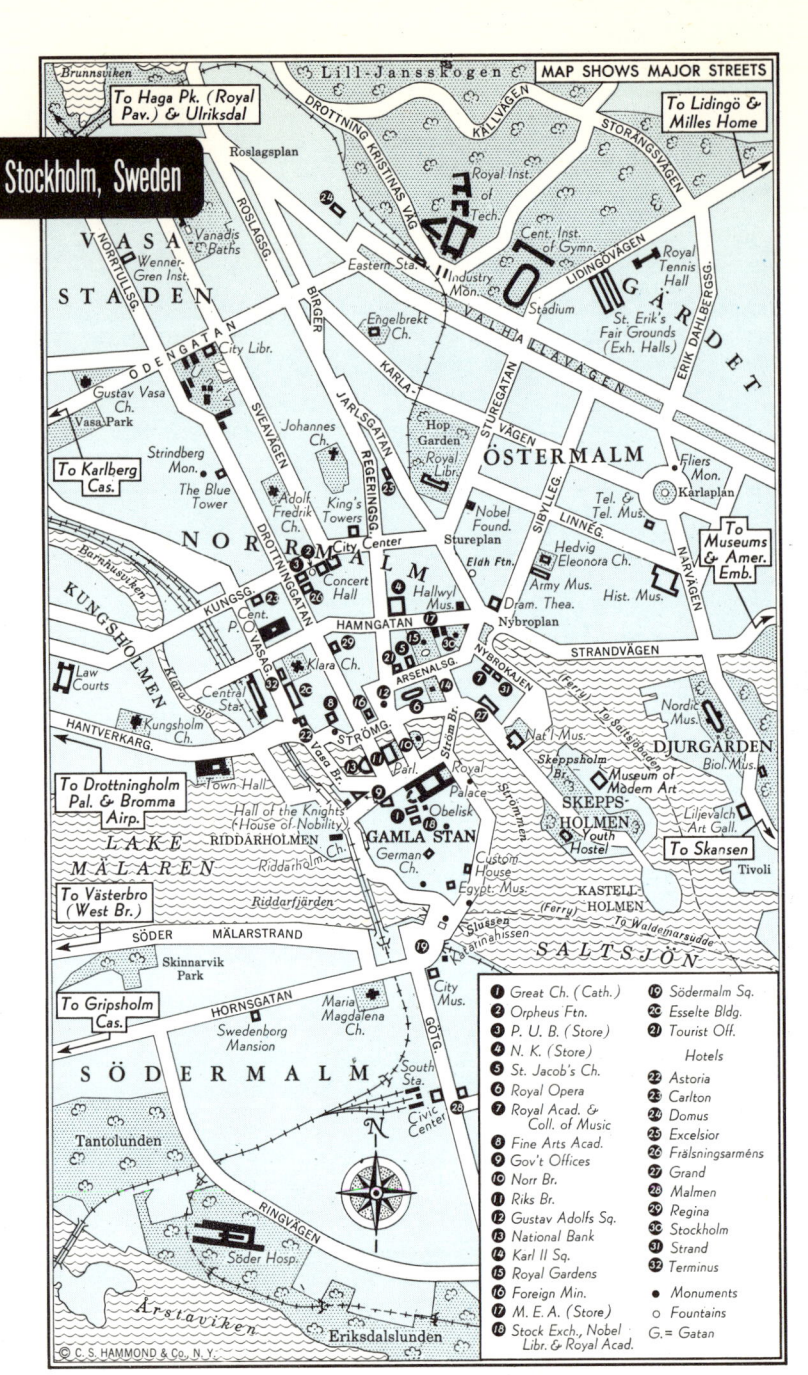

and once was a meeting place for the princes and potentates of much of Europe. The thirteenth-century **Maria Church** has exquisite old furnishings. Popular nearby vacation spots are **Ramlösa Spa, Mölle, Torekov** and the island **Hallands Väderö**, a national park with unusual flora and a wealth of birds. . . . MALMO . . . . across from Copenhagen, Denmark, is one of the oldest cities in this part of the world. Malmöhus Castle: built from 1434-1542, was once a powerful fortress and during its long history has served as a prison, restaurant and now museum. **City Theater** is generally regarded as the most modern in Europe. : . . The university town of LUND is the cultural center of the fertile southern region and well-known for Scandinavia's finest Romanesque **cathedral** dating from the early twelfth century, which contains a number of valuable treasures from the Middle Ages, including a giant astronomical clock. . . . The impressive, fortified **Kalmar Castle** of immense strength, at KALMAR on the southeast coast, the oldest parts of which date from the twelfth century, was once known as "the Lock and Key of Sweden." . . . Almost without exception, the people on the island of OLAND, across the sound from Kalmar, have relatives in the United States.

STOCKHOLM. A row of blazing torches lights up the classic columns of the Concert House every December tenth. Crowds gather in the square as shiny limousines pull up beside Milles' celebrated Orpheus fountain, discharging notable persons from all over the world to take part in the cultural and social highlights of the year — the Nobel Festival. The festival, though, is only one manifestation of life in Stockholm. World-renowned is the entire new trend in style known as Swedish Modern, synonymous with the best in contemporary arts and crafts, and the "City on the Water" is its cradle. Exquisite glassware, fine silver, striking interior decoration — all are influenced by this new trend, visible in the buildings, the sculpture and the museums. The 700-year-old capital, never ravaged by war, shows the influences serving as its foundations: the thirteenth-century Riddarholm Church, burial place of Swedish kings; seventeenth-century Skokloster Castle, overflowing with art, and handsome Hall of the Knights, modeled on French and Italian classicism; and the French-influenced, eighteenth-century, unique Court Theater of Drottningham Palace, and extraordinarily imposing and symmetrically satisfying Royal Palace.

With more than 10,000 islands, the Stockholm Archipelago presents one of the world's most unusual seascapes, a paradise for swimming, fishing and sailing. The two principal centers are Saltsjöbaden and Sandhamn where big regattas take place. . . . Off the east coast of Sweden is the fabulous, legendary island of GOTLAND, the "Pearl of the Baltic." Visby's stately City Wall frustrated the attempts of many invaders, and Bulverket, the remains of another pre-historic fortification, built on poles over a shallow lake, is unlike anything elsewhere. Picture stones, from the pre-Viking era are also unique. Each summer a Miracle Play is performed in the ruins of St. Nicholas' Church, Visby. Some 200,000 migratory sea birds roost on small Stora Karlsö island each spring and the semi-wild "russ" horse, a small, ancient species, is found in no other place but Gotland. On the coast is the famous resort of Snäckgärdsbaden. . . . Picturesque UPPSALA, north of Stockholm, with Sweden's largest university and finest Gothic cathedral, is pervaded with an air of cultural repose. Uppsala Cathedral, whose 400-foot twin spires are equal to its entire length, contains a veritable treasure of textiles and silver and gold objects. On a hill commanding the town, is the sixteenth-century Uppsala Castle, scene of many great historical events, but of the town's prehistoric political importance as a stronghold of the heathen chieftains, nothing now remains but the gigantic burial mounds. A good time to visit here is on Walpurgis Night, the last day in April, when the Uppsala University students stage their traditional welcome to spring. . . . The province of Dalarna has long been a popular vacation region. To a great extent the local people still wear their colorful national costumes and have preserved many old customs.

VASTERBRO BRIDGE, STOCKHOLM — Swedish National Travel Office

MORA, on long, romantic Lake Siljan, is the goal of the big event of the skiing season, the 55-mile competition over the route once taken by King Gustav Vasa. . . . RATTVIK is the site of the unique church boat race in July, in which teams compete in the long, multi-oared boats used to take the lakeside villagers to church. . . . Equally popular in winter and summer among skiers, fishermen and hunters is the beautiful, invigorating Swedish mountain range stretching north from Dalarna, including the holiday centers of STORLIEN, FJALLNAS and VALADALEN. . . . More and more people are discovering the strange and unusual beauty of that vast snow-capped region where, north of the Arctic Circle, the Midnight Sun never sets for forty days and nights — a country of rolling mountains, of endless plains where nomadic Lapps still graze their reindeer herds, of waterfalls, glaciers and rivers. In up-to-date KIRUNA, about 100 miles north of the Artic Circle, is a most remarkable church, built of wood on an architectural theme drawn from the design of a Lapp hut. . . . ABISKO and RIKSGRANSEN are resorts in this area.

Finland

Heart of HELSINKI . . . . . . the lively, modern capital of Finland, is Senate Square, or the Great Square. Since most of the buildings surrounding it were designed in the early nineteenth century by the same architect, the whole square forms a remarkably homogeneous and attractive sight. Architecturally it is Empire, with its neoclassical slanting roofs over bright-colored buildings. The north side is dominated by the magnificent Great Church of Helsinki, with its beautiful columns and minarets, while the old Helsinki University Building is on the western side. The only exception to these Empire buildings is the mansard-roofed Sederholm Residence, built in 1750. On Mannerheim Road, the main boulevard, is the impressive, modern Eduskuntatalo (Parliament House) of red Finnish granite and the Kansallismuseo (National Museum), with its tower, incorporating the facades of a palace, a castle and a church. Just off this road is the railway square, with the famous Rautatie Asema (Railway Station), one of the most beautiful public buildings in Finland; Ateneum Art Gallery and Kansallisteatteri (National Theater). The Mannerheim Museo, a conspicuous yellow wooden house, was the home of C. G. Mannerheim, Marshall of Finland, and is now preserved as a museum with all his trophies and relics. Since the Finns are great sports-loving people,

SKANSEN—OUT-OF-DOOR MUSEUM AND ZOO — Swedish National Travel Office

57

there are a number of stadiums in the capital, but the most important is **Olympic Stadium**, built for the 1952 Olympic Games. The top balcony of the stadium tower commands a wide view of the city, coastal islands and dense forests of the interior. **Suomenlinna**, the Gibraltar of the North, is a group of fortified islands with ramparts protecting the approaches to Helsinki. This island fortress has had a long and stirring history, and the special atmosphere of former centuries can be felt even today. Visitors should also make the t.ip to **Korkeasaari Island Zoo**, rich in northern fauna. Seurasaari island, with its open-air museum and a village made up of original old wooden farm buildings from various districts, is a fine natural park and a popular swimming place. Folk dancing and an open-air theater take place during the summer. The most famous of all Helsinki festivals is the **Sibelius Festival**, held in early June in the Festival Hall of Helsinki University, in honor of Jean Sibelius, Finland's native son.... The tourist cannot help being struck by the profusion of lakes in Finland, and no one should miss taking a cruise through one of the important watercourses on a white passenger steamer. In this way, travel to **AULANKO NATIONAL PARK**, the number one lake resort near Hämeenlinna, Sibelius' native town. Here you can enjoy the excellent beach, a traditional *sauna* (Finnish steambath) or a restful afternoon by the idyllic swan lake....... Former capital **TURKU** .... second largest city in Finland, dating back to about 1150, grew up round its famous **Cathedral**. Its archipelago is considered the most beautiful in the country, and the **Turku Castle** an outstanding landmark. . . . Unique experiences are provided by a thrilling rapid-shooting trip in the north, demonstrations by lumberjacks of their hazardous skills in several log-rolling contests or a trip to **KILPISJARVI**, in the heart of the vast, barren arctic expanse north of the Arctic Circle, where herds of reindeer are tended by colorfully costumed Lapps.

LAPPS AND REINDEER "Finland Travel"

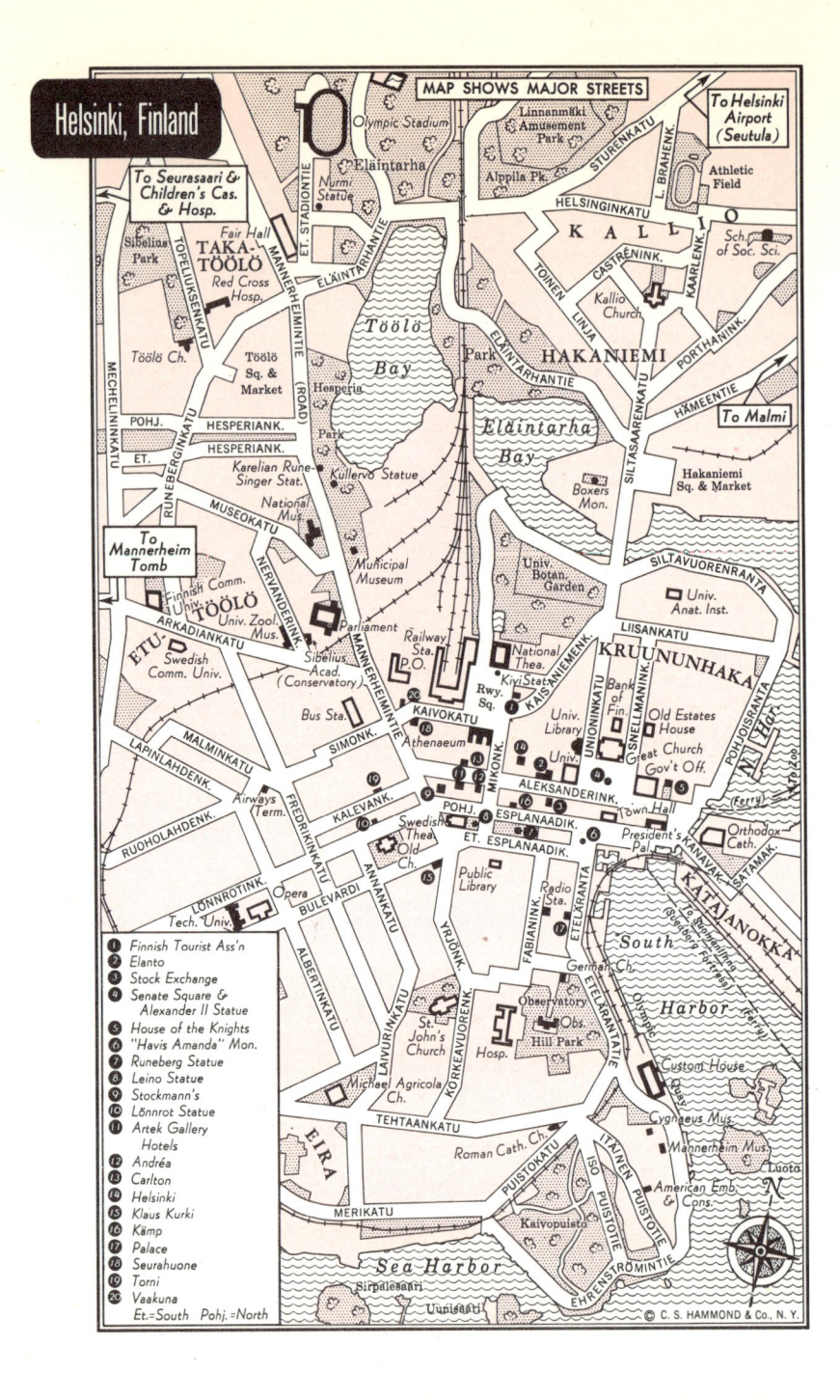

ONE OF FINLAND'S MANY LAKES "Finland Travel"

Switzerland

CHILLON CASTLE, MONTREUX

CROSSROADS OF EUROPE

Matchless scenery, centuries-old towns and traditions and the proud cultural heritage of the world's oldest republic have led travelers to Switzerland for generations. The rigid Swiss national standards of hospitality, superb cuisine, cleanliness and honesty appeal particularly to Americans and enable them to enjoy the details of living while they enjoy abundant scenic and historic charms. The scenery, which usually causes visiting writers to resort to the adjective "incomparable," is an ideal backdrop for the unlimited sport and recreation facilities found throughout the country. Of course, the really outstanding sports are mountaineering and skiing, for which this tiny republic has had a matchless reputation for generations, since fifty 13,000-footers, the most challenging peaks of the entire Alpine region, sparkle skyward in Switzerland's Alpine rampart. Beauty, hospitality, health, sport — and education — make this not only the favorite location for all kinds of international conferences, but also the favorite vacation area for people of all nations.

LINGUISTIC TALENT

In the north and east German is spoken by the natives. It's French in the southwest, Italian in the south and a centuries-old language derived from Latin called Romansch in some valleys in the southeast. But to the traveler, English is the universal tongue in Switzerland. Most educated people speak English.

CULINARY SPECIALTIES

French, German and Italian influences predominate in regions where those languages are spoken, so each region has its specialties: *fondue* and *raclette* (melted cheese dishes) in the French section; sausages, roasts and fried potatoes *(rösti)*, in the German section; air-dried beef *(bündnerfleisch)* and ham, sliced paper thin, in the Grisons; Italian specialties in the Ticino. Swiss pastries and desserts are world-famed. Swiss wines are excellent, especially when ordered in the region where the grapes are grown — always ask for the local wine. Swiss wines, unlike French, are best when new, and in general, white wines are preferred. Swiss brandies are delicious, but highly potent, with Marc, Kirsch, Pflümli most popular. Swiss beer, too, is excellent.

LAND OF WILLIAM TELL, SYMBOL OF FREEDOM

BERN. Throughout the centuries the Bernese have devoted every care to keeping their beautiful and unique city as it was built in the Middle Ages. It is to this tradition and care that we owe one of the best preserved medieval cities in Europe, a town which can be considered one of the loveliest adornments of the continent. For hundreds of years all households had to manage without water; however, as water is a necessity, fountains were erected in most of the streets. These public fountains naturally became the most popular meeting places and at the wide fountain basins busy clatter mingled with the splashing, sparkling water. It would indeed be fascinating if the figures which adorn them could tell us of the many events they have wit-

THE KRAMGASSE AND CLOCK TOWER, BERN

nessed since they first stood on their slender perches. But the figures themselves also all have a history and meaning of their own. Most striking feature of Bern's medieval architecture are the arcades, the arched-in pavements on both sides of the streets. Luxurious, tempting shop displays of intricate mechanical devices and other modern items provide for the window-shopper a vivid contrast as he strolls along under the massive, medieval arcades.

CATHEDRAL, BERN
Bern Tourist Association

TOWN HALL, BERN
Bern Tourist Association

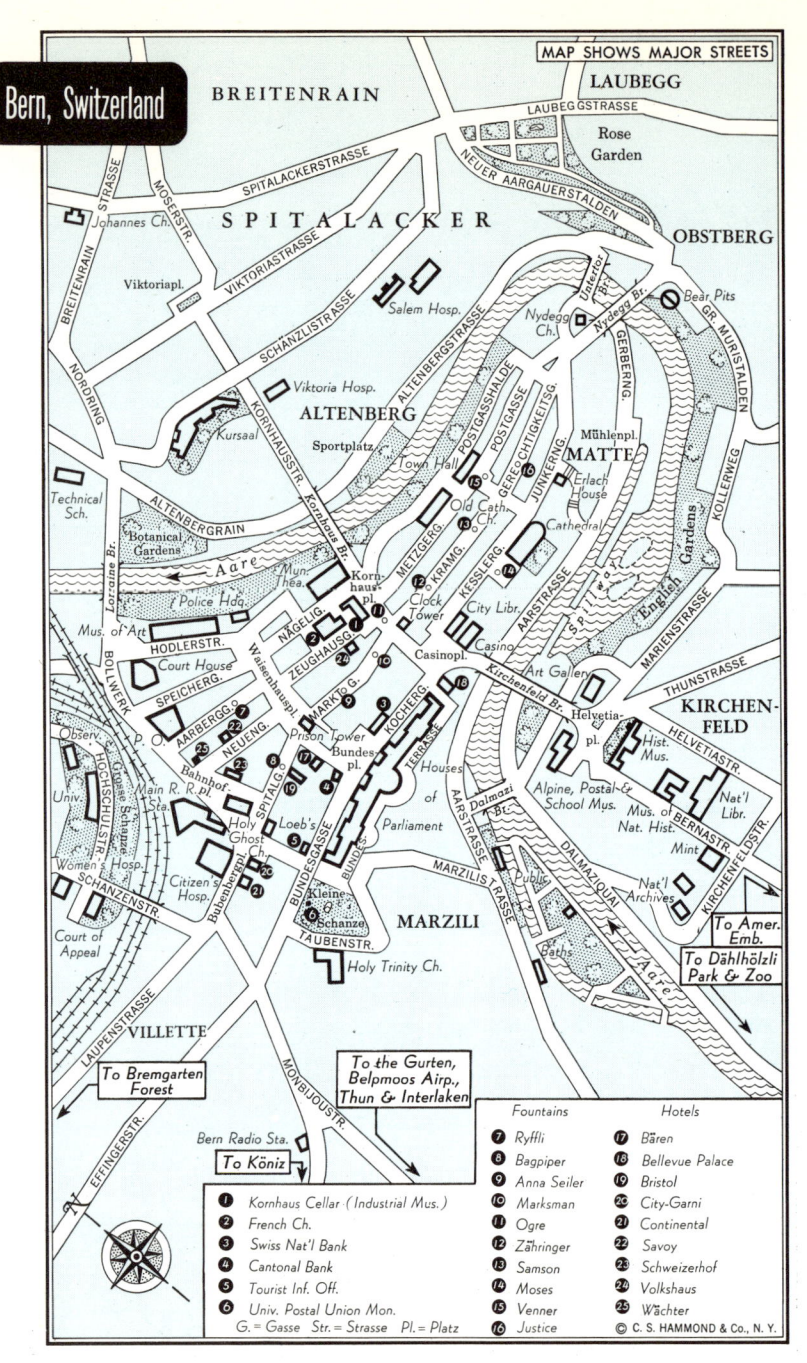

ASSEMBLY HALL OF LEGISLATURE, BERN
Bern Tourist Association

Bern, Switzerland

MAP SHOWS MAJOR STREETS

Fountains
7. Ryffli
8. Bagpiper
9. Anna Seiler
10. Marksman
11. Ogre
12. Zähringer
13. Samson
14. Moses
15. Venner
16. Justice

Hotels
17. Bären
18. Bellevue Palace
19. Bristol
20. City-Garni
21. Continental
22. Savoy
23. Schweizerhof
24. Volkshaus
25. Wächter

1. Kornhaus Cellar (Industrial Mus.)
2. French Ch.
3. Swiss Nat'l Bank
4. Cantonal Bank
5. Tourist Inf. Off.
6. Univ. Postal Union Mon.

G. = Gasse Str. = Strasse Pl. = Platz

© C. S. HAMMOND & Co., N.Y.

60

GENEVA. Since World War I, Geneva has become the international city par excellence. Her broad avenues, busy shopping streets and flower-decked lakeside promenades spread out comfortably around a wide bay. Tall, French-style buildings and innumerable sidewalk cafés lend a cosmopolitan air and even the most casual visitor has a sense of being in the center of things as he sips a smooth drink during the *apéritif* hour, watching the world go by and witnessing history in the making. However, Geneva did not need to wait for the League of Nations to win international recognition. Men began to settle here centuries before the great colonizing priod of the Roman Empire, for the crest of the hill on which the old quarters now rise afforded an ideal strategic position for primitive tribes. She was fairly insignificent, though, until John Calvin, ardent French champion of the Reformed Faith, sought a haven here. As a great religious leader, Calvin attracted famous scholars of his time and received many French, Italian and English refugees, making the city famous as the "Protestant Rome." A favorite residence of foreigners from this time, her reputation was further enhanced with her selection as the seat of the former League of Nations and site of the International Red Cross. Other international associations abound and to the permanent population is added a constantly renewed stratum of political and diplomatic celebrities and their staffs. Consistent with this role is the university's unique School of Interpreters, where linguists are trained for high-ranking jobs in these world organizations. In the late sixteenth century, the craft of watchmaking also began to take root in Geneva, so that by the following centuries Geneva watchmakers had won a remarkable reputation throughout the world, especially for their exquisite enameled and jewel-studded cases, eagerly sought by art connoisseurs as precious collectors' pieces. Today, she is still the world's great watch center and her Watches and Jewels Exhibition, held yearly in August, sets the watch and jewelry style trend for years in advance. Not alone because of her location at the Crossroads of Europe is Geneva an international favorite, but also because of her delightful situation in the midst of verdant hills on the shore of the deep-blue and remarkably transparent Lake Geneva, whose soothing beauty may be luxuriously relished aboard the distinctive, charming lake steamers.

STATUE OF ROUSSEAU Boissonnas

BRUNSWICK MONUMENT Geneva Tourist Association

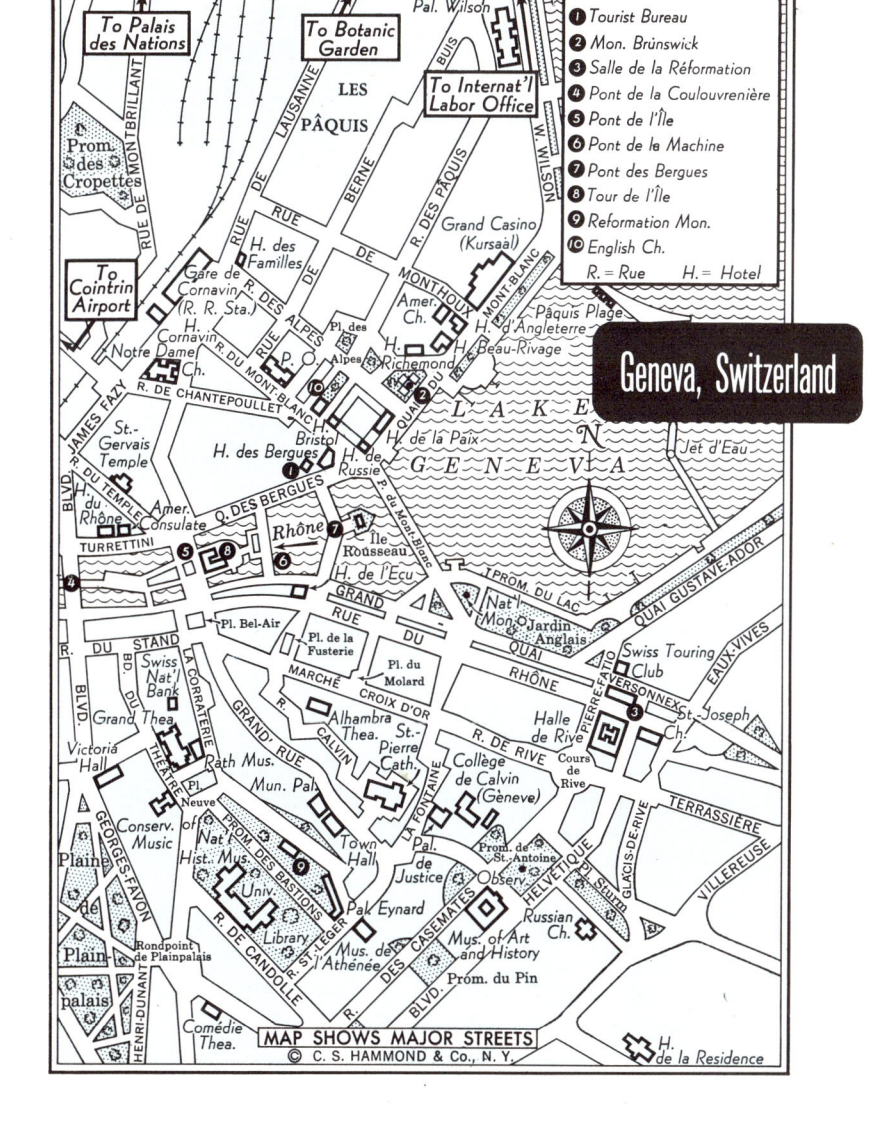

ANCIENT CATHEDRAL OF ST. PIERRE Geneva Tourist Association

LAKE GENEVA

... The northwestern shores of the lake are known as the La Côte district, where the vine has been cultivated for centuries. Most famous of these white vintages are perhaps the Fechy and Tartegnin, crisply cool and rather heady. Center of the La Côte wine production and an active yachting and sailing center as well is **MORGES**, known for its charming **Grape Harvest Festival**. Of remarkable interest is the small parish **Church of St. Sulpice**, built before 1200 by monks of Cluny Abbey in Burgundy, one of the very few surviving Romanesque structures in Switzerland....
LAUSANNE .... centrally situated on the south-facing Swiss shore of Lake Geneva, has achieved unique newspaper fame as the "City of Kings," for a surprising number of royal personages — both reigning and "ex" — have chosen to take up residence here. It also enjoys international repute as an educational and medical center. Built on three hills, the highest of which is crowned by the **old quarter** and the fine **Cathedral of Norte-Dame**, an excellent example of Burgundian Gothic architecture, Lausanne is a city of steep streets and stairways. Unique in modern Switzerland is the watchman who, every evening at 8:30, climbs the 236 steps of the cathedral tower and keeps watch over the city all night, calling the hours at the four corners of the tower. The **Federal High Court of Appeal**, a very fine example of modern architecture, forms a pleasant contrast with the nearby "Château" of **Mon-Repos**, headquarters of the International Olympic Committee. A most delightful excursion is the trip to picturesque **Gruyères**, center of a rich dairy farming country and home of the famous cheese, a perfect gem of a medieval fortified "burg," rising high on a rocky crag at the foot of an old tenth-century castle whose story is a strange intermingling of fact and legend.... To the east of Lausanne lies the Lavaux district, the steeply terraced vineyards producing excellent white wines, which are consumed on the home market, mostly open and as an "aperitif," although they also serve as excellent companions to the local specialty: fried filets of lake perch. At the end of this district is quiet and lovely **CULLY**, a haunt of painters.
... **MONTREUX** ranks among the most famous year-round resorts in the world. The view from the flat, tablelike summit of **Rochers de Naye** is superb, extending over the whole of Lake Geneva, while it also provides excellent skiing. Montreux' celebrated **Chillon Castle** is one of Europe's famed beauty spots and its walls, lapped by the waters of the lake, have inspired romantic hearts and great poets. The origin of the castle is lost in the dawn of history, but it was Peter, Duke of Savoy, known as the "Little Charlemagne," who made Chillon as we know it today, probably with the help of English military architects from the court of the Plantagenets. The impressive stronghold was used chiefly as a defence and a prison and its courtyard is replete with gloomy memories, since it witnessed numberless executions over the centuries, from the countless Jews who were put to death there in 1348 to the 27 "witches" in 1613. Most famous of Chillon's prisoners was Francis Bonivard, Prior of St. Victor Abbey in Geneva and hero of Byron's poem, "The Prisoner of Chillon." The Musée du Vieux-Montreux in one of the ancient buildings of the town, a former convent of the eleventh century, has collections and manuscripts on the history of the district. The thirteenth-century **Church of St. Légier-La-Chiésaz** is a fine example of pure Roman architecture. The nearby quiet market town of **Vevey**, site of John Jacques Rousseau's sentimental best-seller of 1763, *La Nouvelle Heloise,* has one of the most modern beaches in the country and is the site of the twelfth-century **Temple de St. Martin**, noted for the grace of its lines and the remarkable windows by the painter Bieler. Culinary specialties of the entire Lake Geneva region include *fondue*, the cheese dish of Western Switzerland which promotes conviviality and good fellowship; *raclette* (cheese melted on the hoop before an open fire and served with potatoes, pickled onions and gherkins) and country-cured sausages (*saucissons*) and ham. ... Between the lakes of Brienz and Thun, in the Bernese Oberland, lies **INTERLAKEN**, magnificent center for hiking,

LAKE BACHALP NEAR GRINDELWALD

SPIEZ CASTLE, BERNESE OBERLAND

Swiss Government Travel Office

lake bathing and skiing in the Jungfrau region. The little village of Brienz, at which Byron stayed, is famous as a center of woodcarving. At Jungfraujoch you may go Ice-skating in the famous ice palace. . . . Queen of high-Alpine resorts is ZERMATT, at the foot of the majestic Matterhorn and surrounded by the awe-inspiring giants of the Alps. Under the shelter of Matterhorn's proud summit, this town, key to the region in which have been accomplished the most daring exploits of the pioneers of the Alps, developed until it has now become the "metropolis" of mountineering. Take the famous **open-air railway** up to the peaks to Rotenboden in the Gronergrat or the new **chair lift**, which has a ski-lift extension during the winter, to Sunnegga. . . . In southeastern Switzerland on Lake Maggiore, LOCARNO'S mild climate, beautiful surroundings and historic past make it a resort of world-wide repute. The picturesque arcades and attractive shops of the **Piazza Grande** are evidence of the purely Lombard character of the magnificent garden city. The Sanctuary of the **Madonna del Sasso**, which looks down on the town from the brink of a rocky terrace, is one of the architectural jewels of a town rich in splendid buildings and artistic treasures. **Locarno Castle**, of medieval, massive construction and marvelous frescoes, is now an archeological museum. A yearly event is the **International Film Festival**, which transforms Locarno into a meeting place for producers, film stars and journalists. Last, but not least, the **beach** is famous for its fine sands. . . . Southwest of Locarno on Lake Maggiore is ASCONA, originally a fishing village, with picturesque corners, romantic little inns and shady arcades. Bohemian, intellectual and elegant life, art expositions and schools give Ascona and the cafes on the *Piazza* or in the *borgo* (ancient part of the town) a special lively touch. . . . To the southwest lies the romantic village of BRISSAGO, on the shore of this eternally peaceful lake. In character the town is essentially Italian, as shown by the historical **parish church** with its avenue of century-old cypresses and also by a classical early-seventeenth-century chapel, the Madonna del Ponte. . . . At LUGANO, a classic health resort, the art-lover will find many treasures in the collection of paintings — generally regarded as one of the most valuable in Europe — in the **Villa Favorita** in **Castagnola**, including among others, works by Rubens, Dürer, Titian, Velasquez, Gainsborough and Rembrandt. The notable art collection in the **Villa Vallone** in the picturesque village of **Morcote** contains valuable examples of Rumanian folk art and the **Vela Museum** at Ligornetto has works of the famous sculptor, Vincenzo Vela. . . . With its countless sunny holiday resorts and numerous spas, several of which have been in use since the time of the Romans, the Canton of the Grisons is characterized by an extraordinary profusion of woods and forests rising from the warm southern valleys up to the glaciers and regions of everlasting snow. At the climatic mountain spa of ST. MORITZ the mild southern and the invigorating nordic climate meet. . . . Charmingly situated in northeast Switzerland, between the Lake of Constance and the mountain chain of the Santis, ST. GALLEN, one of the greatest centers of the linen trade, ranks among the prettiest towns in the country. The origin of the town dates back over 1300 years, when the Irish missionary Gallus built his cell here, and to this very day St. Gallen remains the guardian of cultural treasures a thousand years old, represented in the world-renowned **Abbey Library**, called the finest rococo interior in Europe. The present **Cathedral**, built 1756-1767, is acknowledged to be one of the masterpieces of baroque architecture. . . . On the Lake of Lucerne — the lake Victor Hugo called "the miracle of Switzerland" — the town of LUCERNE has an atmosphere all its own. Here is the region where Swiss democracy was born and the spirit of the town centers around the deep love of peace and freedom that is so typically Swiss. A top-flight cosmopolitan holiday resort, it still retains all the charm and fascination of the romantic Middle Ages. All travelers will agree with Mark Twain who saw Lucerne as "a fascinating city; with its picturesquely situated hills,

DRYING GRAIN AT OBERSAXEN, GRISONS OBERLAND

A. Steiner

its many gables, towers, turrets and bay windows; and with its old gray city wall, peeping out here and there . . . a delightful sight." The famous **Lion Monument**, on the northern edge, is considered one of the most popular memorials in the world. Commemorating the courage and fidelity of a Swiss regiment that took part in the defense of the Tuileries in Paris in 1792, the "Lion of Lucerne" was designed by the Danish sculptor Bertel Thorwaldsen and carved in a sandstone cliff. Next to the Lion Monument is Lucerne's **Glacier Garden**, a series of potholes worn in the sandstone bed of an ancient glacier. Here, too, is the **Richard Wagner Museum**, filled with mementoes of Wagner's residence here, valuable original scores, manuscripts and a collection of old musical instruments. Among the historical points of interest are the covered **Chapel Bridge** with **Water Tower**, dating from 1333, and the well-preserved **Old Fortifications** and **Musegg Towers**, dating from 1350-1408. Over 500 years ago Lucerne was already noted for its Easter and Passion plays; since 1938 the tradition has found its modern counterpart in the annual **Summer Music Festival**. Extremely rewarding scenic excursions can be made to the tops of nearby mountains—the Pilatus, the Rigi and the Stanserhorn. While here you may also obtain some of the exclusive, engraved glassware produced by the skilled designers and craftsmen of Lucerne. . . . **BRUNNEN** is situated on one of the loveliest bays of the lake, where the country is rich in history. This is the country of William Tell, with many reminders of this romantic, legendary figure, including **Tell's Monument and Chapel** and the natural monument to F. Schiller, author of the play, *William Tell*. In Rütli Meadow, overlooking the lake, birthplace of Switzerland, representatives of three neighboring valleys met and took the oath that formed the Swiss Confederation in 1291 for the purpose of self-defense against a common foe. On December 9, 1315, representatives of the same highlanders, newly victorious over Louis of Bavaria, met at Kapelle Brunnen and renewed the Everlasting League. The **Archives** housing the Charter of Confederation are also located here. This charming town is an ideal center for lake bathing and fishing and for rambles in the mountain. . . .

ZURICH. Center of the Swiss Reformation during the sixteenth century was wealthy and prosperous Zürich, Swiss metropolis and lakeside garden city. She still remains today an international intellectual center, featuring the famous University of Zürich and the Federal Institute of Technology, as well as a number of richly endowed museums, with valuable collections of paintings and sculpture also including those of stained glass, porcelain, weapons and costumes at the magnificent Swiss National Museum. Most artists live in the section called Schipfe, where visitors strolling through its narrow, shadowy alleys will see along the way many painters at their easels. The notable June Festival, highlight of the cultural season, presents outstanding operatic, ballet, symphonic and drama performances by prominent Swiss and foreign masters. Scattered throughout the city are captivating open-air terrace beer gardens; inviting places to spend a few hours of interesting conversation lulled by a background of soft music, after a leisurely walk through the beautiful quiet park, with its rustic bridges, along the banks of the peaceful canal, and watching the slow-moving punts which dot its waters.

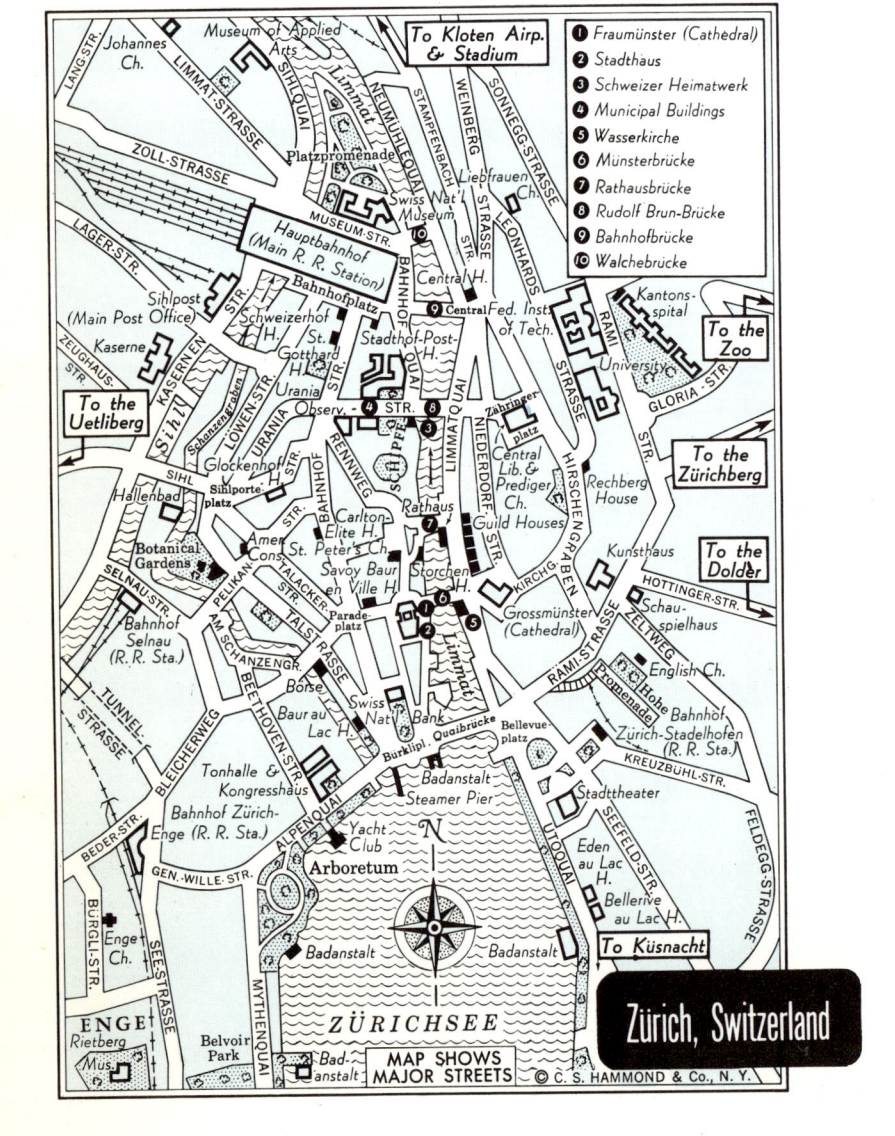

ST. GALLEN CATHEDRAL — Swiss National Tourist Office

WASSERKIRCHE — Swiss National Tourist Office

Austria

MUSIC AND DANCING

Music and dancing, gaiety and wine, ancient castles and mountain scenery — these things mean Austria, land of emperors and dukes, of song and sport. Vienna, enchanting city on the magic Danube, home of the waltz and the thrilling Viennese opera. The sunny vineyards of Lower Austria and the Burgenland, producing the excellent, tasty Austrian wines. The famed **Tyrol** and **Carinthia**, with their magnificent alpine scenery the mecca of expert mountain climbers and skiers. Salzburg and Gastein valley, of picturesque, colorful folk costumes and dancing, center of the fashionable, sometimes exclusive, health-resort spas with their healing medicinal springs. And all set in the background of old medieval towns, regal palaces and ancient customs. From all these intrinsic features, the well-known "Austrian atmosphere" has resulted and is forever being renewed through the jovial open-heartedness of the people, their recognized musical endowment and their hospitable nature. It is this incomparable "Austrian atmosphere" that holds every visitor in its spell.

CHURCH FESTIVALS

Every Austrian village in the summer offers some particular entertainment, especially on Saturdays and Sundays. You will see some of the most beautiful costumes on "Corpus Christi Day" in June and on "Assumption Day" in August. Beginning in mid-summer and into fall, Austrian villages celebrate "Kirtag," that is the combined anniversary of the consecrating of the church and the Harvest Festival. The dates are set locally and announced only a few weeks before taking place.

FROM TYROL TO VIENNA

Climbing a **turreted** hill above Lake Constance (Bodensee) at the far western end of Austria is **BREGENZ**, a city antedating Rome. Even the medieval **city gate** and **city walls** are still there. The **cable car** swinging up the **Pfänder** offers a view across the gabled roofs to the old

HEILIGENBLUT — Böhringer

town and the flowery esplanade of the lake to the shores. An enchanting **boat trip** on Lake Constance (Bodensee) at night and an excursion to the Bregenz Forest, with its charming villages and peasant costumes dating from another age, are favorites with visitors ... **FELDKIRCH,** south of Bregenz, is a medieval town boasting **arcades**, **old gates** and fragments of **antique walls**. The **castle** is seven centuries old but the quality of the **wine**, the **singing** and **dancing** have never been better.... To the east is **ST. ANTON**, a pretty alpine dorf famed for its bracing air, many pleasant walks and the tinkling, jangling passage through its main street, morning and evening, of herds of cows and goats. The **zither players**, **singers** and **dancers** here are of the best.... The historical center of culture and the main junction of the Tyrol, the province world-famous for its beautiful scenery, is **INNSBRUCK,** a Gothic city set on the Inn River at the foot of the majestic Nordkette Range. The **Hofkirche** contains the tomb of Maximilian I, the most elaborate tomb ever erected for a Christian king, and the **Tyrolean Folk Art Museum** has the world's best collection of folk art, costumes, etc. During the summer, native Tyrolean dancing is performed nightly at the **Hotel Maria Theresia**. Innsbruck's **palace** and **gardens** and the **Goldenes Dachl** (Golden Roof) inn are also of great interest. Excursions may be made from here to Berwang, a small remote village nestled in the mountains of the Ausserfern district, which is exceptionally rich in Alpine flora; the Achensee, Tyrol's highest alpine lake and near the 13th century Tratzberg Castle, site of imperial hunting parties in centuries gone by; Neustift, considered Austria's most typical alpine village, and the all-year skiing areas in the **Austrian Alps**. ... Located southeast of Innsbruck at the end of the Ziller Valley, **MAYRHOFEN** is a center of weekly **peasant costume festivals** on Saturday and Sunday from mid-June through mid-September,

INNSBRUCK — Austrian State Tourist Dept.

ZELL AM SEE _{Austrian State Tourist Dept.}

STIFT MELK ABBEY OVERLOOKS THE DANUBE IN THE WACHAU _{Austrian State Tourist Dept.}

with the gigantic annual festival taking place on the last Sunday in July. This beautiful alpine village is also famous for its spring flowers. . . . Closer to the eastern border of Tyrol province is KITZBUHEL, a medieval town now one of the country's most fashionable resorts during both summer and winter. If it's a gay night-life the visitor is seeking, this is an ideal place to go, since this town is famous for its "Tyrolean evenings." A cable car rises from here to the top of the Hahnenkamm . . . Continuing east, LOFER, an enchanting fairy-tale-like village, is very well-known for its beautiful alpine flowers. The Hotel Brau is decorated in typical modern peasant style by Austria's most famous contemporary architect, Clemens Holzmeister. . . . From the typical lake resort and mountain town of ZELL AM SEE excursions may be made to the Krimml Water Falls, the highest falls in Europe. . . . South of Salzburg is the ancient city of HALLEIN with the salt mines (open to visitors) at Dürrnberg. . . . Many-towered SALZBURG, one of Europe's most beautiful cities, is at all times bursting with music, history and natural charm. It is famous as the birthplace of Mozart, whose home may be visited, and for the Salzburg Festival, which starts annually in late July and terminates at the end of August, attracting many eminent musicians, conductors and music connoisseurs from all over the world. The Abbey and Church of St. Peter, with its fourth century catacombs, and many other baroque and Renaissance churches are also worthy of attention. The twelfth-century fortress-castle of Hohensalzburg is one of the best preserved examples of this type of architecture, and includes a park, museum and an excellent view of the city. Other palaces here are the Mirabell Palace and Gardens and the Hellbrunn Castle, with its famous water works. Delightful excursions can be made to Austria's highest mountain, the Grossglockner; the famous town of St. Wolfgang with "The White Horse Inn" of operetta fame; Liechtenstein Gorge and the village of Oberndorf, where Silent Night, Holy Night was composed . . . Between Salzburg and Linz is the SALZKAMMERGUT lake district — a treasure house of well-known holiday spots — romantic, poetic, lovely. Nestling between the mountains and hills, dozens of lakes, both great and small, reflect all the loveliness of this blessed landscape. One of the most daring cable lifts in Europe lays bare the unrivalled panorama from the Feuerkogel, while the new gondola railway from Obertraun opens up the secretive fairy-story world of the Dachstein Giant Ice Caves . . . At LINZ white steamers ply back and forth to Passau along the Danube, Austria's river of fate with her legendary shores, whose scenery changes from clear views over cosy villages to thick, green forest, through farming country, spacious and fruitful . . .

VIENNA. Vienna, dating back to the Roman era and beyond, has become over the centuries a symbol of European culture. Strategically located on the lovely,

RELIGIOUS PROCESSION, TYROL _{Austrian State Tourist Dept.}

Vienna, Austria

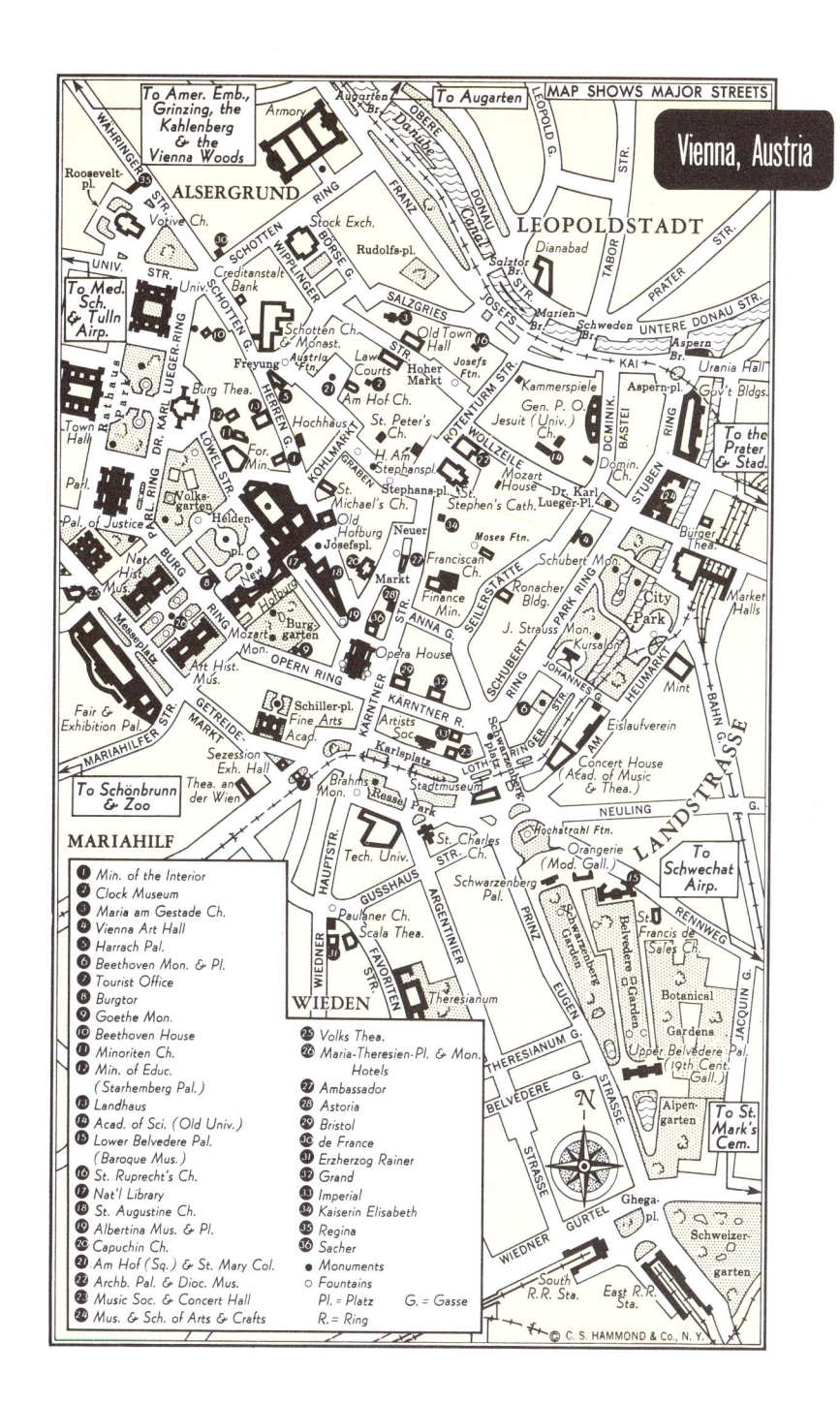

MAP SHOWS MAJOR STREETS

1. Min. of the Interior
2. Clock Museum
3. Maria am Gestade Ch.
4. Vienna Art Hall
5. Harrach Pal.
6. Beethoven Mon. & Pl.
7. Tourist Office
8. Burgtor
9. Goethe Mon.
10. Beethoven House
11. Minoriten Ch.
12. Min. of Educ. (Starhemberg Pal.)
13. Landhaus
14. Acad. of Sci. (Old Univ.)
15. Lower Belvedere Pal. (Baroque Mus.)
16. St. Ruprecht's Ch.
17. Nat'l Library
18. St. Augustine Ch.
19. Albertina Mus. & Pl.
20. Capuchin Ch.
21. Am Hof (Sq.) & St. Mary Col.
22. Archb. Pal. & Dioc. Mus.
23. Music Soc. & Concert Hall
24. Mus. & Sch. of Arts & Crafts
25. Volks Thea.
26. Maria-Theresien-Pl. & Mon.

Hotels
27. Ambassador
28. Astoria
29. Bristol
30. de France
31. Erzherzog Rainer
32. Grand
33. Imperial
34. Kaiserin Elisabeth
35. Regina
36. Sacher

● Monuments
○ Fountains
Pl. = Platz   G. = Gasse
R. = Ring

© C. S. HAMMOND & Co., N.Y.

RATHAUS (CITY HALL) *Austrian State Tourist Dept.*

legend-haunted Danube, Austria's river of fate, this gay, glamorous city of the Hapsburgs is the world's capital of glorious music and bewitching dance. Her beautiful concert halls have resounded to the most majestic music on earth, for she has embraced the brightest galaxy of composers any city has ever known — Mozart, Beethoven, Haydn, Schubert, Schumann, to name only the greatest of them all. And what woman has never dreamed of romantically swirling to the entrancing strains of the "Beautiful Blue Danube" or some other Vienese waltz on a moon-drenched terrace or crystal-chandeliered ballroom in the very city where Johann Strauss composed his lilting melodies. Center of intellectual accomplishment, with her famed university, and other artistic achievement, as well as the home of magical music, Vienna's splendid art galleries and imposing buildings characterize all periods of artistic styles, from the Romanesque through the Gothic, renaissance and early baroque, culminating in the famous Vienna Baroque, to which the city gave its individual style.

PALACE OF SCHONBRUNN ON THE OUTSKIRTS OF VIENNA

J. Walter Thompson Co.

SALZBURG

In EISENSTADT, south of Vienna on the Leitha mountains, the Haydn Mausoleum and the castle of Esterházy are the two often visited chief cultural and historical attractions. Castles from the Middle Ages, such as Forchtenstein, Schlaining and Güssing, or Bernstein castle, now an exclusive pension, all have most interesting collections and are the stage for historical pageant plays. The immense Neusiedler Lake, the only lake on a plain on the continent, in the midst of the famous wine villages, is a popular resort throughout the year. Eisenstadt is in the Burgenland, secretive, ancient border country on the edge of the Hungarian plains . . . GRAZ, the old provincial capital of Styria, called the "Green Land" because of the wealth of beautiful woodlands, has on display the world's largest collection of medieval armor — enough to outfit 30,000 men and horses — a fascinating reminder of the many years of development and the deep-rooted traditions of these Austrian people and cities. Eggenberg Castle, a lovely baroque hunting castle; Lur Grotto, the world's largest alpine caverns, as well as the city parks are other attractions . . . At ADMONT, northwest of Graz at the entrance of the wild, romantic climbing country of the Gesäuse mountains, is an ancient Benedictine abbey, whose priceless library contains more than 120,000 volumes . . . A little west of here is ALT-AUSSEE, a quaint village with an unforgettable view across the lake into the Dachstein Glacier . . . Close by is HALLSTATT, one of Europe's most picturesque lake villages, located near the site of the lake dwellers settlement, which gave its name to the pre-historic Hallstatt Age. On June 9th the "Feast of Corpus Christi," one of the most elaborate Austrian feasts, is celebrated with a lake procession, and weekly peasant costume festivals are held every Saturday and Sunday. Visitors should not fail to have lunch on the lake shore and to visit the local museum, with its choice collection of relics and implements dating back to the Ice Age . . . VILLACH, near the point where the borders of Austria, Yugoslavia and Italy join, contains an interesting Old Quarter and the Paracelsus House. The "Villach Kirtag Festival" takes place on the first weekend in August. Visits can be made to the twelfth-century Cathedral at Gurk; the walled town of the Middle Ages; Friesach, whose townspeople stage plays in the castle during the summer; Europe's best preserved medieval fortress-castle at Hochosterwitz, where on the first Sunday in September the "Kirtag feast" is held in the keep and courtyard, and the pre-historic excavations at Magdalensberg. Popular nearby lake resorts include Velden, Pörtschach and Maria Wörth . . . SPITTAL, with its Renaissance castle and horse market and fine park, is very near Villach. It is a gathering point for mountain climbers, who go by chair lift to the mountain village of Mallnitz, starting place for high alpine tours, and a center for swimmers, who enjoy the Weissensee, one of the most lovely and warmest lakes of the Carinthian Lake Plateau . . . Between Mallnitz and Böckstein, the Tauern tunnel runs right through the mighty barrier of the High Tauern and joins the holiday centers of Carinthia with the Gastein valley, whose world famous radioactive healing springs have been recently enhanced by the amazing cure results of the Böckstein tunnels. In the elegant hotels and pensions of BAD-GASTEIN, Europe's most fashionable spa, and BAD HOFGASTEIN there are about 6000 beds available . . . Neither amateur nor professional photographers will want to overlook HEILIGENBLUT, considered the most photogenic and most beautifully located alpine village on the continent. Situated at the foot of the Grossglockner, it is the home of a famous climbing school. Franz-Josef-Haus may be seen by driving up the Grossglockner High Alpine road . . . South of Heiligenblut is the pretty little city of LIENZ. Utterly destroyed on the last day of the war, its central square, which boasts a pink castle, pale blue houses, arcades, lacy wrought-iron balconies, has been restored completely. The Castle Bruck has a distinguished Roman collection, a splendid Egger-Lienz, Defregger Collection of paintings, a restaurant and a pretty view.

CASTLE OF ESTERHAZY

Portugal

BELEM TOWER

LAND OF SUNNY LEISURE

If you visit Portugal you will like the serious, warm-hearted people who have a friendly welcome for all who come to their shores. It is a land where the visitor may enjoy charming landscapes and curious old towns without ever being aware of the passage of time. Most of the people are farmers and live a life of simplicity rounded out by hard work. The northern half of Portugal is mountainous and the southern half, flat with some hilly regions; the climate is mild, for the most part, and springtime in Portugal is an enchanting season when the countryside is brilliantly covered by a rainbow of colored flowers.

AN EVENTFUL PAST

In many ways Portugal's history is like that of Spain of which it once formed a part. Rome brought Christianity and the Latin tongue; the Moors influenced architecture, music and mingled their blood with that of the local inhabitants. During the struggle with the Moors a national spirit began to emerge. A young French noble, Henry of Lorraine, was granted the "county of Portugal" by the Spanish Alfonso VI as a reward for his military services. The "county" was extended, and by 1140 Portugal had become a separate kingdom. Later King John I married a daughter of England's John of Gaunt. The Treaty of Windsor, concluded at this time between Portugal and England, is still in force and makes England Portugal's oldest ally. The fifteenth century was the Golden Age of Portugal's history. Inspired by Prince Henry, the Navigator, Portuguese mariners embarked upon their famous voyages. Names like Diaz, Cabral, Da Gama and Magellan testify to Portuguese leadership in the Age of Discovery. A new route to India, discovery of Brazil and the circumnavigation of the globe mark the zenith of power that Portugal had achieved in the civilized world. In 1580 Portugal was placed under Spanish rule, but sixty years later independence was regained, although some of her oversea possessions were lost.

THE BULL SURVIVES

The bullfight in Portugal is different from that in Spain. Some Portuguese bullfighters demonstrate their skill on horseback, others on foot, but in either case the bull is never killed in Portugal. Whatever your interest in bullfights is, you will find other opportunities for giving expression to your sporting instinct. If you like fishing, the rivers of the northern provinces are recommended. Resorts in the south afford good swimming, tennis and golf. Winter sports, such as skiing, are held each January and February in the Serra da Estrêla in central Portugal, the country's highest mountain range. Soccer games, the favorite spectator sport, are played every Sunday from October to July at the huge National Stadium in the outskirts of Lisbon.

GENEROUS MEALS

The Portuguese meal is served for the person with a big appetite. Four or five courses are standard — sometimes more! You can't go wrong on fish or seafood. The Portuguese are also fond of sweets and among their favorite desserts are *arroz doce* (sweet rice) and *ovos moles* (sweetened eggs). Also try *porco a Alentejana* (cubes of braised pork served with clams in their shell). *Dobrada* is also tasty and consists of tripe, prepared with white beans and sausages and served in a heavy cream sauce. There are hundreds of wines to choose from, including Madeira, of course, before the meal and port as the

FISHING BOATS, LISBON

finishing touch. *Vinhos da casa* come with the meal and are likely to be very good. Portuguese rosé wines are among the best in the world and go well with any dish. **Mateus Rosé** is the most popular.

THROUGH CITY AND TOWN

LISBON. A noble and gracious city, Lisbón rises tier upon tier above the ship-studded waters of its fine harbor. Located where the river Tagus widens to meet the Atlantic, Lisbon, like Rome, is a city built upon seven hills. It is a place of white or pastel-colored houses, of broad tree-lined avenues and little winding streets overhung by Moorish balconies. Although many of its medieval buildings have been destroyed by earthquakes, Alfama, the older section of the city in the vicinity of the cathedral, still contains many magnificent relics of Lisbon's past history. A number of the city's buildings display excellent examples of Manueline-style architecture, which, influenced by the Age of Discovery, consists of intricate decorations and nautical symbols such as globes, twisted cables and the Templar cross which was displayed on the sails of early ships. The Monastery at Belém facing

CASTLE OF PEND NEAR CINTRA

TWA—Trans World Airline

the sea from the north shore of the Tagus was built by Manuel I to commemorate Vasco da Gama's discovery of a sea route to India. The Tower of Belém, originally a fortress, marks the spot where the great explorer landed after his adventurous voyage. The city of Lisbon is dominated by the Castelo de São Jorge, a fort which majestically crowns the highest of the seven hills and may occupy the site of ancient Roman fortifications. From its high perch, the Castelo looks out upon a breath-taking panorama of sea, harbor and city.

Nightlife is rather restrained here. Friends usually gather in cafes to indulge in pleasant conversation over small cups of strong coffee. The *Fado* Cafes may afford a new experience. The *fado* is a nostalgic ballad sung to evoke sorrowful sentiments. It is usually improvised by the singer who is accompanied by two guitars — one Spanish and one Portuguese. Most night clubs are found in the **Bairro Alto**, the old part of the city, and in the **Alfama**, where the old Moorish buildings still line winding streets. More enlightening perhaps is the **Port Wine Institute** with its amazing list of hundreds of varieties of Port.

South of Lisbon is **SETUBAL**, center of Portugal's all-important sardine industry. Near here are a number of picturesque fishing villages and in Setubal are two interesting 16th century churches. . . . West of the capital on the seacoast is **ESTORIL**, a luxurious seaside resort and winter playground with a very popular **casino**. Popular as a home of ex-kings, it is attractively laid out with masses of flower beds. Take a short walk to **CASCAIS**, a colorful fishing town where each weekday evening a fish auction is held and the bidding is in reverse, in Dutch fashion. Famous also is the **Boca do Inferno**, a huge cave carved out by the sea, into which the waves rush with a deafening

AMOREIRA AQUEDUCT NEAR ELVAS

roar.... A little further up the coast is the resort-fishing village of ERICEIRA with an interesting old fort.... About twenty miles from Lisbon is SINTRA, site of the Royal Palace and Pena Castle perched atop one of the peaks from where you get a magnificent view of land and sea. Nearby are the famous gardens of Montserrate, laid out by a wealthy Englishman in the last century, one of the finest gardens in Europe.... On the way to Sintra is QUELUZ with its great palace, the "Versailles of Portugal." Its formal gardens and park with little lakes and fountains are lovely and the interior is beautiful.... North of Sintra is MAFRA with its rather fascinatingly ugly monastery-palace. This vast edifice has no less than 5,200 doors and 2,500 windows and required 45,000 workers to build it. Its church towers house over 100 bells which may be heard fifteen miles away.... OBIDOS is a fascinating town contained within the crenelated ramparts of its enormous Moorish fortress.... The great church at ALCOBACA, one of the finest examples of Cistercian art in Europe, has the Cloister of Silence and huge monastic kitchens. The tomb here contains the remains of Portugal's immortal lovers, Dom Pedro and Inez de Castro.... Ten miles northeast is BATALHA containing the Church of Santa Maria, Portugal's "Westminister Abbey." Here lies John of Gaunt's daughter, English wife of John I of Portugal. The latter's son, Prince Henry, the Navigator, also lies buried here.... To the east is FATIMA, "The Lourdes of Portugal," one of the best known Catholic shrines in the world. Huge numbers of visitors gather and camp here on the 13th of each month from May to October to commemorate the appearance of Mary as reported by three Portuguese children in 1917.... Nearby is NAZARE with its fishing boats curiously painted and shaped like melon rinds. Most typical of Portuguese fishing ports, its inhabitants may be seen wearing their colorful "Scottish" plaids.... Southeast is EVORA, inhabited by Phoenician, Iberian, Roman and Moor. The Roman Temple of Diana may be seen here as well as the Convent of São Francisco which contains the Chapel of Bones, a structure whose walls are lined with human remains.... Further north is COIMBRA with its famous University (one of the oldest in Europe) and the only university in Portugal. The old Cathedral is reputed to be the finest example of Romanesque architecture in the Iberian Peninsula.... A little north of here is BUSSACO with its famous hotel converted from a former palace and its incredible park with trees of every kind and age including genuine Cedars of Lebanon.... Also near Coimbra is LUSO, a spa with well-known alkaline springs. ... FIGUERA DA FOZ, thirty miles outside the university city, has a beautiful ocean beach with fine hotels and casino. OPORTO ..... to the north, is the country's business and financial center and is also a lively, noisy and bustling port, known for its artistically decorated cafes and its extraordinary Church of São Francisco. The church contains one of the most unusual collections of wood decorations to be found anywhere. This city is internationally known for its wine industry and has wine lodges where Port is tasted, blended and bottled.... Nearby is the pleasant resort of OFIR and, a little further, GUIMARAES, former capital and of great historic and architectural interest. ... VIANA DO CASTELO is a beautiful coastal town in the north near the Spanish border. It is well known as a great lace-making center.

THE AZORES AND MADEIRA

The AZORES consist of nine islands having a temperate climate, although often rather damp and misty. They are well suited for raising grapes, oranges and pineapples. Interesting places to visit are Ponta Delgada and Furnas with its thermal springs on São Miguel Island. The island's volcanic origin makes it quite scenic.... At MADEIRA, in a climate of eternal spring, one can lead a lazy existence and watch the sparkling sea. In some districts there are vineyards which produce the famous Maderia wine. This is really an enchanted land with incomparable mountain scenery and lush, tropical growth. The hotels here are adept at making life effortless and pleasant. Funchal, the capital, lies in a perfect setting overlooking the sea with mountains on three sides in the background. Visitors will enjoy every aspect of the town, the busy narrow streets, picturesque squares, the colorful market and the lovely town park.

CASA DAS BICOS, LISBON

GOSSIP AT THE VILLAGE WELL, RURAL PORTUGAL

Spain

THE ALCAZAR, SEGOVIA

THE LURE OF SPAIN

No single adjective will suffice to describe a country as vast and varied as Spain. Within a few hours a tourist may be transported from regions of perpetual snow in the north to the radiant, sun-drenched provinces in the south. Spain has had a colorful past, and her traditions lend a uniqueness to the character of her people. Winter, spring, summer or fall, all seasons enhance some part of Spain — a land, in fact, with limitless interest for all. But more than this, you will discover that, unlike any other European country, a tour through Spain will impart a mystical experience which will last a lifetime. Spaniards call it being touched by *el alma de Espana* — the soul of Spain!

THE ROMANS CALLED IT HISPANIA

Spain's past is a tale of conquests and reconquests. Originally populated by a primitive race known as Iberians it was later a province of the Roman Empire and governed by Roman pro-consuls. After the decline of the Empire it was overrun by Vandals (Andalusia) and Germanic invaders known as Visigoths. In 711 A.D. Moslems from Africa swarmed up through the south at Gibraltar to occupy parts of Spain for nearly 800 years. The struggle between Christian and Moor continued until the famous monarchs, Ferdinand and Isabel, supplanted the last crescent with the cross in 1492.

BLOOD AND SAND

The great form of entertainment for the Spaniard is the bullfight. Almost every town has its own bull ring. The bullfighters — *toreros* — may become national idols just as ball players attain national renown in our country. Bullfights are usually held on Sunday afternoons (in Madrid and Barcelona they are held on Thursdays also). The bullfight is like a three-act drama. The first act brings on the *picadores* who ride into the arena and thrust steel-tipped shafts into the bull to weary him by loss of blood. During the second act the *banderilleros* exhaust the animal further by placing barbed darts in his shoulder. In the last act the *torero* seeks to tire the bull by having it chase his *muleta* (red cloak) which is manipulated with skill and grace. When the bull is sufficiently infuriated, the kill is attempted which consists of a clean thrust into the back of the neck and downward into the heart. The bull is dragged off by a mule team to the sound of a stirring march while a new bull is released into the ring to begin the drama anew. Six bulls are usually killed in a single afternoon. Some of the best bull rings are located in Barcelona, Seville and Madrid.

Good food and incomparable wines are the glories of Spain. Lunches are served from 2:00 to 4:00. Dinners are never prepared before 9:00 P.M. If you like new delicacies, Spanish food will enthrall you — Spanish dishes are not highly spiced, though well seasoned. A national dish is *cocido*, a stew made with meat, vegetables and garbanzos (chick peas). *Arroz con pollo* (chicken with rice) will delight the palate. *Paella* is the typical dish of Valencia, consisting of fried rice, shellfish, chicken, fish and meat, all deliciously combined. *Caldo* is the national soup of Spain — if soups can attain such distinction! It must be tried at least once. The wines, of course, are as fabulous as they are original in this land of grapes. You may sip the liquid radiance of a sherry from Jerez de la Frontera, from where the name sherry is derived, or you may savor the rich white wine of Málaga. In any case, you will observe that the drink of Spain is her native sherry and

PRADO MUSEUM, MADRID

that there is a sherry to suit every taste. Sherries are typed according to taste and bouquet, fino, amontillado, or oloroso.

THE CITIES OF SPAIN

MADRID. Madrid, Spain's handsome capital, is often spoken of as the "Monumental City" because of its abundance of statuary and impressive public monuments. City gates, bridges and fountains complete Madrid's traditional landmarks. Few towns offer such variety of scenes and so many different moods and aspects. Next to the wide thoroughfares teeming with onrushing traffic, full of noise, dazzling with electric signs, are sleepy little streets and squares steeped in profound peace, haunted by memories of that other Madrid known by the Hapsburg and Bourbon Kings. Though Madrid's actual beginnings are lost in time, the city was known to have been a Moorish outpost until the latter part of the 11th century. Its location at almost the exact geographical center of the Iberian peninsula may have influenced Philip II in choosing Madrid as his capital in 1561. Built atop the New Castilian Plateau, at an altitude of some 2,150 feet, its skyline towers taller than that of any other European city. Here, the climate is often extreme, varying as much as 50 degrees in a single day. In summer, a blazing sun beats relentlessly down from cloudless skies on the barren red plain, while in winter the city is swept by icy winds from the Sierra de Guadarrama. Although Madrid is Spain's capital and its administrative center, it is still considered only a "villa" (town) never having received the official designation "ciudad" (city). Madrid became a Loyalist stronghold during the Civil

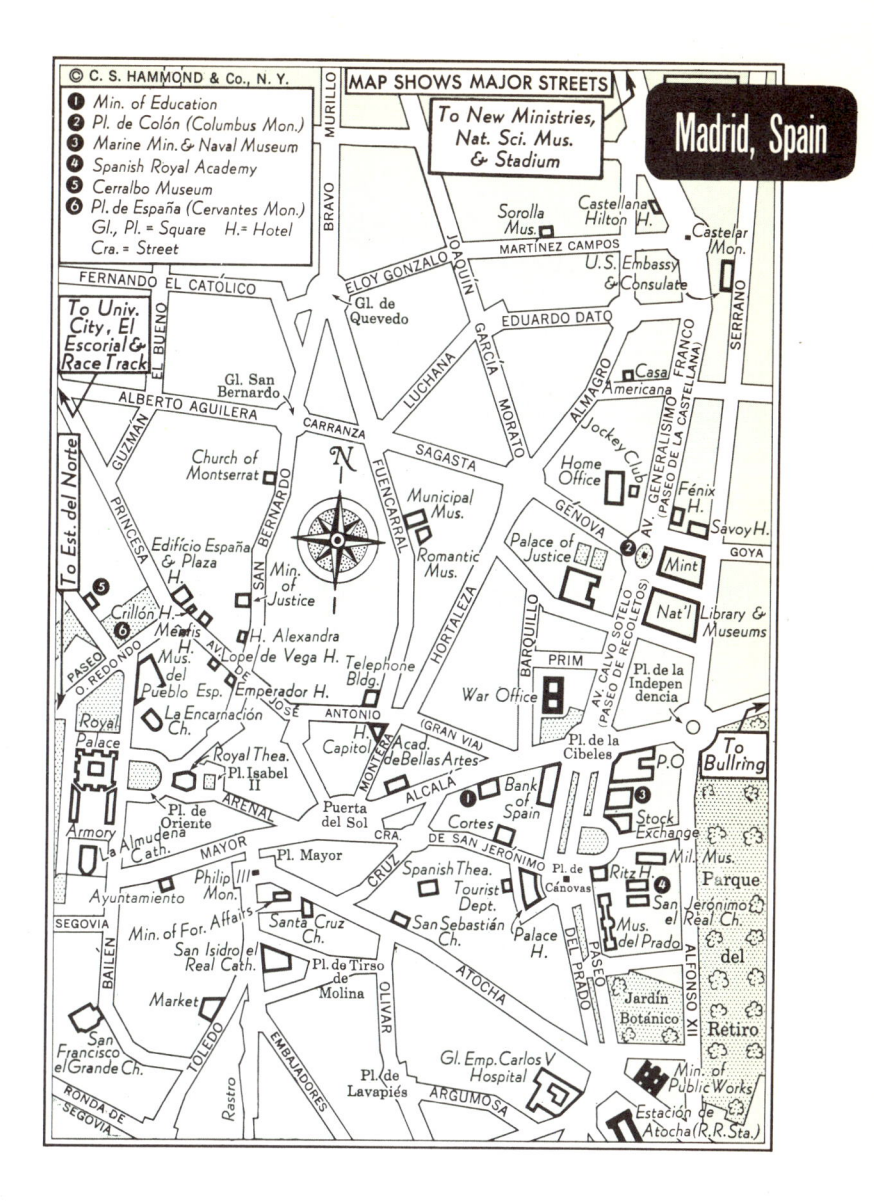

EL RETIRO, MADRID

Philip Gendreau

CASA DE LA REAL PANDERIA

Spanish Government Tourist Office

War (1936-1939) and was heavily bombed by Nationalist forces before its surrender. During the twenty-nine day siege, with four columns of Nationalist troops converging on Madrid, Nationalist sympathizers who awaited their arrival within the city made up the original "Fifth Column." Modern Madrid has its skyscrapers, its towering buildings and its newest source of pride, the Ciudad Universitaria (University City), erected against a background characteristic of Velasquez's canvases. Madrid is an excellent starting point for many very pleasant excursions. For the lover of nature, the imposing Sierra de Guadarrama is close at hand offering good mountain climbing and winter sports facilities in an atmosphere of restful quietness . . . . Also within a short distance from the capital is **ALCALA DE HENARES**, birthplace of such notable figures as Cervantes, creator of the immemorable Don Quixote, and Catherine of Aragón, first wife of much-married Henry VIII of England. Here too, was founded by Cardinal Cisneros, great statesman and cleric of Spain, the University of Madrid, now located in the city proper. Visit the **Palace of the Archbishops of Toledo** and the archives. By all means enjoy a "comida" at the Hosteria del Estudiante. It is a typical 15th century inn; note the huge fireplace, goatskin wine containers and old trappings from the horses of caballeros, as well as the beauty of the interior courtyard with its quaint wall. . . . Former capital of Spain, **TOLEDO** is a city of art, history and romance where El Greco lived. Built by the Moors and recognized as the center of medieval learning, it is today the see of the primate of Spain. Among its notable landmarks are the Cathedral of Toledo, the Moorish Bridge spanning the Tagus River and the Alcázar, once the residence of the Cid, Spain's national hero, and site of the bitter struggle during the Civil War. . . . South of Toledo is **CIUDAD REAL**, (La Mancha), in whose vicinity you may retrace the journeys of Don Quixote and his faithful squire Sancho Panza where they tilted with windmills and made illusion of reality. . . . **AVILA** and **SEGOVIA** are laid in scenic richness. At Segovia, famed for its early Roman history, is one of the finest Roman aqueducts which is still in use. The Suloaga Ceramic Museum has one of the finest exhibits in Spain. Visit the "Segovia Alcázar" (fortress) most typical castle in Spain. Built by Alfonso VI, it has recently been restored. . . . **LA GRANJA** nearby is a splendid 18th century, French-style palace with magnificent gardens and splashing fountains. . . . **AVILA** is noted for its medieval wall, the finest example of its kind. It is still in a good state of repair, turrets and all. Visit the Cathedral and the Monastery of Santo Tomás. . . . The great plains of the province of **CASTILE**, broken here and there by tall sierras or lofty battlements of ancient castles, contains many quaint old towns, some over a thousand years old, such as **AYLLON, SIGUENZA, TORDESILLAS** and **SORIA**. It is in this last city that the splendid red of burnt earth dominates stones, bricks and landscape alike. It is truly the "Red City of Spain." . . . **SARAGOSSA** is a very old city which became famous for the extraordinary defense by its inhabitants against Napoleon.

NORTHERN SPAIN

The northern boundaries of Spain are formed partly by the massive chain of the Pyrenees and the beautiful Bay of Biscay. To the south of these natural barriers is a great land of rolling slopes and cool forests. Basques, Asturians and Galicians inhabit this area, still preserving their regional customs, dialects (the Basques have a language unrelated to any other tongue on earth), and their colorful, picturesque native dress. In this region, the foothills around **SANTANDER** and **ASTURIAS** are not easily forgotten. Bear, wild boar, wolf and deer live in the thickets which abound in this section. Also to be found here are the cave paintings of **ALTAMIRA**, some of the earliest drawings made by the hand of man. . . . Close by **SAN SEBASTIAN** and **BILBAO** are some of the finest golf courses in the world. The **Picos de Europa** are a mountain-climber's paradise and the inland roads are excellent for cycling. Pelota, a regional game, is played with great skill by almost every villager in these provinces. . . . **GALICIA** is situated in the northwest corner of the Spanish peninsula. Inland from the surf that crashes with unrestrained fury against the cliffs of **Cape Finisterre**, is a gentle land of pine trees, heather and vineyards. The *rias* or bays of **VIGO** and **PONTEVEDRA** bear a striking resemblance to the fiords of Norway. The *Gallegos* or natives of this northern province still display their Celtic origins. Dressed in short skirts and beret and making music upon the ancient "gaita" (bagpipe), one would think that the hardy Scot had by some strange accident drifted from his northern home. . . . Halfway between **PONTEVEDRA** and **LA CORUNA** is **SANTIAGO DE COMPOSTELA**, shrine of Spain's apostle and patron saint, St. James. During the Middle Ages a steady flow of pilgrims journeyed over the Pyrenees and along the "French Road" to visit the hallowed sepulchre. Thus it was that along the way many of Spain's monasteries grew in size and reputation as they offered rest and food to the weary traveler. The city contains the famous Portico of Glory, a masterpiece of Romanesque art. The whole province of Galicia is celebrated for its delectable seafood — its lobsters, crabs, shellfish, prawns and shrimp are un-

BULL RING, MADRID

TWA—Trans World Airline

rivaled for their delicate flavor. . . . In the northeast the visitor has three attractions to choose from: BARCELONA, SITGES and COSTA BRAVA.

BARCELONA. Barcelona, in Catalonia, is Spain's chief manufacturing center and its second largest city. Although founded nearly three centuries before the birth of Christ and possessing a share of Roman ruins, Moorish relics and Medieval churches, Barcelona stands apart from

LA SAGRADA FAMILIA, BARCELONA
Spanish Government Tourist Office

other Spanish cities, somehow lacking their quaint charm, their characteristic atmosphere. Essentially a modern city, well planned and well built, it is for the most part given over to commerce and industry. Only in the "Ciudad" (Old Town) with its narrow streets, its 13th century Gothic Cathedral, has passing time moved at a slower pace. Hugging the shores of the Mediterranean Sea, Barcelona spreads in a narrow crescent between the river Besos on the north and Llobregat on the south, the pink-and-white of its suburbs, the vivid foliage of its gardens contrasting strongly with the huge factories, warehouses and spacious harbor installations that make it Spain's most important seaport. The Catalonian Hills, culminating in the 1,745-foot Tibidabo, form an austere backdrop and afford splendid views of the town's extensive panorama. Barcelona is a city of broad avenues, fine shops, attractive restaurants, numerous cabarets and theaters, several bull rings and a noted university. In contrast to this serene setting Barcelona's history has been marked with violence in frequent and passionate political and social uprising. SITGES is the seaside resort of the area with a balmy all-year-round climate. . . . COSTA BRAVA (the Catalonian coast) has the loveliest summer climate in the country.

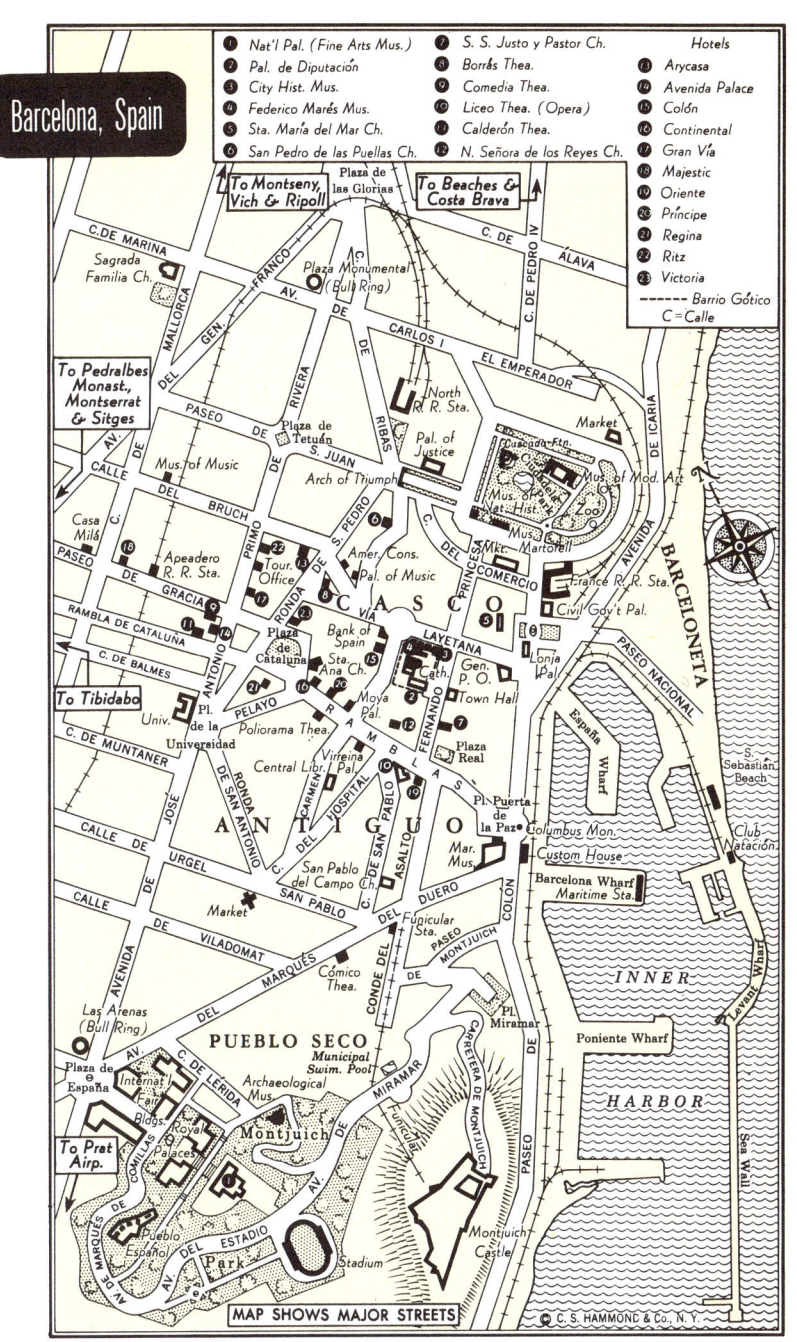

Here pine trees grow even upon bare rocks surrounded by cork, almond and olive trees. The crystal-clear water reflects an amazing variety of hues. . . . Roman ruins at TARRAGONA, great Gothic monasteries at POBLET, green-velvet valleys of ARAN, winter sports at NURIA are made more unforgettable by a friendly people, the Catalonians, who drink their red wine from odd-shaped beakers and know how to cook. . . . Further down the coast is VALENCIA, city of the Cid whose glory is still preserved in epic and legend.

In ANDALUSIA, Spain's plastic beauty dazzles the eye. Its very name suggests magic, mystery and Moorish castles. From her cities the great figures of the Age of Discovery and Exploration embarked upon their voyages to find what lay beyond "the end of the world." Orange groves white-washed villages, bull-fighters, gypsies and the swirl of many-colored

THE CATHEDRAL
Spanish Government Tourist Office

Barcelona, Spain

1. Nat'l Pal. (Fine Arts Mus.)
2. Pal. de Diputación
3. City Hist. Mus.
4. Federico Marés Mus.
5. Sta. María del Mar Ch.
6. San Pedro de las Puellas Ch.
7. S. S. Justo y Pastor Ch.
8. Borrás Thea.
9. Comedia Thea.
10. Liceo Thea. (Opera)
11. Calderón Thea.
12. N. Señora de los Reyes Ch.

Hotels
13. Arycasa
14. Avenida Palace
15. Colón
16. Continental
17. Gran Vía
18. Majestic
19. Oriente
20. Príncipe
21. Regina
22. Ritz
23. Victoria

------ Barrio Gótico
C = Calle

75

skirts blend themselves together to form a vision of chromatic splendor. For two thousand years different civilizations have left their imprint on the Andalusian soil.

SEVILLE . . . . is enchanted: Countless scenes delight the eye and everywhere the atmosphere is redolent of the clinging aroma of orange blossoms from her world-famous groves. The slim elegance of the Statue of the Giralda (the figure of a woman representing Faith mounted atop the bell tower of the Cathedral) which moves like a weathervane in the slightest breeze, and the sweet fragrance from the nearby Patio de los Naranjos (orange groves) will remind the visitor that he has arrived in the land of Bizet's Carmen. The Cathedral here is magnificent and is one of the finest examples of Gothic architecture in the world. The Santa Cruz section is the Spain of the foreigner's imagination with its narrow tiled streets, patios and grilled windows through which a young *senorita* might be wooed to the accompaniment of a plaintive guitar. Christopher Columbus is entombed here and a library contains documents written in the discoverer's own handwriting. . . . The graceful columns of the magnificent **Mosque at CORDOBA** and the splendor of the formidable **Alhambra**, the fortress-palace in **GRANADA**, typify the geometrically beautiful Moorish architecture found throughout Andalusia. . . . Within a few miles from Granada is the **SIERRA NEVADA**, second highest range in Europe, where winter-sports facilities are excellent. These lofty mountains are but a few hours away from the sunny Mediterranean coast, making it possible to ski in the morning and bathe in the warm sea in the afternoon. . . . To the southwest is **MALAGA**, land of the famous grape. The Mediterranean coast from Málaga to Gibraltar enjoys a climate almost unequalled in the whole of Europe. This is due not only to its position on the southernmost top of the Continent, but to the protection by various chains of mountains from the northern winter-cold winds and summer-hot breezes that blow from the high Spanish plateau or tableland. The waters of the Mediterranean, warm enough to bathe in winter, are also pleasantly cool in summer. The sun shines on this coast almost constantly and the bathing is ideal, even in the hottest weather. Sword-fishing here is a favorite sport. . . . Inland, near **RONDA**, the sportsman may practice stalking the Spanish ibex, one of the finest game animals in the world. Ronda itself is one of the most unusual small towns in Spain. Famous as one of the last strongholds of the Moors, you find much Moorish architecture; also what is said to be the oldest bull ring in Spain. There is the former house of the "cid" or Moorish King of the area built on the side of a steep rocky cliff. You enter from street level and keep going down flight after flight, reaching the garden at the lower level and finally a door from which stone steps take you down to the bath at water level. The river which flows through the town provides a crossing for traffic. The city seems to be practically isolated from the rest of the world. . . . **GIBRALTAR**, the "Gates of Hercules," offers an imposing sight of a familiar Mediterranean landmark.

GOATHERD AND FLOCK, MALAGA TWA—Trans World Airline

VACATION ISLANDS

The **BALEARIC ISLES** of **Minorca**, **Ibiza** and **Majorca** afford a change from the irregular features of the mainland. Peaceful coves, gnarled olive trees and towering cliffs provide the setting where a visitor may do nothing but drink in all the serenity of the Mediterranean atmosphere.

Majorca, the largest island, offers many attractions to the visitor. At Valldemosa you can see the room where George Sand and Chopin spent the winter of 1838 and the piano he used. Note the simple beauty of the Monastery with its drawbridge, secret door and lively flower-adorned patio. Watch the native dancers who dance with their hearts as well as with their feet. . . . Motor to **ARTA** and visit the caves where you will marvel at the beauty of nature and forget the outside world, listening to the beautiful music played by a string orchestra from a small rowboat. The beautiful coloring in the stalactites and stalagmites is highlighted by an unusual lighting effect. It's like a glimpse of another world. You'll leave feeling better in mind and refreshed in soul. . . . **PALMA** is an idyllic spot, overlooking the blue bay with its Cathedral spires reaching heavenward, little boats moored in the bay, fishermen coming and going and the blue, blue sky overhead. Nearby is an imposing castle on a hill overlooking the city.

STREET SCENE, CORDOBA TWA—Trans World Airline

Italy

ARCO DELLA PACE (ARCH OF PEACE), MILAN

Italian State Tourist Office

LAND OF SEAS AND MOUNTAINS

Italy is one of the oldest countries in Europe. Her influence on European and world history has been enormous and enduring. Her influence in architecture, sculpture and drama, all the arts and sciences has affected their development the world over, beginning with the ancient Roman Empire before the Christian era, and then, after a lull, the reawakening in the Renaissance. This lovely land, washed by three seas and traversed by magical mountains, offers her visitors not only the finest in art treasures and historical monuments but a gay and charming modern world also. In Rome, Florence, Venice, Capri and the Riviera life is gay and sophisticated, with dining and dancing under the stars, sunning and swimming in luxurious surroundings. There is entertainment to suit every taste whether it be trying your luck in the casinos or simply relaxing and watching life around you. The Italian, and there are two distinct racial types (the northern fair-complexioned and the southern dark-complexioned), has a penchant for individualism which is expressed in everything he does, be it building a house just a little different from his neighbor's or running his business the way he chooses. The Italian is also a romantic and believes happiness is achieved by the sheer joy of living, breathing, sleeping and waking. He loves good music, good food, good wine and the other pleasures of life. Being a warm-hearted people, they welcome the visitor and will gladly, if given the chance, help him to fully enjoy his visit in their sunny land.

THINGS TO DO

A great part of Italy's charm to visitors is that there is always something to see, hear or do. In Italy, everybody goes to the opera and if you are there during the six months season, January through June, you will, too. In addition to La Scala, all the big cities have quality performances. In summer too, there is music. Outdoor concerts are most popular and in Rome and Venice especially the music is excellent. Italy is a Catholic country and it seems that hardly a day passes that there is not a feast or spectacle somewhere in the country, whether it be a local patron saint's day or a national religious day, such as Epiphany, Feast of St. Joseph, Corpus Christi, Feast of Sts. Peter and Paul or Feast of the Assumption. The celebrations are always colorful and well worth going out of the way to see. Sports of all kinds are ever popular, with automobile racing being probably the most exciting. Horse races, dog races and polo matches draw large audiences. The Italian national sport is *calcio* (soccer). Of course, mountain climbing, skiing and other mountain sports are at their best here, as are water sports, including sailing and under-water hunting. Tennis and golf are also popular, with courts and courses invariably set in picturesque surroundings, more often than not in view of the beautiful sea with a backdrop of snow-capped peaks. Another favorite pastime is cycling. A great event is the Grand Tour of Italy, which occurs in June and is followed with excited interest by all Italians.

ITALIAN FOOD IS TASTY

There are good restaurants in every city. From the big city cafes to the tiny, informal little restaurants in small villages, you will find food of high quality served

THE ITALIAN DOLOMITES

Italian State Tourist Office

with wine of equal goodness. The food is a bit starchy, perhaps, but you are on holiday, so forget your diet and enjoy the many tasty dishes. A few of the local specialties include *Carciofi alla Romana* (artichokes seasoned with special herbs and boiled in oil), *Cannelloni* (rolls of pastry, filled with meat and savory, covered with cheese, bechamel and tomato sauce), *Cotoletta alla Bolognese* (a Milanese veal cutlet garnished with melted cheese and covered with a tomato sauce), *Ossobuco* (veal cut across the marrow bone and served with a thick sauce and rice or green peas and mashed potatoes) or *Prosciutto con Fichi o Melone* (ham served with melon or fresh figs). Veal is the favorite Italian meat and is prepared in numerous ways, always good. Eggplant and artichokes are also favorites and equally good. Fish is excellent and there is a great variety. Be sure to try *zuppa de pesce* (a very spicy soup made with a large variety of seafood), especially good in Venice and Genoa. Cheeses play an important role in the Italian cuisine. There is a large selection of soft cheeses such as ricotta, fonina, robiolina, mozzarella, stracchino and bel paese; and of hard cheeses such as provolone, groviera and parmigiano. The spicy gorgonzola mixed with butter and eaten with pears is something to remember. Favorite dessert is fresh fruit, but there are a number of mouth-watering, rich little pastries such as *Mille Foglie* (creampuff), *Sainte Honoree* (chocolate and vanilla whipped cream tart) or *Zuppa Inglese* (cream pie soaked in liqueur and covered with a thick layer of whipped cream).

The vineyards of Italy produce more wine than any other country except France. From the north come the best red table wines, Barolo and Chianti being the two best known. The vineyards which produce Barolo are in Piedmont within a strictly limited district called Le Langhe, which comprises the vineyards of Barolo and a few adjoining parishes. Chianti is the wine of the vineyards of Radda, Castellina and Gaiole, three parishes known as Chianti Ferrese, in the province of Siena. Although Chianti is usually a red wine, there is now a little white Chianti made. There are also a number of good white wines, both dry and sweet, produced. Italians always drink wine with their meals and even in small restaurants you will find an adequate selection for each course. Among other Italian liquors are Brandy, Grappa, Strega and Maraschino. Vermouth forms the basis for a variety of aperitifs.

ROME. Much of the fascination of modern Rome lies in its historic past; in its long association with Christianity; in fragments of its ancient grandeur unearthed from the dust of time. Perhaps no city on earth has enjoyed a longer, more continuous importance, both politically and religiously, than Rome, seat of the Italian government and former capital of the Roman Republic and Empire For this the "eternal city" belongs not to Italy alone but to the world at large. A museum of grandiose proportions, few places have so many objects of religious and historical interest to attract the student, the pilgrim, the artist or the sightseer. This is the "city of the seven hills" founded by the legendary Romulus over seven hundred years before the birth of Christ. It is the city of the Caesars; of Mark Anthony and Marcus Aurelius; of Nero and Diocletion. This is the spot from which civilization spread outward across the face of Europe; the headquarters of the early Christian church and the cradle of the Italian Renaissance. Modern Rome lies within a wide bend of the Tiber River about seventeen miles northeast of the Mediterranean Sea. Its situation is strategically unimportant, the city owing its prominence to purely man-made factors. Originally Rome stood on seven ridges to the east of the Tiber, in the Latium region of central Italy. Gradually through the centuries, the city spread downward to the level of the plain where, by the period of the Roman Empire, it encompassed the entire Campus Martius. The modern city is built literally atop the ancient one, which careful excavations reveal lying as four street levels beneath an accumulation of volcanic ash. Archaeology is a vital part of the Roman scene and much of Rome's expansion and building in recent years has been planned with a consideration to the city's famed ruins. On the Palatine (one of the seven hills) where according to legend, Romulus traced the city's first boundaries, still stand the colossal remains of the palaces, stadia and gardens built first for the wealthy patricians and later for the Emperors. Here it is said that Augustus "found a city of brick and left one of marble." Nearby, the Colosseum is probably the best known, of ancient Roman relics. Below the Palatine is the Roman Forum, once the hub of Roman life. Here it was that the large public meetings and games were held and the triumphant processions of Rome's Emperors and generals returning from conquest passed along the Sacred Way. The top of the Capitoline Hill is reached by a

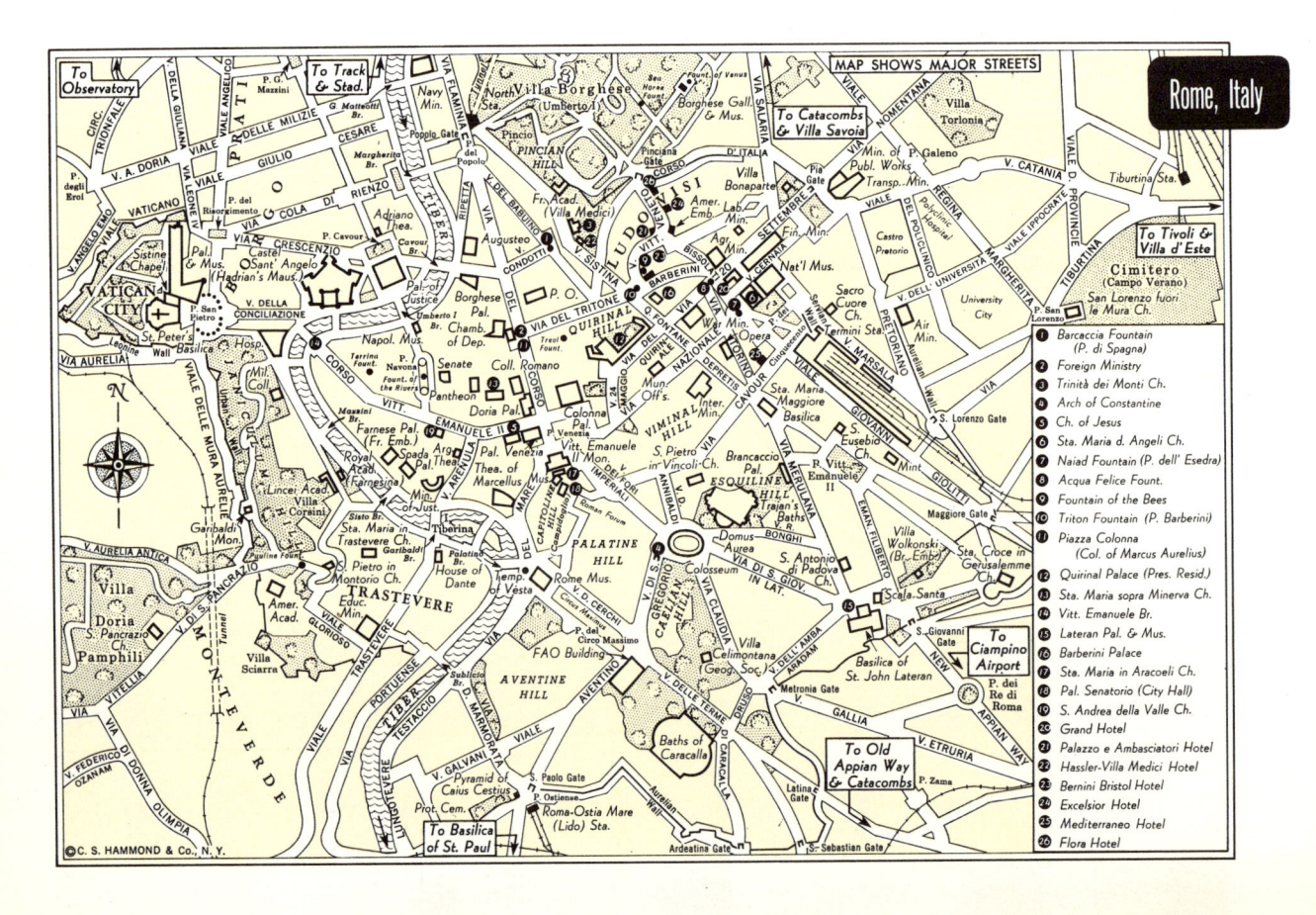

THE COLOSSEUM
<small>TWA—Trans World Airline</small>

broad flight of stone stairs. On the summit is Capitol Square, in the center of which rises the bronze equestrian statue of Marcus Aurelius while in the background the City Hall is flanked by the Piazza Conservatori and the famed Museo Capitolino. Designed by Michelangelo the Museo contains a spectacular collection of Roman sculpture. In the center of the city is the Pantheon best preserved of the ancient monuments; it has been used as a church continuously for more than 2,000 years. Built by Marcus Agrippa to celebrate the victory over Anthony and Cleopatra, and completely rebuilt by Hadrian, both Roman and Pagan gods were worshipped here until its final consecration as a Christian church in A.D. 609. Today it contains the tombs of the Kings of Italy. The Vatican, seat of the papacy, lies to the west of the Tiber. This "City Within a City" contains the Basilica of St. Peter, the world's largest Christian church and the culmination of designs by some of the most celebrated architects of the Renaissance including San Gallo, Peruzzi and Raphael. Michelangelo designed its magnificent dome and Maderna its façade. Before the Basilica is an immense square surrounded by an elliptical colonnade consisting of four rows of 284 columns. Among the various buildings which comprise the Vatican Palace is the Sistine Chapel on the ceiling and the altar wall of which Michelangelo painted his greatest masterpieces; "The Last Judgment" and "The Creation." Next to St. Peters the most famous of Rome's medieval churches are St. John Lateran, Santa Maria Maggiore and St. Pauls Without the Walls.

AROUND ABOUT THE COUNTRY

Most visitors to Italy concentrate on touring her lovely cities with possibly a stop on the Riviera or Capri. However, for those who have the time to tarry awhile, there are picturesque little out of the way villages and towns and incomparable mountain and maritime scenery. As a matter of fact the mountains which form the backbone of Italy seem to rival the sea in providing spectacles as magnificent as any in the world.

NAPLES. "The farther I am from you, the nearer you are to my heart" — this is the passionate, homesick song of the Neapolitan away from his illustrious city, with her mild, caressing climate and striking scenery. Dating back to the Greeks in origin and a source of deep fascination for the rich people of Rome, the city has always been a favored summer resort. Many masterpieces of the Greek and Roman eras are preserved in her National Museum, Europe's most important archeological museum, whose art collection is also famous. A gay, festive city of song, feasting and revelry, with a deep love and extraordinary flair for life, her most beloved festival is the Piedegrotta Feast, a devout homage to a miraculous Madonna and at the same time, a song contest marking the birth of the most catching popular Neopolitan songs of the year. Favorite pastime of her merry-makers is dining on mouth-watering *pizze alla napolitana,* topped

THE ARCH OF CONSTANTINE
<small>TWA—Trans World Airline</small>

later by a tangy sweet *pastiera napolitana* and refreshed with sweet Capri or some other wine, in a charming restaurant overlooking the enchanting bay. The men and women—dark-haired, vivacious and passionate — keep singing and dreaming through the years, eternally in love with their smiling "Napoli."

GAY, SUNNY, COLORFUL CAPRI AND ENCHANTING ISCHIA

Long a honeymoon and vacation paradise, CAPRI is easily accessible by boat from both Naples and Sorrento. A day spent here will be a delight never forgotten. Most of all you will enjoy the boat trip to the famous **Grotta Azurra**, a walk to the point where you can view the **Faraglioni**, the famous rocks jutting out of the water, a drive to the village of **Anacapri**, a visit to **Villa Jovis**, one of the palaces built by the Roman Emperors Augustus and Tiberius, and a visit to **Villa San Michele** built on the ruins of an ancient Roman villa by the author of *The Story of Michele*, Axel Munthe. Though highly commercialized, this enchanting island has lost none of its charm in 2,000 years and its natural beauties remain unspoiled. In the center of Capri is the characteristic "Piazzetta" crowded with open-air cafes where all the tourists sit for hours sipping drinks while the natives sit on the steps of the church that overlooks the square.

Guarding the northwestern entrance to the beautiful Bay of Naples is the island of ISCHIA, noted for its mineral springs and beautiful, everchanging scenery. **Mount Epomeo** towers 2,589 feet high in the center of the island. The port of **Porto d'Ischia** consists of a small perfectly sheltered port surrounded by white oriental-looking houses, steep, narrow streets, villas, gardens and beautiful pine woods. From here the road leads to **Casamicciola**, fa-

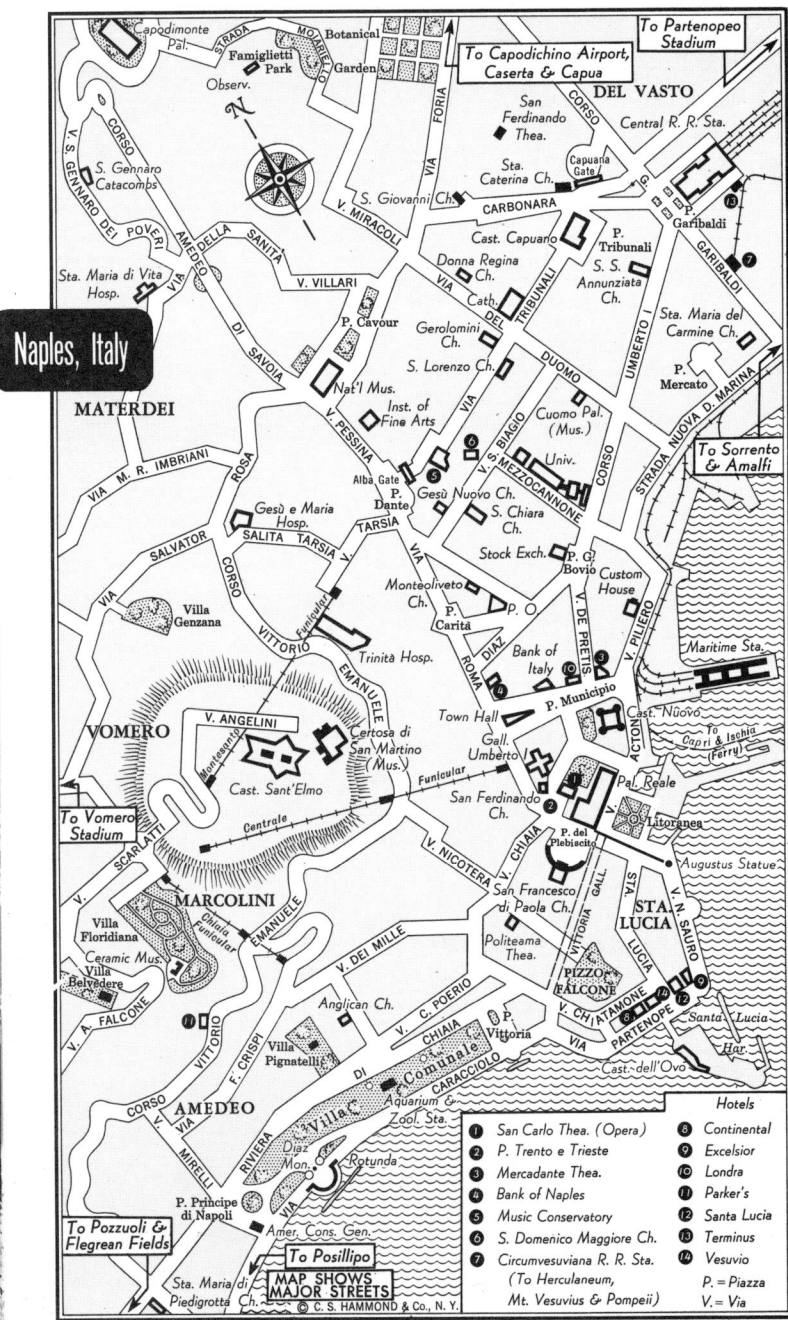

BAY OF NAPLES

CAPRI, VIEW FROM THE ROCK OF TIBERIUS

AMALFI

mous for its mineral radio-active waters. The beach here is especially fine and slopes gently into the sea. All over the island there are lovely walks and an excellent twenty-mile long road circles the island, offering magnificent panoramas. Excellent local wines are to be had, including the fine scented Epomeo.

ENVIRONS OF NAPLES

East of Naples is **Mount Vesuvius** and the ruins of **POMPEII**. A visit here is an absolute must. The story told by the ruins will be hard to believe even after you see them. Excavations into this silent city reveal a way of life cut off almost instantly, but preserved in stone since 79 AD, by Vesuvius' first recorded eruption. Visit the **Amphitheater**, the **Foro**, the various temples, the streets and the houses with magnificent mural paintings predominantly in **Pompeian red**.

SORRENTO, south of Naples, noted as a shopping center and for fine swimming, perches on a high cliff with its houses hidden in parks, orange and palm groves and gardens. Below is the intensely blue sea and the fine beach. . . . **POSITANO** is another picturesque town nearby made famous by the many artists who live here. Dazzling white houses contrast with the clusters of green trees descending towards the sea. Quaint, narrow little streets lead to the beach. . . . **AMALFI** whose name recalls memories of bygone days and the powerful Italian seafaring republic, is an ideal weekend spot. It has an interesting **Norman Cathedral**.

SICILY

PALERMO . . . . located at the foot of **Mount Pellegrino**, is a most beautiful city. Norman art treasures are still preserved there. The most important monuments are: the **Cathedral**, **Palazzo dei re Normanni** (of Arabian origin and restored by the Norman kings), the **Cappella Palatina** (richly decorated with twelfth century mosaics), the **Norman Cathedral of Monreale** (its walls are entirely covered with inlaid marble and mosaics and the cloister is adorned with 200 twin columns), the church of **San Giovanni Degli Eremiti** (of oriental style and famous for its thirteenth century cloister), the **Palazzo Zisa** (in Moslem style) and the magnificent villas and parks with their tropical plants. . . . About seven miles away is **MONDELLO**, the beach of Palermo, which offers good bathing facilities. . . . On the Ionian Sea, **TAORMINA**, enhanced by gorgeous villas and gardens full of rare plants, and pervaded with the scent of orange blossoms, is the most popular winter and summer resort in Sicily. It is situated on a promontory about 300 yards above sea level and gives a magnificent view of the snow-capped volcano, Mount Etna, in the background. There are many monuments worth visiting, including the **Greek Theater**, which stands on the summit of a hill, the fifteenth century **Palazzo Corvaia**, the **Palazzo Santo Stefano**, the **Cathedral** with the seventh century fountain, and the medieval castle. . . . Further along is **CATANIA** . . . . rich in art treasures. The bathing resort here, **La Plaja**, is especially good and is picturesquely set in a thick pine grove.

North of Rome, in the center of Italy, is the beautiful green region of Umbria with its large **Lake Trasimeno**. **PERUGIA**, its capital, has long been a cultural center and is famous for its **Italian University of Foreigners**, founded in 1307. . . . Nearby is **ASSISI**, the native town of St. Francis. It is a picturesque town and has maintained intact its medieval aspect. The **Basilica**, composed of two churches built one above the other, contains the tomb of St. Francis. . . . West of Perugia, in Tuscany, is another charming medieval town, **SIENA**. Here the famous **Palio** takes place every year (July 2nd and August 16th), attracting tourists from all parts of the world. The Palio is a fifteenth century pageant in which the seventeen boroughs of the town are represented. In the museum here is a magnificent collection of Italian primitive paintings. . . . North of Siena is beautiful **FLORENCE** . . . . cradle of the Renaissance. It flourished under the Medicis in the 1400's and al-

TEMPLE OF CONCORD, AGRIGENTO, SICILY

WINDMILL, SICILY *TWA—Trans World Airlines*

most every building in the old part of the city has claim to recognition as a Renaissance shrine. This was the "home town" of Dante, Petrarch, Bocaccio and Galileo and many of Michelangelo's sculptures and Raphael's paintings may still be admired in Florence, each on the spot where it was created. A good place to start sight-seeing is the **Piazza del Duomo** (Cathedral Square). On the same square you can visit the great **Cathedral of S. Maria del Fiore** and admire the splendid dome created by Brunelleschi. Adjoining is the Gothic **bell tower** or **Campanile**, designed by Giotto. Opposite the cathedral is the **Battistero of San Giovanni**, famed for its Ghiberti doors. Other celebrated churches are **Santa Croce**, where Galileo, Michelangelo, Foscolo, Alfieri, Canova and many other great Italians are buried; **Santa Maria Novella**. (thirteenth century) with its charming cloisters; **S. Lorenzo**, one of the masterpieces of Filippo Brunelleschi, and **S. Miniato al Monte**, located on a hill which gives a view of the whole city of Florence. The **Piazza della Signoria** is another interesting square which is in effect an outdoor museum, dominated by the tower of the thirteenth century **Palazzo Vecchio** which can be seen from almost anywhere in the city. The outside of this palace is stern and forbidding, but the interior is magnificent. Directly opposite this palace's main entrance is the **Porch of the Lancers**, which contains many wonderful groups of statuary, including "The Rape of the Sabines" and "Hercules Slaying the Centaur." Toward the Arno is another palace, the **Palazzo Uffizi**, which now contains the National Library, State Archives and one of the world's most famous art galleries. A corridor running from the Uffizi to the **Pitti Palace** (with another famous museum) crosses the Arno, over the **Ponte Vecchio**, the last of six bridges that once crossed that river into Florence.

It is more than a bridge; it's a market place and a cluster of little shops offering all manner of wares in silver, leather, cloth and other skillfully fabricated materials. Near here you should visit the **straw market** where tourists and natives bargain for lovely goods in linen, straw and leather. You should also visit the **Giardino di Boboli**, the lovely garden with its amphitheater where some of the celebrated performances of the **Maggio Musicale** take place during the months of May and June. Nearby is the famous **Michelangelo Square** atop a hill giving a marvelous view of this beautiful historic city of Florence.... In the outskirts of Florence is **FIESOLE** which is famous for its fantastic, rich villas. Situated on a high hill, it gives a panoramic view of Florence and the whole surrounding Arno Valley.

Westward is **LEGHORN** . . . . the seaport of Florence and site of the Italian Naval Academy. Although war damage has left little of historic interest, a visit to **Montenero Sanctuary** is worth while. . . . A half-hour away is **PISA** with its famous **Leaning Tower** and superb Cathedral. . . . About twelve miles northeast of Pisa is the old walled town of **LUCCA**, often overlooked by tourists. A drive to Lucca is well worth while because it gives you a view of the fertile Italian countryside. In Lucca itself you will see the town's picturesque narrow streets. . . . Northwest of Pisa the bustling port of **GENOA** . . . . is a fascinating mixture of the medieval and the modern. The old section, with is narrow winding streets, stairs and bridges hemmed in by buildings dating from the Middle Ages, is the most interesting part.

THE ITALIAN RIVIERA

All three seas of Italy have their individual beauty and characteristic coasts, but the blue of the water seems bluer and the white of the sand seems whiter on the Riviera. Like the adjoining French Riviera, it offers every possible facility for a seaside holiday, from modest little villages to pretentious villas. **SAN REMO** is one of the more fashionable resorts with an excellent climate all year 'round. It has a vast range of amusements, including the Casino, dog shows, motorcycle races and flower carnivals. San Remo is noted for its beautiful flower market. . . . Not far from San Remo is **ALASSIO**, situated at the center of a bay and surrounded by green hills dotted with luxurious villas. It has a lovely sandy beach, a casino and tennis club. . . . On the coast below Genoa **SANTA MARGHERITA LIGURE** is another ideal resort. Here you will enjoy both a rocky and sandy beach. . . . A little further below Genoa, **RAPALLO** is a favorite with both Italians and foreigners. Here festivals, golf tournaments, regattas, horse races, art exhibitions and shows take place all year 'round. . . . Next is **PORTOFINO**. Situated in a very small bay, it is one of the most picturesque and charming towns of the Riviera and is famous for its underwater fishing. Portofino attracts a very cosmopolitan society of artists, movie stars, aristocrats and industrialists, although it is a typical fisherman's village. . . . Further below is **VIAREGGIO**, an elegant, modern resort with smart cafes, shops, bars and restaurants. At Carnival time it is especially gay and colorful.

TURIN AND MILAN

TURIN . . . . became the first capital of the Italian kingdom in 1861. Testifying to this period of greatness are the city's monuments: The **Palazzo Madama**, which was the seat of the first Italian Senate, the **Royal Palace** and the **Carignano Palace**, where the proclamation of the kingdom of Italy took place. On the hill near the city is the **Basilica of Superga**, where many members of the royal

PONTE VECCHIO, FLORENCE *TWA—Trans World Airlines*

family of Savoy are buried. Turin is mainly an industrial city. The Fiat Corporation's factories are here, together with famous distilleries and chocolate factories. . . . West of Turin is **SESTRIERE** in the Cottian Alps. Because of its magnificent snowfields this is one of the leading winter resorts in Europe, beloved by every type of skier. It is also favored in the summer with a dry healthy climate.

MILAN. The second largest city in Italy and its greatest industrial, commercial and financial center, Milan rises imposingly above the rich garden of the Lombard plain. Since 222 B.C. when the original Gallic town fell to the invading Roman legions, Milan has known many aggressors and her history has been one of repeated devastations. Today, few buildings remain from Roman and early medieval times, although it is still possible to distinguish the tiny rectangular nucleus of the ancient town within the boundaries of the modern city. Because of Milan's strategic position at the confluence of numerous rail lines and its importance in the industrial field, it was the target, in World War II, for both German and Allied bombs. Many of its famous landmarks were destroyed or damaged during the war. Perhaps the city's most impressive structure is its Gothic cathedral located at one end of the spacious Piazza del Duomo. Among the largest in Europe, the cathedral is elaborately ornamented with over 100 pinnacles and 4,400 statues of various periods. The main tower, which rises 354 feet above the street, is surmounted by a golden figure of the Virgin. The cathedral's roof, reached by stairs carried up the buttresses, commands an excellent view of the city as well as the

THE CASTEL SFORZESCO
Italian State Tourist Office

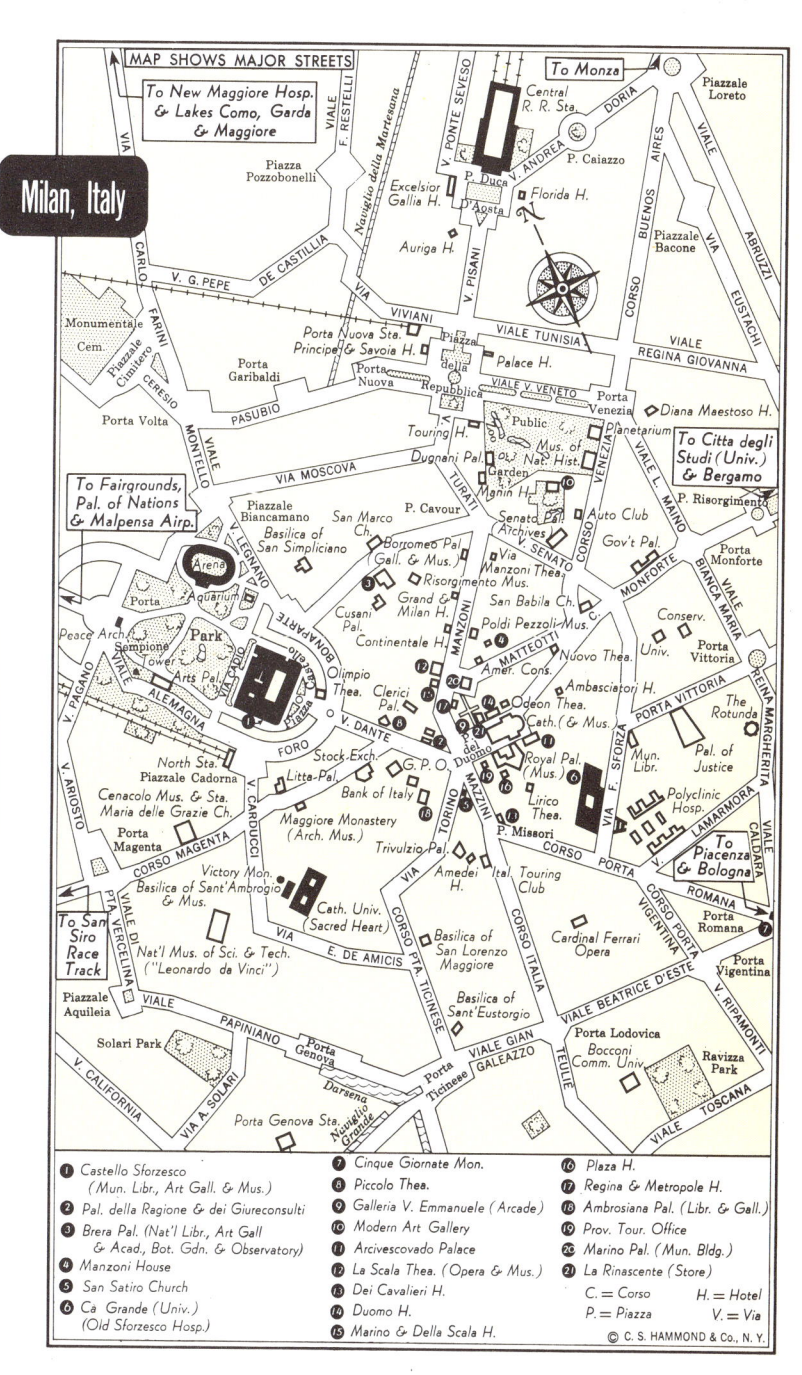

THE CATHEDRAL OF MILAN
TWA—Trans World Airline

surrounding plain with its tidy checkerboard of fields and roads bordered by symmetrical rows of Lombardy poplars. To the south, can be seen the long line of the Apennines stretching along the horizon, while to the north and west rise the snowy peaks of the Alps. Two splendid palaces also face the Piazza del Duomo. These are the palace of the archbishops of Milan and the Palazzo Reale which is built on the site of the Viscontis' mansion. Milan's notable buildings include the church of San Ambrogio, founded by St. Ambrose in the 4th century and restored during the 11th century in the style of a Romanesque basilica; the 15th century Casa dei Borromei with its exquisite Gothic courtyard; the beautiful Loggia degli Osii and the famed 17th-century Biblioteca Ambrosiana. Besides a great treasure of architectural masterpieces, Milan possesses a wealth of painting and sculpture. The renowned Brera picture gallery contains works by such masters as Veronese, Bellini, Raphael, Luini and Bramantino, while Leonardo da Vinci's immortal fresco "The Last Supper" adorns the refectory wall of the convent of Santa Maria delle Grazie. Milan is a noted center of music and the theater, as well as the home of various educational institutions including a university and a school of engineering.

ITALY'S LAKES

The lake region displays amazing scenic contrasts. Luxurious hotels and magnificent villas, built amidst subtropical vegetation, line the lake shores. Rising in the background are dark green hills which gradually merge into rocky mountains covered with snow. These beautiful lakes are either on or very near the Italian-Swiss border. LAKE COMO, just two hours away from Milan, offers many attractions. During the season, April to October, there are yachting races, fashion shows, concerts and of course, tennis and water sports. The town of COMO is well known for its silk industry, one of the finest in the world. Important monuments include the eleventh-century Cathedral, with its Gothic façade and the ancient Palazzo del Broletto. In the surroundings there are many beautiful villas such as the Villa Olmo. . . . CERNOBBIO is probably the most popular and fashionable spring and fall resort on the lake. The small town is linked to Como by boat and streetcar. . . . A favorite center for excursions and sports is BELLAGIO, situated on a promontory in the center of the lake. . . . East of Como is LAKE GARDA, another beautiful and popular resort area, with the tourist centers of GARDONE RIVIERA, where the poet Gabriele D'Annunzio lived, and SIRMIONE, famous for its hyperthermal sulphurous waters. Both are ideal for a vacation or for a long rest. . . . On LAKE MAGGIORE, west of Como, STRESA is the finest climatic resort. The season opens in April and ends in September, which is generally the best month of the year to visit the lakes. Famous for its mountain excursions, walks, swimming and fishing.

CORTINA D'AMPEZZO

ITALY'S MOUNTAINS

The mountains are everywhere in Italy, forming the backbone of this peninsular country and then running across the northern "top" of the country like the crossbar on a "T." Rounded, green-covered mountains, bald, rocky hillocks, regal, snow-capped peaks — all types of mountain scenery can be found in this beautiful land. Mountain climbing is a favorite Italian pastime and the skiing grounds are among the finest in Europe. In northern Italy some of the popular skiing resorts are SESTRIERE (described under Turin), MADONNA DI CAMPIGLIO, SAN MARTINO DI CASTROZZA and SELVA DI GARDENA. CORTINA AMPEZZO, known as the "Queen of the Dolomites,"

LAKE COMO

VENICE

rises 4,015 feet above sea level and can be reached by motor coach from Milan and Venice or by train from Rome, Milan and Venice. Situated in the picturesque Ampezzo Valley and surrounded by the stately **Dolomites**, Cortina is a great international tourist center during the summer and winter months. There are two aerial cable cars to **Mount Pocol** (over 5,000 feet high) and **Mount Faloria** (6,954 feet high), and several chairlifts. Automobile races, tennis and golf tournaments, mountain climbing, fishing, shooting, skiing, skating and bobsledding provide plenty of excitement for vacationists and tourists.

THE QUEEN OF THE ADRIATIC

VENICE . . . . is one of the most unusual cities in the world and traditionally one of the most romantic. Its geographical position, great historical past and incomparable art treasures are the main reasons for its universal fame. Nevertheless, this paragon of cities got off to a rather unromantic start. In the year 425, Attila the Hun drove the people of northern Italy from their homes and literally out into the Adriatic, where they found refuge on a few bare and dismal islands. Settlements, increasing in number, were built up there. As time passed, the security of their isolation enabled the Venetians to become prosperous and powerful. By the end of the seventh century, Venice had become an independent state and her ruler, or doge, one of the strong men of Europe.

Venice today is built on and around about 120 small islands, close together, in the middle of a great lagoon about a mile and a half from the sea. It is cut up by 150 canals and tied together by 400 bridges. The only means of transportation is by foot on the few very narrow streets or in the characteristic gondolas, boats, motor boats and waterborne streetcars (Vaporetto). The most famous bridges are the **Rialto** and the **Ponte dei Sospiri** (Bridge of Sighs). You will want to see the **Piazza di San Marco**, Venice's only large square, paved with marble. Colonnades and arcades enclose this square on three sides and on the fourth is the **Church Campanile of San Marco**, a marvelous example of Byzantine architecture. Across the square is the **Torre dell' Orlogio** and its clock. Two giant bronze Moors strike the hours with sledge-hammers on a large bell. They have been doing it ever since 1497. Not far from the square is the **Palazzo dei Dogi**. A must, of course, is a ride along the **Grand Canal** with its two miles of historic buildings, principally palaces and churches. Robert Browning died in the **Palazzo Rezzonico**. Lord Byron wrote part of "Don Juan" in the **Palazzo Mocenigo**, and Richard Wagner composed the great second act of "Tristan and Isolde" in one of the Palazzi Mocenigo. Each year, in July the traditional **Regata of the Sposalizio de Mare** (Marriage of the Sea) takes place on the Grand Canal. Other palaces along the Canal include the stupendous Gothic **Ca' D'Oro**, the **Ca' Foscari** and the **Ca' Pesaro**. See also the church of **Santa Maria della Salute**, built as an expression of thanks for the end of the plague in 1630. One of the most enjoyable pastimes is a walk through the crowded and narrow alleys, over the arched bridges and into the curious shops of the artisans.

When you've had your fill of the treasures in art and architecture, visit the **Lido**. This beautiful stretch of beach runs along a shoestring island that divides the Venice lagoon from the open sea. It is the most fashionable seaside bathing resort in Italy, attracting a cosmopolitan crowd from all over the world. Here, too, are the **Palazzo Municipale** with the world famous **Casino** and the **Palazzo del Cinema**, where the International Film Festival is held in September each year. The season is from May through September.

Famous islands in the vicinity are: **MURANO**, a village on five small islands, is world renowned for its centuries-old glass blowing art. Marvelous masterpieces of this work in blown glass from the fourteenth to eighteenth century are exhibited in the **Museo Vetrario**. Nearby, the sixteenth century church of **San Pietro Martire** contains paintings by Giovanni Bellini, Tintoretto and Veronese. **TORCELLO**, a small village in the lonely lagoon, was once an important town and still preserves some of its notable medieval monuments. These include the Church of S. Fosca, an octagonal building of the eleventh century and the Cathedral erected during the ninth and the eleventh centuries. **BURANO** is a famous island where the most exquisite laces are made.

Southwest of Venice is one of the oldest and most interesting cities of Italy, **BOLOGNA** · · · · · The **University of Bologna**, founded in 1088, is the oldest in Europe and one of the greatest in the world. The city retains a medieval aspect with its arcaded streets, two remarkable **leaning towers** and hundreds of impressive buildings and churches, all rich in art treasures. Among the many interesting buildings are the **Palace of King Enzo**, the 13th century **Church of San Francisco**, the **Fine Arts Museum** with a fine collection of paintings by Francia, Reni and Domenichino, the **Observatory** and the medieval town hall. Bologna is equally famous for its culinary art. Here, in the restaurants and hotels is found some of the best food in the whole of Italy. . . . A fascinating side trip from Bologna, or from Florence, is a visit to the tiny republic of **SAN MARINO**, atop a mountain in the Apennines.

TOWER OF PISA

Greece

PARTHENON
TWA—Trans World Airline

BIRTHPLACE OF WESTERN CIVILIZATION

Located in the main stream of civilization, Greece has witnessed from time immemorial the clash of men and ideas and the encounters of armies and of cultures. Birthplace of democracy, she has stood for centuries in the defense of Western civilization from the onslaughts of despotism and tyranny. Determined by Greek thought, by the character of the people and the geographical position of the country, its history stretches back more than 4,000 years. It is a fascinating story of great achievement in the face of recurrent adversity. All of modern Greece is a visual history of European civilization, with the grandeur of the world's greatest art treasures scattered across the land, making the entire country an immense exhibition of art. You may follow the evolution of art through the ages, step by step, from the earliest Minoan Period in Crete to the classical period, which produced such masterpieces as the Parthenon, and later to the Christian era when magnificent Byzantine art flourished. Cradle of civilization and birthplace of the gods, land of legend and beauty which has inspired centuries of art and the essence of philosophy, Greece welcomes the world.

NATIONAL DISHES AND DRINKS

Many Greek specialties may be obtained in the "tavernas," or restaurants of a local character. Among the best are *souvlakia* (lamb or pork on skewers) and *dolmathakia* (rice and meat in vine leaves). There are numerous excellent Greek table wines, including sweet dessert wines like "Mavrodaphni," "Samos" and "Santorini," and there are several good brands of Greek brandy. "Retsinato" and "Kokinelli" are national wines flavored with resin, which are served in the "tavernas." Fish has also been an important food in Greece for centuries.

LAND OF MYTH AND MAGIC

ATHENS. Outlined against the sky, overlooking Athens, stands the majestic Acropolis, with its Parthenon, built in the fifth century, B.C., a landmark of extraordinary beauty, grandeur and monumental power, a timeless citadel of the most dynamic period in the history of mankind. During this era of greatness, a remarkable culture flourished in the Greek city states, notably in Athens, which produced the masterpieces that have since inspired art and thought throughout the world. Aeschylus, Sophocles, Euripides and Aristophanes, Ictinus and Phidias, Socrates, Plato and Aristotle — the roll of mighty thinkers and noble artists who walked her dusty, sun-drenched streets is matched by no other city in history. It was here the ideals of democracy were first formulated and Western civilization was born. This heritage of free thought is manifested in the Athenians' pastime: the art of conversation, or more particu-

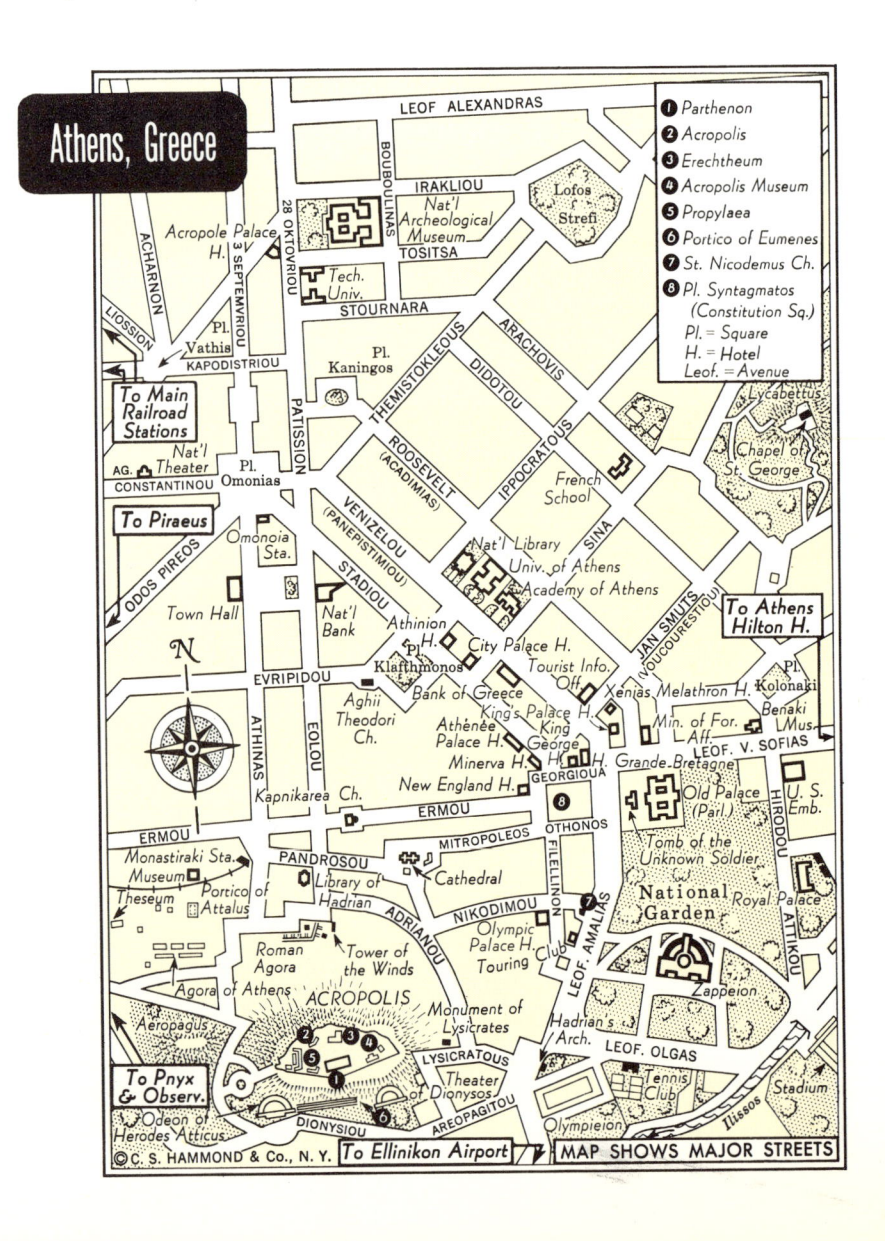

Athens, Greece

1. Parthenon
2. Acropolis
3. Erechtheum
4. Acropolis Museum
5. Propylaea
6. Portico of Eumenes
7. St. Nicodemus Ch.
8. Pl. Syntagmatos (Constitution Sq.)

Pl. = Square
H. = Hotel
Leof. = Avenue

THE FIGHTING EVZONES TWA—Trans World Airline

beauty. **MYKONOS** is the most picturesque of Aegean Islands and most fashionable bathing resort in the Eastern Mediterranean. . . . The mythical birthplace of Apollo and Artemis is **DELOS**, famous sanctuary island of ancient Greece, featuring the primitive **cave-temple of the god and rich houses** with magnificent mosaics. . . . **SANTORINI**, or **THERA**, is the island with an underwater volcano, one of the strangest natural phenomena of the world, into the crater of which ships can sail. . . . Mythical birthplace of Zeus, chief of Olympian deities and god of hospitality, is **CRETE**, the "Great Greek Island" famous alike for its history and its natural beauty. Detailed evidence of the way of life of a civilization going back more than 3,000 years B. C., known as the Minoan period, is to be found in the **Palace of Knossos**. The Herakleion Museum houses a spendid collection of the remains of this wonderful culture. The island's combination of mountain, plain and sea, of luxuriant fertility and of barrenness is characteristically Greek. . . . The resort island of **RHODES**, largest and most beautiful of the Dodecanese, is known as the "Isle of Roses."

larly, debating. Everywhere and at all times, they skillfully discuss all questions, disputing this point, upholding that side, expounding their opinions on everything, expressing their love not only of the spoken word but most of all, their fascination with logical argument. The classical Agora and the Byzantine Hippodrome is the present-day Constitution Square, in front of the Parliament Building, where gesticulating speakers may be seen, during the day and far into the cool of the night, leisurely strolling in pairs or groups or sitting around the tables in outdoor *tavernas,* eating ice cream and sweets, drinking Turkish coffee and the powerful native *ouzo* and discoursing, contending, reasoning. Because of the delightful dry, clear climate, with balmy breezes from the mountains and the sea, and the sociability of these loquacious people, the Athenians live outdoors. In fact, it sometimes seems not a single person has stayed in his own home, for the house is used only for rest; for all other activities — eating, meeting, playing—they go out to the streets, the gardens or the cafés. King of the streets, though, is the donkey, adding still more to the city's unique rural charm. It is this small, proud, plodding donkey who brings in from the bright countryside in his tiny cart the preeminent olives, the glorious Greek grapes and the fragrant royal-hued violets, "the crown of Athens."

On the isthmus linking Peloponissos with mainland Greece is **CORINTH**, with the old paved streets and fountains, made familiar by Paul's sermons and the Epistles to the Corinthians. The ancient city was dominated by the impressive height of **Acro-Corinth,** on which much of the formidable system of ancient fortifications still stands. . . . . . . The seven Ionian Islands are like gems rising out of the blue sea and Kerkyra or Corfu is the loveliest and most splendid of them all. It has a luxuriant vegetation, among which orchards and olive groves abound. The attractive town of **KERKYRA**, capital of the island, surnamed by the Byzantines "the town with two summits," is one of the most picturesque in the country, with its narrow, shaded streets characteristic of the seventeenth and eighteenth centuries. Of the many fine churches, the richest in Byzantine paintings and silver is **Saint Spyridon Church**, near the famous Esplanade. Besides containing many other interesting monuments and providing many marvelous views, Corfu is also a popular resort, because of the fine seashore and the coastal waters abounding with fish, being especially renowned for lobster fishing. . . . The celebrated Isles of Greece, immortalized in the classic stanzas of Lord Byron, are pearls set by nature in the beautiful Grecian Seas, scenes of indescribable

ACADEMY OF ATHENS Papaioannou

PIRAEUS, THE PORT OF ATHENS TWA—Trans World Airline

87

Turkey

LINK OF TWO CONTINENTS

A panorama of seven thousand years of human history — of varying cultures and civilizations — the like of which no other land has experienced, is revealed in every corner of modern Turkey. Dating back to the fourth millennium before the Christian era, people of the paleolithic period, and those of the Age of Caverns, lived on these highlands and along the coast. Then came the Hittites, Lydians, Phrygians, Carians, Dorians, Aeolians, Ionians, Commerians, Bithynians, Persians, Greeks, Romans, Byzantines, Danishmends, Seljuks and finally the Ottoman Turks, who established themselves after the beginning of the fourteenth century. Today, the splendid reminders of this old-world romance, combined with the new-world culture of the modern, Westernized Turkish Republic create an intriguingly unique country — a bridge, both geographically and culturally, between East and West, as well as a bridge to the remote civilizations of the ancient past.

GOURMETS OF THE NEAR EAST

Turkey has always had the reputation of a paradise of good living and gastronomy. A famous old Turkish proverb says, "The spirit gets into a man with the food he eats." For many centuries, the delights of Turkish cooking have enchanted the palate of Westerners visiting the country and Americans generally take with zest to *boreks* (a special preparation of pastry dough with cheese or chopped-meat filling) and *cerkes tavugu* (chicken prepared with a special walnut and red-pepper sauce). You must not miss the *shish kebab* with rice (*pilâv*) and if you prefer vegetables, another specialty is stuffed eggplant (*zeytin yagli patlican dolmasi*) and green peppers (*biber dolmasi*).

ANCIENT GLAMOUR

ISTANBUL. Istanbul — Constantinople — Byzantium — no matter what her name (and she has been called by all three), each conjures up visions of Eastern splendor and might. Only city bridging two continents — Europe and Asia — her shores are washed by the Marmara Sea, the Bosporus and the Golden Horn, whose sparkling waters add still more enchantment to her fabulous fame. Proud jewel of emperors, she was the glittering prize city of the Byzantines, of the Eastern Roman Empire and upon her capture in 1453 — signalizing the end of the European Middle Ages — of the mighty Ottoman Empire. Her great walls withstood many an heroic assault, but when the city succumbed — only three times in her history — she brought such wealth and authority that commanders and kings thought any blood sacrifice worth such dazzling rewards. Today, her breath-taking skyline symbolizes both her impressive past and future influence — a skyline whose magic is the thousands of minarets that, with pious, slender fingers, aspire to heaven and the majestic domes of the 444 mosques that sit like crowns on the summits of her seven hills.

Research seems to have proven that ANKARA . . . the capital since 1923 and a modern metropolis with large boulevards and all kinds of European-style buildings, has been inhabited since paleolithic and neolithic time. However, some archeologists believe that it was first built by the Hittites, who had founded a powerful empire in Anatolia 2,000 years before the Christian era. In 278-277 B. C. the Galatians, having invaded the region, made the city their capital, Galatia, and laid the foundations of the present-day Citadel. During the Byzantine period, the walls halfway to the top were built, and several restorations and reconstructions followed in the Seljuk and Ottoman periods. The Galatians also built the **Temple of Augustus**, although it was originally dedicated to Men, a Galatian divinity. No museum in the world contains so full and rich a collection of Hittite works as the **Museum of Archaeology of Ankara**. Most remarkable of all is the **Mausoleum of Kemel Atatürk**, founder and first president of the Turkish Republic. Founded in 301 B. C., **HATAY** or **ANTAKYA** (ancient Antioch) on the River Asî (Orontes) was the capital of Syria and for centuries one of the principal cities of the world. Caesar and Augustus did much for her prosperity, hence the important ruins dating from the Roman era. . . **IZMIR** · · · · known for nearly 3,000 years as "the first city of the Eastern Mediterranean," is the second port of Turkey and center of a rich agricultural area. Kadife Kale (The Velvet Castle) overlooks the city and commands a breathtaking view of the bay. The walls and towers on the hill were originally built during the reign of Alexander the Great, with traces of additional construction and repairs made during the Ottoman period . . . One of Turkey's most popular resort cities is **BURSA** . . . . a city essentially Turkish, where everything — even the atmosphere — belongs to the past. Biggest mosque in Bursa is Uli Cami (Great Mosque), a great rectangle covered with twenty cupolas. However, two world-famous monuments considered the most magnificent specimens of early Turkish-Ottoman art at its highest are **Yeşil Cami (Green Mosque)** and **Yesil Türbe (Green Mausoleum)** containing the tomb of its builder, Mehmet I. Masterpiece of the mosque is the Mihrat (altar), a jewel of ceramic art. These monuments received their names from their decorations of greenish tiles, made by a secret process lost for centuries, and those adorning the octagonal mausoleum are especially remarkable. To its unchallenged merit as an historic and artistic city, Bursa adds that of a famous spa, and most visitors to the city go primarily to visit these thermal baths. Oldest and most famous, dating largely from the fourteenth century, is **Eski Kaplica (Old Spa)**. Bursa is situated at the foot of a huge mountain called **Uludağ**, a three-fold attraction as a summer resort, an alpinistic center and a winter-sports area, where the streams and lakes abound in trout and the forest with wild game. A delightful trip can be made to **Karacabey Harasi (Ranch of Karacabey)**, where pure Arab horses are bred. Do not leave Bursa without visiting the **Biçakcilar (Covered Bazaar)**, where hand-made Turkish hunting knives and the best Turkish towels and silks are sold, since the city has been famous for its silks

BLUE MOSQUE

Turkish Information Office

AFRICA

The epithet "dark continent" no longer describes Africa, for it has been awakened by the dazzling light of progress; and with this progress has come a vigorous national feeling and dissatisfaction with European rule, resulting in self-government in ever-increasing proportions.

Until recent years, a trip to Africa invariably meant going on a safari to hunt big game. This naturally excluded all but the immensely wealthy. Today, however, with improved methods of transportation and other facilities, the veil has been partially lifted from the face of this exciting continent.

You can now visit famed Casablanca and the infamous Casbah; take a giant step backward in time as you view the magnificent Pyramids and the ageless Sphinx; marvel at the tiny Pygmies in their intriguing villages, contrasting them with the giant Watusi, Africa's tallest people, who sometimes achieve a height of more than seven feet; or visit the inhabitants of the town of Goulimine, where the long blue veils that are worn by both men and women, eventually turn their skin blue.

Another color, gold, describes fabulous Johannesburg, South Africa, the center of the goldfields. No tour is complete without a trip through a mine here and in Kimberly, where more than $1,500,000,000 worth of diamonds in the rough have been taken from the mine since it opened in 1868.

Synonymous with Africa is big game, but the traveler no longer has to go on a safari to encounter these animals; for the continent now boasts marvelous national parks that are truly wildlife sanctuaries. Here the sight of gorillas, giraffes, zebras, lions, rhinoceroses and other beasts provide a thrilling climax to any African vacation.

NORTH ATLANTIC OCEAN
SOUTH ATLANTIC
Mediterranean Sea
Red Sea
Persian Gulf
Caspian Sea
Gulf of Aden
Gulf of Guinea
Sahara
Libyan Desert
Arabian Desert
Nubian Desert
Tibesti Massif
Ahaggar Mts.
Atlas Mountains
Tanezrouft Route
Hoggar Route
Equator
Azores
Madeira
Funchal
Canary Is.
Las Palmas
Ascension
Lisbon
MADRID
Barcelona
Sardinia
ROME
Naples
Sicily
Gibraltar
Tangier
Rabat
Casablanca
Mazagan
Mogador
Agadir
Tiznit
Marrakech
Fez
Meknes
Oujda
Oran
Algiers
Sidi-bel-Abbes
Constantine
Bône
Bizerte
Tunis
Kairouan
Sfax
Gabès
Djerba
Timgad
Biskra
Laghouat
Ghardaia
Touggourt
Ouargla
Colomb-Béchar
El Goléa
Timimoun
Adrar
In Salah
Tamanrasset
Agadès
Zinder
Ghadames
Tripoli
Homs
Hun
Benghazi
Shahat (Cyrene)
Derna
Tobruk
Jarabub
Aujila
Siwa
El 'Alamein
Sphinx & Pyramids
El Faiyûm
Alexandria
CAIRO
Port Said
Suez Canal
Asyût
Nile
Thebes
Luxor
Idfu
Aswân
Abu Simbil
Wadi Halfa
Atbara
Meroe
Omdurman
Khartoum
Blue Nile
White Nile
MOROCCO
IFNI
SPANISH SAHARA
ALGERIA
TUNISIA
SAOURA
OASIS
LIBYA
Tripolitania
Fezzan
Cyrenaica
UNITED ARAB REPUBLIC
Egypt
MAURITANIA
Sudanese Republic
MALI FEDERATION
Senegal
NIGER
CHAD
SUDAN
UPPER VOLTA
NIGERIA
GHANA
TOGO
DAHOMEY
IVORY COAST
GUINEA
SIERRA LEONE
LIBERIA
PORT. GUINEA
GAMBIA
CAMEROONS
CAMEROUN
CENTRAL AFRICAN REP.
REP. OF CONGO
GABON
RIO MUNI
FERNANDO PO
REP. OF THE CONGO
RUANDA-URUNDI
UGANDA
KENYA
TANGANYIKA TERR.
ETHIOPIA
SOMALIA
FR. SOMALILAND
ADEN PROT.
YEMEN
SAUDI ARABIA
QATAR
KUWAIT
IRAQ
IRAN
JORDAN
ISRAEL
LEBANON
Syria
CYPRUS
TURKEY
GREECE
U.S.S.R.
SPAIN
PORTUGAL
ITALY
ALB.
ANGOLA
Katanga
Villa Cisneros
Port-Étienne
Nouakchott
Senegal
St-Louis
C. Verde
Dakar
Bathurst
Kayes
Bissau
Bamako
Niger
Kankan
Conakry
Freetown
Monrovia
Abidjan
Timbuktu
Goundam
Djenne
Hombori
Bourem
Gao
Menaka
Niamey
Ouagadougou
Kumasi
Volta
Accra
Cape Coast
Lomé
Porto-Novo
Lagos
Abeokuta
Ibadan
Benue
Kano
Nguru
Mao
L. Chad
Ft-Lamy
Shari
Logône
Ft-Archambault
Cameroon
Douala
Yaoundé
Príncipe
São Tomé
Annobón
Libreville
Port-Gentil
Lambaréné
Pointe-Noire
Cabinda
Boma
Matadi
Brazzaville
Léopoldville
Luanda
Congo
Cuango
Kasai
Sankuru
Ubangi
Bangui
Uele
GARAMBA NAT. PK.
Aketi
Buta
Aruwimi
Ituri Forest
Irumu
Stanley Falls
Stanleyville
Coquilhatville
L. Léopold II
Lomami
Lualaba
Kindu
Kasongo
Kongolo
Albertville
Manono
UPEMBA NAT. PK.
Bukama
L. Mweru
Jadotville
L. Bangweulu
Kalambo Falls
ALBERT NAT. PK.
Ruwenzori
L. Edward
L. Albert
Murchison Falls
L. Kioga
Elgon
Kampala
Entebbe
L. Victoria
Kisenyi
L. Kivu
Bukavu
Uvira
Usumbura
Kigoma
Ujiji
L. Tanganyika
L. Rukwa
Tabora
Mbeya
L. Nyasa
Kisumu
Nanyuki
Kenya
Nairobi
Ngorongoro Crater
Serengeti Plain
Kilimanjaro
Moshi
L. Eyasi
Lushoto
Tanga
Pemba
Zanzibar
Dar es Salaam
Mafia
Kilwa Kisiwani
Lindi
Mtwara
Mombasa
Malindi
Lamu
Kismayu
Juba
Mogadishu
L. Rudolf
L. Abaya
Jimma
Addis Ababa
Dire Dawa
Harar
Hargeisa
Berbera
Zeila
Djibouti
Assab
Gondar
L. Tana
Aksum
Asmara
Massawa
Port Sudan
Jidda
Mecca
Medina
Riyadh
Dhahran
San'a
Aden
Mukalla
Socotra
Istanbul
Ankara
Kayseri
Izmir
Athens
Crete
Antalya
Beirut
Damascus
Jerusalem
L. Van
Mosul
Baghdad
Babylon
Tigris
Euphrates
Abadan
Tabriz
L. Urmia
Hamadan
Qum
Tehran
Susa
Isfahan
Shiraz
Kerman
Meshed

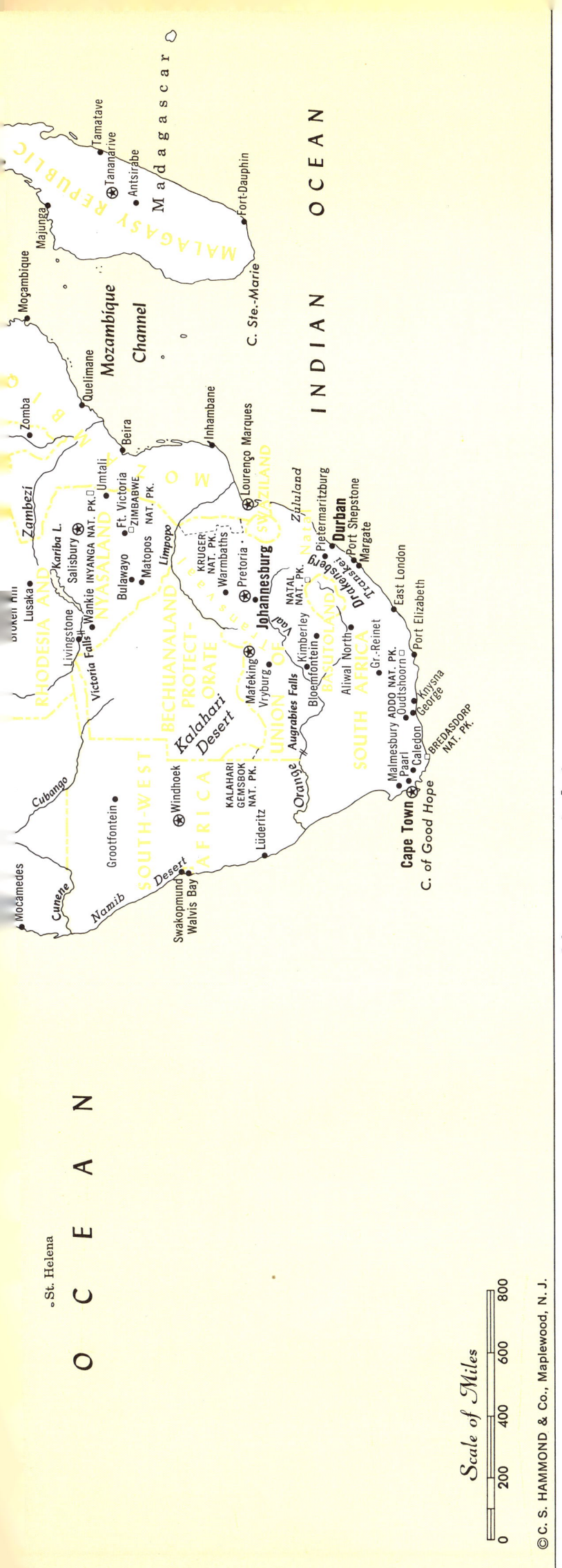

Notes and Itinerary

North Africa

CATHEDRAL IN ANCIENT CARTHAGE

TWA—Trans World Airlines

ISLAM MAGIC AND ANCIENT RUINS

You who want your journey to take you away from the daily round of duties and over-familiar sights, go to North Africa. You will make a journey through history, from Phoenician Carthage to Roman Timgad, to shades of Byzantium at Tebessa and the creations of Arabo-Berber civilization — Fez Tlemcen and the holy city of Kairouan. Geographically the variety is just as great. There are the magnificent, warm Atlantic and Mediterranean beaches and the coast roads winding high above the sea; the gorges and crests of the Atlas mountains whose scenic beauty cannot fail to arrest even the most fervent mountaineer; the oases and the Sahara, a spectacle of overpowering grandeur and simplicity. Gleaming white, serene, mysterious, intense, scintillating, curious, traditional — all this, and more, are Morocco, Algeria and Tunisia. Everywhere, from Marrakech to Tunis and from Algiers to Mogador, the sun, the sky and the sea contribute to the creation of so fascinating a scene that even before leaving it you will feel the pangs of nostalgia.

EASTERN COSTUME

On the streets, some women in North Africa still hide beneath the all-enveloping, cloaklike robe called *djellaba* and mysterious veil. Otherwise, in the home, they wear an overdress of rich material, called a *foquia*, above another magnificent full-length gown called *kaftan*, with embroidered slippers on their feet. The Berber women and men also wear colorful, flowing robes, whose designs indicate the specific tribe from which they come.

MOROCCAN MANNERS

In Morocco, only Mohammedans may enter the mosques; other people are prohibited from doing so and this prohibition sometimes even extends to the immediate surroundings of the mosque. The Medersas or Mohammedan colleges may, on the other hand, be visited and they give a very good idea of Mohammedan religious architecture.

ORIENTAL FEASTS

Oranges of all kinds, including mandarins coming straight to the table from nearby groves, translucent dates called "fingers of light" in Arabic and other fruit are fitting dessert to a meal of mutton or chicken *couscous* in an appetizing sauce, or perhaps, a dish known as *mechoui du sud* (a sheep roasted whole over a wood fire and served with melted butter). Mint tea is the national beverage of the North Africans and along with mint tea or Moorish coffee served in small cups, they serve Arab sweetmeats, including "golden fritters," *zlabias* with honey, "gazelles' horns" sprinkled with sugar and *rahat-lokoum* (Turkish delight) perfumed with rose or lemon.

CASABLANCA. With its contemporary architecture, its broad neon-lighted streets, its extensive harbor installations and its cosmopolitan atmosphere, Casablanca is a modern city; yet its Moroccan setting changed but little in the past six centuries. Outside the city, Berbers and Arabs live in much the same manner as their ancestors lived in the 14th century. Founded by the Portuguese in 1515, Casablanca occupies the site of the ancient city of Anfa, which was destroyed by them in 1465. French forces gained control of Casablanca in 1907. On the ruins of the town which their naval guns had reduced to rubble, the French erected a gleaming new city. Under the direction of Marshal Lyautey, first resident general of Morocco, the city's economic future was secured by the building

MARSHAL LYAUTEY STATUE, CASABLANCA Philip Gendreau

PLACE DU GOUVERNEMENT, ALGIERS French Government Tourist Office

of jetties to protect its exposed position. Its harbor thus sheltered from the northeast winds and the Atlantic, Casablanca has become one of the great ports of the African continent and probably the most spacious artificial seaport in the world. The Cazes airport, also of major importance to the city's commerce, handled much of the Allied military traffic for the North African campaign in World War II. Here in a queer but interesting melting pot including Europeans, Maghrebines, Levantines and Americans, veiled Arab women, wearing flowing robes, are seen frequenting the enormous, strikingly modern **Orthlieb swimming pool**, the world's second largest. . . . A little beyond Cape Blanc, the happy fishing ground of lobster-catchers, looms up the old, clean, quiet Portuguese town of **MAZAGAN**. The remains of the citadel, which the Portuguese began in 1506 and held until 1769,

NEW MEDINA, CASABLANCA *French Government Tourist Office*

PLACE DE FRANCE, CASABLANCA *Philip Gendreau*

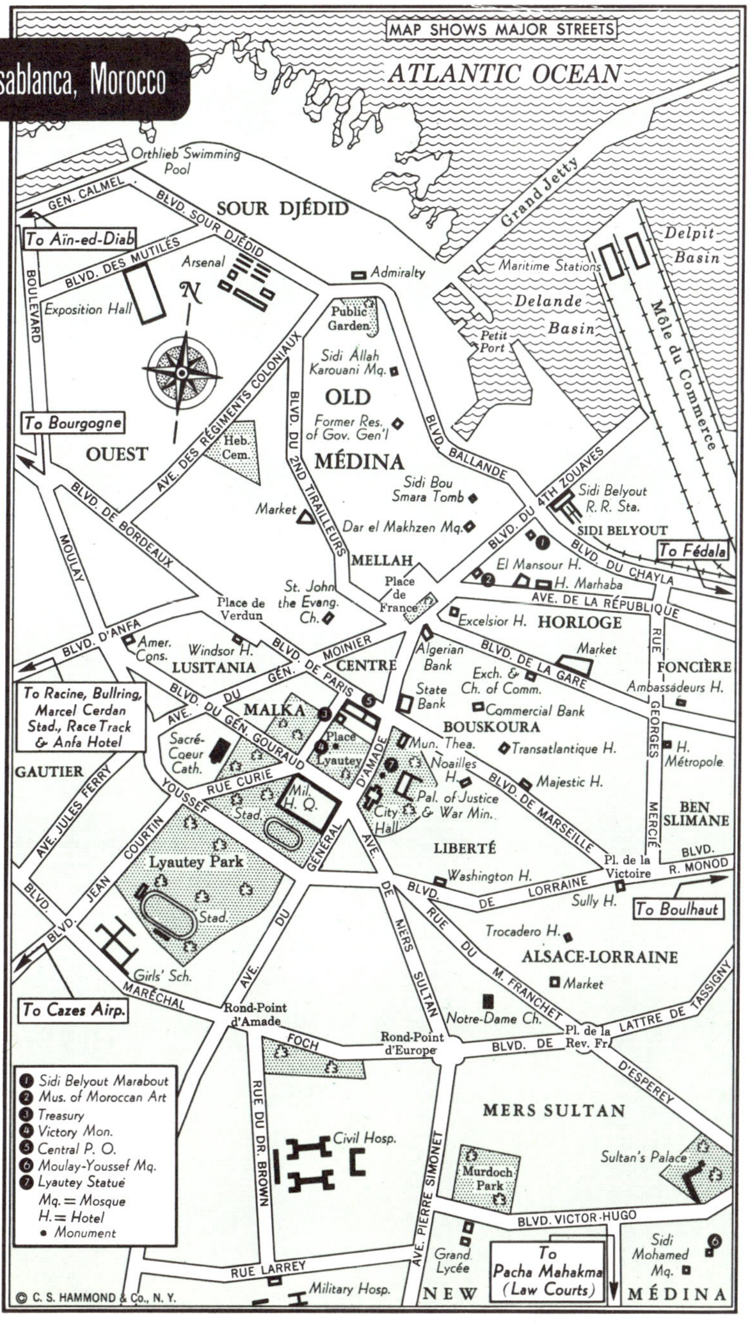

give it a warlike air. The imposing, gloomy **armory** adds to the town's picturesqueness. Once the first port in Morocco, Mazagan still has its **beach**, about three miles long, the finest and most attractive in the country, its **casino** built on piles, one of the most up-to-date **markets**, mild winters and cool summers — a perfect spot for relaxation and rest. . . . **SAFI**, famed for its sardines and pottery, is now the second port of Morocco, but still retains the picturesqueness of the very old trading stations. After going to the wave-splashed **Chateau de Mer** (sea castle) and loitering on the **Potters' Hill**, you will enjoy a rest in the **Place du Rbat**, in the heart of the city, where lanes and impasses form an isle of quiet provincial life. As in the *ksours* in the south, some of these little streets are kinds of tunnels cut out in the high walls of the houses. A change of scenery is afforded by the drive past the black earth of the plains of the Abda-Ahmar and the steep, bare coast to Cape Cantin, the Soloeis of the ancients. . . . Seen from a distance, **MOGADOR**, white and gleaming, seems to float upon the waters. There are few spots affording such strikingly contrasting views. On the one hand the Atlantic; on the other, the woods; between them the dazzling, peaceful waters of the little port, romantic islets and a jewel of a town, iridescent in the filmy mist. This town, built in 1765 after the plans of one Cornut, a captive in Morocco, used to be a privateers' hideout. The **fortress, Portuguese bridge** and the **old port** provide vivid recollections of its romantic, adventurous past. The **Purpurariae** is where Juba II set up the dyeworks which supplied Rome with the most-sought-after purple. In the semiarid country to the east, pert little dark-coated goats graze high in the branches of argan trees, often climbing as high as twenty feet to reach the light-green, olivelike fruit. . . . With so little rain it is scarcely ever troublesome and a temperate climate of remarkable regularity, **AGADIR**, called the "Gate to the South," is probably the finest seaside resort in Morocco. For a glimpse of real Arab village life, visit **Tiznit**, a walled desert town, with the **old mosque** and the peaceful holy spring. Goulimine, further south, is the home of the famous "blue men." The faces, hands and wrists of the men of this tribe have a bluish tinge from the dyed robes they have worn since centuries back. . . . **MARRAKECH** . . . . the great Berber capital and to Moroccans the "city of earthly delights," is a huge oasis at the foot of the snow-clad Atlas peaks. Each Thursday the great *souk* is held outside the city walls when the people of the countryside and the caravans of camel traders come to barter with each other. Within the city walls, the center of activity is the public square of **Djemaa el Fna**, where entertainers attract the inhabitants during the long hours of the night. In this city where each section carries one kind of goods, most fascinating is the **Street of the Dyers**, north of the square, where vivid skeins of newly dyed wool drips from walls and bamboo poles slung from roof to roof across the street. Vying in appeal is another attractive section, the aromatic **spice market**. Near the square is the world-famous **Koutoubia Mosque** with its tall minaret. The lovely **Menara Gardens** are outside the *medina*. . . . The intellectual and cultural capital is beautiful **FEZ** . . . . . founded more than 1,100 years ago, really three cities. The brightly decorated arch of **Bab Bou Jeloud** is the gateway to **Fèz el Bali** (Fèz the Old), where cobbled lanes, so narrow the pedestrian may touch both sides at once, twist between walled courtyards. Within the old city is the tomb of **Moulay Idriss II**, one of Morocco's holiest shrines. The narrow **Bab Moulay Idriss, the Alley of Sanctuary**, is the passageway where thieves, murderers or political refugees are traditionally safe from arrest. Heart of the city is the 1,000-year-old **Karaouine University**, a scholastic center for the whole world of Islam. The nearby town of **Azrou** is a popular winter-sports area. The holy city of **Moulay Idriss** is so sacred to Moslems that no Christian or Jew may spend the night there, although you may visit it during the day. . . . **MEKNES** . . . . west of Fèz, is a trading and business center, with hustle and bustle not found in the other ancient cities of Morocco. It was the incredible "Black Sultan" of the Alaouites, Moulay Ismail, who made it famous. Picking it as his capital in 1672, he wanted to make the city a rival of Versailles by building palaces and government buildings of enormous size. . . . **RABAT** . . . . . The quarters of the seafront offer the spectacle of a very different town from the smiling Rabat of villas and gardens. The tawny **Casbah of the Oudaias**, the color of the rock it stands upon and the oldest part of the city, is a miniature city in itself. Built in the twelfth century as the equivalent of an English feudal castle, the Casbah now shelters artisans and craftsmen who keep alive the old handcrafts passed down from generation to generation. Farther inland is the stately, yet delicate ruin of Merinide necropolis of **Chellah**, built, it is thought, on the site of the Carthaginian and Roman trading stations. . . . In Algeria, near the western border, is the attractive town of **TLEMCEN**, with its lovely scenery of green orchards and the fine remains of the early Spanish period. Neighboring **Bou-Medine** contains the ruins of the thirteenth-century mosque **Mansoura** with its imposing walls and famous minaret. . . . Between Tlemcen and Oran is **SIDI BEL ABBES**, birthplace of the French Foreign Legion. **ALGIERS.** Stretching along a bay for ten miles in the shape of an amphitheater, at the foot and on the slopes of coastal hills, exotic Algiers appears from the sea as gorgeous tier upon tier of brilliant white, so dazzlingly beautiful in the surrounding luxuriant verdure that the Arabs liken her to a diamond set in an emerald frame. Her story, too, is almost as violently exciting as her appearance is ravishing. Founded by Berbers, she became important after Turkish rule was established by the fiery Barbarossa in 1518. From this time she became the chief seat of the Barbary pirates, scourge of the Mediterranean, who menaced shipping or exacted tribute from all those plying the sea until the French captured the city in the last century. A land of mystery, of the white burnoosed Arab and his veiled lady, a land of high adventure, Algiers still retains her spinetingling but exaggerated reputation as the haunt of spies and fugitives and the scene of whispered intrigue. Today, as capital of Algeria and the core of bitter Arab opposition to French rule, her halls and avenues often do resound with the sharp, staccato sounds of noisy street fighting or violent political battles. It is the residence of the Governor General, seat of the Algerian Assembly and a large, busy, prosperous port. Outstanding views of the city's famous bay may be obtained from the balcony of **Saint-Raphaël**, the **basilica of Notre-Dame d'Afrique** and the upper end of the **Casbah**. A progressive, modern city, Algiers has **luxurious shops** in its newer section. In the picturesque seaside region west of the city are the Roman ruins at incomparable **Tipasa**, including **La Grande Basilique Chrétienne (Tomb of the Christians)**, one of the most beautiful archeological sites on the Mediterranean; and the Roman ruins and valuable collection in the museum at **Cherchell**, formerly Cesarea, the capital of an artist king before

ALGIERS

ADMIRALTY BUILDINGS, ALGIERS

becoming the capital of a Roman province. In the **Kabylia**, country of the Berbers and of the impressive Djurdjura mountain range, are curious hill-top villages whose inhabitants jealously guard their ancient way of life.... Southeast is **BISKRA**, a luxuriant oasis and an ideal winter resort as well as a spa and health resort.... **CONSTANTINE**, formerly known as Cirta and dating from Phoenician times, having been a fortress which held out against numerous sieges, is extremely pleasant and attractive, built on a steep rock bordering the Rhummel canyon. Because of its unique position there are many bridges in the town, especially spectacular being the suspension bridge of **Sidi M'Cid**. Do not miss taking a walk through the famous **Rhummel Gorges**. Beyond the thick forest groves northeast of the city is **Bône**, with its beaches, plains, orchards, orange groves and Roman ruins. Algeria has given birth

MODERN FRENCH QUARTER, ALGIERS

TWA—Trans World Airlines

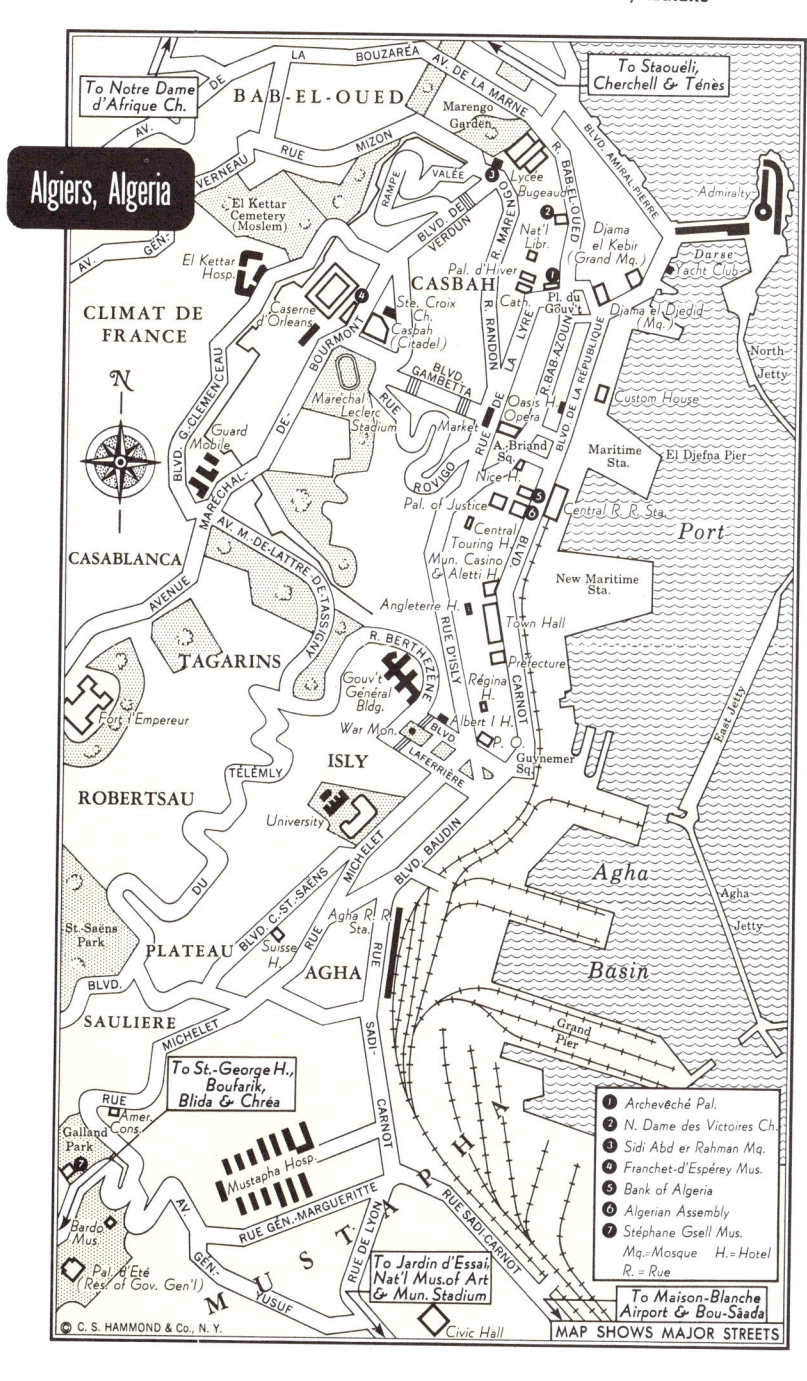

to many famous men, but at their head is to be found St. Augustin, the most illustrious of the fathers of the Christian church, who was born at Thagaste of Berber parents and became bishop of Hippo Regius near Bône. It was in this town that he made his famous sermons and wrote those works which contributed so profoundly to the development of Christian civilization in the West. South of the city, **Timgad**, a striking example of Roman colonization in Numidia and equal in importance to Pompeii, and **Lambèse**, its neighbor, are among the most interesting military cities of the Roman world preserved to us.... Not far from the border of Tunisia are the Roman ruins at **TEBESSA**, whose **Temple of Minerva** is the most remarkable relic of pagan religion in North Africa. The **basilica** here, over-shadowed by the memory of the great St. Augustin, is the greatest and best-preserved of the Christian monuments....

CASBAH, ALGIERS

French Government Tourist Office

95

DESERT, NORTH AFRICA French Press & Information Service

RHUMMEL GORGE, CONSTANTINE TWA—Trans World Airlines

The two important routes across the Sahara connecting North Africa with Central Africa are the **HOGGAR ROUTE** and the **TANEZROUFT ROUTE**, and if you want to have a really rare experience, these vast stretches of unforgettable, attractive country can be crossed without any particular danger. The Hoggar route travels through such places as **Ghardaïa**, the quaint capital of the very barren region of **M'Zab**; the magnificent gorges of **Arak** and **In Guezzam**, with its many prehistoric remains. The Tanezrouft route goes through the oasis of **Beni Ounif**, whose neighboring oasis of **Figuig** has 200,000 palm trees and curious fortified villages; the **desert of Tanezrouft,** "the land of thirst," and the Savannah vegetation near **Aguelhoc** to Gao in Niger. . . . **TUNIS** . . . . . the capital of Tunisia, comprises the modern city set out like a chessboard and the **Mohammedan quarter**, with a very special Oriental character. The position of the town, sheltered by the bay, is most attractive and its fine **mosques** and colorful **markets** are famous. Covered by the dust of Tunisia, the vestiges of the first beginnings of the Christian church in this country have come down to us more intact than in any other country, and notable collections from these remains are in the **Musée du Bardo**. The attractive village of Sidi Bou Said, facing the sea, overlooks the ruins of **Carthage**. The Church of Africa, of which the seat was at Carthage, furnished numerous martyrs, including Felicity, Perpetue and Cyprian, and many great and wise men, including Augustin and Tertullian. The ruins of the **Basilica of St. Cyprian**, at the foot of the red rocks of Sidi Bou Said, offer an entirely unique spectacle. Here, too, is the small, compact **St. Louis Chapel**, raised to shelter the remains of the French king who died at Carthage of the plague in 1270 A. D., after arriving here at the head of the Eighth Crusade. . . . One of the most revered centers of religion in Islam is the holy town of **KAIROUAN**, south of Tunis. The twelve-centuries-old **Grand Mosque** is the principal one in North Africa. . . . Situated in barren surroundings nearby is the gigantic amphitheater of **El Djem**, one of the most impressive Roman buildings in Africa. . . . On the coast is the important fishing village of **SFAX**, whose Mohammedan part of town is still protected by imposing fortified **ramparts**. . . . Further down the coast is the lovely bathing resort of **DJERBA**, celebrated for its climate, the industrious activity of its inhabitants and its Hebrew remains, unique in the world.

HOT SPRINGS NEAR CONSTANTINE TWA—Trans World Airlines

NATIVE BAZAAR, TUNIS TWA—Trans World Airlines

AFRICA

1. Pyramids of Egypt
2. Tunisian rug embroidery
3. Market scene at Monlay
4. Typical mosque in Morocco
5. Camels at rest in Algeria

AFRICA

1. Fishermen near Capetown
2. Dancer at Shembe festival Durban
3. Touching up wall decoration in Ndebele village
4. Giant Protea, national flower of the Union
5. Elephants in Kruger National Park

All photos:
South African
Tourist Corp.

AFRICA

1. Masai natives, Tanganyika
2. Giraffe on the plains of east Africa
3. Scene on the Kenya coast
4. Zebra in Nairobi National Park
5. Lofty mount Kenya, Africa's second highest peak

All photos:
East Africa Tourist Travel Assoc.

All photos:
Br. Information Services

AFRICA

1. Mosque at Kano, Nigeria
2. Gezira cotton, the "white gold" of the Sudan
3. Modern hospital at Kumasi, Ghana
4. The Wana of Wa, a chieftan of Ghana
5. Native weaving in Sierra Leone

Egypt

SPHINX AND PYRAMIDS, GIZA

6,000 YEARS OLD

This ancient African country was a tourists' delight centuries before many other lands were even discovered—attracting tourists with the very same magnetic power luring visitors here today. The pyramids were a source of wonder even in Biblical times; the exuberant cosmopolitanism combined with Oriental mystery of the cities brought pleasure seekers from afar; the healthy climate brought its quota of distinguished personages and the regions of the Upper Nile, with its unequalled examples of age-old artistry and skill, seized the imaginations of romantic travelers. The story of Egyptian civilization is a long one, since from the dawn of recorded history there has been a civilization in the Nile valley, contributing not only learning and inspiration to other countries but exotic pleasure and relaxation to happy visitors from all corners of the globe.

THE NIGHTS OF RAMADAN

Travelers particularly will enjoy visiting Egypt during the Arabic month of Ramadan, the Moslem month of fasting, held during the spring. During this traditional season of remembrance, initiated by the Procession of the Ro'ya and the children's march through the streets, while swinging colored lanterns and chanting traditional songs, the minarets of the mosques are encircled throughout the night by their rings of twinkling lights. Ramadan was chosen as the month of fasting because, according to legend, this is the time the first revelations came to the Prophet Mohammed. From dawn to sunset no food or drink whatsoever may be consumed. To sustain the faster throughout the day, a light repast is taken shortly before dawn and in the small hours of the night, there may be heard the rhythmic beating of a *tablah* (drum), as down the street comes the "Masahharati," awakening the fasters by name for their "Sohoor," as this little meal is called. It generally consists of light foods such as yoghurt, a special kind of beans, fruit and thirst-quenching drinks. At sunset there is nothing more welcome than a glass of *Amar-el-Din*, a delicious and nourishing drink made from sheets of dried apricots, and many people like to break their fast with this. Soon after come the sounds of youthful voices and the sight of swinging lanterns as the children gather together to sing the songs of Ramadan. In some households there are lanterns hanging over the doorways and inside can be heard the chanting of the Koran, and perhaps a glimpse may be caught of a room full of guests, making their Ramadan calls, listening to the chanting and eating the nuts and sweetmeats offered during this month. In some of the older coffeehouses there are recitals from the Arab romances by a minstrel, accompanied on the *rababa*, a small stringed instrument played like the cello. The sunset breakfast, the evenings of pleasant companionship, the songs and the chanting, the lanterns and the lighted minarets — all this makes of Ramadan a happy and a well-loved time.

THE NEW OLD LAND

ALEXANDRIA. When Alexander the Great traced his proposed plan for a new city on the ground of Pharos Island in 332 B.C. the Great Conqueror could hardly foresee that this city, in less than a century, would become the largest and most magnificent in the known world. Alexander never saw the great city he had founded and which still bears his name. Leaving Egypt, he entrusted its construction to his viceroy. Strategically located just west of the Nile Delta on a narrow strip of land between Lake Mareotis and the Mediterranean Sea, Alexandria soon became the "Gateway to Egypt" and the hub of trade between Europe and the Middle East. The rocky island, where stood the wonderful Pharos lighthouse, was joined to the mainland by a narrow causeway and incorporated into the city. Here Euclid wrote his famous geometry; here Hellenistic and Jewish culture flourished. Its two libraries were said to have contained nearly 700,000 scrolls. Through the centuries Alexandria's importance declined with the loss of shipping, due in part to silt closing a channel which linked the city with the Nile. Not until the 19th century did it regain some of its former importance. Today with its modern harbor installations, it is Egypt's foremost port through which most of this country's foreign trade passes. Much of the an-

YACHT CLUB, ALEXANDRIA

cient city now lies beneath the water and the eastern part of its divided harbor is suitable only for small fishing boats. Except for a tall red granite shaft known as "Pompey's Pillar" almost nothing remains of Alexandria's antiquity. Egypt's second city, is not only a vast Mediterranean port but also a delightful seaside resort. Two of the main streets of ancient Alexandria, present-day **Fouad Street** and **Nebi Daniel Street**, were then as now the centers of the commercial, cultural and political life of the city. After Alexander's death, the Ptolemaic Dynasty founded here the famous library and museum, attracting the greatest philosophers and scientists of the ancient world. The ruins of the **library**, the most important of ancient times, are all that remain. Several **necropolises** of the Hellenistic era have been excavated and those of **Mustapha Pasha**, **Chatby** and **Anfoushy**, together with the **Catacombs of Kom El-Chougafa**, are particularly interesting, with their wall paintings, collections of funeral furniture and scenes from ancient mythology. The old lighthouse, built during the time of Ptolemy II in 280 B. C. on the Island of Pharos and counted one of the Seven Wonders of the World, was destroyed by earthquake in 1375. The **lighthouse** which took its place stands at **Ras-el-Tine** in the western part of the city. Not far from the catacombs is another famous landmark: **"Pompey's Pillar."** This great column, erected in honor of the Emperor Diocletian in about 297 A. D. and standing some 88 feet high, is made of a beautiful red granite, polished into an exquisite style, while the foundation is made of blocks taken from more ancient buildings, all with their respective inscriptions. A great deal of the story of ancient Alexandria may be pieced together in the **Greco-Roman Museum**, containing a wonderful collection of sculptures, sarcophagi, mummies, jewelry, coins and figurines, including the famous "Tanagras." In the western part of the city is the vast **Montaza Palace** of ex-King Farouk, with its great corridors, sumptuously furnished rooms and atmosphere of unrestrained luxury, surrounded by the magnificent park, formal gardens

CORNICHE DRIVE, ALEXANDRIA

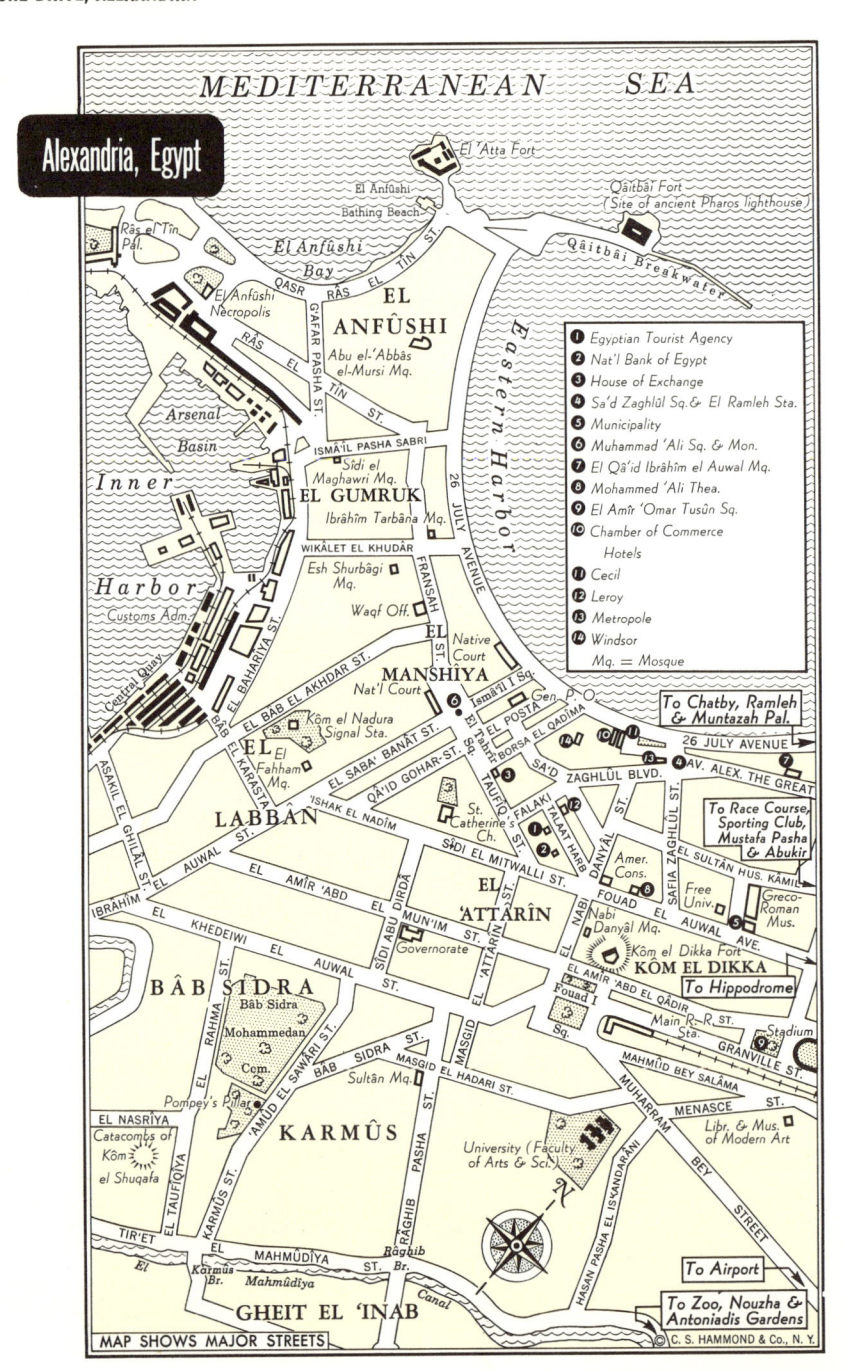

BATHING BEACH, ALEXANDRIA

98

and pavilions. The fine **Abu el-Abbas el-Morsi Mosque**, dating from the thirteenth century, has exquisite arabesque decorations, wall mosaics, wood engravings and teakwood pulpit. The splendid **Corniche**, which runs along the seafront, leads to the famous, gay suburb of **El Raml** or **Ramleh**, called the Egyptian Riviera. Some of its twelve beaches, particularly those at **Stanley Bay** and **Sidi Bishr**, challenge comparison with the smartest bathing resorts in the world. Excursions include **Abukir**, now a delightful fishing village, site of the ancient city of Canope, where Nelson fought Napoleon; **Rosetta**, a medieval town at one of the mouths of the Nile; and the desert cemetery at **El Alamein**, west of Alexandria, where in 1942 General Montgomery outmaneuvered Rommel's Panzers and annihilated the Afrika Korps.

CAIRO. Sophisticated Cairo, on the banks of the ageless Nile, contains vestiges of the more than 8,000 years that civilizations have flourished in this land of sunshine, culture and beauty. She was influenced by Heliopolis, on the right shore of the Nile, and Memphis, on the plateau of Giza, on the river's left bank. In Cairo is an entire throbbing and bustling section of the medieval East with its own history and folklore, its own culture and customs, its own philosophy and its own Arabian Nights atmosphere. In this section of covered alleyways, known as the "**Mousky**," is the famous colorful bazaar of **Khan El Khalili**. Just across the street from one entrance to the Mousky is the great **El Azhar Mosque** and university, religious and educational fountainhead of the entire Moslem world and the oldest university in existence. Founded in 970 A. D. by Gohar, this mosque, whose name means "splendid mosque," with its pure gold ceiling and large columns of gleaming purple and blue tiles, is the greatest work of the Fatimid Dynasty. Here were preserved Muslim science and Arabic language and literature during the dark ages which followed; it is still the greatest center for Muslim culture today. One of the most important monuments in Egypt is the **Mosque of Ahmad ibn Tuln**, built in the 9th century. Not far away is the **Sultan Hassan Mosque**, considered by many as the finest example of Arabic architecture in the world, built during the fourteenth century in the Mameluke period with stones from the pyramids. Conspicuous for the sheer beauty of its architectural design is **Mohammed Ali Mosque**, standing in the middle of the Citadel, with its huge dome, alabaster-faced walls and its delicately slender minarets. In the center of Cairo, on the right bank of the Nile, stands the large, square, white **Museum of Egyptian Antiquities**, or the **Egyptian Museum**. After 84 years of existence, this museum houses the richest existing collection of antiquities. All archeological ages from prehistoric times to the Roman Empire are there represented by specimens of unique value. Three groups of particular beauty and interest are a unique collection of wondrously preserved mummies of different dynasties; the statuary of the Age of the Pyramids (the 28th to 24th centuries B. C.), including the statue of Chephren, a masterpiece of striking vigor; and a precious collection of relics illustrating all ages of Pharaonic history, with the royal trappings of Tutankhamon, a treasure trove so priceless and beautiful that there are those whose sole reason for visiting Egypt is to see it. Situated near the museum is the sprawling **House of Parliament** and east of it is **Abdin Palace**, Farouk's stupendous palace, now a museum. The **Museum of Islamic Art**, still farther east, contains the world's most precious and comprehensive collections of Muslim art, including a priceless exhibition of earthenware water jugs and filters and the most beautiful specimens of the Mamelukes. The **Desert Institute** at Heliopolis, on the eastern desert outskirts of Cairo, founded for the scientific study of the desert and its development, contains sections showing the different desert plants and animals in their natural habitat. The **Opera House**, next to the beautiful **Azbakiya Garden**, on Ibrahim Pasha Square or Opera Square, the "Times Square" of Cairo, was built for the celebration of the Suez Canal's opening, when "Aida," com-

NILE RIVER, CAIRO

Egyptian State Tourist Administration

NATIVE BAZAAR, CAIRO

TWA—Trans World Airlines

EL TAHRIR SQUARE, CAIRO
Egyptian State Tourist Administration

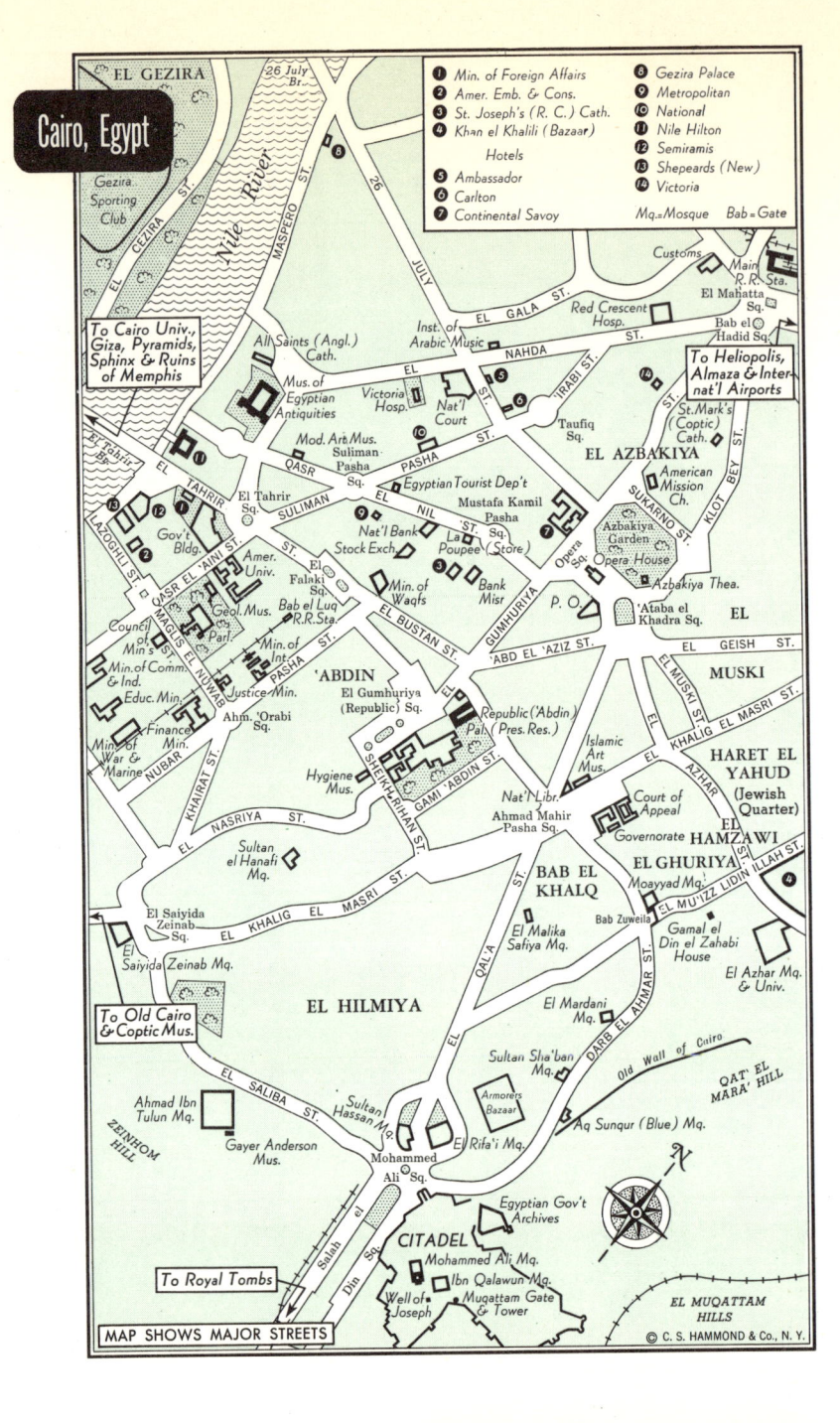

missioned especially for this event, was to be given. However, since Verdi did not complete this notable opera in time, "Rigoletto" was performed instead. . . . In the suburbs are an endless variety of attractions. Of course, the most important and most famous are those stupendous monuments at Giza: the **Pyramids** and **Sphinx**. Occupying the center of the vista is the mysterious figure of the Sphinx, with its head of a man and its body of a beast, lying at the edge of the desert. At its right, a rocky cliff, pierced with tombs, serves as the pedestal to the imposing mass of the Cheops Pyramid, or Great Pyramid, one of the wonders of the world. The Chephren Pyramid, or Second Pyramid, somewhat smaller than that of Cheops, serves as a background to the Sphinx, while the third famous pyramid, that of Mycerinus, is beyond the horizon. These colossal monuments to the great period of Egyptian history were constructed during the Fourth Dynasty, between 2680 and 2560 B.C., and their construction remains a mystery even now. Adjacent to the Giza pyramids are rows of "mastaba" **tombs** in which are buried the relatives of the king and the courtiers who formed the official class of the strong central government. At Sakkara, every visitor stands in admiration before the remains of the buildings around the **Step Pyramid**, by far the most important monument existing on the face of the earth from that date, the Third Dynasty (2780-2680 B.C.). In the midst of that vast enclosure towers the great stepped structure, the first attempt towards the building of a pyramid. The architect Imhotep, the great genius considered in later periods as a God of Medicine, added one mastaba on top of another, each decreasing in size, until the whole building assumed something of a pyramidal form. In Old Cairo are many Christian monuments and memorials of the Coptic Church of Egypt, one of the oldest churches in Christianity, whose members are now racially the purest representatives of the ancient Egyptians. Included are the centuries-old **sycamore tree** under which the Holy Family is said to have taken refuge during its flight into Egypt from Herod; the cave in the crypt of the church of St. Sergins (Abou Serga Church) where, according to legend, they dwelled; **El Mouallakah**, or **Suspended Coptic Church**, with its masterful column of icons, its door of inlaid ivory and its beautifully decorated marble; and the **Coptic Museum**. . . . Upstream on the Nile River, the ancient route through Egypt, is **FAYOUM**, the garden of Egypt, in one of the richest and most beautiful of all the provinces of Egypt. Surrounded on three sides by the Libyan desert, it is separated from it on the north by salty **Lake Karoun**, the Sacred Lake or Lake Moeris of the ancients, made by the Pharaohs an aristocratic residential area. . . . . . South of the lake is the **Pyramid of Illahun**, tomb of Senusert III. From this pyramid came the beautiful jewelry of the princesses, in particular the royal diadem, speaking highly of the skill and taste of the ancient goldsmiths. A beautiful and picturesque excursion

MOHAMMED ALI MOSQUE, CAIRO
Egyptian State Tourist Administration

through date forests and beside waterfalls and gardens takes you to the **Pyramid of Hawara**, tomb of Amenemhat, founder of the Twelfth Dynasty, who began an ambitious project for turning Lake Moeris into **a vast reservoir**. To the south of the pyramid stretches the funerary temple known as the **Labyrinth**, without doubt the most important and most complicated of discovered funerary temples. . At LUXOR and KARNAK, two villages further up the Nile, was the ancient city of Thebes, of which Homer said "that only the grains of sand outnumbered the wealth enclosed within Thebes and its hundred gates." The wealth of the Sudan and the Asiatic countries poured into Thebes, and the Court of Pharaoh was the meeting place of the envoys of all the then known world, who flocked to the capital of the Empire to offer their homage to the King, present their tribute and express their loyalty to Egypt. These mighty monuments speak highly of the great power, skill and engineering ability of the Egyptians. On the right bank of the mighty river is the **Luxor Temple**, the **Karnak Temple** and the **"Avenue of the Sphinxes,"** connecting the two temples. This fabulous, two-and-one-half-mile-long avenue, the greatest thoroughfare of ancient Thebes, built by King Amenhotep III, was of overwhelming grandeur, lined by marble temples, palaces, obelisks encased in gleaming metal and on either side, rows of ram-headed sphinxes, each with a statue of the Pharaoh between its paws. On the opposite bank are the **sepulchral temples** of **Thotmes** at **Deir-el-Bahari**, one of the most remarkable monuments of Egyptian architecture; of **Set I** and **Rameses II** at **Qurna** and of **Rameses III** at **Medinet Habu**. The **Great Hypostyle Hall** at Karnak and the stupendous **Memnon statues** are also representative of the majesty and daring of ancient Egypt. The **Valley of the Kings** contain the royal sepulchres of tombs of the New Kingdom (1567-1090 B. C.), veritable subterranean mansions, or a series of corridors and chambers hewn in the rock, some of which go more than hundreds of feet deep, the innermost of which contains the granite sarcophagus with the golden coffin of the ruler, all decorated with splendid bas-reliefs illustrating the funerary beliefs prevailing during that epoch. Some four hundred **private tombs**, believed to belong to the nobility, are terraced on the desert hill at Qurna. . . . Halfway between Luxor and Aswan is EDFU. Here is the **Temple of Horus**, from the Ptolemaic Period (332-30 B. C.), with its mighty pylon towers, one of the best preserved in all Egypt. Taking 180 years to complete, it is one of their real masterpieces, reflecting both the traditional Pharaonic architecture and a moderation of Greek lines. . . . The last stop on the Nile

VISITING THE PYRAMIDS

Egyptian State Tourist Administration

ASWAN DAM, ASWAN

Egyptian State Tourist Administration

is at ASWAN, famous for its modern and **ancient architecture**, as well as being popular as a health resort because of its magnificent dry, warm climate. The modern masterpiece is the splendid, mile-and-a-half-long **Aswan Dam**, which has added over a million and a half acres of land to cultivation. It is in fact this dam which was responsible for the submerging of the beautiful island of **Philae**. The **Temple of Isis** built there dates from the Pharaonic era down through the Ptolemaic and Roman periods. When the sluice gates are opened between July and October and the water recedes, you may still visit this mysterious and magic home of the "Lady of Enchantment," but in winter only the pylons of the temples are to be seen in the middle of a vast expanse of water. From the famous **Aswan granite quarries** many of the most noted obelisks and statues of ancient Egypt originated, and these quarries are still being actively worked in much the same manner as they were thousands of years ago. . . . The traveler who wishes to really see all of Egypt should visit the OASIS OF AMUN at SIWA, most delightful and most luxuriant of Egypt's oases, in the endless sands of the Libyan desert in the northwest. Throughout conquests, religious upheavals and successive dominations by Alexander the Great, the Romans, Christian monks and the Arabs, the isolated population of Siwa has retained its own individual character, making a living vestige of a people who otherwise belong now only to history. At the beginning of the route leading to the oasis there is situated, on a rise in the ground, a sort of citadel. As the caravan approaches, what at first appeared to be one great building divides itself up into a series of old but solid fortifications and some extremely picturesque **houses**. The houses are, in fact, crowded together one on top of the other in tiers, thus forming a town of eight stories. At the **Temple of Amun**, the ruins of which lie not far away from the spring of Cleopatra, was found the famous oracle of Jupiter-Amun, consulted by Alexander in 331 B. C. His visit left such a great impression that when he was in Asia he sent messengers to consult the priests of Siwa before any important step.

PYRAMIDS, GIZA

TWA—Trans World Airlines

Central Africa

FAMILIAR SCENE ALONG CONGO — Philip Gendreau

THE HEART OF THE CONTINENT

The African continent is to most Americans a land of mystery. No longer remote and inaccessible, but still suffused with the spirit of the frontier, Africa is now available to the modern tourist. You will see strange landscapes, exceptionally interesting animal life and exquisite flora in the most enchanting settings. You will be entranced by Africa's great variety of interest, ranging from scenes of breathtaking beauty to the traditions of the ancient folklore of the natives. You will see such thrilling sights as the dances of the giant Watusis and the homes of the mysterious Pygmy people. And you will never forget your first sight of game in the magnificent national parks, the great wildlife sanctuaries of the world. For the serious hunter, the non-conformist seeking the really rare and unusual and the traveler looking for a remote, serene vacation, the savage beauty of Africa, its fascinating charm and picturesque people insure a never-to-be-forgotten time of your life.

PRIMITIVE, MYSTERIOUS WONDERLAND

After visiting the colorful **market**, serene **La Parc de Bock**, the impressive **Albert the First Monument**, the **native quarters** and the "**Corniches**," from which there are superb views of the city, in **LEOPOLDVILLE**, capital of the Belgian Congo, you may take a **steamer** up the Congo River or Lualaba River, famed in story and song, to **STANLEYVILLE**, in the central part of the country. One of the oldest towns in the Congo, it was founded by the English explorer Sir Henry Morton Stanley, of Stanley and Livingstone fame, in 1883. Considered the most typical of all Congo towns, it is today the center of communciations, not only of the Belgian Congo, but of the whole of central Africa. The town even boasts a fine, large **Stanleyville Cathedral**. It is a good starting point for hunting parties venturing into the interior and because of the picturesque **Wagenia Fisheries** near the Seventh Cataract of the river's rapids and the impressive **Tshopo Falls**, also a favorite tourist center. The **native quarters** are fascinating, as are the nearby Arabicized negro village and other villages like Wamba, where you may be fortunate enough to see a Mabudu dance; **Niangara**, with the artistically decorated native courthouse, and **Gangala na Bodio**, where you will watch the trained elephants working. Unusual scenic attractions include the **Elephants' Way**, the **Wanie Rukula landscape** and the **Mount Hoyo caves** near Irumu.... Another popular **excursion steamer** sails through the beautiful scenery between **KONGOLO** and **ELISABETHVILLE**, on the Congo's most picturesque sector, the last navigable part of its upper reaches. On board the *Prince Leopold* life is pleasant and restful. At the numerous calling places where fuel is taken in, travelers may land and mix with the natives in their exceptionally picturesque and charming environment. The peaceful river flows through the famous **Kisale Lake**, with its luxuriant vegetation of lotus flowers, water lilies and papyrus, and skirts along the **Upemba Lake**, whose shores attract many herds of elephants. At Elisabethville, where visitors enjoy many of the amenities of a European town, are famous **copper smelting sheds** and one of the best appointed and up-to-date **native townships**, where many different tribes can be seen.... **ALBERTVILLE**, built by the Arab slave traders as a port for slaves, is on the shore of **Lake Tanganyika**, deepest lake in Africa, and has many picturesque villages in the neighborhood. A fascinating excursion can be made through the desolate jungle and high into the mountains to the Luvua River and then through dense flat bush country to **Manono**, where huge open **tin mines** employ the most modern machinery. From Albertville clean and well-appointed **steamers** leave for trips on the lake, with a stop at Kigoma, on the east shore in Tanganyika, for a short drive to Ujiji, largest purely native city in east Africa, originally a center of the slave trade and the place where Stanley found Livingstone.... North of Lake Tanganyika is **BUKAVU**, on beautiful **Lake Kivu**. This attractive town is a fine place to enjoy a restful visit by the shores of the lake or to tour Ruanda-Urundi. The lake, situated 5,200 feet above sea level, surrounded by green mountains and containing many wooded islands, is reminiscent of Switzerland. To the north is **Katana**, with a large native market, and to the south is the Ruzizi valley, with **coffee** and **cinchona plantations**. A lovely mountain road leads into Ruanda, where the giant Watusi tribe lives as overlords of the smaller Bantu natives, including the villages of **Nyanza**, where the King of Ruanda resides, and **Kabgayi**, where the White Fathers mission is located. On the northern shores of Lake Kivu is **Kisenyi**, at the foot of the **Virunga Volcanoes**, one of which is still active and makes a "pillar of smoke by day and a pillar of fire by night." A road passes right over the lava flows of 1912, 1938 and 1948. Here the Watusis perform their colorful native dances, the most spectacular in Africa.... **RUINDI CAMP** is in Albert **National Park**, a fully protected nature reserve covering some 2,022,500 acres and offering a great variety of remarkable sites

GORGE BELOW VICTORIA FALLS — British Information Services

102

MAIN CASCADE OF VICTORIA FALLS

British Information Services

and innumerable specimens of a fauna which has almost disappeared from most districts of the Congo. From here you may visit **Rutshuru Falls**, see elephants, hippos and buffalo, as well as pelican and other waterfowl, and drive through **gorilla country** and **bamboo and podocarpus forests**. . . . There are Pygmy villages near **BENI**, a small market town on the edge of the Ituri Forest, and **fine walks** in the neighborhood of lovely **MUTWANGA**, on the slopes of the beautiful Ruwenzori Mountains, whose native name means "Mountains of the Moon." The **American Mission** in Mutwanga is well worth a visit. . . . On the Ruwenzori slopes in Uganda is the **QUEEN ELIZABETH GAME PARK**, the newest and one of the most interesting game reserves in Africa, especially famous for its elephants, although buffalo and hippos also abound and even some lions are found. The game may be seen feeding and watering on the banks of the river. Tours include the **Salt Lake** at Katwe and the fisheries on **Lake Edward**. . . . **FORT PORTAL**, capital of the native kingdom of Toro, is situated in the foothills of the snow-covered Mountains of the Moon. The area of **Bundabugyio**, situated on the Semliki Flats, is famous for crocodiles and is also the center of the **Carnegie Yellow Fever Research Institute**. . . . From **BUTIABA** on Lake Albert, a **launch** sails up the Nile, through a truly tropical setting containing all types of game, to the foot of beautiful **Murchison Falls**. From the top of the falls is a magnificent view of the Victoria Nile. . . . **KAMPALA**, situated like Rome on seven hills, near Lake Victoria, is the commercial capital of Uganda and the native capital of Buganda. Here is the **Tomb of Mutesa I**, former Kabaka (ruler) of the Baganda, a Bantu tribe. Even when the Europeans reached the territory, the Baganda, one of the most powerful of the tribes in eastern Africa, were an organized and comparatively civilized people, with developed political organizations above the average in Africa. The old fort may still be seen on **Old Kampala Hill**, and both the **Anglican and Roman Catholic Cathedrals** are spectacularly situated on the tops of hills. Other places of interest include the **House of the Kabaka**, the **Makerere University College** and the unique **Uganda Museum**. In the rolling Uganda country to the north of Kampala, an export crop of cotton is grown by well-to-do native farmers in long white robes. . . . The incomparable country in western Kenya between **KERICHO**, in a beautiful area of tea plantations, and **NAIROBI** includes the spectacular Rift valley, splitting Africa from south to north, and numerous lakes covered by thousands of flamingos. At Nairobi, the capital, are the **Coryndon Memorial Museum**, with its distinguished collections, and the attractive, modern **Parliament Building**. This town also continues in importance as an outfitting center for African big-game *safaris*. The extremely popular **Nairobi National Park** contains up to thirty species of game, including lion, hippo, giraffe, cheetah and an abundance of antelope and some of the smaller carnivora. One of the most important sites in the world from an archeological point of view is **Olorgesailie**, the only known "living-site" of hand-ax men, dating from approximately 200,000 years ago. . . . The world-famed spectacle attracting most African visitors is the mighty, indescribable **VICTORIA FALLS**, on the Zambezi River, at the northwestern border of Southern and Northern Rhodesia. This is the world's greatest waterfall, twice as high and twice as wide as Niagara. As their discoverer, David Livingstone, remarked in his diary, "It is rather a hopeless task to endeavour to convey an idea of it in words, since, as was remarked on the spot, an accomplished painter, even by a number of views, could but impart a faint impression of the glorious scene." The flood waters come down during April, May and June and the Victoria Falls then are at their best, except that the dazzlingly white mass of spray fills the chasm and towers hundreds of feet into the blue sky, and veils the splendor of the falls to some extent. Take the **Dawn Patrol Flight** and the **trip by boat** up the river to Kandahar Island. . . . In the eastern part of Southern Rhodesia are the **ZIMBABWE RUINS**, ruined fortress city of unknown origin that continues to puzzle scientists. Some say that it was built by the Queen of Sheba, but other scientists claim it was the Empire of Monomatapa.

Union of South Africa

JOHANNESBURG SKYLINE

ROOTS IN GOLD AND DIAMONDS

As truly fabulous as the tales written about it, the Union of South Africa is a modern, progressive country whose cities, carved against the wild, untamed background of mountain and jungle, have their roots in gold and diamonds, and perhaps wealth yet undisturbed by the centuries. The flora and fauna of the country is fabulous and the coasts and mountains offer superlative scenic beauty. But the most provocative feature of this land is her native tribes; their colorful dress, amazing dances, ornate finery and their willingness to perform for a moderate *bansela* (tip) make a visit to their **kraals** (villages) a delight.

WHITE WINE AND LOBSTER TAILS

Richly endowed with basic food staples, fruit and cattle, the Union's cuisine is superb. Fish and shellfish, including the famous lobster tails and rock oysters, are delicious. The variety of fruits is legend; try the delicate Hanepoot grapes or the *spaanspek* or muskmelon, served iced with a syrup made of brown sugar, cinnamon and a dash of the native liqueur called van der Hum. A great delicacy in the Cape Province is penguin eggs. Most typical food is the *braaivleis,* or barbecue, meat roasted over an open fire. The Union produces its own fine wines and brandies, comparable in flavor to their European counterparts.

JOHANNESBURG. With its foundations literally springing from the world's richest reef of gold-bearing ore, Johannesburg is truly the realization of the ancient dream of Eldorado. The "City of Gold," with the raw newness of its massive buildings etched against the sky, is the largest and wealthiest city in South Africa, yet scarcely sixty years have passed since its beginnings. Many a hardy pioneer still living today can recall the early gold rush era when, as a tiny mining camp with a huddled group of prospectors' huts and its streets mere wagon ruts, Johannesburg attracted fortune-seekers from all parts of the world. The city stands on the high, barren Witwatersrand (Ridge of White Waters) of the South African Transvaal, beneath which lies the fabulous Rand "diggings," which at present yield one third of the world's gold supply. South, east and west of the city rise the steel headgear of mines whose shafts probe to depths of more than 8,000 feet to tap the vast wealth of the golden veins. On every hand the dumps, huge and golden, make Johannesburg unique. Now, recent discoveries of uranium are adding to the city's amazing prosperity. Perhaps the greatest symbol of progress is Johannesburg's tallest building, **Escom House,** a vast glass and concrete structure which dominates its surroundings like a watch tower. A tour of the city must include a visit to a gold mine to see the precious metal being extracted 8,000 feet below the surface and to see the thrilling African tribal dances of the native mine workers. They perform in the mine compounds, beating their shields and tossing their high headdresses, while they thump the earth with their bare feet to the throbbing music of the "kaffir pianos," huge wooden xylophones.

HEADGEAR OF GOLD MINE

NATIVES NEAR UMTATA

CONVEYOR BELT AT GOLD MINE

Johannesburg, South Africa

COMMISSIONER STREET — Union of South Africa, Gov't Information Office

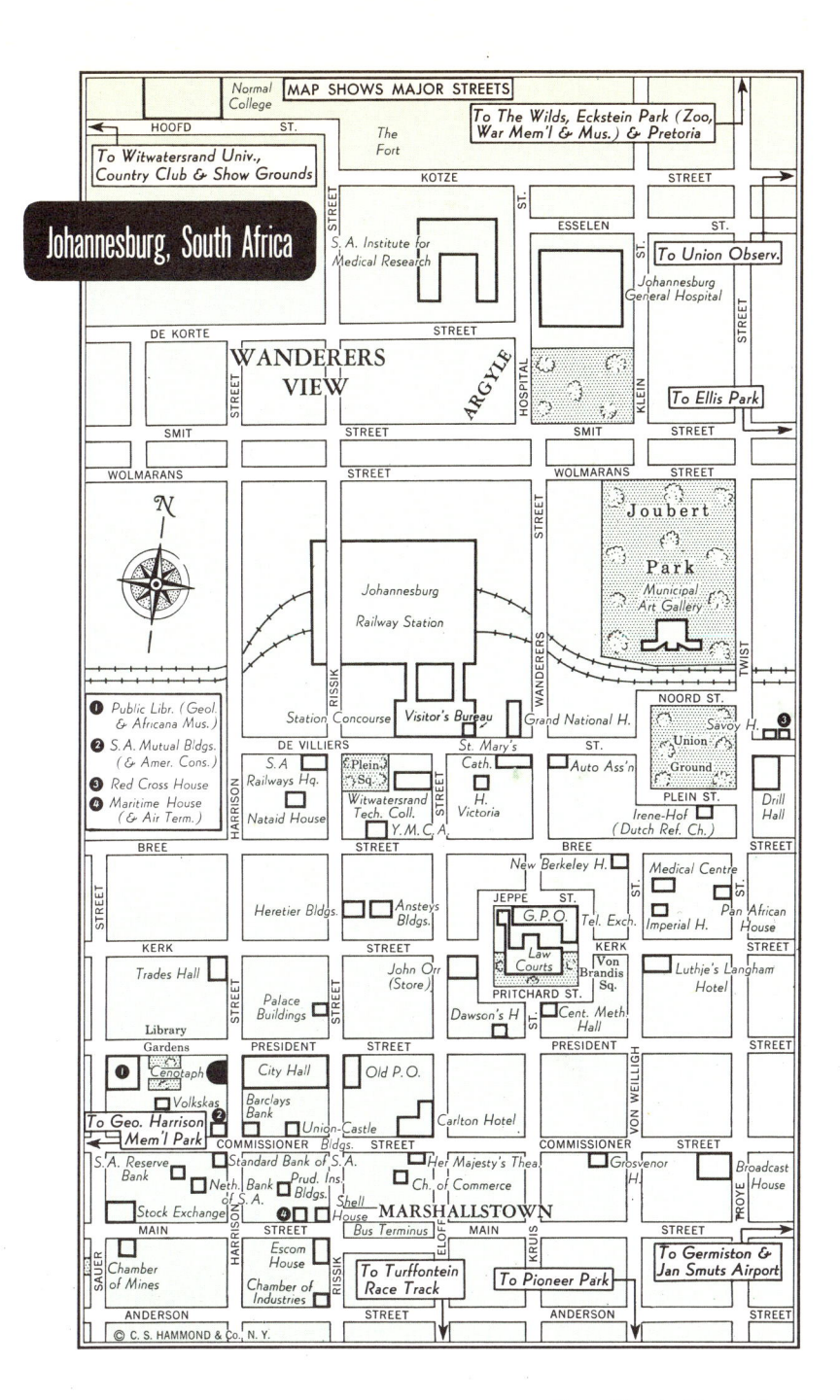

AROUND THE COUNTRY

Cape Province, the land of flowers, vineyards, great forests, wild coasts and historic homes, is the seat of the Union's legislative capital and most famous seaport, **CAPETOWN**. Beloved by seamen of all ages and countries, Capetown is called the "Tavern of the Seven Seas." Built beneath and around wondrous **Table Mountain**, it is beautifully situated facing the bay. Two of the oldest and most historical buildings in the city are the **Dutch Reformed Church**, containing a magnificent pulpit carved by Anton Anreith, whose work adorns many Old Cape buildings, and the solidly built **Old Supreme Court**, a monument to the builders of an earlier age. Visit the **Houses of Parliament, St. George's Cathedral**, headquarters of the **Anglican Church**, and **Government House**. No one should miss the famous **Gardens**, a botanist's paradise, whose seeds were planted by the Dutch East India Company and whose shrubs and trees were brought from every country on earth. The central walk of the gardens leads to the **South African Museum**, world-famous for its plaster casts of Bushman and Hottentots, the Cape's two aboriginal tribes. Nearby is the striking **National Art Gallery**, housing the private old-masters collection of Sir Alfred Beit, as well as a fine group of paintings by South African moderns. Ten minutes drive from the city is the lower station of the aerial cableway to the top of **Table Mountain**. From here one gets a panoramic view of the Cape Peninsula. Near Capetown is the "Groote Schuur" (the Great Barn) where Cecil Rhodes lived and which houses all his treasures. Be sure to take the Marine Drive around the **Cape of Good Hope** and see all the charming resorts on the coast, including world-famous **Muizenberg**. Another must is a visit to the **National Botanic Gardens** at Kirstenbosch.... Driving toward the east one travels through miles of fertile, flower-covered countryside. Here is the famous and incredibly beautiful stretch of coast line known as the **Garden Route**, running from Capetown to Plettenberg Bay skirting the Outeniqua and Tzitzikama Mountains. Along this route you can visit the **Ostrich Farm** at Oudtshoorn, the fabulous **Cango Caves, Wilderness**, a gem among resorts, and the famous cliffs called **Knysna Heads**. This coast is dotted with delightful holiday centers with excellent facilities for swimming, boating, camping and fishing. An interesting excursion into the rolling hills inland brings you to the land of the two million Bantu, called the "Red Blanket People" because of their unique robes... At **KIMBERLEY**, the diamond center of South Africa, one can still visit the **Big Hole**, where diamond mining began. Although it is no longer in operation there are several other nearby mines which can be visited.... **Natal**, land of the mighty Drakensberg and the hamlets of the Zulus, is hemmed by sub-tropical beaches and wonderful surf. **DURBAN** is a modern city of imposing buildings and wide tree-lined avenues. Here European civilization has come to terms with the African, for Zulus may be seen walking the streets dressed in the height of European fashion or colorfully arrayed in tribal

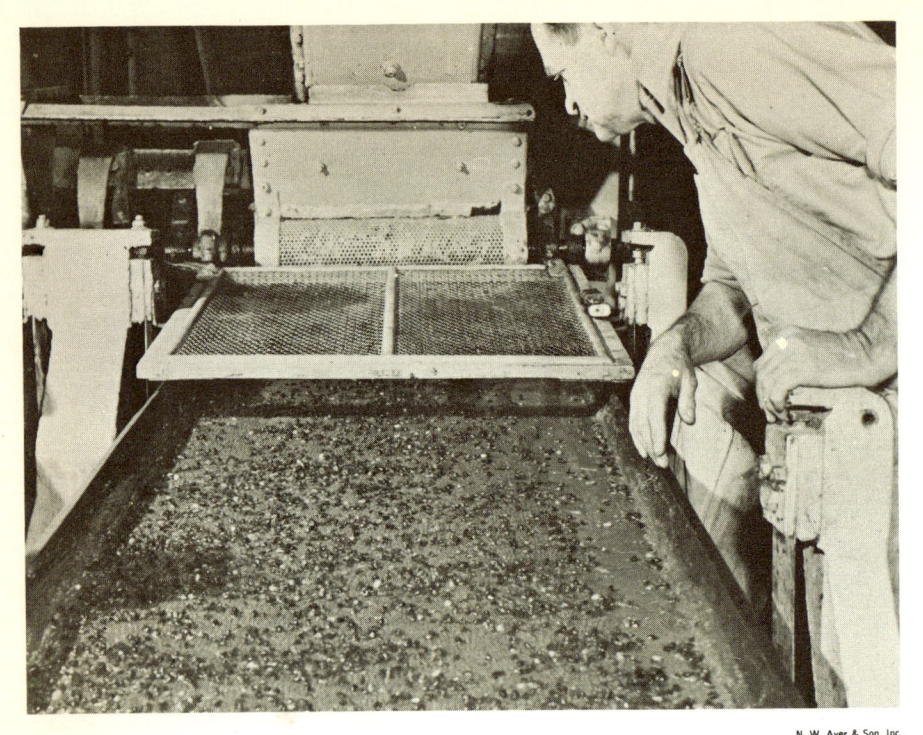

DIAMONDS IN THE ROUGH

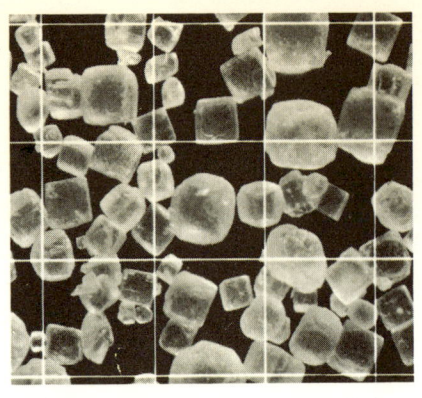

DIAMOND CRYSTAL

dress. Durban has developed as a national playground. Its personality is expressed in its fine race courses, tennis courts, bowling greens, golf courses and modern theaters. Its harbors are a yachtman's paradise and the resorts strung out along the coast make this area the Union's "Riviera.". . . . Northwest of Durban are the scenic roads which lead to the **Drakensberg (Dragon's Mountain)**. No part of South Africa is more varied or profuse in beauty and legend. The roads climb into the kraals of the Zulu tribes and past the caves of the Bushmen. Between May and August the peaks and higher slopes of the Drakensberg are snow-covered; in summer they are carpeted with a host of brilliant veld flowers. There are numerous resorts and the bracing climate encourages one to enjoy the excellent variety of sports, climbing, riding, fishing for trout, swimming. . . . To the northeast, in the heart of Zululand, is **HLUHLUWE,** the great game preserve where you can see the rare white rhinos lumbering about, as well as zebra, giraffe, impala, warthog and other wild beasts. . . . **Transvaal,** that land of gold, big game and dynamic, rich skyscraper cities, lies to the northwest of the Drakensberg. Through its interior runs a spinal column of gold.   Built over this is the city of **JOHANNESBURG.** . . . . . To the north is **PRETORIA,** the Union's beautiful capital, with its magnificent Union Buildings and flowering jacaranda trees which rival the cherry trees in Washington, D.C. . . . Northeast of the capital is **Kruger National Park,** the world's largest wildlife sanctuary. Here, in this great 8,000 square-mile-tract of Bushveld untouched by civilization except for modern tourist camps, one sees the amazing variety of animals native to South Africa wandering at large. . . . The Orange Free State is a province of prairies, waving grain, sheep and cattle. Its lovely capital, **BLOEMFONTEIN** ("Fountain of Flowers"), lies in the heart of the boundless veld. From Naval Hill in the center of the city, site of the Lamont Hussey Observatory of Michigan University and the Franklin Game Reserve, one gets a magnificent panoramic view of the surrounding undulating farmlands and flat-topped hills, or *koppies.* Among the city's many elegant buildings the historic, classical **Raadzaal** and Union's impressive **Court of Appeals** stand out. Nearby is another important **Observatory** at **Mazelspoort,** the Boyden Southern Station of Harvard University, most important one in the Southern Hemisphere.

ESCOM HOUSE

PREMIER DIAMOND MINE NEAR PRETORIA

106

ASIA

Asia, largest of the continents, is like a beautiful patchwork quilt, each piece being important to the whole, yet an entity unto itself. A trip to this great continent of extremes is filled with wonderment and miraculous sights, such as the impressive Himalaya Mountains, with the highest peak in the world, Mount Everest, being 29,028 feet high; Tibet, the highest plateau on earth, and the breathtakingly splendid Taj Mahal of India, which, although built in 1630, still symbolizes the exotic aura that surrounds all of Asia.

The mysterious Orient entices the traveler to its fabulous ports of Hong Kong and Singapore, two of the most exciting cities anywhere; to picturesque Japan, which consists of four lovely islands, and is renowned for its unique culture, charming Kabuki theater, quaint architecture and graceful cherry trees; to Burma, called the "Golden," because of the gold-encrusted pagodas that dot the landscape; and to intriguing Istanbul, formerly Constantinople, with its five hundred mosques and glamorous history of glory and accomplishments.

You are transported to the pages of the "Arabian Nights" when you enter Baghdad, capital of Iraq; in fact your entire vacation in Asia will be memorable for its fairy tale quality and the indescribable magic that envelops this continent.

Often considered the cradle of the human race because the Biblical story of the creation of mankind originated here, Asia was also the birthplace of the great religions, Christianity, Judaism, Mohammedanism and Buddhism, thus making it the site of pilgrimages made by thousands of people every year. The Bible relates the story of the continent from the Garden of Eden to Babylon and Nineveh, and although Asia has changed in this age of modern commercialism, it has never lost its singular appeal.

Map: Asia and Northern Hemisphere

Oceans and Seas:
- ATLANTIC OCEAN
- ARCTIC OCEAN
- PACIFIC OCEAN
- Bering Sea
- Sea of Okhotsk
- Sea of Japan
- Yellow Sea
- East China Sea
- Baltic Sea
- North Sea
- Black Sea
- Caspian Sea
- Aral Sea
- Red Sea
- Persian G.
- Bering Str.

Countries and Regions:
- UNITED STATES (Alaska)
- Greenland
- ICELAND
- IRELAND
- GREAT BRITAIN
- NORWAY
- SWEDEN
- FINLAND
- DEN.
- NETH.
- BELG.
- FRANCE
- GERMANY
- CZECH.
- POLAND
- AUST.
- HUNG.
- RUMANIA
- BULG.
- YUGOSLAVIA
- ALB.
- GREECE
- UNION OF SOVIET SOCIALIST REPUBLICS
- TURKEY
- CYPRUS
- LEBANON
- ISRAEL
- JORDAN
- U.A.R. Syria
- IRAQ
- KUWAIT
- SAUDI
- IRAN
- AFGHANISTAN
- JAMMU & KASHMIR
- CHINA
- Tibet
- Inner MONGOLIA
- MONGOLIA
- Manchuria
- NORTH KOREA
- SOUTH KOREA
- JAPAN
- RYUKYU
- EUROPE

Islands:
- ALEUTIAN IS.
- KURIL IS.
- Sakhalin
- Hokkaido
- Honshu
- Shikoku
- Kyushu
- Wrangel I.
- NEW SIBERIAN IS.
- SEVERNAYA ZEMLYA
- NOVAYA ZEMLYA
- SVALBARD (Spitsbergen)

Mountains and Ranges:
- Kolyma Range
- Stanovoi Range
- Ural Mountains
- Altay Mts.
- Tien Shan
- Kunlun Mountains
- Caucasus
- Elbrus
- Kamchatka Peninsula
- Genghis Khan Wall
- Great Wall
- Khyber Pass

Deserts:
- Gobi Desert
- Taklamakan Desert

Rivers and Lakes:
- Lena
- Ob
- Yenisei
- Amur
- Irtish
- Volga
- Dnieper
- Danube
- Rhine
- Yangtze
- Huang (Yellow)
- Tigris
- Euphrates
- Syr Darya
- Amu Darya
- Lake Baikal
- Lake Balkhash
- Issyk Kul

Cities:
- LONDON, PARIS, BERLIN, Vienna, MOSCOW, LENINGRAD, Stockholm, Riga, Kiev, Odessa, Stalingrad, Istanbul, Ankara, Bursa, Izmir, Antalya, Konya, Kayseri, Antakya, Aleppo, Beirut, Damascus, Jerusalem, Mosul, Baghdad, Babylon, Basra, Abadan, Kuwait, Dhahran, Riyadh, Medina, Tabriz, Tehran, Ramsar, Hamadan, Qum, Isfahan, Shiraz, Persepolis, Susa, Kerman, Meshed, Nishapur, Ashkhabad, Krasnovodsk, Baku, Batumi, Archangel, Perm, Nizhni Tagil, Sverdlovsk, Tyumen, Tobolsk, Magnitogorsk, Orenburg, Aktyubinsk, Chimkent, Tashkent, Samarkand, Stalinabad, Bukhara, Khiva, Mazar-i-Sharif, Herat, Kabul, Ghazni, Kandahar, Peshawar, Attock, Abbottabad, Rawalpindi, Gilgit, Srinagar, Simla, Amritsar, Lahore, Multan, Omsk, Novosibirsk, Tomsk, Kuznetsk Basin, Stalinsk, Krasnoyarsk, Frunze, Alma-Ata, Karakorum, Karakhoto, Ulan Bator, Ulan Ude, Irkutsk, Khabarovsk, Vladivostok, Port Arthur, Tsingtao, Tsinan, Peking, Tientsin, Kalgan, Mukden, Changchun, Harbin, Pyongyang, Seoul, Sapporo, Sendai, Tokyo, Yokohama, Kamakura, Gifu, Nagoya, Kyoto, Osaka, Kobe, Hiroshima, Nagasaki, Okinawa, Shanghai, Nanking, Hangchow, Hankow, Wuhan, Kiukiang, Changsha, Foochow, Kaifeng, Loyang, Sian, Chengtu, Chungking, Minya Konka, Yangtze Gorges

National Parks:
- AKAN NAT. PK.
- TOWADA NAT. PK.
- SHIMOTSU NAT. PK.
- NIKKO NAT. PK.
- FUJI-HAKONE NAT. PK.

North Pole

Notes and Itinerary

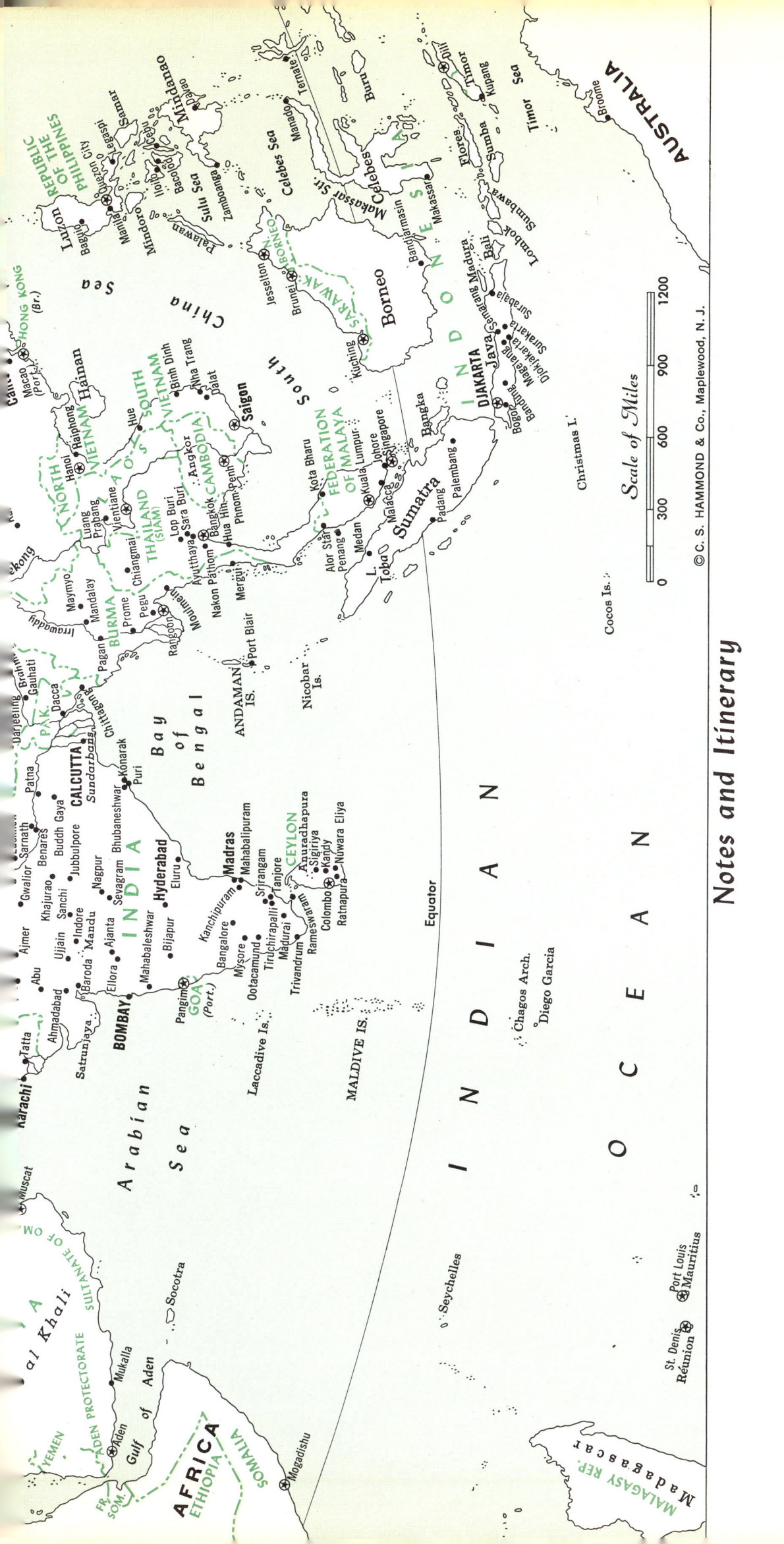

Syria, Lebanon and Cyprus

KEY TO THE NEAR EAST

Located at the eastern edge of the Mediterranean, in the heart of the Middle East, Syria's and Lebanon's central geographic position has made them, since the dawn of history, the highway of nations and the goal of empire builders. In ancient times, when the camel was the principal means of land transport, the great caravans of commerce passed through here, and Damascus, enchanting oasis on the edge of the desert, was the leading international trading post, whose possession was considered essential to the security of all the great empires of the past. Everywhere the traveler goes he will encounter evidences of succeeding civilizations, as the whole history of the human race unfolds before him. Today more than ever, Damascus is the meeting place of world travelers and traders and from a military point of view, still the vital pivot of the entire area. While preserving the ancient relics of the mighty civilizations of long ago, Syria and Lebanon confidently look ahead to even greater glories in the future.

ISLAND BASTION

Another valuable gateway to the Near East is the beautiful island of Cyprus. Although chiefly famous for its strategic importance, its vigorous, irregular scenery, its many sandy beaches, its rare old ruins and its quiet, calm country and port life make it ideal for those seeking a remote, lazy vacation on the exquisite, shining Mediterranean.

FRUITS OF DAMASCUS

Rivers springing from sources in the mountains make their way through lovely valleys, turning wide surroundings into big oases. It is therefore not surprising that apricots, cherries, peaches, grapes, apples, pears and other fruits are particularly delicious and abundant here.

DAMASCUS. To the Arab world, Damascus is the cradle of Islamic culture and the symbol of Islamic glory. As the world's oldest continuously inhabited community, she has always been the highway of nations, and in ancient times the great camel caravans found shelter and comfort in her hospitable khans, or caravan inns. The "street called Straight" (Acts IX:11) is where Paul stayed while in the great and flourishing capital of Biblical times. Little changed today, the broad, gloomy, cobblestoned street is lined with *souks,* or bazaars, where shrewd craftsmen sell the exquisite jewelry and gold or silver thread brocades for which the city has been justly distinguished throughout the ages. At the foot of the peaks of Anti-Lebanon, the copious gardens and orchards, watered by the Barada River, the "Golden River" of the Greeks, make Syria's capital a luxuriant oasis in the surrounding forsaken desert and the succulent "Fruits of Damascus" harvested in this fecund valley have a flavor fit for the gods. The

THE STREET CALLED "STRAIGHT"

Philip Gendreau

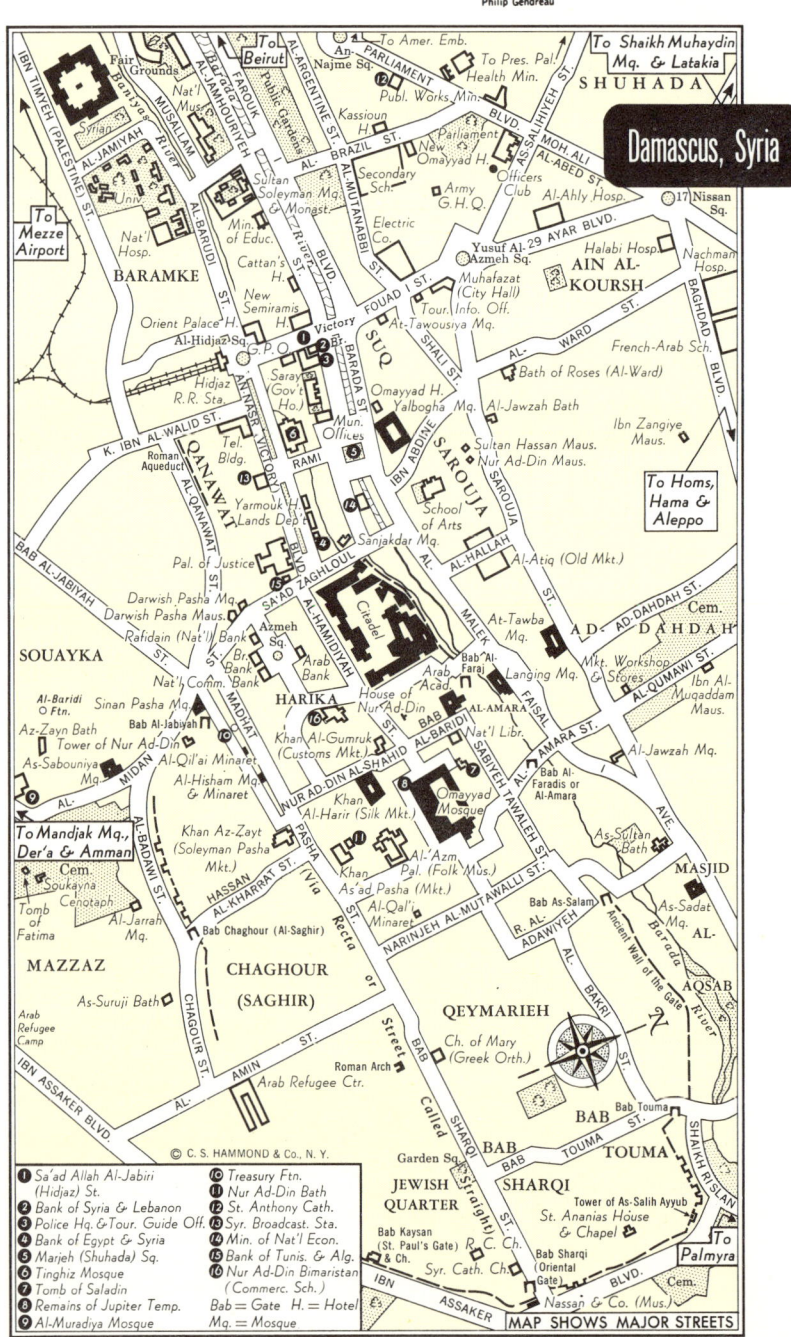

110

glorious fertility and richness in the midst of desolation is said to have caused the Prophet Mohammed to decline to enter this garden city, explaining that no man is entitled to enter paradise twice. HAMA, "the Melodious City," nestling among great willows and poplars on the banks of the Orontes River, has hundreds of rare, fascinating, huge primitive chain pumps or water wheels, called *norias*, incessantly creaking, turning and pumping water for the city. The handsome **Great Mosque**, formerly a Christian church, has remarkably fine minarets and the **Beit el Azm Palace** is famed for its courts and its eighteenth-century paintings. . . . Near the northern border is interesting ALEPPO . . . Syria's largest and most picturesque city, already a renowned city in the days of Nineveh and Babylon and capital of a great kingdom 2,000 years before Christ, possessing a character of its own that has been preserved through countless generations. On a hill in the middle of town, surrounded by a deep moat, is the **Citadel**, a magnificent example of Arab military engineering, dating back to the thirteenth century. Even the ancient city wall, with the **Gates of Antioch, El Hadid (Iron Gate)** and **Quinnesrine**, is still almost wholly intact. You will also enjoy a walk within the walls, through the unique arched *souks* and a stop at one of the picturesque *khans* or ancient caravan inns, like the fine **Khan el Wazir** or **Khan es Saboun**. After visiting the busy, noisy markets, you will enjoy a few quiet hours at the **Dallal Palace**, containing some exquisite woodwork and a beautiful courtyard with fountains; the great **Mosque of Zacharia**, with the most beautiful minaret in Syria, dating from 1290, or the **Aleppo Museum**, with its rare treasures. At St. Simeon are the imposing ruins of a **Byzantine fort** in a picturesque setting and the great **Basilica of St. Simeon**, one of the largest churches in the entire Near East, built in the Syria-Roman style popular in the Antioch region. . . . The ancient port city of LATAKIA, founded by the Greeks over 2,000 years ago, has played a prominent part in history. Today it is the center of the mysterious Nosairia sect, found only in this region. Near the town is the ancient storied **Castle of Sahion**, once an impregnable stronghold. Taken and held for many years by the Crusaders, it was finally reconquered by the Arabs under Saladin.

LEBANON

BEIRUT. "The devastating discord among nations will only cease to compromise peace when Beryte [Beirut], protecting the right to tranquillity in life, rules in spirit over land and sea, fortifies towns with a bulwark of unalterable and eternally valid laws." The world conflicts referred to in this quotation make it seem quite up-to-date, when actually it is by Nonnus, a Greek writer living about the end of the fourth century A.D. The Phoenicians, who inhabited Lebanon as early as 4000 B.C., were noted as traders, not warriors, and gave to the world the first alphabet, the first principles of architecture and the industry of dyes (in particular, that of purple), transparent glass, timber and metallurgy.

CYPRUS

Cyprus is an island in the eastern Mediterranean, lying sixty miles west of Lebanon, with an area less than half that of Wales. The coastline is indented and rocky, but interspersed are long, sandy beaches, accounting for its main attraction for people from other lands, since the bathing all along the coast is excellent. NICOSIA, the capital, lies several miles south of the center of the northern coast. An important monument within the walls is the **Mosque of St. Sophia**, built in the thirteenth century as a church. The younger **Orthodox Cathedral** is famous for its frescoes. Outside the walls, the **Cyprus Museum** displays valuable collections of antique pottery, jewelry and coins, among many others. . . . In the beautiful rugged scenery of the north coast is KYRENIA, a popular summer resort. Guarding the harbor from the crest of the high hill at the pass through the mountains is the twelfth-century **St. Hilarion Castle**. To the east is the wonderful **Bellapais Abbey**, one of the finest examples of Gothic architecture in the Levant, and the **Castle of Buffavento**.

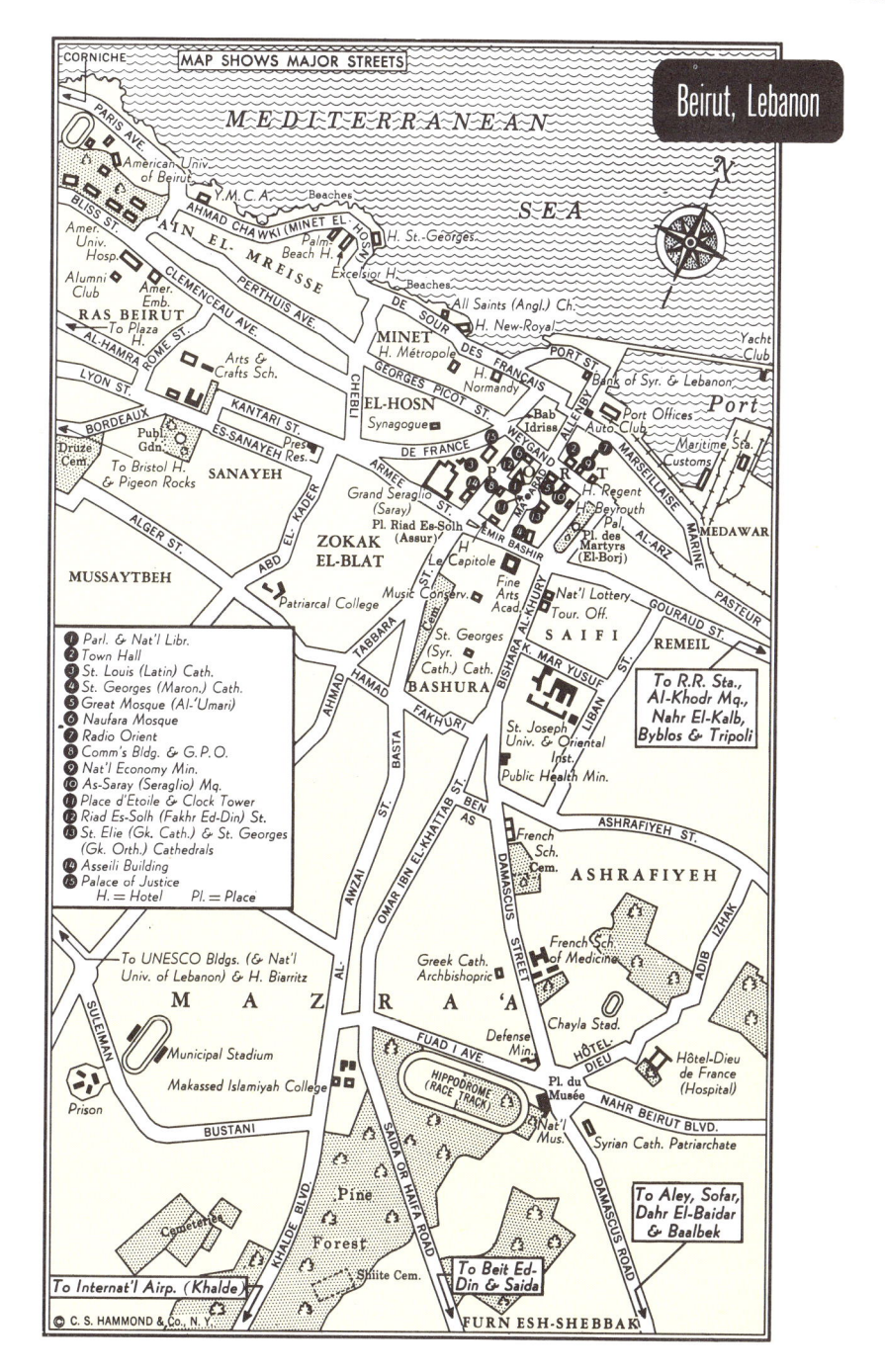

TEMPLE OF BACCHUS

Philip Gendreau

Iran

LAND OF OMAR KHAYYAM

Iran is the new name for ancient Persia, one of the first great empires, land of Cyrus the Great and Darius, which 2500 years ago, extended from India and the borders of Mongolia to Egypt and the Danube. Persians based their brilliant civilization upon arts and traditions old as the pyramids and throughout the lands conquered by them they spread and developed culture. Evidence of her glories fill museums the world over. Her sculpture, pottery, carpets and miniatures, her gardens and her poetry have inspired ensuing generations and civilizations and so her glorious heritage remains. Today the country, reduced in power and size as a result of a series of disastrous wars, faces a bright new future, revitalized by large-scale social, industrial and economic reforms. The cities of modern Iran, improved by great new buildings and broad avenues, carefully preserve their original charm and historic monuments.

SHERBETS TO PILAUS

Rice and lamb, of course, are eaten everywhere. There is an unending variety of rice dishes, **pilaus**; one favorite is chicken, rice, nuts and dates deliciously combined; another is a mixture of fish, chopped fresh dill and other herbs and rice. **Kabob**, skewered pieces of lamb roasted over coals, is delicious.

RELIEF FROM THE APADANA STAIRWAY
Oriental Inst. Univ. Chicago

TEHERAN. Teheran was an insignificant village until chosen as the capital of Persia, now Iran, at the end of the eighteenth century. But history from the beginning mentions Persia. Evidences of her glories fill museums the world over, but especially her own National Museum. Her sculpture, pottery, carpets and miniatures, her gardens and her poetry have inspired ensuing generations and civilizations, and so her glorious heritage remains. Teheran reflects both her own history as a small village and her later fame as the capital of an important Near East country with a rich, exciting past. One section retains a typical Oriental aspect of crooked, narrow streets and clamorous bazaars, while another consists of broad, tree-lined avenues and European-style buildings. In this latter district is the marble royal palace and splendid foreign legations.

AROUND THE COUNTRY

.... In the foothills of the Elburz Mountains, north of Teheran, are a number of pleasant summer resorts overlooked by snow-capped **Mount Demavend**. The evergreen forests here offer good hunting and unforgettable walks and rides in the woods. On the snowy slopes winter sports are popular. ... Across the mountains on the Caspian Sea are two fine, modern seaside resorts, **RAMSAR**, with its beautiful gardens and casino and **BABULSAR**, famous for its caviar. Another historic city, **HAMADAN**, the ancient Ectabana, capital of Media, has a number of ancient monuments, including the supposed tombs of Esther and Mordecai, the tomb of the mystical poet Baba Tahir, the tenth-century stone Parthian lion, and the beautiful new stone Mausoleum of Avicenna, the great Persian philosopher.

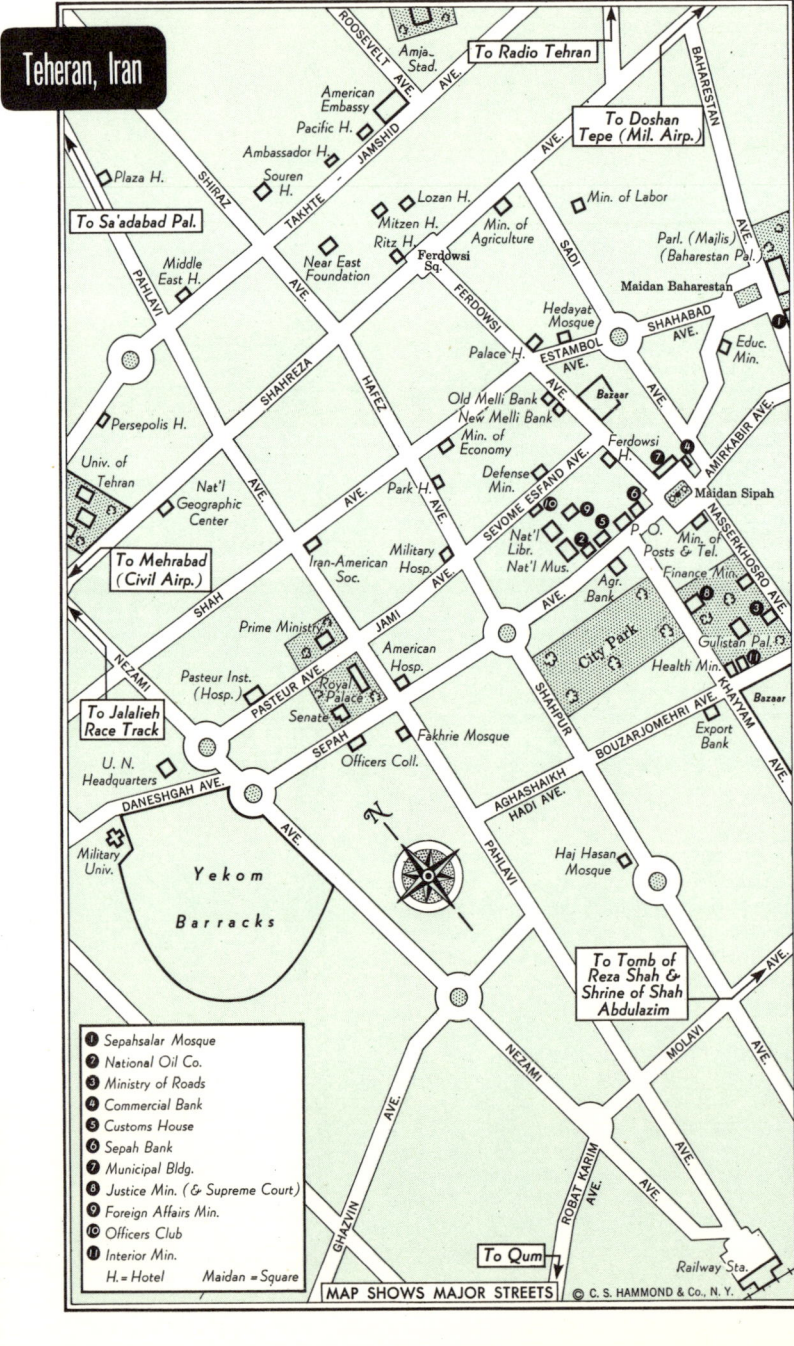

Teheran, Iran

1. Sepahsalar Mosque
2. National Oil Co.
3. Ministry of Roads
4. Commercial Bank
5. Customs House
6. Sepah Bank
7. Municipal Bldg.
8. Justice Min. (& Supreme Court)
9. Foreign Affairs Min.
10. Officers Club
11. Interior Min.

H. = Hotel   Maidan = Square
MAP SHOWS MAJOR STREETS
© C. S. HAMMOND & Co., N. Y.

ASIA

1. Street scene in Hong Kong
2. Japanese shrine
3. Open market at Kokura, Japan
4. Winter scene near Inchon, Korea
5. Village near Yokohama, Japan

ASIA

1. Nazareth, Israel, nestled on a hillside, is a center of pilgrimage
2. Arab street scene
3. The Taj Mahal, tomb of an Indian Empress, is one of the world's most beautiful buildings
4. Floating market at Bangkok, Thailand
5. Traffic officer in Srinagar, Kashmir

ASIA

1. Waterfront at Iskenderun, Turkey
2. Minaret over the Orontes River at Antioch, Turkey
3. Onions growing in the irrigated desert of Arabia
4. Camel and pack meets modern train crossing Arabian desert

ASIA

1. Spring and Autumn Temple at Kaohsiung, Taiwan, China
2. Cultivating rice in China
3. Busy docks at Singapore, one of the crossroads of the world

Iraq

MESOPOTAMIA—"LAND BETWEEN RIVERS"

With the establishment of the Kingdom of Iraq in 1921, Iraq regained her status as a political entity — a status lost in 1258 as a result of the Mongol invasions. Throughout the land a strange variety of monuments testify to its illustrious past, representing a succession of widely different periods in her long history, along the ageless waters of the Tigris and Euphrates, within whose coils, tradition says, the Garden of Eden was found and lost. Ur, Babylon, Nineveh, Samarra — the glory, wealth and learning of these amazing capitals of mighty empires resounds through the ages.

THE PEOPLE

Many of the vicissitudes through which the country has, at various times, passed are reflected in one or another of the modern Iraqi people.... In the cities the racial blending is more subtle and complicated. The races include Kurds, Indo-Iranian by extraction, of the Islamic religion but with a language of their own, whose families are characterized by the strongest possible feudal sense, a rigorous code of honor and considerable freedom of the women; Christians, mostly living in the Mosul district; Jews, the majority of whom live in Baghdad, and many others like the Yezidis, Turcomans and Shebeks.

LOCAL CUSTOMS

Arab tribesmen dress in long shirts made of gray sheeting or unbleached gray cloth, while the women generally wear black *abas* or cloaks made of wool, goat hair or imported silk, although in urban centers, many men wear European clothes. Rice, bread, dates and meat comprise the chief diet of the laboring class.

BAGHDAD. Storied scene of the *Arabian Nights,* Baghdad lies in an extensive desert plain between the ageless waters of the Tigris and Euphrates, within whose coils, tradition says, the Garden of Eden was found and lost. Founded in 762 A.D., she has been from Sumerian times a focal point of desert travel and trade. At the beginning of this century, Baghdad had shrunk to the dimensions of a small Arab market town of twisting lanes and rickety houses of mud and reeds. With the birth of Iraq, the capital has become one of the world's most rapidly expanding cities — broad, imaginative, with flower-lined boulevards and notable new buildings, like the Opera House, Karkh Hospital and wonderful spacious, well-lighted, modern homes and schools.

At KUT, downstream on the Tigris, is one of the numerous barrages constructed to bring water to idle lands. Nearby are the ruins of the fabulous city of Babylon, the Babylon of Nebuchadnezzar, one of the Chaldeans who ruled from 606-539 B. C., nothing being left of the older city of Hammurabi.

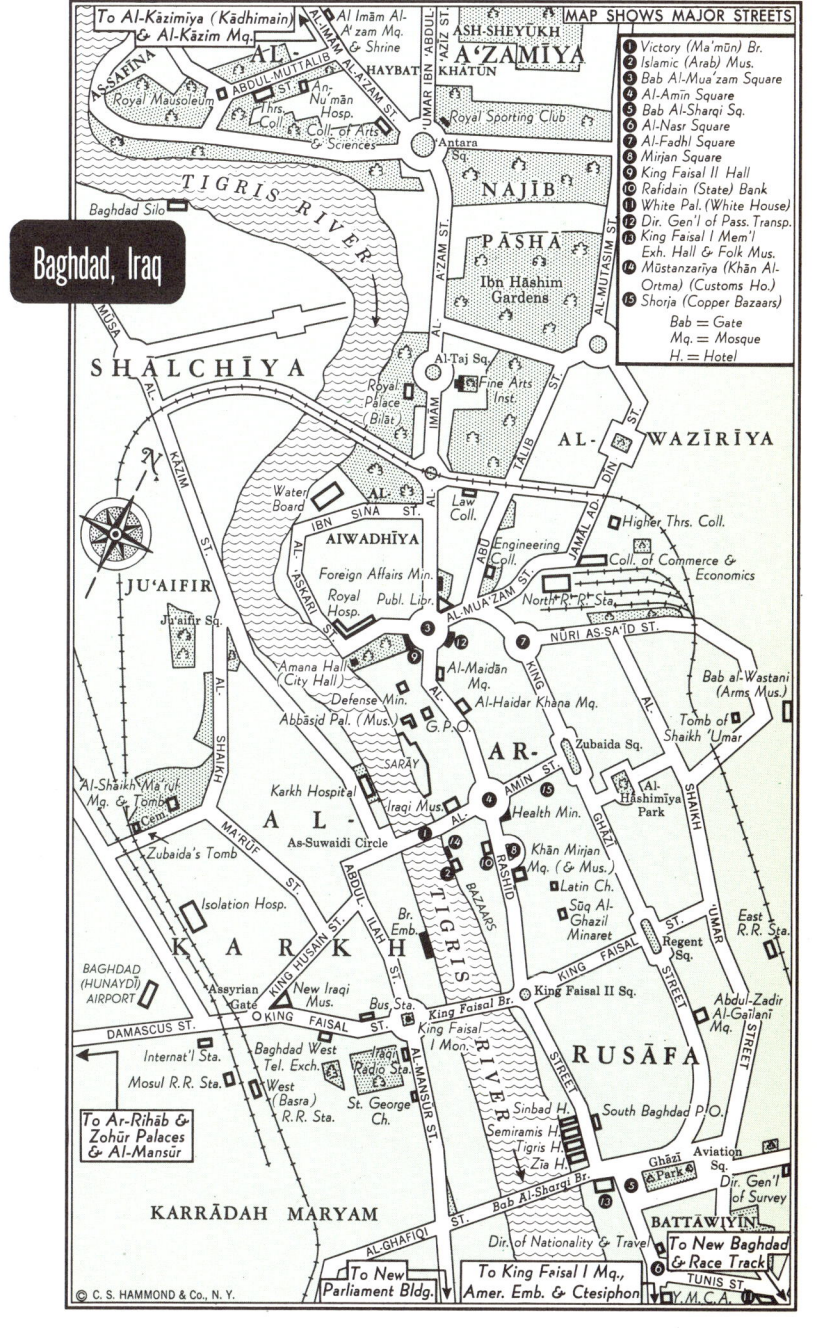

CTESIPHON ARCH
Philip Gendreau

Saudi Arabia

MYRRH, FRANKINCENSE, OIL

Not many travelers from Western countries visited Saudi Arabia before the discovery of its rich oil fields in the 1930's, yet it is an ancient land, as many ruins throughout the country prove. The frankincense and myrrh of the Biblical "Three Kings" could have come from Arabia, as it was an important product of the southern part of the country. . . . Government concessions given to oil and mining companies have brought modern roads, communication and transportation facilities to take the place of the camel and the donkey, although the motor car has not yet eliminated the former as a means of travel for Bedouins and other nomads of the desert, or the motor truck, the latter as a beast of burden. Arabia's cities are crowded places; their crooked streets are beehives of activity. The country has vast deserts dotted with oases, the largest being HOFUF, east of Riyadh. It has seven immense springs and a population of more than 100,000. The walled city of Hofuf has a Governor's palace, a mosque, market place and numerous residences, whose flat roofs are used as sleeping quarters.

ARABIAN BANQUET

Arabs are hospitable; coffee is served on every and any occasion. A typical formal banquet has a whole roast sheep as its main course — served on a huge platter with rice and raisins; dishes of soup, stews, chicken, vegetables, fruit and candies are placed around the platter. After coffee, at the end of the meal, small cups of sweetened tea, flavored with mint, are served. Today, Western-style foods are more likely to make up a menu for foreign visitors. Friday is the Moslem Sabbath, and the month of Ramadan is their lenten season.

ABOUT THE CITIES

MECCA, about 40 miles from the Red Sea and one of Saudi Arabia's two capitals, is the famous Holy City of the Moslem world. Every Moslem's desire is to make a pilgrimage to this birthplace of the Prophet Mohammed at least once during his lifetime, but non-Moslems may not enter the Holy City. . . . MEDINA is the burial place of the Prophet and non-Moslems are also excluded from this second sacred city. . . . JIDDA, on the Red Sea, is about 40 miles west of Mecca and a main stopping place for pilgrims to the Holy City. It has a busy airport outside the city. . . . RIYADH, in the eastern central part of Saudi Arabia, is the political capital with the royal palace dominating the city. . . . DHAHRAN, near the Persian Gulf, is a new city, built by the Arabian-American Oil Co. to house its personnel and their families. It has a hospital, modern stores and the first motion picture theater built in Saudi Arabia.

BOOM DOCK OF ARAMCO
TWA—Trans World Airlines

OIL WELL, SAUDI ARABIA
Philip Gendreau

Jordan

ANCIENT AND HOLY GROUND

Jordan (until recent times the major portion of ancient Palestine) and the River Jordan are familiar and revered names to Hebrews, Moslems and Christians the world over. The founders and leaders of the world's three great faiths knew its cities and pilgrims down through the ages have come to visit its shrines. The Christian especially considers the **River Jordan** a hallowed stream, for Christ waded into its waters to be baptized by John the Baptist. Many sacred songs have been written about the river and its banks. About half of the river's 200 winding miles run through Jordan to its outlet in the Dead Sea. A major portion of Jordan is desert, peopled by Bedouins who raise goats and sheep. Wealth is still rated by these nomadic tribes in the number of camels a man owns, but a modern automobile, standing outside his black tent, is no longer a rare sight. A large part of the Arab world is fast adopting Western ideas and methods.

AMMAN . . . . . . the Philadelphia of Bible times, is the capital of Jordan — an interesting and fast-growing modern city. Arabic-type homes rise on its hillsides; its main streets are filled with buses and passenger cars and are lined with shops, restaurants and business establishments. In contrast to its modernity are its historic ruins giving visitors who view them an idea of ancient Philadelphia. . . . JERUSALEM · · · · southwest of Amman, is partly in Israel and partly in Jordan, the latter part being called the "Old City." It is truly the Holy City, for within its walls are most of the shrines of the Holy Land. The Moslem Mosque of the 7th century, The Dome of the Rock, is built over a rock 58 feet long by 44 feet wide, covering an abyss. Moslems, Christians and Jews each have their own traditions for holding the Rock in reverence. The Church of the Holy Sepulchre is the sacred shrine of Christianity. What is left of Solomon's Wall is known as the "Wailing Place of the Jews" who began the custom of coming here in the Middle Ages to mourn the loss of Jerusalem. Outside the city's walls are the Garden of Gethsemane and the Mount of Olives. . . . BETHLEHEM, to the southwest, has the Church of the Nativity as the sacred shrine of Christendom. It is believed to have been erected on the spot where stood the stable in which Christ was born. . . .

DOME OF THE ROCK

Oriental Inst. Univ. Chicago

CHURCH OF THE NATIVITY

Philip Gendreau

Israel

HAIFA AND BAY FROM MT. CARMEL

LAND OF THE BIBLE

Israel, one of the youngest countries in the world, is a pulsating, modern country, but it is also a link with ancient traditions. The long-sought Jewish homeland, it is the mecca for the Christian pilgrim, as well as the Moslem, who wishes to see the land where his religion was born and tread the same dusty paths, lush valleys and legendary mountains that knew the step of the prophets and seers of old. The redeemed soil of Israel is again a wonderland of exotic plants and delicate wild flowers, of luscious fields and unrivaled orchards. Here East and West meet and the pages of the Bible become reality.

HUMAN KALEIDOSCOPE

Although roughly the size of New Jersey, the heritage of myriad civilizations lives on in Israel — a fascinating paradox of a land which is one nation and, simultaneously, a dazzling kaleidoscope of different national cultures — for 85% of her citizens were born elsewhere and the old customs and old costumes remain. Therefore, although Hebrew is the official language, Yiddish is very common and English is spoken everywhere. Most road signs are in Hebrew, Arabic and French and signs in hotels and interesting sites are also in English.

MILK AND HONEY

From sunny, hillside vineyards come the luscious grapes which are pressed into Israel's famed wines. Jaffa oranges are received joyously all over, and the orange and the grapefruit make the country's national drink "Mitz." In the sub-tropical Jordan Valley clusters of bananas and dates grow, while large watermelons and syrupy sweet figs, exotic guavas, juicy mangoes, all grown in the lovely Galilee, soon find their way to the tables of Jerusalem, Tel Aviv and Haifa. Apples and luscious plums, too, from the orchards of the Sharon Valley and the "Sabra," the wild prickly pear, complete the fruit fare of Israel. The Galilee is also famous for its ancient, gnarled olive groves.

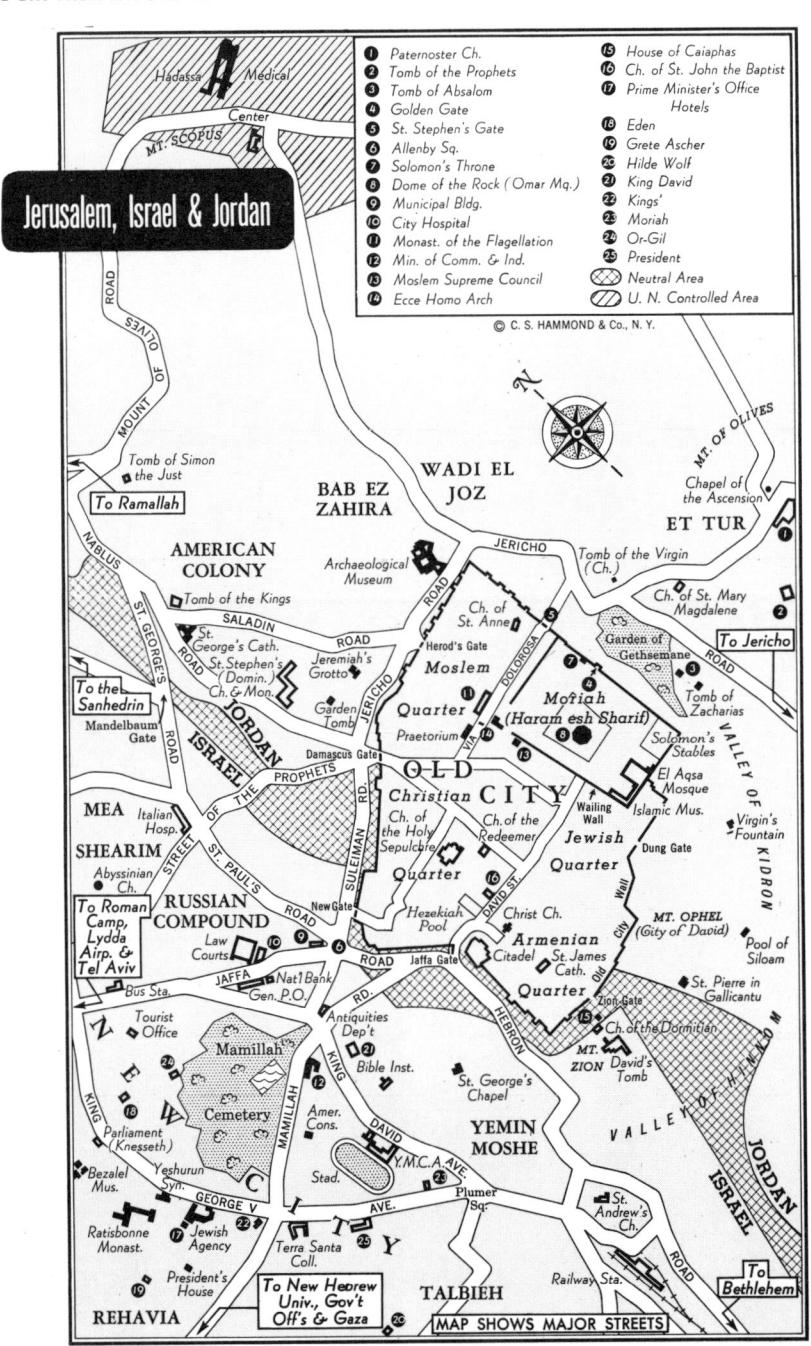

Jerusalem, Israel & Jordan

1. Paternoster Ch.
2. Tomb of the Prophets
3. Tomb of Absalom
4. Golden Gate
5. St. Stephen's Gate
6. Allenby Sq.
7. Solomon's Throne
8. Dome of the Rock (Omar Mq.)
9. Municipal Bldg.
10. City Hospital
11. Monast. of the Flagellation
12. Min. of Comm. & Ind.
13. Moslem Supreme Council
14. Ecce Homo Arch
15. House of Caiaphas
16. Ch. of St. John the Baptist
17. Prime Minister's Office

Hotels
18. Eden
19. Grete Ascher
20. Hilde Wolf
21. King David
22. Kings'
23. Moriah
24. Or-Gil
25. President

Neutral Area
U. N. Controlled Area

© C. S. HAMMOND & Co., N. Y.

JERUSALEM. Throughout three millenia of history, Jerusalem the Eternal, city of David, in the Judean Hills has been revered in the hearts and minds of men. Within her precincts were nurtured the world's greatest monotheistic religions, and her ancient stones have formed a backdrop to some of the greatest dramas on the stage of history. The Holy City of the Jews — site of Solomon's Temple and the Wailing Wall — and Christians alike — scene of much of Jesus' ministry, his death, burial and resurrection — she is also venerated by the Moslems as next in holiness to Mecca and Medina. She envelops such noble shrines as Mount Zion with the Cenacle, probably the scene of the Last Supper, and the traditional Tomb of David; Sanhedria, rock-hewn catacombs where the Sanhedrin, high priests of ancient Israel, were buried; the Mount of Olives; Romena, camp of the Roman Tenth Legion, and the Dome of the Rock, or Mosque of Omar.

MT. SINAI

YESTERDAY, TODAY AND TOMORROW

The seaside metropolis of **TEL AVIV** has merged with aged, oriental **JAFFA** to form a single city . . . . . cultural center of the country as well as the largest city. The Municipal Museum contains modern works of art, mostly by Jewish painters, and Bialik House Museum serves also as a library devoted to Jewish poetry. Theatrical companies with headquarters in Tel Aviv include "Habimah," oldest theatrical company in the country, specializing in classical tragedies and comedies, and "Chamber Theatre," composed mainly of young actors, performing mostly translated drama in a lighter vein. The renowned Israel Philharmonic Orchestra and many chamber music groups give performances regularly. The gay "Adloyada" is the culmination of Purim carnival time, celebrating the rescue of the Jews by Esther in the time of King Ahasuerus, replete with fancy-dress parades, masked balls and dancing in the streets. . . . Between Tel Aviv and Haifa are the seaside resorts of **NETANYA**, with its diamond cutting and polishing factories, and the nineteen-centuries-old port of **CAESAREA**, built by Herod the Great and capital of Roman governors. . . . Israel's main port, **HAIFA** . . . . . is the location of famed Mount Carmel. From the Carmel's breezy summit, the prophets Elijah and Elisha denounced the heathen priests of Ba'al. Today, the slopes house the major church of the Carmelite order and the World Faith Center, with its gold and marble Temple of Justice. Mount Carmel's greatest attraction, besides its huge wonderland of parks, gardens and forests, is its breath-taking view encompassing Acre Bay, the nearby beaches and resorts, the snow-capped mountains of Lebanon, the saffron hills of Galilee and the green-carpeted Valley of Zebulun. . . . The northern guardian of the Zebulun Valley is **AKO** or **ACRE**, one of the most ancient cities in the Holy Land. Surviving successive Egyptian, Canaanite, Phoenician, Hellenistic, Arab, Crusader and Turkish occupations, its massive battlemented walls withstood the onslaught of Napoleon. . . . In the northern highlands of Israel is the lofty summer resort of **TSEFAT** or **SAFED**, mysterious, shadowy, beautiful, where the towering sages of Judaism who explored the depths of Kabala walked through the town's narrow streets 400 years ago, in contrast with today's Artists Lane, gathering place of surrealists, impressionists and other modern artists. Visible from the heights of Safed is a gleaming, harp-shaped body of water almost 700 feet below sea level — the Sea of Galilee or Lake Tiberias. One of the world's oldest spas, whose medicinal hot springs have been an attraction for 2,000 years, its gentle waters also bring swimmers and sailors there throughout the year. On the north shore are the Mount of the Beatitudes, upon the slopes of which Jesus preached the Sermon on the Mount, and Capernaum or Kefar Nahum, with the ruins of the synagogue where Christ is believed to have taught, and also containing a synagogue of the second or third century. . Every Christian pilgrim to the Holy Land visits **NAZARETH**, the boyhood home of Jesus. Built on the traditional site of this home is the twentieth-century Church of the Workshop of St. Joseph. Here, according to legend, at the Virgin's Well, is where the Angel Gabriel first appeared to Mary. . . . The Romans and the Crusaders battled at **MEGIDDO**, southwest of Nazareth, the Biblical Armageddon where you may still visit the stables of King Solomon and venture into a bygone world of temples, high places, fortresses and garrison buildings. . . . The Negev mountains constitute a fascinating world in themselves — of highly variegated shapes, of all colors of the rainbow, of peaks and canyons twisted and contorted by the giant hand of nature. The Negev is no less renowned for its two seas.

ANCIENT SYNAGOGUE AT SITE OF BIBLICAL CAPERNAUM

Philip Gendreau

India and Pakistan

NEW NATIONS—AGE-OLD ROOTS

The two new republics of southern Asia — India and Pakistan — present a picture so varied and a culture so diffuse that to attempt to describe adequately their many fascinating facets would be an impossible task. Even the land ranges from the great extremes of the towering snow-clad peaks in the undulating Himalayan range, through the beautiful, breathtaking Kaghan, Indus, Kashmir or Kulu valleys and the vast plains, plateaus and fertile fields of the Punjab or Central India, to the barren, sandy, desert wastes of Sind and the dark, mysterious jungles of East Bengal and Malabar. The people, too, are just as diverse as their scenic background, including in the rich racial mosaic the tall, fair Kashmiri, the enterprising Punjabi, the chivalrous Rajput, the rugged Pathan, the artistic Bengali and the quick-witted Tamilian. Consequently, most of the world's great religions are also represented, with Buddhism, Jainism and Sikhism, Christianity and Zoroastrianism adding their own particular flavors to the predominant faiths of Hinduism in India and Mohammedanism in Pakistan. This variegated pattern stems from the influences of the many strange, multifarious peoples who have swept into the land, introducing their own cultures upon that highly developed civilization already existing here over 4,000 years ago. Thus, the ancient traditions, picturesque customs and manners and great artistic achievements combine in a scene found in no other region on earth.

ART OF DANCING

Indian classical dance is a highly perfected art, in which the movements of eyes, neck and arms, the grace and beauty of sculpturesque poses and the pattern of sound and cadence woven by the feet constitute a rhythmic whole. In its classical forms, rhythm, music and gesture are fused to convey a single impression. These find purest expression in *Bharata Natyam* — pure dance, not a dance drama — the traditional style prevalent in South India. The artist is usually a woman, and the dancing is done to traditional Carnatic music. *Abhinaya* is one aspect of the dance wherein the dancer interprets a song, especially the emotion and mood of it, by means of facial expressions and sensitive gestures. Today the Indian ballet is represented mainly by three dance forms: the *Kathakali*, *Kathak* and *Manipuri*. *Kathakali*, originating from Malabar, is a highly developed pantomimic dance in which classical, medieval and modern strands have been harmonized into a unique science of histrionics. Literally the word means "story play," enacted through movements of the body, gestures, artistic mime and music. This is usually performed by men, since it calls for virile movements of the body, with the dancers wearing heavy make-up in bright colors, voluminous costumes and much jewelry. *Kathak*, of North India, is more lyrical and less dramatic than *Kathakali*, with the dance rendering episodes from the *Radha Krishna* legend in pantomimic form. Although retaining

GATEWAY TO INDIA, BOMBAY
TWA—Trans World Airlines

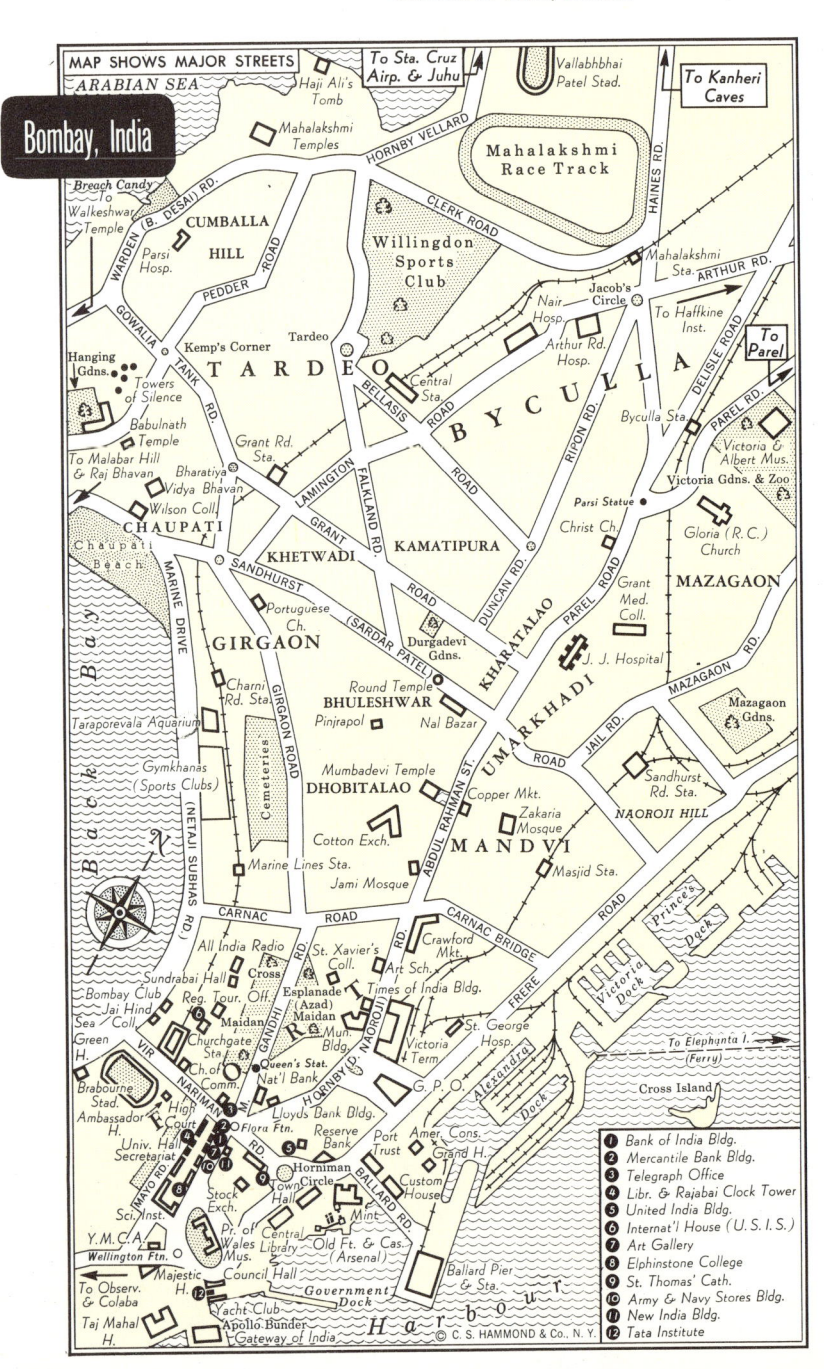

Hindu themes and sentiments, courtly and foreign influences are noticeable in the fleeting footwork and swift movements of the body. Each dance is set to a traditional melody and the movements of the dancer tell the story. In contrast to the classical *Kathakali* and the sophisticated *Kathak*, the *Manipuri* dance is a folk ballet of the east.

ASIAN DELICACIES

Pakistanis are fond of food that is spicy and well-flavored. Among the tasty dishes are a variety of curries and pilaus, especially cooked meat or fish with rice, *kebabs* (fried or broiled meat), *shami kebabs* (fried meat cakes), *kofta* (meat balls), *murgh-i-Mussalam* (stuffed fried chicken) and *shahi tukre* (sweetbreads cooked in milk and honey). The Punjab, where citrus fruits grow in great profusion, is noted for its fruit drinks.

INDIA, VARIED AND INTERESTING

BOMBAY. Bombay, the "Gateway to India" and the principal city of the western region, provides the traveler coming by sea with the first glimpse of the country. Its beautiful harbor is studded with hilly islands, and its palm-fringed shore rises gradually to meet the misty-blue peaks beyond. Besides being India's chief port of entry, Bombay is a modern commercial city, so cosmopolitan in appearance and habits that the visitor feels at home immediately. The city is also an industrial center where throughout the day a constant stream of people flows in and out of its busy textile mills, smart business premises, palatial hotels and streamlined transport. In the evening, the center of interest is the city's splendid promenade by the sea, the Marine Drive, to which sophisticated ladies, elegantly dressed in "saris," lend color and gaiety. Of interest to the visitor are the Hanging Gardens on Malabar Hill which offer a panoramic view of the bay and the imposing buildings of the city below. Also noteworthy is the Parsi Tower of Silence, the Prince of Wales Museum and Art Gallery, the Brabourne Stadium and the seaside resort of Juhu. At Mahalakshmi, Bombay has the best race course in Asia. A good deal of Bombay's local color derives from the mixed nature of its population. Apart from the local inhabitants, there are thousands from other parts of India who come here to make a living. The different customs, languages and even the food eaten can make a fascinating study. . . . Southeast of Bombay is BIJAPUR, splendid capital of a powerful 16th-century Muslim state, whose architecture combines grandeur and grace, as well as ornamentation. Its finest building is Gol Gumbaz, mausoleum of Sultan Muhammed Adil Shah, with its enormous dome, second largest in the world. . . . At SANCHI, site of extensive Buddhist remains, is the imposing Great Stupa, a solid dome of sandstone with profusely carved gateways. . . . Rich in historic associations and architectural beauty, GWALIOR is the site of Gwalior Fort, about two miles long and 2,700 feet wide. Six massive gateways of elaborate design lead to the fort, while within is the splendid **Manmandir Palace**, one of the best specimens of Hindu architecture. . . . Strategically situated on the Yamuna River, **DELHI** · · · · has always been the gateway to the rich Gangetic plains, in addition to commanding the roads to all parts of India. Planned by Sir Edward Lutyens and Sir Herbert Baker, the modern city of **NEW DELHI** . . . . was formally opened in 1931. A refreshing feature is the long, tree-lined road, ablaze in spring with flaming *gulmohur*, yellow laburnum and mellow, cool jacaranda and margosa. According to Fergusson, "the most magnificent palace in the East or perhaps in the world" was the **Red Fort**, with its graceful ramparts. The marble hall, **Diwan-i-Khas (Hall of Private Audience)**, with its graceful arches and flower-inlaid piers, has been immortalized by the Persian couplet inscribed in letters of gold on its walls: "If there be a paradise on earth. It is this, it is this, none but this!" Opposite is **Jama Masjid**, biggest and most beautiful mosque in India, also erected by the Emperor Shah Jahan. Built of red sandstone and white marble, its three striped, bulbous domes and two tall and slender minarets are characteristic of Mughal architecture. Inside the ruined fort of **Purana Qila** is the **Qila-i-Kuhna Masjid (Sher Shah's Mosque)**, an excellent example of Indo-Afghan architecture with the pointed arch, a Muslim feature, combined with brackets essentially Hindu in style. The first great example of Mughal architecture is the beautifully proportioned, impressive **tomb of Emperor Humayun**, built in 1565 of red sandstone with a central dome of white marble. On the road to **Humayun's tomb** is that of **Isa Khan**, built in 1547, the "last true example of the Lodi style of architecture," main features of which are an octagonal building with an enclosing veranda and a hemispherical dome surrounded by eight smaller domes. Commanding a panoramic view of Delhi from the south is the 5-story Qutb Minar, highest stone tower in India, completed in about 1190. Around Princes' Park, west of Purana Qila, stand the mansions of the Maharajas of the former princely states. Still further west are the modern government buildings including the palatial red-and-white sandstone **Rashtrapati Bhavan**, official residence of the President of the Republic, and the fascinating circular Parliament Building, encircled with an open colonnade. Jantar Mantar, the observatory erected in 1725 by Maharaja Jaisingh II of Jaipur, the great astronomer-king, contains six huge masonry instruments to study the celestial bodies. . . . The Western Himalayas offer many interesting hill resorts, chiefly SIMLA, formerly the summer capital of India, known for its splendid view and fine walks. . . . Further downstream on the Yamuna is AGRA . . . . city of the Taj Mahal, known throughout the world for its pierced marble work and beauty of proportion. . In the most ancient and holy city of India, BANARAS, . . . an array of shrines, temples and palaces rise in several tiers from the bank of the Ganges River. At nearby Sarnath, Buddha delivered his "first sermon," expounding the four Noble Truths. The famous Asoka Pillar, whose lion capital has been adopted by the Republic of India as the state emblem, stands here.

CALCUTTA. Calcutta is young as Indian cities go. It owes its origin to an agent of the East India Company who, in 1690, chose this site for a British trade settlement. The settlement prospered both because of its excellent trade position and its importance as the headquarters of British administration until 1912. Today, Calcutta is the second largest city in India. As it has grown up in comparatively recent times, Calcutta has none of the ancient historical monuments that characterize Indian towns. There are, however, more relics here of British rule than anywhere else in India, some dating back to the earliest days of the East India Company's settlement. A modern city, Calcutta offers all the amenities a visitor can desire. In Chowringhee, the densely populated city area, are excellent hotels, cinemas, restaurants, and a shopping center capable of meeting every conceivable requirement. The Maidan, a vast park, two miles long by a mile wide, might be called the lungs of this heavily populated area. Here Calcutta citizens spend much of their leisure time.

TAJ MAHAL — TWA—Trans World Airlines

ELEPHANTS HAULING LOGS

Within the park are beautiful drives, gardens and a section known as the Brigade ground where ceremonial parades are held. The two Dhakuria Lakes, which have a combined frontage of about a mile and are lined with tall palm trees and surrounded by parkland, is another spot popular with the people of Calcutta. Regattas and rowing championships are regularly held on the lakes.

Of the 7,000 temples once located in **BHUBANESHWAR**, on the eastern coast, not more than 100 now remain. Exquisitely carved, they are amongst the oldest in India and exhibit a variety of architectural styles of about ten centuries ago. . . . Center of the sunny south, seat of an ancient civilization, **MADRAS** . . . . . even today retains an old-world charm. Nucleus of the English establishment was **Fort St. George**, completed in 1653, and within it is **St. Mary's Church**, reputed to be the oldest English church in Asia, with its handsome marble tablets. The wide sea-front **Marina** is reputed to be the second-best beach in the world, while lining it are the Moorish-style **Chepauk Palace**; the imposing, sixteenth-century, Italian-renaissance-style **Presidency College** and the modern-Gothic **San Thome Cathedral**, with its beautiful stained-glass windows. Among the temples in Madras, most striking is the **Kapaleeswarar Koil** in Mylapore, "the abode of peacocks." This temple has the characteristic towering pylon, known as *gopuram*, typical of Dravidian architecture. Behind the temple is a large sacred tank surrounded by flights of steps on the

HUGLI RIVER, CALCUTTA

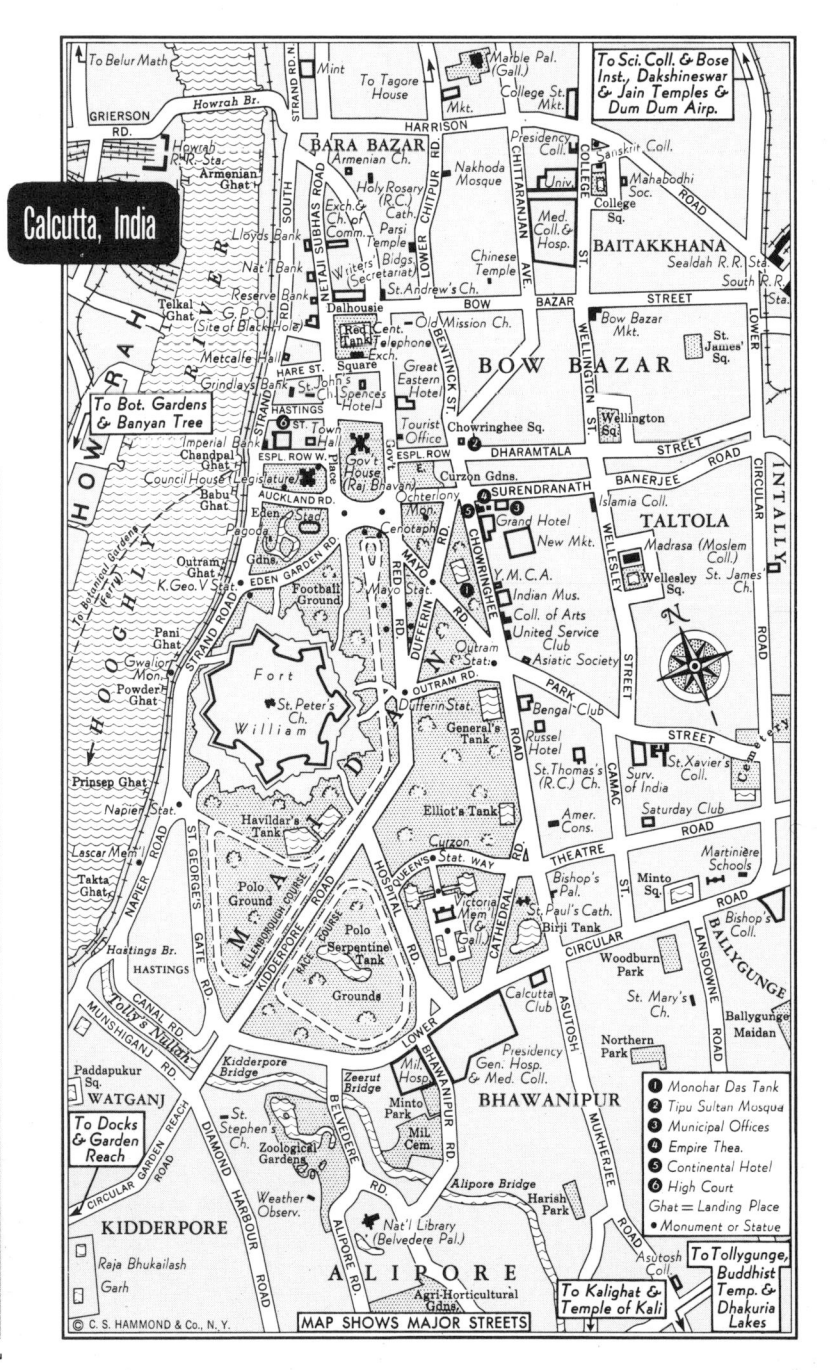

KALIGHAT TEMPLE, CALCUTTA

four sides, where devotees may be seen at all times of day, bathing and cleansing themselves before worship. Across the Adyar River are the headquarters of the **Theosophical Society**, an expansive estate of appealing beauty, offering cool, quiet shelter under the huge banyan tree on the grounds, or in the well-equipped library with its rare collection of palm-leaf manuscripts and ancient books dating back a thousand years. Music forms an integral part of life in South India, which has a rich heritage in this fine art. **Carnatic** music, as this classical type is called, has been kept alive by a long line of artists, quite a few of whom live in Madras, and the cultural life of the city is one busy, stimulating round of concerts and dance recitals, particularly during the Christmas season. . . . A pleasant seaside resort south of Madras is **MAHABALIPURAM**, also known as the Seven Pagodas. The first foundations of Dravidian architecture in India were laid by the ancient Pallava dynasty, who ruled the territory now known as the Madras State during the sixth to eighth centuries A.D. In this small village are the earliest remnants of their monolithic temples, figures and carvings, unique in conception and masterly in execution, all hewn out of the rocks, most important being the **Five Rathas**, the bas-relief on a huge rock popularly known as **Arjuna's Penance**, the **Mahishasura Mandapam**, the **Krishna Mandapam** and the **Shore Temples**. . . . **MADURAI** . . . . further south, has always been a seat of Tamil learning and culture.

KASHMIR

Nestling in the bosom of the Himalayas lies the valley of Kashmir — the tourists' paradise — where hunters, anglers, lovers of hiking and trekking all find their delight. **SRINAGAR** . . . . lies along the banks of the Jhelum, its waters crossed by seven bridges, and near **Dal Lake**, surrounded by the lovely pleasure gardens laid out by the Mughal emperors. . . . For the vigorous traveler, **GILGIT AGENCY** offers excellent mountain climbing, fishing and skiing facilities.

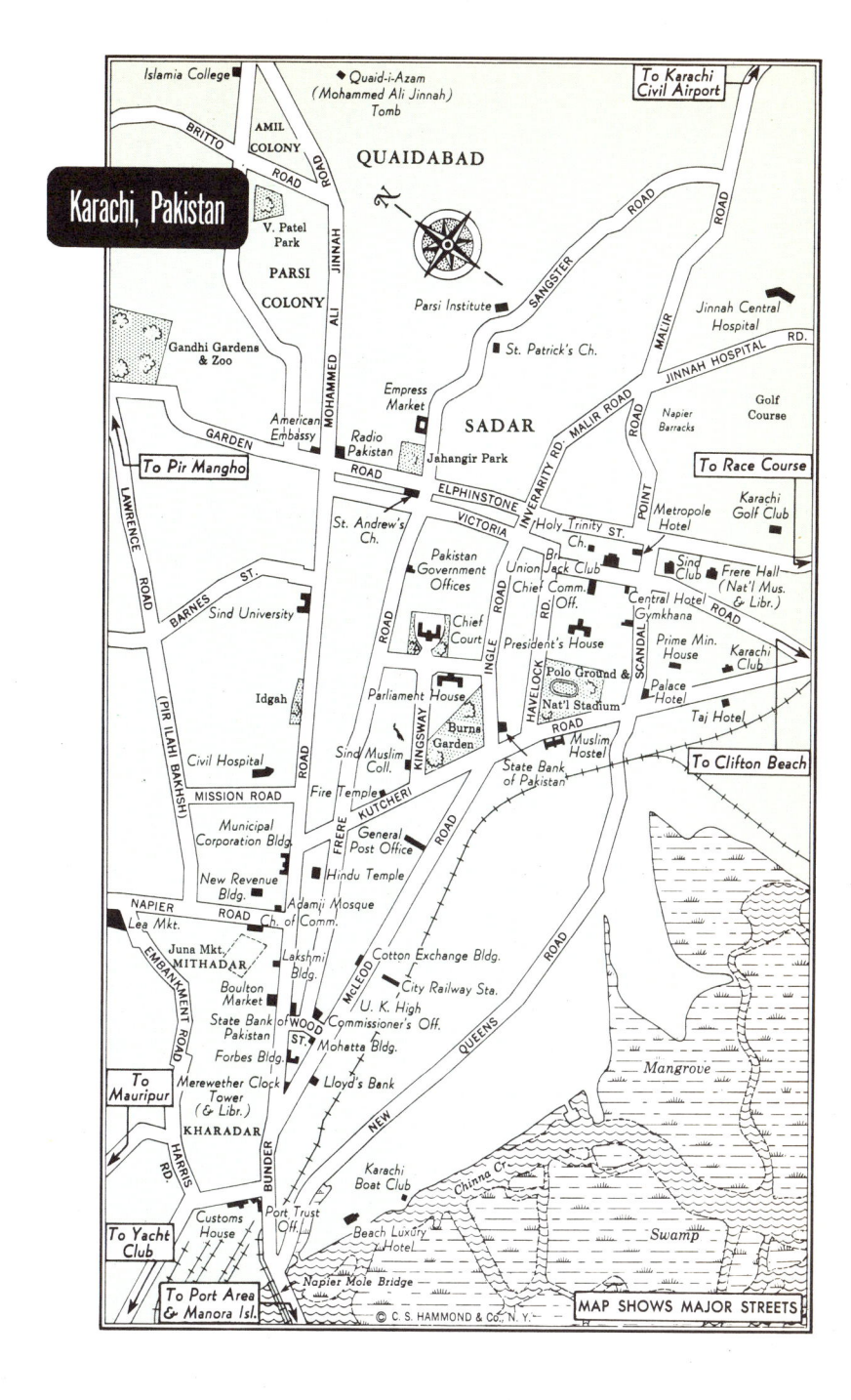

Karachi, Pakistan [map]

PAKISTAN

KARACHI. "From a fishing village to a metropolis" — that is the story of Karachi. Since selected in 1947 as the first capital of the new state of Pakistan, she has more than doubled in size. And only three centuries ago, when known as Kalachi, "the land of the sand dunes," she was just a small fishing port with a long history, including identification as Alexander the Great's Haven, the Korokula of the Greek travelers and the site where the first Moslem invaders landed on this subcontinent. Now a clean, thriving trading center, cooled by a brisk sea breeze, her picturesque past and bright future are both reflected in the donkey and camel carts proceeding side by side with high-powered cars and modern buildings like the Cotton Exhange bordering the same streets as the narrow,

CLOTH MARKET BAZAAR, KARACHI

crowded, stall bazaars. Too, the dedicated crowds paying homage at the tomb of Mohammed Ali Jinnah, founder and first governor-general of Pakistan, are as large as those attending the classic Quaid-e-Azam's Gold Cup race. And the Mithadar (Sweet Water) and Kharadar (Salt Water) Gates still remain from the old wood and mud fort, while the young Pakistani parliament conducts its weighty discussions in English.

At **TATTA**, fifteenth-century capital of the Sammas Rajputs, the Moghul architecture and mosaic tilework decoration reached the acme of artistry. Its greatest monument is the **mosque** begun by Emperor Shah Jahan in 1647, whose main dome has exquisite mosaics of white and blue set in a blaze of bright colors. Among an astonishing array of Muslim tombs along the **Makli ridge** is the **tomb of Mirza Jani Beg**, the last of the Tarkhan rulers, with richly carved surface tracery on the enclosure walls. In contrast, Tatta is also extremely popular with hunters, for the surrounding country abounds with game, including partridge, grouse, snipe, hog and bear. . . . Around the year 3,000 B. C. the Indus Valley Civilization flourished along the banks of the mighty Indus River, in the stretch of territory extending from the Arabian Sea to the Himalayan foothills. Center of this great human endeavor was **MOHENJO-DARO**, the Mound of the Dead, northeast of Karachi. These ruins include the **citadel**, containing a remarkable series of structures, with its massive fortifications. A similar city, but not so spectacular, is at Harappa in the Punjab. . . . An entirely different place is **SUKKUR**, a flourishing market town and site of the world-famed, mile-long **Sukkur Barrage**, longest dam in the world. Close by is the large, single-span **Sukkur Railway Bridge**, built in 1887, one of the first cantilever railway bridges ever constructed. Testifying to the creative excellence of Muslim craftsmen of the Moghul age are many ancient buildings, mosques and mausoleums in the historic city of **MULTAN** . . . . a town of considerable antiquity in the Punjab. The city is, additionally, the only place in the subcontinent where important monuments of the early Arab or pre-Moghul era still remain. Outstanding among the **five famous tombs** of the twelfth to fourteenth centuries is the **tomb of Rukni-Alam**, built between 1320 and 1324. The **old fort** near the city is well worth a visit. . . . **LAHORE** . . . . is a gay, charming and hospitable city — center of Pakistan's cultural and academic life. Modernity glows in a setting of ancient history, as lining the vast avenue of the **Mall** are buildings like the massive building of the **Punjab University**, oldest and largest in the land, and the office of the "Civil and Military Gazette," where Rudyard Kipling worked. Down the road from the office is the huge, unserviceable cannon known to the literary world as **Kim's Gun**. Away from the hum of business, Lahore relaxes in the vast pleasure grounds of the famous **Shalimar Gardens**, built by Shah Jahan, the fifth Moghul emperor, in 1637. Water flows gracefully over three terraces through an artificial channel studded with fountains. The pure marble cascade is embedded with tiny shelves for lamps, so at night when the lamps are lit, the water shines and glistens in the hues of flickering flames. Shah Jahan, creator of the Taj Mahal in memory of his beautiful queen, also built in Lahore one of the first mausoleums of the East — the **tomb of the Emperor Jahangir** — in memory of his father. Rising above the banks of the Ravi River, the red-sandstone mausoleum is surrounded by the spacious **Dilkusha Garden**. **Badshahi Mosque**, built in 1673 by Aurangzeb, the last of the great Moghul emperors, is another memorable monument. Reputedly the largest in the world, designed on the model of the Al Walid Mosque in Mecca, the Badshahi Mosque has an ascetic grandeur and magnificence all its own, with its towering red minarets, vast steps and three superb domes . The **salt mines** at **ATTOCK**, a small town lying on the border between the Punjab and North West Frontier Province, are among the wonders of the world — hundreds of feet of thick seams form lovely caverns of rock salt, resplendent in gleams of flickering light. . . . Another favorite hill station is **ABBOTTABAD** in the midst of the most lovely scenery, where snow-clad mountains gaze down on a panorama of pine-strewn hills, rivers, fields of gold and vivid green and little villages hanging precariously on the hill crests. This is an excellent starting point to tour the **Kaghan Valley**, a region of breathtaking beauty offering pleasant shooting and very good trout fishing. . . . To the north is **TAXILA**, with extensive **remains of three distinct cities** dating from about 190 to 85 B. C. The **Buddhist stupas** and the monasteries at **Mohra Moradu** and **Jaulian** are the best-preserved monuments of their kind in Pakistan. The **Zoroastrian temple**, constructed in the Scytho-Parthian epoch, is another magnificent architectural

SHALIMAR GARDENS, LAHORE
Government of Pakistan

specimen. . . . The rugged hill country of the Khyber Pass is the land of warriors who carry their rifles as nonchalantly as the Westerner does his umbrella, although at the same time, hospitality to the stranger still remains the age-old and inviolate custom. **PESHAWAR** . . . is the center of this frontier tribal country, home of the tall, bearded and large-boned Pathan, of the Afridi and of the Khattak sword dance. A picturesque city, it also remains an important center of trade between Afghanistan and Pakistan and its **Bijori Gate Bazaar** is even yet the meeting place of caravans from many countries. In keeping with its long history, the city's **Museum** has a rich collection of the Gandhara sculptures and Buddhist relics. Ten miles from Peshawar begins the historic **Khyber Pass**. . . . **DACCA** . . . . . the capital of East Pakistan with a touch of medievalism, possesses a number of intriguing historical remains from Moghul times, including the huge **Lal Bagh Fort**, the **Burra** and **Chota Katras (Gateways)** and over a thousand mosques. It also has many fine modern buildings like the outstanding **High Court** and famous **Dacca University**. **SUNDARBANS**, a forest region in the southwest corner of East Bengal, is the haunt of the famous Royal Bengal tiger and, consequently, a mecca for international sportsmen. . . . A rewarding experience for the really hardy and adventurous visitor is a trip to the wild and unexplored **CHITTAGONG HILL TRACTS**, the habitat of primitive tribes of Mongolian extraction who build their houses high on stilts, where the rivers team with fish, the jungle is ablaze with color and innumerable species of wildlife — elephant, tiger, leopard, rhinoceros, bison, deer, python — haunt its shaded depths.

RICHLY ADORNED COURT ELEPHANT AT BHARATPUR
Philip Gendreau

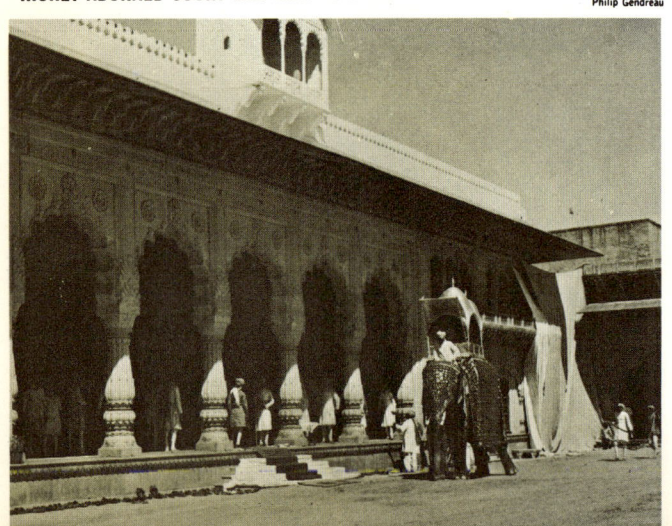

RA KHERIGAR PALACE, JUNAGAD
Philip Gendreau

Ceylon

LANKA: "THE RESPLENDENT"

The charm and fertility of the island of Ceylon has been its bane as well as its blessing. Separated from the continent of India by only a narrow strip of sea and standing athwart the highway along which caravels of East and West quested for commerce or conquest, the island has throughout the centuries attracted the stranger from across the seas. Still blessed with a fertile soil, pleasant climate, magnificent scenery and central position, Ceylon retains today its magnetic pull for peoples of other lands.

CINNAMON ISLE

COLOMBO . . . . . modern capital of Ceylon, is a world-famous port, with luxurious shops, pleasant parks, exotic temples and crowded, colorful bazaars where the East holds sway. The thriving city once offered protection to the trading vessels of the Arabs, Egyptians, Greeks and Romans, and later to the ships of the Portuguese, Dutch and English. Adjoining stately Queen's House, residence of the Governor-General, is Gordon Gardens, site of an old Dutch church where the last Sinhalese king of Kotte was buried, now a miniature park containing a huge rock, relic of the Portuguese occupation, on which is carved the arms of the King of Portugal. In picturesque Victoria Park are birds of bright plumage, flowers of brilliant hues and leafy bowers, including the Madara tree, rarest in Ceylon, whose bark is poisonous and whose wood is said to be an effective charm against wild elephants; balsawood trees, yielding the lightest wood in the world, and magnificent collections of orchids. Of striking architectural beauty, with its great white dome and pillared façade, is the Town Hall. On a hill near Main Street is Wolvendaal Church, a fine cruciform built in 1749 in Doric style, containing many memorials of Dutch rule. In Kochchikadde and Sea Street are shrines sacred to Hinduism, with artistically carved stone pillars and exteriors a mass of grotesque figures, images and symbols, expressions of the age-old art of India. During the Dutch regime, cinnamon was cultivated in a number of gardens outside the city. This is now the fashionable residential quarter. A few miles out from town is the famous Buddhist temple of Kelaniya, a masterpiece of oriental temple construction, held in greatest veneration. Frescoes of exquisite beauty and color adorn the walls. . . . Drowsy, flower-fragrant, set amidst the picturesque hills, KANDY is the famous and beautiful mountain stronghold that was the last part of Ceylon to fall into foreign hands. Heart of the town is the Dalada Maligaqa (Temple of the Tooth), enclosed by an ornamental stone wall and a moat. The Pattirippuwa (Octagon) was at one time a British military prison and is now a library containing a valuable collection of rare old palm-leaf manuscripts. Most striking features of the temple are the many images of Buddha; the elaborate door inlaid with silver and ivory, with two pairs of elephants' tusks on either side, at the entrance to the sanctuary containing the silver-gilt, bell-shaped shrine protecting the Sacred Tooth; and the six inner shrines ornamented with precious stones. Next door is the Audience Hall, with its excellent wall plates and rich carvings on the satinwood pillars. It was here that Ceylon's independence was celebrated in 1948. Kandy's chief glory is the lake, said to have been made by Sri Wickrama Raja Sinha, the last king of Kandy. The famous Kandy Perahera is held in August, when richly caparisoned elephants, tom-tom beaters, Kandyan dancers and chieftains in jeweled costumes walking in stately procession combine to make this the most glamorous pageant in the East. At Peradeniya are the famous Royal Botanical Gardens, containing among their unequalled luxuriance of exotic vegetation a spice collection and the stately Palm Avenue, one of the world's finest collections of palms. . . . Nestling in the bosom of the mountains, NUWARA ELIYA, with its fine invigorating air and picturesque scenery, is a most charming spot. There are attractions to gratify every taste — wild rugged heights and peaceful plains, cataracts and babbling brooks, golf on one of the finest courses in the East, trout fishing and mountaineering. A few miles out are the noted Hakgala Gardens, with giant tree ferns, sunken rose gardens and ornamental creeks. . . . The stupendous domes of dagobas loom large and a 2,000 year-old history unfurls as the visitor approaches the holy city of ANURADHAPURA, for 1,400 years the capital of Ceylon. Devanampiya Tissa, who reigned during the third century B. C., founded the monastery called Isurumuniya, in a setting at once picturesque and peaceful. A white dagoba gleams amidst the green foilage and reflections are cast in the still blue waters, while sculptures of supreme beauty, such as the panel of "Lovers," enhance this ancient rock temple. King Dutugemunu, most celebrated ruler, conquered the Dravidians who held Ceylon in thrall, and the period of freedom that followed was marked by the renaissance of art. The greatest work undertaken by him was the Ruanveliseya, of enormous proportions, with its white dome and gilded spire. A masterpiece of architecture and a striking memorial to the artistic genius of the Sinhalese race, it is the most celebrated dagoba in Ceylon, being regarded by all as a monument of peculiar sanctity. Largest building is the Elephant Stables, whose columns are of such an unusual height that the appellation is quite fitting. In these ancient edifices, the entrance received sculptural embellishments and most characteristic of these were the stone slabs with rounded tops, called guardstones, bearing anthropomorphic representations of serpent deities (Nagas). The moonstone, a semi-circular slab, with its characteristic feature of a procession of animals, is also peculiar to Sinhalese architecture. . . . The enormous mass of granite, forming the rock of SIGIRIYA (Lion Rock) rises abruptly, with beetling brows and precipitous sides, to a height of some 600 feet above the surrounding plain. In the fifth century A. D. King Kassapa transformed it into the most impregnable fortress in ancient Ceylon. Oldest and best-preserved of the ancient paintings in the country, in a cavity on the western face of this rock, are portraits of 21 ladies, the only secular pictures known to ancient Ceylon art. That they are the work of a master painter or painters, opinion is agreed, but experts will never tire of wondering who they are, what they are up to, why and wherefore they were created. At the summit of the rock, where Kassapa had his palace, is a carefully planned drainage system for the palace, massive ramparts even now over thirty feet high

KANDYAN DANCING GIRLS

Ceylon Dept. of Information

MOSLEM MOSQUE, COLOMBO

TWA—Trans World Airlines

Japan

GEM OF THE PACIFIC

No longer a remote country, veiled and untouched by the main currents of the world, and one of the few Eastern countries still open to visitors, Japan is the goal of those with a taste for the mysterious, alluring Orient, for she is fascinating in endless ways. Her land is rich in lofty peaks, verdant plateaus, picturesque cascades, sapphire lakes and health-giving hot springs. Life in Japan is no less colorful, with festivals that have been preserved through the ages, arts that are redolent of her long cultural history and amusements brimming with exotic charm. Those who feel the magnetism of the mellow Oriental civilization happily will fall completely under the spell of this intoxicating land.

JAPANESE FESTIVALS

To every Japanese the New Year is the festival of festivals. Every house front is decorated with the *kado matsu*, a pair of decorative stands of pine twigs and bamboo stalks, all symbolic of good luck. Friends and relatives come to say their New Year greeting and are served two specialties: *otoso*, sweetened Japanese wine, and *zoni*, a soup containing rice cakes and vegetables. The most popular amusements are battledore and shuttlecock by the girls, kiteflying by the boys and card games, called *karuta*, unique to Japan, by everybody. Generally speaking, the festivals held in Tokyo and southwestern Japan are more animated than those of Kyoto and its surrounding provinces, which have a more ancient origin and are more dignified, but not in the least lacking in color and charm.

On social and ceremonial occasions, especially during the New Year season, the long-sleeved, elaborately patterned *kimono* of the Japanese women comes into prominence. As in the case of the *obi*, the sash which holds the *kimono* together, there are various unwritten laws governing the colors and designs of the *kimono* to be used for different occasions.

EASTERN FOODS

Sukiyaki and *tempura* are the two names in Japanese cooking that are gaining international fame with the epicure. The former is a tasty preparation of thin slices of choice meat and vegetables, cooked in sweetened soya sauce, and the latter consists of fresh prawns and fish in season deep-fried in the finest vegetable oil. Japanese wine, called *sake*, is made from rice, and is drunk hot. Japanese beer is regarded by many as being among the best in the world. Japanese green tea is drunk not only at meal times but throughout the day at frequent intervals, and it is customary in the home to serve tea to a visitor regardless of the time of day.
. . . NIKKO NATIONAL PARK, north of Tokyo, is noted for its wonderful harmony of natural beauty and artistic splendor. The high light is **Toshogu Shrine**, built in 1636, one of the greatest monuments in the history of Japanese architecture, with its striking, richly decorated **Yomeimon Gate** and vermilion-painted, crescent-moon-shaped **Sacred Bridge**. Here also are Lake Chuzenji, a favorite for yachting, boating and trout fishing, and its **Kegon Waterfall**, probably the most famous cataract in Japan. In the winter, the wind turns the water into a cluster of gigantic, lacelike icicles. . . . West of Tokyo is the quiet seaside resort of KAMAKURA. Perhaps best-known of its many historic mementoes is **Diabutsu (Great Buddha)**, a superb bronze image measuring 42 feet in height and cast in 1252, standing in the grounds of the Kotokuin Temple. Although smaller than the Buddha in Nara, as a work of art it is considered far superior. The Hachiman Shrine, founded in 1063, has two museums: the new **Art Museum** and the **Kamakura Kokuhokan** (Municipal Art Museum of Kamakura), housing many rare art objects of the time when this city was the seat of government (1185-1336). . . . HAKONE, farther west, forms the southern part of the Fuji-Hakone National Park. A popular mountain and hot-spring resort, it has a superb view across **Lake Hakone** to **Mt. Fuji**, the highest mountain in Japan. Despite its great height, Fuji is not a difficult peak to scale and attracts hordes of climbers during the summer. . . . Glittering cloisonne ware are the prize of NAGOYA · · · · industrial center of central Japan. Nearby Ise-Shima National Park is known for the **Mikimoto pearl farms** in Ago Bay, as well as for its attractive beach scenery. The **Japan Alps** and **Joshin-etsu National Parks** offer pleasure to mountaineers and skiers throughout the year. . . . For about five months from the beginning of May, the unique **cormorant fishing** is to be seen on the Nagara River at GIFU · · · ·

IMPERIAL CITY TOWER, TOKYO

Philip Gendreau

LITTLE GIRL AT THE SHRINE OF NARA

Publishers' Photo S-

Every moonless night the flotilla of fishing boats glides down the river under the light of blazing torches, while teams of clever birds, held with strings by master fishermen, busily duck and dive and come up every few minutes with their catch of "ayu," a troutlike fish. Each cormorant wears a ring around the base of its neck so that it may not swallow any except very small fish. . . . The capital of the country for more than ten centuries (794-1869), KYOTO · · · · often called Japan's art center, is a city rich in historic association and legendary lore. **Nijo Detached Palace**, or Nijo Castle, originally belonged to the Tokugawa Shoguns and the grandeur of its decoration and embellishments is in striking contrast to the simplicity of the **Old Imperial Palace**. An embellishment in red lacquer is added to the beauty of **Heian Shrine**, with its beautiful garden of cherry trees, azaleas and irises. Other celebrated Buddhist fanes are the magnificent **Higashi** and **Nishi Honganji Temples**, both splendid examples of Japanese Buddhist architecture, and **Sanjusangendo**, also called the "Hall of Thousand Buddhas," an elongated temple constructed during the thirteenth century. Originally built as the country villa of a shogun, **Ginkakuji (Silver Pavilion)** has an elegant landscape garden and a ceremonial tearoom. Kyoto is also a city of festivals and colorful fetes, some gay and others solemn and mystical, including the distinctive **Miyako Odori** ("Cherry Dances") at the Kaburenjo Theater. Other fascinating festivals are the "Aoi Matsuri" (Hollyhock Festival) in May, a procession led by an imperial messenger and his suite in full court costume and said to trace its origin back to the sixth century, and the "Mibu Kyogen" in April, consisting of a number of pantomime farces originating in the thirteenth century. However, the **Gion Festival** in July, dating back to the ninth century, is the largest and gayest celebration and one of the country's best-known, with its parades of ornamental floats. . . . NARA, south of Kyoto, was the cradle of Japanese art, crafts and literature. Its **Nara Park**, largest in the country, is a natural woodland where tame deer roam at will. At the foot of Mt. Mikasa is **Kasuga Shrine**, reached along an avenue of antique stone lanterns. The shrine buildings, painted a bright vermilion and hung with some 1,000 metal lanterns, are celebrated for their classic architecture and enchanting setting. **Horyuji Temple**, consisting of a cluster of buildings, each a flawless masterpiece in its respective style of architecture, and housing a wealth of priceless objects of art, is the oldest existing temple in Japan and probably the most antique wooden structure in the world, since it traces its founding to the year 607. Another attraction is **Todaiji Temple**, noted for its big bell and colossal bronze Daibutsu, at 53 feet high the largest of its kind in the world, completed in 749 after repeated trials in casting. . . . The second largest city in Japan is OSAKA . . . . An important center of domestic and foreign commerce from the very early days of Japanese history, Osaka's position was further strengthened when in 1584 Toyotomi Hideyoshi had his residential **Osaka Castle** built here, one of the grandest and strongest castles in the country. **Nakanoshima** is the civic center, while **Sennichimae** and **Dotombori** are the pleasure quarters and **Shinsaibashi-suji** is the busiest shopping street. At the **Banraku Theater**, only one of its kind in Japan, are presented the celebrated Japanese puppet plays, employing the unique "Three-man Puppetry," each of the principal puppets being operated by three manipulators, producing amazing lifelike movements. The spring Sumo tournament takes place at the Prefectural Gymnasium. From here the visitor should take the steamer trip through the romantic **Inland Sea**, a scenic, island-studded waterway between Honshu Island and the islands of Shikoku and Kyushu. . . . A vivid reminder of Japan's grandeur in the feudal days is the stately donjon of **Egret Castle**, with its white walls and gracefully curving lines, at HIMEJI . . . . northwest of Osaka. . . . In HIROSHIMA . . . . where the atomic bomb exploded on August 6, 1945, stands the **Peace Tower**. Miyajima (Shrine Island), scenic gem of the Inland Sea, is noted chiefly for the **Itsukushima Shrine**, whose buildings are connected by corridors or galleries stretching out over the sea, so that at high tide the whole edifice seems to be floating on the surface of the sea. The "**torii**" gate of the shrine, made of camphor wood and over fifty feet high, rises out of the sea nearly 200 yards from the shore. . . . One of the best-known hot-springs resorts is BEPPU, on the eastern coast of Kyushu, the southernmost island. Featured here are hot sand baths on the beach, where people half bury themselves in the sand, soaked with hot-spring water gushing out from below. In the suburbs are numerous "Hells," including boiling ponds of hot-spring water, and bubbling mud.... An exotic port city is NAGASAKI . . . . at the western extremity of Kyushu. The **Uraba Mansion** located here is associated with *Madame Butterfly*. **Unzen National Park**, across the bay, is an internationally renowned summer resort. Among Nagasaki's many outstanding festivals is the October **Okunchi Festival**, when many colorful dances of Chinese origin are performed, of which the *Ja Odori*, or Dragon Dance, is the best. . . . SENDAI . . . . north of Tokyo, is the cultural center of northern Honshu. Well-known scenic attractions are **Matsushima** ("Pine Islands"), a great number of islands, each covered with aged, gnarled pine trees, dotting Matsushima Bay. At nearby Mt. Zao, an ideal ground for skiing, may be seen the "silver thaw," the weird spectacle of rows upon rows of trees coated with scintillating ice, standing like statues in the snow. A rural country from of old, the district still preserves a number of quaint customs and colorful events. Of these the "**Tanabata Matsuri**" or Star Festival is best-known for its gorgeous pageantry, when the whole city becomes alive with colored decorations of various designs. In the "**Nomaoi Matsuri**," or Horse Festival, held in July on the Hibarigahara Plain at **Haranomachi**, south of Sendai, gallant horsemen in ancient armor demonstrate their skill.... SAPPORO . . . . is the center of Hokkaido, the northernmost island. At Sankakuyama are many ski jumps, among which the "**Okura schanze**" is one of the best in the Orient. . . . SHIKOTSU-TOYA NATIONAL PARK includes **Lake Toya**, abounding in salmon trout and crabs, and **Jozankei Spa**, with excellent skiing slopes in the surrounding mountains . . . The small village of SHIRAOI, near Sapporo, is in the Ainu district, where these aborigines of Japan, now found only in Hokkaido, live in accordance with their old customs and manners.

CORMORANT FISHING ON THE NAGARA RIVER

Japan Tourist Assn.

ITSUKUSHIMA SHRINE

Japan Tourist Assn.

THEATER DISTRICT AT NIGHT, TOKYO

Philip Gendreau

TOKYO. An Oriental city that has been westernized, Tokyo, capital city of Japan since 1869, still retains much of her old eastern flavor and charm. Thus, she offers the most impressive exhibitions of unique Japanese attractions like the classical Kabuki dramas and Noh plays and *sumo*, or Japanese wrestling, along with fine modern accommodations, outstanding baseball games in Ueno Park, fashionable stores on Ginza and Nihombashi Streets and the bustling business center of Marunouchi. Since the dress, too, reflects both influences, women wearing *yofuku* (western clothing) may be seen walking along the streets with others in the traditional *kimono*. Geisha dancers and ritualistic tea ceremonies, Oriental art and architecture, Buddhist and Shinto temples, ancient popular festivals, gorgeous landscape gardens and Tokyo's famous cherry trees, lovely pearl jewelry, exquisite silks, costumed dolls, glistening lacquerware, delicate china and carved ivory are just a few fascinating features. In Japan, flower arrangement is a loving art and the people are true artists in the medium, so, throughout the city, unusual floral displays provide an additional pleasing touch to the colorful scene.

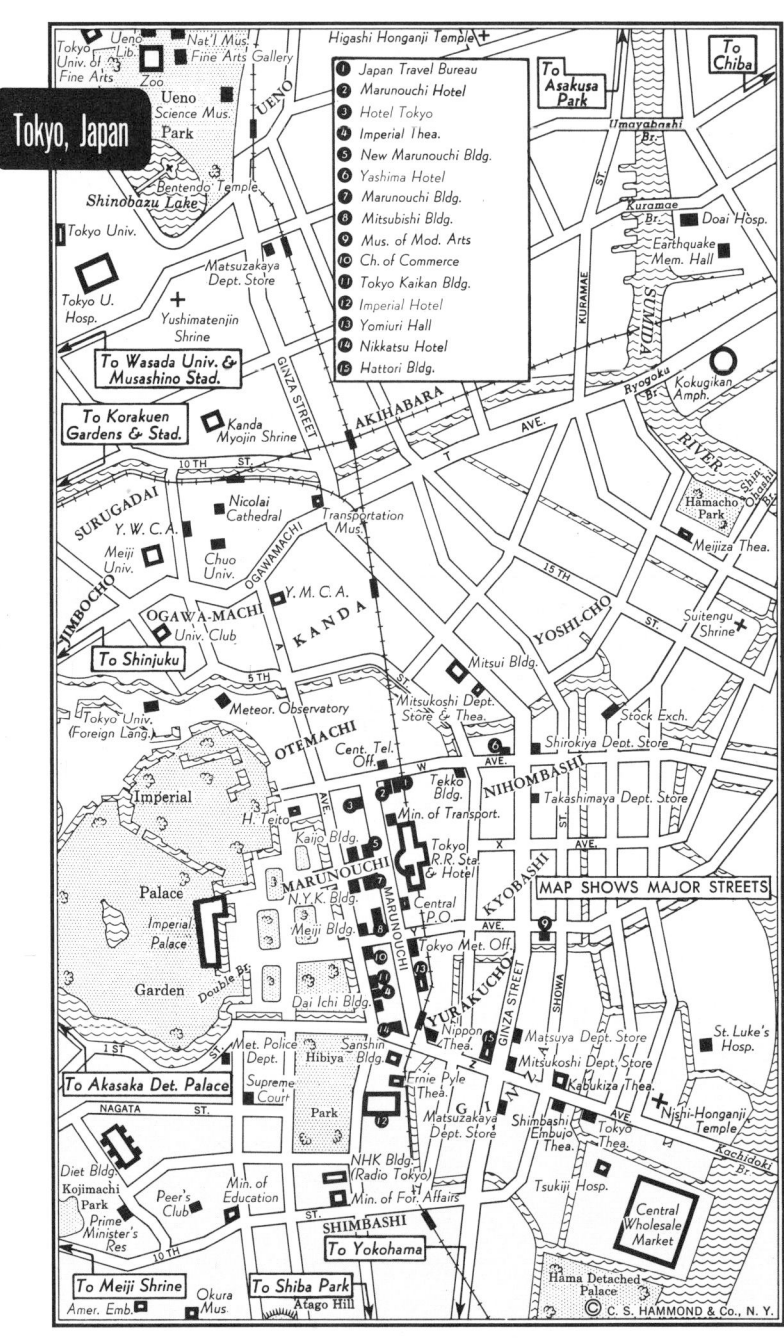

RAISING SILKWORMS

Japanese Govt.

Hong Kong and Singapore

TWO FABULOUS, EXCITING CITIES

Hong Kong and Singapore, two of the most colorful, if not *the* most colorful ports in the world, both lie on islands off the Asian mainland, the one off China, the other off the southern tip of the Malay Peninsula. They are the Occident's gateways to the East and the Orient's gateways to the West. Malays, Chinese, Indians, Pakistanis and Europeans, Muslims, Buddhists and Christians live side by side in peace and goodwill. With justice are these free ports called melting pots of East and West.

AND A VARIED MENU, TOO

With their cosmopolitan populations, Hong Kong and Singapore have, perhaps, the most varied collection of exotic foods in the world. In both cities, a visitor has the opportunity of enjoying a variety of Chinese dishes — and the best. The Chinese people are well-versed in good eating and Chinese food, particularly Cantonese dishes, is probably the best in the world. Cantonese food has been supplemented by Peking, Tientsin, Shanghai, Szechwan and Fukien dishes, including bird's nests, savory soups, shark's fins, stuffed chicken and an almost bewildering list of other delicacies. For the unconventional who like to go "slumming," Hokien Street in Singapore, at night with its brightly lit stalls along the sides of the street, provides the most delightful Hokien Mee (noodles boiled and flavored with prawns, vegetables and spices in a tasty bowl of soup). *Satay* (pieces of skewered meat, grilled with spice) is spoken of with relish among the various communities in Singapore. It is eaten with rice cakes, cucumber and peanut curry.

HONG KONG. Although bearing the official name Victoria, this renowned port is better known by the misnomer Hong Kong, the name of the British Crown Colony of which it is the administrative headquarters. Crowded into a narrow strip on the north shore of Hong Kong Island, it is only a mile from the Chinese mainland and is strategically situated for trade with that country. Hong Kong's island setting is one of the loveliest in the southern seas while its latitude gives it a climate much like that of Hawaii. Silhouetted against a cloud-capped mountain wall, its skyline is a unique mixture of ancient Eastern and modern Western architecture. Buildings, seemingly piled one atop the other, climb to precarious heights on Victoria Peak while others overflow onto land reclaimed from the fringes of its harbor. The narrow streets, the little shops, the docks and crowded quays are a teeming hodge-podge of humanity drawn from the corners of the earth. Bustling with activity, the harbor is a world within itself, pulsing with a never-ending flow of commerce that is the life blood of Hong Kong. Originally founded as a safe base from which opium could be smuggled into China, the city has now risen through legitimate trade to become one of the world's greatest seaports where the twain of Orient and Occident meet and merge in a kaleidoscopic scene.

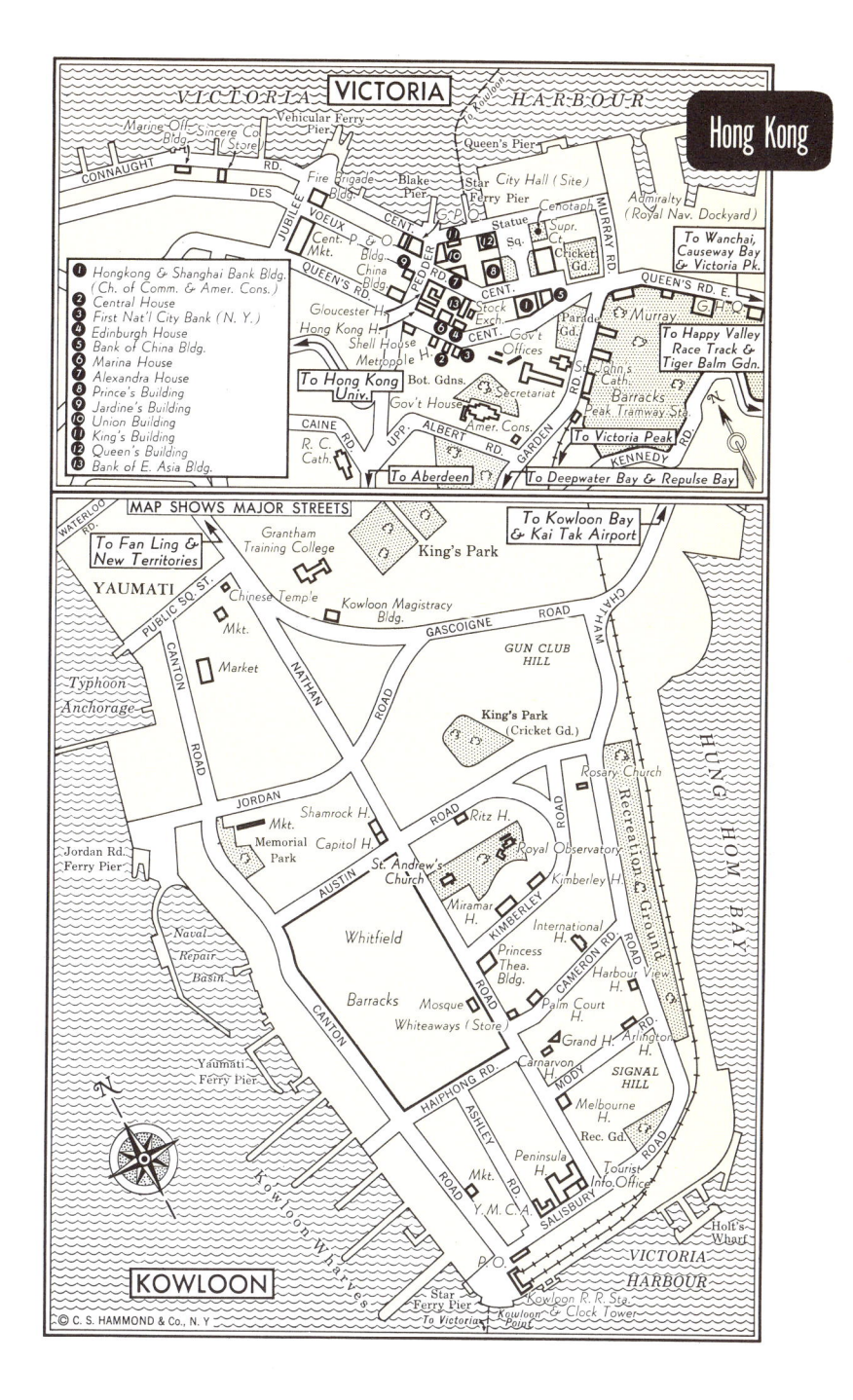

VICTORIA PEAK, HONG KONG

ON THE RIVER, SINGAPORE

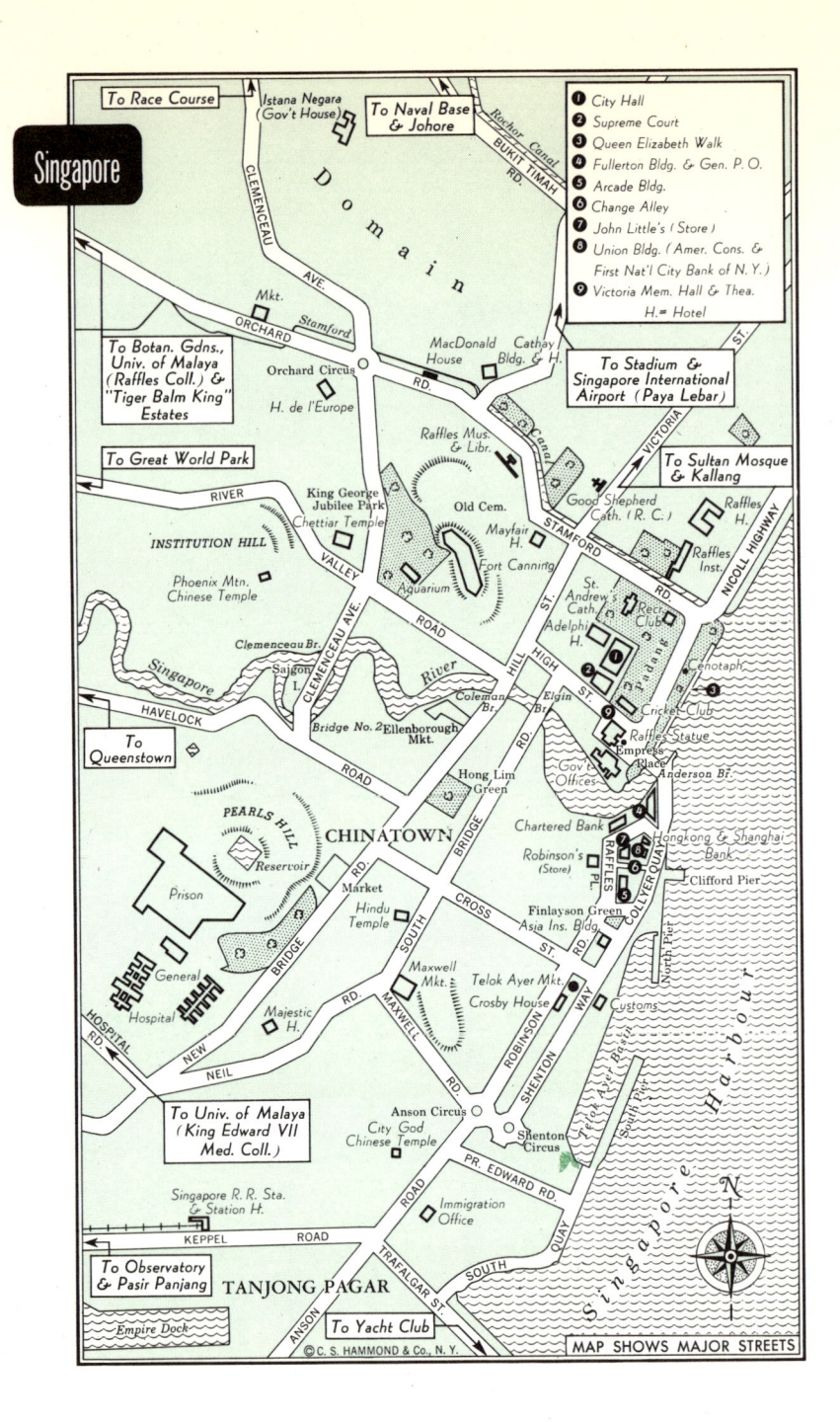

SINGAPORE. One of the most colorful ports in the world, the diamond-shaped island of Singapore lies on the southernmost tip of the Asiatic continent. It is the Occident's gateway to the East and the Orient's gateway to the West. Malays, Chinese, Indians, Pakistanis and Europeans, Moslems, Buddhists and Christians live side by side in peace and goodwill. Singapore is called with justice the melting pot of East and West. The name comes from two Sanskrit words, "Singa Pura," meaning the "Lion City," recalling the time before the arrival of Islam when Indian influence was predominent. Although the history of the colony trails back into the mists of time, it had fallen into obscurity when Sir Thomas Stamford Raffles landed here in 1819 and began to develop it from a mangrove swamp. As the "emporium and pride of the East," Singapore is a fascinating city where beautiful Eastern works of art, lavish carpets, carvings, jewelry, exotic Malay sarongs and Oriental slippers are sought. Famous Change Alley emits an atmosphere and glamour all its own, with a reputation as a bargain hunter's paradise. Comprising a motley collection of roadside stalls, the narrow alleyway is the place to find anything, from a needle to a bale of cloth or a Persian carpet.

BEACH SCENE — Singapore Public Relations Office

SINGAPORE RIVER — Singapore Public Relations Office

128

Thailand

of transportation not so long ago. Today planes and railways have largely supplanted the oxcart and elephant, as means of travel. However, river traffic is still important, and families live their entire lives on small craft floating on the waters of the country. In some rural areas elephants are still trained for heavy work; in the cities modern household appliances are obtainable. Missionaries introduced Western educational systems, medicine and modern methods in other fields. . . . In foods, rice and fish are chief staples; fruits and vegetables are plentiful and in the larger cities many well-known brands of canned goods are available. . . . In sports, Thailand's many rivers and its location on the Gulf of Siam offer opportunities for fresh and salt-water fishing. Outdoor sports have become very popular.

AYUTTHAYA, north of Bangkok on an island at the mouth of the Pa Sak River and a former capital, has interesting ruins. Destroyed in battle in the 18th century were a royal palace, several temples and pagodas. They are among the few relics left of Thailand's earlier times.

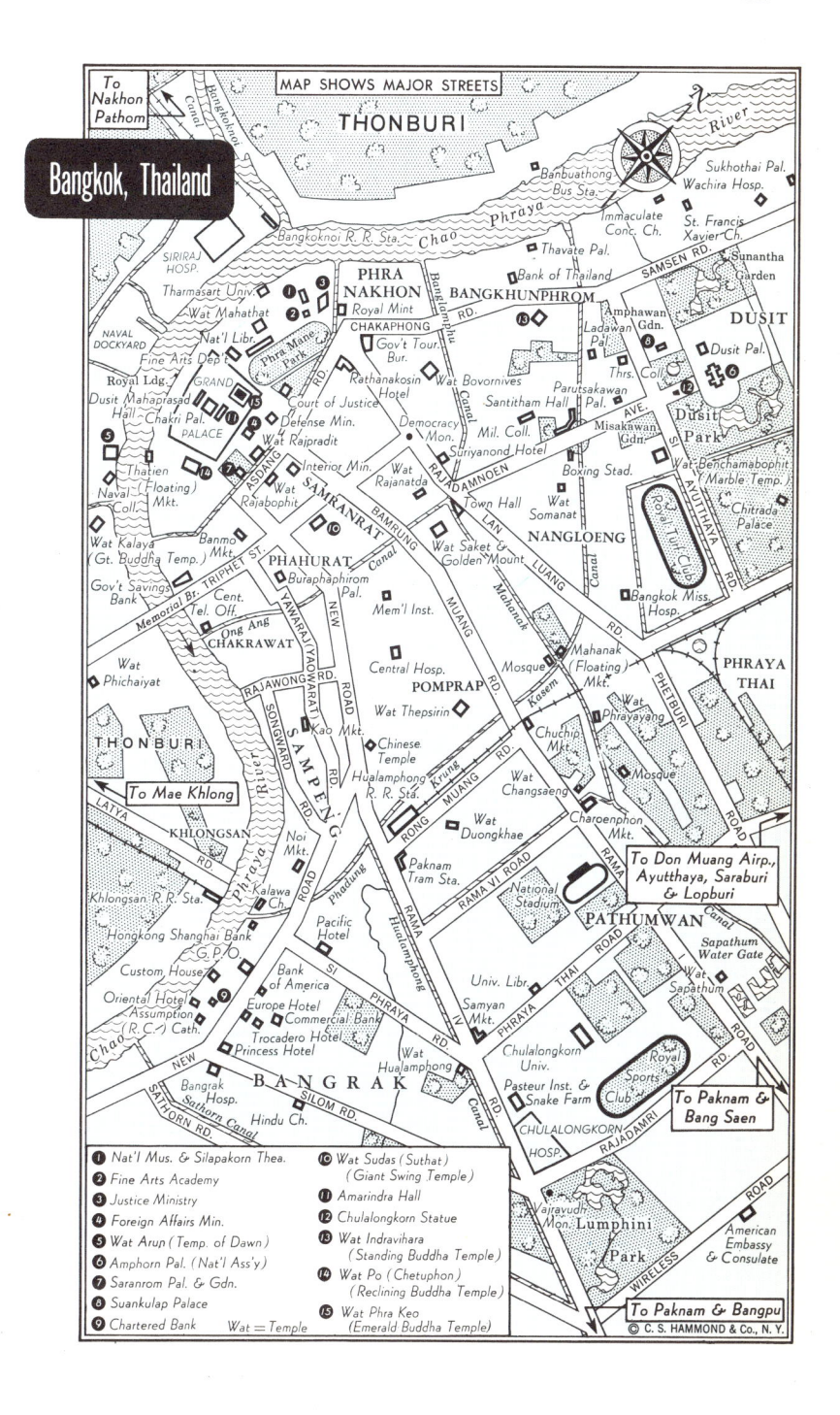

HINDU TEMPLE, BANGKOK TWA—Trans World Airlines

BANGKOK (Krung Thep). Bangkok with its network of canals jutting from the Chao Phraya River is sometimes likened to Venice. Until the innovation of motor vehicles these canals or "klongs" served as the city's principal thoroughfares. Even today, despite Bangkok's modern paved streets the klongs carry a heavy volume of water traffic. They are also the site of fabulous "floating markets" where in the early hours of the morning, sampans laden with fish and farm produce gather, offering their varied wares to Bangkok's housewives who move through the colorful maze in their own little boats. Capital of Thailand (Siam), Bangkok lies in the center of the world's greatest rice producing area. This commodity with tin, teak and rubber are the city's exports. Although too shallow to accommodate the larger ocean-going vessels, the harbor of Bangkok nevertheless attracts ships from every corner of the globe. Probably the city's most noted feature is its Buddhist monasteries with their lance-like spires and roofs of gleaming tile or ornately fashioned teakwood. These monasteries, over 400 in number, serve as homes for the yellow-clad Buddhist monks and also as schools, hospitals, clubs, playgrounds and centers of artistic and educational development. Most famous of Bangkok's shrines is the Temple of the Emerald Buddha containing a beautiful collection of art works associated with Thailand's ruling house, and the Emerald Buddha carved from a large piece of the precious green gem.

OXCARTS TO AIRPLANES

Thailand is one of the most fascinating countries to visit, for it has much to interest the traveler. Ornate temple spires beautify the skyline, and the gentle ringing of tiny bells form a pleasing background. It has cultural traditions several centuries old. The music differs from the Western style, but the dances are graceful and expressive; girls are trained in this art from childhood. In the decoration of silver articles the Siamese craftsman is unexcelled. . . . Oxcarts were one of the chief methods

Indonesia

BATAK VILLAGE, SUMATRA
Philip Gendreau

THE NECKLACE OF THE EQUATOR

Geographically, Indonesia is made up of the largest island group in the world, extending for well over 3,000 miles between the continents of Asia and Australia. Because it is situated across the equator, it has no "seasons" as we do — only wet and dry. But in spite of its tropical position, only a part of the land area suffers the sweltering heat usually associated with the equator. In the people, as well as the land, there is much diversity. In parts of the islands very ancient customs and traditions exist which seem to take one back to the days of the wild tribe, to magic and witchcraft; then above that layer is the gentle animism of the Hindu period. Mohammedanism has also contributed a great share in molding the life and attitudes of the Indonesian. Successive invasions down the centuries, and the seas which separate each island, have produced different physical types, a number of languages and a great variation of customs, dress and folklore. Indonesian scenery will be unforgettable with its volcanic mountains rising from the land, its temples of ancient grace and solemnity, its thriving cities and its blending of the old and the modern.

TAPE AND GOUDEK

Each city of Indonesia has its particular dish. Around the Bandung area *tapé*, the product of a ferment made from rice and applied to the cassava root, is considered a delicacy by the Javanese. Also, when ripe, the *tapé* is toasted until the outside of the pulpy mass is crackly and brown, at which time it is glazed with butter and has the appearance of gingerbread. Another delicacy is a type of gold fish (unlike our household variety). In Djokjakarta the famous dish is *goudek*, a vegetable dish spiced with red peppers and seasoned with herbs, moistened with cocoanut milk and completed by the addition of hard-boiled eggs. It is usually sold in the street by a vendor. *Krupuk* is a typically Indonesian food. Made from rice, wheat or cassava flour mixed with some savory ingredient, such as powdered fish, it is steamed, dried and then baked. It is eaten as a crunchy sort of cracker.

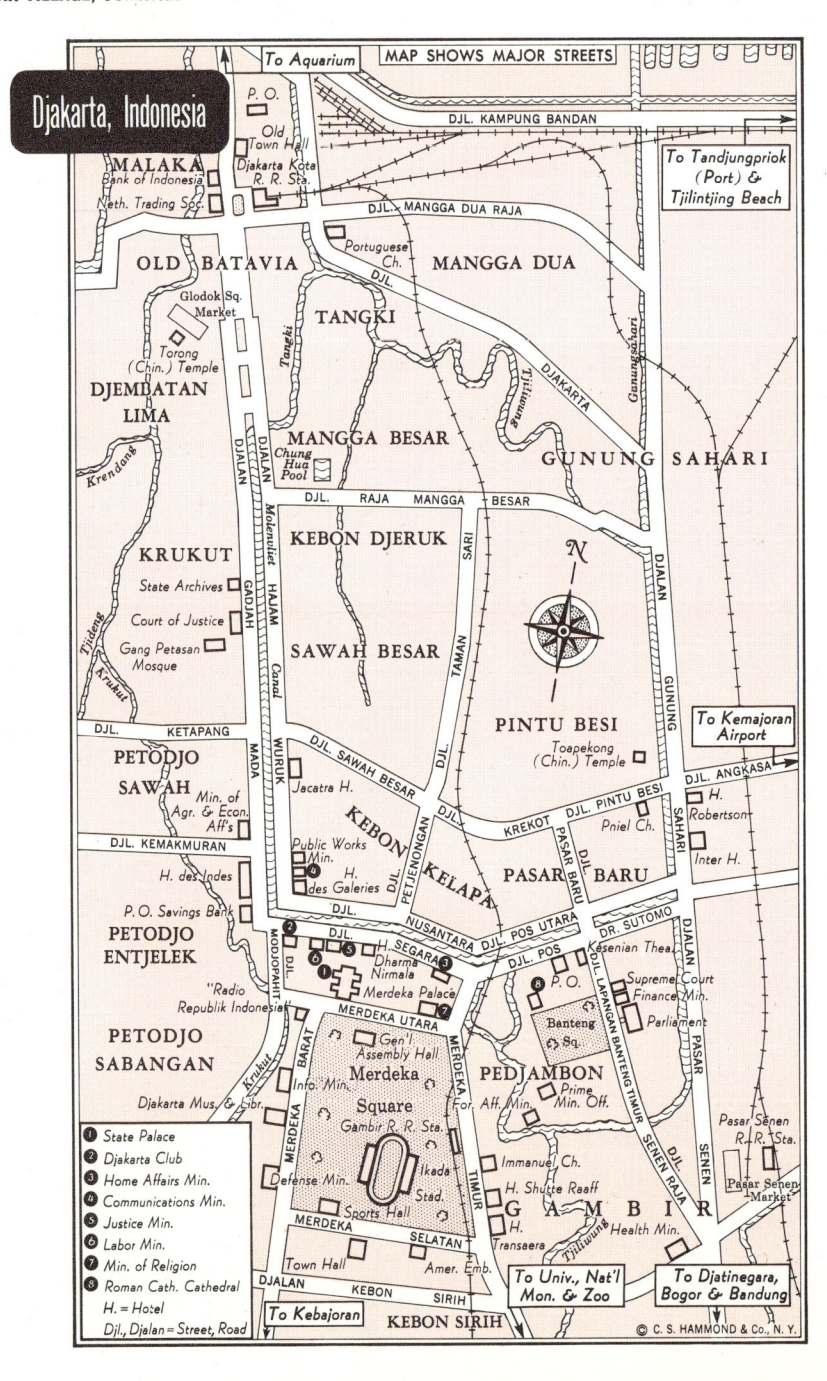

130

The Philippines

RURAL SCENE, PHILIPPINES

EAST MEETS WEST

An Occidental culture in an Oriental setting on tropical islands of great beauty, makes a visit to the Republic of the Philippines something to always remember. The Spanish discoverer, Ferdinand Magellan landed on the island of Cebu in 1521, claimed the archipelago for Spain and named it for his Spanish King, Philip II. Magellan found here a mixed race, with a culture largely Malayan, whose history dated back to very early times. Spain ruled the Philippines for almost four centuries, during which time Christianity and Spanish culture became firmly established. Spain ceded the islands to the United States in 1898 and rapid advances in education were made during that regime. A Commonwealth form of government was set up in 1935, and the Republic of the Philippines became an independent nation in 1946.... Filipinos are a literate people; many converse in Spanish and Tagalog (the national language), and English is spoken, or understood, almost everywhere in the principal islands. A "Filipino" may belong to any one of more than 40 ethnological groups, but the Filipinos themselves prefer to be classed as Malays.

The Philippine archipelago consists of more than 7,000 islands, rich in scenic beauty; nearly 900 of them are inhabited. Forest-covered mountains come down to the sea and waterfalls, wide fertile valleys, coastal plains, navigable rivers, bays and gulfs, white beaches and palm-shaded villages offer a pleasing panorama to the traveler arriving by sea. Inter-island boats maintain regular schedules, and traveling by air between most cities is easy and convenient. There are also many fine roads for the motorist to enjoy; the visitor from the West will find facilities resembling those at home. In most cities American and Continental cuisine of fine quality prevails, and there are many restaurants specializing in Oriental dishes. *Lechon* (roast pig served the Filipino way) is a great favorite; sea foods and native-style curried chicken are much in demand.

AROUND THE ISLAND

LUZON, in the north, is the largest and most important island of the Philippines, yet the primitive and the modern lie very close together; primitive Negritos, who still hunt with bows and arrows, live within 50 miles of cosmopolitan Manila. In northern Luzon the fertile fields in the Cagayan Valley produce the tobacco rolled into the famous Manila cigars and cigarettes. Guided tours of these vast fields include a visit to the factories to see how tobacco is processed. For the sports-lover visiting Manila there is golf, tennis, fishing, or watching horse races, cock fights or movies. To watch the Basque game of jai alai being played, is exciting; it is one of the fastest of all games.... Manila can also offer the visitor a gay night life with fine entertainment, excellent food and dancing to the music of good orchestras for additional enjoyment. Some hotels, restaurants and night clubs are air-conditioned.... QUEZON CITY north of Manila, has been the capital of the Republic of the Philippines since 1948. The city was named for Manuel L. Quezon, first President of the Commonwealth, who desired to build a new and more beautiful capital.... TAGAYTAY CITY, south of Manila, can give you an idea of how the Swiss Alps would look in the tropics: sun-clad instead of snow-clad. The city is located on a ridge overlooking **Lake Taal** with **Taal volcano** rising from the center of the lake — probably the lowest volcano in the world. From the heights of the city the view is magnificent.... BAGUIO, the "City of Pines," some 130 miles north of Manila, lies 5,000 feet above sea level in wooded mountains. It is an ideal vacation resort with good hotels, golf courses and other attractions.... In this vicinity are the famous **Rice Terraces** which wind more than a thousand miles around steep mountainsides. Experts consider them to be a greater engineering feat than the Pyramids of Egypt; they are an awe-inspiring sight. The Igorots built these step-like terraces over a period of 1,500 years.... The market place in Baguio is usually crowded with Igorots and other primitive people, selling their native handicrafts.... LAS PINAS, a quaint town within easy motoring distance of Manila, has in its church an organ made entirely of bamboo wood over 100 years ago — possibly the only one of its kind in the world.... A trip up the **Pasig River** to **Laguna Province** provides an interesting view of life along its shores.... A thrilling experience is a visit to **Pagsanjan Falls**, where skilled boatmen — two to a canoe — take you up to the falls and "shoot the rapids."... From LEGASPI, a busy city in a cocoanut-producing area, the traveler may drive to several scenic spots: **Tiwi Hot Springs**, **Bato Lake** and the **Kagsawa ruins**.... High on **Mt. Mayon** volcano is The Rest House. Wild strawberries growing in the volcanic soil make this a popular place to visit.

VISAYAS is the name given to the central group of islands between Luzon and Mindanao, the larger ones being CEBU, NEGROS, PANAY, LEYTE and BOHOL.... CEBU, on the island of Cebu is a beautiful city. In 1565 Legaspi founded a Spanish settlement on the site of Magellan's landing in 1521. Still to be seen is a Cross, believed to have been planted by the discoverer's own hand, marking the spot where he placed the flag of discovery.... A launch trip to nearby **Mactan Island** is a popular excursion. A

NATIVE TRAFFIC

monument stands on the site where Magellan was killed by a native chief. . . . In the church of San Agustin is a doll-like image said to have been given to a local chief by Magellan; it has been venerated as "Santo Niño" (Holy Child) for four centuries. . . . Cebu's cosmopolitan life blends well. There are golf and tennis clubs and an open-air night club has a natural swimming pool. . . . BACOLOD, on NEGROS ISLAND, is in a large sugar-producing area. Guided tours may be taken through immense fields of sugar cane and the larger mills. A prosperous city, it has beautiful parks, wide boulevards and palatial homes. . . . ILOILO, on the island of PANAY, also enjoys prosperity from the sugar industry. However, it is especially noted for its "pina cloth," fine, silk-like material made from the fibres of a certain type of pineapple plant, native to this region, and woven into wearing apparel. . . . Villa Beach is a popular resort a few miles west. . . . MINDANAO, the second largest island in the Philippine archipelago, is the most southerly of the principal islands. . . . ZAMBOANGA, one of its chief cities, is a charming place to visit. Hanging gardens rise above lily ponds and fountains; boulevards wind through cocoanut groves and rice fields; orchids grow in profusion in the hills, filling the air with their fragrance. Zamboanga is the home of the Moros, who are not a race but a Mohammedan people living much as their ancestors did in villages built on bamboo stilts. Their colorful attire and their handicrafts make a visit to the Mohammedan areas of Mindanao a "must". . . . A trip to TALUKSANGAY will give you the interesting experience of seeing a primitive Moro ceremonial dance, held in the Mohammedan Mosque. . . . A trip to historic Fort Pilar and beautiful Pasonanca Park would be interesting. The gaily colored sails of the Moro's fishing boats, called vintas, dotting the seas, add their charm to picturesque Zamboanga. . . . DAVAO has a beauty typical of the South Seas, yet it is an important seaport and is the center of a large abaca growing area. Abaca is a tough-fibred hemp from which Manila rope is made. The plantations are well worth visiting. . . . West of Davao lies Mt. Apo, the Philippine's highest mountain (9,690 feet), easily seen from the city on clear days. . . . Around the town of DEL MONTE are large pineapple plantations and a canning plant where visitors are welcome. . . . There are other interesting places to visit on the island of Mindanao: Lanao Lake in the province of LANAO, where Moro communities surround the lake; BUKIDNON province, a pineapple plantation area and COTABATO province where native Moro villages are the attraction. Moros are skilled pearl divers and fishermen; beautiful pearls and brightly colored fish are for sale in the native markets, and their metal work and coral jewelry are much in demand.

On the island of JOLO, south of Mindanao, Moros form a large part of the population. Here lived the Sultan of Sulu, once the ruler of the Philippine Mohammedans. Travelers, who come to this southern island, would find a visit to Sulu's Mosque very interesting. . . . The islands of LEYTE, MINDORO, SAMAR and PALAWAN are mountainous, thickly forested and have much of scenic interest to the visitor.

The Philippine islands form a compact group and are considered by many to be the most fertile tropical islands in the world. Less than 50 miles off the coast of northern Mindanao is the greatest ocean depth on this planet. Mt. Everest could be completely submerged in this "deep."

MANILA. With its background deeply rooted in Western civilization, Manila is an Occidental city in an Oriental setting. Manila's streets are lined by modern concrete and steel structures and with its many uniquely Western features it more closely resembles an American city than do the other cities of the Philippines.

PHILIPPINE LEGISLATURE

Philip Gendreau

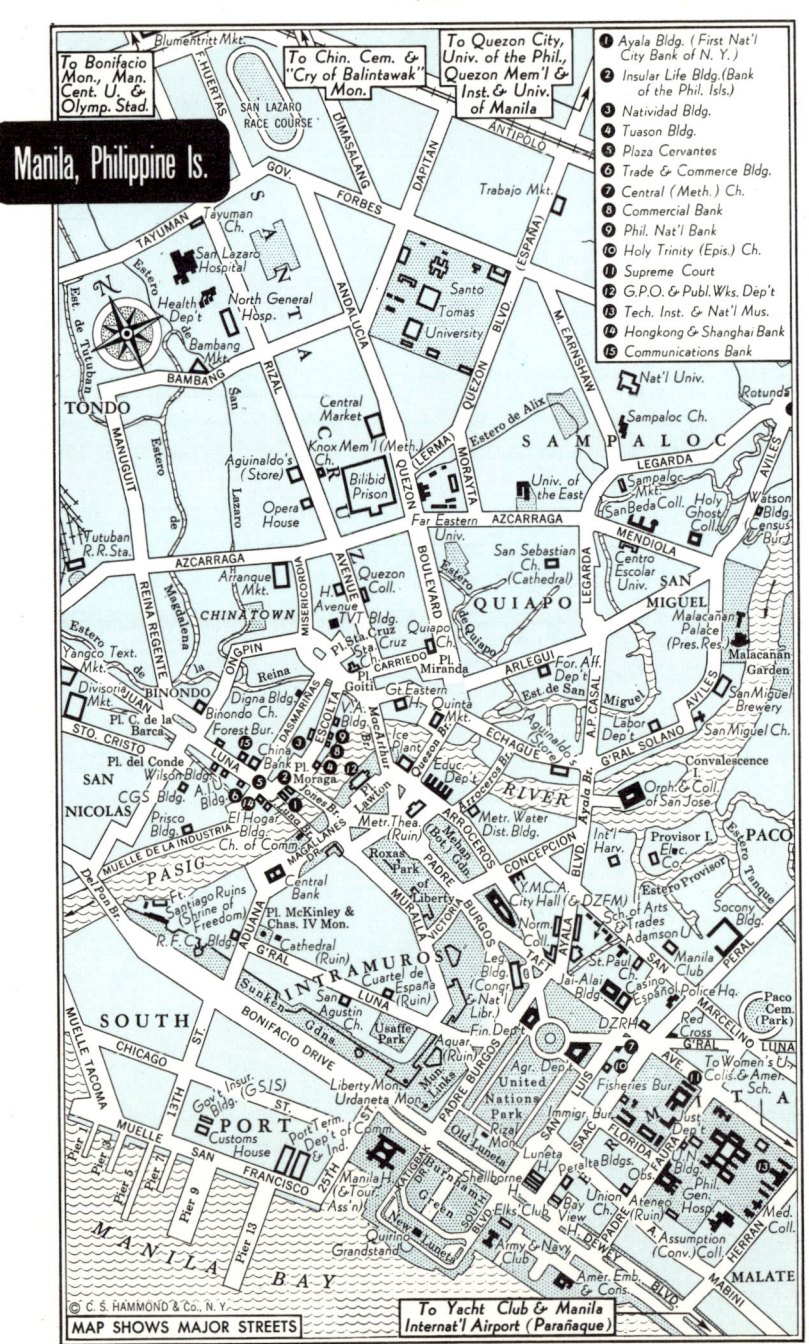

THE PACIFIC

Often called "the sunshine continent" because of its fine climate, Australia is a wonderful place to vacation, since regardless of the time of year, you can enjoy either swimming and fishing, golf on the well-kept courses, or excellent skiing during the winter months. The people "down under" are similar to Americans, although their colorful speech will amuse and fascinate you. Any place except a city or town is called "the bush," and the ones who live there are "bushmen." Wool is the foundation of this country's prosperity, and the sheep from which it comes is called a "jambuck;" while the ranch is a "station." Two trademarks of Australia are the kangaroo, a marsupial peculiar to this continent, and the eucalyptus or "gum tree," found throughout the land and often achieving the height of our California redwoods. Canberra, the capital, and Sydney, the "harbor city," are gay and cosmopolitan, with much to please the sight-seer.

Also rising out of the Pacific are the mountainous "Happy Isles," New Zealand. Here is everything to make a visitor happy: a cool moist climate, exquisite scenery, unsurpassed facilities for sportsmen, and its Polynesian people, the Maori, who are tall, handsome and friendly, and make this a veritable Shangri-la for the vacationer. Although most of the Maoris still live on small farms and keep to their ancient customs, the progressive British population is ambitious and proud of their cities such as Wellington, the capital. This metropolis, built on steep hills overlooking a majestic harbor, has cable cars similar to those in San Francisco to facilitate ascending the hills, as well as all other modern conveniences for present-day living.

On the other hand, life in the Fiji Islands has remained unchanged for more than a century, with East Indians, native Fijians and Europeans enjoying a carefree existence in this South Sea island paradise. Any tourist who wants to "get away from it all" can do just that in delightful Tahiti, where the thatched huts of the picturesque villages, the palm-encircled beaches and the sound of the rolling surf are the main attractions.

Orchids growing wild everywhere, palm trees swaying in the cool breeze, hibiscus, poinciana, and the treasured Bird of Paradise dotting the landscape—all this is Hawaii. Deep-sea fishing, spear-fishing off the reefs, sunning, swimming or surfboard riding at the famous beaches such as Waikiki, feasting on roast pig and poi at a luau, and virtually "going native"—these are the highlights of your Hawaiian holiday. An extinct volcano, the legendary Diamond Head, adds to the magical spell cast by these Pacific Islands, whose charming capital, Honolulu, is truly a city of friendship and love, "Aloha." This famous greeting and farewell word, coupled with the fragrant flower leis that are given to all visitors epitomize the gracious yet simple spirit of this enchanting place.

The Philippines too have a welcome to tourists, "Mabuhay," meaning long life and Godspeed in these islands where, having been under the rule of Spain for almost four centuries, the customs and culture are still predominantly Spanish. Here the traveler encounters great contrast, for cities such as Manila, with its gay night life, hotels and horse races, are mingled with rural scenes of rice fields, coconut groves and sugar cane plantations. These beautiful tropical islands provide the visitor with another varied and exotic vacation in the Pacific.

Hwang
Tsingtao
Seoul
SOUTH KOREA
Sea of Japan
Yellow Sea
Pusan
Hiroshima
Kyoto
Fuji
TOKYO
Sendai
Kamakura
Nagoya
OSAKA
Nagasaki
Beppu
Shikoku
Kyushu
Honshu
JAPAN
Yangtze
Nanking
Wuhan
CHINA
SHANGHAI
East China Sea
Changsha
Foochow
RYUKYU IS.
Naha
Okinawa
Taiwan Str.
Taipei
Canton
Macao (Port.)
Tainan
Kowloon
Victoria
HONG KONG (Br.)
Pingtung
Taiwan (Formosa)
BONIN ISLANDS
Iwo Jima
VOLCANO ISLANDS
Marcus I.
Midway Is.
Kure
HAW
South China Sea
Philippine Sea
Luzon
Baguio
Quezon City
Manila
REPUBLIC OF THE PHILIPPINES
Legaspi
Samar
Palawan
Iloilo
Bacolod
Cebu
Negros
Sulu Sea
Zamboanga
Mindanao
Davao
MARIANA ISLANDS
Garapan
Saipan
Tinian
Agana
Guam
Wake I.
International Date Line
Micronesia
Ulithi
Yap
Eniwetok
Bikini
MARSHALL ISLANDS
Kwajalein
PALAU ISLANDS
TRUK IS.
Ponape
Kusaie
CAROLINE ISLANDS
TERRITORY OF THE PACIFIC ISLANDS
Celebes Sea
Borneo
Manado
Ternate
Equator
Makassar Str.
Melanesia
Bairiki
Tarawa
GILBERT IS.
Nauru
Ocean I.
ADMIRALTY ISLANDS
New Ireland
Celebes
Buru
Amboina
Ceram
Makassar
Hollandia
NETHERLANDS NEW GUINEA
TERR. OF NEW GUINEA
New Guinea
Goroka
Madang
Rabaul
Kokopo
New Britain
Bougainville
Choiseul
Lae
Wau
PAPUA
SOLOMON IS.
Santa Ysabel
Malaita
ELLICE IS.
INDONESIA
Lombok
Flores
Dili
Timor
Sumbawa
Sumba
Kupang
Arafura Sea
Torres Str.
Port Moresby
Samarai
Solomon Sea
Honiara
Guadalcanal
SANTA CRUZ IS.
Vanikora
Fongafale
Funafuti
Polynesia
Timor Sea
Darwin
Arnhem Land
Gulf of Carpentaria
Cape York Pen.
Great Barrier Reef
Coral Sea
Espiritu Santo
NEW HEBRIDES
Malekula
Vila
Efate
Ahau
Rotuma
FIJI
WALLIS IS.
Matautu
Lambasa
Vanua Levu
Ba
Nandi
Levuka
Viti Levu
Suva
ISLANDS
Birdum
NORTHERN TERRITORY
Cairns
Townsville
Flinders
OCEAN
Broome
New Caledonia
Bourail
Nouméa
Plum
LOYALTY IS.
I. of Pines
Tongatapu
Great Sandy Desert
WESTERN AUSTRALIA
Alice Sprs.
QUEENSLAND
Rockhampton
Great Dividing Range
Gibson Desert
AUSTRALIA
LAMINGTON NAT. PK.
Brisbane
Southport
Stanthorpe
Grafton
Norfolk I.
Kingston
SOUTH AUSTRALIA
Great Victoria Desert
Coober Pedy
L. Eyre
Darling
NEW SOUTH WALES
Lord Howe I.
Abrolhos Is.
Geraldton
Kalgoorlie
Port Augusta
Broken Hill
Newcastle
SYDNEY
North Cape
North I.
Auckland
INDIAN
Nullarbor Plain
Great Australian Bight
Pt. Pirie
Adelaide
Mildura
Murray
Katoomba
Canberra
Kosciusko
MT. BUFFALO NAT. PK.
Tasman Sea
Perth
Darling Range
Fremantle
Port Lincoln
Victor Har.
VICTORIA
NEW ZEALAND
Rotorua
Taupo
EGMONT NAT. PK.
TONGARIRO NAT. PK.
Kangaroo I.
Daylesford
MELBOURNE
Wilson's Promontory
Wellington
Busselton
Denmark
Albany
Mt. Gambier
Warrnambool
Bass Str.
Launceston
NELSON LAKES NAT. PK.
Hanmer
MT. COOK NAT. PK.
Christchurch
CHATHAM IS.
TASMANIA
MT. FIELD NAT. PK.
Hobart
Port Arthur
South I.
Timaru
Queenstown
FIORDLAND NAT. PK.
Dunedin
Half-moon Bay (Oban)
Stewart I.

Notes and Itinerary

Australia

"DOWN UNDER"

Australia is a young, vigorous country of rugged individualism. As many American GI's found out during the last war, the people of our two countries are very much alike, and Americans visiting this friendly nation will feel right at home. In a land of sunshine and temperate climate, these people are outdoor-minded and sports-loving. Australia is noted for its beaches, and the snowfields in the Australian Alps are even larger than Switzerland's. Especially fascinating to the visitor are the strange animals and plants common only to this small continent, like the well-known kangaroo; the koala, the original "Teddy bear"; the mixed-up platypus and the dingo, or wild dog; the speedy emu; the highly popular kookaburra, often known as the "laughing jackass," and the bird-world's greatest mimic—the lyre bird; the gum tree (eucalyptus), in some places towering higher than the California redwoods; the freak bottle tree (baobab), which stores water in its trunk, and the jarrah, one of the world's hardest woods. Another distinctive feature of the country is the approximately 50,000 aborigines living in the far north, in Central Australia or on reservations. One of the most primitive peoples in existence and the oldest living species of man, they live the life of the Stone Age.

ABOUT FOOD

Passion fruit is an Australian specialty; no fruit salad is served without it and it is used in icings and fillings as well. However, if you want to sample the real national dish, order crayfish or steak and fried eggs.

ROUND A CONTINENT

SYDNEY. Of all cities outside the United States, visiting Americans probably feel most at home in Sydney. With the same language and heritage, plus similar characteristics of youthful vigor and rugged vitality, Australia is much like our own country, anyway, and with her skyline and tempo of living, fashionable stores, good night clubs and up-to-date theaters, Sydney resembles an American city more than any other "down under." Cradle of Australia and her largest city, as well as the third city of the British Commonwealth, this trade and transportation center is situated on one of the world's finest and most beautiful harbors, dominated by her famous landmark, the Sydney Harbour Bridge. Because of her relatively venerable age in relation to other Australian settlements, she embraces old historical buildings situated along the picturesque winding streets that follow the former cattle-wagon paths near the harbor in addition to new modern buildings along the outskirts of this area. Sydney is also a well-known resort, with no less than twenty-one ocean surf beaches and at least half a dozen other beaches on the harbor or Botany Bay — all free to the public.

Southwest of Sydney is **CANBERRA**, the garden city and capital of Australia, located in a broad valley in the foothills of the Australian Alps. A planned, model city, built from the design of Walter Burley Griffin, an architect from Chicago, its wide, sweeping avenues, brilliant gardens and modern buildings give a magnificent setting to the nation's Parliament. The big, low **Parliament House**, with its uncluttered, dignified lines, the fortress-

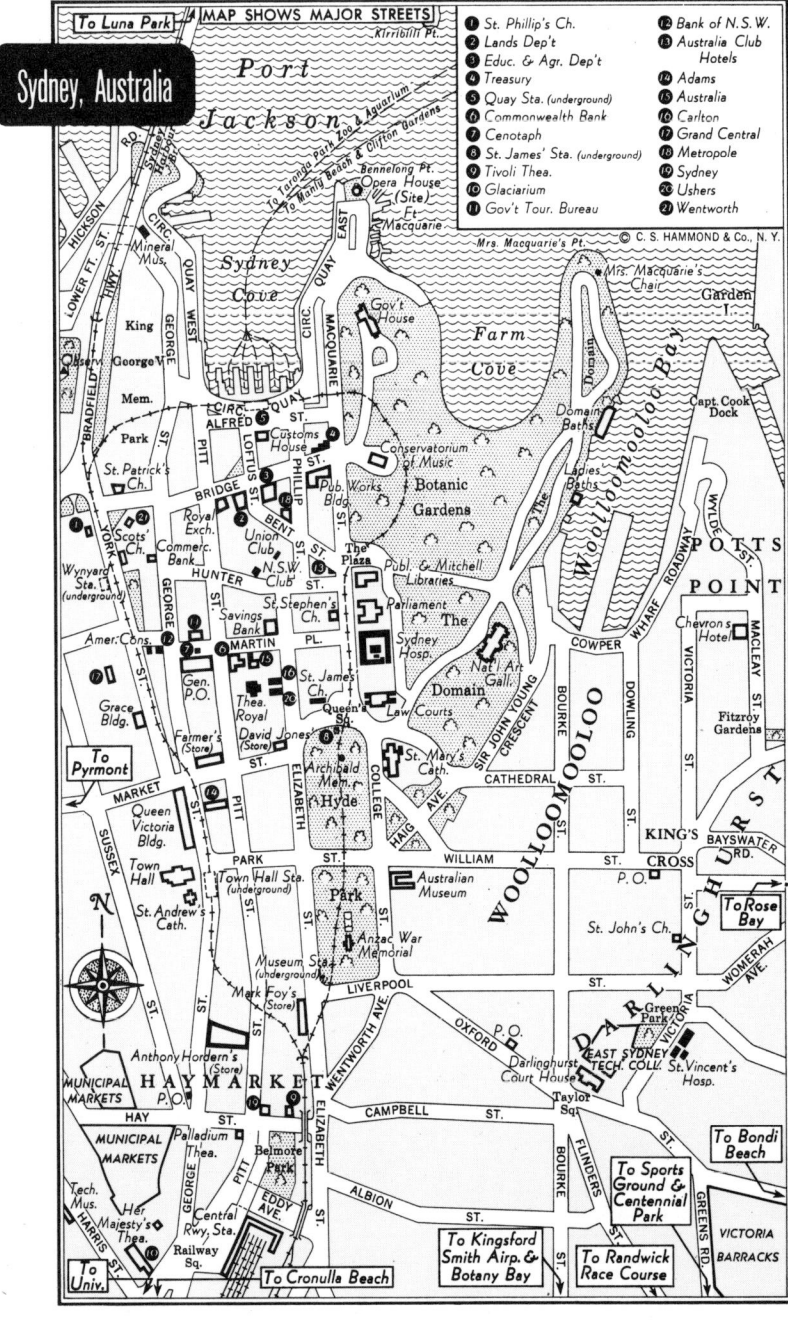

SAILING, SYDNEY HARBOUR
Australian News and Information Bureau

AUSTRALIA

1. A koala bear, the original "teddy bear"
2. Beach scene with excursion steamer on Great Barrier Reef
3. Girl with beautiful, natural-color coral
4. Typical Queensland bush scene with Kerry fat cattle

AUSTRALIA

1. Rose garden near Parliament House, Canberra
2. Artesian well in western Queensland
3. Two gray cockatoos, native to Australia
4. Beach scene at Sydney

AUSTRALIA

1. Watson's bay, a quiet seaside cove
2. Girl with young red kangaroo
3. Stockman and his dog with flock in new South Wales
4. Rawlinson Range, a flat tableland, typical of central Australia

AUSTRALIA

1. Weather station near Mt. Koskiusko
2. Girl with Wallaby
3. Pink cockatoo, one of the more exotic native birds
4. Riding a giant tortoise on the beach

like Australian War Memorial Museum, the Governor-General's and Prime-Minister's residences and the other public buildings are Canberra's main attractions.

MELBOURNE. A great industrial and financial center of Australia, Melbourne also is one of her chief ports. Despite the heavy industrialization, though, the city has an air of quiet and dignity reminiscent of Boston, coupled with an attractive symmetry of wide streets, pleasant parks and beautiful gardens. In Fitzroy Gardens is Captain Cook's Cottage, where Australia's discoverer lived. It was re-erected after shipment intact from Yorkshire, England. All these elements combine to produce an excellent background for leisure as well as work. And Melbourne is not staid and dull; on the contrary, recreation is most important to her. It is here that the Melbourne Cup race is run in November — one of the country's greatest sporting events and a day of national festivity — and the finals of the Australian Rules season are played in September — one of the world's fastest football games. Thus, it is fitting that Melbourne was chosen as the site of the 1956 Olympic Games, and for the first time in history the symbolic Olympic flame was carried by plane from Greece into the Southern Hemisphere, to the Melbourne Cricket Ground, beginning the sixteenth modern Olympiad.

HOBART, on the island of Tasmania, the heart-shaped pendant to Australia known as the Island State or the Apple Isle, is backed by one of the most beautiful settings of any city. Besides this spectacular setting on the Derwent River, overshadowed by towering **Mount Wellington**, its winding, hilly streets, old narrow byways of the convict days and the small docks used by the fishing fleets, all contribute to its intriguing character. A trip from Hobart to **Port Arthur**, on the densely wooded Tasman Peninsula, will take you past a wild rugged coast to the ruins of what was the most famous of Australia's penal settlements. . . . The capital city of South Australia, famed for its wheat and fine wines, is **ADELAIDE**, called the "city of churches." Backed by the **Mount Lofty Ranges**, the city proper is separated from the suburbs by an attractive "green belt" of more than 1,700 acres of **park, garden** and **sport grounds**. There are also several excellent beaches, such as **Victor Harbour**, and exciting deep-sea fishing in the waters of **Spencer Gulf**. Here in the heart of the wine country, at Barbossa Valley, visitors may take part in the **Barbossa Harvest Festival**. Another interesting trip may be taken to **Mount Gambier**, where an extinct volcano has formed four wonderful lakes. Adelaide's Museum and Art Gallery houses a notable collection of Australian art. . . . Inland is the unique town of COOBER PEDY, which because of the continual heat is built beneath the surface of the earth. Its opal mines are renowned. . . . At the isolated settlement of ALICE SPRINGS, in the heart of the lonely, sparsely settled lands of the interior, are vast aboriginal reservations, the haunts of buffalo and crocodiles. . . . The famous **Golden Mile,** richest strip of land in the world, is in the desert city of **KALGOORLIE**, Australia's most productive gold-bearing region. . . . PERTH, the largest city on the west coast, is the center of the timber and mineral area. With more sunshine than any other city in the country, it is famous for the gay, varicolored wildflowers, like the green and red kangaroo paw, that carpet the surrounding hills in the spring. The University of Western Australia was the first free university in the British Empire. From here visits can be made to the tall timber area, specifically the Karri and Jarrah forests, in Australia's southwest corner and the fascinating and extensive caves in the Yallinup district. . . . North of Perth is the all-year-round seaside resort of GERALDTON . . . Forty miles offshore in the Indian Ocean are the **ABROLHOS ISLANDS**, the southernmost coral isles in the world, where swimming enthusiasts are attracted by the beaches and **warm, clear water** and gourmets by the outstanding **sea food**. . . . Still farther up the coast is BROOME, home port for the pearl luggers of the Indian Ocean. . . . DARWIN, in the northern cattle-raising region, is one of the world's last frontier towns, reminiscent of the unsophisticated towns

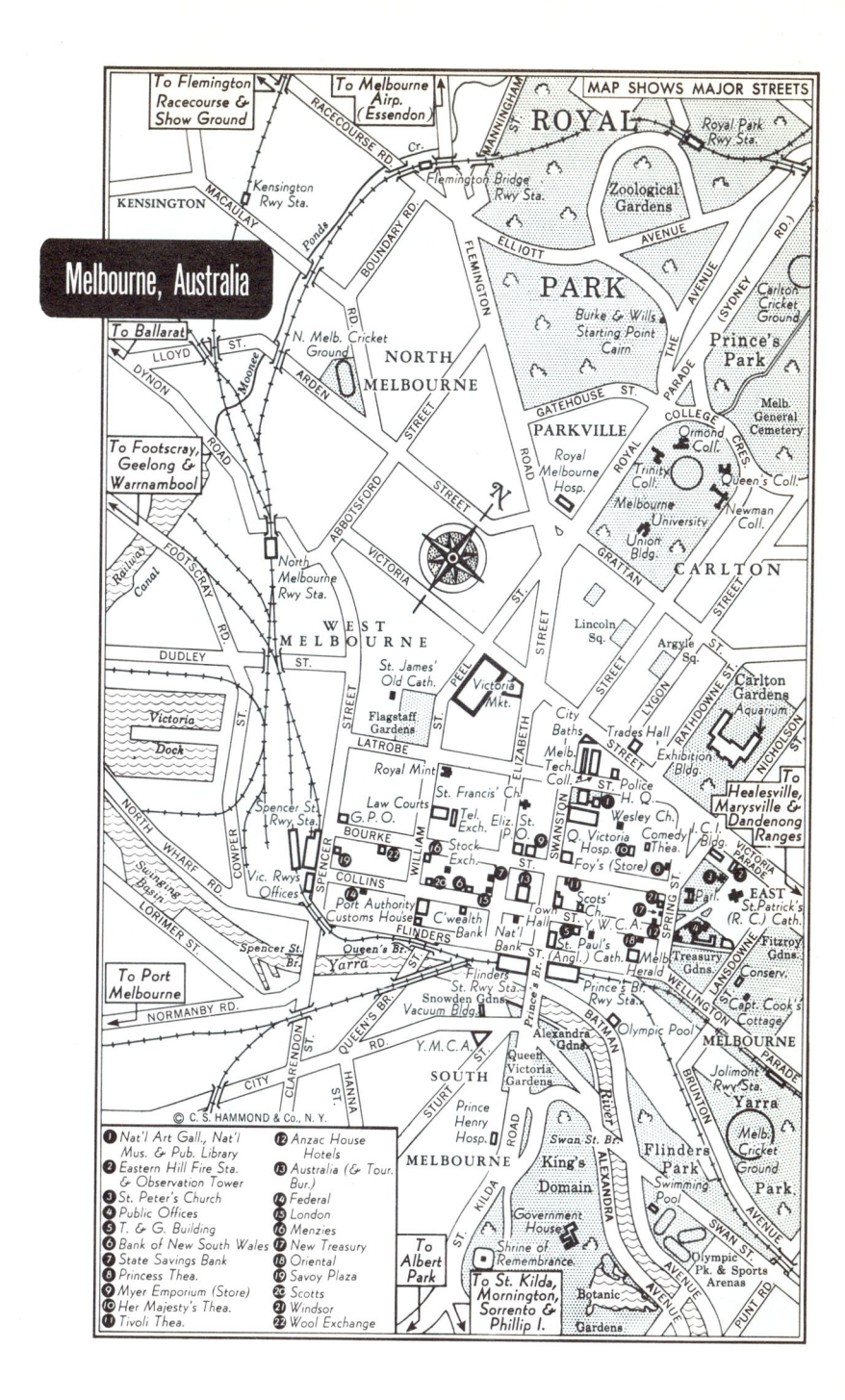

WOOL DROVING ON KANEMBLA SHEEP STATION, NEW SOUTH WALES

Philip Gendreau

of the old American Wild West. Here are found some of the world's real adventurers: the pearl divers of the Arafura Sea, the crocodile hunters of Arnhem Land and the gold prospectors from the lonely inland. This town is also the favorite with big-game hunters, since from Darwin experienced Northern Territory guides conduct **shooting parties** in search of buffalo and crocodiles. . . . The railroad trip from **CAIRNS**, Queensland's northernmost port, to the Atherton Tableland provides many awe-inspiring views as the train slowly climbs up round the mountainside from the coastal plains below, with its bright tropical foliage and yellow and green canefields. The Barron Falls, although not as magnificent as some of the world's other famous falls, are just as beautiful as the others and are one of the continent's greatest sights. . . . Dotted with gardens bright with tropical flowers and shrubs and enjoying a climate that is the envy of the rest of Australia, **BRISBANE**, capital of the sugar-cane state of Queensland, is a city noted for its friendliness and **gorgeous scenery**. Although not a city of outstanding buildings, the City Hall is magnificent. The rolling **Darling Downs** are a richly productive growing region. Visits may be made to **Lone Pine Fauna Preserve** and the tropical fruit farms at **Oasis Tourist Gardens and Redlands**. The south coast beaches, especially Southport, **Surfers' Paradise** and **Coolangatta**, are favorites with vacationers. . . . One of the world's major scenic attractions is the **GREAT BARRIER REEF**, the mighty coral formation fringing Australia's east coast for 1,200 miles. **Brilliant coral** lies just below the surface of the sea and the water between the white-beached, palm-fringed islands teem with strange **tropical fish**, making this an ideal region for a lazy carefree vacation, especially for naturalists, anglers and sightseers. . . . **NORFOLK ISLAND**, an Australian possession 930 miles east of the continent, is being developed as a tourist resort, since it has an equable climate and fine scenery. Many of the island's inhabitants are descendants of the mutineers of the renowned ship *Bounty*.

YORK STREET, SYDNEY

LAKE MALYYULLUMBO

ABORIGINES

CITY HALL, BRISBANE

138

New Zealand

HOME OF THE MAORI

A mountainous country, New Zealand is halfway between the Equator and the South Pole. Attractions for visitors from across the seas include the art and culture of the Maori — the Polynesian people who established themselves here six or seven centuries ago and now share the rights, privileges and responsibilities of citizenship with the New Zealanders of European descent — the beauty and grandeur of the country's magnificent scenery; and the fine sports activities. There are hundreds of miles of sandy beaches, good climbing, skiing and skating, rivers well-stocked with salmon and trout, and good shooting, especially for deer.

DINING

New Zealand cooking is typically British and since mutton is quite plentiful, there are many dishes featuring it. All kinds of sea food are available in delicious dishes.

FISHING, SKIING AND MOUNTAIN CLIMBING

AUCKLAND. Auckland, largest metropolis of New Zealand, is a two-ocean city in the north of the North Island, her eastern flank touching the Pacific, while her western boundary is embraced by the Tasman Sea. A subtropical city, she closely resembles a British provincial town, nevertheless, and Aucklanders still proudly, warmly call themselves British. The city is in an extremely beautiful location, for she is built on hills, many of which are extinct volcanoes, among the world's finest examples of spatter cones. A number of these sixty volcanic hills, once used by the Maoris as forts, are now parks of great beauty, with sheep, or four-legged lawn mowers, grazing serenely on the undulating slopes and summits. In one of these, the Domain, is the fine War Memorial Museum, commemorating those Anzacs who served in both World Wars and containing one of the best existing Maori collections. A sprawling city that has grown like Topsy, Auckland has virtually no apartment buildings and almost everybody lives in one-story bungalows with yellow walls and red roofs. Thus, as you gaze out over the outstretched city from the surrounding hills, before your eyes spreads one vast, bright, scarlet sea.

WELLINGTON . . the capital, is on North Island. It has a large and attractive harbor — in this case set in a natural amphitheater of steep hills. Besides the fine baroque **Parliament Buildings**, the **National Art Gallery** and the **Dominion Museum**, with an extensive Maori art collection, are located here. Its **Alexander Turnbull Library** is one of the best historical reference libraries in the world, with a notable collection of early editions and manuscripts. Standing off the west-coast beaches of **Paraparaumu** and **Waikanae** is a fragment of original New Zealand **Kapti Island**, one-time haunt of lawless whalers and traders, of pirates, murderers

ARTS BUILDING, UNIVERSITY COLLEGE
New Zealand Embassy

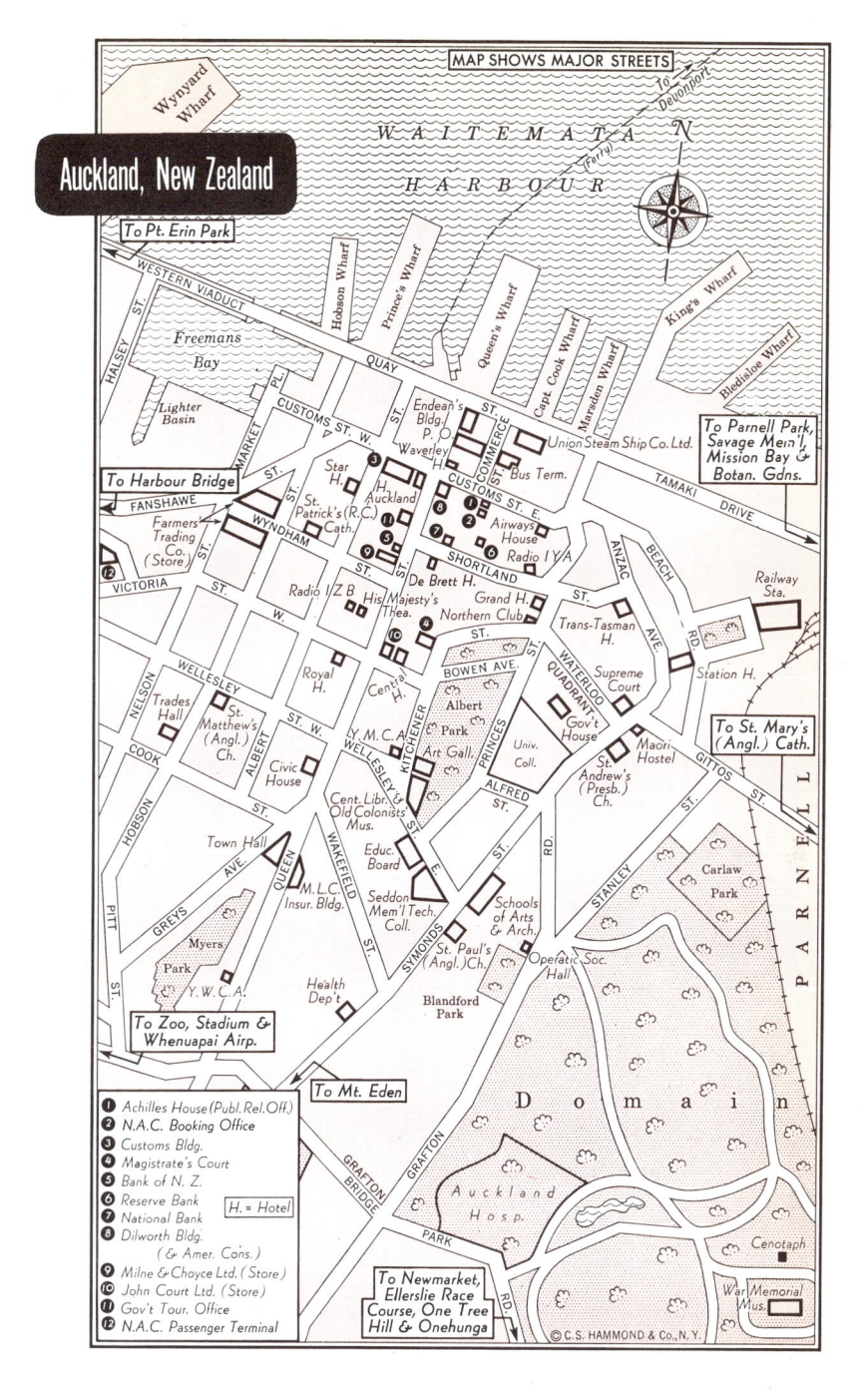

and head-hunters. Now a sanctuary of recovered nature, the luxuriant, evergreen bush, with its dense undergrowth of shrubs, vines, ferns and giant tree-ferns, is slowly extending to cover the island and the forest is once again alive with native birds like the kiwi and the weka, which cannot fly; the musical bellbird and tui; the alert and friendly fantail; the kaka, green and brown parrot of the forest, and the kea, or mountain parrot. A wide variety of trees and shrubs, ranging from those associated with the low country to rare mountain and subalpine species, may be found in **Egmont National Park**, encompassing the beautiful lone peak of Mount Egmont, rising sheer from the rich, fertile plains on the west coast of North Island. A true volcanic peak built up over a long period of time into one of the most perfectly shaped mountains in the world, it is a favorite with skiers. . . . With its parks, tree-lined avenues, street names and imposing **Cathedral**, CHRISTCHURCH . . . . . the city of the plains, nearly halfway down the east coast of the South Island, is regarded as the most English of New Zealand cities. It is laid out in neat, straight lines on the plains, with the grassy-banked Avon River breaking the geometric pattern as it wanders through the city It has public gardens peerless in New Zealand and many fine private gardens. Alpine climbers speak in high praise of the climbing in the region of **Tasman Park**, including the great Tasman Glacier, largest in the dominion with a total length of over eighteen miles and an average width of one mile and a quarter, considered by ski experts to provide one of the finest skiing grounds in the world; majestic Mount Cook and a number of other lofty peaks and extensive glaciers. Unique among famous glaciers are the two nearby great rivers of ice, **Franz Josef Glacier** and **Fox Glacier**, which, born among the snow and ice fields of the Southern Alpine Chain, descend through dense forest for the major part of their journey. Giant piles of stone pancakes — rock formations and caves — are stacked high along the west coast at **Punakaiki**, near Greymouth. Close by, the sea rushes with great force into a famous blowhole between rocky barriers, sending up waterspouts sometimes 150 feet into the air. . . . HANMER SPRINGS, north of Christchurch, is a popular spa and TIMARU, south of Christchurch, is a favorite seaside resort. . . . DUNEDIN, farther down the coast, was founded under the auspices of the Free Kirk of Scotland and has strong associations with Edinburgh, whose Celtic name it bears. Besides a wide range of industries, it has the **University of Otego** and many fine churches. Sea food is inexpensive and good and the city is enviably near the oyster beds at Stewart Island. St. Kilda and St. Clair are fine, long, sweeping beaches. . . . From South Island's chief tourist center of QUEENSTOWN, west of Dunedin, visitors go skiing on famous **Coronet Peak** and fishing in snow-fed rivers, providing fine salmon catches, as well as rainbow and brown trout. Largest, grandest and wildest of New Zealand's parks is **Fiordland National Park**, encompassing the Southern Fiords in the extreme southwest, having no counterpart elsewhere in the world. So wildly broken is this fiord country, it was not until 1888 that Quintin McKinnon, an intrepid explorer who had long searched for some way through the maze of huge canyons and mountain walls, discovered after many attempts the one passable saddle, later named in his honor **McKinnon's Pass**, and the doorway to fiordland was finally unlocked. The canyons through which this **Milford Track** trail, called the "World's Wonder Walk," winds its way are huge chasms among sheer walls of the mountain, chiseled and sculptured from the solid rock by glacier ice of some prehistoric era. Now, in strange contrast to the manner of their making, a fairy forest of trees, shrubs, ferns and hanging mosses, marking the dramatic change to subtropical conditions, fills these gorges and climbs high among the clefts and crevices surrounding them. **Sutherland Falls**, near Milford Sound, is the highest waterfall in the Southern Hemisphere. . . . Fast becoming one of the country's favorite resorts is little OBAN on Stewart Island, known to the Maori as "Rakiura," or "Isle of the Glowing Skies," one of the great scenic attractions of the dominion. Clothed in dense forests, with hundreds of delightful bays and havens, this lovely isle has a remarkably mild climate throughout the year. **Port William** was a favorite anchorage for old whaling ships, while **Paterson Inlet** is a base for the modern Antarctic-bound whalers.

MAORI MOTHER AND CHILD

MT. COOK, NEW ZEALAND'S HIGHEST PEAK

New Zealand Embassy

CHIEF OF THE ARAWA TRIBE, NEW ZEALAND

SOUTH AMERICA

Fun, fiestas and fabulous scenic grandeur epitomize a visit to South America. Whether you gaze in wonder at the Indian ruins in Peru, reminiscent of 1533 when the Spanish explorer Pizarro conquered the Incan capital of Cuzco, or revel in the modern luxury that is Buenos Aires, the cultural center of the continent, the unmistakable magic left by the early Spanish and Portuguese settlers is all around you.

On the pampas, or treeless, grassy plains of Argentina, today as in the past are found the picturesque gauchos, who continue to wear their ancestral costume of short boots, black sombreros and baggy pants, as they do the work of present-day cowboys, yet sing the same romantic songs as their counterparts did many centuries ago.

Some places, such as Caracas, Venezuela, are true studies in contrasts, for you find a blending of the old Spanish colonial architecture with the contemporary structures of a thriving metropolis.

Others, such as Brasilia, which just recently replaced Rio de Janeiro as capital of Brazil, are actually "cities of tomorrow." This ultramodern city, built on a man-made lake, is shaped like a swept-wing plane, and it was erected from Brazil's prairie land in order to attract the people away from the crowded coastal areas.

Traveling from remarkable Angel Falls, the highest waterfall in the world, to the snaky Amazon, the longest river on earth, South America is teeming with extremes to excite the imagination of the visitor.

The Latin people too are exciting, warm and friendly—like the climate—and their pace of life is not so hurried as ours in North America. They are a happy breed, gay and fun-loving, and the contagion of their carefree existence assures the tourist of a delightful holiday.

ATLANTIC OCEAN
Caribbean Sea
PACI
WEST INDIES
St. George's
Grenada
Margarita I.
Tobago
Port of Spain
Trinidad
Serpents Mouth
Aruba
NETH. ANTILLES
Willemstad
Gulf of Venezuela
Coro
Puerto Cabello
La Guaira
Cumaná
Barcelona
Maturín
Caracas
Maracay
Valencia
Barquisimeto
Maracaibo
Lake Maracaibo
Trujillo
Guanare
Valera
Mérida
San Cristóbal
VENEZUELA
Soledad
San Fernando
Puerto Ordaz
Ciudad Bolívar
Cerro Bolívar
El Callao
Angel Falls
Orinoco
Llanos del Orinoco
Puerto Carreño
Puerto Ayacucho
Guiana Highlands
La Gran Sabana
Roraima
Santa Elena
Tumereng
Bartica
Georgetown
New Amsterdam
Nieuw Nickerie
Paramaribo
Albina
St. Laurent du Maroni
Cayenne
BRITISH GUIANA
Kaieteur Falls
Totness
Essequibo
SURINAM (DUTCH GUIANA)
FRENCH GUIANA
Bôa Vista
Branco
Santa Marta
Barranquilla
Cartagena
Calamar
Magangué
Mompós
Gulf of Darién
Gamarra
Cúcuta
Bucaramanga
Puerto Berrío
Chiquinquirá
Honda
Tunja
L. Tota
Bogotá
Villavicencio
Girardot
Magdalena
Cauca
Antioquia
Medellín
Manizales
Armenia
COLOMBIA
Buenaventura
Cali
Palmira
Huila
Neiva
Popayán
San Agustín
CANAL ZONE
Colón
Portobelo
Panamá
Balboa
PANAMA
Santa Clara
Gulf of Panamá
Tumaco
Pasto
Esmeraldas
Tulcán
Otavalo
Ibarra
Sto. Domingo
Quito
Cotopaxi
ECUADOR
Manta
Jipijapa
Ambato
Baños
Santa Elena Bay
Guayaquil
Riobamba
Alausí
Salinas
Gulf of Guayaquil
Cuenca
Tumbes
Loja
Talara
Piura
Caquetá
Negro
Santa Isabel
Japurá
Amazon
Iquitos
Marañón
Andes
Chiclayo
Cajamarca
Ucayali
PERU
Trujillo
Chimbote
Pucallpa
Yungay
Tingo Maria
Huarás
Huánuco
Cerro de Pasco
Mountains
Pativilca
La Oroya
Tarma
LIMA
Callao
Huancayo
Machu Picchu
Cuzco
Ayacucho
Pisco
Ica
Abancay
Sicuani
Nasca
Juliaca
L. Titicaca
Puno
Chacaltaya
Arequipa
Copacabana
La Paz
Guaqui
Tiahuanaco
Mollendo
Moquegua
Altiplano
Tacna
Arica
Iquique
Potosí
Tarija
Juruá
Purús
Pôrto Velho
Madeira
Manaus
Guajará Mirim
Riberalta
Beni
Guaporé
Trinidad
Mamoré
BOLIVIA
Cochabamba
Santa Cruz
Oruro
L. Poopó
Sucre
Pilcomayo
Chaco
Puerto Guaraní
Fuerte Olimpo
Corumbá
Paraguay
Mato Grosso
Cuiabá
AMAZON
Santarém
Tapajós
Xingu
Mouths of the Amazon
Marajó I.
Pará
Belém
Equator
Tocantins
Araguaia
BRAZIL
São Luís
Parnaíba
Fortaleza
Natal
João Pessoa
Recife (Pernambuco)
Caatingas
Garanhuns
Maceió
Paulo Afonso Falls
Penedo
Aracaju
Salvador (Bahia)
Ilhéus
Campos
São Francisco
Goiás
Brasília
Goiânia
Pirapora
Diamantina
Cordisburgo
Araxá
Lagôa Santa
Belo Horizonte
Ouro Prêto
Andradina
Ribeirão Prêto
São João del Rei
Vitória

Notes and Itinerary

Venezuela

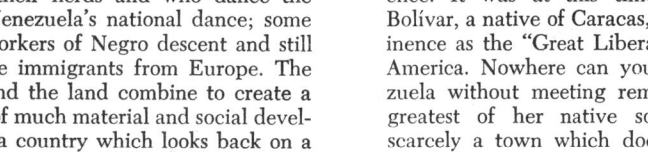

PALACE OF THE ACADEMIES, CARACAS

Pan American Union

COUNTRY OF MODERN DISCOVERY

This land of oil and iron is also a land of orchids and diamonds, of snowy Andean peaks and emerald jungles, of the mighty Orinoco and the world's highest waterfall. Much of its splendid, rugged scenery is being explored today for the first time, while its wealth of resources is still being discovered and developed, for the "Age of Discovery" in Venezuela is far from over. But this country is more than mere geography and resources. It is people — nearly 5 million of them. Some are sophisticated city dwellers whose ancestors founded the larger cities during colonial days; others are farmers who cultivate the fertile mountain valleys; some are *llaneros* (cowboys) who ride the plains tending their herds and who dance the *joropo*, Venezuela's national dance; some are oil workers of Negro descent and still others are immigrants from Europe. The people and the land combine to create a country of much material and social development, a country which looks back on a proud cultural heritage and forward to a future filled with limitless possibilities.

Venezuela's past properly begins with the name of Alonso de Ojeda who, in 1499, sailed into Lake Maracaibo, where, seeing Indian pile-dwellings over the water, he named the land Venezuela (Little Venice). To colonize a part of this land, Charles V of Spain granted a contract to a German firm, the Welsers, and while they accomplished valuable explorations, they so antagonized Spanish authorities that the contract was terminated. Venezuela later became part of the Viceroyalty of New Granada. Early in the 19th century when Napoleon had overrun Spain, attempts were made to secure independence. It was at this time that Simón Bolívar, a native of Caracas, rose to prominence as the "Great Liberator" of South America. Nowhere can you go in Venezuela without meeting reminders of the greatest of her native sons. There is scarcely a town which does not have a statue of the Liberator in the center of its plaza. So if you would like to enrich your trip, take a good biography of Bolívar with you and become acquainted with the "George Washington" of South America and his native land.

PLATOS TIPICOS

Each section of the country has its own traditional dish, but the national dish is *hallaca,* a sort of boiled pie with a cornmeal cover and filled with meat and a dozen other ingredients. Other unusual dishes include *pastel de Maracay* (turtle meat potpie) and *pabellón* (rice, meat and fried bananas). Try some of Venezuela's fruit—**chirmoyas**, **zapotes** and **granadillas**.

EXTRA CURRICULAR ACTIVITIES

In Caracas you can play golf and tennis, swim in the pools of various clubs, ride horseback and bowl. The beach resorts of Macuto, near La Guaira, offer surf bathing and deep-sea fishing. Other excellent beaches are Catia de la Mar, Choroni and Margarita Island. Big-game hunting is good in the **Guiana Highlands** as well as in the *llanos* of Guárico State, where the jaguar lives along with land tortoise, deer, fox and tapir. The rivers which wind through the country are stocked with eels, stinging ray and fighting fish which make delicious eating. Here too, in the lagoons inhabited by brightly-plumed herons, the huntsman will find a large specie of Moscovy duck often weighing as much as 20 pounds.

THE PORT CITY

LA GUAIRA is the country's principal port dramatically situated along a narrow strip of Caribbean coast. This ancient city, founded in 1589, rises from the harbor on terraced ledges hewn from rock, with **La Silla Peak** rising behind it. This city is connected to the capital by the **Autopista**, an amazing superhighway which cost about 7 million dollars per mile, and is a masterpiece of engineering.

OIL FIELD, LAKE MARACAIBO

The capital, CARACAS comprises two distinct sections: the ancient town, with its baroque style of architecture, and the new city, composed of modern suburbs spreading into the surrounding hillsides. All the great landmarks of Caracas are retained in the "historic quadrilateral," covering 12 blocks in the town's center. This Spanish colonial "city of red-tiled roofs" contains an abundance of charm and interest. Most of the attractions are within a few blocks of the **Plaza Bolívar**. Paved with mosaic and shaded by arched trees, it is a favorite gathering place. On the east side of the Plaza is a **colonial cathedral** which displays within its interior paintings by such masters as Rubens and Murillo. The **Palace of Justice**, facing the plaza, stands on the site where the Declaration of Independence was signed in 1811. The **Church of San Francisco** is the oldest and most interesting in the city with an altar lavishly carved and covered with gold. Nearby is the **Bolivarian Museum** where many relics of the Liberator are kept. Especially interesting is a medallion with a miniature of George Washington and a lock of his hair which was sent to Bolívar by the Washington family. The **Casa Natal**, where Bolívar was born, is an aristocratic colonial home which has been made into a national shrine. The **National Pantheon** contains the remains of Bolívar. Behind the tomb rises a great white marble likeness of him. At the side of the tomb are memorials to the great historic figures of Miranda and Sucre. In the suburbs is located the impressive ultramodern **University City**. The stadia here are large enough to accommodate the Olympic Games. **Miraflores Palace** is the presidential residence. Nearby is **Calvary Hill** from whose crest an excellent view of the city and valley may be had. You can see bullfights in season at **Nuevo Circo**. Half a century ago Caracas was a modest agricultural center, but today the old Caracas is vanishing and the city is fast becoming one of the great capitals of the world. When Diego de Losada founded this city in 1567, the entire area was covered with forests but now massive structures of steel and concrete mingle with century old churches and on every hand the venerable landmarks of the past give way to the future.

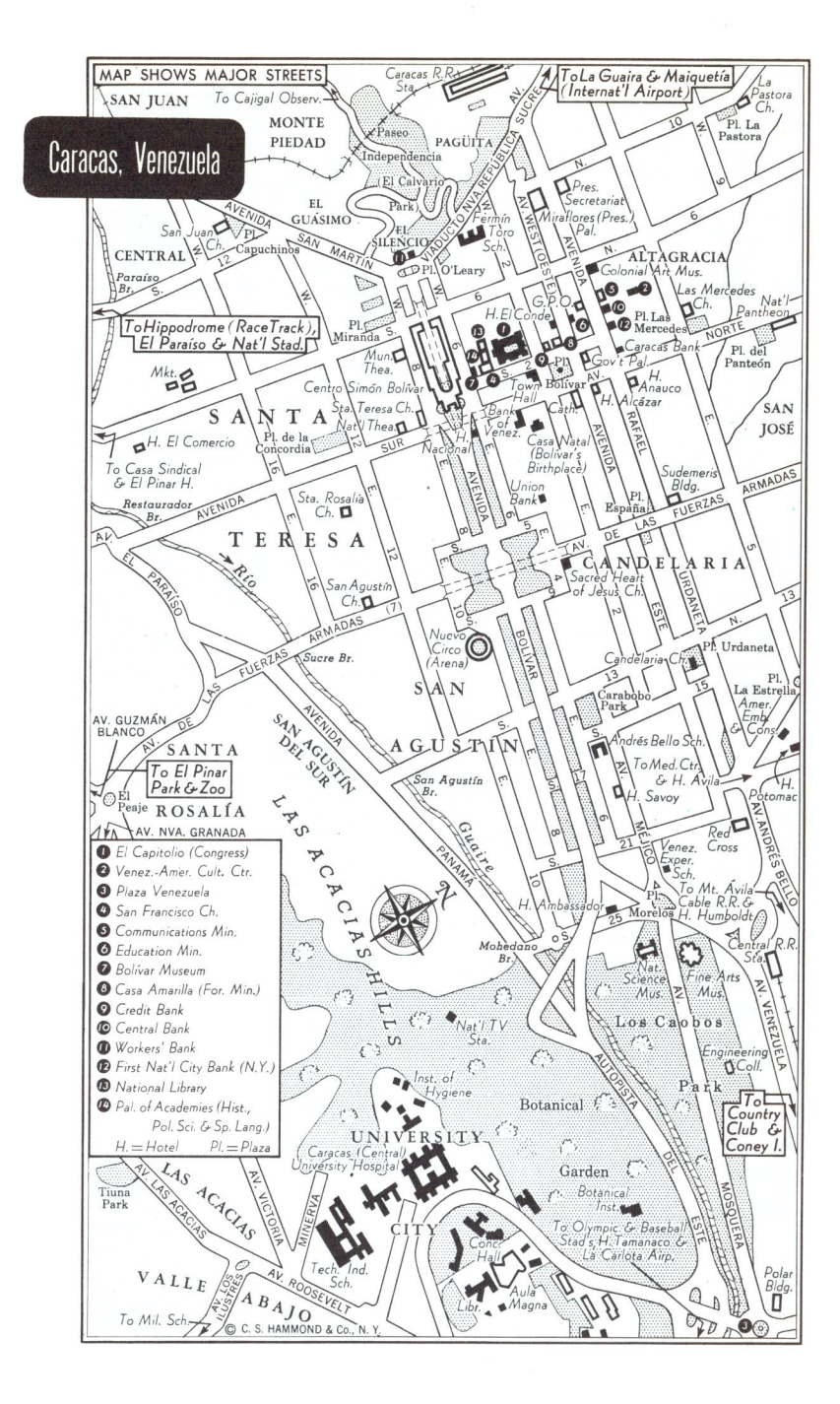

AVENIDA BOLIVAR, CARACAS

Hamilton Wright

TOURING THE COUNTRY

While Caracas is undergoing an almost complete change its surroundings are the same as when the conquistadores founded the city over 390 years ago. El Avila, with its majestic peak rising in lofty grandeur some 10,000 feet in the air, serves as a spectacular backdrop to the capital. . . . About 70 miles west of Caracas is **MARACAY**, center of the rich coffee and sugar region. In the **Plaza de Tacarigua** you may see life-sized replicas of the most interesting pieces of sculpture of the aborigines of the country. This was the city of the firm dictator of the early 20th century, Juan Vicente Gómez. It was he who beautified the city with broad boulevards, a great bull ring (Sevillian style) and the **Hotel Jardín**, where he used to give sumptuous banquets. Aptly named the "garden spot" of the country, the city is bordered by beautiful **Lake Valencia** on the south and the **Las Delicias** hills on the north. . . . Further to the west is **VALENCIA**, a city perfumed by the scent of lemon and orange blooms. Rambling houses, with iron-studded doors and grilled windows, built around cool patios, present a forbidding aspect to the narrow streets which stem from flower-filled plazas. Many of the country's wealthy maintain homes here. The **Battlefield of Carabobo** is but a short drive from the town. Here the patriot army commanded by Bolívar broke forever the Spanish hold on Venezuela. . . . To the north of Valencia is **PUERTO CABELLO**, second most important port of the country. The town is built on a protected harbor in which the water is so quiet it is said that a ship can be moored by a hair (cabello) — hence the name. Its ancient fortresses will remind one of the days when protection was needed against the pirates of the Spanish Main. Another place in the vicinity is **Playa Gañango**, a beautiful beach where famous deep-purple grapes the size of wild cherries grow in abundance. . . . Southwest from the port city is the thriving agricultural center of **BARQUISIMETO**. Great producer of pineapples, sugar cane and sisal, it has risen to become the third city of the Republic. . . . **MARACAIBO** is the second city of the country and today is synonymous with oil. This lazy, sprawling, sun-baked city, with its contrasting Spanish colonial and Indian quarters, has been transformed in four decades into a thriving metropolis complete with Rockefeller supermarkets, Sears Roebuck stores and American-type hotels. This "City of Palms" contains excellent beaches along the picturesque lakeside. Here one may see the light fishing skiffs of local construction, manned by fishermen softly singing Creole songs. On the other side of Lake Maracaibo are the oil derricks which have brought so much wealth to Venezuela. One of the phenomena of the area is the intermittent silent lightning seen over the Catumbo River, far to the south. . . . A trip to the eastern section of the country to visit the city of **CIUDAD BOLIVAR** is worth while. Capital of the largest state in Venezuela, it is located 200 miles up the **Orinoco River** on the narrows of that great waterway. This busy port was founded in 1532 and originally was called **Angostura**, home of the famous bitters. Later the name was changed to honor the country's national hero. River boats, dugout canoes paddled by Indians from the interior and shallow draft steamers from the **Río Apure** are always seen along the waterfront. In the center of the city, facing the **Plaza Bolívar** the Congress of Angostura met to proclaim the Republic of Gran Colombia and elect Bolívar president. The Alameda, the main thoroughfare of the city, is shored against the river by a huge, thick wall, at the end of which stands an old Spanish castle, now used as a warehouse for products of the region. Directly across the river and connected by a ferry is **SOLEDAD**, starting point for all places north of the Orinoco River. . . . Two excursions will prove exciting to lovers of the unusual. The first is a trip by air to view the world's highest waterfall, **Angel Falls**. The more daring may try a trip to the foot of the falls by jeep. The other excursion is a trip to **MARGARITA ISLAND**. Known as the "Isle of Pearls," it is one of 70 that make up the state of Nueva Esparta. This is the center of the pearl industry. History has it that Columbus brought Queen Isabella a necklace of Margarita pearls when he returned from his third voyage. Also located here is the **Cueva del Bufón** (Clown's Cave) where pirates were supposed to have hidden their treasure. None has yet been found!

ANGEL FALLS

Hamilton Wright

Colombia

OLD FORTRESS, CARTAGENA

THE LAND OF EL DORADO

Everyone has heard of the pot of gold at the end of the rainbow. The lure of easily-acquired riches was particularly strong in the 16th century when Spanish explorers of Colombia's wild terrain were spurred to superhuman efforts by the legend of El Dorado (the Gilded Man). The legend has to do with an Indian chief living high in the Andes who made a practice of propitiating the gods by covering his entire body with powdered gold and washing it off in the waters of a crater lake, into which precious jewels were also cast as sacrificial offerings. Even today attempts have been made to find the half-billion dollars worth of treasure which supposedly lies at the bottom of Lake Guatavita. But the early explorers, in their vain search for this wealth, overlooked the real treasures of Colombia. Today the country is the principal source of the world's emeralds; her rivers and mines abound in gold, platinum and silver; her forests hold large supplies of rubber, dyewoods, hardwoods and balsam, and her soil nurtures the wild orchid. Indeed, one cannot begin to measure Colombia's treasures without also including her magnificent scenic beauty, her romantic history and her proud culture.

COLOMBIAN MEALS

You will find a wide variety of good foods in Colombia ranging from delectable native dishes to sophisticated foreign fare. Baked bananas are a standard dish. Native fruit such as *nisperos* or *granadillas* (passion fruit) are a real treat. Colombian tamales are always tasty, made of corn meal, meat, vegetables and seasoning. Native dishes are usually highly spiced, but delicious. No meal is ever complete unless it is topped off by an aromatic demitasse of Colombian's excellent coffee.

CITIES AND SIGHTS

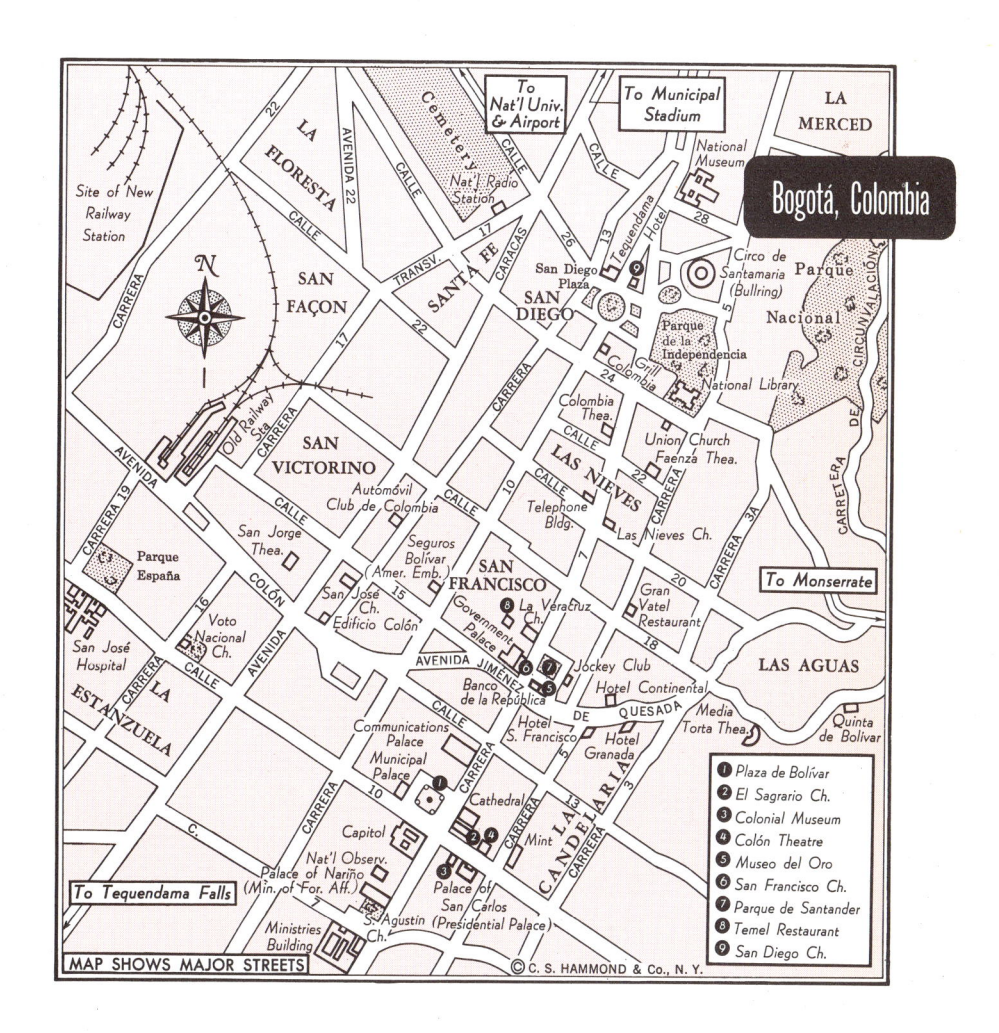

The city of **BARRANQUILLA** is the gateway to Colombia. If your hobby happens to be fishing, then Barranquilla is the right place to go. Great schools of fish feed at the mouth of the **Magdalena River** as it sweeps out into the **Bocas de Cenizas** (Mouths of Ashes). The **Pradomar Beach Club** at Puerto Colombia will arrange for the hire of fishing launches. . . . West of Barranquilla is the walled city of **CARTAGENA**. Any tour of the city should begin with the massive walls. Within the city you may visit the **Church of San Pedro Claver**, named for the gentle father who, back in slave trading days, devoted his life to caring for the slaves brought to Cartagena. Outside the walls is the **Fortress of San Felipe Barajas**, once the strongest fortress in the New World, which defended the city against the repeated attacks of the freebooters who sailed the Spanish Main. Nearby are the ruins of the **Convent of Santa Cruz de la Popa** with its charming image of the Virgin, famous in Cartagena's legends. Here on February 2nd each year a procession of townsfolk carry lighted candles up the hill to say prayers to the Blessed Mother. . . . For many years the main means of transportation within Colombia was the Magdalena River. Even today flat-bottomed paddlewheelers ply up and down its shores. Wide stretches of jungle alternate with open country and alligators are a common sight, sunning themselves on the sand bars. Monkeys chatter in the trees and birds of brilliant plumage fly through the green foliage. Here fishermen wield their huge nets from boats in midstream in the same manner that has been practiced for generations. . . . MEDELLIN, Colombia's second city in size, is delightful for its mild climate and its facilities for gracious living. A favorite resort for tourists, its streets are overhung with trees and bordered by beautiful mansions and gardens. The massive **Metropolitan Cathedral** on the **Parque Bolívar** is said to be the largest all-brick church in the world. A short drive from the city will bring you past the impressive fincas (country estates) where you see coffee of the finest quality being picked and behold the orchid garden with its mass of fragile, exotic flowers.

THE CAPITAL

BOGOTA is located on a fertile, four hundred square mile Andean plateau known as the Sabana de Bogotá. Until the inauguration of Colombia's first commercial airline in 1920, Bogotá was probably one of the world's most isolated capitals. To reach the city from Barranquilla on the coast, entailed traveling by boat for more than a week up the Magdalena River and then continuing on by rail across the mountains. Here, the city's inhabitants could at one time boast they spoke the purist Spanish in the Americas. Bogotá was founded in 1538, by Gonzalo Jiménez de Quesada and the ragged, half-starved survivors of an epic trek from the fever-ridden coast, through dense jungles and up the Eastern Cordillera of the Andes. Today, the 8,500-foot high plateau basin in which the city lies, is one of the most densely populated regions of Colombia and Bogotá's Techo Airport links the city with important centers of both Europe and the Americas. Old Bogotá centers around Plaza Bolívar. Still retaining its colonial appearance, this section of narrow streets and overhanging balconies runs from the south to the east of the main plaza. Within this area is one of the finest of the city's colonial mansions, the **Palacio de San Carlos**, home of Bolívar when he was president of Gran Colombia. To the north and west is the modern section. Here you may visit the Banco de la República to see the Museum of Gold where 5,000 hand-wrought gold and silver articles evidence the high degree of craftsmanship of the Colombian Indian. Bogotá's richest church, the **Church of San Francisco**, is adorned with lavish gold altars of breath-taking splendor. Overlooking Parque de la Independencia is the stunning modern building of the **National Library**. Following the winding road above Parque, you arrive at the gates of the **Quinta de Bolívar**, the quiet country home of the Great Liberator. The house has been made into a museum of Boliviana and the spacious gardens are kept as they were when he lived here. Nearby is the amphitheater called **Media Torta** (Half Cake) which is filled every Sunday morning with people who come to watch programs of folk music and dancing. On the northwestern edge of town is University City, a splendid group of buildings which house the National University. . . . Southwest of Bogotá is CALI, a charming city full of friendly people famous for their zest for living and their fondness of sports. Cali's churches are particularly beautiful and reflect the religious nature of the inhabitants. The **Church of La Merced** contains a large stone image of the Virgin de los Remedios (Healing Virgin) which is reputed to have been found already sculptured in a nearby valley. There is a legend which relates how the image returned mysteriously to the original valley several times until a priest painted trees, flowers and birds on the altar to make the Virgin feel at home. Here, also, is the birthplace of one of Colombia's greatest authors, Jorge Isaacs. His romantic novel, *Maria*, is a masterpiece of Colombian literature, and through it the beauty of the **Cauca Valley** has gained world-wide fame. . . . One hundred miles south of Cali is the historic city of POPAYAN. Here there are many churches, as well as monasteries and cloisters, of classic Spanish architecture. The **Church of San Francisco** is especially famed for its carved pulpit and celebrated bell whose resonant tones have been called the "Voice of Popayán." From this picturesque city the visitor looks up to the snowclad summit of the Puracé. Popayán prides itself as being the "cradle of great men." No less than seven presidents, besides many great prelates, scientists and artists, number among her sons. Settled by many noble Spanish families, coats of arms may still be seen over the doorways of many of the city's fine old mansions.

SIMON BOLIVAR STATUE, CARTAGENA

BULL FIGHT, BOGOTA

Ecuador and Peru

INDEPENDENCE PLAZA, QUITO — Hamilton Wright

AT THE EQUATOR AND BELOW

Ecuador, a country that straddles the equator, is a land of interest and surprises. Here you will learn that the best "Panama" hats are made not in Panama, but in Ecuador around Jipijapa; that the kapoc in pillows comes from Ecuador's giant ceiba trees; that model airplanes are made of Ecuadoran balsa, the world's lightest wood. Streets "paved" with cocoa beans spread in the sun to dry and Indians dyed from head to foot with flaming red stain are some of the surprises that will make a trip to Ecuador unforgettable.... Peru, also, is a country of great surprises and interest. It is culturally the oldest of the South American nations. For centuries it was the leading political power on the continent, first as the center of the Incan Empire and later as Spain's foremost vice-royalty in America. Here you will see throngs of Indians gather at the capital to celebrate Christian holidays in a manner reminiscent of Incan worship. You will learn that an important industry is the production of guano, a natural fertilizer, deposited by sea birds, and so vital to the country that no visitors are allowed to trespass upon the "bird sanctuaries" where it is produced. The odd, the unique and the picturesque all await the visitor who makes the trip to Ecuador or Peru.

RIVALRY AND INTRIGUE

The area of both Peru and Ecuador once formed part of the vast Incan Empire. Divided between two brothers, Huáscar and Atahualpa, a struggle ensued for control of the entire empire, in the course of which Huáscar was killed. This civil unrest greatly aided the Spanish conquest. Led by Francisco Pizarro, the Spanish forces met those of Atahualpa in what is now Peru. When the great Incan refused to acknowledge the supremacy of the Spanish king and the Christian religion, Pizarro ordered his men to fire upon the Incan warriors and Atahualpa was taken prisoner. Although the Emperor paid a tremendous ransom in gold and silver for his release, he was charged by the Spaniards with various crimes and put to death. With its leader dead, the Empire crumbled under the fierce onslaught of the Spaniards. After Pizarro's triumph, expeditions were sent southward to explore other regions. Ironically, Pizarro was slain by his own men.

MEALS FROM TWO COUNTRIES

Ecuador has many native dishes that may please the gourmet. Try *locro*, a soup made of potatoes, or *llapingacho*, a cheese and potato cake which, when decorated with a fried egg, is called *llapingacho montado* or "with a rider." Corn on the cob is called *choclo*, corn meal mush, one of Ecuador's staple foods, is *mote*. Guayaquil can provide you with *serviche*, a sea food platter you will long remember.... While in Peru sample *anticuchos*, deliciously barbecued beef heart. *Picadillo a la criolla* is a Creole hash made as only Peruvians can. For sea food, try *tortillas de camarones* (shrimp omelet) or *escabeche*, the country's typical fish platter.

THE LAND OF THE EQUATOR

Of increasing tourist interest in Ecuador is GUAYAQUIL.... Here "chocolate-paved streets," where brown beans of cacao are laid to dry on the roads, present one of the most unusual sights in the world. The city's main boulevard is the **Malecón Simón Bolívar**. Crossing the city is **Avenida 9 de Octubre**. On or near these two thoroughfares you will find the principal public buildings and stores of the city. The many shops here and in the Public Market offer a fascinating array of handicrafts. At the southern end of the Malecón is the statue of the **Indian chieftain and his wife, Guayas and Quil**, who were supposed to have commited suicide when the Spaniards invaded their country. A good starting point for sightseeing is **La Rotonda**. Here a colonnade partially encircles the famous **Statue of Generals Bolívar and San Martín**, whose epochal meeting took place on this spot in 1822. Be sure to see the **sorcerer's pole**, a carved totem pole, located at the central arcade of the City Hall. It is one of the most prized relics in South America.... Westward, on the coast, is **SALINAS**, noted for its fine bathing and excellent fishing. Santa Elena Bay provides unequaled facilities for surf bathing. Fishing for black marlin, swordfish or sailfish is exciting sport from April to December. Here visitors may indulge in the intriguing pastime of hunting treasure in the form of Spanish pesos and doubloons which are still washed up on the beach from sunken Spanish galleons by the "Easter Tides" in springtime.... **PLAYAS**, 60 miles from Guayaquil, is another favorite resort.... One of the most exciting rail journeys in the world is that from Guayaquil to Quito where the train climbs a zigzag course, gaining 11,000 feet in about 100 miles, over the Andes. On the way the train stops in **RIOBAMBA**, noted for its weekly fair when the Indians bring their intriguing wares. From here the train passes through the Avenue of Volcanoes and down into the valley to **AMBATO**, the garden city of Ecuador and a fascinating market town. Nearby is Cotopaxi, the highest active volcano in the world. Throughout the trip the scenery is breathtakingly beautiful. Llamas and exotic birds and flowers and red-ponchoed shepherds brighten the landscape.... To the north lies **QUITO**, the capital.

Nearly everything in the city exudes an air of antiquity — magnificent old churches, sleepy little plazas basking in the sun and narrow cobbled streets lined with graceful arcades. Begin your tour of the city early in the morning and you will see the rosy sunlight reflected on glistening snow-capped mountains. You will see also the Indians dressed in brilliantly colored ponchos, still chattering the ancient Quechua tongue as they trudge down from the hills with their market wares, bearing the weight of their burdens by a strap slung across their foreheads. Heart of the city is the **Plaza Independencia**, dominated by the stately **Cathedral** with gray-stone porticos and green-tile cupolas. Wander down **Calle de la Ronda**, one of the oldest streets in the city, past **Santo Domingo Square**, the principal shopping district and on to **Parque Alemeda** where you will find the oldest **astronomical observatory** in South America. Largest of Quito's churches is the **Church of San Francisco**, occupying a full block on the plaza of the same name. It is built on the exact spot where Atahualpa's palace once stood. A strikingly massive edifice, this church is built of stone, with two great bell towers crowning its Renaissance façade. Among its many treasures is a group of statues of the Virgin Mary and the twelve apostles carved by a humble Indian named Roughface.... About ten miles from Quito is the **Equator Line**. The granite monument which marks it was erected in 1924 to commemorate a survey taken to measure the arc of the meridian. Here you may stand astride the famous line with one foot in the Northern Hemisphere and the other in the Southern.... South of Quito is the lovely Los Chillos Valley with its large colonial haciendas, lush and beautiful trees and flowers and mineral springs. In this beautiful setting is the Quito Country Club.... West of Quito is the village of **SANTO DOMINGO DE LOS COLORADOS**, home of the fabulous Colorado Indians. Believing the color of blood to be a protection against evil spirits, the men of this tribe paint themselves from head to toe with a brilliant red dye; they wear their hair plastered down in a stiff fringe resembling a helmet rather than hair.

PERUVIAN JOURNEY

LIMA. Capital of Peru and for centuries the viceroyalty of Spain's vast colonial empire in South America, Lima is a city of proud tradition where on every hand are found the remains of its once fabulous culture. On January 18th, 1535, the great conquistador Francisco Pizarro inscribed its circumference with his famous sword of Gallo, naming his new capital Ciudad de los Reyes—"City of Kings"—in honor of the Epiphany. Later the city became known as Lima, a mispronunciation of Rimac, a river on whose banks the city was founded. Its original checkerboard pattern of 117 squares, designed to provide shade on at least one side of the street at all times, still survives as do many of the colorful names by which the streets were designated. In 1746, a shattering earthquake destroyed most of Lima and its port of Callao, six miles distant on the Pacific coast. Today few of the city's buildings antedate this disaster. Although Lima lies within a few degrees of the equator in a region whose climate should under normal conditions be tropical, the city enjoys little equatorial heat.

BULL RING, LIMA
Pan American-Grace Airways

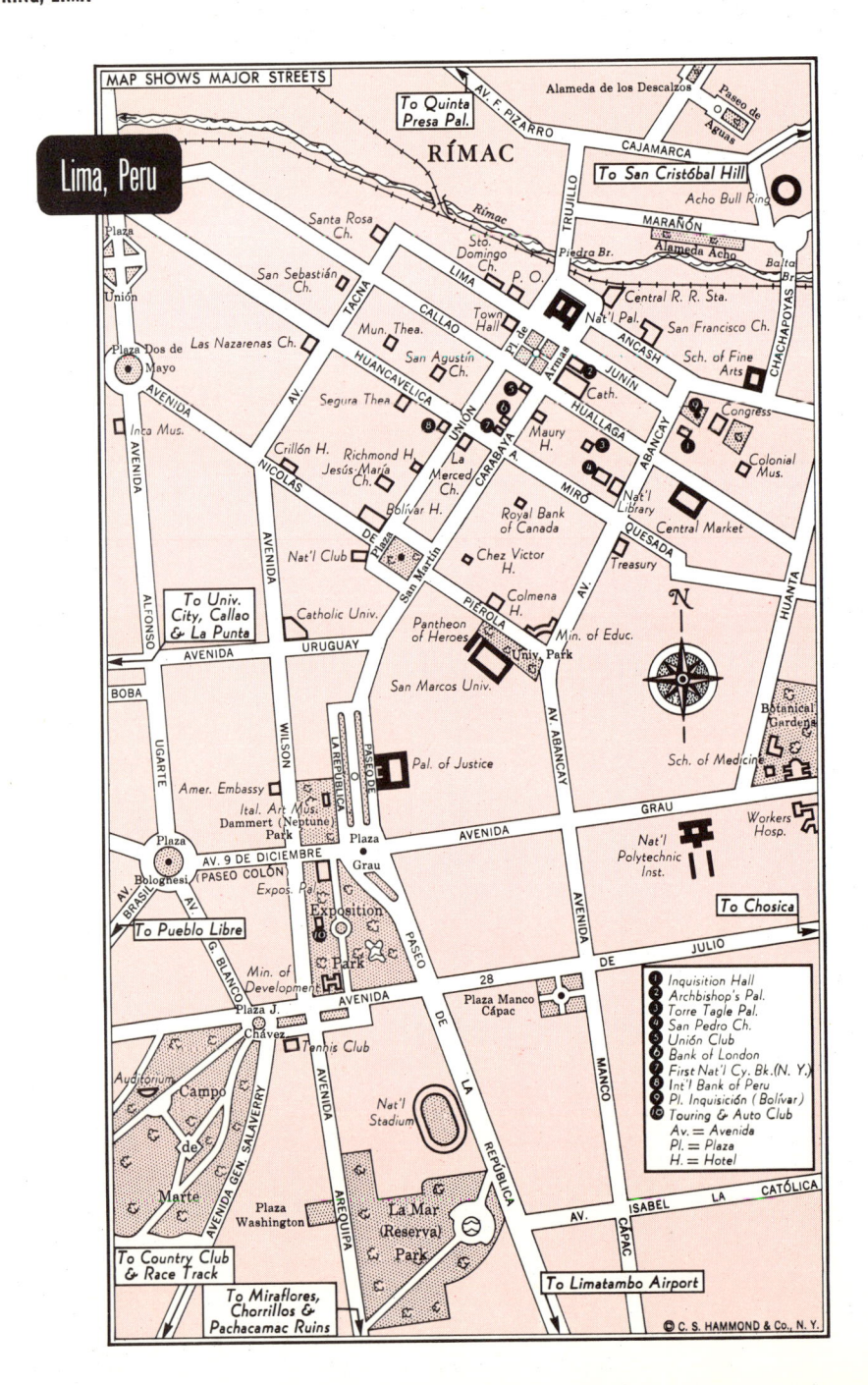

LA MAR PARK, LIMA
Pan American-Grace Airways

150

From May to November, thick clouds caused by the antarctic chill of the Humbolt Current, shroud the bald peak of San Cristobal and obscure the sun. Though little rain falls in the arid coastal region about the city, fog and the heavy mist known as the "Garua" drift inland from the Pacific during the winter months. Situated on the Rimac River, it is the center of Peru's political and social life. Originally the center of town, the **Plaza de Armas** is surrounded by the City Hall and other official buildings. On the west side of the Plaza is Lima's Cathedral. Here lies the mummified body of Francisco Pizarro, enclosed in a glass-paneled case behind which a stone mural depicts his exploits and life. Early Lima gloried in churches, and so it is that churches are encountered everywhere. Most interesting perhaps is the **Church of San Francisco** with its mural of tiles and its marvelous architecture executed in authentic Renaissance style. Equally famous is the **Church of San Agustin** whose superlative façade reflects the luxury of Lima's colonial past. Nearby is the **Palacio de Torre-Tagle**, the finest example of colonial architecture in the country with its balconies, massive doorways and carved lions, all echoing the Lima of the viceroys. It is now Peru's Foreign Office. Today the **Plaza de San Martín** marks Lima's center about which are clustered the city's theaters, public buildings, hotels and restaurants. The shopping section is located nearby on **Jirón Union**. While in the city you will want to visit the **University of San Marcos**, oldest in the Americas and originally governed by the Dominican Order. Here, also, is located the **Pantheon of the Heroes**, containing the tombs of the most outstanding men of Peruvian history. To visit the interesting suburb of **San Lázaros** you will cross the old stone bridge over the Rimac River, built by a famous Marquis in the 17th century, and one of Lima's most durable landmarks.... Interesting excursions around Lima include the beautiful suburbs of **Miraflores**, the busy port of **Callao** where you can enjoy the sun and the sea on the large beautiful beaches of **La Punta**, and a trip to **Pachacamac** to see the Incan ruins.... AREQUIPA, second city of Peru, nestles at the foot of majestic, snow-capped El Misti. Quaint old buildings and ancient churches here are constructed of a pearly white volcanic material and the streets are filled with Indians in gaily colored dress, laden llamas ambling side by side with modern automobiles and street cars, making this busy commercial town most picturesque. There are many local items for sale in the markets, including leather articles, pottery, native textiles and llama wool rugs and throws.... High in the Andes on the shore of beautiful Lake Titicaca is PUNO, from where boats cross the lake to Bolivia. The ancient city of CUSCO is located in south-central Peru at an elevation of 11,024 feet. This city justly deserves its title of "the Archaeological Capital of South America." Throughout the city are found the ruins of Incan temples, fortresses, palaces and other structures. On a hill overlooking Cusco from the north is the **fortress** of Sacsahuaman, an excellent example of Incan architecture. Near the **Plaza de Armas**, the principal square of the city, is the site of the **Temple of the Sun**, the Incan house of worship. A short distance from the city are the **fortress of Ollantaitambo** and the ruins of the city of **Machu Pichu**. The latter, for centuries unknown to the Spaniards, was only discovered by archaeologists in 1911. A magnificent ancient stronghold, it has become one of the wonders of the continent.... Of uncommon interest to tourists is the town of HUANCAYO, southeast of Lima. Its picturesque architecture, temperate climate and fascinating Sunday market, largely attended by Indians from surrounding areas, attract many visitors. It is probably the most unusual market in Peru.

MT. COTOPAXI-PAN AMERICAN HIGHWAY

Hamilton Wright

CONVENTO DE LA MERCED, CUSCO

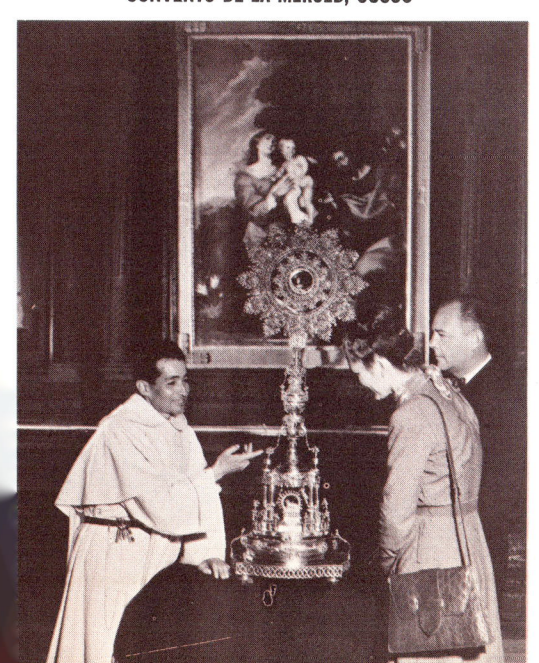

"VICUNA SHOP," LIMA

Pan American-Grace Airways

Brazil

SUGAR LOAF, RIO

COLOSSUS OF THE SOUTH

The fourth country in the world in terms of continuous territory, Brazil is also the largest country in the world with a Latin culture. Brazil is unique both culturally and ethnically, for its peoples during the last four centuries have produced a culture and nationality in which are blended the Portuguese heritage with its Celtic, Nordic and Moorish strains. The folkways of the Negro and the Indian, the European elements from Italy, Spain, France and Germany; all these influences have combined to create the Brazilian of today. His country is a land of exuberant vegetation, of golden beaches fringed with silvery breakers, of quiet gardens and throbbing waterfalls. But Brazil is also a land of the future. Its rivers hold the restless power of twenty million horses, and its mountains provide an inexhaustible treasure-chest of resources which pump the lifeblood of industry into the country's thriving wonders — the longest river in the world, its two waterfalls higher than Niagara, its unrivaled harbor of Rio — all of which justify Brazil as being a land of spectacle and splendor.

FOOD A LA BRESILIEN

It will prove to be fun to seek out restaurants which specialize in native Brazilian dishes. Try *feijoada completa* (black beans and meat cooked in a sauce flavored with herbs and onions), *vatapá* (usually fish or shrimp cooked in a sauce of peanuts, palm oil and cocoanut milk), or the many *picadinhos* (hashes served in a variety of ways with wonderful, piquant sauces). Brazilian cookery is at its best in Bahia, where Creole specialties of African and Portuguese origin are unsurpassed. Many of Brazil's tropical fruits may be delightful to you: *fruta do conde* (custard apple), *mamão* (papaya) and mangoes. In addition to the popular *cafézinhos* and chocolate, there are many refreshing drinks prepared from the cocoanut.

WHERE FOOTBALL IS SOCCER

Futból (soccer) is the most popular sport in Brazil and can be watched all over the country. Horseracing and auto racing are major sports in Rio. Don't fail to visit the huge Maracanã Stadium in this city, the largest in the world. Brazil is a fisherman's paradise — lakes, rivers and the Atlantic abound in endless varieties. Game is abundant, both large and small; big-game hunters go to Mato Grosso for jaguar, puma, tapir, wild pig, ostriches, crocodiles and giant stork. Facilities for golf, tennis, horseback riding and water sports are found at all leading resorts.

THE NEW CAPITAL

BRASÍLIA. On April 21, 1960, Brasília became the new capital of Brazil. President Juscelino Kubitschek brought to reality the dream of a century to move the capital inland, away from the crowded coastal section. At a cost to the government of 250 million dollars spent on the initial phase of construction and an expected expenditure of another 200 million, the city was built to accomodate the two Houses of Congress, the Supreme Court, and the executive branch. The officials and their families numbered 15,000 on "moving day," but they eventually hope to attract half a million people to this metropolis carved from a wilderness. Already new highways link Brasília to Rio de Janeiro and the city's modern airport is of utmost importance to its existence and growth. The buildings are of contemporary design.

CITIES AND SIGHTS

RIO DE JANEIRO. Surmounting the 2,310 foot summit of the Corcovado, Landowski's great sculpture of Christ the Redeemer, erected to commemorate Brazilian independence, looks serenely out across land-locked Guanabara Bay. In the distance guarding the portals of the South Atlantic, the towering eminence of the Sugar Loaf, Rio de Janeiro's most imposing landmark thrusts its great rock dome above a crescentic sweep of incredibly blue water. The wooded slopes and granite faces of mountains rise from

PALACE OF THE DAWN, BRASILIA

CHRIST STATUE, RIO

a flat beach-scalloped plain. Here amid one of nature's most spectacular settings, the city of Rio de Janeiro lavishly spreads her panorama of red tiled roofs and pink walled houses, of rococo façades and the starkly denuded shafts of apartment dwellings, of flower filled parks and sprawling factories, of 20th century skyscrapers and mile upon mile of palm-lined boulevards. The beauty of the city, its innumerable parks and plazas and miles of scenic drives are the result of years of scientific city-planning. The city's main thoroughfare is **Avenida Rio Branco.** Walking up this broad, tree-shaded avenue, with its patterned mosaic sidewalks, one is struck by the advanced modern design of its imposing buildings. **Rua do Ouvidor,** one of the principal shopping streets, is lined with fashionable shops and jewelry stores displaying Brazil's wealth of gems. At the end of **Avenido Rio Branco** is the **Monroe Palace.** At the end of this avenue the scenic beach drive, **Avenida Beira-Mar,** begins at **Paris Plaza** and follows the sinuous curve of beaches among which is the famed, crescent-shaped **Copacabana** with its beach promenade of black and white mosaic. Near the beginning of the drive you may turn off and visit the **Lapa** district, reminiscent of Paris' Montmartre, with its cafés, cabarets and night clubs. Continuing along the sea front is the parklike **Gloria Section,** with fine hotels, residences and the **Cardinal's Palace.** Aristocratic **Paysandú Street,** guarded by stately rows of royal palms, ends at **Guanabara Palace,** former official residence of the President and now the City Hall. While touring around **Botafogo Bay** you will come to a point of land called **Morro da Urca.** Towering above this is the gigantic dome of **Sugar Loaf Mountain.** A great thrill will be the ascent to the summit (1,200 feet) by cable car made in two stages from the station at **Praia Vermelha.** The panoramic sight here will be unforgettable. Beyond the beaches you may take the interesting **Circuit of Gávea,** skirting **Lagôa Rodrigo de Freitas,** a large lagoon. On the shore is the race track of the **Jockey Club,** scene of the national sweepstakes and the famous automobile races held in June. Driving along **Avenida Niemeyer,** which cuts into thick forests, you will come to various golf courses and polo fields; thence into **Tijuca forest** with its crystal waterfalls, the **Emperors' Table** and many other beauty spots. Especially worthwhile is the impressive **National Museum,** occupying the former imperial palace, set in the midst of a lovely park, the **Quinta da Bôa Vista.** Here, too, is located the **Zoological Garden** with its marvelous collection of multicolored Brazilian birds. Of interest to music-lovers is the **Municipal Theater** which enjoys a brilliant opera season from May through August, and where the famed Toscanini first won acclaim as a conductor. Rio has over 200 churches all noteworthy for their richly decorated interiors. Among these is **Our Lady of Penha** which is famous for its

COPACABANA BEACH, RIO
Pan American-Grace Airways

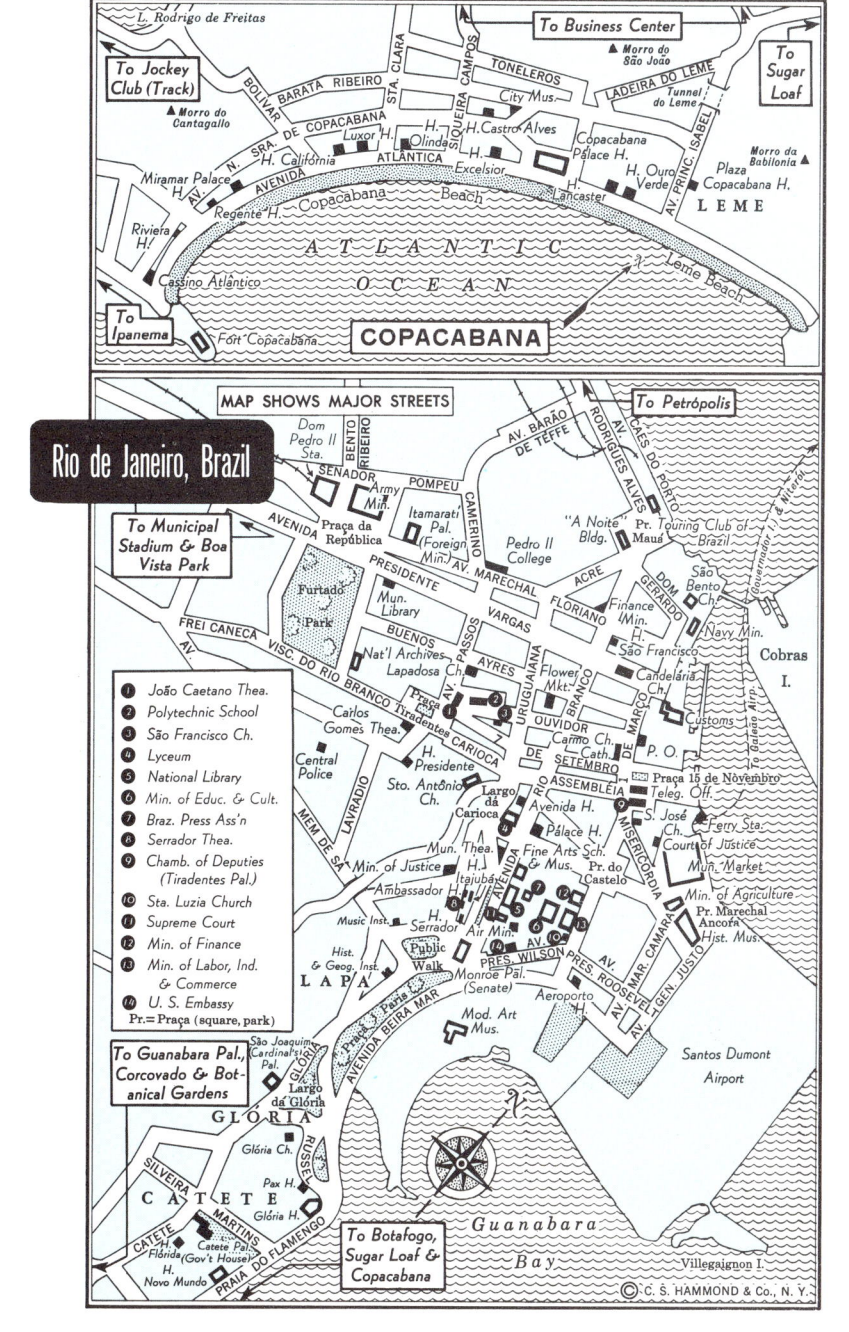

RED BEACH, RIO
Brazilian Gov't Trade Bureau

153

365 steps and annual religious festival in October. But Rio is more than scenery, marble and cement. The traveler who spends the four days before Lent in Rio will never forget the Carnival celebration which literally sweeps the people off their feet in a wave of indescribable merry-making, masquerading and pageantry to the continuous accompaniment of the Samba — and all without benefit of hard liquors, the sale of which is banned during the festivities. During the remaining 361 days the Cariocas (natives of Rio) indulge in countless diversions from the cafézinhos (little cups of black coffee) they sip throughout the day in shaded sidewalk cafés to the daily lottery which entices the entire population to play through the ever-present posters which advise the public with the slogan *"Fique Rico"* ("Get Rich"). . . . The trip from Rio to PETROPOLIS is an exhilarating experience and affords a magnificent view of Rio harbor. Once in the town the cobblestone streets and mountain streams which wind through the town like man-made canals will put the tourist in mind of Switzerland without snow. Here you will find the **Palace of Dom Pedro II**, the **Rio Negro Palace** and the **Pantheon of the Sovereigns** where rest the remains of the Emperor and his wife. The **Hotel Quitandinha** is a complete resort in itself. An enormous edifice of Norman-Swiss architecture, it has the **Organ Mountains** for background and, in the foreground, a large artificial lake. . . . A short distance from Petrópolis by car is the delightful resort of TERESOPOLIS, named after the wife of Emperor Dom Pedro. At a higher altitude, this twin resort spreads over many valleys and has the needle-pointed peaks, the **Finger of God**, dominating every view. . . . Further to the north is the mountainous state of MINAS GERAIS (General Mines). This was the land of Brazil's "Wild West" in the days of the bandeirantes (adventurers) and the "gold rush" of the 1690's. One of its chief cities is OURO PRETO, the museum city of colonial art and architecture still preserving its 18th-century mansions of mining magnates. At the height of its golden era Ouro Prêto's wealth was fabulous, and lest the Portuguese Crown use it up, the townspeople magnificently embellished their churches, though not their homes. The city's churches are all in exquisite 18th-century style, most notable of which is the **Igreja de São Francesco de Assis**. Also of interest is the church of **Santa Ifigenia**, founded by an African chieftain. . . . The first of Brazil's planned cities, BELO HORIZONTE . . . . derives its name from the "beautiful horizon" formed by the Curral d'el Rei mountain range. Filled with modern skyscrapers and ultramodern buildings, this city truly symbolizes the new Brazil. . . . North are LAGOA SANTA and CORDISBURGO, both of great anthropological interest because of the discovery of the "Lagoa Santa Man" in one of the numerous caverns located here. . . . DIAMANTINA, 200 miles from Belo Horizonte, is the center of the diamond-mining region. The mines have yielded millions of carats since the 18th century, including the Getulio Vargas diamond weighing 726 carats and the third largest ever discovered. . . . Southwest of Belo Horizonte is the pleasure resort of POCOS DE CALDOS with its many hot sulphur springs and Brazil's most fashionable watering place. . . . Located further north on the coast is BAHIA (Salvador) . . . . . This is the city "with something different," full of color and movement, set amidst the blended fragrance of coffee, cacao, church incense and tropical blooms. A place of majestic churches, of art and learning implanted by the Jesuits, it is also flavored by the primitive folklore of Africa — preserved in the music, dances and voodoo rituals of present-day descendants of Sudanese slaves. Baiana negresses skillfully balance fruit-filled baskets on their heads as they move gracefully through the streets. Some of the most beautiful churches are located near old colonial mansions, and a trip through Baixa do Sapateiro, named in honor of shoemakers, will make the past come alive again. . . . Further up the coast is RECIFE . . . . . the "Venice of Brazil." The reefs of coral which enclose the harbor gave the city its name. Here ruins of old Dutch forts, such as the one of **Buraco**, attest to the Dutch occupation of this territory in the 17th century. Of particular interest is the **Church of St. Francis of Assisi**, built in pure 18th-century style and noted for its "Golden Chapel," rich altars, carved rosewood furnishings and pictorial tiles imported from Portugal. Several bridges, notably the Bôa Vista, constructed of wrought iron, lead to a section rich in historical interest. Highlight of a pleasant excursion is a trip to OLINDA, suburb of the city, where you will see the **Monastery of São Francisco** with its carved rosewood sacristy and the **Fort of St. Francis**, popularly called the "Cheese Fort." Along the coastline it is interesting to watch fishermen launch their *jangadas*, whose red, blue and green sails dot the harbor. But before leaving be sure to taste the delicious pineapples for which the area is famous. . . . At the top of Brazil is BELEM . . . . capital of the state of PARA. Although 60 miles below the equator the city is not oppressively hot. Huge mango trees spread a canopy of shade over the streets and the numerous sidewalk cafés. Here tourists may charter a boat to MARAJO ISLAND. During the rainy season, native hunters lasso and harpoon man-eating crocodiles and alligators which infest the waters. . . . If you have the wanderlust and yearn to see a different world, take a trip up the Amazon to

WATERFRONT MARKET — Brazilian Gov't Trade Bureau

OURO PRETO — Brazilian Gov't Trade Bureau

RECIFE — Brazilian Gov't Trade Bureau

MANAUS..... To glimpse only a part of the Amazon is the experience of a lifetime. This is the land of backwoodsmen and rubber-gatherers whose huts dot the clearings on higher land. Here you can see the flight of herons, parrots and salmon-pink birds, accented by vivid splashes of color from tropical plants. When one reaches Manaus it is a surprise to find an attractive and modern city. Once the rubber capital of the world, it remains the commercial center of the Amazon Valley. Dominating the city is the **Opera House**, built by the rubber barons at an astonishing cost, and decorated with objects of art from Europe.... Returning to Rio again and moving southward one comes to **SÃO PAULO**. Often compared with Chicago, São Paulo like her North American counterpart is a vast manufacturing and processing center. Less than fifty years ago, a small provincial town, São Paulo today ranks as the largest industrial city in South America. Located at the very heart of the major coffee, cotton, livestock and mineral producing area of Brazil, the city's enormous development has been due largely to an abundance of hydro-electric power and her close proximity to the export terminus of Santos. Modern highways which link the city with the mineral deposits of Minas Gerais and to the mighty Volta Redonda steel mills also contribute to her growth. Within her ever-lengthening perimeter more than 5,750 mills and factories turn out a diversity of goods ranging from automobiles and heavy machinery to chemicals and plastics. Besides her new wealth of factories and skyscrapers, São Paulo has many handsome public buildings, flower-filled parks and beautiful residences. Among her notable institutions is the University of São Paulo. The business section is known as the **Triângulo** (Triangle) and contains banks and important business houses. The most fashionable shopping street is **Rua Barão de Itopetininga**. On the outskirts of the city is **Ipiranga Hill** where Dom Pedro I proclaimed Brazil's independence with the immortal cry of "Independence or Death." A fascinating place to visit is **Butantán Institute**, six miles from the center of the city. Better known as the "Snake Farm," this unique institution is engaged in developing antisnakebite serums as part of its broad scientific research. The city's many churches include ancient and interesting ones such as Santo Antonio, where, it is said, girls pray for husbands. The Municipal Stadium has an ampitheater which seats 80,000 spectators and can put on a show with over 10,000 participants (a new and larger stadium is to be built in the future).... A trip to **SANTOS** .... is worth while via the fine modern highway of **Via Anchieta** which links São Paulo with the coffee port. It is from these docks in Santos that the world's coffee cups are filled. No one should leave this region without a trip to a coffee *fazenda*.... Typical of the extreme south of Brazil is the state of **RIO GRANDE DO SUL**. Here the valiant figure of the *gaucho* (cowboy) still dominates the land. Picturesque in baggy trousers tucked in tooled-leather boots with silver spurs together with poncho, broad-brimmed hat and indispensable sheath knife, they relax with harmonicas and guitars while they sing and dance the *chimarrita*, a distinctive part of Brazil's folklore.... Worth a special trip is a visit to the crowning glory of Brazil's natural wonders, **Iguassú Falls**, where the Iguassú River plunges over an escarpment in the form of a two-and-one-half-mile crescent, bathed in rainbow hues, to a gorge 230 feet below.

ANHANGABAU PARK, SAO PAULO

Bolivia

LLAMAS ON THE ALTIPLANO
Pan American World Airways

COUNTRY OF ANCIENT CULTURE

Bolivia offers the visitor the opportunity of discovering one of the most fascinating yet little-known countries of the Americas. Here you can see life as it was lived centuries ago. You can gaze upon ruins which some archaeologists have estimated to be over 10,000 years old, or you may vacation on the shores of Lake Titicaca, sacred lake of the Incas, which is shrouded in pre-historic Indian legends. Nowhere else in the world will you see such colorful Indian festivals and witness such strange rites with their mixture of the pagan and the Christian. Here, too, you can watch primitive dances and hear plaintiff songs sung in an ancient language accompanied by weird music played on instruments that were old when the Spaniard came. Once within the country you will become acquainted with the haughty llama, Bolivia's beast of burden, who refuses to carry a load exceeding a certain weight. Only after a visit to this land will you come under the magical spell which only Bolivia knows how to cast.

BOLIVIAN COOKERY

Many native dishes may be sampled in Bolivia. Try *lla-uchitas*, a Bolivian tidbit somewhat like a filled cookie. They are easier to eat than to pronounce! Another popular dish is *empanadas de queso*, or cheese turnovers, fried in hot fat. *Salteñas Bolivianas* are delicious turnovers made with meat.

BEFORE AND AFTER PIZARRO

Around 600 A. D. the civilized Aymará Indians lived at the southern end of Lake Titicaca. About 600 years later the Incas, highly civilized themselves, conquered the region and incorporated the Aymarás into their empire. Within a few hundred years the Spanish conqueror, Francisco Pizarro, began his conquest of the Inca Empire. The Indians would not submit, however, to the exploitation by the Spaniards. Twice during the 17th century there were native uprisings. Once the city of La Paz was besieged by Indians who tried to force the town into submission by damming a river and then exploding the dam so as to flood the settlement, a technique they had learned during their enslaved labor in the silver mines. But the Spanish had come to stay, and with their tight hold on the country the Indians' courage was transformed into stoic passivity. Although the Indian's physical resistance was subdued, his cultural spirit was never wholly conquered by the impact of Spanish domination. Even today he may still be seen playing his ancient *zampona* at a fiesta, or dancing the traditional *sicuri* while wearing his gigantic ostrich feather headdress. Such is the strength of the customs that emanate from his dim and remote past.

TOURING BOLIVIA

LA PAZ. Situated in the Altiplano region of western Bolivia, at more than two and a quarter miles above sea level, the air of La Paz is crisp, its natural setting spectacular. To the east, Mount Illimani towers, its rugged slopes clad in the snowy robes of the Royal Andean Cordillera. About the narrow green-carpeted valley in which the city lies are gathered the bare mineral-colored peaks of lesser mountains. From the valley floor, the steep canyon walls rise almost perpendicularly above its cluster of red tiled roofs, its dignified Legislative Palace, and its Greco-Roman cathedral. In 1548, to celebrate the end of a long and bitter struggle between Pizarro and de Almagro, rival conquerors of Peru, the city of La Paz was established. Translated into English the inscription which graces its elaborate coat of arms reads: "With discords and with stubborn rages at length in harmony compounded, the town of peace was thereon founded—a monument for future ages." Belying the name, the history of La Paz, until the end of the 19th century, was far from peaceful. Exploited by the Spaniards, besieged by Indians, torn by revolutions, unsettled by long periods of political antagonism, yet here a new country emerged from the chaos and in July, 1809, Bolivia declared her independence. Today, although Sucre continues as the official capital of Bolivia, several branches of the government make La Paz their headquarters and the city has become the principal center of her country's industry, commerce and communications. Of principal interest in the city is Santo Domingo Church where native plant forms are sculptured around the pillars of the entrance. The Cathedral located here was begun in 1835 and has only recently been finished. The Prado in the southern section

GOLF COURSE, LA PAZ

La Paz, Bolivia

Map legend:
1. Government (Pres.) Pal.
2. Military Club
3. Bishop's Pal.
4. San Augustín Ch.
5. Mercantile Bank
6. Mining Bank
7. Central Bank
8. Chamber of Comm.
9. Agriculture Min.
10. State Gov't Offices
11. Villaverde House
12. Cirbol (Radio Boliviano)
13. Obelisk
14. Cathedral
15. Gen. Post Office
16. Club La Paz
17. City Hall

INDIANS SELLING SOUVENIRS — Rob Gerstmann

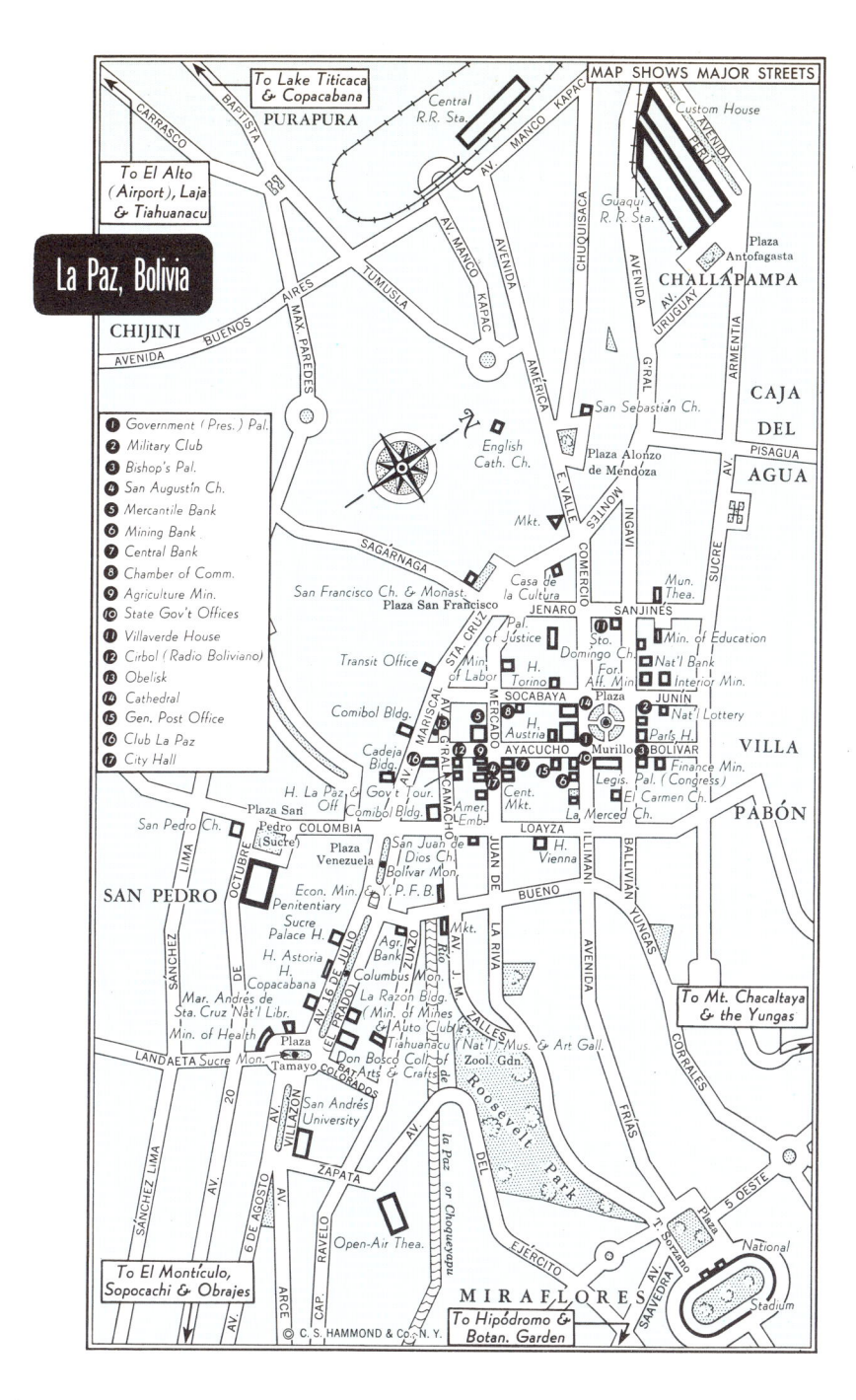

is a wide avenue with flower beds in the center and spacious walks. Nearby is **El Monticulo Park**, known for its fine view of the city and the surrounding mountains. If you want an idea of what a colonial nobleman's house looked like, visit the former residence of the Marquis of Villaverde with its armorial bearings over the door. In the **Miraflores district**, east of the capital, is the **stadium** built to accommodate 50,000 people; international soccer matches are played here every year. A common sight around La Paz and its suburbs is the **Aymará Indian**, wearing his woolen, peaked cap with long ear flaps, a homespun poncho and sandals. The Aymará woman wears her black hair divided into two braids, and on top of her head is set a round, felt "derby.". . . A short distance from La Paz lies **Lake Titicaca** with **Mt. Illampu** in the distance. The **Islands of the Sun and Moon** (Titicaca and Coati) and other parts of the lake's basin abound in Incan and pre-Incan remains. The visitor wishing a glimpse of Indian ways of life may hire a **balsa**, or native fishing craft, constructed of weeds lashed together to form a boat. If you like trout fishing, you may get the trout of your life in the waters of the lake. The average catch is around 25 pounds; the record is 36½ pounds. . . . A short distance away is **COPACABANA**. The first week in August this town is thronged with pilgrims who come to worship at the renowned shrine known as the **Virgin of the Lake**. . . . Three hours from La Paz is the village of **TIAHUANACU**, rich in archaeological lore. It is believed that the ruined city is the work of the Aymará Indians. Here stands the monolithic gateway or **Portal of the Sun** with its puzzling symbols. Also located here are the **ruins of the Palace of Kalassaya**, covered by ancient silence. The Aymará civilization, which flourished here 1300 years ago, presents one of the most baffling mysteries in South American archaeology. . . . Although the government has its headquarters in La Paz, the legal and official capital is **SUCRE**, the "garden of Bolivia." Interesting to visit are the **Cathedral**, with its jewelled statue of the Virgin of Guadelupe, and the **Government Palace** on Plaza 25 de Mayo. Once a "stop-over" for the Spanish conquistadores traveling between Lima and Buenos Aires, the city retains a lordly and aristocratic air, preserving many of its Castillian traditions and customs as well as its fine colonial buildings. . . . To the northwest of Sucre is the mining city of **ORURO**. Here are found Bolivia's famous "devil dancers" wearing their awesome masks with horns as they perform during the pre-Lenten carnival season. . . . South of Oruro is **POTOSI**, Bolivia's important tin center. The name of the city has become a word in the Spanish language synonymous with untold wealth. The principal public buildings are the **Casa de Moneda**, or mint, built for coining silver from adjacent mines and the old **cabildo** or town hall built in the 16th century. While here, one should visit the quaint colonial **Church of San Benito**. Near the town is the fabulous **Cerro Rico** (Rich Hill) from which two billion dollars worth of silver has been taken since it was first opened by the Spaniards. . . . If hunting is your sport, then you will want to visit **SANTA CRUZ**. Here you can experience life in the tropical jungles and still enjoy modern comforts — even if a bit on the rustic side. Tigers, panthers and deer inhabit the area around this town.

COCHABAMBA-SANTA CRUZ HIGHWAY

Paraguay

PARAGUAYANS WEAVING BASKETS

Pan American Union

"PLACE OF THE GREAT RIVER"

Towering palms, delicate orchids and ever-present orange trees will not be the only sights that the visitor will encounter in this rural, inland country lodged between the two giants of the continent. It is also a land where the golden-skinned salmon is caught, where trees grow so hard they are called *quebrachos* (ax-breakers), where the people sip their tea from gourds and where one may observe Indian women contentedly smoking big black cigars. It is a land where the old Indian tongue, Guaraní is still the language of the "man in the street," and where milk is delivered to your doorstep on a burro. Exquisite lace, so fragile it is referred to as "spider web" cloth, is the secret art of the Paraguayan women whose skillful hands perform a seeming feat of magic. Such a panorama of the colorful and curious awaits the visitor who enters the borders of Paraguay.

PARAGUAYAN FOOD

The tourist should certainly sample *sopa Paraguaya*, a delicious corn cake, as well as *albóndigas con chipá guazú*, a combination of meat balls and corn pie. If you have a sweet tooth try *cocereva* (candied grapefruit). No trip to Paraguay is complete unless you have tried the aromatic *yerba maté*, a drink which has made Paraguay famous.

CAPITAL AND COUNTRYSIDE

Capital and most important city is ASUNCION . . . . river port and commercial center of the country. The wide streets and regular blocks give the city a distinctive charm, especially after a downpour, when the cobblestones take on a shiny black appearance. Orange trees line the broad avenues and buildings have courtyards filled with magnolia, jasmine and rose plants. The spirit of Paraguayan life will be captured in one of the several markets of the town. Outside such places oxen rest from dragging the loaded carts and gray donkeys with hobbled feet stand blinking in the sun. Inside is a scene of cheerful confusion: Servant girls mill around with their baskets, trying to outbid or at least outshout each other. Squatting stolidly on the ground by their wares are the merchants, mostly women who have ridden in from the country sidesaddle on the little donkeys waiting outside. With ruffled skirts and blouses, their heads wound in long black shawls, they await their customers, speaking Guaraní with their neighbors and now and then sipping maté from a gourd. A visitor may wander through the crowd looking for samples of the exquisite *ñandutí* lace; this fabulous product, of which there are over a hundred and twenty varieties, is woven in patterns bearing such poetic names as "flower of the bewitching thistle," "monkey-eyelash" and "flower of the wild guayaba tree." Of course the majority of marketgoers come to buy fruit, vegetables, fish and meat. The visitor who cannot wait for his food may enjoy his meal on the spot if he is patient enough to sit on a bench and wait for a tasty stew while it is being prepared over the coal fires. Having had an intimate glimpse of everyday life in the capital, you will want to visit some of the sites of the town. Impressive buildings are the **Congressional Palace**, designed in severe Spanish colonial style, and the **Government Palace** nearby, which was modeled by an Italian architect in Renaissance style. Across the street from the latter is the **Cathedral** with its two square bell towers and imposing arcades. The clock on one of the towers is the city's official timepiece. The most prominent church in Asunción is **La Encarnación**, reminiscent of the Milan cathedral. Also of interest is the **Oratory of the Virgin of Asunción**, modeled after Les Invalides in Paris and containing the remains of Paraguay's paternal despot, Carlos Antonio López, and his son. The visitor will enjoy a trip to some of the city's fine parks. Standing on the highest part of the city is **Parque Antonio López**. From here spreads out a panorama of town, bay and river. The sun, when it sets beyond the distant reaches of the marshy, wooded **Chaco**, is an unforgettable sight. Another lovely park occupies the former **estate of Bernadino Cabellero**, one of Paraguay's heroes. Here the visitor may see plantings of coffee and yerba maté and of lapacho, a tree with a purple or pink flower, which yields a particularly hard wood. . . . The countryside around the capital is ideally adapted for horseback riding, and visitors say an orange never tastes so delicious as when plucked from a roadside tree and eaten, still warm from the sunshine, in the saddle. Continuing on horseback one sees cattle grazing in the fields or standing in quiet little streams. Crossing a brook the horse may stop halfway, facing upstream to drink, while a vulture looks on morosely from a fallen tree. Women are seen along the roads enveloped in black shawls with donkeys laden with oranges or maté. One may have a baby in her arms while holding a black umbrella. Another may be trying to lessen the rigors of a trip to market by smoking a large cigar. . . . Four miles from Asunción is the suburb of TRINIDAD. Here the estate of the former dictator López has been converted into a **Botanical Garden** which, because of its wide variety of plants, is one of the finest in the Americas. Extending over an area covering more than two square miles, it encloses bays, lagoons, virgin forests and the sloping hills of a nine-hole golf course, Roman and Japanese landscaped gardens, pergolas overgrown with roses and jasmine and examples of Paraguayan wildlife, both animal and vegetable, are all found here. . . . Not far from the capital is the town of CAPIATA. Here the church is thought to be the work of the Jesuits. It has fine bells, delicately carved altars and a renowned, life-sized **figure of Christ on the Cross**. . . . . The town of ITAUGUA, on the same road, is given over to the making of ñandutí lace. Here even the old women and little children carry their frames with them and work as they walk. . . . A pleasant excursion is one to SAN BERNARDINO, about 35 miles from Asunción. Located on the shores of **Lake Ypacaray**, it is Paraguay's most popular resort and health center, equipped with a country club and fine hotels. . . . Travelers to Paraguay should also make a point to admire the wildlife of the Chaco, with its many brilliant birds, by taking a motor launch up the **Pilcomayo River**. The round trip can be made from Asunción in one day and is well worth the extra time it takes.

Uruguay

PARQUE RODO, MONTEVIDEO

Pan American World Airways

"RIVER OF THE PAINTED BIRDS"

La República Oriental del Uruguay was so named in the colonial days because of its situation on the east bank of the River Uruguay, which in turn was named by the Guarani Indians, who once inhabited this region. Rolling grain fields, orchards and pastures are richly carpeted with intense green, contrasting with black, newly turned earth. A belt of sandy lowlands extends southward down the Atlantic seaboard from the Brazilian frontier to the Río de la Plata estuary. Thus, the country is noted for its beautiful pastoral scenery, its many fine beach resorts and its capital, Montevideo, one of the most modern cities in the world. It is the smallest republic in South America but it is one of the most advanced, politically and socially, in the world. A true welfare state, Uruguay has rightly been called the "social laboratory of the Americas." Its bountiful natural resources, its advanced social and political organization and the liberality of its laws have become well-known far beyond its frontiers, and tiny Uruguay occupies an honored place among the American nations.

CULTURE

While indigenous influences played a great part in the cultural development of many Latin American nations, such was not the case in Uruguay. The foundations of Uruguayan culture were laid during the colonial era with strong emphasis on the contributions of the mother country, Spain. In the centuries that followed, the culture of Uruguay became more generally European in expression. Contemporary Uruguayan culture is a national culture that has developed from the native creativeness of the Uruguayan people. It is national in the sense that it expresses the character of the Uruguayan people but cosmopolitan in that it is not limited in scope or bound by traditionalism.

GOOD LIVING

There are few places where such abundance and variety may be found as in Uruguay. Excellent European and Creole dishes, sea food and good native wines are served. Steaks and grills of fine flavor cut from beef grazed on natural pasture are essential dishes. Vegetables and fruits also have excellent flavor, such as lettuce, peaches, apples, pears and really delightful tangerines, to mention only a few. The Uruguayan string beans and *pastel de carne* (Uruguayan meat pie) are two especially popular dishes.

BANDA ORIENTAL

MONTEVIDEO. Montevideo, the capital of Uruguay, lies on the north shore of the Río de la Plata on Montevideo Bay across from El Cerro, a low mountain that is supposed to have given the city its name. When Magellan's ships sailed into the Río de la Plata in 1520, a lookout on seeing El Cerro shouted in Portuguese "Monte vide eu!" (I see a mountain!) Largely because of its salubrious climate but also because of its fine natural facilities for sea and river bathing, Montevideo has become one of the most popular summer resorts in South America. Stretching along the shore of the river for several miles are splendid bathing resorts which attract not only the people of Uruguay but also those of neighboring countries. Within Montevideo are three well defined districts, kept more or less distinct by zoning regulations. The Ciudad Vieja (Old Town) built on the peninsula is the commercial and financial center. Even today, this old section retains its colonial atmosphere. Spreading out from the peninsula is Ciudad Nueva (New City), in which most of the modern architectural development has taken place, including the handsome buildings of the national government, office buildings and churches. The third district in the city is residential, containing beautiful homes with large flowering gardens which front on broad shady streets. Montevideo's transit system connects all sections of the city. Center of the Old City is the **Plaza Constitución**, the city's original square, on **Sarandí Street**, which with **Avenida 18 de Julio**, is a principal thoroughfare. Bordering the plaza are two of Montevideo's oldest and most interesting structures, the Cathedral and the **Palacio del Cabildo** (City Hall), whose severe lines suggest the dignity of colonial times. Also in the downtown section is the **Plaza Independencia**, the social center, in which is an heroic monument by Zanelli of General José Artigas, Uruguay's national hero — one of the many fine sculptures in the capital. Not far from this plaza is the **Teatro Solís**, one of the finest and largest theaters in South America, in which the great dramatic and operatic artists of the world appear. A symphonic center of first rank, Montevideo inaugurated its famous **orchestra of the Servicio Oficial de Difusión Radio Eléctrica (SODRE)**, Official Broadcasting Service, in 1931. In the New City, spreading out from the peninsula, most of the modern architectural development has taken place. Special attention is reserved for the **Legislative Palace**, a magnificent structure where the General Assembly meets. The lower part of the building is of gray granite, while the two upper floors provide a color contrast of rose marble crowned by several symbolic groups and decorative motifs. Very impressive are the modern lines of the **Hospital de Clínicas**, near **Parque José Batlle y Ordóñez**. A unique feature of this park is one of the country's best-loved monuments, the life-sized bronze group, **El Monumento a la Carreta** (The Cart),

PLAZA INDEPENDENCIA, MONTEVIDEO

Gendreau

by the noted sculptor José Belloni, commemorating the Uruguayan pioneers. This group demonstrates an unusual and interesting treatment of a public monument; it is not set on a raised pedestal but follows the contour of the ground. Thousands of fans jam the **Estadio Centenario (Centenary Stadium)**, also in this park, to watch the game of soccer — the country's number one sport. In this district, too, is the **National University**, one of America's top-ranking institutions of higher learning. The numerous gardens throughout the city are one of its most striking features. The **Prado**, Montevideo's oldest and most beautiful park and a popular rendezvous, is a vast expanse of glades, gardens and lakes traversed by a picturesque little stream, containing a wonderful rose garden of some eight hundred varieties, which has given to the metropolis the name of the "City of Roses." **Parque Rodó** contains the **Gran Teatro Municipal de Verano (Open-Air Summer Theater)**, the **National Museum of Fine Arts**, with works by living artists, and **Ramírez Beach**, most popular urban beach. At the end of summer, Montevideo explodes into Carnival, when the city is full of noise and fun, with a great parade, gay popular dances and small stages, called "Tablados," set up in neighborhood squares and featuring local talent. In the fall comes **Semana Criolla (Creole Week)**, with a rodeo, barbecues and entertainment by the "Sociedad Criolla," consisting of traditional songs, dances and games. Largely because of its salubrious climate, but also because of the fine natural facilities for bathing, Montevideo has become one of the most popular summer resorts on the continent. Some of the world's finest beaches fringe the coast. **Pocitos**, adjoining the capital, is one of the most popular, while the social favorite is **Carrasco Beach**, with one of the largest beaches on the Uruguayan coast.... The well-known aristocratic residential resort of **PUNTA DEL ESTE**, on the Atlantic east of Montevideo, is the gathering place of the swankiest cosmopolitan smart set and goal of sport fishermen. There are two beaches, Las Delicias and San Rafael, and boats take fishermen either to **Gorriti Island** for silver porgies or trolling nearby for bonitos and bluefish. A most colorful pageantry is offered on rocky **Isla de Lobos (Seal Island)**, permanent refuge for thousands of seals.... Northeast of here is **ROCHA** on Rocha's Lake, when great shoals of black sea drum, white bass, silversides, bluefish and pompanos come in. Not far from the Brazilian border is the marvelous artificial forest of **Santa Teresa National Park**, including a large number of exotic trees from different parts of the world. At the center of the park is star-shaped Santa Teresa Fortress, begun in the eighteenth century by the Portuguese, completed by the Spaniards who won it in battle and restored by the Uruguayan government. Erosion has produced some odd effects on the land near this historic fortress.... West from Montevideo is **MERCEDES**, standing on the south bank of the Rio Negro, thirty miles above its junction with Rio Uruguay. It is one of the cleanest and neatest cities of the interior — where hilly plains stretch endlessly into the distance — a favored health resort and a picturesque center for yachting and fishing, especially for dorados, surubies, a kind of deep-water catfish, and the tararira.... Third city of the republic is **SALTO**, farther up the Uruguay. There is some wine production and large-scale beef farming here, but these industries are minor compared to the great orange and tangerine groves surrounding the city, giving it the title of "City of Oranges." Above Salto the river runs between high banks, with many rapids, and a favorite excursion is by launch to one of these, the **Salto Chico**. Another favorite is the trip to the picturesque, majestic waterfall of **Salto Grande**, making this an important fishing center also, since dorados, mendoles and the giant dientudos continually climb the waterfall, a curious, fascinating spectacle.

RACE TRACK, MONTEVIDEO

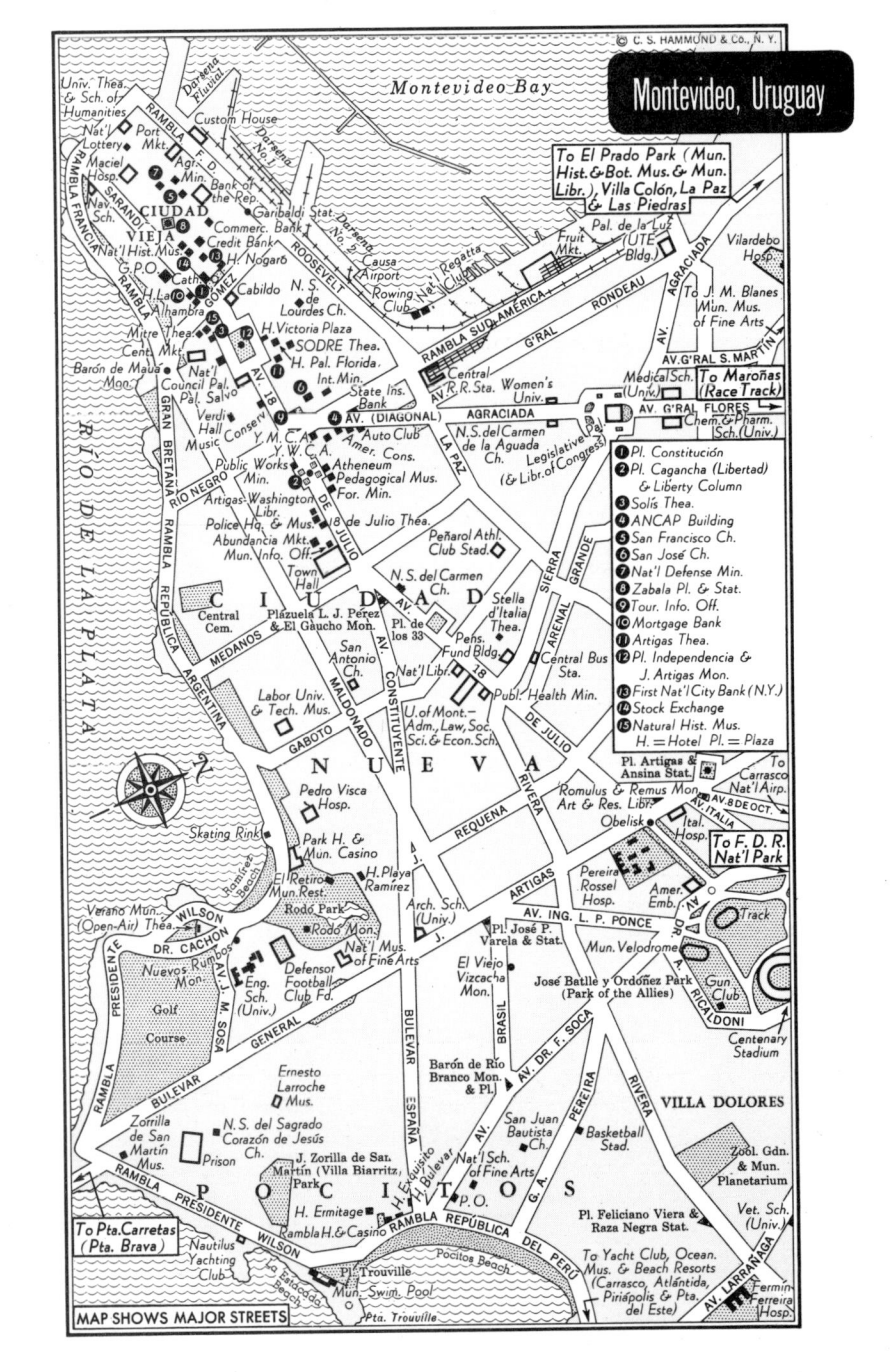

Gendreau

SOUTH AMERICA

1. Man and woman in native dress—Peru
2. "La Boca" section of Buenos Aires—Argentina
3. City of Caracas—Venezuela
4. Street scene, Buenos Aires—Argentina
5. Girls weaving straw hats—Ecuador

SOUTH AMERICA

1. Gaucho and his horse—Uruguay
2. Llamas serve as beasts of burden—Bolivia
3. Huasos (cowboys)—Chile
4. Vina del Mar, a famed resort on the Chilean coast

SOUTH AMERICA

1. Volcano Santiago near Managua—Nicaragua
2. Farm and farmhouse—El Salvador
3. Urca and yacht area, Rio de Janeiro
4. Oxcarts on way to quartz mines—Brazil
5. Washing clothes—Brazil
6. Native children—Brazil

SOUTH AMERICA

1. Display of native handicraft, Santiago Atitlán —Guatemala
2. Children in native costume, Medellin—Colombia
3. Church and market place—Chichicastenango— Guatemala
4. Andes Mountains—Venezuela
5. Ancient ruins at Machu Picchu—Peru

Chile

CHILE'S NORTHERN COASTLINE — Hamilton Wright

THE LONG AND SLENDER COUNTRY

A spectacular display of wonderful scenery awaits the visitor to Chile. From the great chameleonlike desert in the north to the frigid reaches of the south, it is unsurpassed for its infinite variety of eye-filling beauty. The great fishing grounds off the scalloped coast of northern Chile, the towering snow-capped mountains, magnificent lakes and glacier-fringed fiords of the central region, and the internationally famous Viña del Mar, the luxurious playground city of the coast, are but a few of the vacation features offered by the varied terrain of Chile. Twenty-six hundred miles in length from the borderline of Peru to the cold, bleak Tierra del Fuego in the Antarctic, it is in no place more than 221 miles wide. Yet traversing this narrow strip of land are two great mountain ranges topped by the highest peaks in the world next to the Himalayas. The Chileans have often been called the "Yankees" of South America for their enterprise and self-reliance and for their ready sense of humor.

In no other country will you find such a delightful blending of Anglo-Saxon names: Bernardo O'Higgins, Arturo Prat, Augustín Edwards, Vicuña Mackenna — all great Chileans with whom you will become familiar as you journey through the country.

SEA FOOD, MEAT AND WINE

Beef and fowl are excellent, but the fish and shellfish are superlative. Besides lobster from Robinson Crusoe's Island, tender oysters, crab and shrimp, there are many foods not found in other countries. *Cochayuyo* (seaweed) is very popular. *Erizos* (sea urchins), *locos* and *ostiones* (shellfish and conger eel) are only a few of the many delicacies to tempt you. The native dishes include *empanadas* (meat-filled cakes), *pastel de choclo* (a combination of corn, meat, chicken and vegetables baked in a clay bowl) and *cazuela* (a stew with chicken, corn, vegetables and rice). The Chilean wines are world-famous; their excellence is partly due to being properly aged in vaults long before they appear on the market. *Pisco*, a colorless grape brandy, is very popular. It is customary in Chile to take tea at around 5 P. M.; the dinner hour is usually around 9 P. M.

FROM DESERT TO ICEBERGS

One of the principal ports in the northern third of Chile is ARICA in the region of the Atacama desert. Here an international railway begins it tortuous trip across valleys, dangerous curves and steep inclines to Bolivia. Within the city a spectacle of note is the great cliff of El Morro, rising 600 feet out of the ocean and the site of a memorable battle of the War of the Pacific. The church of San Marcos here was built by the same man who constructed the world-famous tower in Paris, Alexander Gustave Eiffel. A strange sight to see is the old American ship, the S. S. Wateree, lying high and dry a mile from town in the Atacama desert, swept there by a tidal wave in 1868. . . . A little further south is the town of IQUIQUE from whose shore line extends the best deep-sea fishing waters in the world, waters which abound in swordfish, needlefish, yellowfin tuna and striped marlin. In the center of the city is Plaza Arturo Prat, named for Chile's great naval hero. . . . Moving on through ANTOFAGASTA, great copper and nitrate center of Chile, and through some smaller cities, one comes to the capital, SANTIAGO . . . . The North American is often struck with an inexplicable sense of the familiar when he first views the Chilean capital, for in its hustle and bustle, in the shiny newness of its maze of lofty skyscrapers, there is a similarity between Santiago and many of the cities of California or Texas. While in superficial appearance the city is both functional and modern, it possesses many fine examples of Spanish-colonial architecture and a history which goes back more than 400 years. The fourth largest city in South America, Santiago lies at the foot of towering snow-capped mountains in the very heart of Chile's paradise vale, the fertile central plain which furnishes the nation with the bulk of its agricultural produce. The Mapocho River winds through the center of the city and one of its arms which dried up when the

SANTIAGO
Hamilton Wright

SANTA LUCIA HILL, SANTIAGO
Pan American Union

river was walled, furnishes the foundation for the Avenida Bernardo O'Higgins or "Alameda" as it is also called. This thoroughfare is Chile's "hall of fame" because of the many great statues which are found along its shady walks. You may begin a tour of the city by climbing **Cerro Santa Lucía**, a little hill rising from the center of town like a castle in the air. In one shady corner, near the small **museum of folk art and primitive arms**, stands a **statue of Pedro de Valdivia** pensively overlooking the city which he founded in 1541. At the foot of Cerro Santa Lucía, and facing Avenida Bernardo O'Higgins, are the **National Archives** and the **National Library**. The library contains one of the finest historical collections in the world and is said to be the largest in South America. Adjoining the library is the **Museum of Natural History** where you will find interesting records of the colonial era, the war of independence and a fine collection of archaeological relics. Further along the **Alameda**, a large open space forms **Plaza Bulnes** and **Plaza Libertad**. This area is known as the **Barrio Cívico**, where an imposing group of buildings houses the capital's civic and administrative offices. One block behind Plaza Libertad is the presidential residence where, every morning, the colorful and ceremonial changing of the Presidential Guard takes place. Between the Alameda and the Mapocho River is the main business district which centers around the **Plaza de Armas**. Branching out from the Plaza are crowded one-way streets where you will find department stores, luxurious hotels, bookstores and newspaper offices. To the southeast of the Alameda is the **Cousiño Park section**, centering around the city's popular playground and athletic field. Not far away is the Club Hípico race track —one of the finest in South America. If you have time, wander through the **General Cemetery** on La Paz Avenue under the century-old cypress trees. The many monuments to Chile's heroes will add to your knowledge of this country's illustrious past. Few cities have as many art exhibits as this one. Exhibits may be seen at the galleries of the **Fine Arts Museum** and the salons of the **Bank of Chile**. . . . There are a number of resorts near Santiago offering facilities for sports or relaxation. **FARELLONES**, high in the Andes, and **LA PARVA**, a new ski center, are popular with skiing enthusiasts and provide some of the best skiing accommodations in the world. . . . If at all possible try to visit a *fundo* or farm in the great **Central Valley** of Chile. Here you will see the Chilean *huasos* (cowboys) perform thrilling feats at their rodeos. Dressed in colorful sombreros, wide-brimmed hats, and wearing fringed leggings, they are justly famed for their excellent riding ability. . . . Northwest of Santiago is the "Pearl of the Pacific," **VALPARAISO**. The starting point in the port section is Plaza Sotomayor, dominated by another statue of Arturo Prat, naval hero of Iquique. This port once saw the "Golden Hind" of Sir Francis Drake while he was waging war against the Spaniards and was where Admiral Farragut first saw sea action as a cadet of fourteen aboard the U. S. Frigate Essex. On the south of the plaza is the Intendencia, Palace of the Governor of Valparaíso, a stately building of French architecture. Three blocks below O'Higgins Plaza, palm-bordered **Avenida Brasil** runs parallel to **Avenida Pedro Montt**. The central market, a gay and colorful affair, is on Avenida Brasil. Here you will find the British Arch commemorating the centenary of Chilean independence; a **statue of Lord Cochrane**, the British naval officer who built up the Chilean navy; and a **statue of William Wheelwright**, the North American who did much to develop transportation in Chile. A short drive along Avenida Altamurano takes you around Punta de An-

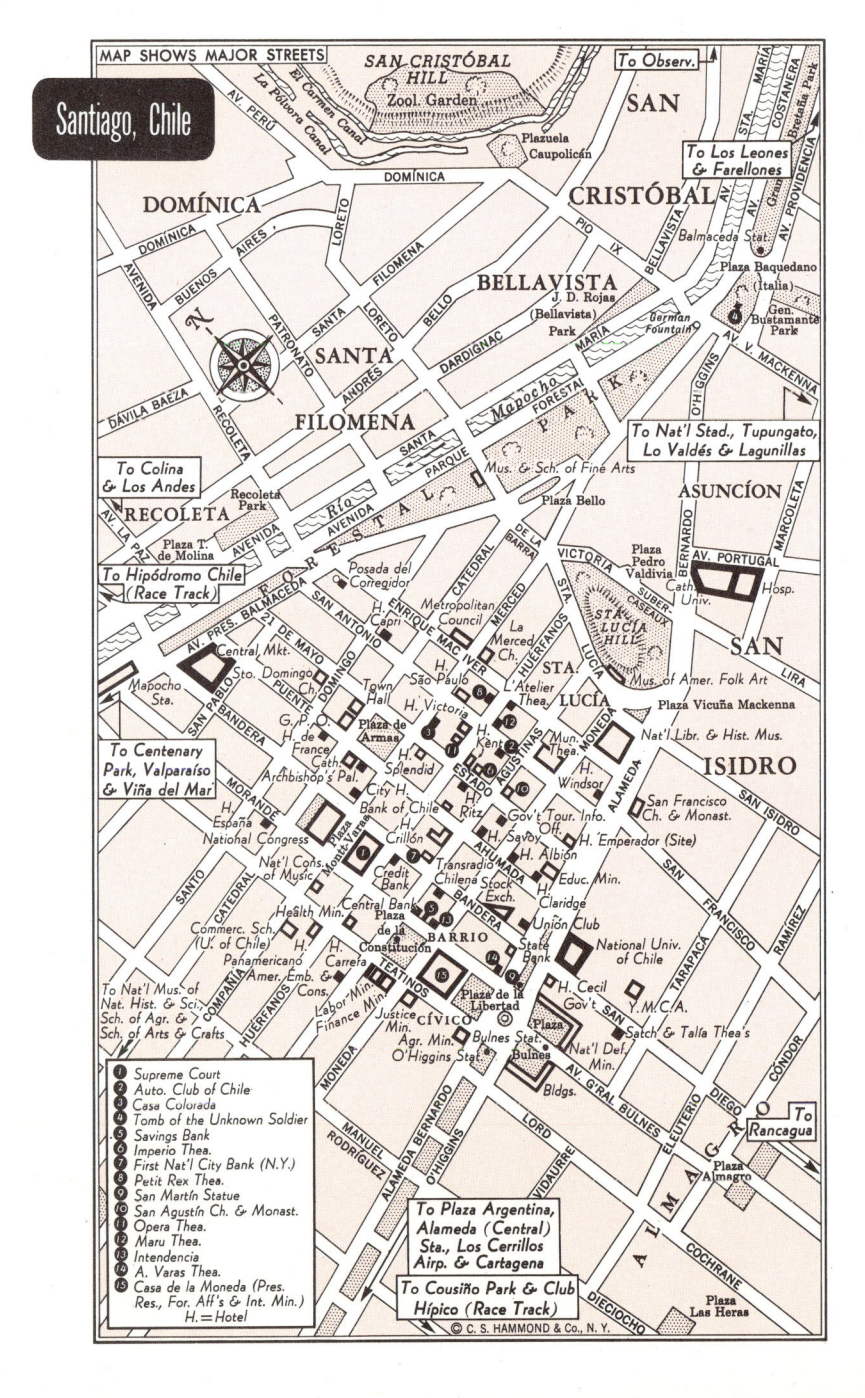

THE CASA DE LA MONEDA
Pan American Union

162

geles, with its lighthouse, to the sheltered beach of **Las Torpederas**. Beautiful flowers spill over the rocky shore line including masses of geraniums and poppies said to have been planted there by an American from California. . . . Show place of the nation, and major attraction on the coast of Chile for tourists, is **VINA DEL MAR**, six miles northeast of Valparaíso. The South American "Cote d'Azure," Viña del Mar is famous for its dazzling beaches of fine, white sand, white sand washed by waters cooled by the Humboldt Current; for its fine even climate and luxurious hotels and for its sumptuous **Casino Municipal** surrounded by terraces and gardens. The city is especially lovely when the jacaranda trees are in bloom, and when the fragrance of roses, honeysuckle, oleanders and wisteria mingles with the fresh sea air. There are facilities for all kinds of sports here. Horse racing during January and March at the **Valparaíso Sporting Club** is one of the most popular events of the season. International polo matches are attended by the cream of society, as are the exciting yacht races. . . . You can visit the very island on which Defoe based his immortal story when you are in Chile, for it lies 360 miles due west of Valparaíso in the **Archipelago Juan Fernández** and may be reached during the tourist season (November to March). The island, often called **Robinson Crusoe Island**, is covered with vegetation quite different from that of the mainland and is permeated with the sweet odor of sandalwood. This island and the others of the group are believed to be the remains of a large coastal island or of a lost continent. Long the haunt of English and Dutch buccaneers who plied the coast, they are famous for the excellent sea food found in the waters offshore. The only settlement on the islands is **San Juan Bautista on Más a Tierra**. It lies at the foot of a large hill overlooking Cumberland Bay. This spot is known as **Selkirk's Lookout**, for it was here that Alexander Selkirk, the marooned British sailor, kept his lonely vigil for signs of an approaching ship. . . . An interesting excursion from the capital is a trip to **PORTILLO**, Chile's most famous winter resort. Its ski grounds, over 9000 feet high in the Andes, attract professional skiers from all over the world. . . . From Portillo a day's trip takes you to the magnificent statue of **Christ of the Andes**. Twenty-six feet high, the imposing figure stands on a granite column surmounted by a globe on which the continents are set in bronze. The following words are engraved on its base: "Sooner shall the mountains crumble into dust than the Argentines and Chileans break the peace to which they have pledged themselves at the feet of Christ the Redeemer." . . . To the far south is **PUERTO MONTT**, where big three-masted whaling vessels, steamers and freighters lie at harbor. It is from here that ships follow the Southern Cross, which hangs in the sky like a brilliant lantern, until it seems as though they could go no further as they penetrate the Antarctic region. Here the newer cities of **AYSEN** and **PUNTA ARENAS** are to be found. The former is situated near **Laguna de San Rafael**, one of the nation's wonders. Surrounding the lake are great forests and three spectacular glaciers, one of which reaches the icy waters of the lagoon only to crumble into small icebergs.

CHRIST OF THE ANDES

RODEO

VINA DEL MAR

Argentina

PLAZA DEL CONGRESO, BUENOS AIRES

A LAND OF CONTRASTS

Argentina provides the traveler with every conceivable type of enjoyment. One may ski or fish in the Andes, golf in the Córdoba Sierras or swim in the ocean at one of the seacoast resorts. If it's a gay, fashionable holiday or a vacation of opera, symphony and art the tourist is seeking, all hopes will be realized in Argentina's up-to-date capital, glamorous Buenos Aires.

PAST AND PRESENT

Although the famed *gaucho* — that nomadic plainsman, untamed, like the wild horses and cattle he hunted—has passed into folklore, the romance of Argentina's past may still be recaptured in the beautiful homes, churches and public buildings of intricate old Spanish architecture in the colonial cities or in the primitive Indian country of the northwest. Besides the Indians of the northwest, whose remote, simple life is unchanged from that of hundreds of years ago, the most colorful Argentinians are the modern cowboys—still called gauchos—of the pampas, who preserve the typical costumes of their proud, romantic predecessors: baggy *bombachas*, short boots and black sombreros. Like their American counterpart, they are magnificent riders and ropers, and their lonely, haunting songs, in a rhythm matching the gait of their horses, are sung as they ride the wide, grassy plains.

EAT, DRINK AND BE MERRY

Argentina is noted for its fine meat dishes, especially those featuring the different cuts of *bife* (beefsteak). Their delicious charcoal-broiled steaks, chicken or lamb roasted on a spit and *parrillada*, a mixed grille of liver, kidneys, etc., are obtainable in any part of the country. The barbecue is the Argentine's favorite form of entertainment. Sea food specialties include Chilean lobster, large shrimps and a sea food chowder. Typical Creole dishes prepared in country style are *asado con cuero*, lamb or beef barbecued in the hide, and *puchero*, a glorified stew prepared in Spanish style. No visitor should fail to try *mate*, the national tea, or omit the excellent Argentine wines and cheeses. Argentine cooks do not try to overpower the flavor of their delicious beef and lamb, and although their Creole dishes are deliciously spiced, they are not overly so.

ROUND AND ABOUT THE COUNTRY

BUENOS AIRES. Many travelers after visiting Buenos Aires with its culture, its elegance and its subtle charm, leave under the conviction that the Argentine capital is the Paris of the Americas. Like Paris, Buenos Aires is a city of many different aspects; it is a modern city of steel and concrete, of skyscrapers and dreams; it is a city full of cozy spots which offer characteristics of the XIX century in the grace of its patios and the artistic beauty of its entrance halls; and it is a merry and daring city with regard to its theaters, cinemas and night clubs. Buenos Aires is a marvelous sight situated on the bank of its great river and surrounded by the vast plains of the Pampas. When Captain Sancho del Campo landed on the bank of the River Plata where the city was founded, he exclaimed, "How good is the fresh and healthy air one breathes in this place." This marked the birth of the new city and established its prophetic name. Almost from that very instant it started to grow, with the certainty of becoming what it is today—the nation's commercial and industrial, as well as its political and cultural capital. Today, Buenos Aires astounds the world with its constant expansion, its building activity, its intellectual centers, museums, industries, polyclinics, social works, palaces, universities and churches. Yet here, nature stubbornly refuses to be overcome by progress. It makes itself manifest everywhere amid cement and stones, to form parks and wonderful green gardens thus providing many oases, for dreamers, children and lovers. Chief point of orientation for sightseeing is the Plaza de Mayo, the heart of the city with the historic Cabildo (Town Hall), where the independence movement was initiated; the pink-hued La Casa Rosada (Government Palace), the official residence of the President, noted for its statuary and rich hall furnishings, and the Cathedral, containing the tomb of "The Liberator," General José de San Martín. The Avenida de Mayo leads to the Palacio del Congreso (Congress Hall), seat of the legislature. North of the plaza is the shopping, theater and commercial district, including the famous Calle Florida, the city's most fashionable shopping street, and Calle Corrientes,

CHAPAD MALAL ESTANCIA, NEAR BUENOS AIRES

street of theaters, restaurants (serving especially fine steaks, the national specialty, and *carbonada criolla,* meat stew with rice, a specialty of Buenos Aires), cafés and night life, with buildings that are monumental specimens of modern architecture. South of the Plaza de Mayo is the old **San Telmo** section—a quiet, picturesque corner of colonial landmarks like the churches of **San Ignacio de Loyola,** almost unchanged since colonial days, and **Santo Domingo,** well-known in Argentine history, and the **Casa de Liniers.** Paseo Colón will take you to the waterfront and the industrial section, predominantly Italian, called the **Boca,** having a life of its own by day and by night with its sea food and Italian restaurants frequented by sailors and workingmen, its Bohemian corner and popular art center. The **Balneario Municipal (Municipal Bathing Beach)** is the city's playground and resort area during the bathing season running from December through March. North of the commercial district is the show section of the capital, including first the **National Museum of Fine Arts;** the **Cemetery of Recoleta,** containing vaults of every possible style of architecture, and beautiful **Palermo Park,** famous for its **Rosedal** (rose garden), **Zoological Gardens,** a number of exclusive sports clubs (among them clubs for polo; soccer, the national game, and *pato,* a sort of basketball played on horseback) and the **Hipódromo Argentino,** with its internationally known Palermo race track; and beyond that, the residential section, **Belgrano,** distinguished by its cobblestone streets and tiled sidewalks, aristocratic mansions and parklike setting. A score of museums and libraries center around the **University of Buenos Aires;** the **National Museum of Fine Arts;** the important **Natural History Museum;** the **Teatro Colón,** one of the world's great opera houses, having its own National Symphony Orchestra, opera and ballet companies, and the **Mitre Museum** or **Casa Mitre,** former home of the country's first president, with quiet patios and *salas* typical of the colonial era.... Thirty-five miles south of Buenos Aires, on the Río de la Plata, **LA PLATA (Ciudad Eva Peron)** . . . . is the center of the meat-packing industry (tours are conducted through the plants) and a main port. It is also famous for its schools for women. It was geometrically planned as a model city and is unique with its handsome public buildings, wide streets and modern improvements. The **Museum** is outstanding for its rich collection of fossils of prehistoric animals.... Still further south along the coast is **MAR DEL PLATA** . . . . . . called the "Pearl of the Atlantic" and queen of Argentina's ocean resorts, summer playground of the country's "smart set" and internationally famous for its luxurious casino. The sea food served here is excellent. Its five miles of beaches include fashionable **Playa Grande,** with its private clubs and extensive estates; **Parque Camet,** with its attractive golf course and polo grounds, and **Bristol Beach,** with the fabulous **casino,** which can accommodate up to 20,000 persons, including one huge room where more than 65 tables can play at one time, and featuring also a gymnasium and ice-skating rink. Preceding the season, which begins the end of December, is the annual "Spring Week" of sports tournaments and activities held the first part of November.... Southwest of Buenos Aires is the important tourist center of **TANDIL** . . . . Built on hills and set among hills, it is a quiet, pleasant resort with fine views of sierra scenery and clear, refreshing air.... The quaint town of **SAN CARLOS DE BARILOCHE** is the principal center for visiting **Nahuel Huapí National Park,** most popular of the seven national parks extending along the Chilean border in the Andean Lake region. Among the many attractions in the park are famed **Lake Nahuel Huapí;** beautiful **Lake Traful,** a fisherman's paradise; **Isla Victoria,** a must for nature lovers with its rare and interesting species of flora and fauna, and **Cerro Catedral,** where thrilling international skiing competitions are held. This region is the mecca for Argentine ski enthusiasts.... North of Buenos Aires, up the Paraná River, is **ROSARIO** . . . . the second city of Argentina. It is, like Buenos Aires, a modern, well-planned city with attractive public squares, excellent boulevards and wide streets.... Up the Paraná is the beautiful colonial city of **SANTA FE** . . . . . . one of the country's oldest and richest in historical and architectural interest. It was in its **Cabildo (Town Hall)** that the Constitution of 1853 was

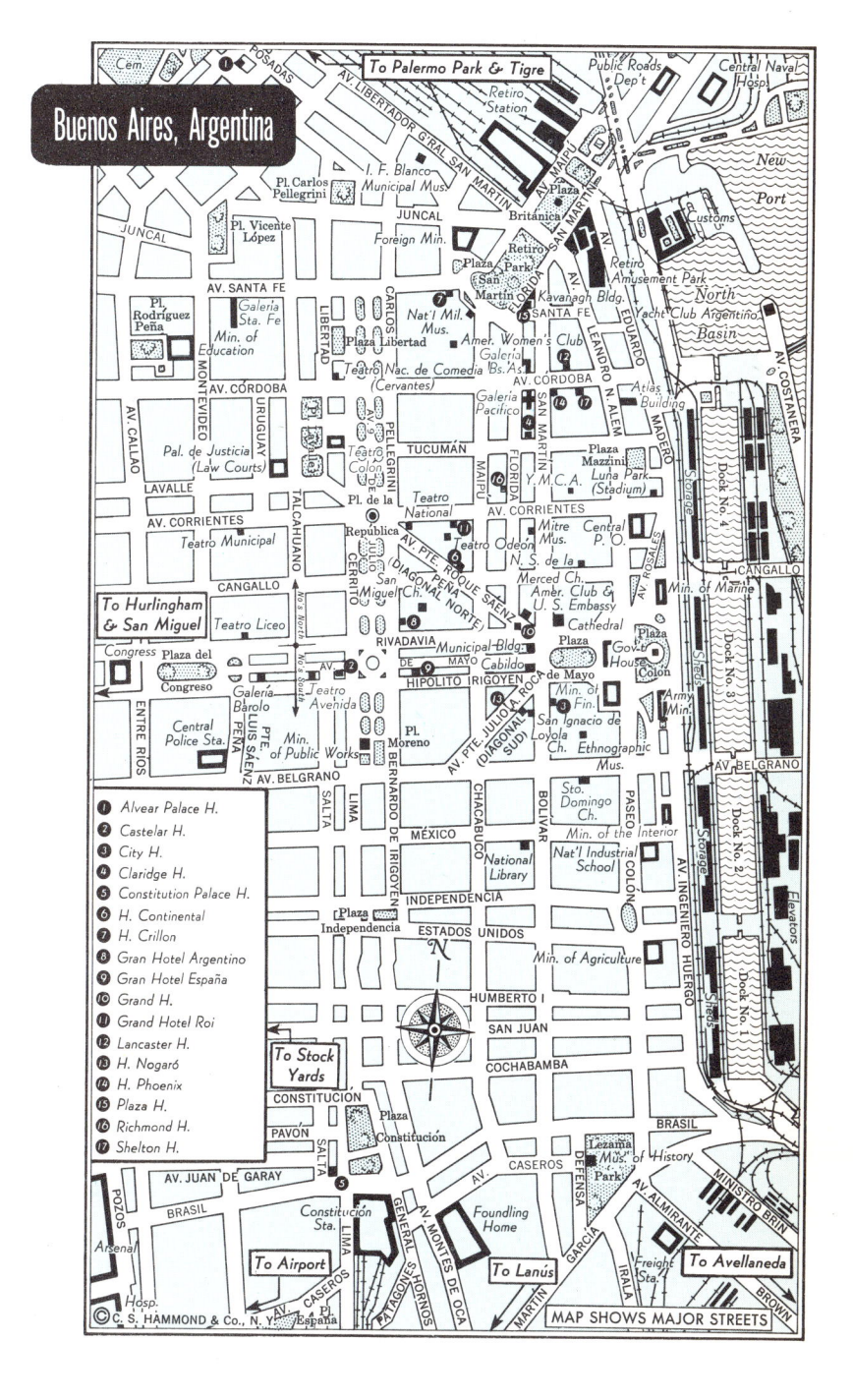

PLAZA 25 DE MAYO, BUENOS AIRES

NAHUEL HUAPI PARK

SKIING, NAHUEL HUAPI PARK *Moore-McCormack Lines*

adopted, with the delegates taking their oath of allegiance upon the crucifix preserved in the famous church of San Francisco. Santa Fe is a university city, but it also has theaters and a race course. Most of its best buildings are in the eastern section, grouped around two plazas: the **Plaza Mayo**, including the Casa de Gobierno, begun in 1660, and the **Plaza San Martín**, whose buildings are of modern origin.... When you reach POSADAS . . . . . on the Alto Paraná River, you are in Misiones Territory—a remote arm of forested lowland which, before the coming of the Jesuits in 1617, was the home of the Guaraní Indians. Not far from Posadas are thirty ruins of old Jesuit missions and no one should fail to see those at **San Ignacio Miní**, which at its height of prosperity in 1713, contained 4,356 people.... From PUERTO IGUAZU you may drive to the Iguazú Falls, one of the great sights of South America. Here the Iguazú River thunders over a double-horseshoe escarpment more than two miles wide to a narrow gorge 230 feet below. Among the 275 separate cataracts are projecting ledges carpeted with tropical growth. The town itself, at a height of 200 feet above the river, affords a magnificent view of the Iguazú . . . CORDOBA . . . . . surrounded by mountains known as the "Argentine Switzerland," is Argentina's all-year-round vacationland. This city, geographically in the center of the country, was a religious and intellectual center for more than two centuries. For this reason it has been called the Argentine Rome or "learned city." The **Universidad Mayor de San Carlos**, founded in 1613, was the first in the country and one of the first in America. Many of the colonial buildings, with the graceful portals, carved wooden balconies and wrought-iron grilles for which Córdoba is famous, making them reminiscent of old Spain, are still standing in the section around the **Plaza San Martín**, including the **Cathedral**, one of America's finest examples of Spanish colonial architecture; the house of **Viceroy Sobremente**, constructed in 1700 and now a museum; the church of **La Merced**, famous for its hand-carved colonial pulpit and candelabras, and the impressive colonial **mansion of the Allende family**. Another enjoyable spot is the beautiful **Parque Sarmiento**, with its zoo, waterfall and fine views of the city. The **Sierras of Córdoba** attract many visitors from the city who wish to swim, ride, shoot or golf. Among the most popular and attractive resorts near Córdoba are **Capilla del Monte** with its curious rock formations and spectacular gorges; **Jesús María**; **Mina Clavero**, a charming town noted for its natural waters, and **Alta Gracia**, one of the country's most popular summer and winter resorts. The whole province of Córdoba is famous for its pastries called *alfajores*.... The southern terminus of the old Inca Empire is the city of TUCUMAN . . . . . In this city, on Plaza Belgrano in 1812, a decisive victory over the royalists was won by patriot forces, and in 1816, at the **Casa Histórica**, the Congress of the United Provinces of Río de la Plata drafted and proclaimed Argentina's declaration of independence. At Villa Nogues, up the mountainside, are fine buildings of European style, summer homes of the well-to-do residents.... From here the Pan American Highway follows the ancient route of the Incas to Cuzco, Peru, through ROSARIO DE LA FRONTERA, a popular resort; tradition-steeped SALTA; JUJUY, with its famous **Tumas de los Reyes** (Baths of the Kings), and the remote Indian villages along the route.... On the route from Buenos Aires to Chile, at the foothills of the Andes, is the historic city of MENDOZA . . . . center of the nation's thriving wine and fruit industry. It was from here that José de San Martín set out with his Army of the Andes to cross the cordillera and help to liberate first Chile and then Peru, and today an astonishing monument to him crowns the **Cerro de la Gloria**, a hill in one of the public parks. Visitors will also enjoy visits to the sun-drenched vineyards and the large wineries. Grapes from Mendoza Province are among the finest in the world and each year, in March or early April, the city holds a gay harvest festival known as the Fiesta de la Vendimia. The **Moyano Museum of Natural History** is known for its collection of Argentine plants and animals.... PUENTE DEL INCA, west of Mendoza, is named for the extraordinary **natural bridge**, one of the marvels of South America, spanning the Mendoza River. This is also a resort noted for its thermal springs and mineral waters and for its superb ski courses. From here excursions may be taken to the base of **Mt. Aconcagua** (23,000 feet), the loftiest peak in the Western Hemisphere, and to the statue of Christ the Redeemer, the "Christ of the Andes," marking the frontier between Argentina and Chile and symbolizing eternal peace between them.

IGUAZU FALLS *Gendreau*

BEACH, MAR DEL PLATA *Gendreau*

NORTH AMERICA (Exclusive of the United States)

Although younger than the United States as a nation, Mexico's culture goes back much further; for when the Spanish conquered this land, they found an advanced Indian civilization here, and the Aztec customs, arts and architecture, coupled with the charm of Old Spain, still prevail today, spelling romantic enchantment for the visitor to this country, which touches our own on its southern boundary.

Many up-to-date places are found here also. Mexico City, the oldest city in North America, is modernistic and progressive in appearance and attitudes. Most of the population that are pure whites of Spanish descent live in this metropolis; while the Indians remain primarily in their picturesque villages, untouched by time.

Another "must" on any trip to Mexico is the glorious coastal resort of Acapulco, situated on a beautiful oval bay, surrounded by magnificent mountains; this scenic grandeur is unsurpassed anywhere in the world.

Connecting Mexico to South America are six small republics: Guatemala, El Salvador, Nicaragua, Costa Rica, Honduras and Panama, plus the British Crown Colony of Honduras—all of which are "happy hunting grounds" for the sight-seer interested in relics of the ancient Mayan civilization that flourished here long before Columbus landed. The primitive native life, lofty volcanoes, dense forests, banana plantations, quaint Spanish missions and the incomparable charm of the blue Caribbean that laps at the shores of these narrow little countries, all add to the glamour you encounter on a vacation to this part of the globe.

At the other extreme, Canada, reaching geographically from the northern border of the United States to the frozen Arctic, shares a similar way of life and background with the United States, but it still has political ties with Europe.

One third of the Canadian population continues to speak French, and a trip to Quebec is like seeing the France of the past, for little ox-drawn carts and religious shrines are evident everywhere, and the inhabitants still use hand looms for weaving and continue to practice other handicrafts also.

For the sportsman, Canada is truly a haven, since hunting of moose, deer, raccoon, grouse, duck and partridge is ever popular, while the deep-sea fishing too is excellent, especially off the Nova Scotia coast. Winter sports such as skiing attract many vacationers to this "land of the maple leaf," as does the splendor of Banff National Park in the Canadian Rockies, and gorgeous Lake Louise, a famed international luxury resort. Whatever diversity of enjoyment you seek, Canada is sure to please you.

ARCTIC OCEAN
ATLANTIC OCEAN
PACIFIC
U. S. S. R.
Siberia
North Pole
Wrangel I.
Chukchi Sea
Bering Sea
Bering Str.
Gulf of Anadyr
St. Lawrence I.
Nunivak I.
Pribilof Is.
Beaufort Sea
Gulf of Alaska
U. S.
ALASKA
CANADA
UNITED STATES
GREENLAND
ICELAND
IRELAND
GREAT BRITAIN
Greenland Sea
Denmark Strait
Davis Strait
Baffin Bay
Hudson Bay
Hudson Strait
Foxe Basin
QUEEN ELIZABETH ISLANDS
Ellesmere I.
Victoria I.
Banks I.
Baffin I.
Southampton I.
Labrador
Ungava
Newfoundland
Great Bear L.
Great Slave L.
L. Athabasca
L. Winnipeg
L. Superior
L. Michigan
Chicago
Seattle
Vancouver
San Francisco
Denver
Minneapolis
Detroit
Cleveland
Pittsburgh
Toronto
Ottawa
Montreal
Boston
New York
Philadelphia
Washington
Indianapolis
St. Louis
Anchorage
Fairbanks
Juneau
Whitehorse
Yellowknife
Churchill
Winnipeg
Edmonton
Calgary
Regina
Saskatoon
Quebec
Halifax
St. John's
Reykjavík
Godthaab
Thule
Bermuda

Notes and Itinerary

Canada

FAVORITE NORTHERN VACATIONLAND

Canada, with its beautiful scenery, its rivers, lakes and seashore, its opportunities for sport of every kind has long been a favorite vacationland with its neighbors to the south. **OTTAWA**, ... a capital of stately dignity and pleasant homes, is situated in a beautiful setting at the meeting of the Rideau and Ottawa Rivers. The Italian-Gothic Parliament Buildings, housing the Senate and House of Commons, include a **Peace Tower** with carillon and a **Memorial Chamber** honoring Canadians who died in World War I. Other interesting public buildings are the **Confederation Building**; the **Justice Building**, headquarters of the Royal Canadian Mounted Police; the **Supreme Court Building** and the **National Art Gallery**, with an excellent collection of works by Canadian artists. Of the many churches, two outstanding ones are the **Basilica of Notre Dame** (Roman Catholic) and **Christ Church Cathedral** (Anglican). The **Central Canada Exhibition**, noted for its exhibits of agriculture, livestock and industry, is held here annually in **Landsdowne Park**. The city also is prominent in the winter sports of skiing, skating and hockey.

THE MARITIME PROVINCES AND NEWFOUNDLAND

The hunting of moose, deer and game birds, fishing for trout and salmon, sailing, canoeing, swimming in lakes and ocean, horse racing, tennis and golf for years have lured sportsmen to **NEW BRUNSWICK**, while the many historical sites and beautiful scenery delight students and photographers. Samuel de Champlain and Sieur de Monts first viewed New Brunswick's mighty river — the **Saint John** — in 1604, when they saw it tumbling into the Bay of Fundy over its eleven-foot drop. . . . **FREDERICTON**, on the Saint John River, was designated as capital by Sir Thomas Carleton on what is now St. Anne's Point when London established the province of New Brunswick in 1734. The present site of the city was hewn out of the wilderness by Loyalists fleeing the American Revolution. It is also the center of the **Handicraft Division of the New Brunswick Department of Industry and Reconstruction**, attracting hundreds of visitors each year. With the laying of the cornerstone of **Christ Church Cathedral** in 1845 began the erection of the first new cathedral foundation on British soil since the Norman Conquest. The buildings now occupying **Parliament Square** were erected in 1880, soon after the disastrous fire which destroyed Old Province Hall. On the square are the **Assembly Chamber**, containing portraits of King George III and Queen Charlotte executed by Sir Joshua Reynolds; the **library**, featuring a copy of the Domesday Book as well as one of the two complete sets of the Audubon bird paintings now in existence, purchased from Louis Philippe of France, and the **Old Government House**, long the official residence of the governor, now the barracks and district headquarters of the Royal Canadian Mounted Police. . . **SAINT JOHN**, city of the seven hills, at the mouth of the river whose name it bears, holds the distinction of the first city to be incorporated in British America, having received its charter in 1785. While the modern city is of Loyalist origin, it was the site of the fort of La Tour, fur trader of the seventeenth century, and scene of many a battle of fur-trade rivalry. Among its churches two stand out as especially worthy of note: **Trinity Church**, the first building of the Church of England, opened on Christmas Day in 1791, displaying among its treasures the communion service sent by George III and one of the six royal coats of arms of the Hanoverian Dynasty rescued from the American Colonies, and **Old Stone Church**, built in 1824 from stone quarried in Bristol, England, displaying the colors of the Third New Brunswick Medium Brigade, Royal Canadian Artillery, founded in 1793, the second oldest artillery militia unit to be organized in the Empire outside the British Isles. The **Court House**, dating from 1830, has a spiral stone staircase unsupported by pillar or post, and the **New Brunswick Museum** preserves the historical records of the province. . **ST. ANDREWS**, in the extreme southwest, is a fashionable summer resort. Of historical interest is the **old blockhouse**. . . . East of Saint John, **MOSS GLEN** is the home of the famous Dykelands Pottery of Kjeld and Erica Deichmann. . . . Near the Fundy coast and **New Brunswick's National Park** is the industrial city of **MONCTON**, where visitors may see the tidal bore and the magnetic hill. . . . **SACKVILLE**, home of **Mt. Allison University**, also includes **Fort Beausejour**, with its museum. . . . On Northumberland Strait, sheltered from the cold waters of the Gulf of St. Lawrence by Prince Edward Island, are the villages of **COCAGNE, BUCTOUCHE** and **RICHIBUCTO**, combining sea bathing and scenic beauty with such excellent native sea foods as oysters, clams and lobsters. . . . At **ST. LOUIS DE KENT** is an exact reproduction of the celebrated **shrine of Notre Dame de Lourdes**, while at **ROGERSVILLE** is a **Trappist Monastery** of unique interest. . . . In the extreme northeast are **SHIPPIGAN** and **CARAQUET**, commercial fishing towns where the traditional blessing of the fleet is a colorful event. . . . The **BAIE DE CHALEUR**, discovered by Jacques Cartier, offers beautiful beaches and resorts, with the added attractions of salmon fishing in the Restigouche and deep-sea fishing offshore. . . . **CHARLOTTETOWN**, capital of **Prince Edward Island** and its largest community, has been called the birthplace of Canada, and rightly so, for here in the **Old Provincial Building** in 1864 twenty-six representatives of Prince Edward Island, New Brunswick, Nova Scotia, Ontario and Quebec first discussed union. The furnishings of the **Confederation Chamber** remain exactly as they were when the historic meeting took place. One of many charming residences of the city is **Government House**, the official residence, erected in 1834. Two institutions of higher learning are located here: **St. Dunstan's University** and **Prince of Wales College**, while the **Island Regional Library** is the center of the excellent library service available to all schools in the Province. **St. Dunstan's Basilica**, the **Soldiers Monument** and **Fort Edward Battery**, guarding Charlottetown's fine harbor, are other points of interest. The Provincial Exhibition and Old Home Week, held annually in August, offer agricultural and other competitive exhibits, horse racing, vaudeville and midway fun. . . . **SUMMERSIDE**, second largest town, surrounded by typically beautiful scenery, is the center of the oyster industry. . . . . Sometimes called "the beginning of America," **NOVA SCOTIA** is the site of the oldest settlement north of the Gulf of Mexico. Many attractions are offered to the tourist: swimming, bathing, sailing, tennis, golf, hockey and other sports, carnivals and festivals. . . . . There are three National Historic Parks in the Province: the **FORTRESS OF LOUISBOURG**, once termed the "Dunkirk of America," on **Cape Breton Island**, site of the fortress built by the French to protect the entrance of the St. Lawrence River; the restored **PORT ROYAL** at **Lower Granville**, erected on the original site of the Port Royal Habitation, built in 1605 by Sieur de Monts and Champlain and destroyed in 1613; **FORT ANNE** at Annapolis Royal, a combination of both French and English fortifications, since it changed hands seven times during the struggle between the French and English for the control of Canada. A large building erected at Fort Anne in 1797 holds a **museum of historic exhibits and a fine library**. . . . Memorial Park at **GRAND PRE**, scene of Evangeline, includes the old French willows, Evangeline's well and the chapel, all surrounded by lovely flower gardens. The ancient village church, once known as the Church of the Covenanters, is surrounded by old graves and has old box pews and a high pulpit. In the distance is beautiful **Blomidon Mountain** with its famed **Look-off**. . . . **CAPE BRETON HIGHLAND NATIONAL PARK**, in one of the outstanding scenic regions of North America, has a rugged and picturesque coastline, indented by deep bays and inlets providing excellent harbors. Inland lie the beautiful **Bras d'Or Lakes**, where at Baddeck begins the **Cabot Trail**, continuing through scenery reminiscent of the Highland country of Scotland, to Ingonish and then on down the coast, where steep hills rise to a height of 1400 feet. . . At **ENGLISHTOWN** is the grave of Angus MacAskill, the Cape Breton giant who stood seven feet nine inches tall and weighed 425 pounds. . . . **HALIFAX**, capital city of Nova Scotia, is situated on the hills surrounding its harbor, one of the finest on the Atlantic seaboard. This lovely city is rich in historic sites, parks and other points of interest, including St. Paul's, the oldest Protestant church in Canada; **Point Pleasant Park** with the **Martello Tower**; the Public Gardens, unexcelled on the continent; the **Old Town Clock**; **Province House**, a Georgian masterpiece of architecture; **Memorial Tower** in Point Pleasant Park, commemorating the first Elective Assembly of the Dominion; **Citadel Hill**, with its old barracks and squat buildings, from which a magnificent view may be had over the harbor, and Dalhousie University. **DIGBY** is a well-known summer resort overlooking Annapolis Basin where all types of sport may be enjoyed. . . . A cool and healthful summer resort, **YARMOUTH**, on the south coast, is a headquarters for deep-sea fishing and beautiful drives. . . . **SHELBURNE**, shipbuilding town on the east coast, is known as the "birthplace of yachts," where the *Malay*, winner of the Bermuda Trophy, and the *Halegonian*, winner of the Havana Trophy, were built. Donald McKay, one of the most famous builders of wooden ships, learned his trade in the shipyards of this city. At the entrance to the harbor is McNutt's Island, with one of the oldest lighthouses in Nova Scotia, the **Cape Roseway Light**. . . . **LUNENBURG**, further north on the coast, is the home of the greatest deep-sea fishing fleet in America, including the *Bluenose*, undefeated champion of the North Atlantic fishing fleets and winner of four International Schooner Races. . . . Latest of the provinces to join the Confederation of Canada, **NEWFOUNDLAND** became the tenth province in April, 1949. Besides having an old and interesting history, it has long been famed as a vacation spot for sportsmen. One of the oldest cities in the New World, **ST. JOHN'S**, the capital of Newfoundland, has had a romantic history. First a rendezvous for fishermen of many nations, it began to take on the characteristics of a commercial center in 1547, though still retaining much of its old-world atmosphere. . . . **CORNER BROOK**, at the mouth of the Humber on the west coast, is the second city of Newfoundland and center of the pulp and paper industry, while **BELL ISLAND** is the great iron-mining center.

PARLIAMENT HILL, OTTAWA

Canadian Govt. Travel Bureau

QUEBEC

From Quebec went forth the explorers, traders, missionaries and voyagers, who helped to open up the inner regions of this vast continent. Since these original settlers were from France, the visitor feels as though he had stepped into a foreign land, upon seeing, for example, the wayside shrines, ox carts, outdoor ovens and other quaint reminders of Old France. Largest of the provinces, it is an all-year paradise for the vacationer. Fishing and hunting are popular attractions, for the streams and lakes abound in trout, bass and pike, while the **Restigouche River** in eastern Quebec is internationally famous for its salmon fishing. Canoe trips can be taken on the network of fresh-water lakes and streams and steamer trips on the St. **Lawrence** and the **Saguenay**. A well-known motor trip is the one around the Gaspé Peninsula, where rugged scenery of cliffs and ocean combine with quaint fishing villages and such natural wonders as **Percé Rock** and **Bonaventure Island**, sea-bird sanctuary. Quebec has seven provincial parks, possibly the two best known being the **Shickshock Mountains** of the Gaspé area and **Laurentide Park**, famous for its golf courses, fishing, hunting and canoeing facilities, in addition to its attraction as a winter-sports center. There are two national historic parks in Quebec. One of them is **Fort Lennox**, the well-preserved remains of one of the largest fortresses constructed in Canada during the last two centuries. Situated on the Richelieu River, that ancient war and trade route to the south, this fort, first built by the French, changed hands frequently during the various wars. Its final fall to the British in 1760 was the prelude to the fall of Montreal and finally, all of Canada. The other historic park is restored **Fort Chambly**, one of several forts constructed on the Richelieu River to protect the French settlers from Iroquois raids. When the first fort, built of wood, was destroyed by fire, it was rebuilt of stone. It, too, fell to the English in 1760. Captured by the Americans during the American Revolution, it was evacuated and burned. An interesting museum is maintained here.... Called the "Gibraltar of America," QUEBEC, the capital city, sits perched on its high rock, looking up and down the St. Lawrence and dreaming of its past, for it was the center and bastion of New France. Here came the governors and intendants and the regiments of soldiers to protect the colony and from here went the settlers of Montreal and Three Rivers. It is a city of remembrance, with its quaint houses, narrow, winding streets, old market places, where the visitor may wander on foot or ride in that curious two-wheeled vehicle called a *caleche*. Among the most important historic sites are the **Ursuline Convent and Chapel**, where votive lamps have been burning continuously through three centuries; **Hotel-Dieu Hospital**, with interesting exhibits of antique silver and other treasures; the **Plains of Abraham**, including the **monument to Wolfe and Montcalm**; the

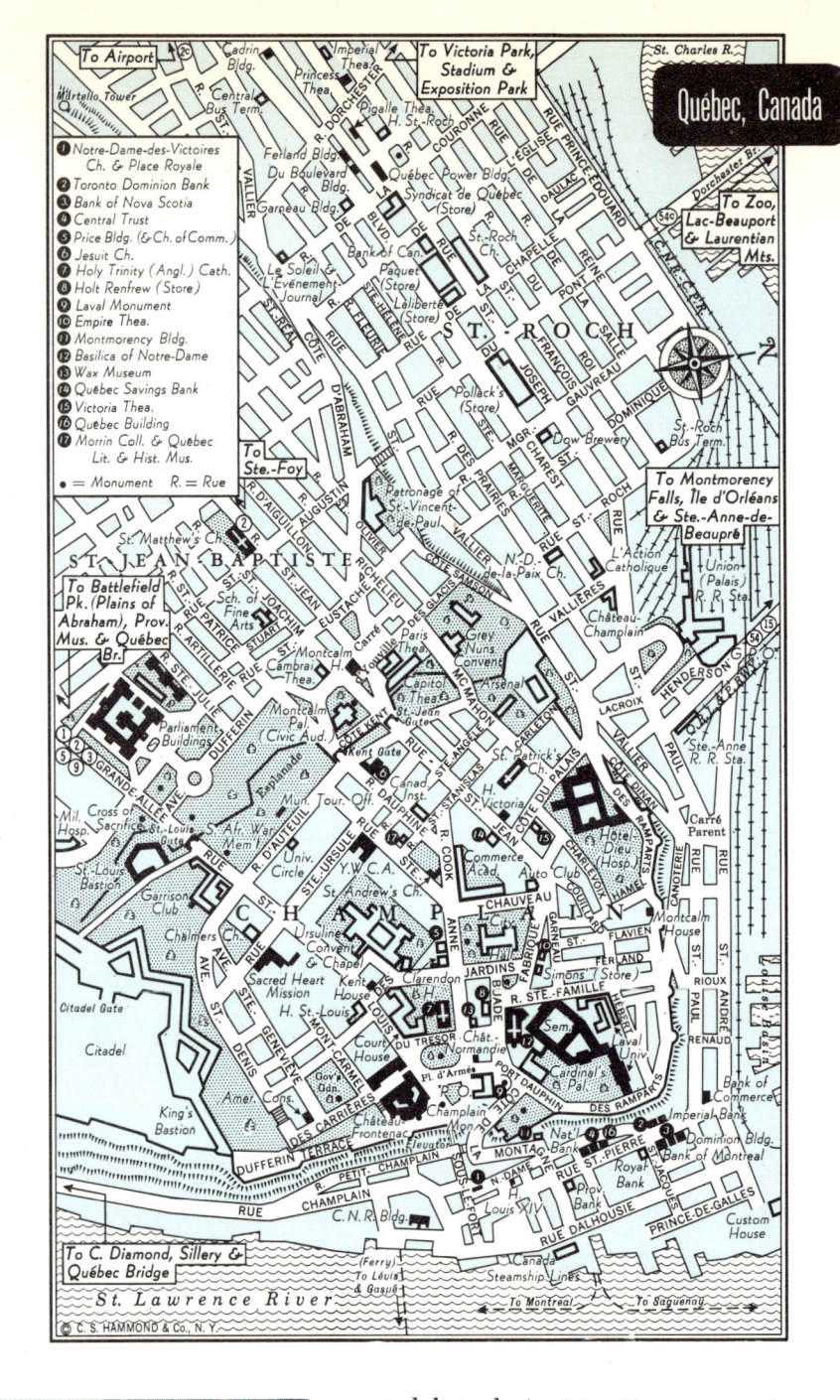

ST. LOUIS GATE, QUEBEC

Citadel and battlements, City Gates and Martello Towers, all part of the city's defenses; Quebec Seminary and Laval University; Basilica of Notre Dame, oldest church in the city; the Church of Notre-Dames-des-Victoires, with its exquisite woodwork and valuable paintings; the Cathedral of the Holy Trinity (Anglican); the Chapel of the Franciscans (White Sisters), where there is a magnificent display of fine needlework; the stately Parliament House; City Hall, on the site of Canada's first school, and the Provincial Museum, with its interesting exhibits. The Lower Town, at the water's edge, is also fascinating. The famed Chateau Frontenac is only one of many hotels offering fine entertainment and good food, with a French and French-Canadian cuisine. All the traditional summer sports may be enjoyed in the city and its environs, while in the winter skiing, skating, curling and sleigh riding take their place. The trip to Sainte-Anne de Beaupré, world-famous shrine of healing, winds through old French farmlands and villages and past the beautiful Montmorency Falls, dropping over a cliff twice the height of Niagara. . . . **MONTREAL** . . . . metropolis of Canada, is a young-old city, for although dating from the seventeenth century, it is a more modern city than Quebec. Towering over the buildings is Mont-Royal, with its great Cross, around which the city is built, both on an island beside the St. Lawrence River. Attractions include Notre Dame Church; St. James' Cathedral; the old Place Royale, where *voyageurs* were hired to go out in search of furs; the Chateau de Ramezay, now a museum; McGill University, with the stern beauty of its Scottish baronial architecture; the modern buildings of the University of Montreal; the Oratory of St. Joseph, now the tomb of miracle-working Frere Andre, and the Wax Museum. The stores of the city offer the cream of Quebec handicrafts, imported fine china, woolens and glassware. From Montreal cruises may be taken to the lower St. Lawrence, where the history of old Quebec unfolds before your eyes, and up the Saguenay, and motor trips to the Laurentians through quiet and ancient settlements of quaint houses. . . . In **THREE RIVERS**, once a great fur-trading center where the Indians came every summer, but now noted for its great pulp and paper industry, are very ancient buildings almost in the shadow of huge woodpiles.

MC GILL UNIVERSITY, MONTREAL

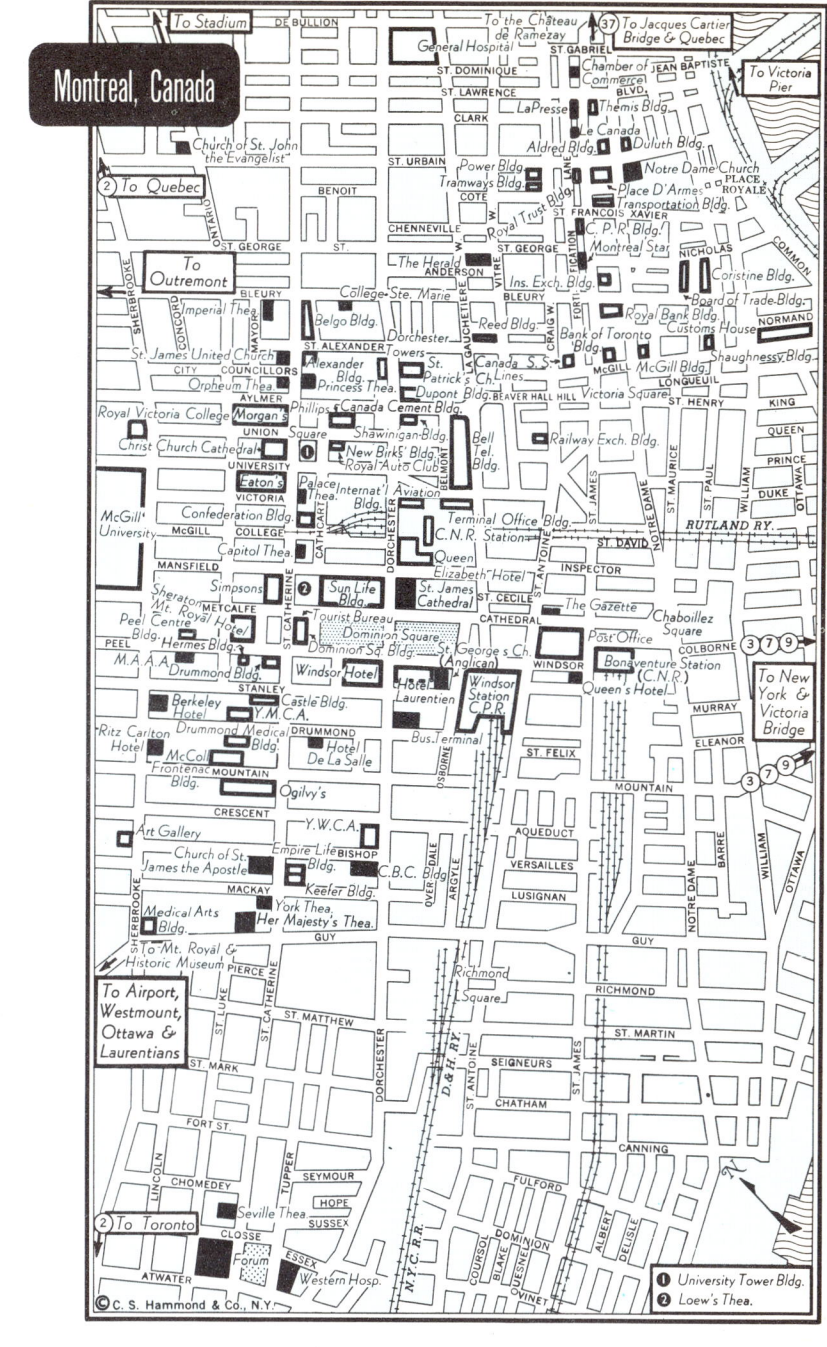

Canadian Natl. Railways

ONTARIO

In the early days, this province was part of the vast fur empire of the French. The Hurons, principal nation with whom the French traded, had their villages on the shores of Georgian Bay in a district known as Huronia. As is then to be expected, it is rich in historic sites — records of the struggles to form an empire and to convert the Indian to Christianity. All Indians in this region now live on the Indian Reserves and almost none of them is Huron. The fur trade through the years remained an important industry, however,

173

and trading posts were established, some of them on the sites of present cities and towns. The visitor to Ontario, whatever his tastes in recreation, will find ample opportunity to gratify them. There are major fishing regions, such as **Muskoka Lake**, the Georgian Bay—Bruce Peninsula area, with **Manitoulin Island** in the bay, **Kawartha Lakes** and **Algonquin Park** in Central Ontario, where trout — rainbow, lake and brown — bass, pickerel and the Great Northern pike may be found; **Lake Nipissing**, one of the best pickerel lakes in Canada, with bass, muskie, trout and pike plentiful in the rest of northern Ontario; the region around Hudson Bay and northwestern Ontario, lying along the northern shores of Lake Superior and the Manitoba border, including the beautiful **Lake of the Woods**. In most of these regions the hunter will be pleased to find deer and moose in quantity and smaller game in abundance.... Other attractions Ontario offers to the visitor are bathing, swimming, boating, camping, picnicking and hiking in the national parks. **Point Pelee National Park** in the southwest offers the study of trees and flowers, small game and birds. The park's marshes give food and shelter to thousands of migrating waterfowl.... **Georgian Islands National Park** is rich in history, for it was here the Hurons had their villages, and traces of those Indians and the missions may be found. Beausoleil Island was for years the home of the Ojibwa or Chippewa Indians. Interesting caves and rock pillars, formed by erosion of limestone cliffs, from which small trees and shrubs sprout, gave to Flowerpot Island its name.... **St. Lawrence National Park** is located in the "Thousand Islands Region" — one of the most picturesque regions of the North American continent—and thirteen of these islands have been set aside as a park. Here the government has provided wharves, pavilions and beach facilities for the vacationer.... **Fort Wellington** at Prescott, on the St. Lawrence, a fortification of the War of 1812, is now a historic park. Although never besieged during that war, it figured in later incidents of the nineteenth century. Particularly interesting are the blockhouse and the caponier, or listening post, outside the fortification, which was reached through a subterranean passage.... **Fort Malden** at Amherstburg, another historic park, was constructed on the banks of the Detroit River between 1797-1799. For the next forty years it was one of the principal frontier posts and figured in the War of 1812. The government maintains an interesting museum at this site.... **TORONTO**........ Indian for "The Meeting Place" — is the provincial capital and the commercial, industrial and cultural metropolis of central Canada, a city of great wealth with beautiful residential districts. Some of the most interesting places are the **monument in Exhibition Park**, marking the site of Fort Rouille, first recorded white settlement established by the French; the oldest **civil clock**, topping St. Lawrence Market, once City Hall; the old **lighthouse on Fleet Street**, which marked the harbor entrance for nearly a hundred years; the **blockhouses of Fort York**, with bullet scars of the War of 1812; the memorial to Zebulon Pike, of Pike's Peak fame, who died when a magazine blew up; **Holy Trinity Church**, more than a century old; the **memorials to Queen Victoria** and to **Robert Raikes**, the founder of Sunday Schools, in Queen Park; the **memorial plaque** commemorating the invention of standard time, in the Sons of England Building; **Colburne Lodge** in **High Park**, the home of John G. Howard, Esq., who bequeathed many acres of park land to the city; unique **Casa Loma**, home of Sir Henry Mill Pellat, nineteenth century financial king, a spectacular stone castle with secret stairways, wine cellars, elegant rooms; the **Parliament Buildings** and **Supreme Court**; the **University of Toronto**; **David Dunlop Observatory**; **Royal Ontario Museum**, and the **Art Gallery**. The open-air Shakespearean Festival and the Canadian National Exhibition, with its many exhibits, are held in Toronto each year.... Once the capital of united Upper and Lower Canada, **KINGSTON** is a town of historic interest. Founded by the Empire Loyalists in 1783, the **first mill** and the **first newspaper** in the province were started here. It is also the home of **Queens College**. Fort Henry was one of the strongest fortifications in Canada after Quebec and Halifax.... **HAMILTON**, a transportation center on Lake Ontario, has one of the finest landlocked harbors on the Great Lakes and one of the most modern Canadian **art galleries**.... **SAULT STE. MARIE**, a large manufacturing city, is also a site of much historical interest. ... **STRATFORD** is the home of the Stratford Shakespearean Festival.

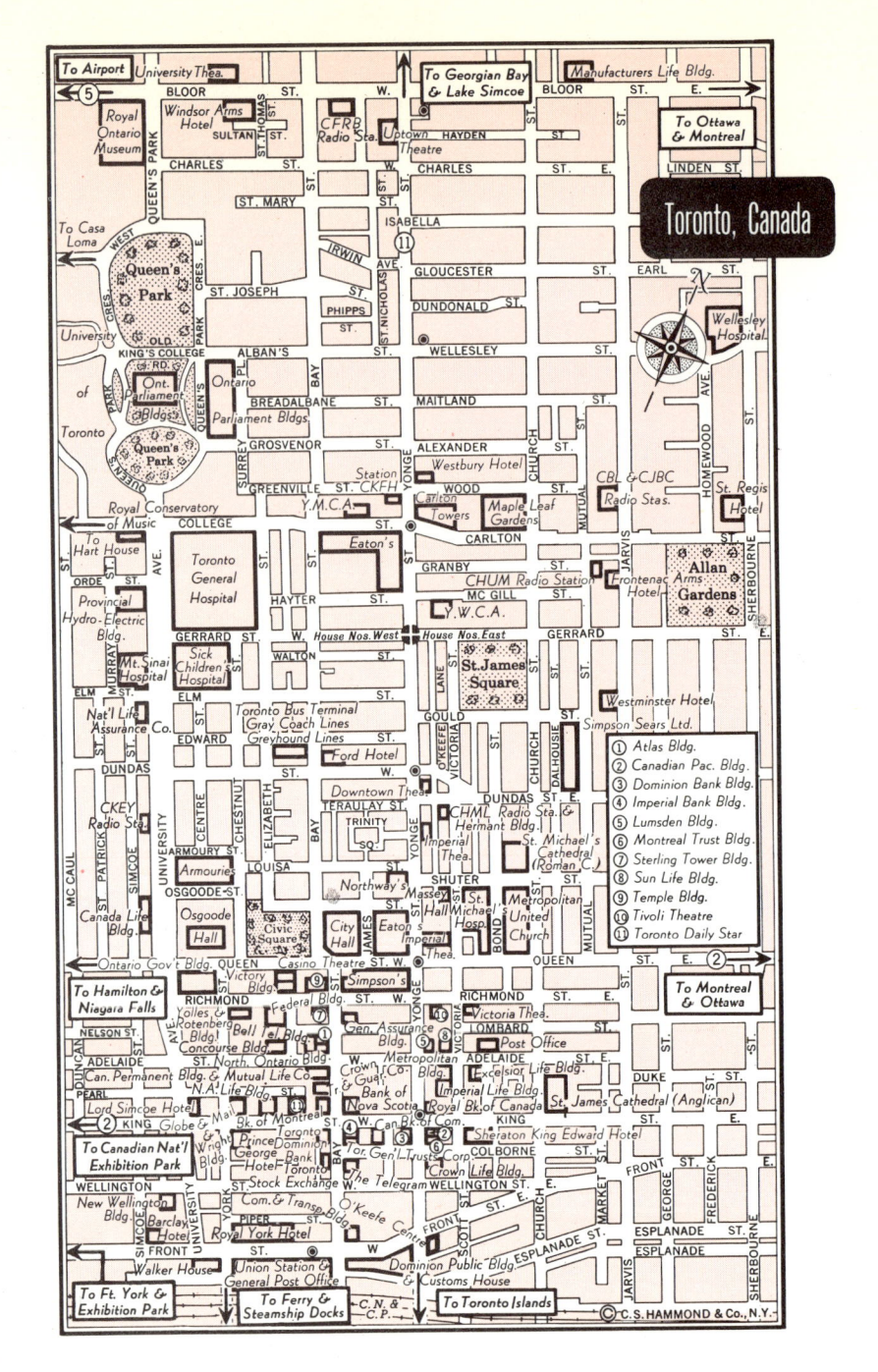

THE PRAIRIE PROVINCES

Manitoba, Saskatchewan and Alberta form the innermost part of Canada. They have physical features in common: their plains — the great grain bowl of the country — rivers, lakes and scenic beauty and in the two westernmost provinces, the foothills and peaks of the Rocky Mountains. **MANITOBA** offers excellent hunting for moose, caribou, deer and small game; fishing for trout, pike and rock bass; canoeing; camping and hiking. **Whiteshell Provincial Park**, located in the eastern part, studded with two hundred lakes and rivers, has facilities for swimming, boating and fishing. Here the vacationer may explore the **Land of the Granite Cliffs**, which rise steeply from the water, covered with forests of poplar, birch and tamarack, interspersed with picnic grounds shaded by clumps of pine. . . . In **Riding Mountain National Park**, in midwestern Manitoba, the visitor finds all the fishing, motoring, hiking and riding he could wish. Big game such as elk, deer, moose, bear and wolf, as well as small game, make the hunter happy. Waterfowl such as duck, swan and geese abound. There is an exhibition herd of buffalo, that former rover of the plains. . . . The **Trout Festival** is held in northern waters, while in Hudson Bay white whale is hunted. **The International Peace Garden**, in southern Manitoba, is of interest. **WINNIPEG** . . . . . founded by Lord Selkirk's colony of the Red River Valley, is the capital of the province. The classic beauty of the **Manitoba Legislature Building**, with the famous **Gold Boy** atop the dome, is one of the city's chief attractions, while the **Civic Auditorium**, with its museum and art gallery; the **Cenotaph**; the city's first **post office**; the gate to old **Fort Garry** and the many churches are other points of interest. The music festival, annual **Canoe Club Regatta** and **Red River Exhibition** are events attracting many visitors annually. The **trip up Lake Winnipeg by steamer** is interesting and beautiful. . . . **THE PAS**, the gateway to the north, holds the Trappers Festival, attended by Indians and trappers from all over the north country. Near here is the **Nelson River**, one of the famous trout-fishing areas of the world. . . . **FLIN FLON**, noted for its mines of copper, zinc, gold, silver, cadmium and salinium, has an interesting history. . . . The wheat city of **BRANDON**, in the south, is noted for its **Provincial Fair**, with livestock and other interesting exhibits. . . . **SASKATCHEWAN** is the middle Prairie Province. Within it are four regions: the open plains of the south and going northward, the parklands, commercial forest lands, lands of rivers, lakes and streams and in the northeast, the "Land of the Little Sticks." In the south lies the great grain-growing region, reclaimed from the wild grasses and buffalo of early days. In **Prince Albert National Park**, in a vast region of rocks, woods and water at almost the exact geographical center of Saskatchewan, the recreational facilities are practically unlimited, with thousands of crystal lakes tied together by little rivers, providing hundreds of miles for canoe trips. Along the shores of **Lakes Waskesiu, Kingsmere** and **Crean** are fine beaches for swimmers, while sport fish abound in their waters. The forests contain various species of big and small game, with a small herd of buffalo brought from Alberta. On **Lake Lavallee** are the pelican rookeries, one of the quaint birds of the north. Golf, tennis, hiking and riding are popular diversions provided by park authorities. At **Montreal Lake** is a trading post of the Hudson's Bay Company and Cree Indian reserve. Two other parks, **Cypress Hills** and **Moose Jaw**, provide similar recreation. . . . **REGINA**, the capital, has its white-walled, dark-domed **Legislative Building** rising amid man-planted trees. . . . **PRINCE ALBERT**, fourth largest city, is the gateway to both the commercial forest region and the "Land of the Little Sticks," a sub-Arctic territory merging into the Northwest Territories. . . . **ALBERTA**, the Foothills Province, is the most westerly of the Prairie Provinces, named for the wife of the Governor-General of Canada, Her Royal Highness, Princess Louise Caroline Alberta. Of greatest interest to the visitor are the scores of lakes and streams affording sport to the angler. Here he may fish for several varieties of trout, including the Loch Leven, found nowhere else in western Canada. The game, overflowing from the national parks where it is protected, includes elk, grizzly, black and brown bear, caribou, deer, antelope, Rocky Mountain sheep, goat, cougar and wolf. In the autumn, when the birds fly south, duck and goose are also popular. . . . It is in the national parks that Alberta's scenery can be most admired. **Banff National Park** is the oldest and second largest of Canada's national playgrounds. Its mountain peaks pierce the sky; its beautiful valleys with their green forests and lakes delight the visitor. The vast **Columbia Ice-Field**, at the northern end of the park, is a remnant of the ice age. Here also are the resorts at **Banff** and **Lake Louise** with their hotels, Banff Springs and Chateau Lake Louise, of international fame. Other points of interest include **Cascades Rock Garden**; the government museum near Bow River Bridge, with its exhibits of the flora, fauna and geology of the region; the hot **mineral springs**, equal to any on the continent, and **Moraine Lake**, in the **Valley of the Ten Peaks**. In the park there is varied entertainment for the visitor, including hiking, riding, swimming, climbing, boating, tennis, golf, skiing and fishing. . . . On the highway to **Jasper National Park** is seen the **Athabaska Glacier**, largest to issue from the Columbia Ice-Field. Through Jasper, largest of the seven parks in the mountains of western Canada, on the **Athabaska Trail**, passed the explorers and fur traders of history. As a matter of fact, the park owes its name to Jasper House, a fur-trading post of the North West Company. Within its borders are many beautiful lakes, among them **Lac Beauvert**, with its jade-green waters, **Medicine Lake**, **Pyramid Lake** and **Maligne Lake**. **Maligne Canyon** is a remarkable example of erosion and the waters of **Miette Hot Springs**, having a wide reputation for their medicinal qualities, are the hottest in the Rockies. At **Jasper Park Lodge** is one of the finest golf courses on the continent. The wildlife sanctuary, one

JASPER NATIONAL PARK, ALBERTA

Canadian Natl. Railways

TUMBLING GLACIER-MT. ROBSON, B.C.

of the largest, provides a home for big and small game of the mountains. . . . The **"Bad Lands"** of the Red Deer Valley wonderfully illustrate the effects of the erosion of wind and rain on rock. . . . Set apart primarily as a wildlife reserve, first in the country to be so designated, **Elk Island National Park** is the home of Canada's national herd of plains buffalo. Purchased from two Montana ranchers, it is one of the relatively few existent herds of this almost extinct animal. **Elk Island Park** contains numerous elk and is also one of the most important bird sanctuaries in western Canada. . . . The Waterton Lakes National Park, another charming playground, adjoins Glacier National Park in Montana, forming with it the **Waterton-Glacier International Peace Park**. At the head of the valleys are cirques forming mountain lakes, while the beautiful coloring of the rock is one of the park's outstanding features, with outcroppings of reddish shales darkening to wine and purple, green and gold. Boating on **Upper Waterton Lake** is a fine way to view the spectacular scenery. Excellent fishing is available in the lakes and streams, where several varieties of trout and whitefish are found. There is golf on the park course, horseback riding over mountain trails to the various lakes and motoring on the excellent highways. The wildlife sanctuary contains many species of big and small game like Rocky Mountain sheep, black bear, elk, deer, Rocky Mountain goat, beaver and squirrel. . . . Alberta's capital city, **EDMONTON**, is the focal point of the mining and fur-producing regions of the Arctic and an agricultural distributing center. Its airport is the hub of traffic to Alaska and northern Canada from southern Canada and the United States. . . . **CALGARY**, in the center of fertile ranching lands, is the scene of an annual roundup, the famous Calgary Stampede.

BRITISH COLUMBIA, THE YUKON AND NORTHWEST TERRITORIES

Separated by the Rocky Mountains from the rest of Canada, **BRITISH COLUMBIA** is almost a country by itself, providing striking scenery, an excellent climate and four beautiful national parks, where camping, boating, swimming, canoeing, climbing, cycling, hiking, riding over mountain trails, fishing and winter sports may be enjoyed. **Kootenay**, divided by the valleys of the Vermilion and Kootenay Rivers, includes the **Radium Hot Springs**, the "Iron Gates" at Sinclair Canyon, Marble Canyon, the "Paint Pots" and an iceberg lake. **Yoho**, an Indian word meaning "It is wonderful," is noted for the **Yoho and Kicking Horse valleys; Seven Sisters, Bridal Veil and Twin Falls; Daly Glacier**; the **Natural Bridge** over Kicking Horse River; interesting peaks and beautiful lakes. **Glacier** comprises a magnificent alpine region of immense peaks, many of them 10,000 feet, ice-fields, glaciers — **Illecillewaet Glacier** is the largest — deep canyons and foaming streams. One of the most primitive of the Canadian national parks, it is of special interest to the mountaineer and nature lover. Therefore, **Mount Revelstoke**, on an alpine plateau near the junction of the Columbia and Illecillewaet Rivers, including meadows dotted with small lakes, is an all-season playground, offering skiing as a winter sport. From Lookout Station, a vast panorama spreads for miles. One of its natural phenomena is the **Ice Box**, a great cleft in the rock strata containing ice and snow even in midsummer. **Kamloops** is a town, not a park, but it is also a region famous for its trout fishing, skiing and hunting. The region of the north is a beautiful but rugged country offering excellent sport in hunting and fishing, while seventy-mile-long **Lake Okanagan**, on the Washington border in the south, is another vacation paradise. . . . The capital of the province is **VICTORIA**, on Vancouver Island, a quiet, regal city with shaded curved streets, stately homes and vivid gardens. The gray-stone Parliament Buildings overlook the inner harbor and the cathedral rises from the calm seclusion of the Bishop's Close. Famed Beacon Hill Park affords vistas of the Olympic and Coast ranges and roads in all directions lead to good fishing. In the shops may be found fine china, woolens and linens of international reputation, while its hostelries provide excellent food and entertainment. . . . **VANCOUVER**. . . . on a fine harbor, is British Columbia's metropolis. Its shops are excellent; the sheltered waters of English Bay are fringed with fine beaches, and hunting, fishing and exploring excursions, golf, tennis, riding and bowling are easily available throughout the year. Chinatown makes a fascinating tour and no visit is complete without a trip to the great, natural Stanley Park forming one side of the harbor entrance. . . . The **YUKON** and the **NORTHWEST TERRITORIES** are Canada's Arctic regions and as such do not hold much appeal to the average vacationist although the Yukon is familiar to most through stories of the gold rush of the 1800's and the poems of Robert Service.

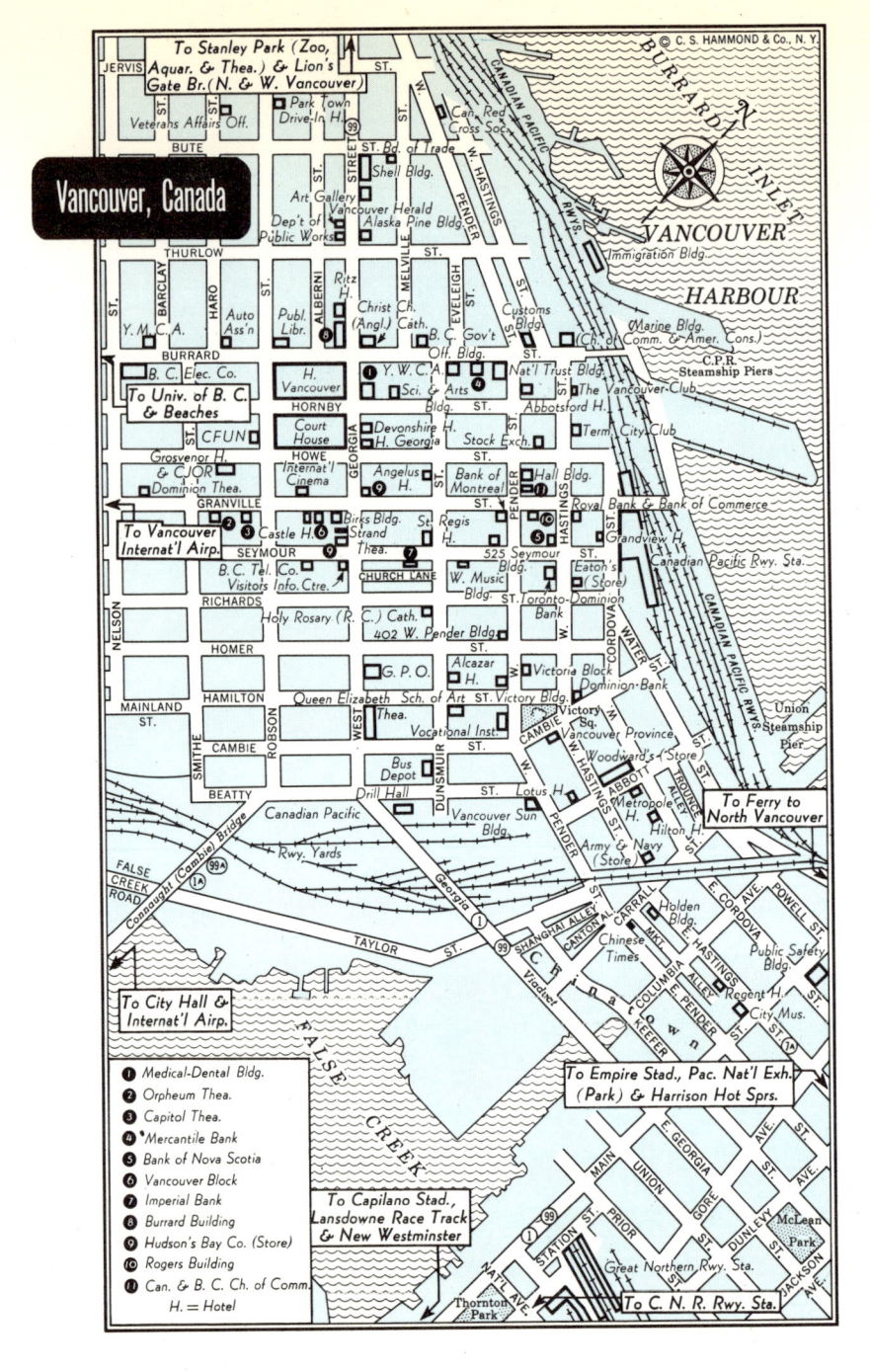

NORTH AMERICA

1. PEACE TOWER and Canadian Parliament Buildings, Ottawa, Ontario
2. PERCÉ ROCK and scenic Gaspé Peninsula, Province of Québec
3. CHÂTEAU FRONTENAC famed hotel and landmark of Québec, capital of Québec Province
4. VAST WHEAT FIELDS stretch across the Prairie Provinces of Manitoba, Alberta and Saskatchewan
5. INDIAN TOTEM POLE, a relic of the past, stands in Stanley Park, Vancouver, B. C.

NORTH AMERICA

1. Mountain town of Taxco, Mexico
2. Communications Building, Mexico City, Mexico
3. Burros carrying wood to market, Guanajuato, Mexico
4. Cathedral San Juan Bautista, Puerto Rico
5. Church, Cockburntown, San Salvador, Bahamas
6. San Juan Hill, Santiago, Cuba

NORTH AMERICA

1. **JASPER NATIONAL PARK** largest of seven parks in the mountains of western Canada
2. **LARGE-SCALE MINING OPERATIONS** are uncovering the vast mineral wealth of northern Canada
3. **DRUMLINS**, elongated mounds of glacial drift as seen from the air over Labrador
4. **LITTLE FISHING VILLAGES** dot both the Atlantic and Pacific coasts of Canada where fishing is a major industry.

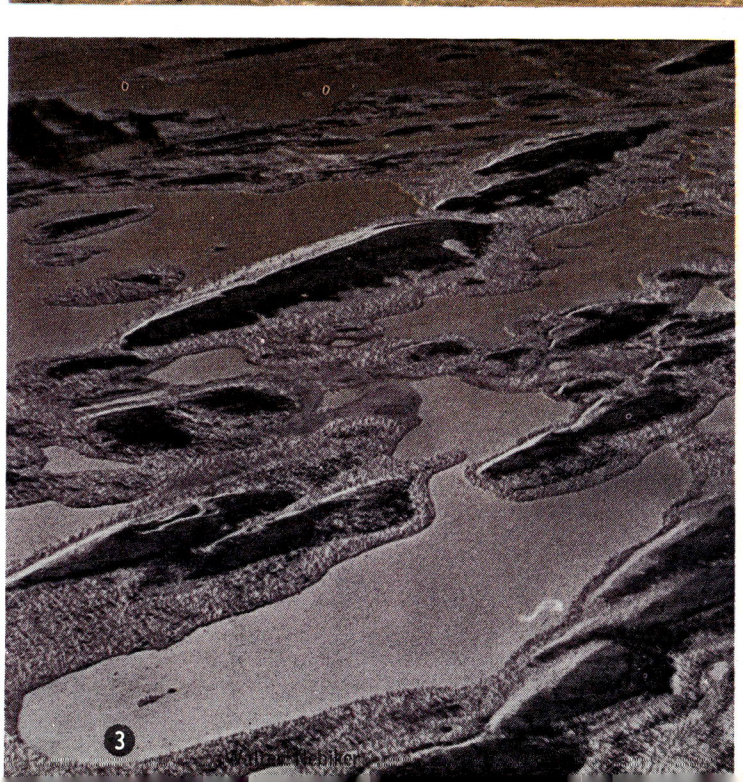

NORTH AMERICA

1. Horse-drawn sightseeing coaches, Victoria, B.C., Canada
2. Red cliffs of the Gaspé, Quebec Province, Canada
3. Mt. Rushmore National Memorial, South Dakota, U.S.A.
4. Falls of the Niagara River are shared by United States and Canada
5. Marine Studios, Marineland, Florida, U.S.A.

Mexico

ADVENTURING IN MEXICO

When the Spaniards first landed on the unexplored Mexican coast they found a fabulous country and called it New Spain. Visitors today will still find Mexico a fabulous country, whether they be tourists or scholars, businessmen or artists. Mexico is truly all things to all people. Here ancient ruins exist in close proximity to modern, progressive cities. Lakes, forests and imposing volcanoes present scenes of unmatched beauty. Wonderful churches and cathedrals vie with one another for the supremacy of Mexico's landscape. And most interesting of all are the people whose customs and dialects vary from place to place. Especially interesting is the Indian population, many of whom still speak the ancient Mayan or Aztec tongue and live much the same way as their renowned ancestors did. Whatever the visitor's interests are, he may be sure of bearing away with him some treasured memory from this land of old and new.

THE EAGLE AND THE SERPENT

Legend says that in 1325 the Aztecs, searching for a place to settle, came to a lake. Here they saw an eagle perched on the stem of a native cactus, which was growing out of a rock. The eagle held a serpent in its talons. Taking this as a good omen, the Aztecs founded their capital here — Tenochtitlán, site of present-day Mexico City. Less than two centuries later the famed Spanish conqueror, Hernán Cortés, landed and subjected the entire region in about two years. From the time of this conquest to the establishment of independence Mexico was governed as the Viceroyalty of New Spain. After nearly three hundred years of Spanish control, the Mexicans first anounced their desire for freedom in 1810, when a Mexican priest, Miguel Hidalgo, declared independence with the rallying cry of "El Grito de Dolores." After Hidalgo's defeat and execution, the patriotic cause was taken up by José María Morelos, and the Declaration of Independence was formerly signed in 1813. Later in the century Benito Juaréz, who became president in 1858, forcibly opposed the setting up of a French Empire in Mexico under the puppet-ruler Maximilian. After much guerilla warfare, Maximilian was captured and shot by Mexican soldiers and the Empire came to an end.

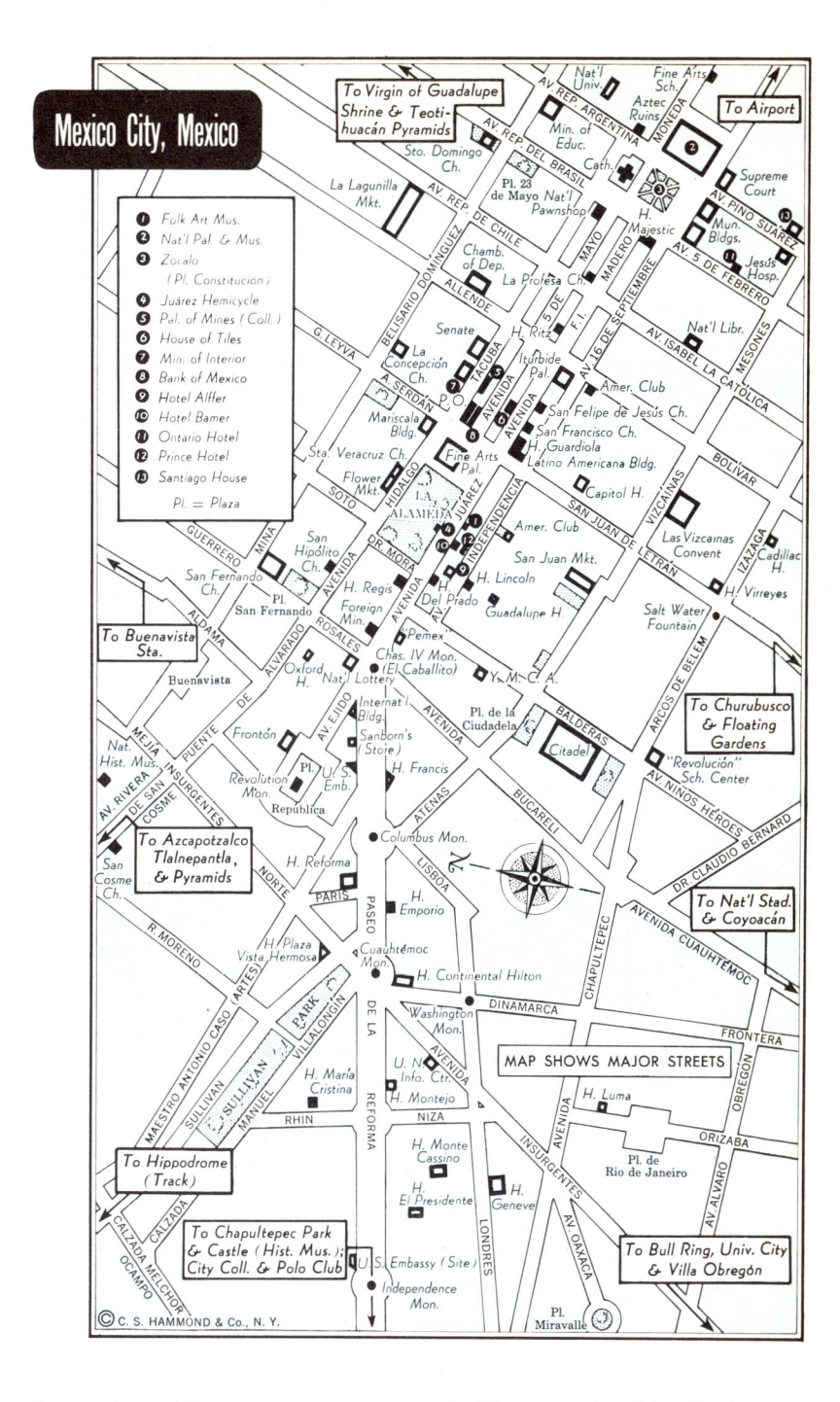

MEXICAN MEALS

Mexican *tortillas* and tamales are famous as typical native foods, but while in Mexico you will want to try some of the other dishes whose renown has been confined to the borders of the country. A savory dish is *pollo en estofado* or Mexican stewed chicken made with cinnamon, olives and other seasoning. Another tasty dish is *cembollos rellenos* (stuffed onions) which will easily prove to be a meal in themselves. If you like salads, try *ensalada de guacamole*, a delicious mixture of eggs, tomatoes, olives and avocados. While in Mexico you may want to sample *penuche*, a type of delicious candy. Wines are plentiful and good. Tequila is an alcoholic drink made from the maguey plant and is known as the national drink of Mexico.

INTERESTING CITIES OF MEXICO

MEXICO CITY . . . . . . the capital, is a modern metropolis which has sprung from the ancient center of the Aztec Empire. The Spanish conqueror Cortés had the main square of the city constructed on the central plaza of the Aztecs. Known today as **Plaza de la Constitución**, it is popularly referred to as the **Zócalo**. On the east side of this plaza is the **National Palace**, now containing various government offices, but once the site of Cortés' residence. Above the central portal of the Palace hangs the **Liberty Bell** rung by the patriotic priest Hidalgo in 1810. Every year on the night of September 15 crowds swarm into the plaza to hear the President ring the bell and give the celebrated *Grito de Dolores* from the balcony. **The National Museum**, on the northeast corner of the Zócalo, has an extensive collection of Indian handicraft and relics. The most prized item is the Aztec calendar stone weighing over twenty-four tons and testifying to the scientific attainments of Aztec culture. To the east of the Museum is the **National Institute of Fine Arts**, with its valuable collection of church paintings including such masters as Murillo, Zurbarán and Rubens. Also in the Zócalo quarter is the **School of Medicine**, interesting because it was originally constructed as the headquarters of the Holy Office of the Inquisition, where the cells of its victims may still be seen. Also noteworthy is the **Palace of Fine Arts**, a large ornate building executed in white marble with yellow domes. Its great weight pressing upon the spongy lake bed of the city has caused the building to sink six feet. Mexico City's main boulevard is the **Paseo de la Reforma**. This walk is interrupted at intervals by circles or *glorietas*, adorned with monuments and flowers. At the end of the walk is **Chapultepec Park**. It was on the hill in the center of the park that the great Aztec Emperor, Montezuma, had his summer palace. **Chapultepec Castle** was begun here in 1783 and later used as a residence by the ill-fated Emperor Maximilian and his wife. Located within many public buildings throughout Mexico City are the forceful murals of such world-famous Mexican painters as Rivera and Orozco. The latter has done an impressive mural on the walls of Chapultepec Castle.... Fifteen miles from the center of the capital is XOCHIMILCO and its wonderful "floating gardens." Visitors may hire flower-decorated boats and drift along the canals of this "Venice of Mexico." The islands here were originally Aztec settlements constructed on floating rafts of twigs and reeds, covered with earth and planted with gardens. Later, as the waters of the lake went down, the plants took root so that the islands were held fast.... A short distance northeast of the capital is the pre-Aztec city of SAN JUAN TEOTIHUACAN. At the center of this ancient spot rises the **Pyramid of the Sun**, nearly 220 feet high, ruins of a residence of an ancient dignitary revealing halls, stairways, a chapel and altar. Pottery, jade ornaments, weapons, and human masks made of nephrite may be seen on display in the **regional museum** nearby.... The religious center of Mexico is the **Shrine of the Virgin Guadalupe**, four miles north of the capital. According to legend, the Virgin appeared to an Indian boy and told him to gather roses from a barren hill. The boy obeyed and carried the miraculous blossoms to the bishop in his cloak. When the mantle was opened a portrait of the Virgin was discovered upon the cloth of the Indian boy's garment. This portrait, framed in gold, is set above the altar in the church erected in honor of the official patroness of the Mexican people.... About 80 miles south of Mexico City is PUEBLA. Laid out by the Spaniards in 1531, it is the most characteristically Spanish city of the Republic, often called "the royal seat of the Spanish Empire," for from its beginning it has clung to Spanish tradition. Keeping an eternal vigil over the **Valley of Puebla** is **Popocatépetl** (Smoking Mountain), famous in Mexican legend and song. Interesting to visit in the city is the **Church of San Francisco** with its graceful towers and glazed tile. The famous **Chapel of Our Lady of the Rosary** nearby is one of the finest examples of ultra-baroque in the world. One of the most refreshing spots in Puebla is the **Agua Ozul**, a huge outdoor swimming pool fed by natural warm sulphur springs. In this town the national costume of Mexico originated, the "china poblana." Legend says that a Chinese princess, arriving in Mexico, adopted the native dress and further enhanced it by embroidering it with colored glass.... One of Mexico's most beautiful resorts is ACAPULCO, on the Pacific coast. Here fishermen may glory in the abundance of sailfish and marlin. Glass-bottom boats offer the tourist a marvelous opportunity to study the magnificent underwater life. Not only can you swim in the blue waters, but also water ski and sail to your heart's content along the fabulous beaches. While here, it is thrilling to witness the courageous diving feats of the young boys who perilously dive from a high cliff into an exceptionally narrow channel below.... Northeast of Acapulco is the quiet town of OAXACA with its colonial homes and green-stone buildings. The lovely **Church of Santo Domingo** is supposed to be one of the finest of its type in the Americas. Commanding a beautiful view of the city is the **Cerro del Fortín**, a site at which lovely rites recalling those of the ancient goddess of harvest are held every year. This hillside is topped by a massive bronze **Statue of Benito Juárez**, the Oaxacan Indian who rose to be president of the Republic. If time permits, an excursion to the surrounding areas should not be overlooked, including one to MITLA to see the Zapotecan ruins known as the "City of the Dead." Another interesting trip is to **Monte Alban** where the fabulous tombs of the past may be seen.... North of Oaxaca is the bustling port city of VERACRUZ. Here there are beaches so wide and sand packed so hard that automobiles may travel along them for miles. The warm climate and unexcelled coastline provide excellent facilities for surf bathing or just basking in the sun. Here you may sample the famous regional drink made from coconut or guanábana. Offshore is the island of **Sacrificios** where a famous pirate allowed his rebellious captives to die of starvation. Not far from Veracruz is **Boca del Río**, famous for its delicacies prepared with shrimp, oysters and crab meat. From this port city deep-sea fishing is a popular attraction which constantly lures fishermen who come from all parts of the world to try their luck.

PYRAMID OF THE SUN

J. Walter Thompson, Co.

Guatemala

LAKE ATITLAN

Guatemala Tourist Bureau

TRADITIONAL HOME OF "PAXIL"

The Indian Garden of Eden, Guatemala maintains the charm of bygone days. Two-thirds of the population are descendants of the ancient Mayan civilization and still tread the same fertile valleys and tree-clad mountains beloved of their forebears. These proud people maintain their ancient customs, language and their gorgeous costumes. Their fascinating, colorful native life and the many ancient Mayan ruins comprise the main tourist attraction of the country. Of course, the land itself, largely mountainous, is of great beauty with numerous lofty volcanoes, sweet-smelling pine woods, dense forests, turquoise-blue lakes and fertile plateaus. And wherever you go in Guatemala, you will hear in the background the tinkling music of the marimba playing folk tunes.

GLORIES OF COLONIAL SPAIN

Then there is the modern, cosmopolitan society of the Spanish Guatemaltecans, many of whose forefathers were among the brave band of three hundred who placed the country under Spanish domain in 1524. In the cities still stand many fine examples of colonial Spanish architecture, and in many cases, as in Antigua, buildings leveled by earthquakes have been rebuilt in the same grand style.

ABOUT FOOD

Continental foods of excellent variety and quality, especially Italian and Spanish, are served in the larger places. You will certainly want to try some of the local specialties, such as *Gallo en chicha* (chicken in a very special sauce), the Guatemalan version of *enchiladas* and *tamales*, and several of the many concoctions made from bananas or plantains. As in all tropical countries the variety of exotic fruits is infinite.

IN THE CAPITAL

In 1776, the year of our War of Independence, GUATEMALA CITY . . . . was founded as capital of Guatemala. Built on a high plateau, in an ideal climate, it is a clean and attractive city with gleaming modern buildings standing shoulder to shoulder with stately old colonial ones. Parque Central, a park bright with flowers, forms the hub of the city. Facing it is the National Palace, the official seat of government. Its arched courtyards, fountain-fed patios, murals and magnificent mahogany-paneled reception rooms are open to the public. Other notable buildings include the University, the National Archeological Museum, the beautiful colonial cathedral and the little chapel atop the Cerro del Carmen, from where there is a fine view of the surrounding green hills and volcanoes. In Minerva Park is a unique relief map of the country. Elevated platforms allow one to look down and get a bird's-eye view of the country. The market here is especially exciting with a lavish display of fruits, flowers and native handicraft. Golf, polo and tennis are popular in the capital and there are excellent facilities for sailing, swimming, fishing and other sports within easy reach.

ROUND AND ABOUT THE COUNTRY

A short drive from the capital, via lovely Lake Amatitlán, is the fascinating resort town of ANTIGUA at the foot of Agua volcano. Capital until 1774, when it was almost leveled by an earthquake, it preserves many interesting ruins. Around them the city has been rebuilt entirely in the old Spanish style, with pastel-hued houses fronting on narrow cobbled streets and the whole framed against a backdrop of blue-green volcanoes. The Palace of the Captains, the University, several monasteries and convents are among the restored buildings of interest. . . . A trip to the HIGHLANDS is absolutely essential, for here are the majestic mountains, the deep sheltered valleys and gorges, the scented pines, the land of the Mayans. In the midst of this splendor lies Lake Atitlán, probably the world's most beautiful mountain lake. . . . PANAJACHEL, on the northern shore of the lake is a luxurious resort. From here launches carry you to the primitive Indian villages which line the 70-mile shore line of the lake. Each village has distinctly different characteristics in dress, customs and handicrafts, and one never tires of observing their unique ways of life. . . . North of Atitlán, high in the mountains, is CHICHICASTENANGO, most famous of Guatemalan resorts. Market days, Thursdays and Sundays, are absolutely amazing and are the reason for "Chichi's" popularity. Squealing pigs, strutting turkeys, hand-loomed textiles, beautiful pottery, exotic fruits and colorfully clad Indians overflow the market place. Special rites are performed at the old church of Santo Tomás and the scent of flowers and incense and the sound of marimba music fill the air. . . . From QUEZALTENANGO, second city of the country and itself a picturesque city, may be taken many interesting excursions, down into the coffee plantations of the warm coastal lands, or up into the cool Cuchumatanes Mountains. . . . In these mountains, near HUEHUETENANGO are the ruins of Zaculeu, outstanding relics of the Mayan civilization. . . . To the north of the capital, COBAN is a charming old town famous for its shadow-work textiles and silverwork, particularly the Cobán wedding chains. . . . Further north, in the real jungle country of orchids and chicle trees, FLORES is a fascinating town built on an island in the middle of beautiful Lake Petén-Itza. Nearby are the ruins of Tayasal. . . . On the Caribbean coast, PUERTO BARRIOS, chief port of the country, offers unsurpassed deep-sea fishing. . . . From here a trip across Lake Izabal and down the Río Dulce to LIVINGSTON will take you through lush tropical forest and give you a glimpse of the great variety of exotic wildlife and vegetation that grows along the coast. You might even sight a Quetzal, that brilliantly-plumaged, long-tailed bird whose traditional love of liberty caused it to be adopted, appropriately, as the national bird of Guatemala.

Honduras

HOW DEEP IS THE OCEAN

Honduras, the largest of the Central American Republics, is an enigmatic country, fascinating to travelers and explorers, and an often-used setting for tellers of intriguing tales. Columbus, alleged to be the first white man to see the country, named it *Honduras*, the Spanish word meaning "depths." Although historians claim the explorer chose this appellation because of the deep waters found offshore, Columbus, viewing its towering mountains, could have sensed the mysteries churning within the canyons of the land. Bordering on the Caribbean Sea and on both the Atlantic and Pacific Oceans, this 59,000-square-mile country, is the most mountainous of the Central American Republics.

AT FIRST GLANCE

Sightseeing in this country of changing contours, bordering on Guatemala, El Salvador and Nicaragua, reveals that its history is as colorful as its topography. Indian and Spanish names disclose the origin of towns and cities. Its architectural chronicle is carved in the stone ruins of its Mayan dwellers, the ornate, romantic façades of its Spanish conquerors and in the uncluttered, modern structures of its now progressive, mestizo population.

WHAT'S COOKING?

The menus of its hotels and restaurants include many native dishes. Typical among them are tortillas (flat corn cakes), enchiladas (tasty meats or vegetables rolled in tortillas), tamale pie (tamal and chile), *tapado* (a stew of smoked beef, vegetables and coconut milk) and *mondongo* (made of tripe and beef knuckles).

WHAT YOU WILL SEE

TEGUCIGALPA, the capital and chief comercial city of Honduras, is situated on a plateau 3200 feet above sea-level against a background of wooded mountains. Its name allegedly derives from the Indian for "silver hills"; extensive silver and gold mining is carried on in the nearby hills. The city really comprises two towns: low-lying Comayagüela and Tegucigalpa proper, with the Choluteca River between. Two masonry bridges connect the two sections. Tegucigalpa is quite hilly and at several points streets of stairs connect one level with another; its pastel stucco houses and white public buildings stand out brightly against the verdant background of mountains. Comayagüela, resting at the foot of the mountains, is level and broad. Here is located the National University and the National School of Fine Arts, the center of contemporary Honduran art. Tegucigalpa's main square is **Parque Morazán**, named for the nineteenth-century national hero, where are located the **Cathedral**, the beautiful **Palace of the Central District**, built of Honduran marble and hardwoods, and the **National Museum**, housing four divisions dedicated to archaeology, history, natural history and national products. Within walking distance are the Presidential Palace, the House of Congress and other government buildings and churches. Along the river is **Concordia Park**, where you can see replicas of striking monuments in the Mayan ruins of Copán. Climb up to the **Paseo La Leona**, the beautiful tree-lined promenade, 700 feet above the city, on the steep slope of El Picacho. .... SAN JUANCITO, northeast of the capital, is the site of the Rosario silver and gold mines; the $2,000,000 worth of silver and gold taken out annually is transported by mule trains down the hills to Tegucigalpa. The mines are reached by a thrilling mountain road which winds tortuously through some of the most glorious scenery in the country. . . . The second largest city in the Republic is SAN PEDRO SUIA, the center of the banana and sugar-growing industries. A briskly modern city, it is in close proximity to the Mayan **ruins of Travesia** and to La Lima, headquarters of the United Fruit Company. . . . About a three-hour drive from Tegucigalpa over the winding, steep mountainside takes you to COMAYAGUA, once the capital of the Republic, in a rich, agricultural valley. Now a small, quiet, provincial town, it has preserved its colonial air in elaborate churches and low houses. Its three-hundred-year old **cathedral** contains priceless Old-World relics and paintings, including a solid silver tabernacle and candelabra which were gifts of Philip IV of Spain and Murillo's "Martyrdom of St. Bartholomew." . . . Beyond **Siguatepeque Mountain** is sparkling **Lake Yojoa**, one of the beauty spots of the Central American cordillera. Serene among pine-covered mountains, Yojoa is an ideal camping, fishing and hunting site. . . . West of this lake region is SANTA ROSA DE COPAN, largest city in the north of the country and the center of the prosperous mining and cattle-raising district, as well as the site of the tobacco, coffee and straw-hat industries. . . . Not far from here, near the border of Guatemala, are the ruins of COPAN, the second largest city of the old Mayan Empire and the probable cultural center of the whole region. One of the most representative sites of baroque Mayan art in the hemisphere, Copan is now the center of Honduras' pre-Columbian art studies. Here you will see the spacious courts, temples, palaces and stairways of the ancient city. There are many examples of the remarkable stone carving of the Mayas, huge heads of animals, representations of gods and hieroglyphs. . . . Traveling east from Copan one comes to the Caribbean Coast cities of Honduras: La Ceiba, Tela, Puerto Cortés and Trujillo, the principal ports of the north coast. . . . . . ROATAN is the Honduran port of entry and capital of the fabulous Bay Islands. Lying 10 to 40 miles north of the Caribbean coast, these Islas de la Bahía, as they are known locally, consist of three large islands, Roatan, Utila and Guanaja. Often referred to as an earthly paradise, they are covered with lush forests, mahogany and fig trees and coconut palms. Many of the islanders are British by ancestry, consequently English is the language spoken with greatest fluency. Their secluded beaches are wonderful for swimming, fishing and exploring. Nearby is PORT ROYAL, famed in buccaneer days. Strategically situated in the emerald-green foothills on the eastern end of Roatan, it is the site of an old buccaneer town, tumbled-down forts and a real pirate's cave.

REPLICA OF MAYAN CIVILIZATION, CONCORDIA PARK, TEGUCIGALPA Philip Gendreau

El Salvador

IZALCO VILLAGE AND VOLCANO — Philip Gendreau

LOVELY TO LOOK AT

Comparable in size to the state of Maryland, the garden republic of El Salvador is a traveler's treasure house. Covering the lower slopes of the Central American cordillera, it is landscaped with verdant mountains, active volcanoes, crater lakes, green forests, tropical valleys and beaches washed by the blue Pacific.

THROUGH THE HOURGLASS

A tour of the cities and towns of this small, oblong-shaped country wedged between Guatemala and Honduras is a journey through the present and a pilgrimage into the past. Ancient ruins clinch El Salvador's claim to the great pre-Hispanic civilizations of the Mayans, Toltecs and Aztecs; many cathedrals and opulent homes reflect the Spanish influence and its latest buildings reveal the economic strides and comparative political stability of the twentieth-century republic.

THE INSIDE STORY

Called the most progressive city in Central America, **SAN SALVADOR** . . . . . . the capital, is situated in the **Valle de las Hamacas** (Valley of the Hammocks) at the foot of the San Salvador Volcano. The valley's name suggests the numerous earthquakes that have shaken the city, the effects of which are indicated by its modern rather than colonial appearance. San Salvador is laid out in the form of a cross, with four spacious avenues meeting at its center. **Plaza Bolívar**, formerly called Parque Barrios, is the city's principal square and the site of its **National Palace**. Other buildings of major importance in the area are the **National University**, the **Archbishop's Palace**, the **National Treasury** and the **Presidential Mansion**. The oldest church is the **church of La Merced**, one of the few buildings not destroyed by the earthquakes. In its tower is the bell which the famed Father Delgado rang in 1811 to proclaim the country's independence from Spanish rule. The **National Museum** houses an interesting collection of jade and pottery relics from the Mayan ruins. Five miles outside the city stands the famed National Stadium, built especially for the Central American Olympic Games in 1935, now used for baseball and soccer. Akin to its historical and religious atmosphere are El Salvador's many holidays and fiestas. Of prominent significance is the one honoring the patron saint of the republic, El Salvador del Mundo (The Saviour of the World). Booths are set up in the main plaza, where handicrafts from all parts of the country are sold, allegorical floats are paraded through the streets and Indians perform traditional native dances. . . . West of San Salvador is **SANTA TECLA**, or **NUEVA SAN SALVADOR**, founded two years after the 1854 earthquake. Situated in an idyllic valley, Santa Tecla's mild, healthful climate attracts many wealthy plantation owners and prominent families. Above the town stand the **laboratories of the Coffee Growers' Association of El Salvador**, where all phases of coffee growing are studied. Higher, on the road to the San Salvador Volcano, live the mountain flower gardeners who sell in the capital's market places. Early in the morning the women may be seen descending the steep roads dressed in their native costumes, carrying their blossoms to market in baskets balanced on their heads. . . . At the very rim of the San Salvador crater is a popular resort, **EL BOQUERON**. Commanding a spacious view in every direction, it is an artist's and photographer's paradise. From El Boqueron can be seen **Lake Ilopango**, San Salvador's playground. Towered by the 6,000-foot volcano of San Vicente, the lake's shores are dotted with vacation homes, hotels and Indian fishing villages. . . . Northeast of the lake is one of the country's most beautiful spas, **LA TOMA**. . . . North of the lake is **COJUTEPEQUE**, an old sixteenth-century town which has twice been the capital of the republic. Annually, on August 29, Indians come from near and far to the Cojutepeque fair to trade their native handicrafts. . . . Still further north is **ILOBASCO**, where most of the Salvadorean **dolls** are made. During the Christmas season the open-air stalls in San Salvador's markets are filled with these tiny dolls, some as small as a grain of rice, representing the Wise Men, shepherds, angels and the Christ Child. Besides dolls, the Ilobascans make **pottery** of every kind. Since all of its inhabitants work in clay, many of El Salvador's well-known sculptors have been Ilobascans. . . . Unlike most of the other cities of the country, **SAN VICENTE**, to the east, has endeavored to preserve its historical old buildings, making it a jewel of Spanish colonial architecture. . . . **SANTA ANA**, west of San Salvador and second only to it as a business center, lies in a large and fertile valley almost surrounded by a gigantic amphitheater of mountains. Its **cathedral** is one of El Salvador's finest examples of Spanish Gothic. Near the Santa Ana Volcano is Lake Coatepeque, whose musical name means "Eye of the Sea." Famous for its mineral waters, the lake is known as "the Vichy of Central America." Completely hemmed in by wooded hills, this rustic weekend resort has excellent facilities for bathing, fishing and sailing. The other nearby lake, Guija, is especially interesting to archaeologists because of the ancient ruins along its shores and on its islands. . . . **ACAJUTLA** is the most popular seashore resort in El Salvador and the port serving the western and central regions of the republic. The stretch of coast between Acajutla and La Libertad is the famous **Balsam Coast**. Here grows the special variety of balsam tree from which is extracted the valuable medicine and perfume base, "balsam of Peru." . . . Lying at the foot of the active Izalco Volcano, **IZALCO** is really two towns — one Indian, the other *ladino* (mixed Indian and Spanish) — merged into one, with each retaining its distinctive characteristics. The natives of this town and the nearby Indian villages retain the dress and customs of olden times, and many still speak their Indian language. The most interesting geographical feature, however, is the volcano. Besides being the most active in Central America, it is — with the exception of two others in Mexico — the most recently formed as well. Because the flames of its regular eruptions can be seen nightly at sea, the natives have given it the appropriate title of "Lighthouse of the Pacific."

Nicaragua

THE CRADLE OF A POET

The Republic of Nicaragua, bathed by the waters of the Caribbean and the Pacific, is 2nd largest of the Central American republics. It is a land of lakes, dormant volcanoes and tropical jungle. Through her ports have passed such men as Francis Drake and John Hawkins on their way to sack wealthy Granada. Two centuries later came Admiral Nelson, heading an unsuccessful naval expedition. Finally the famous "forty-niners" arrived, walking unmindfully over the deposits of gold in Nicaragua, on their way to seek the precious metal in California. Today one hears English spoken in the Caribbean ports of Nicaragua by descendants of British settlers and Jamaican Negroes, both of which became the first permanent colonists. But above all, Nicaragua is the land of Rubén Darío, the world-renowned poet whose lyric verse comes readily to the tongues of Spanish-speaking peoples.

COLUMBUS STOPPED HERE

Columbus sailed along the coast of Nicaragua on his last voyage in 1502. He had met heavy seas along the Honduran coast and when he found calm waters at the cape he named it Cabo Gracias a Dios (Cape Thanks To God), as it is still called. Spanish conquerors sent from Panama under Gil González Dávila arrived in 1519. They were received by an Indian tribe that lived around Lake Nicaragua. The chief of this tribe, Nicarao, consented to be baptized and ordered his subjects to be baptized as well. It was from him, it is believed, that the country came to be known as Nicaragua.

AROUND THE COUNTRY

MANAGUA . . . . capital of the country, differs from all other Latin American capitals in that it has not been built around a single main plaza. The principal park, **Parque Central**, in spite of its name is on the northern edge of the town close to **Lake Managua**. It is interesting to observe the life of this tropical city by strolling along the downtown streets and walking along the palm-lined **Malecón** overlooking the lake. Across the street from the Parque Central is **Parque Darío** containing an artistic monument to her greatest son and immortal poet. At the base of the Statue of Rubén Darío is the gondola of Poetry which bears the goddess of Fame proclaiming the glory of the poet to the four winds. A block from **Avenida Roosevelt** (named to commemorate the late president's sixtieth birthday) on **Calle Central** is the large public market with its vast array of agricultural products, native foods and handicrafts. Among the cultural institutions you will want to visit are the **University of Nicaragua** and the **National Museum**. In the southwestern section of the capital, in **El Cauce Park**, are the **Huellas de Acahualinga**. These are footprints of human beings and animals which are probably the very earliest trace of man yet discovered in Central America. South of the city is the **Campo de Marte** a large parade ground which contains the country's fine military academy. Not far beyond is the President's Palace done in Moorish style and looking down over the expanse of the capital. Beyond is the new residential section of **Las Piedrecitas** with its beautiful gardens and terraces. Here a magnificent view may be had of **Lake Asososca, Lake Managua** and **Lake Jiloá** with the old volcano, **Momotombo**, in the distance. . . . **TIPITAPA** is a spa on Lake Managua about 14 miles from the capital. This spot promises to become the most important resort in the country. The Tipitapa water is hot and sulphurous and has become a favorite watering place. If you enjoy fish dinners, by all means take advantage of Tipitapa's restaurants. Freshly-caught fish from Lake Managua are roasted and served in a variety of ways. . . . About 50 miles from Managua is the beautiful city of **LEON**. This city cherishes its tradition of learning and culture and has the distinction of being the boyhood home and resting place of Rubén Darío. Be sure to visit the 18th century Cathedral, completed after a century of construction and one of the largest in Latin America. Here the remains of Nicaragua's poet rest in an impressive tomb. Other interesting colonial buildings are the **Palacio Episcopal** and the **Instituto Nacional**, the latter occupying an ancient monastery. Walking along León's cobbled streets you will admire the typical houses of Spanish architecture, built around a central patio and roofed with red tiles. Still used in the streets are yokes of oxen drawing high-wheeled carts just as they appeared in colonial days. . . . If possible, take a short trip to the seaside resort of **PONELOYA** where you will find beautiful, broad beaches, colorful sunsets and the **Peña del Tigre** (Tiger Rock), a cave in which, according to an old story, two lovers once hid and were devoured by a tiger. . . . Southeast of the capital lies **GRANADA** on the edge of Lake Nicaragua. This was the wealthy city of colonial times that was so often sacked by English, Dutch and French pirates. Still clinging to its traditional ways, it is a leisurely old town full of old-world charm and simplicity.

MANAGUA MARKET

Costa Rica

BANANA PLANTATION *Publishers' Photo Service*

LAND OF TRANQUILITY

Costa Rica is a beautiful and enchanting country and her delightful climate, natural beauties and unique atmosphere of serene joy and calm endear her to the hearts of all visitors. Hospitality is the keynote of this "Land of Eternal Spring," and whether you are in search of a restful vacation just admiring the lovely scenery or more exciting diversions, you will be warmly welcomed.

BOOKSHOPS AND FESTIVALS

Costa Ricans, predominantly Spanish in origin, are a happy people, very fond of music, dancing and sports. There is great merrymaking during the annual carnivals in San José during December and January, at which time one can see bullfights a la Costa Rica — the bull is never killed. The high degree of culture is attested to by the preponderant number of bookshops. As a matter of fact, Costa Rica reportedly has more per square mile than any other country. The Spanish touch is apparent in the cooking, and native dishes, especially in San José, are deliciously prepared. Be sure to try their specialities, such as *palmito* or *pejivalle* (fruits of palm trees used in a variety of dishes), *gallo pinto* (rice and beans) or *paella* (deliciously flavored rice, meat and vegetables).

THE HAPPY CAPITAL

In the heart of the central plateau lies SAN JOSE, the "Happy Capital," one of the most attractive cities of Central America, with broad, clean streets and beautiful gardens at every turn. The architecture is an attractive mixture of traditional Spanish and modern. Make a point of visiting the **National Theater**, a really magnificent edifice with marble balconies and carvings. Its foyer decorated in gold and adorned with Venetian plate mirrors is awe-inspiring. The **National Museum**, a converted fortress built around a landscaped quadrangle, features rare old pottery and well-planned special exhibits. Visit the **Zoo**, the Country Club, the Metropolitan Cathedral, **Legislative Assembly**, the Union Club, principal social center of the country, and make a tour of the national **liquor factory** where you can sample the delicious **crema de nance**. In the heart of the city is the **Parque Central**, a beautiful park with mosaic sidewalks and many huge tropical trees. Make a point of taking a drive along the **Paseo Colon**. One of the three main arteries of the city, it is a wide modern parkway flanked with magnificent chalets and mansions. At the **National Stadium** are played all the important soccer (football) and other outdoor-sports matches. Visit the **National University**, one of the finest in Latin America. Another must is a visit to the famous orchid exhibit in the **La Mil Flor** garden.

ROUND AND ABOUT THE COUNTRY

The central plateau, where the great majority of people live, is a very picturesque land with charming little villages, extensive coffee plantations and magnificent scenery.... **LA CATALINA**, only thirty minutes by car from the capital, is a lovely mountain resort, a bit of Switzerland transported, where one can enjoy horseback riding, swimming, hunting and mountain climbing.... **HEREDIA**, six miles from San José, is the center of the coffee industry. It is reminiscent of cities in southern Spain with its church towers, red roofs, grated windows and its flower gardens surrounded by white adobe walls. Visit one of the numerous **plantations** in the area.... Westward is **ALAJUELA**, a resort town and the sugar capital. It is famous for its **flowers** and for its **market days** on which you will see the best examples of these quaint little hand-painted **ox carts** still in use in the rural areas.... Near Alajuela is the **Ojo de Agua**, a picturesque swimming pool fed by cascades from numerous springs in the vicinity.... North of Alajuela is the **volcano Poas**, 9,000 feet high. Its crater, largest in the world, encloses a vast sulphur lake from which intermittently erupts a geyser 2,000 feet high.... Southeast of San José is historic **CARTAGO**, the first city founded by the Spaniards and formerly capital of the country. Here is still preserved the atmosphere of the colonial period. The **Basilica of our Lady of the Angels** is a favorite national shrine. On Sundays the **market** is most colorful, and one can buy earthenware and leather and wood articles from the country folk who bring their wares in their little carts.... East of Cartago is the beautiful **OROSI** or **ENCHANTED VALLEY** through which runs the tumultous **Revantazón River**. The valley can be explored by car or horseback and at the far side, across the mountains, is the famous **Orosi cataract** which falls from a height of 300 feet over the crest of a mountain. Also in the valley is the **Church of Orosi**, an old Spanish mission which preserves important relics and artistic treasures.... Nearby are the famous ruins of **UMARRAS**, site of another Spanish mission.... Northeast of San José, **IRAZU VOLCANO**, towers 11,300 feet high. One can drive clear up to the mouth of the crater and the panoramic view from the top is breathtaking. On a clear day can be seen both the Atlantic and the Pacific.... Coastal towns are in real tropical climate and do not enjoy the ideal year round weather of the central plateau villages.

Panama and the Canal Zone

LAND OF THE POLLERA

Panama is typically Latin and the architecture, national customs and the beautiful costumes are reminiscent of Old Spain and the early "conquistadores." The land is one of many contrasts in scenery, people, customs and costumes. From the cosmopolitan cities near the Canal Zone to Chiriqui Highlands in the west or the Darien region in the east, one passes through picturesque villages where ox carts or horses are the standard transportation, quaint coastal fishing villages and beautiful mountain scenery. Of particular interest is the Panamanian Carnival which takes place annually during the four days before Ash Wednesday. Then the Montunos or country people troop to Panama City and the streets are gay with celebrants, the women attired in their beautiful *pollerá*, the extravagant, bouffant dress worn on festive occasions when dancing the national folk dance, the "Tamborito."

GASTRONOMICALLY SPEAKING

There is a great variety of dishes and native drinks and both hotel and restaurant food is excellent. Be sure to try some of the typical and delicious Panamanian dishes like *puerco con patacones* (pork with deep-fried banana slices), *sancocho* (thick soup with chicken and vegetables) or treat yourself to an *empanada* (tasty little pies stuffed with meat, fish or chicken).

HISTORIC PANAMA CITY

Is built near the site of the original city sacked by Morgan the Pirate in 1671. Architecturally the city is Spanish with an admixture of modern. Narrow streets open onto great plazas planted with lovely flowers and tall palms. As in most Panamanian towns, the houses, built of concrete or stone, inevitably have grillwork balconies and are built around a patio. Culturally the city has a cosmopolitan air because of the continual stream of visitors from other lands that throng the narrow streets, gay cafés and fascinating shops. Central Avenue is the shopping center and its many shops and bazaars are filled with a galaxy of souvenirs and gifts from practically every country in the world. Among the many churches in the city, the most interesting include the twin-towered **cathedral**, San Francisco, San José with its magnificent **Golden Altar** which was formerly in Old Panama and was ingeniously saved by a monk who camouflaged it with black paint so Morgan and his pirates would ignore it, and **Santo Domingo** with its incredible flat arch made entirely of brick and mortar and with no internal support. Other points to see include Bolivar Plaza with its monument to the great Liberator, the very impressive **President's Palace** with lovely patios and tame egrets wandering about, and the native market, always very busy and very colorful. On the waterfront stands a great monument to the French and their struggle to build the canal. The promenade here, Las Bovedas affords a magnificent view of the bay. One can visit the **dungeons** in the nearby Palace of Justice.

ROUND ABOUT THE COUNTRY

A sightseeing highlight is a tour of the ruins of Old Panama, one of the great historical landmarks of the Americas. Here it was that all the gold and treasures from the fabulous land of Peru were stored awaiting transshipment to Spain. It was a flourishing trade center until, at its peak, it was attacked and reduced to smoking ruins by Morgan in 1671. On the way to the ruins you pass through the lovely **suburbs** of Panama and the ever-popular **dog track** and **race track**. At the boundary of the old city still stands the famous **King's Bridge**. . . . On the Atlantic side of the Isthmus is the "Gold Coast" and **COLON**, a veritable melting pot of all nations, and one of the world's greatest commercial centers. Colon's **Front Street** far surpasses even Central Avenue in the capital for its amazing variety of wares from the world over. Night life here is absolutely "frenzaic," with every conceivable type of entertainment, food and drink. Points of interest in the city include the beautiful **Hotel Washington** with its lovely lawns and large swimming pool, the **cathedral**, the magnificent statue to **Columbus**, the **Stranger's Club** and Colon's magnificent **Municipal Building** and Plaza. . . . From either Colon or Panama one crosses freely into the **CANAL ZONE**. On the Atlantic side one can visit **CRISTOBAL** with its palm-shaded avenues, clean modern buildings and air of efficiency, a direct contrast to its cosmopolitan twin city, Colon. The **docks** and the **residential section** are the chief tourist attractions. Near here one can visit the **Gatun Locks**, Mount Hope, Silver City and the various U. S. Army bases, including **Fort Davis**. . . . On the Pacific side **BALBOA** is the administrative center for the canal. The **Administrative Building** contains an interesting museum and excellent **murals** depicting scenes from the building of the canal. Be sure to visit the Orchid Gardens. . . . Adjacent to Balboa is **ANCON**, of interest because of its tropical housing project. . . . Other places of interest nearby are the U.S. Army posts and **Naval bases**, **Miraflores Locks**, **Pedro Miguel Locks** and the experimental tropical gardens at Summit. . . . On the way to **Madden Dam** you cross **Las Cruces Trail**, a part of the old stone highway to Old Panama. This is in the heart of the **Jungle Preserve**, a fascinating area of dense tropical growth. . . . **PORTOBELO**, northeast of Colon, is now just a small native village but it contains interesting ruins of the Spanish city that flourished here until it was sacked by Morgan in 1668. . . . From here the route leads to the **SAN BLAS ISLANDS**, the incredibly beautiful emerald islands where the San Blas Indians still live in primitive fashion according to their ancient tribal laws and customs. . . . The **CENTRAL PROVINCES** of Panama comprise an area of rolling plains, dotted with tiny thatched adobe "ranchos" and colorful towns and villages. The costumes of the natives are especially attractive and one can find many treasures among the native handicrafts. . . . In Panama Bay is **TABOGA**, Island of Flowers, an ideal resort with excellent fishing and swimming. . . . For those whose interests incline toward hunting, fishing and the outdoor life, the **CHIRIQUI HIGHLANDS** offer the best in hunting and **trout fishing**. This is the sugar and coffee country and the hills and slopes of the towering volcanic peaks abound in a great variety of **birds** and **wild game**. Trout streams at the base of 11,000-foot **El Volcan** offer unexcelled rainbow and native trout fishing.

REMAINS OF THE OLD CHURCH, PANAMA CITY

Publishers' Photo Service

Bermuda

POETIC ISLANDS

A graceful string of coral islands set in the bluest sea, the radiant beauty of semitropical foliage, sweeping pink sandy beaches, sailing craft gliding in and out of sheltered harbors and a beaming sun showering down golden hours — this is Bermuda, oldest British colony, situated due east from North Carolina, home of the glorious, fragrant Bermuda Easter lily, of colonial formality and ceremony, of unique, pastel-tinted cottages, of gaily costumed, dancing "Gombeys" — the ultimate in pleasure and health resorts, about which one famous resident has written: "You'd think that Nature lavish'd here/ Her purest wave, her softest skies,/To make a heaven for love to sigh in,/For bards to live and saints to die in!" — Tom Moore.

BERMUDA LOBSTER

The Bermuda lobster is one of the most cherished local dishes. It resembles a large crawfish and can be broiled or boiled, or served as lobster thermidor or Newburg. Cassava pie is the *pièce de résistance* of Christmas dinner and beloved by Bermudians, who wouldn't think of Christmas without it. The root of the cassava plant is used to make a thick, sweetish pie crust, covering cubes of cooked pork and chicken. Sweet potato pudding, not like the United States sweet potato pie, is the Bermuda dish for Guy Fawkes Day, November 5, while salt cod and bananas is the traditional Sunday breakfast dish. In addition to the well-known vegetables, be sure to try such local triumphs as pawpaws and cristophenes.

ISLAND HOPPING

HAMILTON, capital of Bermuda, is the cultural and shopping center as well. **Front Street**, where the liners and freighters dock, **Queen Street** and **Reid Street** form the shopping center, and every visitor should take some time browsing through shops along here. Bermuda and Bermudians have established a distinguished record in sailing circles the world over and the magnificent Royal Bermuda Yacht Club, the patriarch of Bermuda racing and the most exclusive club in the colony, has an impressive location on **Albuoy's Point**, an attractive park on Hamilton Harbour. The **Colonial Parliament** and the **Supreme Court** both meet in **Sessions House**, with its famous clock tower. Tourists enjoy the spirited debates of the Parliament, the oldest in the world except for those of England and Iceland, and the sessions of the wigged and very British court. Another landmark is the majestic **Cathedral**, built of native stone, but with liberal use of stone imported from Scotland, Normandy, Nova Scotia and Indiana as well. The library is in **Par-la-ville**, a fine old house whose gardens, dating from the middle of the nineteenth century when this was the home of William Perot, are among the loveliest in the colony. The **Bermuda Historical Society Museum** has interesting collections of old furniture, china and silver, mementos of Bermuda history and oil paintings of early settlers. The beautiful **Government House**, residence of the Governor, and **Admiralty House** near Spanish Point, residence of the ranking British admiral, are open to tourists several times a year. The center of tennis activity — a popular, year-round sport — is the **Bermuda Tennis Stadium**, a few minutes' walk from Front Street. From Hamilton, an excursion may be taken to the **Sea Gardens**, the coral reef encircling Bermuda, to watch the strange coral formations and varicolored fish from the glass-bottomed boats . . . At the far eastern end of the colony is quaint **ST. GEORGE**, the oldest settlement and the capital until 1815. Venerable **St. Peter's Church**, probably the site of the oldest Anglican church in the Western Hemisphere, has communion silver valued at $250,000, a cedar altar so old it looks like mahogany and a gallery where the slaves used to sit. The beautiful little park, **Somers Garden**, is where the heart of Sir George Somers, leader of the company to first set foot on Bermuda, is buried, although his nephew took his body back to England. On Old Maid's Lane, the street where poet Tom Moore lived while in Bermuda, is an entrance to famous **St. George Hotel** . . . Take the delightful ferry trip across St. George's Harbour to **ST. DAVID'S ISLAND**, to see the unusual St. David's Islanders, an interesting mixture of American Indian, Negro and Irish ancestry, and to visit the **lighthouse**, from which there is a wonderful view . . . There are a number of points of interest around **HARRINGTON SOUND**, west of St. George's Island, including several beautiful caves where the stalagmites and stalactites have assumed many lovely and spectacular effects, with **Crystal Cave** and **Leamington Cave** the most popular; **Tucker's Town**, where many wealthy Americans and Britishers have their homes and the location of the world-famous golf course at the **Mid-Ocean Club**; the **Lili Perfume Factory**, which visitors may tour; the deep natural fish pool at **Devil's Hole** and the **Bermuda Government Aquarium**, with probably the finest collection of tropical marine fish in the world, and the adjoining **Government Museum** . . . The entire **SOUTH SHORE** of Paget, Warwick and Southampton is dotted with many magnificent pink-coral beaches, Bermuda's greatest attraction, including the small deserted coves and the formal facilities like **Elbow Beach Surf Club**, **Breakers Club**, **The Reefs** and **Princess Beach Club**. During the spring, the oleanders along the South Road make the view of the breaking surf even more beautiful and many tourists prefer to take the trip along here by carriage . . . Also in **SOUTHAMPTON** is **Gibb's Hill Lighthouse**, producing one of the best views of the islands you can find — dramatic in daytime, romantic by moonlight. . . . **Somerset Bridge**, in **SANDYS**, connecting the main island with Somerset Island, with a draw just large enough for a sailboat mast to pass, is said to be the smallest drawbridge in the world. About a quarter of a mile from here are the **Cathedral Rocks**, where the coral cliff has been worn by the ocean until it resembles Gothic architecture.

ROYAL BERMUDA YACHT CLUB

Bermuda News Bureau

The Bahamas

QUEEN'S STAIRCASE, NASSAU
Bahamas News Bureau

VACATIONER'S HIDEAWAY

One-time haven of adventurers, buccaneers and blockade-runners, and now one of the world's most celebrated international playgrounds are the Bahama Islands, just east and southeast of Florida. Here life is deep-rooted in gracious, leisurely Old World traditions — charming background for an excitingly different vacation in a vast island paradise of exotic ever-blooming flowers and year-round beauty on land and sea. There is a very special quality of softness to the Bahamas, meeting place of the world's elite — in the pastel pinks and yellows of old houses, in the velvety sands of the beaches, in the very air itself.

ABOUT FOOD

Specialties of the Bahamas cuisine are the conch salads, with lettuce, tomatoes, peppers and onions, and conch fritters. Of course, the fish dishes are delectable and Nassau is especially noted for its fine sea foods. One of the unusual sea-food favorites is green turtle pie. In addition to these, Bahamians use coconuts and pineapples — their own, which, although small, are deliciously tender and juicy — in a variety of ways.

NASSAU, ETC.

NASSAU, the capital of the Bahamas, on the island of NEW PROVIDENCE, is characterized by its wealth of historic charm, modern sophistication and tropical atmosphere. Here, where the international set play, pirates once held sway. Throughout Nassau — and, indeed, the entire Bahamas — you'll find thrilling reminders of the swashbuckling seventeenth-century existence. Here, for instance, is rugged **Fort Charlotte**, still commanding the approaches to the harbor. The **Queen's Staircase**, with sixty-six bricked treads cut in the solid rock, said to be the work of slaves, leads to the back of another old fort, **Fort Fincastle**. The first glimpse of this charming colonial capital after disembarking from the ship at Prince George's Wharf will be the view of the beautifully proportioned **post office**, House of Assembly and other government buildings at busy Rawson Square in the heart of downtown Nassau. The wharf, itself, is another charming part of the city, where eager native boys dive for coins tossed into the water. The picturesque **markets** scattered along the wharves, including the informal open-air native market in Rawson Square, are well worth visiting. A trip through Nassau's busy harbor to the **Sea Gardens** is one that should not be missed. Through the glass bottom of the boat may be seen an underwater panorama of exotic and gaily colored fish, darting among feathery sea plumes, pastel-colored fans and weird formations of coral. There's nothing more relaxing or more typically Bahamian than another kind of ride, in a fringed-topped carriage, past quaint Bay Street shops, through an avenue of royal palms and past the beautiful homes of Bahamians and winter visitors, where gardens of bougainvillaea, hibiscus, frangipani and passion flower overflow pink walls. Another short ride — this time on another boat — from Prince George's Wharf to Hog Island brings you to **Paradise Beach**, Nassau's most famous. On all the soft sands and crystal-clear Bahamian waters, like the magnificent beaches at **Fort Montagu**, the Bahamas Beach Club, Rose Island and others, you will enjoy the world's finest sea bathing and sailing. The bay is superb for water skiing, and the Bahamian waters offer a thrilling challenge to the fisherman to match wits with amberjack, kingfish, bonito, tuna, marlin, tarpon, bonefish and other scrappy fighters. You can also enjoy golf at the smart Bahamas Country Club, tennis on championship courses, horse racing at **Hobby Horse Hall** and polo matches at **Clifford Park** . . . HARBOUR ISLAND, at the northern tip of Eleuthera, with its secluded beaches, provides an ideal setting for those who want a quiet vacation. One of the oldest settled islands, as well as one of the most popular, it has always been noted for its seamen and ships. On the ocean side is the famous **Pink Beach**, one of the Bahamas loveliest . . . The largest island, ANDROS was once a pirate rendezvous. Since it is low, swampy and cut through by mangrove-bordered creeks, there is good duck shooting here and for years it has been the breeding place of flamingos. . . . The quaint, three-hundred-year-old villages and superb beaches on ELEUTHERA make it the best-known and most populous island after New Providence . . . To BIMINI came the pirates of one century and the rum-runners and the bootleggers of a later date. And nowadays come the greatest big-game fishermen of the world, seeking blue marlin, white marlin, giant tuna and many other varieties. Here also is the legendary "Fountain of Youth" which Ponce de Leon sought . . . LITTLE EXUMA and GREAT EXUMA are parts of a chain of numerous cays, noted for their beauty. Because there are several good harbors, this is a favorite of the Bahamas with yachtsmen . . . Most southerly and third largest of the Bahamas, INAGUA has wild horses, the largest flamingo rookery in the colony, duckshooting and great salt ponds.

British West Indies

ENGLISH HARBOUR, ANTIGUA

IN A PLACID SEA

If you are looking for some place to spend a quiet, lazy vacation of swimming, fishing, sailing or just picnicking on a wide beach under a bright tropical sun, then by all means go to the British West Indies, where the landscape is magnificent, life is easy and the pace slow. For a vacation spot that is really off the beaten path, go to the Windward or Leeward Islands, or if you prefer a little more popular place, try Barbados, "the Riviera of the Caribbean," or fascinating, cosmopolitan Trinidad.

TROPICAL DRINKS

Rum is the national drink on all the islands in the British West Indies. Barbados planters punches and rum punches are famous, and so are the fresh lime squashes and gin slings. The green swizzle is a Trinidad specialty made from Carypton (an Angostura product). Less extensively used but worth trying are poncha crema, sorrel cocktail, soursop punch and granadilla punch.

LAND OF THE FLYING FISH

"Warm, favoured lands that never know the biting northern cold, where endless summer ever reigns with glories manifold." This is BARBADOS, the Caribbean Island lying farthest east. The most English of the West Indian Islands, both in scenery and in the character and habits of its inhabitants, it has in consequence received the affectionate sobriquet of "Little England." However, the abiding charms of Barbados are the sunshine and the sea which encircles this tropical isle with a belt of the deepest blue. BRIDGETOWN is a busy port, a blend of the old and the new, with narrow, winding streets and byways with quaint names giving it a picturesque atmosphere. Bathsheba, a seaside resort on the east coast with fine stretches of beach, is where the flying fish fleet returns usually at about two in the afternoon. In this area the hills run nearer to the coast, and the scenery is more rugged and picturesque than in any other part of the island. Hackleton's Cliff at an altitude of approximately 1,000 feet, commands a splendid view of this coast.

LAND OF THE CALYPSO

African rhythms, Hindu temples, Moslem mosques — cosmopolitan in appearance — this is amazing TRINIDAD. The capital is PORT OF SPAIN . . described authoritatively as the cleanest and healthiest city in the West Indies. One of the wonders of the world is Pitch Lake, 114 acres of asphalt, glamorized in fantastic stories and legends. Popular shore excursions are drives along the Saddle, a road built by American Seabees during World War II, through the grapefruit orchards, cocoa estates and bamboo groves of Santa Cruz valley, and the North Coast Road, 1,000 feet above the blue Caribbean, with a sweeping view of about 100 miles. Maracas Bay is Trinidad's popular picnic beach, while others almost equally popular are at Toco, Manzanilla, Mayaro and Balandra, a perfect half-mile-long crescent. Shop for bargains in British goods and French perfumes on Frederick Street and Marine Square and for filigree jewelry and Oriental treasures in the Hindu bazaars.

UNSPOILED, TROPICAL EDEN

TOBAGO'S coastline is deeply indented, girdled by sun-baked beaches and coconut groves, and the scenery is undescribably beautiful, from the coral shore of the southwestern lowlands to the loveliness of volcanic hills and valleys in the north and east. The pattern of life is simple, woven in soft tones of informality and ease; sea bathing, horseback riding through coconut estates, tennis, deep-sea fishing and hiking are the main recreations. Robinson Crusoe Hotel, within fifteen minutes walk of SCARBOROUGH, the main town, is noted for its delicious "Creole" dishes and Castle Cove Beach Hotel specializes in Chinese dishes.

*VOLCANIC ISLES

The four colonies making up the WINDWARD ISLANDS form part of the chain of islands known as the Lesser Antilles. GRENADA, "Spice Island of the West," whose capital is ST. GEORGE'S, is the most southerly and the most populous of the group. It is very picturesque, with volcanic mountains and a great many streams and springs, and breathtaking landscapes thrill the sightseer at every turn. . . . . ST. LUCIA is very mountainous, with forest-clad volcanic cones rising sheer out of the sea on the west coast and sulphurous springs nearby. The capital is CASTRIES. . . The most striking feature of mountainous and densely wooded ST. VINCENT is the volcano, Soufriere (4,048 feet), on the northern shore, which was active as recently as 1902. . . . . The most northerly island of the group is DOMINICA, having a continuous range of mountains running the whole length of the island.

HISTORICALLY RICH

The British colony of the LEEWARD ISLANDS is divided into four presidencies. The western part of the island of ANTIGUA, one of the presidencies, is composed of volcanic rocks, while the remainder consists of plains just above sea level on which sugar cane is widely grown. English Harbour is the site of an old naval dockyard where Lord Nelson once had his headquarters. Barbuda, a dependency of Antigua, is a flat coral island with a large lagoon on the west. There is deer, duck and pigeon shooting on Barbuda and excellent fishing and bathing round the coast. . . . ST. CHRISTOPHER, generally known as ST. KITTS, is of volcanic origin and very mountainous, and NEVIS resembles it in general characteristics. St. Kitts is known for that remarkable old fortress called Brimstone Hill, famous during the eighteenth century as the "Gibraltar of the West Indies." On Nevis, hot mineral springs with valuable medicinal properties, which made the island a fashionable health resort in the eighteenth century, are found near CHARLESTOWN, the town where Alexander Hamilton was born. There is good bathing and sea fishing on both these islands and a limited amount of shooting when migratory birds visit them from July to September. . . . Also of volcanic origin, MONTSERRAT has rugged forested hills.

*As a result of the formation, in 1958, of the West Indies Federation within the British Commonwealth, certain regroupments have taken place among the British Caribbean colonies.

Cuba

FIRST COLONY

Lying off the Florida Keys, Cuba is a traditional vacationland for visiting Americans. For excellent swimming, exciting deep-sea fishing or just relaxing in the bright sunshine, no place surpasses it. In addition, there is Havana — beautiful, gay, sophisticated Havana — with its modern conveniences, urban enjoyments and bright festival air. And for a glimpse of the old life, when Cuba was the first colony in the New World, there are the mellowed churches, venerable palaces and imposing fortresses still standing in every part of this sunshine island. Truly, the modern visitor of today can well agree with Christopher Columbus when he wrote: "This land is the most beautiful that eyes have ever seen."

ABOUT FOOD

Cuba has many delectable typical dishes, of which these are the specialties: *arroz con pollo* (rice and chicken), *cangrejos moros* (Moorish crabs), *congri* (rice with black beans), filet of Pargo, *picadillo* (Cuban version of beef hash), hot tamales, avocado salad.

THE CAPITAL

HAVANA . . . . . on the northwest coast, is the capital and largest city in Cuba. A modern, cosmopolitan city, with wide boulevards and buildings of ultramodern architecture, it has yet retained all the interesting aspects and charms of colonial times. Facing the **Plaza de Armas**, around which the original city was founded in 1519 at the western end of the channel, are a number of old buildings: **El Templete**, a small chapel in Tuscany style, built in 1828 to commemorate the first mass and first city council held on that site; **La Fuerza Castle**, second oldest fort in the New World, begun in 1538 and now the **National Library**; **Lieutenant-Governor's Palace**, today the seat of the Supreme Court, and City Hall, which for centuries was the home of the island's Spanish governor-general, both fine examples of colonial architecture. **Morro Castle**, famous fort across the channel at the entrance to Havana harbor, constructed in 1589-1597 and containing many interesting and exciting relics of the past, and across from it, **La Punta Fortress**, built in 1589, recall exciting episodes, pirate attacks and the short war with England. Not far west, quaint, old **Cathedral Square** has been restored to its original glory. **Columbus Cathedral**, for which the square is named and an excellent example of Spanish baroque, contains a wealth of treasures in gold, silver and precious stones, paintings and gorgeous vestments. On either side and opposite the Cathedral are **colonial mansions** that once were the homes of Cuba's nobility. The colonial structure of perhaps the greatest architectural value is **San Francisco Convent**, dating from the 16th century. In the patio of Santa Clara Convent, used for offices now, are still to be seen the 300-year-old section of a street with three of the original houses, including the first market, bathhouse and village pump. Adjoining the old colonial city rises modern Havana—vast, beautiful and sumptuous. A handsome structure combining various architectural styles, the **Presidential Palace** contains beautiful paintings by leading Cuban artists. However, the remarkable feature of this palace is the glass tiled dome. The **National Capitol** is impressive for its sumptuous decorations, noble proportions and rich materials like marble, stone, gilt, bronze, precious woods. **Central Park** is the starting point of Havana's night life and on the east side of the park is **Centro Asturiano**, with its beautiful ballroom, all-marble stairs and tiled bar. Another night spot is **Casino Nacional**, a lavishly fitted palace with gorgeous interior decorations and at its entrance, a fountain of graceful nymphs that is famous as a fine work of art. In the upper part of the Paseo de Martí (Prado Boulevard), a gay, historical boulevard called the "Champs Elysées" of Havana, are the open-air cafés where orchestras feature typical native music. For those interested in sports, there are all kinds of games to be seen, including boxing matches, dog shows and others at the magnificent **Sports Palace**; horse racing at the outstanding **Oriental Park Hippodrome**; jai-alai, probably the speediest game in the world, at **Frontón Jai-Alai** and **Frontón Havana-Madrid**; and many others like polo, baseball and sailing. La Concha Beach, in Marianao, is the most popular in the neighborhood. On the cultural side, there are concerts by the **Philharmonic Orchestra of Havana** and other world-famous artists at the Auditorium Theater. Magnificent residences border the avenues, such as the **Avenida de los Presidentes**, in the aristocratic section of Vedado and particularly along First and Fifth Avenues in the wealthy, exclusive section of Miramar. Other points of interest are the **University of Havana** and "Jesús de Miramar" Church, the largest church in Cuba, considered a model of Roman architecture and enriched with imposing murals. The Carnival, which takes place in Havana during the Lenten season, is a unique, fascinating spectacle. The special feature is the parade of *"Comparsas,"* based on the traditional slave celebration of their one day of freedom granted every year.

ROUND ABOUT THE COUNTRY

The **ISLE OF PINES**, off Cuba's southern coast, is called "Treasure Island," since it is believed to be the locale of Stevenson's immortal novel. A pirate rendezvous in bygone days, it is today a popular vacation area because of its healthful climate; extensive beaches, like Bibijagua

SANTIAGO DE CUBA HARBOR

Beach with its black sand; tropical vegetation; abundance of hunting and fishing; and fine boating, especially on the Las Casas River... West of Havana is **PINAR DEL RIO**, from where visits can be made to spectacular Viñales Valley, the loveliest in Cuba, popularized by painters and photographers, and the tobacco fields of Vuelta Abajo, where the world's best tobacco is grown... **MATANZAS**, east of Havana, has been called the "Cuban Athens," because of its social and cultural refinement. Facing an enchanting bay, with a marvelous scenic background of sloping hills, the serene grandeur of the **Yumurí Valley** and the banks of the Canimar River, it also has nearby the wondrous **Bellamar Caves**, whose crystallizations produce an incomparably beautiful gamut of colors... A famous beach, distinguished and cosmopolitan, **VARADERO BEACH** is renowned for its brilliantly blue waters and silvery white sands. Visitors may tour the Jose Arechabala, S. A. Industries, an important liquor and candy factory... **SAN MIGUEL DE LOS BANOS**, frequently called the "Vichy of America," is a few miles away. Located among picturesque mountains, it has five mineral-water springs... Yachting is the main attraction at the shipping port of **CIENFUEGOS**, called the "Pearl of the South." Each year it is the scene of the Inter-Club Rowing Races. Historic Jagua Castle and Hanabanilla Falls, the most beautiful in Cuba, are located here... The wealthiest storehouse of fishes and variety of species in Cuba is in **CAIBARIEN**, on the north shore, and the richest fishery of all is Los Ensenachos Key. On the nights of the 24th and 25th of December, the famous *Parrandas de Noche Buena* festival takes place... In **SANCTI SPIRITUS** the original narrow streets and architecture, denoting the Moorish influence, still prevail, casting a singularly attractive appearance of ancient beauty, so much so that most of it has been reproduced on canvas by noted painters. Facing the Plaza Mayor is the church, containing a charming "Chapel of The Rosary," and the Museum has numerous historical treasures... **TRINIDAD**, on the south coast, has preserved, as none other in the New World, its colonial atmosphere and charm of the past. Recommended especially are the ancient palaces of the Iznagas, Canteros and Borrells and the Conde de Brunet. Several old families, such as the **Torrados, Frías and Palacios**, possess wonderful collections of antique works of art. Especially Trinitarian are the "parrandas" composed of a group of young men who parade the streets at night, with violin and guitars, intoning songs beneath the grilled windows of the young ladies.... The first metropolis of Cuba, **SANTIAGO DE CUBA**..... is now second only to Havana in importance. It was in this vicinity that the principal events of the Spanish-American-Cuban War took place, now commemorated by landmarks and monuments at famous San Juan Hill.

COLUMBUS CATHEDRAL, HAVANA

Jamaica

MEMORABLE ISLE

Jamaica is an island of legends, the intermingling of many old races, the modern accent of fabulously chic visitors. In this loveliest of islands is found not only scenic beauty, but also an ideal climate throughout the year, excellent sport facilities, a restful environment, friendly native people and the hospitable social life of the largest British colony in the West Indies. Jamaicans say that anyone who has been to their island must return again. Perhaps they are right—for visitors nostalgically remember that great houses still survive from old planter days, the natives sing pensive ditties, orchids hang from trees and the rum is the best in the world.

FOOD

The fish is superlative, the bananas grow large and are colored by a pretty pastel palette and here is an *embarras de choix* of vegetables. You can pluck oysters fastened to the roots of mangrove trees under water.

FAMOUS, FASHIONABLE RESORTS

The main metropolitan area of Jamaica is the capital, KINGSTON . . . . Among its many attractions is the sprawling Institute of Jamaica, with its library, museum, history gallery, lecture hall and vivarium. Besides shopping in the stores with attractive prices, visit the perfume factory and one of the bottling and blending plants of the famous Jamaica rums. Near this commercial area is the largest open-air native market in the West Indies. There are excellent facilities for sportsmen, including deep-sea fishing, especially for marlin; riding in the delightful mountains; golfing on courses like the smart Liguanea Club, in the foothills of the Blue Mountains; yachting at the Royal Jamaica Yacht Club and exciting polo, besides racing, on one of the world's most picturesque polo fields at renowned Knutsford Park, the "Ascot of the Caribbean," where the brilliant Racing Carnival is celebrated in December and January. Nearby are the ruins of Port Royal, once the "wickedest place on earth," in its brawling heyday an opulent rendezvous of seventeenth-century pirates and buccaneers. At suburban St. Andrew are the Hope Botanical Gardens, with their wealth of tropical plants, trees, orchids and bougainvillaea. An amazing, winding drive of several miles through the Blue Mountains will take you to Newcastle and its exciting panoramic view of Kingston and its harbor. . . . The north coast, around the sleepy little fishing village of OCHO RIOS, is noted for its excellent hotels and guest houses, its unexcelled facilities for water sports, like Roaring River Beach, and golf at the Upton Country Club. Fern Gully is a cool and narrow canyon of breathtaking beauty, in which one motors between awesome phalanxes of giant ferns and other exotic vegetation. . . . On the northwest coast, MONTEGO BAY, with its amazingly clear sea water, is internationally known as the fashionable center of the Caribbean. It is praised for its many excellent beaches, including the celebrated "Doctor's Cave" or "White Sands" Beach, said to be the world's finest. Many picturesque sugar-cane and coconut plantations are located nearby. . . . Near the old town of FALMOUTH, east of Montego, is Good Hope Ranch, surrounded by coconut groves and banana plantations visible for several miles, a fine example of the old great houses of the West Indies. Visitors should take the horseback ride from the ranch through the weird and legendary Cockpit Country. An unforgettable experience is the boat trip out into Oyster Bay and the brilliant phosphorous lagoon, one of the most concentrated in the world, where the movement of a fish or a hand in the water creates vivid streaks of light like liquid fire. . . . In the central highlands are the popular resorts of CHRISTIANA and MANDEVILLE, "the English village," with its serene atmosphere and rather British appearance, complete with village green. Pleasant drives take visitors to the excellent bathing beaches and deep-sea fishing facilities of the south coast and the alligator hunting and river fishing on the Black and Cabaritta Rivers. . . . At nearby LACOVIA is the famous "Bamboo Avenue," whose gracefully intertwined bamboo trees form a two-mile continuous natural archway. . . . On the northeast coast, an area noted for the almost unreal beauty and brilliance of its tropical flowers, plants and trees, is lovely PORT ANTONIO, a center for swimming and deep-sea fishing. For the exhilarating and unique experience of "river rafting," embark on a bamboo raft guided by a native pilot over a sinuously curving stretch of gentle rapids on the Rio Grande. The mysterious Blue Lagoon, of "unfathomable" depth, is world-famous because of its intensely blue water. . . . The Jamaican dependencies, the CAYMAN ISLANDS, consisting of Grand Cayman, Cayman Brac and Little Cayman, are becoming increasingly popular as tourist resorts.

"BAMBOO AVENUE," NEAR LACOVIA

TROPICAL LANDSCAPE — Jamaica Development Board

Haiti

UNIQUE REPUBLIC

The Hispaniola of the Spanish, the Saint-Domingue of the French has become Haiti, where whistles of the master's whip are no longer heard, where life is gentle and pleasing in the shade of mysterious mountains. The western part of the island of Hispaniola, it is, next to the United States, the second oldest independent state and the only French-speaking republic in the Western Hemisphere, with a potential prosperity far in excess of other lands of equal area. Americans will love this fascinating little republic for the special qualities making it really unique — the independence of the people, their intriguing, unusual cultural heritage and their exceedingly interesting and checkered history.

CULTURAL TRADITION

The unique combination of cultural traditions found in present-day Haiti is typified in the country's unofficial language — Creole. This tongue — the only one that has been created spontaneously in the Western Hemisphere — is based on the Norman French of the sixteenth-and-seventeenth-century buccaneers.

OLD RECIPES

Dine on flaming lobster *Sauce Ti malice* or turkey prepared with shrimp according to a recipe that comes down from the buccaneers. Try the Haitian version of a boiled chicken dinner, known as *Bouillon Poulet*. Other specialties include *Black Rice* — studded with tiny mushrooms known as *Djon-Djon*.

FASCINATING CULTURE AND HISTORY

PORT-AU-PRINCE . . . . . the capital, is an orderly city of wide streets, green parks and a mixture of French colonial and modern architecture. There are two main plazas: the **Champs de Mars**, a combination park, military field and recreation center, and the **Place de l'Indépendance**, laid out in gardens of tropical flowers surrounding the tomb of the great heroes, Dessalines and Pétion, who forged the republic. Public buildings of interest include the beautiful, domed "**Casa Blanca**," the presidential palace, containing the famous hall of busts; the French-influenced **Treasury** and the very modern **Postal Palace**. Since Haiti, of all the Caribbean islands, has developed the only distinctive art culture, those interested in this unique aspect of the tiny republic should visit the **Centre d'Art**, where primitive paintings and some sculpture of young Haitians are shown. Another fascinating cultural characteristic is the fact that the dances and songs of present day differ little from those of the slave period and have preserved the rhythmic qualities and beauty of African folk art. Performances are given by the **Troupe Folklorique Nationale** at the open-air **Theatre de Verdure**, by the bay, and by courtyard gatherings of natives presenting the original voodoo dances under the spell of the sacred drums. Many rare documents and relics are on display in the **Museum**, among them the famous diamond crown of Emperor Soulouque, who ruled the country a century ago. The most exciting and exotic of all Haitian festivals is the three-day, pre-Lenten **Mardi Gras**. A traditional carnival made up by the people themselves, the ceremonies are full of symbolism and magic . . . In the mountains behind Port-au-Prince, known as the Haitian "Alps," is **PETIONVILLE**, full of fanciful decorated villas. From here you may see the thatch-roofed native houses and peasant women walking gracefully along the road to market with baskets full of fruit and vegetables skilfully balanced on their heads. Dine and dance at Haiti's best night club, the "**Cabane Choucoune**." . . . Farther up the mountains are the famous year-round resorts of **KENSCOFF** and **FURCY** . . . Southeast is the cool **FORET DES PINS**. Unique in the Caribbean, it covers 150,000 acres where one can find strawberries, green parrots and, if you are lucky, the rare "L'oiseau musicien" singing his three mysterious notes . . . On the southern peninsula is the historic port of **JACMEL**, where the streets are like stairways, with famous, coconut-shaded **Carrefour Raymond**, most beautiful of Haiti's beaches . . . From **SAINT MARC** on the northern peninsula you may visit the enchanting island called **Ile de la Gonâve**, a paradise for nature lovers and fishermen. According to legend, it was here that the Lost Dauphin, Louis XVII, was hidden and died . . . Historic **CAP-HAITIEN**, on the north coast, was the wealthy colonial capital and still retains some of its earlier aspect, with its balconied houses and short, narrow streets. Dating from that period are the centennial **Cathedral** and the **Justinian Hospital**. When Napoleon sent his brother-in-law, General Leclerc, to quell the rebellion, his beautiful sister established there her luxurious court and the ruins of **Pauline Bonaparte's regal palace** still are on view. After the successful revolt, Henri Christophe, the fabulous revolutionary personality and former slave who inspired Eugene O'Neill's *Emperor Jones*, proclaimed himself King Henri I. On top of a mountain peak 3000 feet above sea level, he built the grim, majestic, impregnable fortress, **Citadelle Laferriére**, a spectacular masterpiece of architecture designed by Henri Besse, a local engineer. Completed in 1817 with the help of 200,000 conscripted former slaves, out of which 20,000 lost their lives, it was here, in 1820, that King Henri committed suicide by shooting himself with a golden bullet. At the foot of the mountain lie the ruins of his pleasure palace, **Sans-Souci**, modeled on the royal chateau of Saint-Cloud near Paris, where the king lived with a fantastic nobility created by him.

SANS-SOUCI PALACE, CAP-HAITIEN

Philip Gendreau

Dominican Republic

LAND OF DISCOVERY

This tiny country, the first of the New World to be sighted by Christopher Columbus, is being discovered all over again, this time by her North American neighbors, as an ideal place to spend a blissful holiday playing on magnificent beaches and in tropical-blue waters and gay night spots. The eastern part of the island of Hispaniola, the Dominican Republic is well-known for its spectacular, ultra-modern hotels, casinos and night clubs, providing every conceivable convenience to enhance an already luxurious life in this Caribbean tourist's delight.

DOMINICAN DISHES

The usual cuisine is Creole or American, with these favorite Dominican dishes: *arroz con pollo* (chicken and rice); plantains cooked with wine and spices or sliced and fried like potato chips; *salcocho,* a stew made of local vegetables and different kinds of meats; *pastelitos,* pastries filled with meat, fish or preserves; roast pig; *pinonate,* a confection of cocoanut and milk, and *rosquetes,* a pastry made with oranges, guayaba, cherries and papaya. They also serve excellent beers and rums.

THE OLD AND THE NEW

Founded by Bartholomew Columbus, brother of the discoverer, as Santo Domingo in 1496, CIUDAD TRUJILLO . . . . the oldest city in the Western Hemisphere, is today a modern, progressive, clean metropolis. No other city in America has the distinction of having been the starting point of so many discoverers and conquerers, since here lived Cortez, Pizzaro, Velazquez, Alonso de Ojeda, Juan de Esquivel, Ponce de Leon, Balboa, De Soto and many others. And of all the islands and countries in the Caribbean, the Dominican Republic has more of its history colored with the exploits and legends of Columbus than any other. Naturally, therefore, there are many of the aged buildings still standing here. Foremost of these is the Primate Cathedral of America (Santa Maria la Menor), the oldest cathedral in the New World, built about 1523. Here, amid a fabulous array of silver and gold ornaments, jewelry and art treasures, including the crowns of Ferdinand and Isabella and a silver carillon made by Benvenuto Cellini, the remains of Columbus lie in state within an awe-inspiring marble monument. Overlooking the harbor stand the moldering ruins of the Palace of Alcazar, built in 1510 for Diego, the discoverer's son. Not far from the sea are the ruins of San Nicolas de Bari, the first hospital in the Americas, built in 1503, with its exquisite arches and columns. Of interest, too, to every citizen of every country in this New World, is the new Columbus Lighthouse, the largest man-made monument in the world, and also the Columbus Ceiba, the tree to which he chained his ships. Since most of the city was destroyed by a hurricane in 1930, many of the buildings are ultramodern and especially interesting are the beautiful new homes, the luxurious up-to-date hotels and the brand-new campus at the University of Santo Domingo, the oldest university in this hemisphere. In contrast to these man-made buildings are such natural marvels as the nearby caverns, with Indian carvings, going deep into the rock and surrounding a virtual sunken tropical Garden of Eden. Visits to Haina Sugar Mill, where the natural cane is processed into the sweet white crystals, or to one of the breweries are interesting observations. Colorful peasants still vend their wares in the Mercado Modelo, a model market unique in Latin America, and along the Calle Conde, principal shopping street, wonderful hand-wrought curios await the shopper. Ciudad Trujillo also maintains an ambitious cultural program, including regular concerts by the National Symphony Orchesta. At delightful "Perla Antillana" Park gay crowds gather to watch exciting horse races and polo matches, and a new stadium furnishes the most modern facilities for soccer, baseball, football and outdoor pageants . . . BOCA CHICA, on the south coast east of Ciudad Trujillo, is the unsurpassable water-sports resort. Fishing for tarpon, marlin, sailfish, snook, bonefish, wahoo and many other thrilling species and water skiing in the shelter of the coral reef are especially popular. This town is also famous for the delicious sea food served there. Nearby, a mangrove island has been transformed into an interesting tropical aquarium, aviary and zoo . . . The most famous seaside resort on the north coast is SOSUA . . . Nestling on the fragrant, pine-clad slopes of the central mountains are the two most fashionable resorts of the interior, JARABACOA and CONSTANZA, where especially fine horseback riding is available. Usually unheard of in the tropics, fine apples, pears and grapes are grown in the vicinity of Jarabacoa, while the mountain air of Constanza is constantly scented with the roses and carnations cultivated there . . . A good base for exploring the north coast of the island, the part where Columbus first landed, is SANTIAGO, north of the mountain resorts . . . Worth seeing, too, are the colorful flamingos at ENRIQUILLO LAKE, 135 feet below sea level.

COLUMBUS CASTLE, CIUDAD TRUJILLO

Dominican Republic Tourist Office

Puerto Rico

CROSSROADS OF THE CARIBBEAN

Roughly rectangular, Puerto Rico is the smallest and easternmost of the four islands known as the Greater Antilles. About one-hundred miles long and thirty-five miles wide, this island is three-quarters mountainous. Puerto Rico is, in fact, a mountain crest, volcanic in action. The Atlantic side of the island is rimmed with a coastal plain eight to thirteen miles in width, while the plain on the Caribbean side narrows from eight to two miles. This contrast in topography creates colorful resorts throughout the entire island, offering a wide choice in vacation activity, but not in climate. The ever-prevailing tradewinds bequeath it a mildness comparable to New England's late spring and early summer.

CUISINE CUE.

Hotels feature many popular American dishes as well as Puerto Rican specialties. Among the latter is *lechon asado* (barbecued pig), native as the hot dog is to the U.S.A., and *arroz compollo*. Bananas are served in a variety of ways, each more tasty than the last. While all types of liquors and wines are available, the island's light rum is an international favorite. Popular, too, is Puerto Rican coffee, as a demitasse or *con leche* (with milk).

AROUND THE ISLAND

The capital and metropolis of Puerto Rico is SAN JUAN. The city proper is situated on an islet, two and one half miles long by one half mile wide, and connected to the mainland by three bridges leading to **Santurce**. Founded in 1519 by Ponce de León, San Juan is the oldest city flying the American flag, and nowhere on American soil is there such a concentration of ancient and historic buildings. In its infancy San Juan was protected by a ring of walls — "Casco" — meaning shell. The term is still used in reference to the old, walled part of the city, which still retains much of its colonial charm. The architecture is Spanish with some adaptations to adjust to the tropical climate, principally heat-proof massive walls, shutters, high ceilings and immense doors. Except for the installation of electric lights, many of the narrow, crowded streets have undergone little change through the centuries. Here are the monuments of its early struggles: **La Fortaleza**, San Juan's first fort built in 1533, and now the residence of the governors of the island; **San Juan Gate**, where the early governors landed from Spain amid much pageantry; **Casa Blanca**, built in 1523 as a fortress residence for the family of Ponce de León, and which was owned by them for two centuries. Well-restored and beautifully terraced, it is now the residence of the commanding officer of the Antilles Forces of the U. S. Army. In this old section of the city is the **Cathedral of San Juan Bautista**, originally built of wood and thatch in 1519. The burial place of Ponce de León and rebuilt many times, the Cathedral has survived storm, enemy and earthquake. Close by is the **Church of San José**, housing old-world religious treasures. . . . Standing in close proximity to this old section of the city and facing San Juan Bay is the **United States Customhouse**. Erected in 1931, it is called the most beautiful customhouse in America. Its two interior courtyards are surrounded by arcaded galleries and are the setting for lily pools and varicolored tropical plants. . . . Continuing toward the Bay one comes to the **Arsenal**, the Royal Navy Yard during Spanish Days and from which the Spanish troops sailed in 1898 at the end of the Spanish American War. It now serves as office for the Insular Department of Labor and other governmental agencies. . . . Perhaps the most beautiful spot in San Juan is **El Morro**, for centuries Puerto Rico's chief defense. Known originally as **Castillo de San Felipe del Morro**, this fortress was started in 1539 and situated on the rocky headland of the harbor facing the Atlantic Ocean. Rich in defensive history, its surrounding green, rolling fields are today part of the military reservation of Fort Brooke. . . . Ever since its foundation, San Juan has been the center of Puerto Rico's governmental, intellectual, commercial and financial activities. On its main thoroughfare, **Avenida Ponce de León**, may be seen the **Insular Capitol**, the seat of the Government and the Island Supreme Court. The entire exterior of this handsome structure is executed in white Georgia marble, while the materials used for interior decoration include both American Tennessee and Italian marbles. . . . Outgrowing its islet some forty years ago, San Juan leaped the Condado Lagoon and overflowed into the section now known as SANTURCE, which is subdivided into the **Condado and Miramar sections**. The Condado section is purely residential and contains some of the recently built luxurious hotels, including the Caribe Hilton. Miramar, also residential, includes a progressive business center and practically everything that can be bought in San Juan can now be purchased in Santurce. . . . The second largest city of Puerto Rico and the largest on its southern coast is **PONCE**, with the world's most photographed fire station. In addition to its fine residential sections blooming with tropical flowers, Ponce has gardenlike plazas, first-class hotels, restaurants, theaters, modern stores and a large public market. Its streets are wide and its atmosphere is South American. . . . The third largest city is MAYAGUEZ, center of the famous needlework industry. Situated at the foot of the Cordillera Central, Mayaguez overlooks **Mona Passage** which separates Puerto Rico from Santo Domingo. Distinctly Spanish in character and customs, this city is the site of **Farragut School**, the first educational institution erected under American sovereignty. In the outskirts is the **Orchid Museum** featuring over 1500 varieties.

Your visit should certainly include a visit to **El Yunque**, the beautiful, lush tropical rain forest where you can swim in the beautiful mountain-top swimming pool fed by the purest spring water.

GOLF AT EL MORRO

Hamilton Wright

Virgin Islands

WATER FRONT, CHARLOTTE AMALIE

Philip Gendreau

PIRATES' HIDEOUT

That hardy explorer, Christopher Columbus, made a second voyage, in 1493, to the New World he had visited the year before. This time he cruised around the islands in the eastern Caribbean Sea. He saw they were lush and beautiful, and looking for fresh water, landed on an island he called Santa Cruz (Holy Cross), which the French during their occupancy translated to Saint Croix. Carib and Arawak Indians, who inhabited the islands, fiercely resented invasion by these strangers; they fought hard for their rights, but without success. The group we now know as THE VIRGIN ISLANDS was claimed for Spain by Columbus.

THE BRITISH VIRGIN ISLANDS

Somewhat off the tourist path are the islands of the British group. TORTOLA is about twelve miles long and three miles wide, with lovely mountain scenery, a fine harbor and inviting beaches. ROAD-TOWN, the capital of the colony is located here. It is a yachting center, but unless you arrive in your own yacht, you can only reach the island by motor launch from St. Thomas — a two-hour trip. There are few guest houses on Tortola and, as they are small, reservations are advisable. All water sports are available and beach picnics most enjoyable. An especially attractive beach is on the northern side of the island at Cane Garden Bay; to reach it you travel by donkey or horseback. Here you may visit a 200-year-old rum distillery. Should you desire to sample some fine old rum on the premises, it will be served to you in calabash shells, but if you wish to buy some to take away with you, you must have your own bottles. . . . ANEGADA and VIRGIN GORDA are each about ten miles long. The former is a low-lying island, the most northerly one of the Lesser Antilles.

THE VIRGIN ISLANDS OF THE UNITED STATES

Having begun to attract visitors from other lands less than ten years ago, it is only in that short time that catering to tourists has become big business. However, efforts are being made to keep the beauty and charming atmosphere of colonial days. On the island of ST. THOMAS, CHARLOTTE AMALIE, the capital of the territory, has become a famous tourist resort, although retaining much of the color of its Dutch and Danish days. Many old mansions, built by sugar barons and rum distillers — left vacant and neglected for many years — have been restored and are now attractive homes of permanent residents. Some of the old estates are fine guest houses, with beautiful views from their terraces and gorgeous flowers in their gardens. Many homes of recent construction have been designed to blend with the old. The ideal climate of St. Thomas, combined with the available comforts of modern living, are bringing a growing number of permanent residents. In Charlotte Amalie you will find several old churches of architectural interest; Fort Christian, built in the seventeenth century, overlooking the Emancipation Gardens; a Danish Cemetery, where old stones tell some of the history of the island; Market Square, where farmers bring their products from their fields on donkeys; a 200-year-old hand-carved Italian marble Wishing Well near the square and many attractive shops on tree-shaded streets or occupying old warehouses of buccaneer days. Stop at Government House to sign the visitors' book and note the murals on the grand staircase. . . . CARENGE is the "Frenchtown" of St. Thomas, where live descendants of refugees who came to the island from Saint Barthelemy, fleeing the slave riots of the early 1700's. . . . In a drive around the island, a main point of interest is the tower on the top of Bluebeard's Castle, from which you get a magnificent view of Charlotte Amalie and its beautiful harbor. The tower was built and fortified in the seventeenth century, but the castle has been restored and is now a fine hotel. Another point from which a wonderful view may be obtained is Rosendahl Hill, looking across Drake Channel to the British Virgin Islands. Along the shores of Magen's Bay, on the north side of the island, archaeologists have found traces of an unknown civilization. Go where you wish — stop at any island for a swim or sightseeing — and be sure of a warm welcome. Spring and summer are the best seasons for cruising or touring, as rates are lower, the waters are clear and usually calm and the trade winds keep you cool and comfortable. . . . Carnival time on St. Thomas is also in the spring, sometimes lasting a week. It is a gay time indeed — parades with huge floats, native bands, dancing in the streets, masked balls and hospitality the keynote. . . . The island of ST. JOHN has not quite caught up with the pace of a modern tourist resort, although it is expected to reach that status when proposed plans for future development are carried out. . . ST. CROIX — beautiful, charming, peaceful, a wonderful contrast to the turbulence of the early days after white men came to the island. Spanish, Dutch, French, English and Danes each took possession of the island at various periods, usually by force. Denmark had the longest rule, although not continuous, until acquired, through purchase, by the United States. St. Croix's scenery is varied — a rocky coastline, fields of sugar cane, gorgeous flowers and forested mountains. Outdoor and water sports, gracious hospitality, a leisurely social life and a comfortable year-round climate make a delightful change from the usual busy pace of modern centers. . . . In CHRISTIANSTED you find the architecture and charm of a seventeenth-century town. The peaked-roofed houses, beautiful archways, patios and gardens filled with lovely flowers and shrubs make Christiansted a most colorful town; it well deserved to be designated a National Historic Site and became officially so in 1952. . . . FREDERIKSTED also has beautiful old homes with graceful balconies and gardens brilliant with tropical foliage. Tours are conducted through some of the old estates. . . . SALT RIVER has changed little since Columbus landed there in 1493. A museum contains an interesting collection of Carib and Arawak Indian relics.

French West Indies

TOUCH OF FRANCE IN THE CARIBBEAN

Once France's vast empire in the New World stretched from ocean to ocean, covering over half of North America, all of Hispaniola and most of the Greater Antilles in the Caribbean. Now the only piece still left are these islands and French Guiana in South America. Of all the Caribbean islands, these French possessions have the closest ties with the homeland, actually being departments of the continental country.

FRENCH FOOD, TOO

In the excellent restaurants, the visitor can eat as he wishes, either in incomparable French style or in the Creole, which is a good deal more spicy and highly flavored. In any case, the local cooking is a gourmet's delight. At Pointe-a-Pitre, Guadeloupe, and Fort-de-France, Martinique, the market is very well supplied with the specialties of the island: yams, Carib cabbage, sweet potatoes and delicious tropical fruits, pineapple, mangoes, corrosols, sapodillas, bananas, breadfruit. The delicious French wines are sold, also.

Guadeloupe

FAMOUS COAST LINE

Guadeloupe is famed for the beauty of its shores: deep inlets on the west, rosy sands on the north, white beaches on Grande-Terre and jagged cliffs at the Pointe des Châteaux. Actually consisting of two islands separated by a salt river (Rivière Salée) four miles long, Guadeloupe proper is of volcanic origin and very mountainous, whereas Grande-Terre, the section to the east, is relatively low and composed mainly of coral and limestone. The old historic capital, BASSE-TERRE, lies at the foot of La Soufrière at the extreme southwest of the main island. For those who like climbing and mountain walks, there are exciting explorations in the thick forests (Victor Hugo Trail, Merwart Trail). Access to the highland forests can also be had by the traces, or rides, from Pointe Noire to Sofaïa or La Boucan and from Petit Bourg to Bouillante. Such excursions lead through dense forest and along torrential mountain rivers, lined by graceful bamboo trees. Among the splendid scenery, that seen during the classical excursion to La Soufrière is especially fine. Hot springs of all kinds abound on Guadeloupe, with the thermal center at Dolé. Those at Bouillante, another popular spa, bubble out of the sea itself. The most unusual attraction of all is the "Valley of the Ancient Caribs" at Trois Rivières, an exhibition of Carib Indian art (the Roche Graves Pre-Colombiennes), like the unique sculptured rocks associated with age-old legends. No visitor should leave Guadeloupe without seeing, too, the beautiful islands of Les Saintes, offering, in their roadstead of limpid waters, in the calm and mildness of their scenery, an epitome of all the grace of the Antilles. . . . Foremost city of Guadeloupe is POINTE-A-PITRE on the island of Grande-Terre, a sugar and rum export center considered as one of the safest as well as one of the most picturesque of West Indian harbors. There are excellent restaurants specializing in French and Creole cuisine, especially La Pergola-du-Gosier, famous with gourmets for many years. Nearby beaches are of surprising variety, with some of white coral sands, as Gosier, Sainte-Anne, Saint-François, Moule and Port-Louis, and others of honey-colored sands, like Cluny and the Grande Anse at Deshaies. The hot springs at La Ravine-Chaude—only half an hour's drive away—and Sofaïa enjoy a well-established and merited reputation.

Martinique

"LAND OF FLOWERS"

That is what the Carib Indians called the island of Martinique. Others have been enchanted with it, too, for instance the magnificent painter, Paul Gauguin, who wrote, "Nature is so rich, the climate so warm, though lightened with cool breezes, that I cannot describe to you how enthusiastic I feel." The surface of the island is hilly, mountainous and covered with exuberant vegetation; the flowers are brilliant, the fruits splendid, while the colorful towns lie at the heads of picturesque creeks and on the flanks of mornes or knolls. There's a strong and fascinating flavor of French colonialism in Martinique that visitors never forget. In the capital city of FORT-DE-FRANCE the small cafés, sidewalk bookstores and multihued dress of the French-speaking inhabitants create a continental atmosphere reminiscent of far-off Paris. The Salon Martiniquais and the School of Applied Arts show interesting works by local painters and sculptors, as well as some from France and foreign countries, and the latter also has folklore and archaeological displays. The Empress Josephine was born at Trois Ilets and a beautiful marble statue to her memory graces the capital's "savanna" or park. Rising from the waters of the southwest coast is Diamond Rock, a natural phenomenon, commissioned a British ship in the eighteenth century, which for ten years successfully held off the French forces, but now stands guard over the lovely beach lying opposite. Beyond the picturesque fishing villages on the shore north of Fort-de-France are the ruins of St. Pierre, once the Paris, now the Pompeii of the New World. Here, in May, 1902, the former gay capital was wiped out by the eruption of nearby Mt. Pelée. Out of almost 30,000 inhabitants, only one man survived — a prisoner in an underground dungeon. At the southeast corner of the island is Savane des Petrifications, one of the four petrified forests in the world. Sailing and boating—in fact, all nautical sports — are much in favor, and excellent regattas are organized by the Yacht Club, which plays an important part in the life of the island.

FORT-DE-FRANCE, MARTINIQUE

Philip Gendreau

Curaçao

WOODEN SHOE SAMBA

Thirty-eight miles northeast of Venezuela lies CURACAO, busiest port in the Caribbean, and most important of the six islands forming the Netherlands West Indies or Netherlands Antilles. An autonomous part of the Kingdom of the Netherlands, these Antilles are divided into two groups, the Leeward or ABC group comprising Aruba, Bonaire and Curaçao, and the Windward Isles of St. Maarten, Saba, and St. Eustatius. Curaçao, with its 115,000 inhabitants and covering an area of 173 square miles, is the largest and the seat of the central government of the Netherlands Antilles. Like a tulip dropped among tropical bougainvillaea, Curaçao is Dutch in character and seems incongruous amid the Spanish-cultured countries of the Caribbean.

APERITIF

Her people being a mixture of many different nationalities, Curaçao's menu is international. Each of its leading hotels specializes in one type of cuisine. Regardless of its specialty one will be able to get the island's most famous product, the orange-flavored liqueur, Curaçao.

TOUR DU JOUR

WILLEMSTAD, situated on its landlocked, clover-shaped harbor, the city is bisected by St. Anna Bay which flows into the busy Schottegat Basin, both of which are sufficiently deep to accommodate large cargo vessels and ocean liners. Barring entrance to the harbor in the heart of the city is the floating causeway known as Queen Emma. Supported by a string of pontoons, this bridge of boats is towed parallel to the quay by a steam launch whenever a vessel enters or leaves the harbor. Equally as quaint are the brightly painted red, green, yellow, pink and blue houses and buildings that line both sides of the channel. The oldest quarter of the city is called the Punda. The two principal streets of this section are Heerenstraat and Breedestraat, where are located the city's leading shops, banks and offices. Other points of interest are the Governor's House at Fort Amsterdam and the Legislative Council and Court of Justice with statues of former Queen Wilhelmina and Peter Stuyvesant, who was Governor of Curaçao from 1643 to 1661. (It was through Governor Stuyvesant that Curaçao became linked with New Amsterdam, the present city of New York, when he became its governor in 1646.) . . . In Punda also is Mikve Israel Synagogue, built in 1732, and said to be the oldest synagogue in the Western Hemisphere. . . . Magnificently located on top of Ararat Hill overlooking Willemstad is the F. D. Roosevelt House, the official residence of the Consul General of the U. S. in the Netherlands West Indies. This superb building was presented to the United States by the people of Curaçao in 1950 in recognition of the beneficial cooperation between the two countries during the last war. . . . Before leaving for other sections of the island a tourist will certainly enjoy visiting the colorful Native Schooner Market where skippers of Caribbean schooners bring their wares from the South American mainland and sell them directly from ship to customer. . . . Pietermaai and Scharloo are the residential sections of the city, and well worth seeing for their ornate and colorful Dutch architecture. . . . The section of the city on the west side of the bay is called Otrabanda, a combination of residential and business areas. Here one finds the famed Curaçao Museum, a government-restored example of old Dutch architecture. It houses many valuable antiques, valuable paintings and furniture of the colonial period. Here one also may see exhibits of Curaçao's recent industrial and economic history. In its spacious gardens are found specimens of all trees and plants growing on the island. . . . East of the city on the bay-studded southern coast is the internationally famous Caracas Bay where the larger cruise ships stop for refueling. (So close to the shallow oil fields of Venezuela, Curaçao has become the home of the world's second largest refinery.) Nearby is Spanish Water Bay with its popular Boca Beach, the haven of water-sport enthusiasts. . . . The most famous beach resort on the island is Piscadera Bay, to the west of Willemstad. Originally built as a recreation center for the Royal Dutch Shell Company, it has been enlarged on a luxurious scale to accommodate visitors to Curaçao's shores. . . . Unlike the southern coast with its many bays, the northern coast is cliff-lined and crowned with St. Christoffel Hill, 1,230 feet high. The mountain range is composed of limestone, a famous formation of which is Boca Tabla, or Devil's Mouth Grotto, pounded by the trade-wind driven surf.

MAIN SHOPPING STREET, WILLEMSTAD

WILLEMSTAD'S FLOATING MARKET

UNITED STATES

On July 4, 1960, the flag of the United States was officially changed to accommodate a star for the 50th state, Hawaii, the jewel of the Pacific Islands; while Independence Day of 1959 saw the addition of the 49th star in recognition of the statehood of Alaska, one of the fastest growing of the United States.

Here is located Mt. McKinley, the highest mountain in North America, with McKinley National Park near Anchorage being second in size to Yellowstone, and famed for its fine specimens of wild animals and birdlife. Fishing, the chief sport of the state, attracts many vacationists, and big game hunters are excited by Kodiak Island, the home of the Kodiak bear, the world's biggest carnivorous animal. Those seeking the unusual will enjoy Barrow, the largest Eskimo village, where whaling, glaciers, igloos and tremendous ice packs are part of the usual scenery; or they might prefer to visit Fairbanks, the center of the gold-mining fields.

In contrast to Alaska, Hawaii, with its delightful climate, is a lavish setting in which to spend a leisurely lazy holiday, lolling on the beautiful beaches and enjoying the lush landscape of the Islands.

"See America first" is applicable to the older states as well as the two new ones, for the diversity of vacations is unlimited in this great land. From the six New England states, with their historic landmarks of a proud Colonial heritage, to the Pacific coast states, rich in mementoes of the Spanish explorers and the Gold Rush days, the sight-seer can step back into the romantic days of the past. Or, he can enjoy the unmatched scenic beauty of the country today, with the snow-peaked Rockies in the West and the lofty Smokies in the South. The spectacle of the fabulous 200 mile-long Grand Canyon of the Colorado River is unrivalled anywhere, while Yellowstone and Yosemite National Parks will always be as popular to tourists as the majestic Niagara Falls is to honeymooners.

The winter sports enthusiast can enjoy his favorite pastime skiing down the snow-clad mountains of New England, or at the renowned resorts of Lake Placid, New York, and Sun Valley, Idaho.

For pure pleasure-seekers, what can surpass Las Vegas, Nevada, with its fabulous gambling casinos, million-dollar hotels and top-flight nightly entertainment? In this same vein Florida, "the sunshine state," and especially Miami, couples gay night life and luxurious accommodations with a glorious climate, ideal for bathing, sunning and fishing the year-round. California too enters the competition for vacation wonderland, due to its magnificent beaches, sun-drenched desert playgrounds and the glitter of Hollywood to attract thousands of tourists to the Pacific Coast.

Not to be overlooked are Washington D.C. and New York City. The former, the nation's capital, is recognized as one of the most cosmopolitan cities in the world, boasting such magnificent buildings as the Capitol, the White House, Smithsonian Institute, Lincoln Memorial and Washington Monument, to name just a few; and famous the world over for its glorious abundance of lovely cherry blossoms in the Springtime.

"Melting pot of the world" with people representing every nation on the globe living within its boundaries, and with the United Nations making its home here, New York truly is unique. Not only is it the entertainment and financial capital of the country, but with its skyscrapers, subways and myriads of cultural and amusement centers, this is the perfect place to spend a holiday. New York, the world's largest city, is a symbol of the ambition, achievements and indomitable spirit of the American people.

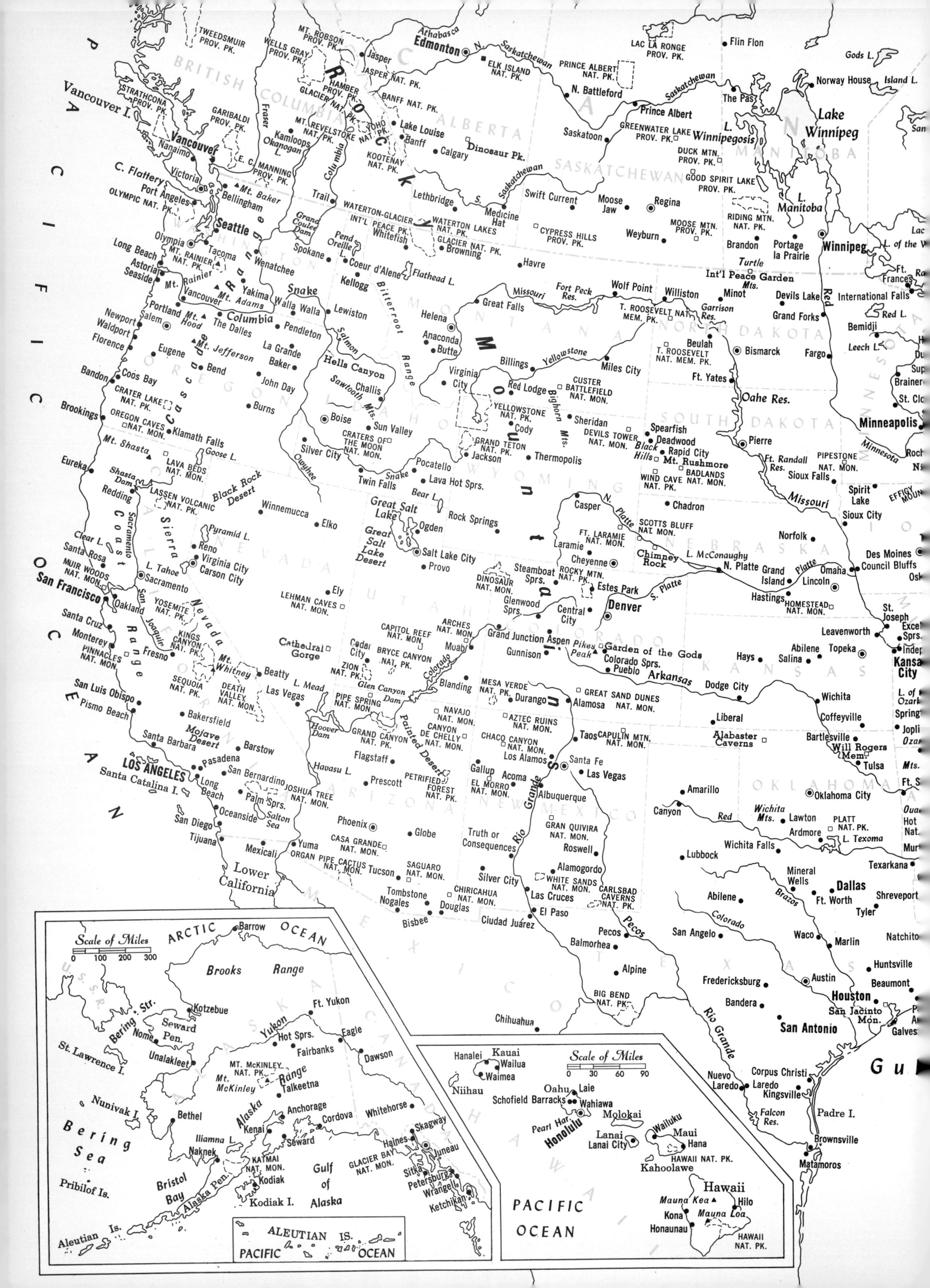

PACIFIC OCEAN
BRITISH COLUMBIA
ALBERTA
SASKATCHEWAN
MANITOBA
CANADA
ROCKY MOUNTAINS
TWEEDSMUIR PROV. PK.
MT. ROBSON PROV. PK.
WELLS GRAY PROV. PK.
Athabasca
Edmonton
N. Saskatchewan
ELK ISLAND NAT. PK.
LAC LA RONGE PROV. PK.
Flin Flon
Gods L.
Norway House
Island L.
PRINCE ALBERT NAT. PK.
Jasper
JASPER NAT. PK.
HAMBER PROV. PK.
GLACIER NAT. PK.
BANFF NAT. PK.
N. Battleford
Saskatchewan
The Pas
Prince Albert
Lake Winnipeg
STRATHCONA PROV. PK.
Vancouver I.
GARIBALDI PROV. PK.
Fraser
MT. REVELSTOKE NAT. PK.
YOHO NAT. PK.
Lake Louise
Banff
Kamloops
Okanogan L.
Columbia
Calgary
Dinosaur Pk.
Saskatoon
GREENWATER LAKE PROV. PK.
L. Winnipegosis
DUCK MTN. PROV. PK.
KOOTENAY NAT. PK.
Vancouver
Nanaimo
E. C. MANNING PROV. PK.
GOOD SPIRIT LAKE PROV. PK.
Victoria
C. Flattery
Port Angeles
OLYMPIC NAT. PK.
Mt. Baker
Bellingham
Trail
Lethbridge
S. Saskatchewan
Medicine Hat
Swift Current
Moose Jaw
Regina
L. Manitoba
RIDING MTN. NAT. PK.
Seattle
Grand Coulee Dam
WATERTON-GLACIER INT'L PEACE PK.
WATERTON LAKES NAT. PK.
CYPRESS HILLS PROV. PK.
Weyburn
MOOSE MTN. PROV. PK.
Brandon
Portage la Prairie
Winnipeg
Olympia
MT. RAINIER NAT. PK.
Tacoma
Long Beach
Astoria
Seaside
Spokane
Pend Oreille L.
Whitefish
GLACIER NAT. PK.
Browning
Havre
Turtle
Int'l Peace Garden
Mts.
Wenatchee
Coeur d'Alene
Kellogg
Flathead L.
Mt. Rainier
Yakima
Mt. Adams
Vancouver
Portland
Mt. Hood
The Dalles
Columbia
Snake
Walla Walla
Lewiston
Bitterroot Range
MONTANA
Missouri
Fort Peck Res.
Wolf Point
Williston
Garrison Res.
Minot
Devils Lake
International Falls
Red
Newport
Salem
Waldport
Florence
Pendleton
La Grande
Baker
Great Falls
Helena
Anaconda
Butte
T. ROOSEVELT NAT. MEM. PK.
NORTH DAKOTA
Beulah
Bismarck
Grand Forks
Fargo
Red L.
Bemidji
Leech L.
Eugene
Mt. Jefferson
Bend
OREGON
Bandon
Coos Bay
John Day
Salmon
Hells Canyon
Challis
Sawtooth Mts.
Billings
Yellowstone
Miles City
Ft. Yates
MINNESOTA
Brainerd
St. Cloud
CRATER LAKE NAT. PK.
Brookings
Burns
IDAHO
Virginia City
Red Lodge
CUSTER BATTLEFIELD NAT. MON.
Oahe Res.
Minneapolis
OREGON CAVES NAT. MON.
Klamath Falls
Boise
Sun Valley
YELLOWSTONE NAT. PK.
Cody
Sheridan
Bighorn Mts.
DEVILS TOWER NAT. MON.
Spearfish
Deadwood
SOUTH DAKOTA
Mt. Shasta
Goose L.
Silver City
CRATERS OF THE MOON NAT. MON.
GRAND TETON NAT. PK.
Jackson
Thermopolis
Black Hills
Rapid City
Mt. Rushmore
Pierre
Minnesota
Eureka
LAVA BEDS NAT. MON.
Owyhee
Pocatello
Snake
Twin Falls
Lava Hot Sprs.
WYOMING
BADLANDS NAT. MON.
WIND CAVE NAT. PK.
Ft. Randall Res.
PIPESTONE NAT. MON.
Sioux Falls
Shasta Dam
Redding
Black Rock Desert
LASSEN VOLCANIC NAT. PK.
Bear L.
Casper
N. Platte
Chadron
Missouri
Spirit Lake
EFFIGY MOUNDS
Winnemucca
Elko
Great Salt Lake
Rock Springs
Sioux City
Sacramento
Coast
Sierra
Pyramid L.
Reno
Ogden
Great Salt Lake Desert
FT. LARAMIE NAT. MON.
Laramie
SCOTTS BLUFF NAT. MON.
NEBRASKA
Norfolk
Clear L.
Santa Rosa
MUIR WOODS NAT. MON.
L. Tahoe
Virginia City
Carson City
NEVADA
Salt Lake City
Provo
Cheyenne
Chimney Rock
L. McConaughy
N. Platte
Grand Island
Platte
Omaha
Des Moines
Council Bluffs
San Francisco
Sacramento
Oakland
Ely
UTAH
Steamboat Sprs.
DINOSAUR NAT. MON.
ROCKY MTN. NAT. PK.
Estes Park
Denver
S. Platte
Lincoln
Hastings
HOMESTEAD NAT. MON.
Santa Cruz
San Joaquin
YOSEMITE NAT. PK.
Nevada
LEHMAN CAVES NAT. MON.
Glenwood Sprs.
Central City
COLORADO
St. Joseph
Monterey
PINNACLES NAT. MON.
KINGS CANYON NAT. PK.
Fresno
Range
CAPITOL REEF NAT. MON.
ARCHES NAT. MON.
Grand Junction
Aspen
Pikes Peak
Garden of the Gods
Colorado Sprs.
Pueblo
Arkansas
Leavenworth
Topeka
Abilene
Salina
Hays
KANSAS
Kansas City
Mt. Whitney
SEQUOIA NAT. PK.
DEATH VALLEY NAT. MON.
Beatty
Cathedral Gorge
Cedar City
BRYCE CANYON NAT. PK.
ZION NAT. PK.
Moab
Gunnison
San Luis Obispo
Pismo Beach
L. Mead
Las Vegas
Glen Canyon Dam
PIPE SPRING NAT. MON.
Colorado
Blanding
MESA VERDE NAT. PK.
Durango
GREAT SAND DUNES NAT. MON.
Alamosa
Dodge City
Wichita
Bakersfield
Mojave Desert
Barstow
CALIFORNIA
Hoover Dam
GRAND CANYON NAT. PK.
NAVAJO NAT. MON.
CANYON DE CHELLY NAT. MON.
Painted Desert
AZTEC RUINS NAT. MON.
CHACO CANYON NAT. MON.
Taos
CAPULIN MTN. NAT. MON.
Liberal
Alabaster Caverns
Coffeyville
Bartlesville
Will Rogers Mem.
Tulsa
Santa Barbara
Pasadena
LOS ANGELES
Long Beach
Santa Catalina I.
San Bernardino
JOSHUA TREE NAT. MON.
Palm Sprs.
Flagstaff
Havasu L.
Prescott
PETRIFIED FOREST NAT. PK.
Gallup
Acoma
EL MORRO NAT. MON.
Los Alamos
Santa Fe
Las Vegas
Albuquerque
Rio Grande
NEW MEXICO
Amarillo
OKLAHOMA
Oklahoma City
Oceanside
Salton Sea
San Diego
Tijuana
Mexicali
ARIZONA
Phoenix
Globe
Yuma
CASA GRANDE NAT. MON.
ORGAN PIPE CACTUS NAT. MON.
Tucson
SAGUARO NAT. MON.
GRAN QUIVIRA NAT. MON.
Truth or Consequences
Roswell
Canyon
Red
Wichita Mts.
Lawton
PLATT NAT. PK.
Ardmore
L. Texoma
Wichita Falls
Lubbock
Lower California
Tombstone
Nogales
Bisbee
Douglas
CHIRICAHUA NAT. MON.
Silver City
Alamogordo
WHITE SANDS NAT. MON.
Las Cruces
CARLSBAD CAVERNS NAT. PK.
El Paso
Ciudad Juárez
Pecos
Pecos
Balmorhea
Alpine
MEXICO
TEXAS
Mineral Wells
Dallas
Ft. Worth
Texarkana
Shreveport
Tyler
Abilene
Brazos
Colorado
San Angelo
Waco
Marlin
Natchitoches
Huntsville
Beaumont
Fredericksburg
Austin
Bandera
Houston
San Jacinto Mon.
Galveston
San Antonio
BIG BEND NAT. PK.
Chihuahua
Rio Grande
Nuevo Laredo
Laredo
Corpus Christi
Kingsville
Falcon Res.
Padre I.
Brownsville
Matamoros
Gulf
Scale of Miles
0 100 200 300
ARCTIC OCEAN
Barrow
U.S.S.R.
Brooks Range
Kotzebue
Bering Str.
Seward Pen.
Nome
Ft. Yukon
Yukon
Hot Sprs.
Fairbanks
Eagle
Dawson
ALASKA
CANADA
St. Lawrence I.
Unalakleet
MT. McKINLEY NAT. PK.
Mt. McKinley
Range
Talkeetna
Nunivak I.
Bethel
Alaska
Anchorage
Cordova
Whitehorse
Bering Sea
Iliamna L.
Kenai
Seward
Skagway
Naknek
Haines
Juneau
KATMAI NAT. MON.
GLACIER BAY NAT. MON.
Gulf of Alaska
Pribilof Is.
Bristol Bay
Kodiak
Kodiak I.
Sitka
Petersburg
Wrangell
Ketchikan
Alaska Pen.
Aleutian Is.
ALEUTIAN IS.
PACIFIC OCEAN
Hanalei
Kauai
Wailua
Waimea
Niihau
Scale of Miles
0 30 60 90
Oahu
Laie
Schofield Barracks
Wahiawa
Molokai
Pearl Har.
Honolulu
Wailuku
Maui
Hana
Lanai
Lanai City
HAWAII NAT. PK.
Kahoolawe
HAWAII
Hawaii
Mauna Kea
Hilo
Mauna Loa
Kona
Honaunau
HAWAII NAT. PK.
PACIFIC OCEAN

Notes and Itinerary

The United States

Pacific Coast States

Think of any type of vacation you can, then think of the Pacific Coast states Stretching over 1,200 miles from Mexico to Canada, with a 2,730 mile coastline, coast ranges, valleys, towering mountains, deserts, lakes, rivers, giant cities, hidden coastal villages — it's all here and much more. A vacation to this vast, diverse playground which offers the utmost in recreational facilities and accommodations is a vacation never to be forgotten.

CALIFORNIA

No matter how exacting your specifications, they can be met, for California is blessed by nature in many ways. An equable climate, the health-giving sun of the southern California deserts in winter, the curative properties of her mineral springs, a thousand mile shore line bathed by the blue Pacific and ranges of majestic snow-capped mountains are to mention but a few. A land rich in historical landmarks from the early Spanish missions to the glamorous days of the "Gold Rush" to the present time — California is, indeed, a vacationist's paradise.

POINT LOBOS, CALIFORNIA

LOS ANGELES. Los Angeles, popularly known as "L.A.," is the nation's third largest city. Situated on the southern California coast, it possesses a metropolitan area so vast it encompasses almost seventy outlying cities and nearly three times that many smaller towns and villages. Altogether Los Angeles spreads out over an area of 452 square miles. A decentralized metropolis, one community seemingly melting into another, it was once described by a humorist as "19 suburbs in search of a city." This great sprawling mass is tied neatly together into one great urban package by an amazing network of roads and superhighways. Los Angeles began its history as a sleepy little pueblo founded in 1781 by Felipe de Neve, the Spanish governor of California. The total population of El Pueblo de Nuestra Senora la Reina de Los Angeles de Porciuncula, as Los Angeles was then known, consisted of eleven Indian and Mexican families. Until 1881 its growth was unspectacular; then, with the coming of the railroads and the land-booms that followed, Los Angeles rapidly expanded its perimeter, swallowing up neighboring towns at a phenomenal rate. The growing of citrus fruit, the discovery of oil, the making of motion pictures and the manufacture of aircraft, all contributed to its spectacular development. An exceptionally fine climate and the grandeur of its setting, with the San Gabriel Mountains on one hand and the blue waters of the Pacific on the other, make Los Angeles a popular spot with tourists. In downtown Los Angeles, the new Civic Center with the gleaming white tower of City Hall is one of the city's most impressive groups of buildings. Nearby, Pershing Square serves as the nearest thing to a general business center. The Plaza, the original heart of the city, and the Old Mission Church, its most historic building, are preserved as relics of early pueblo days. Olvera Street, too, recalls the past. Crowded with little shops, gay with colored lanterns and Latin music, the narrow street, closed to all but pedestrian traffic, is a replica of a Mexican street of a century ago. Avila Adobe on Olvera Street is Los Angeles' oldest building, dating back to 1818. Wilshire Boulevard runs westward for some 17 miles, passing Hancock Park, where the famous La Brea Tar Pits have yielded the remains of prehistoric monsters trapped millions of years ago in the oozing asphalt pools. The boulevard leads on through Beverly Hills, home of many notable screen stars, to Santa Monica, where it ends at the Pacific Ocean. Hollywood, the city's most famous district, lies northwest of the downtown area. The large motion picture studios are located here as well as the western headquarters of most of the major radio and television networks. The main streets of the glittering film capital are Sunset Boulevard and Hollywood Boulevard, while the busy intersection of Hollywood and Vine serves as its main center. The Hollywood area is probably Los Angeles' biggest tourist attraction. Just north of Hollywood proper lies Griffith Park, which includes within its 4,253 acres an observatory, a planetarium and a zoo. Due south of the center of Los Angeles is SAN PEDRO HARBOR, the world's biggest and busiest man-made harbor. Just west of San Pedro is LONG BEACH with its famous Rainbow Pier, enclosing a 32-acre lagoon, and Signal Hill, one of the great oil producing areas of the West Coast. Forest Lawn Memorial Park, a burial ground which ranks as a major sightseeing attraction, is northeast of the city proper in GLENDALE. Just east of the city is PASADENA, noted for its Rose Bowl, and superb Huntington Library and Art Gallery in the suburb of SAN MARINO just to the south. A little further south is San Gabriel Mission. A visit through one of the major movie studios in CULVER CITY or BURBANK is a top tourist attraction. Be sure to visit Disneyland, a recently added children's "wonderland come to life." Twenty-five miles east of Los Angeles is POMONA, where the Los Angeles County Fair, largest in the nation, is held annually in late September. The San Fernando Valley lies to the northwest of downtown Los Angeles. The nearby mountains offer excellent winter sports. Baseball, football, fights, wrestling and midget-car racing are found at the following stadia and arenas: Olympic Stadium; Pan Pacific Auditorium; Memorial Coliseum — home field for U.C.L.A., U.S.C. and the Los Angeles Rams football teams. If interested in horse racing, go to the spectacular Santa Anita Track at Arcadia or the Hollywood Park. There are 26 universities or colleges in the Los Angeles area. They include: University of California at Los Angeles (U.C.L.A.) in Westwood Village, University of Southern California on University Avenue, California Institute of Technology at Pasadena. Santa Catalina Island, called the "Magic Isle," is a scenic mountain rising out of the Pacific Ocean 25 miles off the southern California coast. It is renowned for its deep-sea game fishing, and through glass-bottomed boats may be viewed the wonders of fantastic submarine gardens. . . . To the south of Los Angeles is the SAN DIEGO-CORONADO area which includes San Diego Bay and the surrounding territory. In and around San Diego, the birthplace of California history, are many interesting and unusual places. San Diego is the center of extensive Navy activities. Here, is Balboa Park, one of the show places of the world; Torrey Pines Park; the marriage place of Ramona, famous in song, story and on the screen; Mission San Diego de Alcala, founded in 1769, first of the 21 missions that stretch northward along the coast on the famous California Mission Trails; numerous beaches and beach cities — CORONADO, LA JOLLA, MISSION BEACH, Silver Strand Beach Park and Point Loma. Below the Mexican border, just a few miles away is colorful TIJUANA. The famous fresh-water fishing lakes of San Diego County, Lakes Hodges, Wohlford, San Vincente, Henshaw and Cuyamaca, are reached via the ESCONDIDO gateway. Palomar Observatory, with the world's greatest telescope, and Palomar

LA JOLLA

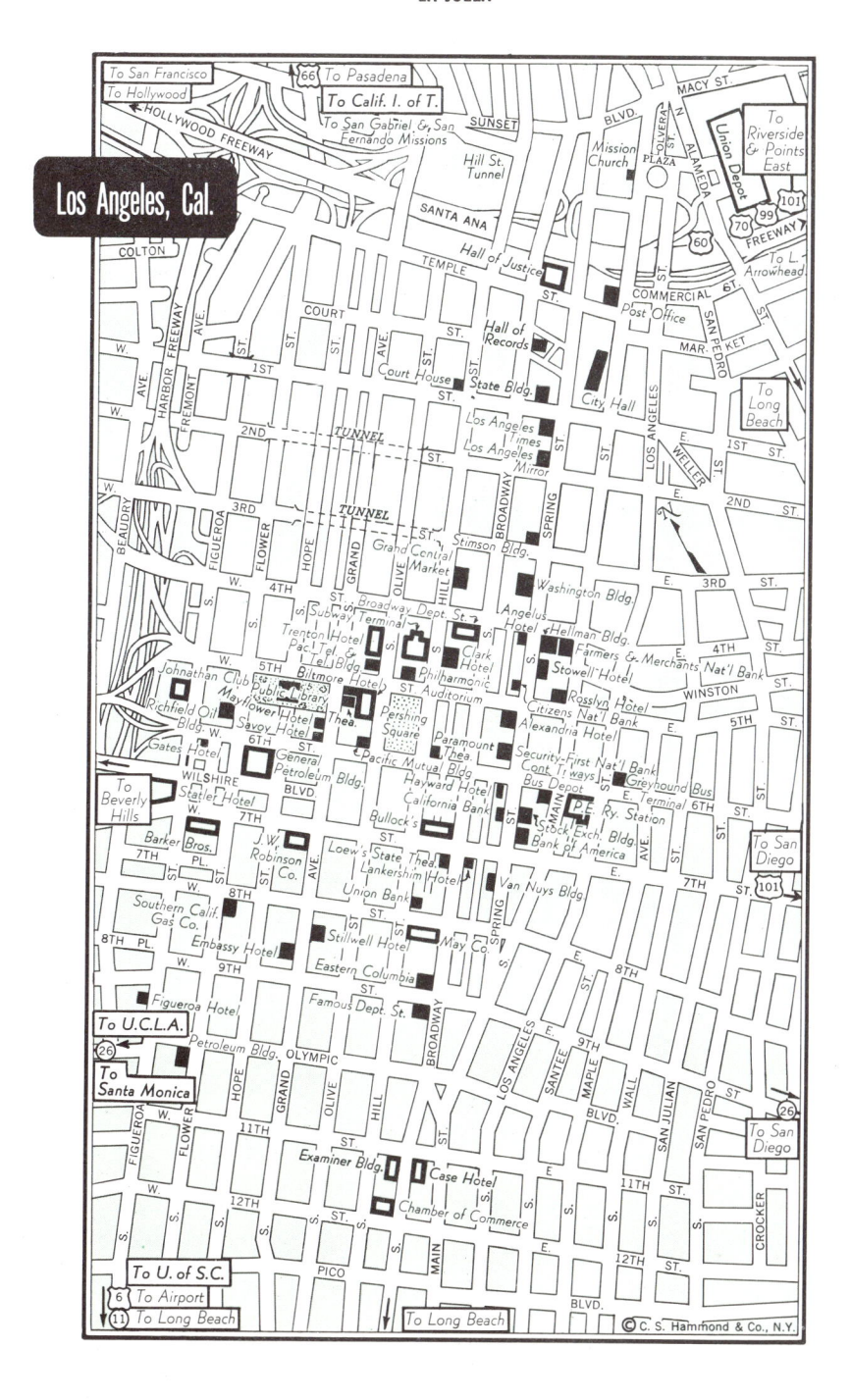

All-Year Club of Southern California

Los Angeles, Cal.

Mountain State Park are reached out of OCEANSIDE and Escondido. Lake Elsinore, with its hot mineral springs, is the "Scenic Health Resort of California." To the south and to the east are a number of other fine mineral springs. Mt. San Jacinto Recreational Area, a summer and winter resort area, is a favorite with teachers and music lovers because of its permanent music and other cultural facilities. It is the gateway by trail to the summit of Mt. San Jacinto. At the summit is Mt. San Jacinto State Park, surrounded by a vast wilderness area. At the foot of the mountain to the east nestles PALM SPRINGS and other desert resort centers. The Palms to Pines Highway circles the mountain from the desert side. Between BEAUMONT and San Jacinto are a number of fine mineral springs. . . . Northwest of here, and to the east of Los Angeles lie the San Bernardino Mountains. Here, you will find Lake Arrowhead and Big Bear Lake Resorts, situated among the pines of the San Bernardino National Forest. Year-round recreation facilities of all types are available at both resort communities. Along and adjacent to the "Rim of the World Drive," from Lake Arrowhead to Big Bear Lake, are many other resort communities, including **BLUE JAY, RUNNING SPRINGS, GREEN VALLEY LAKE** and **SNOW VALLEY.** Some of the finest facilities and snow conditions for winter sports during the winter months are found in this region. . . . North along the coast from Los Angeles you come to the Santa Barbara area. SANTA BARBARA, nestling between the mountains and the sea, owes much of its charm to its old Spanish atmosphere — rich in heritage and flavor of the "Days of the Dons"—Mission Santa Barbara, "Queen of the Missions," the Court House and other buildings of Spanish architecture and numerous historic adobes. Old Spanish Day Fiesta, in which the entire community participates, is held annually at the full moon in August. The Botanic Garden and Museum of Art and Natural History are of particular interest. The smooth sandy beaches and aquatic sports in the harbor are the chief recreational attractions. . . . To the north is the Los Padres National Forest with numerous recreational areas and the Sespe Game Preserve. Continuing north, the PISMO BEACH area includes many beach resort communities. You will enjoy year-round camping facilities, excellent surf fishing and clam digging for the famous Pismo clam. A few miles to the north is the Mission San Luis Obispo de Tolosa. . . . In southeastern California and extending into Lower California and Mexico is the Colorado Desert. Included in the desert area are Imperial Valley and Coachella Valley, noted for its date gardens. Both are famous irrigated agriculture areas. Located here, also, is the Salton Sea. In the northern part of the Colorado Desert is Palm Springs. To the west of Palm Springs is the Joshua Tree National Monument, rich in desert vegetation and wildlife. Nearby is the oasis of Twentynine Palms, a health resort. North of the Colorado Desert extends the great Mojave Desert. Here you will find many dude ranches and the health resorts of BARSTOW, VICTORVILLE and MOJAVE. To the north and bordering the Nevada state

MISSION SAN DIEGO DE ALCALA

SUTTER'S FORT

Sacramento Chamber of Commerce

line is **Death Valley National Monument.** Here you can see the greatest contrasts in altitude, scenery, coloring, mineral and chemical formations of any place in the United States. Here is the lowest point in the United States, 280 feet below sea level. Death Valley's history, starting with the Gold Rush of 1849, is as fascinating as its weird and colorful scenery. . . . **INYO-MONO** playgrounds, including **Owens Valley, Mammoth Lakes, June Lake** and **Mono Lake,** is an outstanding recreational region stretching along the eastern slope of the Sierra Nevada for more than 200 miles. It is a section of beauty and mystery, of purple mountain ranges, golden desert spaces, tumbling streams and hundreds of gemlike lakes in stately surroundings of crag and pine — a section whose historical storehouses are filled with a wealth of pioneer lore and Indian legend. To the west the Sierra Nevada reach their greatest height. **Mt. Whitney,** with an altitude of 14,495 feet, is the highest point in continental United States and in sharp contrast Death Valley, to the east, is the lowest. **Mono Lake,** 6,420 feet above sea level, the "Dead Sea of America," contains no living thing except a species of shrimp. The entire Inyo-Mono region is famous for its trout fishing. Here, too, is the habitat of the golden trout. . . . The **San Joaquin Region,** with its fertile valleys, foothills and rugged mountains, is another one of the finest of the state's recreational areas. Hundreds of crystal-clear, gemlike lakes dot the vast reaches of the Sierra, and it is in this region that practically all the remaining stands of the Sierra redwoods, the *Sequoia gigantea,* are found. In the southern section of the region are **Red Rock Canyon** of scenic interest, the **Kern River Canyon** and the recreation centers at **Hart Memorial Park, Mt. Breckenridge** and **Mt. Frazier.** North of **BAKERSFIELD** are **California Hot Springs** and **Camp Nelson.** From the valley is reached **Kings Canyon, Sequoia** and **Yosemite National Parks, Millerton Lake National Recreation Area** and the recreation areas of the Sequoia, Sierra and Stanislaus National Forests. Sequoia National Park was created for the preservation of its vast groves of "big trees," the *Sequoia gigantea.* The **General Sherman Tree,** largest and oldest of all living things, rises to a height of 272 feet, has a diameter over 36 feet and is estimated to be between three and four thousand years old. Directly north, Kings Canyon National Park has some of the wildest and most beautiful scenery in the United States — massive peaks, glacier cirques and lake-covered plateaus 10,000 to 14,000 feet above sea level — "Wild as the Himalayas," a region of superlative unspoiled mountain wilderness. Millerton Lake National Recreation Area is the result of one of the huge construction projects of the Central Valley Project. Waters of the lake are backed up by **Friant Dam.** Along the 43 miles of lake shore line are beautiful wooded areas. Yosemite National Park lies to the west of Lake Mono. Glacier-carved **Yosemite Valley,** with its towering cliffs of sheerest granite, is so massive and high that it is difficult to appreciate the scale on which they were sculptured. The **Mariposa Grove of Big Trees** and **Glacier Point** are renowned features. **Ski Lodge at Badger Pass** is a major snow-sports area. A short distance southeast of Yosemite is the **Devil Postpile National Monument.** It consists of peculiar vertical and curved basaltic columns 60 feet high and ranks with the famous Giant's Causeway of Ireland.

LAKE ARROWHEAD

All-Year Club of Southern California

SAN FRANCISCO. San Francisco's exhilarating individuality is so well-known as to be almost legendary. Haunted by memories of this wonderful city, people all over the United States harbor intense desires to return permanently to San Francisco and never tire of extolling her virtues to those unfortunates who have never felt her allure. A city of supreme and exotic beauty despite her fogs, her cool, even temperature is a continually refreshing source of pleasure. Her delightful setting amidst sparkling waters and high hills is inspiring. And the cable car, jaunty little relic of bygone days and still a cherished mode of travel over the peaks and dips of the steep hills, is the symbol of San Francisco. Coit Tower stands like a sentinel on storied Telegraph Hill, the lookout station of early days. And no one would dream of leaving San Francisco without sipping cocktails in the twilight at the "top of the Mark" — the Hotel Mark Hopkins — with its magnificent fifty-mile panorama of sparkling cities, mighty bridges and the Golden Gateway to the blue Pacific. Truly a storybook city, San Francisco is colorful and cosmopolitan, with an international flavor contributed by her communities of foreign descent. Appropriate indeed is it that the United Nations was born in 1945 in San Francisco's Opera House. In the vicinity of Broadway live San Franciscans of Chinese, Japanese, Spanish, Basque, French, Italian, Hawaiian, Mexican and many, many other ancestries, languages and ways of life. The Latin Quarter for instance, near Telegraph Hill, is a city-within-a-city, a bit of Italy, medieval in parts, warm, sunny, with its markets, flowers and lovely churches. It's the brassy part of town, some of it, for within is the onetime Barbary Coast. Something of the brazen old flavor remains today, with many of the same gaudy buildings still standing, some with their original decor. The city is famous as a gourmet's paradise, where dining out is a custom. Feasters enjoy Chinese Pea Pod Chow Yuk, Italian *pastas* and *cappuccino,* French onion soup and frogs legs *doré,* Mexican *chiles rellenos,* Spanish-Basque *arroz a'la Valenciana,* Armenian shashlik and many other little-known, international delicacies. It was for just this reason that Caruso, of the golden voice and lusty appetite, said, "There is a diabolical mystery to your San Francisco. Why isn't everyone fat?" And no one has ever been able to answer. Her cosmopolitan character is mirrored, too, in her wealth of cultural activity. Stage-struck San Francisco has recently been undergoing a notable renaissance of the theater, outbidding all other cities, except New York, in dramatic art. In the field of music, she has long been outstanding, with the triumphant San Francisco Opera Company, the Pacific Opera Company, the Cosmopolitan Opera Company, the renowned San Francisco Symphony and her unique summer musical repertoire. Most notable of all, perhaps, is the magnetic attraction she has long held for writers ever since Bret Harte, Jack London and Robert Louis Stevenson reveled in her virile, invigorating atmosphere. Romance? It's everywhere, in this "most exciting city known to man," as mystery writer Leslie Ford has described it. Romance comes in the Golden Gate with ships and trade winds, climbs Nob and Russian Hills and Twin Peaks, lives in the breathtaking views, prowls little Chinatown alleys and strolls the waterfront, beckoning to adventure in the city that's a world in herself. San Francisco is a convenient base for trips into adjacent areas. These include an easy trip to **Muir Woods** and the great redwood grove just beyond Golden Gate Bridge to the north.... An exploration of the chain of towns across the bay to the east includes: **OAKLAND** where you can see **Lake Merritt**, a salt-water lake in the heart of the city, **Lakeside Park** with its Children's Fairyland, **Snow Museum** and the **Municipal Rose Gardens**. Regional parks adjoining Oakland include **Redwood**, **Round Top** and **Lake Temescal**. Other places of interest are **ALAMEDA** with the

MISSION DOLORES, SAN FRANCISCO
Redwood Empire Association

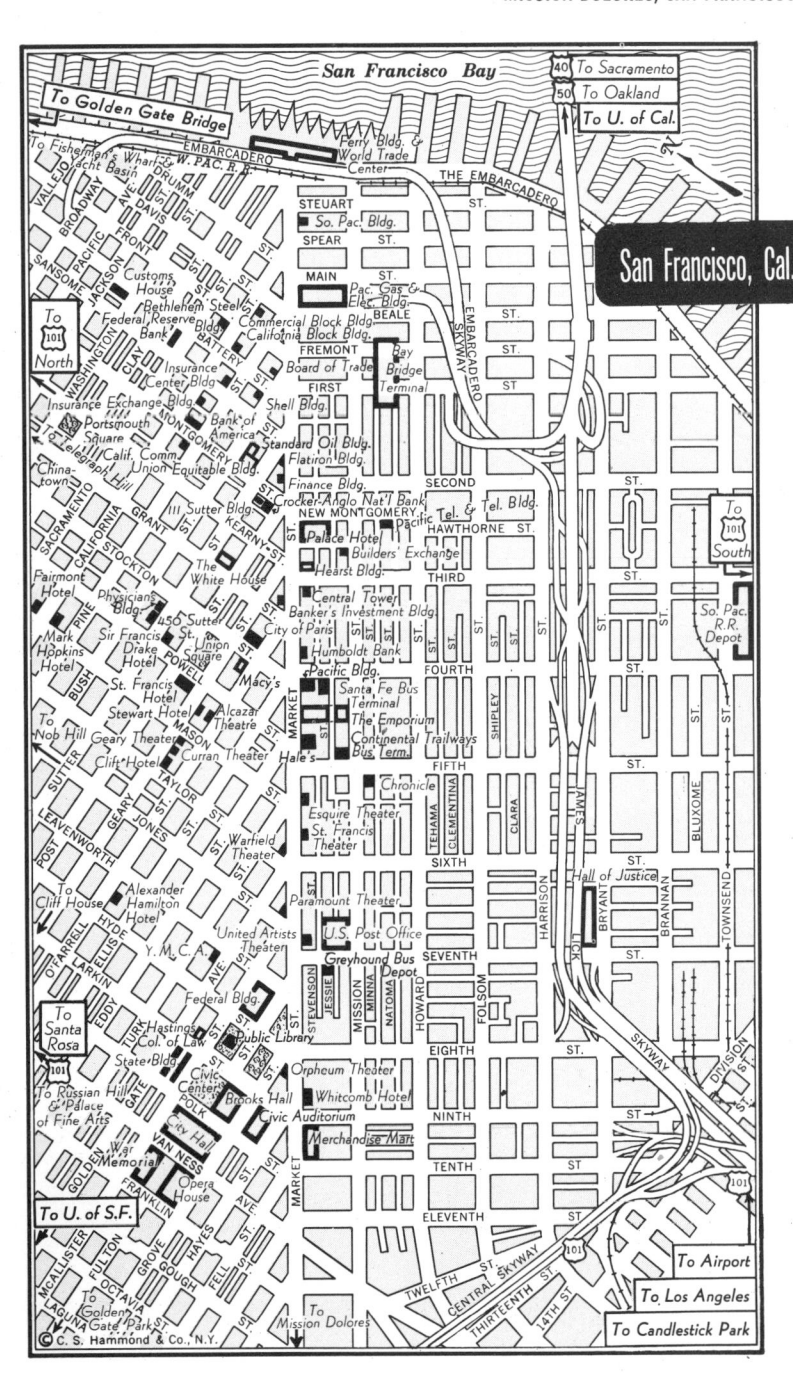

FISHERMAN'S WHARF, SAN FRANCISCO
San Francisco Chamber of Commerce

204

Alameda Naval Air Station; BERKELEY, home of the University of California and the Golden Gate Fields Track for horse racing; RICHMOND, major sea-port. A trip down to PALO ALTO, home of Stanford University, takes you through a chain of handsome suburban communities which include SAN BRUNO and SAN MATEO. A trip southward to the Monterey Peninsula, termed the "Circle of Enchantment," takes you to a world-famed playground, with the nationally known Pebble Beach and other golf courses, and numerous recreational facilities. Historically, old MONTEREY was the capital of California under three flags and the birthplace of the state's constitution. Several state historic monuments and numerous adobes are reminders of this era. Today, Monterey typifies the spirit of the Riviera of the Pacific. The picturesque commercial fishing fleet; Point Lobos State Park; Pacific Grove and the Hopkins Marine Station; Carmel-by-the-Sea, with its artist colony; Mission San Carlos Borromeo de Carmelo, where rests Junipero Serra, father of the missions, and Pfeiffer-Big Sur State Park, all add to the visitors' interest in this area. . . . The Santa Cruz Mountain Area, with redwood-covered mountains dotted with summer homes and resorts, is a favorite playground of the San Francisco Bay region. Here are located the Big Basin Redwood State Park and the county-owned Felton Grove of Big Trees. Ocean bathing, pier and deep-sea fishing at SANTA CRUZ add to the attractions. . . . The Mother Lode Country is a reminder of the discovery of gold and the "Gold Rush" which followed. Starting at Mariposa in the south, State Highway 49 traverses the Mother Lode to GRASS VALLEY, NEVADA CITY and to SATTLEY on the north. Ghost towns and historical markers are reminders of that glamorous era and make it easy to follow the paths of those pioneers. Near PLACERVILLE is COLOMA where gold was discovered in 1848.

SACRAMENTO . . . . . capital of California, lies in the southern part of the immensely fertile Sacramento Valley. Here is Sutter's Fort Historical Monument and many other historical points of interest. . . . North of San Francisco, SONOMA, lying in the Sonoma Valley, the "Valley of the Moon" made famous by Jack London, is the site of the last of the 21 California missions, Mission San Francisco de Solano. . . . The Redwood Empire (*Sequoia sempervirens*) embraces that part of California in a 10- to 30-mile-wide belt starting across the bay north from San Francisco and extending northward along the coast to Oregon. Resorts of all types are found throughout the region along with many of the beach, lagoon and redwood state parks. Near DYERVILLE, 33 miles south of EUREKA, is the world's tallest tree, Founder's Tree (364 feet). The streams of the region afford some of the state's finest fishing for trout, steelhead and salmon. A forest of petrified giant redwoods, natural steam geysers and the heart of California's light-wine industry are among the many attractions of the region. . . . The region around Clear Lake has been aptly termed "The Switzerland of America." The lake is the largest body of fresh water lying wholly within the state. Its elevation is 1,350 feet, with volcanic mountains that rise to a height of 4,000 feet surrounding it. Boating is excellent and the usual recreational activities are available. . . . The Lake Tahoe region lies within three national forests: the Tahoe and Eldorado in California and the Toiyabe in Nevada. It is one of the state's most popular playgrounds. (See description under Nevada). Donner Pass, one of the country's most outstanding snow-sports areas in winter, lies northwest of the lake. The Feather River and Yuba River region is a region of rivers and streams of jewel-like lakes and gorgeous scenery. Mines and ghost towns, reminders of the gold rush, abound. LA PORTE and JOHNSVILLE are the birthplaces of skiing in the United States. . . . Lying between Siena City and the Feather River is the Lakes Basin Recreational Area, where, within a radius of a few miles, are some 35 lakes which afford excellent fishing. . . . In Lassen Volcanic National Park stands Mt. Lassen, the most recently active volcano in continental United States. The last eruption occurred in 1915, the scars of which still remain. Volcanic activity is evidenced by geysers, bubbling mud pots, a boiling lake, hot and cold mineral springs, Cinder Cone, a mountain of volcanic ash, and others. . . . Mt. Shasta marks the conjunction of the Coast Range with the Sierra Nevada. It is 14,161 feet in height, rises a sheer 10,000 feet above its surrounding ranges and its snow-covered summit is visible for more than 100 miles from valley highways. It is the center of an outstanding recreational area. Shasta Lake and Shasta Dam are in this region, as are Castle Crags and Burney Falls State Parks. . . . The Trinity Alps is a region of rugged mountains, rushing streams and lakes. Most of it can be characterized as primitive or wilderness, accessible only by hiking or packing in. It is a paradise for the fisherman and the hunter. . . . If you are looking for a dude or guest ranch vacation, California has a large number. They are located in all sections of the state — in the mountains, valleys, foothills and along the coast. One of the many things which makes the state so interesting to the visitor is California's love of a fiesta. Approximately one thousand such colorful and entertaining celebrations are held throughout the year in all sections of the state. Special foods in southern California include: pink beans (frijoles) simmered, then fried with cheese; Japanese sukeyaki; barbecued spareribs; fresh fruit and vegetable salads. In San Francisco and the northwest: Columbia salmon; smoked salmon; jerked salmon; abalone steak; Dungeness crab; croppino; Oriental foods and teas.

OREGON

Nature endowed Oregon with fertile valleys, great mountains, snow-capped

CALIFORNIA REDWOODS

Southern Pacific Photo

VIEW OF HELL'S GATE CANYON AND THE ROGUE RIVER
Oregon State Highway Commission

peaks, vast sweeps of forests, an ocean to make her climate perfect, rivers and lakes fed by mountain snows and valley rains. She filled her woods with game, her streams with fish. This was the glittering paradise that started the covered wagons rolling westward with their cry "On to Oregon!" The paradise that the pioneer found is yours today in a visit to Oregon. Fishing, hunting, skiing, boating, swimming, mountain climbing, horseback trips, golf — these are only a few of the pleasures at your choice.

You've never seen beaches quite like the Oregon beaches, for here mountain, forest and ocean meet. Spurs of the Coast Range, heavily wooded, come down as a great drop curtain for the stage of hard, clean sands. Each beach has its legend — the forgotten treasure of early Spanish or Russian ships, the mountain-high shell-mounds of the Indians and relics of the earlier peoples. Southernmost are the popular BRANDON and COOS BAY sections. Northward there are WALDPORT on the Alsea River, the picturesque old fishing town of NEWPORT on Yaquina Bay and the famed Tillamook beaches. Northernmost are the Clatsop beaches — CANNON BEACH, a 12-mile strand, ideal for horseback riding and bicycling, and SEASIDE, where the End of the Trail Monument marks the conclusion of the Lewis and Clark expedition in 1805. A pleasure unique is the hunt for agates which are found in profusion in the sands after each high tide around AGATE BEACH. At the mouth of the Columbia River, near ASTORIA, horses are used to haul in the great salmon seines, sometimes as long as 2,000 feet. . . . PORTLAND · · · · · the Pacific Northwest's "City of Roses," straddles the Willamette River, on the south bank of the Columbia River about 75 miles east of the Pacific Ocean. With Mt. Hood in the background, it is one of our most photogenic cities. Spanning the Willamette River is St. Johns Bridge, cathedral-like in appearance, and listed by many as one of the seven most beautiful bridges in the world. The Sanctuary of Our Sorrowful Mother, the world's outstanding memorial to universal motherhood, is a mecca for nearly a half million pilgrims and visitors annually. Sacajawea, the "Bird Woman" credited with leading the Lewis and Clark expedition to the Pacific Northwest, is one of the many statues and fountains to enjoy in Portland. Visit the colorful International Rose Test and Sunken Rose Gardens. Lambert Gardens, consisting of ten gardens of unparalleled beauty, is a paradise of flowers from April until late in the fall. Forestry Building, world's largest log cabin, houses the Gallery of Trees, where you can get a complete picture of the forests products industry. . . . South of Portland lies the Willamette Valley, one of the richest agricultural areas in the world, between the Coast and Cascade Ranges. SALEM, capital of Oregon, is in the middle valley. The University of Oregon is at EUGENE, and Oregon State College at CORVALLIS. Willamette University, at Salem, founded in 1842, is the oldest American educational institution west of the Missouri River. BREITENBUSH SPRINGS is a resort with some fifty mineral hot springs. . . . One of the world's most scenic drives, the Columbia River Highway takes you eastward from Portland through the great gorge the river has cut in the Cascade Mountains. The Vista House at CROWN POINT, 750 feet above the river, is among many lookout points You pass Multnomah Falls which drops 620 feet down the wall of Columbia gorge in a misty recess of green moss and delicate ferns, and 10 more spectacular waterfalls in the next 11 miles. In the gorge visit **Bonneville Dam** and its ingenious fish ladders which lead around the dam and enable the salmon migrating upstream to by-pass the obstacle. After the town of HOOD RIVER you approach THE DALLES, where the Columbia rushes through an eight-mile narrow channel. . . . The entire Cascade Mountain Range from one end of Oregon to the other is dotted with lakes set like jewels in the timbered mountains. Crater Lake, one of the true wonders of the world, is a great body of water 2,000 feet deep and six miles across set in the crater of a once gigantic volcano 8,000 feet high in the Cascades of southern Oregon. It has been set aside in Crater Lake National Park for the enjoyment of the tourist. Its water is of an indescribable blue, mirroring the trees and mountains around the lake's great rim. Visitors may enjoy the scenic values of Crater Lake in winter amid a fantasy of snowy splendor. Just to the north is Diamond Lake, one of Oregon's premier rainbow-trout waters. . . . The Oregon Caves or Marble Halls, southwest of Crater Lake near the California state line are famous for their Ghost Chamber, King's Palace and Dante's Inferno rooms. Continuing northward in the Cascades from Crater Lake are Three Sisters and Mt. Jefferson, beauty spots that are uniquely their own. . . . Just a short distance east of Portland is the most famous of Oregon's alpine playgrounds, Mt. Hood, where the government has erected Timberline Lodge at the 6,000-foot level above Government Camp. For magnificent views of Mt. Hood and the Cascade Range, ride the Skiway from Government Camp to Timberline Lodge — a treetop trip on the world's largest and longest (3.1 miles) tramway. . . . To one who loves wide open spaces and solitude, central and southeastern Oregon offer everything. On the dry plateau near JOHN DAY, the John Day Fossil Beds State Park permits a glance into the early eras of the earth. Fossils have been unearthed there of huge mastodons and miniature horses, of giant sloths and saber-toothed tigers. In this area are Hart Mountain Antelope Refuge and Malheur Migratory Bird Refuge. Owyhee Canyon, in extreme southeastern Oregon, is a chasm of stark, grim, rugged beauty. . . . The Wallowa and Blue Mountains area of northeastern Oregon is another tourist playground. The Anthony Lakes in the Blue Mountains are a choice summer and winter playground in the BAKER-LA GRANDE area. Wallowa Lake is the heart of this area. Lying at the edge of the Wallowas, along the Idaho state line is the Grand Canyon on the Snake River, deeper than the Grand Canyon of Arizona. . . . Northwest of the Blue Mountains is PENDLETON, where every September it is host to the Pendleton Round-Up, a three day rodeo and Indian ceremonial which is one of the gayest and most colorful pageants of the northwest. . . . Clams, giant crabs, sea bass and perch, cod, sole, salmon and halibut provide epicurean treats which make Oregon famous for its sea-food dishes.

WASHINGTON

Washington, the "Evergeen State," which a little more than a century ago was part of the Oregon Territory, is an ideal vacation spot. Here, you will find America's coolest summer climate, magnificent scenery, mountains, verdant forest, ocean beaches, lakes, rivers, unrivaled recreational facilities and modern cities and towns. It's cool, it's green, it's great — in Washington state.

SEATTLE. Seattle, the metropolis of the Pacific Northwest and gateway to Alaska is situated on Puget Sound, along the crescent-shaped, pier-lined rim of Elliott Bay. It is a city of changing vistas; of broken hills, sharp ravines and numerous watercourses. Visible to the west across the blue waters of the Sound, are the distant snow-mantled mountains of the Olympic Range, while to the east and southeast rise the Cascades, their deeply forested slopes dominated by the symmetrical, glacier-ridged cone of Mount Rainier. Nearby are found unrivaled recreational facilities which include fishing, sailing, camping, mountain climbing and year-round winter sports. Within a short distance of Seattle lies the vast untouched wilderness of northern Washington or the magnificent fringes of Pacific seacoast. Seattle's climate, tempered by the warm ocean currents, knows no extremes of heat or cold. Though fog is not uncommon in this region and the rainfall heavy, particularly in winter, the resulting growth of plants, flowers and trees is lush and verdant. Rivaling Seattle's beauty of setting are its outstanding commercial advantages. Its deep and sheltered harbor, the large docks and warehouses lining its waterfront, have long contributed to its importance as a port. During the years 1942 to 1946, great numbers of fighting vessels slid down the ways of its shipyards on Harbor Island at the entrance to Elliott Bay. In World War II, Seattle formed a vital link in our Pacific supply lines; from here thousands of troops embarked for bases in Alaska, the Aleutians and the far-flung islands of the Pacific. Hydroelectric power, generated by dams along the Skagit River of northern Washington, furnish ample electricity for Seattle's rapidly expanding industry, while recent development of western Canadian oil resources have made the city an important refining center. Seattle is the world's largest fur market and the home of the Boeing Airplane Plant—pioneers in the production of larger-type aircraft. Today, four great railroads and eight airlines serve the city. Toward the end of the 19th century, Seattle gained wide renown as a point of departure for the

MT. HOOD, OREGON'S HIGHEST PEAK
Oregon State Highway Commission

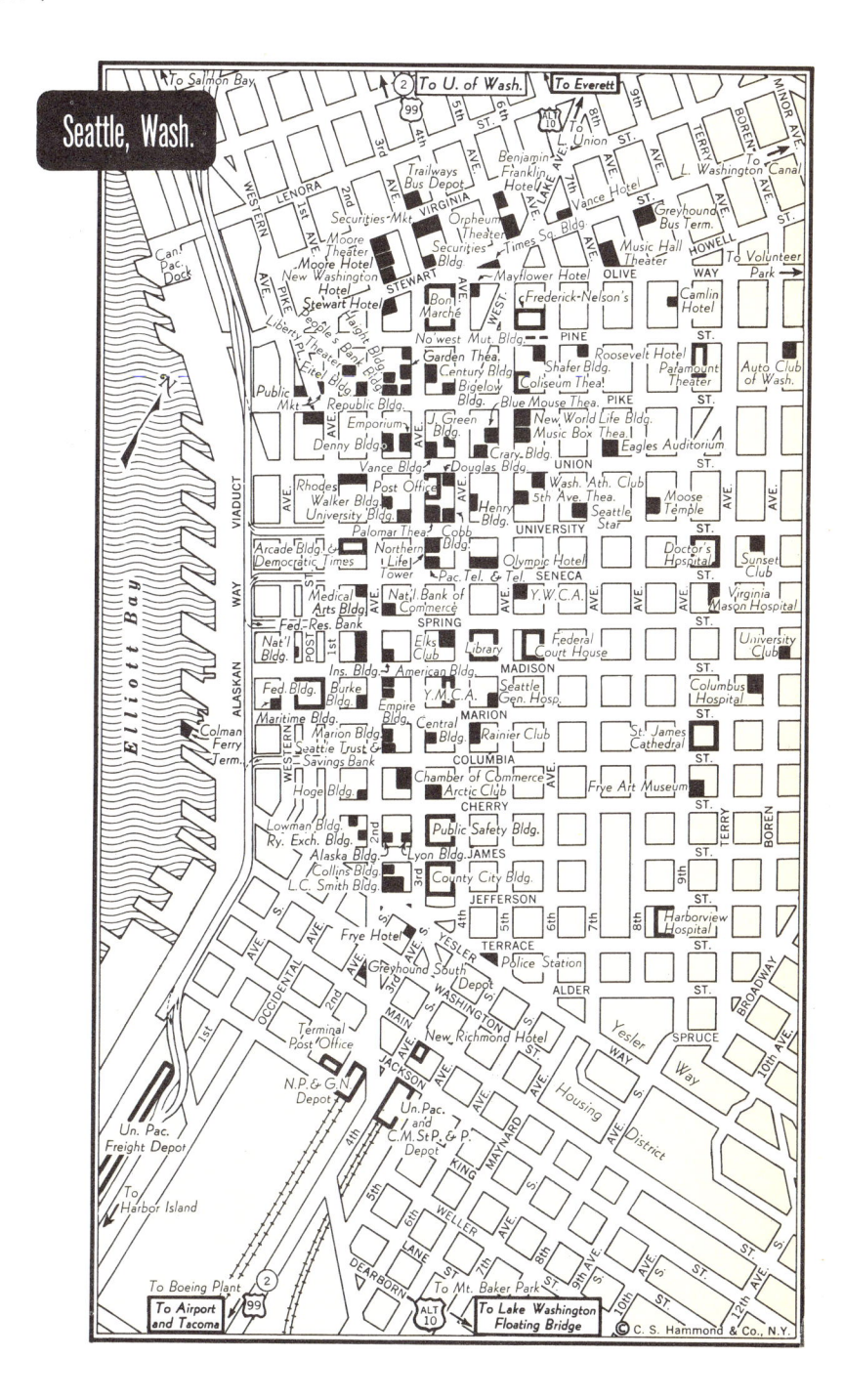

MT. RAINIER

J. Walter Thompson Co.

frenzied hordes rushing to the Yukon in search of gold. Though now the gambling joints, cheap saloons and gaudy dance halls have vanished from the scene, Seattle's waterfront still retains some of the flavor of bygone days. Here ship chandlers, picturesque curio shops and the fish and oyster booths are to be found. Lake Washington, 22 miles long and 4 miles wide, lies to the east of Seattle and is connected to Puget Sound by the Lake Washington Ship Canal. From Seattle a number of interesting side-trips may be taken. North of Seattle and east of BELLINGHAM in the Cascade Range lies Mt. Baker, elevation 10,750 feet. At the 4,000 foot level is Mt. Baker Lodge and Resort, a haven for skiers as the snow remains all year round. LYNDEN, near the Canadian border, is a bit of Holland in Washington. Dutch customs and language are still cultivated there. . . . Directly west of Seattle, across Elliot Bay on the Kitsap Peninsula, lies the thriving community of BREMERTON and the home of the Puget Sound Navy Yard, second largest in the United States. Puget Sound, famous for its fighting salmon, also offers visitors fine salt-water swimming beaches and excellent boating facilities. . . . Surrounded by the azure waters of Puget Sound are the San Juan Islands, an enchanting paradise for the nature-loving pleasure seeker. These islands offer an ever-changing panorama of wooded slopes, hidden bays, narrow inlets and distant mountain peaks. San Juan Island, Orcas Island and Lopez Island are the three largest of the group and have modern tourist resorts of every type. Located on San Juan Island, FRIDAY HARBOR has the University of Washington's Oceanographic Laboratory. . . . The Olympic Peninsula, on which is located the Olympic National Park, is one of the last frontier areas in the United States. In the northeastern section Deer Park offers a magnificent panorama of Juan de Fuca Strait and Vancouver Island. Olympic National Park, dominating the center of the peninsula, is a unique wilderness of coniferous rain forest, wildlife, alpine-flower meadows, glaciers and trout-filled lakes and streams, set in one of the most rugged mountain masses in the entire country, the Olympic Mountains. Surrounded by this fortresslike stronghold is Mount Olympus, 7,923 feet high, quite similar to the one in Greece. An interesting trip is the 364 mile Olympic Loop through the foothills that offers such attractions as a 50-mile ride along the beautiful Hood Canal, a visit to the little city of PORT ANGELES with its famous salmon and crab grounds, and a view of crystal-clear Lake Crescent, which lies in the shadow of Mount Storm King in the northern end of the park. The wettest winter climate in the continental United States prevails on the west side of the park. Here, an extraordinary junglelike forest growth has developed with giant conifers reaching 200 feet or more into the sky, mosses softly carpeting the forest floor and upholstering tree trunks and fallen trees, with draperies hanging from the branches — all permeated with a misty green light. This belt stretches from sea level to a height of about 5,000 feet. . . . South of the park is LONG BEACH on the Pacific Ocean, with more than 28 miles of sandy beach where visitors can drive cars or ride horseback on a firm surface or just relax comfortably in the sunshine. . . . About 20 miles south of Seattle lies TACOMA . . . . lumber capital of the world and a busy industrial and commercial city and port. West of Tacoma is SHELTON, a logging town, where the daily speech is spiced with lumberjack expressions. . . . About 30 miles southeast of Tacoma lies the vast mountain forest playground Mount Rainier National Park, "the mountain the Indians called God," a mecca for sight-seers, camera enthusiasts, mountain climbers, fishermen and skiers. Mount Rainier, located on the western edge of the Cascade crest line, towers to a height of 14,408 feet and its glacial systems, which conceal all but the more rugged crags and ridges, are greater than those of the Swiss Alps. Set in a parklike paradise of flower-carpeted mountain meadows, giant forest, glacial rivers and cascading waterfalls it is a never-to-be-forgotten sight of awe-inspiring beauty. Mt. Rainier presents a difficult climb over ridges of crumbling lava and pumice and along inclined and deeply crevassed ice fields and glaciers. Saddle-horse trips will take you to the points of greatest scenic interest throughout the park. For those who have the time to spare, a week's pack trip over the Wonderland Trail is a unique experience of primitive and beautiful nature. The

DAFFODIL FARM, ORTING, WASHINGTON

trail completely encircles the mountain. Relatively good trout fishing may be enjoyed in park lakes and streams. Situated on the north side of Mt. Rainier is **Paradise Valley**, said by some to be the greatest single scenic attraction in the entire Pacific Northwest. Nearby you can see the great **Nisqually Glacier**, the famous **Silver Forest** and the beautiful **Narada Falls** dropping 168 feet to the **Paradise River Canyon**. Farther south **Spirit Lake**, backed by **Mt. St. Helen**, is another scenic area. Throughout the Cascades you will find snow-capped mountain peaks and sparkling lakes, each offering its own scenic beauty to the tourist. **Snoqualmie Pass** is a spectacular stretch of road drilled through rock tunnels and hewn into canyon walls; it is a spot of record snowfalls—up to 400 inches a year. Twenty-five miles east of **ELLENSBURG** is the **Gingko Petrified State Forest**. To the north is **WENATCHEE**, the world's apple capital. . . . **SPOKANE** . . . . . a great trading center, is the hub of the "Inland Empire." **Spokane Falls** is a never-to-be-forgotten sight, particularly in the spring and early summer. The falls are beautifully illuminated during the period of high water. In the city is located **Gonzaga University**. Spokane is the center of a superlative land of lakes and dashing trout streams. Within a circle of 50 miles surrounding the city are 76 mountain lakes. Summer homes, cabins and camps nestling on forest-bordered lake shores, in glens and shaded woods, and on rocky cliffs, offer comfortable accommodations. Northeast of the city a scenic drive leads to the top of **Mt. Spokane**. . . . Spokane is the nearest large city and the main gateway to **Grand Coulee Dam**. Here you will thrill to the sight of man's greatest handiwork. Five hundred feet high, the biggest concrete structure ever raised on earth, the dam impounds the waters of the mighty Columbia River, forming **Lake Roosevelt**, 151 miles long, which extends to Canada on the north and provides a man-made navigable waterway and water playground. . . . South of here, at the bend of the Columbia River, near **PASCO**, the **Hanford Atomic Energy Plant** is one of the largest nuclear fission projects . . . . . . **Baked salmon, goeducks, large native clams, Olympic pan roasts and an oyster-catchup mixture on toast are favorites and specialties of Washington.**

Rocky Mountain States

The Rocky Mountain states encompass the huge mountainous area that divides the continent. This is the land of snow-capped peaks, dark canyons and battlemented mesas. The mountains, called the Rockies, are actually a vast system of various ranges, each one different in detail or structure, each one of ever-changing hue and color depending on the time of year and time of day. They provide unlimited recreational activities, whether it be hunting or fishing, skiing down snow-covered slopes or just enjoying the majestic mountains and valleys. Added to this mountaintop land are an exhilarating climate and dramatic historic associations — the saga of the westward movement, the Lewis and Clark Expedition, the Oregon and Mormon Trails, frontier forts and mining boom towns, Indian wars and cattle wars. The Indians have changed a great deal since the time when they valiantly defended their homeland but you can always find an ancient chief (not always really a chief) willing to pose in full regalia for a picture while his grandsons are off going to school or earning a living in the contemporary fashion. The latest newcomers and perhaps the ones most perfectly at home in the mountain valleys are the Basque sheepherders who tend their flocks on mountain pastures. Whether you come to enjoy the scenic wonders and wilderness of the national parks, the Western atmosphere of thrilling rodeos and dude ranches or the pleasures of a modern resort, you will find the Rocky Mountain states a treasure chest of things to do and see.

COLORADO

DENVER. In 1857 a trapper built a cabin where two streams come together. It was a good place for a home, with plenty of wood, water and grass. When the gold rush started to the Pike's Peak region, more settlers came. It was a convenient base for mining operations, a good place to live, a good place to trade. Denver is a great metropolitan city for the same reasons it was settled in the early days. Bright sunshine and clear, dry air make Denver's climate healthful and invigorating. Pleasant seasonal

BUFFALO ON GOVERNMENT PRESERVE, MOIESE, MONTANA

Philip Gendreau

changes occur, but one thing remains constant: Colorado sunshine. No cloudy, dreary spells — no excessive cold or heat. A city of fabulously green lawns, nourished by water from the giant backdrop of snow-covered peaks, mile-high Denver is the natural gateway to a thrilling scenic treasury. Winter unfolds a dazzling panorama of white splendor, enticing to the sight-seer, irresistible to the skier. In the spring, carpets of wild flowers in the valleys contrast with the wonder of white-tipped peaks in the high country. Brilliant blue skies frame the lush green beauty of summer. And fall ushers in a spectacular fairyland of color, as entire mountainsides turn to shimmering gold. 25,000 acres of canyons, mountain trout streams, lakes and recreational areas are included in the Denver Mountain Parks. A visit to the parks might include a drive to the summit of **Mount Evans** on the highest auto road in the country, a stop at Buffalo Bill's (William Cody) grave on top of **Lookout Mountain** and possibly a summer concert at **Red Rocks Amphitheater**, a colorful outdoor arena among dramatic sandstone formations. For downtown sights, there is the neo-Greek **Civic Center**, with various government buildings like the handsome **City and County Building**, which faces the gold-domed **State Capitol** from across a broad esplanade. Other places of interest nearby are the **United States Mint**, which coins a good portion of the nation's money; the **Denver Art Museum** (in the City and County Building) and the **Colorado State Historical Museum**. . . . CENTRAL CITY, thirty miles west of Denver, is the scene for the **Central City Play Festival**, a major attraction in the West. The old mining town's **Opera House** has been rehabilitated from the dim past in order to stage dramas and operas with outstanding stars from the East. . . . About 65 miles northwest of Denver is **Rocky Mountain National Park**, 405 square miles of mountain splendor, glacial lakes, rugged peaks, flower-bright upland meadows and a variety of wildlife. The park is one of the country's largest and best mountain playgrounds, with over 65 peaks with elevations above 10,000 feet. ESTES PARK is a resort town at the entrance to the park. . . . For ski facilities **Berthoud Pass** and **Arapahoe Basin** lead a long list of popular ski areas, all within 100 miles of Denver. You will, of course, find numerous ski centers throughout the Colorado Rockies, slopes for both novice and expert, ski jumps, single and double chair lifts that carry you silently to the tips of breath-taking mountain peaks. ASPEN and STEAMBOAT SPRINGS are two other outstanding Colorado ski centers with facilities and winter carnivals. . . . South from Denver, COLORADO SPRINGS is noted both as a resort town and a health center. Fabulous resort hotels like the **Broadmoor** have an ideal location with the Rockies as a backdrop. . . . It is not far to MANITOU SPRINGS, where you can take the cog railway to the summit of **Pike's Peak**, the 14,110-foot mountain that was the goal for wagons heading west to the Colorado goldfields. An automobile road also climbs the high peak for a vista that is hard to surpass. Within easy driving distance is the **Royal Gorge** of the Arkansas, a mighty chasm gouged in solid granite. A highway bridge spans the gorge 1,053 feet above the river and an incline railway descends at an angle of 45 degrees to the bottom of the canyon. Also of scenic interest, a few miles west of Colorado Springs, is the **Garden of the Gods**, a natural park with grostesque shapes in red sandstone particularly striking in the morning or evening sun. . . . To the south near ALAMOSA is **Great Sand Dunes National Monument**, a vast expanse of sand covering an area of sixty square miles. The dunes rise in knife-edged slopes and peaks sometimes 1,500 feet high. . . . To the west a delightful drive through the San Juan Forest and Wolf Creek Pass will take you to DURANGO, center of one of the most scenic regions of the state. Further west in the southwest corner of the state, **Mesa Verde National Park** includes thousands of acres of canyons and mesalands set aside for the preservation of many ancient cliff dwellings and surface pueblos. The mesa itself rises a sheer 2,000 feet from the floor of Montezuma Valley. The most spectacular Indian dwellings are found along the walls of the deep canyons left exactly as they were when deserted in the thirteenth century. The National Park Service has an extensive program of talks and guided tours which give an accurate picture of the lives of the prehistoric inhabitants. . . . To the north, the **Black Canyon of the Gunnison National Monument** includes eleven miles of the most picturesque portion of the fifty-mile gorge. GUNNISON is the headquarters for the famed trout streams of central Colorado. . . . **Colorado National Monument** is a half-hour's drive west of GRAND JUNCTION. The 18,000-acre area is seamed with canyons, honeycombed with caves and unusual rock formations. . . . In the northwestern part of the state Colorado shares with Utah **Dinosaur National**

ASPEN, COLORADO

Loey Ringquist

Monument, a fantastic land only partly explored as yet, with rich fossil beds of prehistoric animals. To complete the circuit of the state you can recross the continental divide in the north over the scenic highway U.S. 40 to make the return trip to Denver.

WYOMING

CHEYENNE · · · · capital of Wyoming, is probably the first stop for travelers entering the state from the southeast. The name always conjures up images of Indian attacks, bad men in gunfights, vigilantes and cattle wars, for the city has always been closely allied with the Old West. The spirit of those rip-roaring days is recaptured in the **Cheyenne Frontier Days Celebration.** It is held in the last week of July and is undoubtedly one of the best shows of its kind. . . . To the north **Fort Laramie National Monument** preserves the remains of old Fort Laramie, one of the most important posts when westward was the course of empire. Built in 1834, it offered protection and furnished supplies to trail-blazing fur traders and the immigrant trains which followed. It also served as a station for the Pony Express and as a military base in the conquest of the Plains Indians. A number of buildings have been restored to their appearance just before the fort was abandoned by the Army. . . . The trading center of CASPER, to the northwest, has several points of interest nearby. The **Casper Mountains** are both a scenic area and a winter-sports playground. To the north, the **Teapot Dome oil fields** recall to mind the national scandal of the 1920's. To the west, **Hell's Half Acre** is a great depression filled with deep caverns, pits, spires, towers and other architectural effects. Pioneers using the Oregon and Mormon Trails left a "register of the desert" by carving their names on **Independence Rock,** to the southwest of Casper. . . . In western Wyoming the mountains of the Grand Tetons are rightfully called the "Alps of America." At **Grand Teton National Park** the mountain chain is at its scenic best. There are no foothills to soften the bold peaks which rise almost vertically 7,000 feet above a comparatively flat valley floor. The range borders the west side of **Jackson Hole,** an excellent place to view the mountain scenery, especially when mirrored in the depths of Jenny and Jackson Lakes. The log-cabin church at **MOOSE** frames a view of the Tetons in its altar window, an appropriate altarpiece for the mountain church. The Teton range includes twenty peaks over 10,000 feet, the highest being **Grand Teton,** which reaches a height of 13,766 feet. There are higher mountains in the world but few offer as great a challenge to mountain climbers. Knifelike ridges, Matterhorns and polished rock walls carved by the glaciers entice mountain climbers from all over the world. You don't have to be an expert, however, to enjoy the mountains. Less arduous trails lead along the glacial lakes or to the mountaintop glaciers. Horseback and foot trails provide occasional glimpses of elk, big-horn sheep and moose, as well as the more common small-game animals. Dude ranches and lodges in the park area and near **JACKSON** supply accommodations for extended visits. . . . **Yellowstone National Park,** in the northwest corner of Wyoming, is nature's greatest variety show. Here in a hissing arena geysers, hot springs and boiling pools spout and spray, performing nature's own "spectacular" amid the rugged Rockies. Large geysers like the well-known **Old Faithful** throw tons of water several hundred feet into the air while growling pools and roaring mud volcanoes perform supporting roles. The colors of the terraces formed by springs and geysers vary from sparkling shades of pink and red to tans and yellows. If there were no geysers or other hot-water phenomena Yellowstone Park would still warrant national park status. One reason would be the **Grand Canyon of the Yellowstone River** with the **Great Falls,** a thundering cataract that drops 300 feet — twice that of Niagara — in a dazzling water display. The park area is also primitive; it remains as nearly as possible as nature executed it. Uncut forests spread over a vast area providing a home for elk, deer, antelope and bears who have become as famous as the geysers. Lakes and streams are stocked for trout fishing. . . . **CODY,** to the east of Yellowstone, was founded by Col. William F. Cody, known more widely as Buffalo Bill. The town's big rodeo and stampede is held the first week in July. . . . Mention should be made of a unique feature of northeast Wyoming — **Devil's Tower National Monument.** This great tower rising 1,200 feet above the plains has the appearance of a gigantic tree stump, even to the barklike outer surface of fluted volcanic rock. A close inspection is worth while for anyone entering or leaving the Black Hills.

MONTANA

When the Lewis and Clark Expedition of 1805 and '06 traversed what is now the State of Montana, they found mile after mile of rolling plains and soaring mountains, hundreds of still lakes and clear streams — a vast land inhabited only by the Indians. Fur trappers and miners followed in later years but for a long time the Indians ruled the plains. Their last victory in striving to keep their lands was the **Battle of the Little Big Horn River,** near **HARDIN,** where General Custer and 300 troops met disaster. The Indian cause was lost, however, for the weight of the U. S. Army soon scattered the Indians. . . . **MILES CITY** is the center for the vast livestock ranches sprawled over eastern Montana. To the north is the Missouri River on which the Lewis and Clark Expedition traveled. They would not recognize one section of the river, however, for the **Fort Peck Dam** has created a large

FREMONT COUNTY, WYOMING

Standard Oil Co. (N. J.)

man-made lake that serves both as an irrigation project and as a recreational lake. Nor would they have realized what great oil wealth lay beneath the surface of **Williston Basin** to the east. . . . Western Montana is dominated by the Rocky Mountains, the site for the mineral wealth that makes Montana "the treasure state." **BUTTE**, in the south, is known as "the richest hill on earth," for beneath the city itself are 2,000 miles of tunnels where copper ore is mined. . . . The ore is shipped to **ANACONDA**, 26 miles away, for processing. The gigantic smokestack of the **Washoe Smelter** is the world's largest. East of Butte, **Lewis and Clark Cavern State Park** offers guided tours of limestone caves, while to the south the old mining town of **VIRGINIA CITY** has been restored as the "Williamsburg of the West." . . . Throughout the mountainland of western Montana dude ranches flourish. Whether you spend a vacation at one of the ranches especially set up for visitors or at one of the operating stock ranches, you will enjoy the outdoor life amid unforgettable scenery. There is plenty of opportunity for horseback trips, overnight camping and a chance to see how a cattle ranch is run. In addition to normal dude activities, almost every Montana ranch boasts excellent trout fishing in nearby streams and lakes. Those visitors who like hunting will enjoy a fall trip when the mountain dude ranches offer pack trips to big-game country for elk, moose, deer, antelope and even grizzly bear. . . . For lake resort pleasure **Flathead Lake**, near **POLSON**, is the largest fresh-water lake west of the Mississippi; it offers fishing, boating and camping facilities. . . . Located in northernmost Montana, astride the continental divide, is **Glacier National Park**. The vast park contains more than sixty glaciers and 200 beautiful lakes. The peaks are alpine in character, shaped by glaciers much larger than those visible now. Cataracts and cascades fall from "hanging valleys" to collect in sparkling lakes like **Lakes McDonald** and **St. Mary**. The spectacular **Going-to-the-Sun Highway**, which crosses the main ridge at Logan Pass, provides a good view of the mountain scenery but for a closer view of the glaciers and a better appreciation of the wilderness, a trip on foot or by horseback over some of the 1,000 miles of trails is recommended. Glacier National Park continues as **Waterton Lakes National Park** on the Canadian side, a symbol of the friendship of the two nations. For an illuminating picture of the life of Plains Indians a trip to the **Museum of the Plains Indians** at **BROWNING** cannot be too strongly recommended. Exhibits of Indian lore, history and art are some of the finest to be seen. Genuine Indian handicraft may also be purchased at the same building. . . . The best skiing facilities of northwest Montana are located on snow fields around **WHITEFISH**, on the western border of Glacier Park.

IDAHO

Idaho is probably the most varied of the Rocky Mountain states. It has mountains to be sure — some 22 separate ranges rising to elevations as high as 12,000 feet — but it has also rivers that foam white in their fury to race through bottomless canyons, weird lava flows and extinct volcanoes, vast forests and rolling wheatlands. . . . The Panhandle of northern Idaho is a region of lovely lakes and great evergreen forests. Near **SANDPOINT**, Lake Pend Oreille is not only a scenic delight but also ideal for fishing for prize landlocked salmon and Kamloops rainbow trout. Hunting in the nearby mountains is considered excellent. Along with Lake Pend Oreille, **Priest Lake** to the north and **Coeur d'Alene** to the south make up "the big three" of resort lakes of Idaho. . . . East of Coeur d'Alene is the silver, lead and zinc mining region; guided tours of the **Sunshine Mine** at **KELLOGG** are available. . . . South from Coeur d'Alene U. S. Highway 95 descends 2,000 feet to **LEWISTON** in a series of spirals offering excellent scenic views. . . . The deepest gorge in America is the **Grand Canyon of the Snake River** extending along the Idaho-Oregon border. The average depth of this chasm is 5,500 feet but at **Hell's Canyon** the canyon bottom is almost lost from sight; it measures a depth of 7,900 feet at a point near **Hat Point**. But unlike the Grand Canyon of the Colorado, the gorge is very narrow — less than 100 feet in some places. A panoramic view of this chasm can be had at **Kinney Point** near **CUPRUM**. For a closer view, boat trips to the northern end of the canyon from Lewiston are available. Another "white water" canyon has been formed by the Salmon River, a tributary of the Snake River. Accessible scenic portions of the Salmon Canyon may be reached from **CHALLIS**. . . . In southern Idaho the capital city of **BOISE** was founded during the gold-mining rush of 1862. Nearby **Arrowrock Dam**, one of the highest irrigation dams in the world, is part of a vast irrigation system that brings water to the fertile Snake River basin. . . . East of Boise, in the rugged alpine-like Sawtooth Mountains is the famous Sun Valley resort, one of the most popular of western ski centers and one which has done much to promote winter sports in general all over America. There are a number of ski runs ranging from beginners' slopes to the difficult slopes of **Baldy Mountain**. Facilities are excellent — whether it is a ski lift to take you up to the top of a run or a nice warm lodge at the bottom. Swimming in an outdoor warm-water pool, dog sledding, sleighing and ice skating are some of the sports to be enjoyed. The mountains of the Sawtooth Range are pleasant at any time of the year, however, and are at their spectacular best around **Mount Hyndman** (12,078 feet). . . . Until such time when space travel is more than a remote possibility a trip to the moon can be enjoyed in facsimile version by visiting **Craters of the Moon National Monument** near **ARCO**, for here indeed is another world of desolate wonder, with cinder buttes, lava flows and strange pock-marked terrain. This moonlike area was the scene of volcanic activity off and on during geologic history, the latest being about 500 years ago. Lava flows spread out in billowy waves, iridescent and glossy as seen in formations like the **Blue Dragon**. Other curious features are the lava bombs, masses of molten lava which were thrown into the air and hardened on the way down, and tree molds where the lava cooled around trees that were in the path of the lava flow. . . . To the south, between the cities of **TWIN FALLS** and **JEROME**, the Rim to Rim Bridge spans the Snake River, offering a

DEVIL'S TOWER NATIONAL MONUMENT

J. Walter Thompson Co.

212

vast panorama of the fertile Magic Valley country. The nearby falls of the Snake River, **Twin Falls and Shoshone Falls**, are somewhat reduced in their splendor due to irrigation projects but during the spring they regain their power; the flood-swollen waters plunge 212 feet at Shoshone Falls.

UTAH

Nature was in a lavish mood when she ladled out to Utah a wealth of scenic wonders. But scenic beauty was not the sole concern of early Utah settlers. It took men of vision, ingenuity and leadership to create a civilization in such an apparently hostile land. It is always a pleasure to come into **SALT LAKE CITY** . . . . from the mountain pass or from across the salt plains. That in 1847 there was nothing but an arid valley seems hard to believe. Yet such it was when Brigham Young, the Mormon leader, decided to build a new Zion. First-time visitors to Salt Lake City will enjoy the wide streets, clean atmosphere and wonderful setting. The city's great attraction is **Temple Square**, the center of Mormonism, or the Church of the Latter-Day Saints, as it is called. The six-spired **Mormon Temple** is closed to the non-Mormons but the interesting **Tabernacle** building next to it can be visited and the famed organ and choral recitals enjoyed. Not far from Temple Square is the **State Capitol**, overlooking the entire valley. **Great Salt Lake**, to the west of the city, is one of America's largest lakes. More notable is its salt content — six to eight times saltier than the ocean's. Bathing in this briny sea is an aquatic experience; you can float with ease but find swimming difficult. **Promontory Point**, nearby, was the place where the two sections of the first continental railroad were joined with the ceremony of driving the golden spike. To the west of the lake, the **Bonneville Salt Flats** are known for the world's fastest automobile speed runs. . . . Also of interest near Salt Lake City are the open-pit copper mines at **BINGHAM CANYON**. . . . The **Wasatch Mountains** of northern Utah provide excellent alpine terrain for skiing and outdoor recreation. Canyons such as the 1,000-foot deep **Ogden Canyon** traverse the north-south range. **OGDEN** has the popular **Ogden Snow Basin** as a ski center, while the slopes of **Alta, Brighton** and **Ecker's Hill** are favorite haunts of Salt Lake City skiers. . . . For scenic drives do not miss the **Alpine Scenic Loop**, near **PROVO**, which leads to **Timpanogos Cave National Monument**. . . . In southern Utah the mountains give way to plateau country where nature displays her brightest colors and most awe-inspiring rock formations. Beginning in the southwest the first great national park is **Bryce Canyon National Park**. It is not a canyon in the usual sense but rather a series of amphitheaters a thousand feet deep, covered with a bewildering assortment of stone pinnacles, towers and spires alive with glowing colors. Scenic drives amid spruce, aspen and pine traverse the park, and trails lead along the rim and descend to the bottom of the canyon for a closer view of the strange rock sentinels. . . . To the west, near **CEDAR CITY**, is **Cedar Breaks National Monument**, a vast bowl of eroded sandstone. Here you will see a labyrinth of ridges and magnificent architectural forms, tinted in all the colors of the spectrum. The cliffs are white and orange at the top, breaking into deep rose and coral further down. Other shades of chocolate, yellow and purple are visible depending on the light and shadow. . . . Further south is **Zion National Park**, a realm of majestic stone temples and cathedrals in a 2,000-foot gorge. You can enter by way of **Mt. Carmel Highway**. The highway parallels the canyon wall, passes through a mile-long tunnel which is pierced with huge windows that look out on a scene of awe-inspiring beauty. The cliffs and monuments soar to heights over 3,000 feet and are especially impressive when seen from below. The names of the features are often taken from religious text — the **Three Patriarchs, Angel's Landing** and the **Great White Throne** — and are in keeping with their actual appearance. . . . Less accessible but no less impressive are the national monuments of southeastern Utah. U. S. Highway 160 leads south from **CRESCENT CITY** past **Arches National Monument**, a series of wind-and-sand-eroded arches and windows. A side road near the movie-location town of **MOAB** leads to breathtaking views of the Colorado River at **Dead Horse Point** and **Grand View Point**. . . . Further southwest of **BLANDING** are several prehistoric cliff dwellings and three natural bridges within a six mile radius. It takes a little hiking to reach them but they are well worth the exertion. South from Blanding the road becomes more rugged while the scenery increases in dramatic quality. This section is **Monument Valley**. From out of the level red plain rise huge monoliths and skyscraping needles of rock, like towering sentinels of the desert. **Rainbow Bridge National Monument**, the world's largest natural bridge and perhaps the least accessible of America's wonders, is near the Arizona border. Horseback trips from **MEXICAN HAT** in Utah or Rainbow Lodge in Arizona do reach the monument, however, and both the adventure of the trip and the beauty of the colossal arch reward those who brave the desert.

ENGELMANN SPRUCE, BOISE NATIONAL FOREST

U. S. Forest Service

The Southwest

The Southwest, land of enchantment and contrast, possesses an ever-changing panorama of vast mesa and towering mountains; of forested retreat and cactus-guarded desert. Wind and water have carved giant forms from a media of colored sandstones and shales. Here also is a cultural crossroad with three civilizations blending into a distinctive way of life — Indian, Spanish and English. Settlements range from modern metropolitan centers, touched by the romance of the Conquistadores and the vigor of the frontier, to sprawling cow towns and Indian pueblos where Hopi and Zuñi have lived for centuries amid what appears to be a barren land. Besides the scenic wonders and historic places of interest, there is lots to see and do. There are Indian ceremonials where tribal dancers in resplendent costume perform primitive dances, thrilling rodeos and local festivals either of Spanish or Old West origin. Resort centers with dude ranches or more luxurious guest ranches provide varied entertainment with horseback trips and outdoor life, while the bigger cities offer more sophisticated pleasures. Ski slopes on the mountains of Nevada and northern Arizona are only a few hours drive from warm, sun-drenched valleys. You will want to bring back some of the authentic handicraft items; Navajo rugs and blankets, Hopi and Zuñi inlaid jewelry, Hopi Kachina dolls, Indian pottery and beadwork. There are also Mexican hand-tooled leather work, and southwest apparel that is both comfortable and distinctive. Don't miss the pleasures of an outdoor barbecue or overlook sampling Indian and Mexican foods.

NEW MEXICO

First visited by white man in the expeditions of Spanish explorers seeking the Seven Cities of Cibolá. They did not find the cities of gold but they did establish a vast empire for Spain. **SANTA FE**, capital of the state, was the seat of government for this empire ten years before the landing of the Pilgrims. The Palace of Governors, erected in 1610, served the royal governors and their successors for three centuries. The low adobe structure has been restored to its original appearance. Santa Fe's churches are excellent examples of Spanish-American ecclesiastical art and architecture, with the **Mission of San Miguel de Santa Fe** probably the most interesting. The Museum of Navajo Ceremonial Art contains a complete collection of Navajo sand paintings. . . . **TAOS**, seventy miles to the north, is actually three separate villages — the old Indian pueblo of **San Geronimo de Taos** dating from the 16th century, the farming section, Ranchos de Taos, with the massive-walled **Mission of St. Francis of Assisi**, and the artist colony of Don Fernando de Taos.

MONUMENT VALLEY
McLaughlin and Co.

. . . In northwest New Mexico are several ruins of ancient Indian civilizations which reached their zenith around 1100 A. D. The Indian villages contained terraced buildings with as many as 1,200 rooms. The larger and more impressive are to be seen at Pueblo Bonita in **Chaco Canyon National Monument** and **Aztec Ruins National Monument**. Complex masonry walls and underground ceremonial chambers or kivas built by Stone-Age architects and masons remind visitors of the similar ancient ruins in Egypt and Asia Minor. . . . **ALBUQUERQUE**, southwest of Santa Fe, is one of the fastest growing cities of the Southwest. The Old Town of early Albuquerque, founded in 1706, displays the characteristic traits of the Spanish settlements with flat-footed adobe buildings. The pueblo architecture of the **University of New Mexico** in the new city is in keeping with that early style. From Albuquerque it is only a short drive to reach neighboring Indian pueblos of **Jemez, Zia, Laguna** and others. At the Acoma Pueblo, 60 miles west of the city, 1000-odd members of the Acoma tribe live atop the 357-foot sandstone tableland reached only by foot trail. The Indians were fierce in defending their homeland against the

WHITE SANDS NATIONAL MONUMENT
New Mexico State Tourist Bureau

INTER-TRIBAL INDIAN CEREMONIAL, GALLUP, NEW MEXICO

New Mexico State Tourist Bureau

Spanish, yet aided the padres in building the imposing **Church of San Esteban Rey** atop the mesa. All the materials for the church and burial grounds had to be carried on the backs of the Indians up the steep rock-cut trail. . . . Further west Highway 66 leads to the city of GALLUP where the Inter-Tribal Indian Ceremonial is held every year in mid-August. The colorful ceremonial brings thousands of Indians from all over the southwest to display their native dances: The Taos perform the Hoop, Deer and Horsetail Dances; the Hopis, the Butterfly Dances; Zuñi, the Eagle Dance, and so on during the four-day festival. Parades, an all-Indian rodeo and riding contests round out the program. Indian artisans display the finest specimens of pottery, silver jewelry, weaving and other handicrafts. You may watch Navajo artists making sand paintings, a strange ritual art in which different colored sands are arranged in stylized paintings. . . . To the south of Gallup is **El Moro** or Inscription Rock, a sandstone mesa where interesting footnotes to history have been recorded. Travelers beginning with Don Juan Onate, returning from the Gulf of California in 1605, have left their inscriptions on the rock. . . . In southern New Mexico near ALAMOGORDO is **White Sands National Monument**. The shifting sands create an endless pattern of rippling beauty as far as the eye can see. The sands are actually deposits of gypsum piled into great dunes, ranging from 10 to 60 feet high. . . . To the southeast is one of the most impressive sights of the region — **Carlsbad Caverns**. Here in bottomless passageways is a weird kingdom which took nature 60 million years to fashion. The main corridor of the caverns is immense but it does not prepare the visitors for the beauty of the chambers beyond. These chambers — the **Green Lake Room, King's**

CARLSBAD CAVERNS
New Mexico State Tourist Bureau

RUINS OF THE MISSION CHURCH AT PECOS PUEBLO
New Mexico State Tourist Bureau

Palace and **Queen's Chamber**—are unparalleled in their splendor. Stone draperies give a truly regal touch to the rooms. In the **Big Room**, the largest open space found underground anywhere in the world, are intricate formations; giant pinnacles reach up to meet their mirrored image hanging from the ceiling; "lily-pads" of stone grow from pools of water. Delicate tints of minerals in the rocks add to the spectacle. Another attraction of Carlsbad Caverns is to stand watch in the summer evening as millions of bats swarm from the entrance arch, spiral upward and disappear for a night's foraging. At dawn they return to a cavern not open to the public, to hang upside down deep within the earth.

ARIZONA

The Grand Canyon State has an invaluable resource in her sunny, dry climate. It has made Arizona a new-found vacationland. TUCSON, major city of Southern Arizona, is popular with winter visitors who come to enjoy the exhilarating winter climate. Adobe buildings with flowered patios, reminiscent of the days when Tucson was a Spanish town, still grace parts of the town but the atmosphere is more closely allied to the American West. The annual celebration is the **Fiesta de los Vaqueros**, one of the top events of the championship rodeo circuit. The **University of Arizona** is famous for its work in archaeology and anthropology. About seven miles south of the city is **San Xavier Mission**, a particularly distinguished example of mission art and architecture with a carved facade, twin towers supported by flying buttresses and a richly decorated interior. An attraction near Tucson is **Saguaro National Monument**, seventeen miles east of the city. The tract covers a weird leafless forest of fluted giant cacti, the saguaro. Here the amazing desert giants grow in grotesque shapes above typical Sonoran desert vegetation surrounded by the scarred and furrowed slopes of three mountain ranges. Spectacular at any season, the forest is especially beautiful in May when the towering columns are crowned with creamy-white blossoms which later turn to brilliant scarlet, edible fruits. . . . TOMBSTONE, southeast of Tucson, was one of the wildest mining towns of the West in the 1880's. Rich silver strikes like those at Lucky Cuss and Goodenough Mines attracted miners from all over. Along with them came the gamblers, dance-hall girls, gunmen and other questionable persons who wished to join in the spoils. After a decade of boom, Tombstone became almost a ghost town when flooding ended mine operations. Today the town is curious as a relic of the roaring West. Points of interest are the **Bird Cage Theater**, former variety theater, gambling establishment and bar, now a museum and restaurant, and **Boothill Graveyard**, where notorious gunmen were buried, as the name implies, "with their boots on." . . . The capital of Arizona, PHOENIX, lies in the center of the fertile Salt River Valley. The name of the city is appropriate, for like the legendary phoenix bird it rose from the ashes of an ancient city. The warm, sunny climate makes Phoenix a popular winter resort area and also a rich agricultural center. Vacationists come to enjoy the desert and mountain country, staying either at one of the more luxurious inns complete with swimming pools and elegant furnishings, or at one of the more modest dude ranches where the accent is on a more rugged outdoor life. During the winter season there are a succession of local celebrations — a championship rodeo in February, the Fiesta del Sol in March and the Pioneer Reunion in April. An interesting side trip from Phoenix is the scenic drive along the **Apache Trail**, State Highway 88, following the winding Salt River, with deep chasms and man-made lakes. . . . To the north is FLAGSTAFF, hub of the many marvels of Northern Arizona. The city not only meets the needs of travelers but also the Hopi and Navajo Indians from nearby reservations. The normal influx of vistors is swelled during the **Indian Pow Wow** every July 4th when 20 tribal nations from seven states gather for parades and ceremonial dances. The exhibit of Indian art in the **Museum of Northern Arizona** and **Lowell Observatory** are additional local attractions. About 15 miles northwest of the city, the **Arizona Snow Bowl** in the high San Francisco Peaks can offer seasonal skiing with a ski-tow, trails and ski-lodge. For the sights around Flagstaff the list is both long and varied. Beginning in the south there is what many persons consider the most beautiful canyon in Arizona — **Oak Creek Canyon**. Not as well known as Grand Canyon, it is still a magnificent spectacle; you can drive through it on Highway 89A following the winding creek past green forests set against 2000-foot red-stone canyon walls. You will pass scenery that you may recognize, for many movies have been filmed here. Special features are **Tuzigoot National Monument**, an ancient Indian pueblo, and nearby **Montezuma Castle**, a well-preserved adobe ruin perched high in a canyon wall. Closer to Flagstaff to the southeast are the **Walnut Canyon Cliff**

SUPERSTITION MOUNTAINS

Phoenix Chamber of Commerce

216

Dwellings and Meteor Crater where an interplanetary missile crashed into the earth, leaving a mile-wide crater. A drive to the north will bring you to Sunset Crater National Monument, a 1000-foot-high volcanic cinder cone whose pock-marked summit is tinted with hues of dull red and orange. Further north are the Wupatki Ruins which date from the 12th century. Here, too, is the celebrated Painted Desert, a magnificent stretch of escarpments, mesas, flat buttes and dunes, all delicately shaded by nature in pastel colors. It is best seen in the early morning light when the formations come to life as the sun rises in the east. The desert actually covers some 300 miles of northeast Arizona so they may be seen at other vantage points. The Petrified Forest, just east of HOLBROOK, combines the natural wonders of the world's largest group of petrified wood along with the fantastic landscape of the Painted Desert. . . . Nothing you have read or heard will quite prepare you for the spectacle of the Grand Canyon. This titanic gorge, 4 to 18 miles wide and over 200 miles long, has been carved by the mighty Colorado River. Standing on the South Rim as the sun comes up one sees the distant caps of the opposite rim take shape and become alive with color. Later, as the sun rises mountains emerge from the purple gloom of the canyon. Throughout the day the changing light causes the whole panorama to slowly alter, giving varying impressions, each succeeding one different than the last. Views alone are not all there is to the Grand Canyon. There is the interesting story of how it all came about: the millions of years of building that created the plateau and the slow unrelenting erosion — the cutting of the tremendous chasms which still goes on. Fascinating, also, is the history of the discovery by the Spanish and the story of the first trip down the roaring Colorado made by Major J. W. Powell and his party. No trip to the Canyon is complete without a journey to the bottom of the gorge. As you descend on muleback over Bright Angel or Kaibab Trail the chapters of geologic history unfold until you reach the turbulent river. You can cross the gorge to the North Rim for an overnight stay, returning the next day. . . . Of a smaller scale but no less impressive is the Canyon de Chelly National Monument in the Indian country of northeast Arizona. The canyon contains a number of cliff dwellings, located in natural crevices, high in smooth, massive, red-sand-stone canyon walls. White House Ruins is particularly impressive, set like a jewel in the sculptured, brilliantly colored rock wall.

NEVADA

Predominantly a mining state in high, sunny land of the Great Basin region, her history and development can be read in the discovery of rich veins of gold, silver and copper which created boom towns overnight. But one of the richest strikes to enliven the interest of the nation is not in silver and gold but in legalized gambling. **LAS VEGAS** is presently undergoing the biggest boom that Nevada has seen since the silver strikes of Comstock

ST. FRANCIS CHURCH, PHOENIX
Phoenix Chamber of Commerce

ON THE TRAIL, GRAND CANYON NATIONAL PARK
Virgil Gripson

217

LAKE MEAD

Lode. Gambling exists elsewhere in the state but not done up in such a bright package. Swank million-dollar hotel establishments like the Desert Inn and the Sands, the Sahara and Flamingo line a section called "the Strip," on the outskirts of town. Both "the Strip" and downtown area offer the best in big-time entertainers from Broadway, Hollywood and television, along with deluxe accommodations and fine foods, in addition to high-stake gambling. The idea of combining hotel, night club and gambling casino all into one is not new, for the old mining boom towns had such establishments in cruder versions. The appeal is the same, however, and there is no place in America quite like it. It is a 24-hour festival, exciting and brightly lit, capturing the fancy of blasé Hollywood stars and gray-haired retired schoolteachers alike. . . . Only 30 miles from Las Vegas is **Hoover Dam,** an engineering marvel that harnesses the mighty Colorado River. You can drive along the crest of the giant dam as well as visit the powerhouses at the base which supply electricity for three states. Lake Mead is a consequence of Hoover Dam. The Colorado bulges out behind the concrete structure to form a broad expanse of water 113 miles long, providing excellent recreational facilities as well as water for the parched soils of the desert. To the west of Lake Mead in the **Valley of Fire State Park** red sandstones have been wind-whipped and honeycombed into fantastic shapes and near animal-like forms. For those visiting the Las Vegas area who prefer mountain terrain there is the **Charleston Peak** area with an 11,910-foot peak, 35 miles west of the city. Ski slopes attract visitors during the winter and high recreation grounds offer respite from the noonday desert sun in the summer. . . . To reach western Nevada, you will have to traverse basin country marked by a series of north-south jagged mountain ranges. In between are valleys where herds of white-faced cattle graze on open ranges like the 25,000-acre-spread of Bing Crosby's near **ELKO.** Other times the open country is almost desert, barren except for sagebrush and mesquite. The Las Vegas Bombing and Gunnery Range in southeast Nevada is in country like this. Here in a large restricted area, the Atomic Energy Commission carries out nuclear experiments. . . . In the southwest corner of Nevada are grouped a number of points of interest. **RENO** regards itself as "the Biggest Little City in the World." It is little in population, numbering around 33,000 even if you count those temporary citizens awaiting divorce decrees. It does have a big-city atmosphere, however. Like Las Vegas, its brightly lighted downtown section is jammed with gambling casinos and night clubs. In the daylight the city reveals itself as a neat, clean city with parks along the Truckee River and an excellent school in the **University of Nevada.** Just 20 miles from Reno is historic **VIRGINIA CITY,** site of the richest silver strike ever made in the world — the famed Comstock Lode. Almost a billion dollars in precious metals were mined before the

TRUCKEE RIVER, RENO, NEVADA

218

lode was virtually exhausted. At its zenith in the '70's the town had no equal in the West for making millionaires and for making pleasure. Bret Harte and Mark Twain once worked for the town's newspaper; their later stories are often based on the wild doings of this fabulous city now almost a ghost town. Still standing are **Pipers Opera House** where audiences acclaimed Edwin Booth and Sarah Bernhardt; the **Bucket of Blood Saloon** and the **Crystal Bar**, survivors from over 100 saloons of more prosperous days. . . . North of Reno the turquoise-blue **Lake Pyramid** lies in a desert-mountain setting. The lake takes its name from the 475-foot tufa rock pyramid that juts out of the deep-blue waters. **Anaho Island** is a bird sanctuary for thousands of pelicans, sea gulls and cormorants. Nevada's second largest lake, **Lake Tahoe,** is shared with California. It is south of Reno in the eastern Sierra Nevada Mountains and is one of the most beautiful. Deep blue in color, it is surrounded on all sides by snow-capped peaks and evergreen forests. A scenic drive encircles the lake and a number of uncrowded resort centers like **TAHOE CITY** and **MEEKS BAY** dot the shore. Both sides of the lake are popular with skiers. Double chair-lifts at **Squaw Valley** in California and at **Reno Ski Bowl** in Nevada carry snow enthusiasts to high altitudes where the snow lasts for half the year.

North Central States

NELSON GALLERY OF ART, KANSAS CITY, MISSOURI

Massie—Missouri Resources Div.

WEST NORTH CENTRAL STATES

The states included in this section are a part of the world's richest larder — one vast productive area capable of feeding the nation and peoples in other lands as well. Travelers crossing the agriculture belt will find broad fields, blue skies with white scudding clouds bringing a promise of needed rain, red barns and white farm houses in seas of tall corn and ripening wheat. To the west and north the corn fields give way to wheat and then the drier range land where cattle graze. Even the larger cities have their roots in the soil; most of the talk is about crops, weather, the price of cattle, for their lives depend on the prosperity of the farms. This rich country was bought from the French under the Louisiana Purchase in 1803. The Americans didn't even know what they bought so they sent an expedition under Lewis and Clark to explore the country. Their journey up the Missouri and over the Rockies to the West Coast is a New World saga. Here, forested hill regions, such as the Ozarks and Black Hills, provide ample rugged country of scenic beauty. Flat-topped mesa and buttes in warm colors relieve the monotony of the plains. The northern wilderness and lake country, especially in Minnesota, provide virgin country, excellent for fishing and hunting and outdoor activities. The history is tied closely to the development of the West.

Regional foods include dishes that early settlers and frontier men lived on; Dakota and Buffalo steak, country hams, fried catfish, hoe cakes (cornmeal), Minnesota wildfowl with wild rice, Squaw dish (omelet with bacon, eggs and corn), venison shoulder and Buffalo berry jelly.

MISSOURI

The crossroads city of **ST. LOUIS** . . . . lies along the crescent-shaped bend in the Mississippi River just south of the junction of the Missouri River. It was named in honor of the French Monarch, Louis IX. The river town began as a fur-trading post in 1763 and has grown into one of the leading cities of the nation. The old city on the banks of the river is being developed under federal government auspices and includes **The Old Rock House,** the city's oldest building. A few blocks away is the **Old Cathedral,** a yellowed limestone edifice over 100 years old on the site of the first church in St. Louis. The **Old Courthouse,** nearby, has a slave block in one entrance. Opposite the Union Station is the fountain,"**The Meeting of the Waters**", by Carl Milles. The most important recreational and cultural center for the city is 1400-acre **Forest Park,** west of the downtown area. It includes, in addition to the usual recreational facilities, the **Jefferson Memorial,** with Jefferson manuscripts and relics, and Charles Lindbergh's trophies. The St. Louis Zoo, also in the park, has a notable feature in the Chimpanzee Circus. Cultural attractions in Forest Park are the **Art Museum,** one of America's finest, with a wide collection of painttings and other art work and the **Municipal Opera Theater,** outdoor amphitheater which holds nightly summer performances. Shaw's Garden on the south side of town, is both unique and internationally famous, has remarkable plant exhibits ranging from water lilies and rare orchids to cactus and plant curiosities that are Botanic freaks. At the Anheuser-Busch Breweries, to the east, one can see the age-old process of brewing beer in its most up-to-date fashion and sample the final product. Mississippi River cruises are available aboard one of the regular packet steamers or on the modern streamlined excursion steamer the S.S. Admiral. . . . Perhaps not as famous as St. Louis but well-known to all readers of "Tom Sawyer" by Mark Twain is the Mississippi river town of **HANNIBAL.** Mark Twain's boyhood home is still there along with the white-washed fence, Becky Thatcher's house and other landmarks which appear in Twain's writing. . . . **COLUMBIA,** in the Daniel Boone country west of St. Louis, is the seat of the University of Missouri, known for its School of Journalism. . . . **JEFFERSON CITY** in central Missouri is located on the bluffs

219

above the Missouri River, providing a splendid setting for the **State Capitol.** The walls of the House lounge are decorated with farm murals by Thomas Hart Benton. . . . Southwest from here is the dragon-shaped **Lake of the Ozarks,** created by the damming of the Osage River. Whole towns were submerged in the waters of the new lake making a weird lake bottom for fishermen and swimmers. The lake with its many coves and turns has a shore line of over a thousand miles so there is ample room for the vacationists. The **Ozark Hills** region which covers southwest Missouri and parts of neighboring states are famous for their scenic beauty of gentle rolling hills and rugged rock promentories above clear streams, of redbud and dogwood trees along quiet country roads. Fishing is excellent; an Ozark specialty is float fishing on James, White and other rivers. On the eastern edge of the Ozarks, the **Big Springs** country is another attraction. Here tremendous volumes of water pour forth from moss-covered rocks. One of the longest, in Big Springs State Park near **VANBUREN,** flows at a rate of over half a billion gallons per day. The Ozark area is populated with hill folk who are descendants of Scotch-English pioneers from the East. They have preserved many of the slowly dying folk crafts and customs; their Saturday night square dances are in the old traditions with untiring "callers" and "fiddlers," and are not encumbered with electric guitars or Brooklyn cowboys. . . . In western Missouri **KANSAS CITY** . . . . . used to be a wild outfitting post for wagon trains heading west over the Santa Fe and Oregon Trails. Today it is a key transportation center, the gateway to the West and Southwest for 12 trunk-line railroads, Trans World Airlines and five other major airlines. It is also a leading livestock and grain market as is evident from massive grain elevators and sprawling stockyards on the edge of the city; the annual stock shows draw thousands of exhibitors and spectators. **Swope Park,** third largest municipal playground in the nation, contains the outdoor **Starlight Theater,** where nightly summer musicals are given, a zoo, golf courses and other recreation facilities. **William Rockhill Nelson Art Gallery** is a handsome building housing an excellent Chinese art collection. Opposite **Union Station,** with its great 8-story-high lobby, stands **Liberty War Memorial** which affords a wide view of the city from its tall shaft . . . . **ST. JOSEPH** to the north was the starting point for the Pony Express Riders in the early days

KANSAS

Although Kansas may be without the rugged grandeur of mountain ranges or thrilling seascapes it does possess a pastoral beauty that can be just as enthralling — golden wheat fields stretching as far as the eye can see, the vast apple orchards of northeast Kansas in full bloom and tall grain elevators and silos serving as skyscrapers above the checkerboard pattern of the fields. The whirring harvester combines moving across the fields of ripened wheat are fascinating to watch. Visitors interested in history will find reminders of the days when the state was called "Bleeding Kansas," the scene of undeclared civil war over the slavery question. Kansas was also a part of the Wild West when differences of opinion were too often settled by the quickest draw.

In eastern Kansas, **LEAVENWORTH,** originally a frontier post to protect wagon trains, is now the U. S. Army's largest military post. A Command and General Staff School is maintained here as well as a federal penitentiary. To the south, **KANSAS CITY** . . . . (often confused with Kansas City, Missouri) is a major stockyard center. Tours of the meat packing plants are available. . . . At **TOPEKA,** further west, the State Capitol is famous for the John Steuart Curry murals of abolitionist John Brown. In Gage Park are two attractions, the Reinisch Gardens and the Old Settlers Memorial Cabin. . . . John Brown lived at **OSAWATOMIE** to the south. The simple home, now part of a state park, served as a station on the "Underground Railway" for fugitive slaves. . . . **ABILENE** was once a roaring cowboy town, the northern terminus of the cattle drives over the Chisholm Trail. Today it is best known as the boyhood home of President Eisenhower. The Eisenhower house

CARL MILLES FOUNTAIN, ST. LOUIS — Massie—Missouri Resources Div.

has been set aside as a museum. West of Abilene, the area around **SALINA** and **MINNEAPOLIS,** are several weird rock foundations. . . . Lake Kanopolis in central Kansas is one of several artificial lakes created by damming the rivers of Kansas, thus making up for nature's omissions. . . . **DODGE CITY** in the western part of the state was once the cowboy capital of the world. The stories and legends of its wilder days have given yeoman service to the "Westerns" of Hollywood. **Boothill** near the City Hall was once the burial ground for victims of gun fights. Burials were often quick and unceremonious, the deceased was interred wrapped in a blanket, his boots still on.

NEBRASKA

In the early pioneer days of the nation the principal route of the westward movement was across Nebraska to the passes in the Rocky Mountains. Through the great Platte River Valley passed Astorian fur traders seeking the pelts of the northwest. Later the settlers moved along this route following the Mormon and Oregon Trails. With the passage of the Home-

KANSAS LANDSCAPE

Standard Oil Co. (N. J.)

stead Act of 1863, giving free land to those who would work it, the land boom was on. Today **Homestead National Monument**, near BEATRICE in southeast Nebraska, encloses the 160-acre claim of Union soldier Daniel Freeman. Some of the original buildings have been restored. . . . An important stop for wagoneers heading west in those early days was the town of OMAHA on the Missouri River. The **Union Pacific Museum** commemorates the first transcontinental railroad which commenced from that city. Also in Omaha is the **Joslyn Memorial** About ten miles west of Omaha is Father Flanagan's **Boy's Town**, a novel social undertaking for homeless boys. The project which covers 1200 acres is actually an incorporated village complete with post office, shops and farms, most of which are managed by the boys themselves. . . . The skyline of LINCOLN, to the southwest is dominated by the white stone shaft of the modern **State Capitol Building**. The 400-foot buttressed tower, a pleasing departure from conventional capitol buildings, is crowned with a gold glazed-tile dome and bronze statue of the Sower, symbol of the plains. In the wing of the building the **State Historical Museum** includes Indian and pioneer relics and a large gun collection. On the University of Nebraska campus is located the **Nebraska State Museum**. Two collections make this museum of interest to visitors. The **Art Collection** contains a good cross-section of paintings of American artists. The second is the **Hall of Elephants** in the science section, where there is a large collection of fossil and mounted elephants, including a large mammoth. . . . At HASTINGS, further west, the **House of Yesterday** is a museum for Western Americana:

early vehicles, weapons and pioneer furnishings. . . . In western Nebraska **Scotts Bluff National Monument** is a landmark of the great plains. It is a huge sandstone tableland towering above the Oregon Trail.

SOUTH DAKOTA

The **Black Hills** of western South Dakota are under-valued by the name. In reality they are mountains, highest in the United States east of the Rockies. From the surrounding prairies and plains they appear black against the distant skyline, which on closer approach turns to purple and soon to the deep green of pine and spruce which clothe them. In the southern part of the Black Hills, **Wind Cave National Park** is noted for the beautiful box-formed crystals of calcite left in the caves when the limestone rock dissolved. The largest herd of American Bison on the continent roams in **Custer State Park**. Further north, in the heart of the Black Hills, **Needles Highway** winds past granite monoliths hundreds of feet high. A popular attraction of the Black Hills is the **Mount Rushmore National Memorial** where the faces of Washington, Jefferson, Theodore Roosevelt and Lincoln have been carved into the side of a granite

THEODORE ROOSEVELT NATIONAL MEMORIAL PARK

Greater North Dakota Assn.

221

mountain. The scale of this monumental sculpture by Gutzon Borglum is in the proportions of a man 465 feet tall. The work of blasting away thousands of tons of granite took 14 years. Black Hills' city of **LEAD**, one of the original old gold-rush towns, is the site of the **Homestake Mine**, the nation's principal source for the precious metal. Guided tours of the surface workings in the summer show how tons of ore are processed for a few ounces of gold. Nearby **DEADWOOD**, wild-West town of truth and dime-novel fiction — once claimed as residents such heroes as Wild Bill Hickock and Calamity Jane. These colorful figures of the West have long been dead, buried in the cemetery on the hill above town, but they are remembered in the "Days of '76" celebration held in Deadwood. At **SPEARFISH** the famed Black Hills Passion Play presents the immortal story of the last days of Christ. On the east of the Hills, at **RAPID CITY**, the South Dakota School of Mines has an excellent Geology Museum displaying giant fishes and reptiles from the prehistoric sea that once covered the Dakotas. On a hill outside of town are huge stone statues of antediluvian monsters. An Indian Museum and Range Days rodeo are other attractions. . . . The **Badlands National Monument** 60 miles east of the Black Hills are a startling contrast to the cool forest, sparkling streams of the Hills. Desolate, arid, eerie — almost devoid of vegetation the Badlands cover a wasteland of 640,000 acres. In early morning or late afternoon jagged peaks, turrets, spires and steep canyons of colored ocean sediments create an unbelievable world that well could be Dante's *Inferno*.

NORTH DAKOTA

The Badlands of western North Dakota, not to be confused with those in South Dakota, consist of numerous flat-topped buttes and mesas cut by erosion into fantastic shapes. The best scenic views of the Badlands can be seen at **Theodore Roosevelt National Memorial Park**, with a north unit near **WATFORD CITY** and a south unit which includes a petrified forest at **MEDORA**. Teddy Roosevelt came to the area for his health and once operated the **Elkhorn Ranch** north of Medora. Also in Medora is the **De Mores Historic Site**, a 28-room chateau museum of a French nobleman who made a fortune in cattle during the time of Roosevelt. . . . **BISMARCK**, in the center of the state, has for its **State Capitol Building** a tall modern structure that is a relief from the usual imitation of the national capitol. The state's **Historical Society Museum** has a fine collection of relics of the early pioneer days. Nearby **Fort Lincoln State Park** in **MANDAN** is the site of the old infantry and cavalry posts from where Gen. Custer left to meet the Sioux in his "last stand" at Little Big Horn; the old fort has been reconstructed along with several Indian earth lodges. To the south, **Standing Rock Indian Reservation** includes the site of Sitting Bull's grave at **FORT YATES**. . . . Upstream from Bismarck, on the Missouri River, U. S. Army Engineers are completing **Garrison Dam**, the largest earth-filled

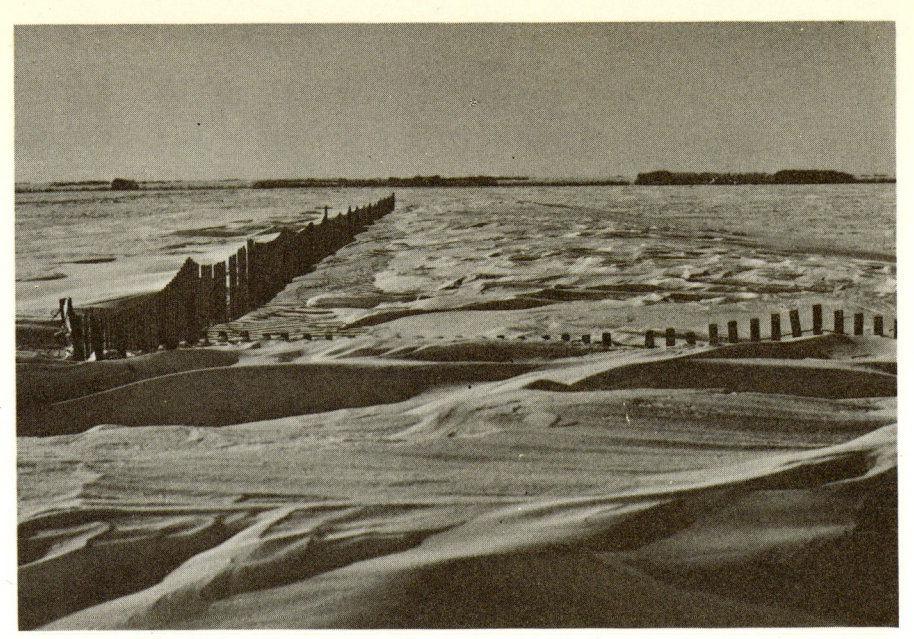

SNOWDRIFTS NEAR LARIMORE, NORTH DAKOTA
Standard Oil Co. (N. J.)

dam in the world. . . . On the Canadian boundary the **International Peace Gardens** commemorate a hundred years of peace between the United States and Canada. Near the Peace Gardens are **Souris National Migratory Bird Refuge**, to the west, and **Turtle Mountain Indian Reservation**, to the east. The Sun Dance performed by Chippewa Indians attracts visitors every June. . . . **Devils Lake**, the state's largest, is a recreational center with water sports, camping and picnic grounds.

MINNEHAHA FALLS, MINNEAPOLIS
Minneapolis Chamber of Commerce

LAKE MINNETONKA

Minnesota Division of Publicity

MINNESOTA

The 10,000 sparkling blue lakes and towering pine forests make Minnesota a vacation paradise for sportsmen and vacationists that is hard to surpass. Legend has it that the thousands of lakes were caused by the footprints of Paul Bunyan, giant lumberman whose exploits are a fascinating part of American folklore. At BEMIDJI, fishing and hunting center, the **Paul Bunyan Water Carnival** celebrates the end of the summer season. Giant statues of Bunyan and his blue ox "Babe" stand on the town lake shore. BRAINERD, to the south, also claims Paul Bunyan as a native product and holds an annual colorful pageant in his name. . . . **Itasca State Park**, southwest of Bemidji, is a pleasant vacation spot with lakes, outdoor recreational facilities, plenty of wild life and the source of the Mississippi River. . . . The gigantic, awe-inspiring open-pit iron mines near HIBBING are interesting to visit. The nation's largest iron-ore deposits, the three ranges Mesabi, Vermilion and Cuyana, send a continuous stream of loaded freight trains to the ore ports on Lake Superior. . . . A large part of the northeast Minnesota forest has been set aside in the **Superior National Forest**. Canoe trips through this wilderness prove to be a rewarding experience for modern-day "voyageurs," properly outfitted to meet the demands of days of paddling and portage over miles of uninhabited country. Canoe trips start from towns on the north shore of Lake Superior, Hovland, Grand Marais and Tofte, or inland at Tower or Ely. Detailed information and maps can be obtained from forest and travel organizations at Duluth. The **North Shore Drive** from Duluth to the Canadian border is a scenic highway where on one side are the horizon blue waters of Lake Superior with low silhouetted ore boats and fishing craft. High on the other side tower the forests of **Misquah Hills** through which tumble countless streams. . . . DULUTH serves as the gateway to the vacation country of northeast Minnesota but is economically more important as a transshipment point for grain and iron ore. The **Aerial Lift Bridge** spanning the ship-canal entrance to Duluth Harbor is an attraction, along with loading operations on the piers. . . . Minneapolis and St. Paul, Minnesota's twin cities to the south, are friendly rivals on the Mississippi River. Both cities have pleasant residential areas among crystal lakes, numerous parks and tree-lined boulevards. ST. PAUL · · · · has a slight

SPLIT ROCK LIGHTHOUSE, LAKE SUPERIOR

ROUND HOUSE AT FORT SNELLING, ST. PAUL

RAPIDS is Palisades-Kepler Park with limestone cliffs along the Cedar River.... To the west of Cedar Rapids are the **Amana Villages**, established by a religious sect of German immigrants in 1855. The original settlement was a communal enterprise and remained so for about 70 years. The seven villages are now organized in a joint stock corporation with less stringent rules over its members. The products of the villages include wool blankets and furniture of early-American design, noted for their craftsmanship, farm products and refrigerators. The quaint homes and craft shops of German design are of interest. German-style foods such as hearth-baked breads, Amana smoked hams and kuchen or coffeecake are a specialty.... Along the highways near **TAMA** one can purchase Indian handicrafts such as bead work and basket work skillfully made by Sac and Fox Indians from the nearby reservations. **DES MOINES** in the center of the state is the state capital and perhaps the farm capital of the nation. The **Iowa State Fair** held here is one of the world's premier agricultural expositions. Farmers from Iowa and neighboring states bring in

advantage as the State Capital. Key attractions are the **Capitol, Como Park** and **Indian God of Peace** statue in City Hall. The nine-day Winter Carnival held every year is climaxed by a firework display on the ramparts of a medieval ice castle built in Como Park.... **MINNEAPOLIS**...... has in the way of scenic views the **"Grand Rounds,"** 61 miles of boulevards encircling the city, **Minnehaha Falls** and the **Falls of St. Anthony.** The city's cultural attractions are extensive: the **Walker Art Galleries**, emphasizing modern art; **Minneapolis Institute of Art**, with a well-balanced collection of traditional art, and the **University of Minnesota Art Gallery.** Northrup Auditorium is the concert hall for the **Minneapolis Symphony Orchestra,** one of the five top-most symphony orchestras in the nation. In July the famous Aquatennial takes over the city with colorful parades, water shows and Mardi Gras atmosphere.... Northeast of the Twin Cities the St. Croix River threads its way through striking rock cliffs at the **Dalles of the St. Croix.** Further south is another scenic part of Minnesota that has become famous through the poem of Longfellow — that part of the Mississippi called "Hiawatha Valley." The famous Mayo Clinic, known the world over for medical research and treatment facilities, is at **ROCHESTER** in southeast Minnesota.

IOWA

This land of plenty is a state which although predominantly agricultural is not without points of interest. In eastern Iowa, near **MC GREGOR**, there are scenic river bluff views and lotus-filled bayous. The **Pikes Peak** area has colored sand cliffs and several Indian effigy mounds. There are many Iowa State Parks which provide camping and fishing facilities along stocked streams and lakes. East of **CEDAR**

PAUL BUNYAN MONUMENT, LAKE BEMIDJI, MINNESOTA

224

UNITED STATES

1. The Alamo, San Antonio, Texas
2. Williamsburg Capitol, Williamsburg, Va.
3. Cranbrook Foundation, Detroit, Mich.
4. Vicksburg Memorial, Vicksburg, Miss.
5. New York Skyline, N. Y.   Photo by TWA

UNITED STATES

1. Autumn landscape, Peacham, Vermont, U.S.A.
2. Soo Canal, Sault Ste. Marie, Michigan, U.S.A.
3. Monument Valley, Utah, U.S.A.
4. Mardi Gras parade, New Orleans, Louisiana, U.S.A.
5. Church ruin, Jamestown, Virginia, U.S.A.

UNITED STATES

1. Auburn, Natchez, Miss.
2. Washington's Headquarters, Valley Forge, Pa.
3. Mission, San Diego, Calif.
4. Iron Lace House, Savannah, Ga.

UNITED STATES

1. Cliff Palace—Mesa Verde National Park
2. Everglades National Park provides a refuge for bears and other wildlife
3. Cape Hatteras, known as "the graveyard of the Atlantic," is our country's only National Seashore
4. Sunrise Lodge—Mt. Rainier National Park

their prize livestock of powerful horses, prima donna steers and giant hogs, and agricultural products of grains, fruits and oversize vegetables; the womenfolk compete for honors in delicious baked goods, jams and preserves. The huge midway of rides and thrills adds a carnival flavor to the proceedings.... **Drake University** at Des Moines holds the **Drake Relays**, a national track event.... In northeast Iowa are the lake resorts of **Spirit Lake** and **Okoboji Lakes** offering the usual summer sports of swimming, boating, golf and fishing.

EAST NORTH CENTRAL STATES

The five states that cover this part of the Mid-West, east of the Mississippi and north of the Ohio Rivers, once made up the Northwest Territory, the first step in the expansion from the 13 original states. Long before white men settled here, however, the Indians had utilized the open country for the growing of Indian corn and had hunted game in the forests. The first white visitors were the French explorers followed by the *voyageurs* who came to barter the trinkets of civilization for priceless furs. The English who arrived later to dispute French possession of the fur country were closely followed by a large group of settlers who came from east of the Appalachians, to clear farmlands, build lumber mills and found towns. With the opening of the **Erie Canal** in 1825 the water route to the **Great Lakes** was complete. Immigrants poured westward to the agricultural lands of Ohio, Indiana and Illinois. Loggers came to cut the virgin timber of Michigan and Wisconsin. Finally, in modern times, the pioneers of the automobile industry chose this site to erect the mile-long assembly plants and giant steel mills that have transformed cities like Detroit into major industrial centers.

Visitors will find different kinds of scenery in this region. The Great Lakes give a maritime flavor to the states bordering their shores. In the northern woods and lake country are well-known vacation spots, and while the rich agricultural prairies to the south do not offer the "spectacular vistas" usually described in guide books, they are, nevertheless, impressive to one unfamiliar with the huge rolling farms of the Corn Belt. In late summer the rural and state fairs provide an excellent opportunity to see the agricultural bounty of the land.

For regional specialties in food the accent is both on quality and quantity, for skimping is frowned upon in this land of plenty. So be prepared for local provender in man-sized portions. State specialties are planked Michigan whitefish, Great Lakes perch, fried Michigan smelts, Wisconsin roast goose stuffed with apples and Indiana chicken pot pies. German and other European dishes are special treats to visitors to those communities which have retained an Old-World character. Kassler Rippchen (smoked rib chop) with Sauerkraut, blood sausage and jellied pigs feet are a few of the dishes available. Special mention should be made of Wisconsin's non-processed cheeses.

STATE CAPITOL, DES MOINES, IOWA
Greater Des Moines Chamber of Commerce

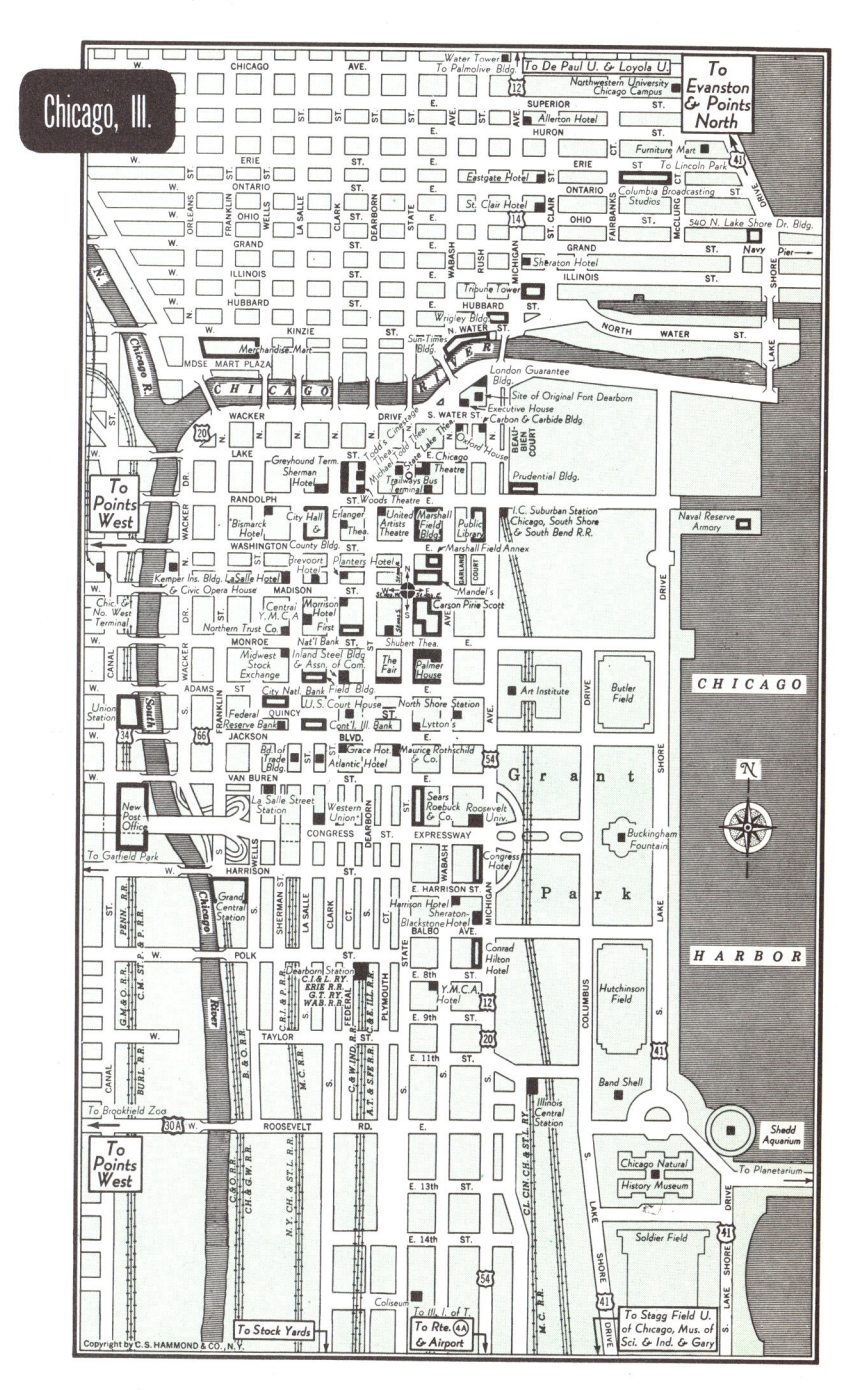

CHICAGO'S SKYLINE SEEN FROM LAKE SHORE DRIVE

Chicago Park Dist.

ILLINOIS

CHICAGO. Chartered in 1833, Chicago is relatively young as cities go, yet its growth has been phenomenal. In keeping with its motto—"I Will"—Chicago has risen from a remote frontier outpost to become the nation's second largest city with a population of over 3½ million people. The great fire of 1871, which completely wiped out the business district, scarcely interrupted the city's progress. The tremendous task of rebuilding—in steel and stone instead of wood—started immediately, and by 1877 recovery was complete, with the Old Water Tower and the legend of Mrs. O'Leary's cow kicking over a lantern about the only remnants of the older city redeemed from the ashes. Standing at the nation's transportation crossroads, Chicago has become the business capital of mid-America—the most productive, the best balanced region on earth in terms of industry, commerce and agriculture. In the words of the poet Carl Sandburg, Chicago is:

> "Hog Butcher for the World,
> Tool Maker, Stacker of Wheat,
> Player with Railroads and the
> Nation's Freight Handler."

More people or more tons of freight can be transported to the rest of the nation from Chicago in less time, at less cost and with fewer transfers than from any other major city. Today, its 22-mile lake front is lined by great masses of towering buildings in a striking setting of handsome parks, broad boulevards, white sand beaches and the sparkling waters of Lake Michigan. The stretch north of the Chicago river is particularly impressive with its apartment houses, big hotels and such landmarks as the Tribune Tower, the Wrigley Building and the Palmolive Building. Here is found the Furniture Mart with its office and display facilities for the nation's leading home furnishers; the Merchandise Mart, the second largest office building in the world; the nationally famous Marshall Field's department store with its spectacular dome composed of millions of pieces of Tiffany glass, and the Chicago Campus of Northwestern University with its schools of law, medicine and dentistry. At the northern end of Lake Shore Drive is Lincoln Park — 25 acres of which house the Lincoln Park Zoo of TV fame with its extensive collection of birds, mammals and reptiles representing almost every part of the earth. The zoo's many attractions draw an average annual attendance of more than four million men, women and children. The center of Chicago's downtown section is an area, seven blocks long by five blocks wide, known as the Loop—the heart of the city—where elevated railway lines actually loop around the financial and commercial buildings. South of the Loop, the Chicago Board of Trade rises 44 stories and is topped by a massive statue of the goddess Ceres—an appropriate symbol, since the building contains the world's largest grain exchange. Here one may witness the various types of grain being bought and sold by means of rapid and—to the layman—often mysterious signals. East of the Loop, stretching along Chicago's filled-in shoreline, is Grant Park with its formal gardens and the Chicago Institute of Art. Works of Goya and El Greco are among the masterpieces in the Institution's collection of paintings. The Chicago Institute is also a leading art school of the Middle West. For scientific museums, Chicago offers The Chicago Museum of Natural History, the Shedd Aquarium and the Adler Planetarium — each outstanding in its field and all located on the south side of Grant Park. Further south, Michigan Avenue leads to the University of Chicago with its handsome Gothic buildings and its 100-acre campus. The University's Stagg Athletic Field is an atomic age landmark. Here beneath one of its stands the first controlled nuclear chain reaction was demonstrated. To the south and southwest are two widely scattered points of special interest—the Union Stockyards, center of the world's livestock marketing and meat packing industries, and the Brookfield Zoo with its fine natural-habitat exhibits of animals. The city's amazing development could not have been accomplished without great citizens as well as great circumstances. Chicago has always been fortunate in the industry and dynamic vitality of its people. To them and to their leaders—the business giants of the past and the capable leaders of the present—the city owes a large measure of credit for its remarkable record over the years.

South from Chicago the Illinois River cuts through **Starved Rock State Park**, an area of great scenic beauty: bluffs, gorges and rock formations that were the backdrop for an interesting history of Indians and French explorers. Marquette and Joliet erected a fort here in 1682. The

ADLER PLANETARIUM

Chicago Park Dist.

226

name comes from the legend of a group of Illinois Indians who suffered starvation rather than surrender to a warring band of Iroquois. . . . In northwest Illinois, at **GALENA** in 1860, lived a former Army captain and unsuccessful businessman named Ulysses S. Grant. At the end of the Civil War, Grant returned to Galena a famous general. The pleasant brick home, presented to him by the local citizens, is now preserved as a State Memorial. . . . **Black Hawk State Park**, near **MOLINE**, marks the hunting grounds of the Sac and Fox Indian tribes. Chief Black Hawk, born and raised here, led the Indians in the war against the white settlers that blazed over western Illinois and southern Wisconsin in the 1830's. The **Hauberg Collection** of Indian relics is located at Black Hawk Watchtower, the highest point in the park. . . . **SPRINGFIELD**, the State Capital, is well-known as a Lincoln shrine. Lincoln came to Springfield in 1837 as a backwoodsman, with few earthly possessions and with some experience as a member of the State Legislature. Establishing himself in law practice in the new State Capital, he married and became a prominent citizen. In the unpretentious white frame house on Jackson Street, Lincoln and his family spent 17 happy years. The building and furnishings remain today just as they were when Lincoln received the Republican Notification Committee. After Lincoln's assassination, his body was returned in state to Springfield. The **Lincoln Tomb**, marked by a tall marble shaft, is in Oak Ridge Cemetery. . . . Twenty miles northwest of Springfield is the reconstructed village of **New Salem** where Lincoln lived his formative years. On the banks of the Sangamon River stand the pioneer cabins, the general store where Lincoln worked, the cooperage, tavern and gristmill. Each building is furnished with authentic heirlooms of the period. Reconstruction was facilitated by the fact that New Salem did not prosper but became a ghost town shortly after Lincoln left, remaining undisturbed until it was rebuilt. . . . Southwest of Springfield, at the junction of the Illinois and Mississippi Rivers, are the wooded hills of **Pere Marquette State Park**, largest in the state. . . . In southern Illinois, **Giant City Park** receives its name from the high vertical blocks of stone which are arranged in a street-like pattern to resemble the handiwork of giants.

RECONSTRUCTED VILLAGE OF NEW SALEM—LINCOLN'S BOYHOOD HOME

MUSEUM OF SCIENCE AND INDUSTRY, CHICAGO

INDIANA

The "Hoosier State," as Indiana is often called, has a homey quality that is one of the state's main assets. Except for the hilly southern part, the state is mostly level prairie country punctuated by occasional low ridges. The physical scenery is restful, in keeping with the natural friendliness of the people. The expression, "grass roots American," usually reserved for use by political orators, can perhaps be best used to characterize the agricultural country of Indiana. . . . In southwest Indiana, at **NEW HARMONY** on the banks of the Wabash River, an agricultural community was founded in 1814. The Settlement differed from others in that it practiced celibacy and outlawed private property. The settlers were Germans, religious followers of George Rapp, and their colony flourished for ten years. The lands were then sold to the Scottish socialist Robert Owen, who planned a more permanent colony based on communal living without religious overtones. The colony failed but it did establish a reputation for education and for granting equal rights to women. A few relics of these early experiments are to be found in New Harmony. A Golden Rain Festival held every June attracts visitors. . . . To the east, the **Nancy Hank's Lincoln Memorial** at **LINCOLN CITY** includes the grave of Lincoln's mother and the log cabin of Lincoln's boyhood. Further east is the village of **SANTA CLAUS** where it is Christmas all year 'round; the post office handles many thousands of letters to keep alive the legend of St. Nicholas. A candy castle and toy village are a delight to youngsters. . . . **VINCENNES**, territorial capital of Indiana and the oldest city in the state, was an important frontier outpost. It was named after the French nobleman Sieur de Vincennes who built the post fort. The French were succeeded by the British and finally by the Americans under George Rogers Clark. The **George Rogers Clark Memorial**, a Greek-Doric temple, has been erected at the site of the old fort in honor of Clark's achievements. A souvenir of Vincennes territorial capital days remains in the **Old Territorial Legislative Hall**. The plain exterior and simple country-made furniture reflect the pioneer days. . . . Indiana has its own resort and health spas with three mineral springs at **FRENCH LICK**, 45 miles east of Vincennes. . . . **INDIANAPOLIS** is internationally known for the Memorial Day racing classic — the 500-mile race at the **Indianapolis Motor Speedway**. This grueling race not only provides the thrill of high-speed racing but also acts as a testing ground for new auto improvements; innovations such as balloon tires, rear-vision

227

mirrors and four-wheel brakes were first introduced here. Other attractions in the capital city are the **Scottish Rites Cathedral**, **World War Memorial Plaza** and the **James Whitcomb Riley Home**. . . . In northwest Indiana the large iron and steel works at GARY provide guided tours. One cannot help but be impressed by the giant blast furnaces, towering smokestacks and harbor activity of this industrial area. **Indiana Dunes State Park**, to the east, is a lake shore vacation spot matching Cape Cod for windswept sand dunes and natural scenery. . . . SOUTH BEND, 30 miles east, is an industrial city famous as the seat of the **University of Notre Dame**.

OHIO

Once a pioneer state of the Northwest Territory, Ohio is now part of the great industrial heartland of the United States. One of the wooden forts which protected the early settlements has been reconstructed at FORT RECOVERY on the Indiana state line. The fort was originally built by General Anthony Wayne in 1793. . . . At DAYTON, in western Ohio, the Wright Brothers produced the first successful airplane. The U. S. Air Force aeronautical laboratories, at **Wright Field**, have continued to give Dayton a prominent position in airplane development. Also of interest in Dayton are the **Dayton Art Institute**, with specialties in Italian and Oriental art work, and **Deeds Carillon** in **Dayton Carillon Park**. East of Dayton, at YELLOW SPRINGS, **Antioch College** is an outstanding school for progressive education where academic study is alternated with practical experience. . . . COLUMBUS, the state capital, is also the seat of **Ohio State University**, a leading institution of higher learning in the Mid-West. The **Ohio State Museum**, located on the campus, contains various collections dealing with Ohio history. . . . South of Columbus, near CHILLICOTHE, the **Mound City Group National Monument** preserves interesting remnants of an age-old Indian civilization. A three-foot embankment encloses a group of 23 burial mounds containing altars and human remains. Little is known of the prehistoric Indians who once inhabited the area. The most impressive of the many Indian mounds in the area is that of **Serpent Mound**, southwest of Chillicothe. Built of earth, it curls like an enormous snake for 1300 feet. Its exact purpose is unknown. . . . For recreational facilities, the **Hocking Parks**, east of Columbus, offer pleasant hiking, camping and picnicking facilities among streams, waterfalls and hardwood forests. . . . The first white settlement in Ohio was founded in eastern Ohio in 1772 at Schoenbrunn Village, now NEW PHILADELPHIA. The settlement has been authentically restored to appear as it did 175 years ago as a Moravian mission colony. MARIETTA, further south on the Ohio, was the first settlement to survive and become a permanent city. . . . AKRON, part of industrial Ohio, is the nation's rubber capital, processing about 40 per cent of the world's raw rubber supply. The **International Soap-box Derby** held every August at Akron is the climax of soap-box racing held throughout the country for boys under twelve. . . . On the shores of Lake Erie is CLEVELAND, Ohio's largest city, an iron and steel center and key port for much of the Great Lakes shipping. For an over-all view of the city, visit the **Terminal Tower** on **Public Square**. Modern parkways encircling the metropolitan area provide a pleasant motor tour of the harbor, nine city parks and the lake front. At **The Mall**, in the downtown section, are the **Cleveland Museum of Art**, the **Municipal Stadium** and **Severance Hall**, home of the Cleveland Symphony Orchestra. Cleveland's many national groups unite each year to hold an annual festival of flower displays, folk music and native dancing at **Cultural Gardens** in **Rockefeller Park**. . . . At the western end of Lake Erie, **Marblehead Peninsula** and **Lake Erie Islands** are popular summer vacation spots. **Perry's Victory National Monument** on South Bass Island commemorates the naval battle fought off Put-In-Bay during the War of 1812. Further west, TOLEDO'S **Museum of Art** has one of the world's best collections of ancient and modern glass along with other art treasures.

MICHIGAN

The State of Michigan is known throughout the world as the producer of that chrome-plated symbol of modern civilization, the automobile. For a look at the production techniques of the modern auto-

LOCKERBIE—HOME OF JAMES WHITCOMB RILEY AT INDIANAPOLIS

OPEN HEARTH FURNACES AT FORD'S ROUGE PLANT, DEARBORN

motive industry, a visit to DETROIT is highly recommended. In a behind-the-scenes tour of any one of the large auto-making corporations one can watch autos take shape as they move along the assembly line. At peak production a glistening new car rolls off under its own power every 20 seconds. Best known of the large assembly lines is probably the **Ford River Rouge Plant** in DEARBORN, part of the industrial Detroit area. Tours start at the Ford Rotunda where displays tell the story of the automotive industry. In contrast to the ultramodern features of the Rotunda, pages from an early American book of history are unfolded in the calm and peaceful atmosphere of **Greenfield Village**. An old windmill, a blacksmith shop, replicas of the homes of Stephen Foster, Noah Webster and William McGuffey are reminders of the days when life was a lot simpler than today. Only horsedrawn carriages roll down the streets past the Wright Brothers Cycle Shop where the airplane was born, and past Menlo Park where Thomas Edison gave meaning to electricity. **Edison Institute Museum** contains fascinating collections of early Americana with displays ranging from the silverware of Paul Revere to the trimotored airplane that carried Rear Admiral Byrd across the South Pole in 1928. Among other sights in Detroit are the **Detroit Institute of Arts** and the **Detroit Public Library**, facing one another on Woodward Avenue. **Belle Isle Park**, located in the Detroit River between the U. S. and Canada, is a popular recreation area with picnic grounds, drives, sport events and summer concerts. . . . The cultural center of **Cranbrook**, 20 miles north of Detroit, is made up of six institutions including the well-known **Academy of Arts**. The impressive buildings and grounds include a fountain designed by the late Carl Milles, noted Swedish sculptor. . . . ANN ARBOR, west of Detroit, is the seat of the **University of Michigan**, a leading university of the Mid-West. A visit to the campus in the fall would not be complete without witnessing a big-time college football game in **Michigan Stadium**, the largest college-owned stadium in the world. . . . EAST LANSING is the home of Michigan's second largest college, **Michigan State University**, with a campus of modern buildings and spacious grounds. . . . The **Furniture Museum** in GRAND RAPIDS attracts travelers interested in interior decoration; on display are fine examples of period furniture produced by native craftsmen. . . . May is the time of the **Tulip Festival** at HOLLAND, southwest of Grand Rapids. Wooden shoes complete the colorful Dutch costumes worn by local citizens, 90 per cent of whom are of Dutch descent. A scrubbing of Eighth Street marks the beginning of a four-day festival featuring parades, folk dances and huge flower exhibits.

Michigan's 11,000 lakes and its long shore line bordering four of the Great Lakes make the state a water wonderland that is popular with swimmers, fishermen, boating and nature enthusiasts. Inland, sparkling streams such as the Sturgeon, Muskegon and Au Sable echo through cool shaded forests. In the western part of the lower peninsula, the area around Traverse Bay is a popular resort land.

TRAVERSE CITY is the center of this country of water-skiing, lake-trout trolling and other sports. The **National Cherry Festival**, held when the bay region orchards are brilliant with blossoms, attracts large numbers of visitors annually. . . . The **National Music Camp** at INTERLOCHEN, southwest of Traverse City, is host to more than a thousand music students from all over the country. Numerous concerts in country surroundings make up the summer program. . . . For a snow holiday Michigan offers a wide variety of winter sports including ice fishing on the Great Lakes, ice skating at the many rinks and lakes, and skiing on snow-covered slopes. In the lower peninsula no one area holds a dominant position as *the* winter sports center. The possible exception to this may be CADILLAC, where the **Caberfae** skiing facilities are outstanding. . . . In the straits of Mackinac, separating the two peninsulas of Michigan, lies the pleasant, historic island of **Mackinac**. This island resort, which has flown the flags of three nations, was important in the War of 1812 as a fortress and later as the headquarters of John Jacob Astor in the booming fur-trade days. Today the island is a scenic attraction noted for the tree-lined bluffs with huge summer homes — some dating from the gay nineties. Splendid formal gardens and long verandas are special features of the famous **Grand Hotel**. . . . Visitors to the **Soo Canal** at SAULT STE. MARIE find the passage of the long ore boats through the **locks** a fascinating experience. Annually, more tonnage passes through this canal than through the Panama and Suez Canals combined. . . . To the west of Sault Ste. Marie, in the wilds of the upper peninsula, the **Tahquamenon Falls** are well worth visiting. The falls are reached by excursion boats from the mouth of the Tahquamenon River or by combination railway and boat tour from SOO JUNCTION. . . . The upper peninsula recreation area centers around MARQUETTE. Good fishing waters provide a variety of species from wall-eyed pike to trout and perch; hunting includes both large and small game with deer and bear as the big prizes. . . . IRON MOUNTAIN on the Wisconsin state line offers to snow enthusiasts two toboggan slides along with ski tows and lodge facilities. . . . **Isle Royal** in Lake Superior is a National Park of untouched wilderness. Since no cars or wheeled vehicles of any sort are allowed on the island, visitors, touring the 44-mile-long island, must follow the trails on foot. The island's beauty lies in the

ORE BOATS, SUPERIOR, WISCONSIN

Philip Gendreau

mixed forests of birches and evergreens, the deep fjord-like bays and harbors. Moose as well as coyote, mink, beaver and rabbits are among the fauna of this island sanctuary.

WISCONSIN

The northern gateway to Wisconsin's vast reservoir of recreational areas is **SUPERIOR**. The city shares an extensive harbor with its "twin," DULUTH, Minnesota. The tall grain elevators and massive iron-ore loading piers give testimony to the great wealth of the region.... **Pattison State Park**, ten miles south of Superior, has Wisconsin's highest falls in **Big Manitou Falls** with a sheer drop of 165 feet.... Located offshore from BAYFIELD, the **Apostle Islands** are known for their fine fishing waters and scenic red cliffs.... Northern Wisconsin lake and woods country is such a large vacationland that detailed descriptions of each fishing and resort location is impossible. **RHINELANDER** is a center for the lake district known for its record-size muskellunge fish. **WAUSAU**, to the south, in the more mountainous country of the **Rib Mountain State Park**, can offer stimulating snow sports of skiing and tobogganing as well as the usual summer fare.... **GREEN BAY** was the site of Wisconsin's first settlement of French fur traders who arrived in 1634. The **Neville Museum** has special exhibits of this early history. The **Roi-Porlier-Tank Cottage** in Tank Park is Wisconsin's oldest standing house.... In southern Wisconsin where the Wisconsin River has eroded a channel through the sandstone bedrock are the **Wisconsin Dells**, a scenic attraction capitalizing on the water-sculptured rock formations. Sight-seeing can be done at both the Lower and Upper Dells on foot or in a more leisurely way aboard sightseeing boats.... Further south, near BARABOO, the blue waters of Devils Lake are surrounded by quartzite bluffs that climb to heights of 600 feet. The whole area is rich in geologic history — the glacier age leaving its trademarks of glacial striae and tumbled rocks.... **MADISON**, Wisconsin's capital, is ideally located on the isthmus between lakes Monona and Mendota. The **University of Wisconsin** shares the spotlight with the State Capitol to give Madison a lively cultural and intellectual life. The nearby tree-lined lakes give urban Madison a country resort flavor. Picnickers and bathers need not travel far to reach sparkling lakes and shady groves.... Wisconsin was settled by immigrants from Europe so that it is not surprising to find various communities retaining an Old-World character. Southwest of Madison is **NEW GLARUS**, a Swiss settlement famous for cheese and laces and to the west, **MINERAL POINT**, a mining town, predominantly Cornish. **MILWAUKEE**, on Lake Michigan, has many Swiss and Germans, expert brewers, hence the famous Milwaukee beers. Milwaukee has other points of interest beside the breweries, however. It has a magnificent lake front, many fine parks, a zoo and two art galleries. The Milwaukee Symphony Orchestra is world famous.... To the south is **RACINE**, where the functional Johnson Wax Building will interest students of modern architecture. It was designed by Wisconsin-born Frank Lloyd Wright, pioneer of modern architects.

South Central States

The four states of this section do not form a homogeneous region; in fact, each state is usually quite distinct from its neighbors. Louisiana is French-speaking, bayou country; Arkansas, predominantly mountainous; Oklahoma, Indian territory of the Great Plains, and Texas — well, Texas is different from any place in the world.

LOUISIANA

NEW ORLEANS. Having flourished in the past under both French and Spanish rule, New Orleans with its colorful history, its saga of pirates and gentlemen-gamblers, its legends of duels at dawn and black magic at midnight, is undoubtedly one of the most romantic cities in the United States. Serving as a gateway to the Mississippi Valley and with access to almost 15,000 miles of navigable waterways, New Orleans is also one of the nation's leading ports. Though the city lies 110 miles upstream from the Gulf, it is easily reached by large ocean vessels. Spreading along a wide crescent-shaped bend of the Mississippi River, its terrain is flat, unbroken by even the smallest of hills and scarcely more than a foot above the level of the sea. Thick mounds of earth hold back the waters of the Mississippi and ships anchored along the levees, high above the surrounding streets, present a strange picture. New Orleans is a city of contrasts where, on one hand, modern skyscrapers rise above their foundations of piles driven deep into the Mississippi muck, and on the other hand are found the delicate iron lace, the stuccoed walls, the balcony-hung streets of the Vieux Carré. Canal Street, one of the widest business streets in the nation, sharply divides the old from the new. The heart of the French Quarter or Vieux Carré is Jackson Square, formerly the Place d'Armes, where the flag of the United States was raised for the first time over the Louisiana Territory. The formal ceremonies surrounding the Louisiana Purchase took place nearby, in a room of the cabildo— an ancient Spanish government building which today serves as a museum. Flanking Jackson Square are the two beautiful, block-long Pontalba buildings. Excellent examples of Creole architecture, these were the first American apartment houses. Also on Jackson Square is St. Louis Cathedral. Originally a Spanish provincial church, the brick and stucco Cathedral built in 1794 is now somewhat altered from the original design by the many changes made over the years. The Old Absinthe House on Bourbon Street is famous as the one-time haunt of the pirates Pierre and Jean Lafitte. The U.S. Customs House at Decatur and Canal Streets is interesting for its Egyptian architecture. This old building once served as a Confederate prison. The French Market, which covers six city

ST. LOUIS CATHEDRAL

Bur. of New Orleans News

blocks, is a traditional New Orleans haunt for early risers and late merrymakers desiring "coffee and doughnuts." The New Orleans Mardi Gras is probably the city's greatest tourist attraction. This prelenten bacchanal begins early in January with masked-balls and other festivities. As the season progresses, the carnival spirit grows in intensity to break forth in a full week of unrestrained revelry. The merrymaking is climaxed on Shrove Tuesday when King Comus—the Lord of Misrule—reigns over the city.

New Orleans' high position in the gastronomic world is based on her reputation for Creole cooking, a happy combination of French and Spanish cuisine, plus Negro and Choctaw Indian influences. Creole dishes spiced by piquant herbs are especially inspired in the preparation of the plentiful Louisiana sea foods: shrimp, oysters, crabs, crayfish and pompano. Jambalaya (rice cooked with crab meat, shrimp, ham and sausage), bouillabaisse, Pompano en Papilote are but a few of the more famous dishes. The luxurious restaurant features the spectacle of flaming dishes like crepes suzettes, cherries jubilee and café brûlot. . . . **BATON ROUGE**, Louisiana's capital city, northwest of New Orleans, is marked by the tall capitol building, one of the most impressive in the country. The observation tower offers a splendid panorama of the city and the meandering Mississippi River. Baton Rouge is in the heart of the magnolia country. The heavy fragrance of the snow-white blossoms fills the air from April to June. . . . North of Baton Rouge, near **ST. FRANCISVILLE**, are several antebellum homes that are reminiscent of the Old South. Set in beautiful landscaped grounds and gardens these mansions are often masterpieces of design, furnished in

BALCONY OF IRON LACE, NEW ORLEANS
Bur. of New Orleans News

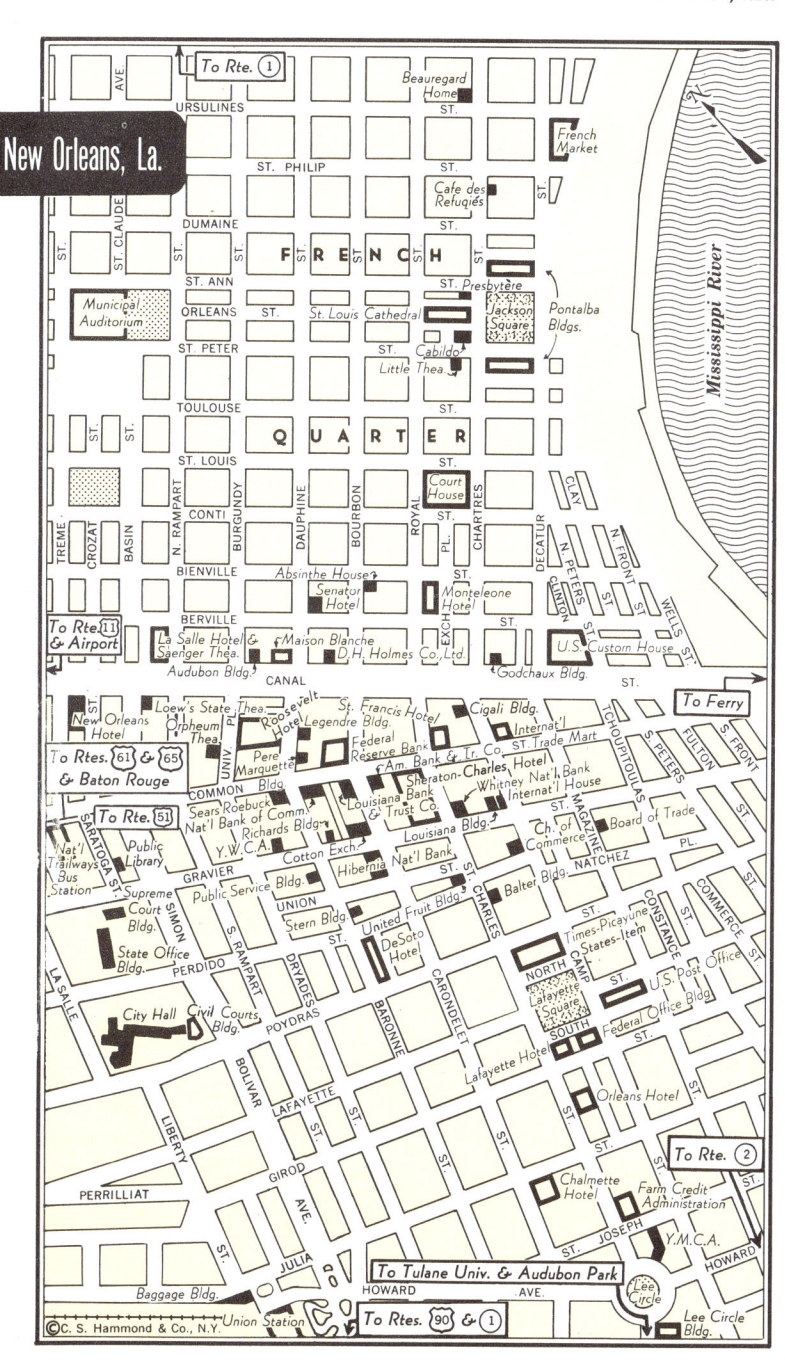

AUDUBON PARK
State of Louisiana

CHICOT STATE PARK, VILLE PLATTE, LOUISIANA

Louisiana State Pub. Photo

the finest European originals. Two of the outstanding homes are **Afton Villa** and **Greenwood**, north of St. Francisville....
In the intricate network of bayous west of Baton Rouge is the alluring Acadia land, the home of the descendants of French peasants expelled by the English from Nova Scotia. The Acadians found refuge in the quiet bayou country of French-speaking Louisiana, took up homes, have multiplied and now are an integral part of the tropical bayou country. Their curious patois of French and English, their customs and handicrafts have been preserved for the span of two centuries. The story of the Acadians is familiar to most Amercians through Longfellow's epic poem *Evangeline*, the story of two lovers separated in the banishment. The couple had their real life counterparts in Emmeline Labiche and Louis Arceneaux. Their reunion on the banks of Bayou Teche, contrary to the poem, did not end happily, however. Louis had by that time despaired of finding his love again and had taken another wife. **Evangeline Memorial State Park**, near **ST. MARTINVILLE**, is the locale of the Evangeline story. No finer setting could have been chosen than this shadowy land of deep green and soft grays, where sunlight glances with a golden touch on stately age-old live oaks and tranquil depths of bayous.... South of St. Martinville, **NEW IBERIA** has a fine plantation manor, **The Shadows**. At nearby **AVERY ISLAND** the **McIllhenny Mansion** and **Jungle Gardens** attract visitors in the spring. The island among the salt marshes produces not only rock salt and peppers for the famous McIllhenny tobasco sauce but is also a snowy egret sanctuary. Other wildlife refuges in the marshy coast of Louisiana such as **Sabine Migratory Waterfowl Refuge** provide a semi-tropical haven for millions of heron, Canadian geese and wild ducks. Fishing for tarpon and other deep-sea fish is a big-time sport for several coastal centers, **LAKE CHARLES, MORGAN CITY** and others. Inland fishing and hunting for all parts of Louisiana is excellent.... **ALEXANDRIA** in central Louisiana is the headquarters for **Kisatchie National Forest**, a natureland of bayous surrounded by forests of virgin pine, cypresses and moss-hung oaks.... **SHREVEPORT** plays host to the citizenry from all over for a spring festival "Holiday in Dixie" which includes rodeos, parades and exhibits saluting the advent of spring. The State Fair held here in the fall is also a big event.

ARKANSAS

The green and golden hills of Arkansas begin where the plains country of the Mississippi Valley leaves off. Two separate mountain systems provide Arkansas with unlimited outdoor recreational opportunities with scenic panoramas from 2000-foot peaks, tumbling mountain streams where small mouth bass lie waiting to rise to the bright colors of the angler's fly, and miles of hiking trails in pine-clad mountains. The **Ouachita Mountains** of central Arkansas are popular with fishermen and campers desiring the quiet wilderness of the forested hills. **Petit Jean State Park**, near **MORRILTON**, is just one of the many mountain retreats where scenic beauty is likely to make the sportsman forget his goal of a prize catch. At the edge of the expansive **Ouachita National Forest** is the resort and health spa of **Hot Springs National Park**. The health-giving mineral waters were first enjoyed by white men in the expedition of Hernando de Soto but the value of the mineral baths had been known to Indians long before the coming of the Spaniards. In 1832 the U. S. Government established the springs as a national park, the first such park in the nation. Today a visitor can enjoy a single or series of baths at one of the elegant hotel establishments or at one of the spick-and-span government bathhouses. The resort also has round-the-clock entertainment ranging from mountain climbing on foot or on horseback, to the sophisticated pleasure of night clubs. Top-flight fishing and all kinds of water sports can be enjoyed on nearby **Lakes Hamilton, Catherine** and **Ouachita**. In passing, mention should be made of the nation's only diamond mine located to the southwest near **MURFREESBORO**. The admission price allows the visitor to try his luck in finding a rough diamond in the open crater.... **LITTLE ROCK**, state capital, has the distinction of owning three capitol buildings. The **Territorial Capitol**, now restored, was constructed in 1820 from hand-hewn oak logs and cypress siding; the reconstruction project includes several frontier homes complete with gardens and furnishings of the period. The **Old State House** is an ante-bellum building of classic design, considered one of the finest in the country. The present **Capitol** is of Arkansas white marble and is known for its photomural rotunda and the mineral and historical exhibits housed in the building.... To the southeast in the rice-growing Grand Prairie country, **STUTTGART** is well-known as a duck hunting center.

The fall migration of enormous flocks of wild ducks brings about a corresponding gathering of duck hunters at the public shooting grounds. . . . In northern Arkansas are the Ozark Mountains, the second mountain system of the state. The southern continuation of the Ozark hills gives Arkansas some of the same scenic grandeur that is described in the Missouri section. **EUREKA SPRINGS** is a center for this rugged mountain country, rich in springs, caverns, lovely glens and waterfalls. Handicraft items such as wood carvings, quilts and hooked rugs are popular with tourists who visit this hillside town. Arkansas also shares with Missouri the wide waters of Bull Shoals Lake and Norfolk Lake, although the giant dams are actually in Arkansas. **BELLA VISTA** in the northwest corner of the state is a popular resort town with giant springs and underground caverns. The town's **Wonderland Cave** includes a night club in one of the larger caverns. **FORT SMITH**, to the south, located between both the Ouachita and Ozark Mountains, was once a frontier post, now a commercial and industrial center. Part of the old fort of 1818 still stands as a museum. The annual Arkansas-Oklahoma Rodeo held here is an outstanding event.

OKLAHOMA

The "Sooner State" as it is called was originally reserved for the Indian tribes displaced by the westward movement. Pressure for homestead lands, however, forced the government to open up the rich lands of the Cherokee Strip for white settlement. At noon on April 22, 1889, as the signal guns went off a great mass of homeseekers in wagons, on horseback and on foot rushed to stake out land claims. Some of the more anxious settlers had previously slipped into the territory unobserved and staked choice claims, thus earning for themselves the name "Sooners," a term which eventually became the state sobriquet. Today most of the Oklahoma rolling plains are devoted to agriculture, either crops or cattle, but some of the lands have produced another richer yield in black gold — petroleum. Some of the richest oil wells were on lands formerly held by Osage Indians who have become rich through royalties they received from oil production on their land. Most of Oklahoma's Indians, except for older generations, live in much the same way as the white people, go to public schools and colleges, work on farms or in the oil fields or, as in some cases, go on to high offices in the state and nation. One of Oklahoma's most famous citizens was part Cherokee Indian. He was the homespun philosopher and humorist, Will Rogers. At **CLAREMORE** in northeast Oklahoma, the state has built the **Will Rogers Memorial** as the burial place for one of the best-loved Americans. The stone building that houses Rogers' personal possessions stands on the hill where he had planned to build a ranch house for his retirement. . . . To the southwest, the modern city of **TULSA** considers itself the oil capital of the world. It appears to be true when one sees the extensive refineries and oil fields that surround the city. The biennial International Petroleum Products Exposition held here would tend to reinforce the impression. But of more interest to visitors will be the **Philbrook Art Center**, a private mansion now a museum, and **Gilcrease Foundation** where excellent examples of Indian art and paintings of the Old West by Remington and Russell are displayed. An extensive collection of books, manuscripts and letters on art and history of the region supplement the art works of the Gilcrease museum. . . . **OKLAHOMA CITY** . . . . in the center of the state is the capital and a strange one it is, for beneath the city is one of the largest oil pools in the nation. Oil rigs erected to tap this rich deposit have appeared on the lawns of private homes and even on the grounds facing the Greek temple front of the State Capitol. . . . To the south near **SULPHUR**, **Platt National Park** is an attraction with over thirty large mineral springs which, like those at Hot Springs, Arkansas, are under federal government supervision. The curative waters, which in some cases spout forth as artesian wells, combine with mountain streams, cliffs and bluffs and scenic drives lined with wild flowers to make the park one of the state's most pleasant vacation spots. . . . Further south are two Oklahoma lakes also popular with vacationists, **Lake Murray**, near **ARDMORE** and **Lake Texoma**, to the east. . . . A drive through **Wichita Mountain Wildlife Refuge** in the western part of the state will yield sights of herds of buffalo and Texas longhorns grazing by the roadside.

TEXAS

This mighty empire of the Southwest sprawls across the map of the United States taking up a vast territory. It is a land of rolling plains, sleepy rivers, rugged mountains and wide gulf beaches. It is also a land of superlatives — largest in size, greatest producer of oil, cotton, livestock and so on *ad infinitum*. Texans are famous for elaborating the virtues and his-

OLD STATE HOUSE, LITTLE ROCK

Little Rock Chamber of Commerce

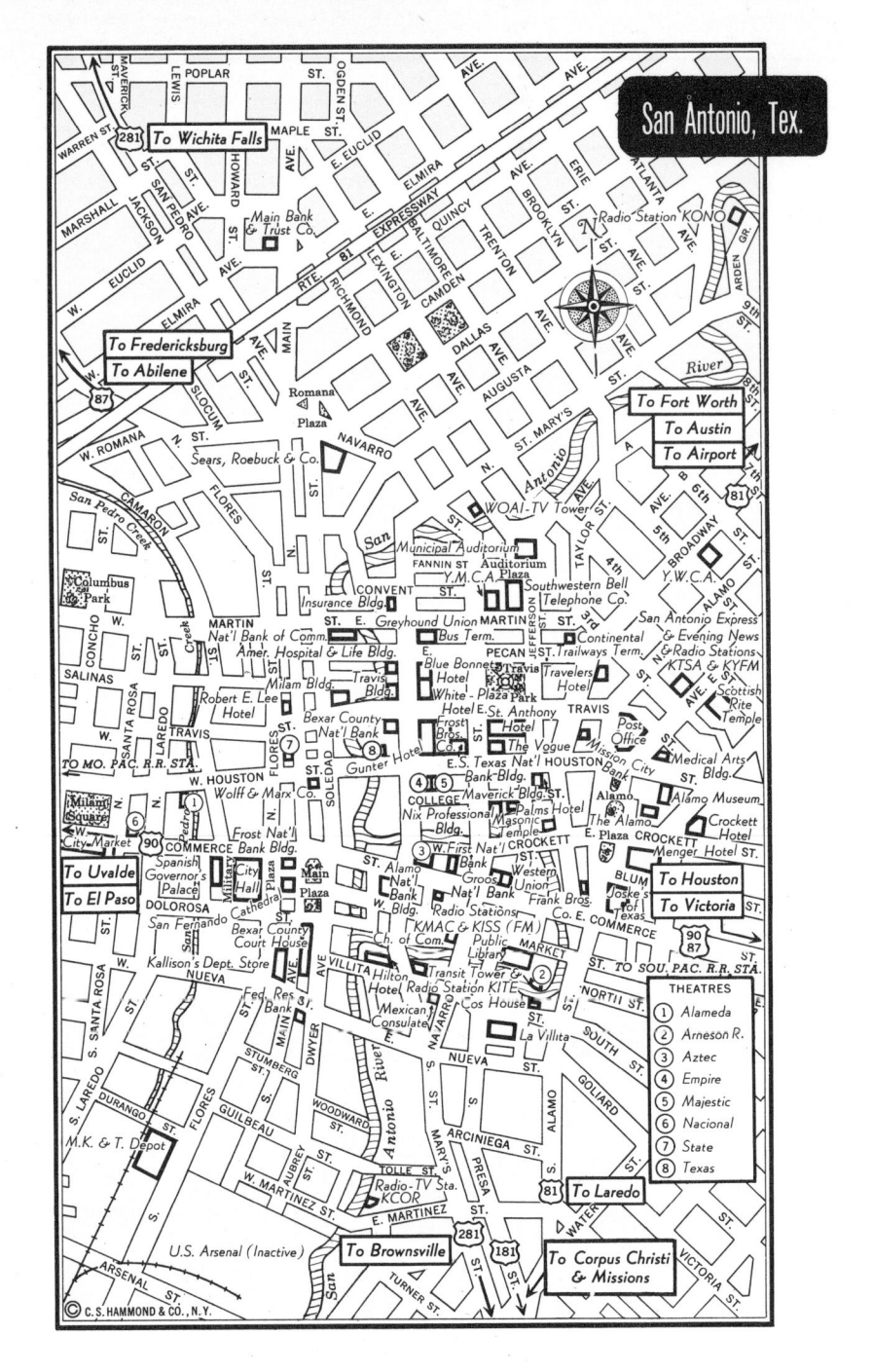

tory of their state so that it is difficult to separate fact from fiction. Texas has been under six flags and its life still bears the imprint of Spanish and Mexican history. The land is studded with old Franciscan missions, forts and battlefields that tell the history of early settlements and the fight for independence. . . . **AMARILLO** is the center for the high plains country of the Texas Panhandle, once desolate range land, now prosperous with oil fields and productive farms; the annual rodeo on the 4th of July is a local attraction. . . . Near **CANYON** to the south, **Palo Duro Canyon State Park** is located in the deepest, most rugged part of a 120-mile canyon noted for rock formations and colored walls. In western Texas, the expression "West of the Pecos" used to denote that region beyond the Pecos River which was without law. Law, of course, has now reached the area but the open country is still forbidding at times. Cactus displays grotesque angular shapes against the gray sands, and isolated mountain ranges loom on the horizon which seems devoid of all habitation. At the westernmost tip of Texas, **EL PASO** has grown to be an important center for people who live in or visit the sun-drenched southwest. The city's international flavor is evident everywhere; in the adobe shops, filled with native hand-tooled leather goods and silver jewelry, hand-loomed Mexican rugs and pottery; in the highly spiced Mexican foods and in the ability of local citizens to speak either Spanish or English with ease. A trip across the Rio Grande to the town of **JUAREZ** is a must for visitors who want to get a glimpse of Old Mexico. . . . **Big Bend National Park**, to the southeast, is a great untamed mountain wilderness along the U-shaped bend of the Rio Grande. Driving from **MARATHON** to the park one first catches sight of a haze-shrouded sawtooth mass on the horizon — the Chisos Mountains which rise to over 5,000-foot elevation. The highway leads to a great rocky Basin surrounded by mountains such as the castlelike Casa Grande. There are improved trails from the park headquarters in the Basin to the Window on **Lost Mine Peak**. Or, one can hire horses to ride to the **South Rim** for an awe-inspiring view across the Rio Grande to Mexico. Deer and antelope are frequently seen along the trail. The **Santa Elena Canyon**, **Hot Springs** and **Boquillas** area, outstanding attractions of the park, provide splendid all-day motor trips from the Basin. Accommodations are limited at the lodges in the park so reservation should be made in advance during the busy summer season. Outdoor clothing is recommended and as a precautionary measure motorists should have filled gasoline tanks and food for the longer trips. . . . **BROWNSVILLE** on the lower Rio Grande enjoys a Mexican atmosphere like the other border towns of El Paso and **Laredo**. The annual **Charo Days Festival** held the week before Lent is a gay celebration with the Latin influence predominant. **SAN ANTONIO** is rich in historic sites. Here is the fortress-mission of the **Alamo** where a handful of Texans fell, including Bowie and Crockett, in battle against over 3000 Mexican troops under Santa Anna. The long, low, white Governor's Palace and La Valita, a block of early Spanish homes where native crafts are preserved, are of interest along with the **San Fernando Cathedral**. The landscaped banks of the winding San Antonio River are a pleasant feature of the downtown area. The Spanish missions to the south of the city are elegant symbols of the work of the San Franciscan Missionaries. Here among the cloistered arches, workrooms and walled patios they patiently instructed the Indians in various crafts and religious teachings. **San Jose**, the "queen of the missions," is world-renowned for its beauty of form and sculptural detail. . . . **BANDERA**, 50 miles northwest, is a typical town of the Old West which has become a center for dude ranches where non-Texans can enjoy rural Western life with modern comforts. . . . The larger cities of Texas are always somewhat of a shock to visitors prepared for something more in keeping with a Hollywood "Western." **AUSTIN**, the state capital and seat of the University of Texas, has its own inland water playground in the **Highland Lake** nearby. **FORT WORTH**, to the north, is a big livestock market for Texas. **Trinity Park** with the Will Rogers Memorial Coliseum and other exhibit halls is the site for the Southwestern Exposition and Fat Stock Show each year. Also in the park is a notable **Botanic Garden** with more than 10,000 rose bushes. **DALLAS** . . . . , to the east of Fort Worth, is a streamlined modern city whose wealth comes from cotton and oil. More sophisticated than other cities of the southwest, Dallas has become a style leader. The luxurious store of Nieman-Marcus rivals New York's most fashionable and expensive shops. **Fair Park**, where the Texas State Fair is held, is an attraction with the Hall of State, a museum of Texas history. Dallas also has a fine symphony orchestra. **HOUSTON** . . . . , largest Texas city, is booming with new skyscrapers, lavish stores and such flamboyant establishments as the Shamrock Hotel. The wealth of its citizens has earned the city the title of "millionaires' city." Chief visitor attraction is **San Jacinto Battlefield** fifteen miles east of the city. A 570-foot monument topped by a lone star commemorates the victory which won Texas her independence. An added attraction to the park is the old **battleship Texas** anchored in a slip of the Buffalo Bayou. . . . The city of **GALVESTON** is one of several resort Gulf cities which can offer seashore relaxation, deep-sea fishing and sailing. . . . Regional food specialties of Texas include a variety of Mexican dishes, chili con carne, *pollo villeno* (baked chicken with highly seasoned ground beef), tamales, *tortillas*, *tacos* and enchiladas. A different barbecue-sauce recipe can be had from each area.

The Southeast States

RALEIGH TAVERN, WILLIAMSBURG, VIRGINIA

Virginia State Chamber of Commerce

The Southland has often been pictured in fiction and the popular imagination as a large amorphous region of unreconstructed Southern colonels, cotton plantations and dull countryside. Actually the South is made up of a variety of landscapes, occupations and cultures. Each state is different in many ways. Agriculture, admittedly, is dominant but busy industrial centers have been built to process the enormous reservoir of raw materials. The tobacco fields of Virginia are quite different from the newly-arrived, productive beef-cattle ranches of the Gulf States. The peoples of this land have separate histories; some are of English descent, others of French origins, each one producing a rich and varied culture. For scenic variety there are the coastal beaches, the rolling hills of the eroded Piedmont and the great mass of mountains which make up the Appalachians. There is plenty to see and do in the Southland. Historic sites are not dull ruins torn from the pages of history; the important ones often are places for creative pageants and dramas. The period costumes are not gathering dust in museums but are worn on special days by local townspeople anxious to display their heritage. For sports and recreation there is no end to the list of national and state parks with excellent facilities. Metropolitan centers provide their share of night life, carnivals and luxurious living.

For regional foods the Southland has its own specialties. Fried chicken is served in several ways, each state regarding its own recipes as the best. Hominy grits, black-eyed peas, red beans, baked hams, spoon bread and hot breads are served almost everywhere. Hog jowls and turnip greens are usually found in the mountainous areas while pecan pie and shrimp pie are Gulf State dishes. Hush puppies (flat corn-meal cakes fried in hot fat) is one of Florida's contributions along with baked pompano (often with shrimp stuffing). Sweet potato pie with two crusts originated in Georgia. Kentucky is famous for its bourbon whiskey and mint juleps, while throughout the Southland native corn whiskey is made.

VIRGINIA

Mt. Vernon is familiar to every American and countless foreigners as the beloved plantation home of the first President of the United States. A short drive from the city of Washington brings the visitor to the white columned mansion overlooking the Potomac River. The classic proportion of the 18th-century mansion stands in the midst of a manorlike village with outbuildings, guest houses, gardens and slave quarters. Here Washington lived the life he most enjoyed — that of a prosperous squire. Mt. Vernon is, of course, just one of the many 18th-century tidewater plantations. **Stratford Hall** further down the Potomac was the ancestral home of the Lee family, birthplace of Robert E. Lee. It is easily reached from **FREDERICKSBURG**, historic town which is linked closely with the Washington family. In the vicinity of Fredericksburg are the battlegrounds of four separate important engagements of the War Between the States. . . . To the west loom the beautiful Blue Ridge Mountains. In Shenandoah National Park, **Skyline Drive** winds its airy way along the crest of the ridge for 100 miles. Near the southern terminus of Skyline Drive lies the pleasant town of **CHARLOTTESVILLE**, native home of Thomas Jefferson. The third President was an architect of buildings as well as nations, for in his home of **Monticello** he built an imposing example of his artistic ability. The original buildings of the University of Virginia in Charlottesville were also designed by Jefferson. The serpentine garden walls and the classic Rotunda are notable exhibits. . . . **RICHMOND** on the James river is closely associated with the Civil War since, as the capital of the Confederacy, it was the prime object of the Union attack. The monuments to the leaders and soldiers of the southern cause are numerous. The former Confederate White House is now Richmond's **Confederate Museum**. The State Capitol, patterned after the Maison Carre at Nimes, France, is the work of Jefferson. Richmond has one of of the finest museums of the south in its **Virginia Museum of Fine Arts**. For a side glance of modern Richmond a visit to a tobacco company plant is recommended. . . . East of Richmond on the York Peninsula are three sites of national historic importance. **WILLIAMSBURG**, 18th-century capital of the Virginia colony, was the center of culture and commerce for over 80 years. As early as 1693 the College of William and Mary was chartered. Williamsburg declined after the capital was moved to Richmond in 1779 to become a quiet county seat and college town. An ambitious undertaking, however, has restored Williamsburg to its colonial grandeur. Reconstruction of destroyed structures and restoration of those still standing were carried out with strict adherence to original plans and details wherever possible. The story of this restoration is fascinating in itself. For this story as well as the history of Williamsburg, the official orientation center provides films and literature. In the restored area are the **Governor's Palace**, the dignified **Capitol**, several taverns, craft houses and many fine homes. Authentic atmosphere is attained by dressing the guides in costume and providing meals in the 18th century manner. . . . Nearby **JAMESTOWN** was the site of the first permanent English settlement in America. The ivy-clad brick ruins of the **Old Church** are the sole remnant of Jamestown remaining above ground. The area is part of Colonial National Park. **YORKTOWN**, the third historic site, is east of Williamsburg on the bluffs overlooking York River. Here at Yorktown the American and French armies conducted the final siege which established American Independence. The fortifications, **Yorktown Custom House** and several other historic houses are worth visiting.

Not all of Virginia is history. Virginia seashore resorts contribute their share of entertainment. **VIRGINIA BEACH**, a dozen miles from the busy Navy port of **NORFOLK**, is a popular ocean spot.

NORTH CAROLINA

The Midsouth vacationland spans a variety of landscapes ranging from the coastal dunes to the mountains of the west. **Roanoke Island**, one of the chain of islands that are strung along the coast of North Carolina, is an historic site. It was here that the first English attempt to found a colony in America ended in tragedy and mystery. In 1587, at **Fort Raleigh** a group of 117 colonists under the leadership of John White prepared a settlement following an abortive previous attempt. Virginia Dare, first child of English parentage, was born in the colony that same year. Shortly after White returned to England for supplies. His return was delayed until 1591 and by then the colony had completely disappeared. To this day no explanation can be found as to the fate of those first colonists. The fort and building have been restored as a national monument and in an open-air theater nearby *The Lost Colony* pageant is performed. On the mountainous sand dunes of Kitty Hawk a second, more modern event took place. Here the Wright brothers achieved fame in the first successful flying machine. The **Wright Memorial Monument** commemorates their flight with a pylon of granite. . . . South of these two sites a modern highway leads along the narrow offshore islands to Cape Hatteras, long synonymous with storms and ship hulks. New navigation aids, however, have reduced the danger. This virgin stretch of sand is now preserved as a National Seashore with new improvements making it more accessible yet retaining the distinctiveness of the old shore. . . . Inland, the tobacco lands rise gently to the industrial Piedmont Plateau. At the edge of the Piedmont are the cluster cities of **RALEIGH, DURHAM** and **CHAPEL HILL**. Within twenty-five miles of each other, these towns contain the capitol of the state, at Raleigh, the state's biggest colleges and important manufacturing plants. Duke University, dominated by the University Chapel's high Gothic tower, is located at Durham. The University of North Carolina, at Chapel Hill, has an exceptionally fine campus. The state capital of Raleigh has two places of interest that reflect the modern South. The **State Fair Arena** is an immense modern structure composed of two parabolic arches from which a saddle-shaped roof is suspended. Evidence of the atomic age may be found in the **Nuclear Reactor** on the campus of the State College. The building is open to the public for demonstrations of atomic processes. . . . To the west **WINSTON-SALEM** is the best place for visitors to see tobacco auctioned and cigarettes made by modern machinery. . . . The Southern Appalachian Mountains which stretch across western North Carolina have only recently been made accessible to visitors. This beautiful area of mountain forest has been the homeland of the mountain people who have lived apart for many generations. Their plain and simple life is rich in folklore, music and handicrafts. The mountains are crossed by a **Blue Ridge Parkway**, a splendid drive through hardwood forests and wild flowers, especially colorful in the spring with rhododendron, laurel and azalea blooming along the roadside. In the fall the gold and scarlet of the leaves cover the slopes in a flamelike mantle. **Mt. Mitchell** is just one of the many peaks above 6,000 feet which give an alpine character to the landscape of the Blue Ridge. At **ASHEVILLE** in the midst of mountain gardens is the fabulous **Vanderbilt Palace of Biltmore**. Too big for its inheritors, it is now open to the public. . . . **The Great Smoky Mountains**, the southern end of the Appalachians, receive their name from the smokelike mist which rises from the thick forests. This whole area is largely virgin timberland, forming a green sanctuary of untold splendor. This was the land of the Cherokees, the most intelligent and advanced of all Indian tribes. The descendants of those Cherokees who were able to avoid the forced move to Oklahoma live on the Qualla Reservation; their handicrafts of baskets, rugs and wooden articles are sought by tourists.

SOUTH CAROLINA

South Carolina's biggest attraction is the beautiful harbor city of **CHARLESTON**. Here is the picturesque and romantic South at its best. Historic monuments combine with old mansions and nearby tropical gardens to attract visitors from far and wide. The gardens outside of Charleston are the big attraction in the spring months. **Cypress Gardens** offer paddle-boat tours along waterways arched over with moss-hung trees. **Middleton Gardens** are more formal in their beauty with statuary suggesting the gardens of Versailles. **Magnolia Gardens** with 25 acres of azaleas and camellias are nearby. . . . In Charleston the old houses of the Battery area are attractive with their light pastel colors and graceful ironwork. From anywhere in the Battery section **Fort Sumter** can be seen guarding the harbor as it did in April, 1861, when the first shots of the Civil War were fired. Of the various fine churches in town St. Michaels has achieved extra distinction in that her church bells have crossed the Atlantic five times. **Charleston Museum** contains a fine collection of pre-Civil War antiques and artistic interiors. During the spring festival, tours are arranged for visiting some of the old mansions. Three houses, however, are open all year long: the Manigualt Mansion, the Heywood-Washington House and Pringle or Miles Brewton House.

Rice was once the staple crop of the Carolina coast so it is a traditional dish of the area, to be found combined with sea food or chicken in many pleasant ways. She-crab soup is a dish that is probably limited to the Charleston area.

GEORGIA

This largest state east of the Mississippi River has a variety of landscape. The Blue Ridge and Smoky Mountains extend into the northeast section of the state providing breath-taking vistas, turbulent trout streams, lakes in a pleasant summer vacationland. Further south, **ATLANTA**, in the fabled *Gone With The Wind* country, is an historic city. The **Cyclorama**, one of the largest paintings in the world, records the Battle of Atlanta. . . . On the coast of Georgia near the Carolina boundary is the city of **SAVAN-**

WRIGHT MEMORIAL, KITTY HAWK, NORTH CAROLINA

North Carolina News Bureau

NAH. The town was laid out in a classic pattern by General Oglethorpe in 1733. Some of the old residences reflect the Roman pattern of the streets by their Classical Revival architecture. The **Telfair House** is a good example of this style. It houses the **Telfair Academy of Arts and Sciences**, one of the finest art museums in the South. Savannah resembles Charleston in many ways. Gardens with magnolia trees and flaming azaleas, old mansions and the waterfront areas are often compared with those of Charleston. **Factor's Row** is the interesting waterfront portion of Savannah. . . . From Savannah to Florida the Georgia mainland is separated from the sea by a series of islands called the "Golden Isles." These flat, secluded islands are covered with the trees of the Southland, live oaks, magnolias and cedars, while the waters are warmed by the southern sun. **Tyler Island** is the favorite beach resort of Savannah. Here on the clean white sands are held oyster roasts, a local specialty. The oysters are roasted in a small oven or pit, removed from the shells when done and dipped in a savory sauce before eating. Of the islands further south only **Sea Island** and nearby **St. Simons Island** are open to the public. Both are pleasant resorts for the sand and sun enthusiasts. . . . The **Okefenokee**, a vast swamp covering 660 square miles, extends across southern Georgia into Florida. Most of the primeval swamp is a National Wildlife Refuge. It is accessible from several places, however. Boat trips from **FOLKSTON, FARGO** or **WAYCROSS** penetrate the maze of trees and untamed wilderness. The number and variety of wildlife is endless: bears and alligators of the more exciting species as well as the graceful egret and heron.

FLORIDA

Florida adds a chapter to history that recalls the explorations of Spanish conquistadores, the search for a mythical Fountain of Youth, and the colorful days of the Spanish Main. **ST. AUGUSTINE** played an important part in that history, beginning with the landing there of Ponce de Leon in 1513. The ancient buildings of this oldest city in the United States still preserve a part of Old Spain in their overhanging balconies, grilled windows and walled patios. The **Oldest House** in the United States is St. Augustine's most famous building. It is a two story building of wood and coquina (a local limestone) with low ceilings, hand-hewed beams and large fireplaces reminiscent of the Middle Ages. The **Old Spanish Treasury** is another interesting building with a patio of rare plants along with the rare furnishings of the interiors. The **Cathedral of St. Augustine** is in the style of the Spanish Missions that are usually found in the southwest United States . . . Near St. Augustine on Anastasia Island, the Alligator Farm with some 6,000 specimens is a local curiosity. On the same island can be seen the Coquina Quarries which have furnished the shell rock for St. Augustine's buildings since 1600. . . . Further south are the **Marine Studios of Marineland** an outstanding attraction of the coast. Here one can watch at close range the activities of giant sharks, porpoises, sawfish and other marine life. The high spot of a visit is at feeding time when the porpoises perform for their meals. . . . In central Florida **ORLANDO** has become a winter resort in addition to being a fine residential city. Stately live oaks and palms grace the parks and boulevards and subtropical plants blossom in lush gardens. **Cypress Gardens** near **WINTER HAVEN** have become the show place of the many gardens of Florida, receiving national attention with movie and magazine acclaiming her beautiful gardens. The still waters of the lagoon reflect the beauty of the azaleas, camellias and gardenias. Water-ski shows have been added to the natural scenery as an additional attraction. . . . A few miles to the south near **LAKE WALES** is **Bok Tower**, an imposing structure housing one of the finest carillons in the world. The tower itself is a thing of beauty. Built of steel and faced with coquina rock from Florida's coast and Georgia marble, it rises 230 feet above Mountain Lake Sanctuary. . . . The fabulous "Gold Coast" of Florida is an example of man's improving nature. The excellent climate, white sandy beaches and warm waters of the Gulf Stream were gifts of nature, but enterprising men have added the royal palm trees, gardens, lavish homes and hotels. **PALM BEACH** is the fashionable resort center of the coast. Here are the lavish estates of the wealthy, luxurious hotels, exotic shops and art studios. The Royal Palm Way with its double row of stately palms is impressive. Further south Greater **MIAMI** is a newer resort center, attracting the big names of the entertainment and business worlds. **MIAMI BEACH** is unique with hundreds of waterfront hotels, each with its own beach,

ROOKERY, EVERGLADES NATIONAL PARK

Florida State Advertising Comm

BEACH NEAR JACKSONVILLE

Bodden Fotos

swimming pool, cabanas and sun deck. For those who have had enough sunbathing there are sightseeing boats which cruise among the islands and lush estates of **Biscayne Bay.** Fishing boats are available for the more active vacationers. Night-club life is gay and lively with big-time entertainers. **In Hialeah Park,** the race track is well-known for its beauty as well as the impressive bets placed there.... South of the lively resort center of Miami, highway US 1 leads to the Florida Keys. The highway connects a chain of islands that stretches out into the Gulf of Mexico for 100 miles. **KEY WEST** at the end of the chain is a picturesque "Caribbean" city that once prospered on ill-fated ships that grounded on the outlying reefs.... Also in southern Florida is **Everglades National Park,** a vast wilderness of swamp and hammocks filled with all sorts of wildlife, including alligators, bears, giant turtles, heron and egrets. Trails such as **Anhinga** and **Gumbo Limbo** lead into the wilderness for a short distance so that visitors may observe the wildlife at close range.... The west coast of Florida has its share of vacationlands. Attractive **SARASOTA** is the winter quarters for the Ringling Brothers, Barnum and Bailey Circus. The price of admission will allow a visitor to wander around the grounds where the acts for the spring tour are being rehearsed. The Ringling Museum of Art, established by John Ringling, contains one of the world's best collections of baroque paintings; it includes works by Titian and Tintoretto, Raphael and Rembrandt and many others. The Ringling Residence overlooking Sarasota Bay is a magnificent mansion set in well-kept grounds. As a reminder of the source of the wealth that enabled Ringling to collect works of art there is the Circus Museum. Here are displayed the retired parade wagons in all their splendor, along with other interesting circusiana, including scale models, old lithographs and posters.... At **TARPON SPRINGS** may be seen a demonstration of sponge fishing. The celebration marking the return of the sponge fleet at Eastertime is a colorful affair to witness. Music and a festive crowd of friends and relatives line the docks to greet the brightly painted boats as they arrive.

ALABAMA

This state is not without its own seasonal celebrations. Mardi Gras time in **MOBILE** is a big event with parade floats, masked balls and generally a good time for all. This carnival originated in Mobile and not in New Orleans as one might believe. The city itself has lots of fine old homes with French and Spanish touch still remaining in the lacelike ironwork. For flowers, the Azalea Trail starting at Bienville Square has few equals, with 17 miles of streets blazing with flowers and numerous gardens along the route opened to the public. To the south of Mobile, the Bellingrath Gardens are another top flower attraction covering some 800 acres.... The mansions of Alabama are of course interesting. The coastal region is notable for the wrought-iron work of the Gulf style while the fine homes found in the interior are usually Greek Revival style. **Magnolia Grove** in **GREENSBORO** is a fine example of one of the ancestral homes done in this style.... For a glimpse at the new Southland a visit to **BIRMINGHAM,** "the Pittsburgh of the South," should dispel any preconceived opinion of the South as being purely agricultural.

MISSISSIPPI

On Mississippi's Gulf Coast, the present shore road that follows what used to be the **Spanish Trail** is now a pleasant marine drive through resort towns and colorful ports with shrimp-boat fleets.... The names of the Gulf cities of **BILOXI** and **PASCAGOULA** are taken from the Indian tribes that once made their homes there. The beaches seem endless; white sands glisten against a background of flowers and moss-draped oaks. The calm waters between the shore and the low islands are popular fishing grounds; the migratory fish pour through the channel passes in consecutive waves. Near Biloxi, **Beauvoir,** the home of Jefferson Davis, has been restored to its former condition. **PASS CHRISTIAN** is one of the more beautiful of the Gulf resort towns with many stately homes fronted by classic white pillars.... **NATCHEZ** on the Mississippi River was perhaps the first to display her ante-bellum homes to visitors as an annual event. Today the **Natchez Pilgrimage** is almost a national institution. In March the show places of the South, **Rosalie, Dunleith** and **Stanton Hall** among many others, are opened to the public. These mansions are furnished and decorated with a lavishness unmatched in the South. Carrara marble mantles, enormous mirrors from France, giant ballrooms paneled in rich woods, along with many other fine treasures, make a tour of the homes an impressive event.

Period costumes and a Confederate Ball help to awaken a feeling of Natchez's heritage. . . . North of Natchez the city of VICKSBURG rests on the high bluffs above the river. In the Civil War this important river town was put under concentrated attack by Union Armies under General Grant. The long seige and final surrender are remembered in the Vicksburg National Military Park, well marked to present a clear picture of the struggle for the city. The U. S. Waterways Experiment Station, also in Vicksburg, contains a model of the Mississippi River System used for research in problems of drainage and flood control.

TENNESSEE

The Mississippi River country is quite different from the mountain country of eastern Tennessee. At MEMPHIS King Cotton rules in the world's largest cotton market. The Memphis Cotton Carnival held in May is an annual affair. At NASHVILLE, the State Capitol of Greek architecture stands on a hill which commands a splendid view of the city and surrounding country. Fort Nashborough, the frontier post which grew into the city of Nashville, has been authentically reconstructed. In Centennial Park there is a full-sized replica of the Parthenon of Athens. . . . A few miles northeast of Nashville is Andrew Jackson's home, the Hermitage. Jackson built the present mansion while President; the furnishings remain as they were in the days of "Old Hickory." The general and his wife are buried here. . . . Norris Dam, near KNOXVILLE, has become a tourist attraction, both for the impressive structure and for the large resort lake created by the dam. Nearby OAK RIDGE is a new city whose significance in the atomic age is known everywhere. The Museum has exhibits explaining atomic energy.

KENTUCKY

Of the many wonders of the world, Mammoth Cave has continued to attract visitors consistently. The caves contain miles of passageways at different levels with underground waterways, falls and a lake. The lowest level, Echo River is an interesting world of strange inhabitants, blind fish and transparent crayfish. The rock formations, of course, have been given fancy names but nevertheless are impressive; the so-called Frozen Niagara is noteworthy. . . . Lincoln's Birthplace Memorial stands near HODGENVILLE. A stone monument encloses a simple cabin that is said to be the birthplace of Lincoln. . . . The Bluegrass Country of Kentucky around LEXINGTON is the land of the world's finest thoroughbred race horses. Here may be found the famous stud farms with their velvety pastures, well-kept barns and, of course, horses — the young playful foals, mares and handsome stallions. The great annual event of racing circles is the Derby at LOUISVILLE'S Churchill Downs. People from all over the world attend this classic of horse racing. . . . In eastern Kentucky the Cumberland Gap forms the historic gateway to the West, through the forested Cumberland Mountains. A toll road climbs Pinnacle Mountain for a breath-taking view.

WEST VIRGINIA

The mountain state of the East. The scenic Allegheny Highland covers a million and half acres of park, forests and vacation retreats. On the western boundary formed by the Ohio River is HUNTINGTON, the state's largest city, noted for its parks, churches and residential district. . . . At CHARLESTON, to the east, the gold-domed Capitol Building is an impressive sight. . . . Southeast of the capital a new turnpike provides an unparalleled scenic drive through West Virginia's rugged mountains. At the terminus of the route is WHITE SULPHUR SPRINGS with the fabulous hostelry of Greenbrier. This has been a popular resort since antebellum days and still retains many of the customs and traditions of the Old South. . . . Northeast from White Sulphur Springs to Maryland stretches the Monongahela National Forest, an uncrowded recreation area of clear mountain streams and forest-clad mountains. ELKINS, the forest headquarters city, presents an annual pageant, the Forest Festival. Smoke Hole Caverns, limestone caves found near PETERSBURG, and Seneca Rock near MOUTH OF SENECA are two popular attractions. Seneca Rock consists of glistening white sandstone which rises spectacularly in towers over 1,000 feet high. . . . CHARLES TOWN, in the eastern panhandle, was founded by Charles Washington, a brother of the nation's first President. It is a charming city with many fine old homes built and lived in by close relatives of Washington. The most famous of those that have been restored is Harewood. East of Charles Town lies historic HARPERS FERRY where in 1859 Abolitionist John Brown made his daring raid on the Federal Arsenal. The enginehouse which served Brown as a fort is now a museum.

Middle Atlantic States

The Middle Atlantic States offer travelers the unique combination of great urban areas of unlimited cultural and entertainment facilities, along with wide expanses of rural and often completely wild country. The beaches lining the great coastal plain and the lakes and streams of the Appalachian upland offer countless resorts for outdoor recreation; many of these vacationlands are only a short distance away from the metropolitan areas. The large cities of the East, like New York, Philadelphia and Washington entertain a year-round stream of guests. Historic landmarks abound in this area particularly those shrines dating from Colonial and Revolutionary times. An airline flight across the Middle Atlantic States traverses in minutes the same terrain that weary Continental and Civil War soldiers marched, fought and died over. The ribbons of rivers seen from the plane were the early highways that opened up the interior westward beyond the Appalachians.

NEW YORK

NEW YORK has been called capital of the world for just about everything, finance, shipping, culture and now with the United Nations located here, it has the added distinction of being the world's political capital. The staggering statistics on New York's 8,000,000 people, hundreds

THE PARTHENON IN CENTENNNIAL PARK, NASHVILLE, TENN.

Tenn Conservation Dept

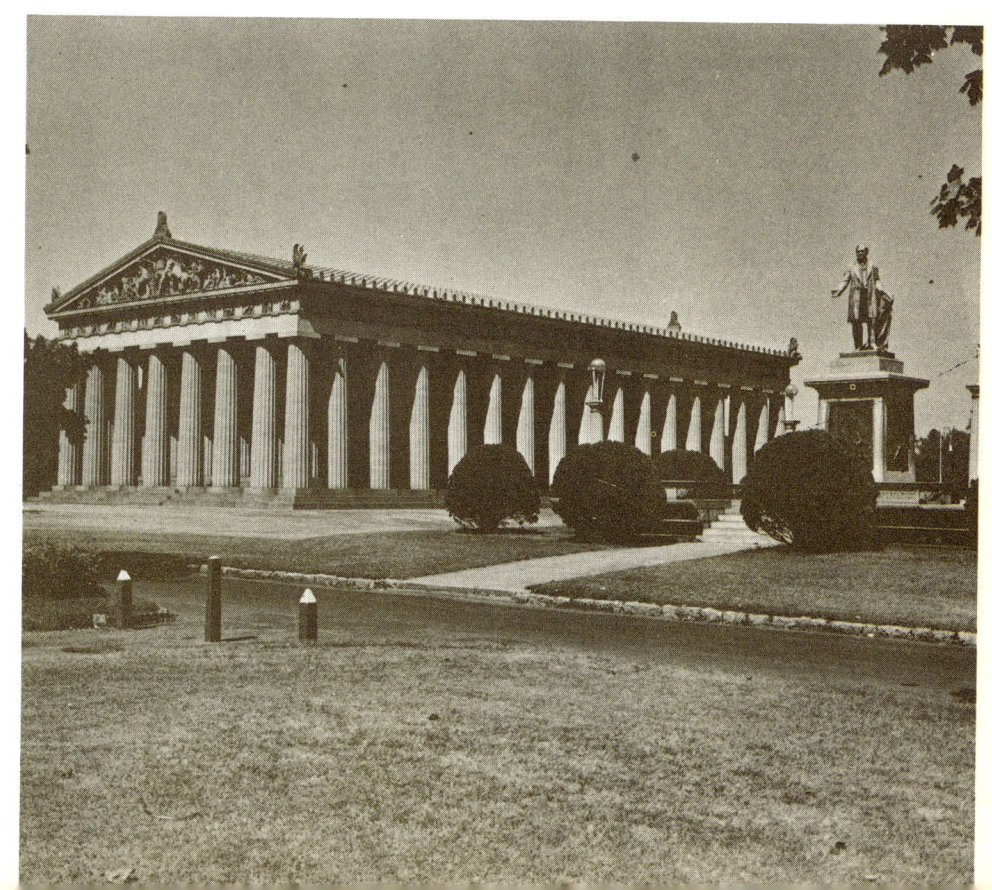

of miles of streets and utility arteries, schools, churches, etc., are apt to overwhelm the visitor. Accepting the fact that New York is big, the best over-all picture of the city can be obtained by either a steamer tour around the island or by a trip to the observation tower of the Empire State Building.... New York has not, of course, always been a giant of a city. It had its humble beginnings as a small Dutch settlement at the southern tip of Manhattan. The site of that settlement is now overgrown with the towers of the financial district. **Wall Street** takes its name from the protective wall built by the Dutch. **Battery Park,** on the very tip of the island, is a good place to begin a tour of the city. It offers a fine view of the busy harbor and contains one of the city's oldest landmarks, **Castle Clinton,** once a fort, later an exhibition hall where Jenny Lind made her American debut. From the Battery ferry boats leave hourly for the **Statue of Liberty** on Bedloe's Island. The monumental figure has been a symbol of freedom for two generations. The giant ferries that shuttle to **Staten Island** from the Battery provide an inexpensive and pleasant way to view the city sky line and harbor.... North of Battery Park, in the canyons of the financial district, is the famous **Trinity Church.** The present church was built in 1846 but the parish itself is New York's oldest (founded in 1697). The churchyard, which is real estate worth about $500 a square foot, has some of the city's oldest graves, Alexander Hamilton's and Robert Fulton's among the more famous.... For a brief look at the activities of the nearby investment houses a visit to the galleries of the **New York Stock Exchange** on Broad Street is recommended. Also in the downtown area are: the **Federal Hall Memorial,** site of Washington's inaugural; **Fraunces Tavern,** an authentic colonial building; and **Chase Manhattan Bank,** where money of all ages is on display.... North on Broadway at City Hall Park are found **St. Pauls Chapel,** the oldest church in the city, and **City Hall,** considered an architectural masterpiece by many.... East of City Hall Park is New York's oldest and most famous big river span, **Brooklyn Bridge.** The twenty-year history of the construction and the interesting tales that are connected with the bridge form a saga by itself. North of the bridge is the **Lower East Side** with many nations represented in its crowded tenements. The area is changing, however, as the various districts lose their distinctive national characteristics with American-born generations growing up and housing developments replacing the more dilapidated sections. **Chinatown** is still a big sightseers attraction but actually there is little to see there. An authentic Chinese dinner, however, may be had at one of the recommended restaurants, making a trip worth while. **Greenwich Village,** about a mile north of City Hall, was once a residential suburb, later a literary and art center. It is now a place to live for many professional and career workers, students, would-be artists and hangers-on. It has some attractive old houses both quaint and handsome, some notable restaurants and night clubs and an outdoor art show that attracts wide interest. Heart of the area is **Washington Square** with a few remaining old buildings on the north side. New York University has its downtown campus here. **Little Italy** to the south of the square is also in a period of change with whole blocks marked for razing to make way for new building plans.... For shoppers, real or window variety, 34th Street and Fifth Avenue offer the biggest department stores and the swankiest shops. **Empire State Building** at the intersection of 34th Street and Fifth Avenue, already the world's highest structure, has been boosted to even greater heights with the addition of a television tower. The top is now 1,472 feet above the street. On Fifth Avenue at 42nd Street behind protective lions is the **New York Public Library.** Besides housing one of the greatest book collections the library offers concerts, lectures and exhibits.... The newest attraction in New York is the **United Nations Headquarters.** The striking modern buildings are set in a handsome landscaped plaza along the East River from 42nd to 48th Streets. The Secretariat building, a majestic slab of marble and glass, towers above the curved walls and low dome of the General Assembly building. The interiors of the buildings are as bold and interesting as the exteriors. The visitors' main entrance is through the General Assembly building where trained guides are available for special tours. The UN Bookshop has on sale various handicraft items from member nations that make fine souvenirs.... Due west on 42nd Street is **Times Square,** entertainment center of New York, with motion-picture houses, theaters, restaurants and hotels. Bright and gaudy and somewhat cheapened by shooting galleries and souvenir stands the area is impressive at night when the giant signs and trick displays compete with each other in a blaze of neon pyrotechnics. On the side streets are the "legitimate theaters," as they are known in New York. Here are staged the musical and dramatic shows. Best guide to

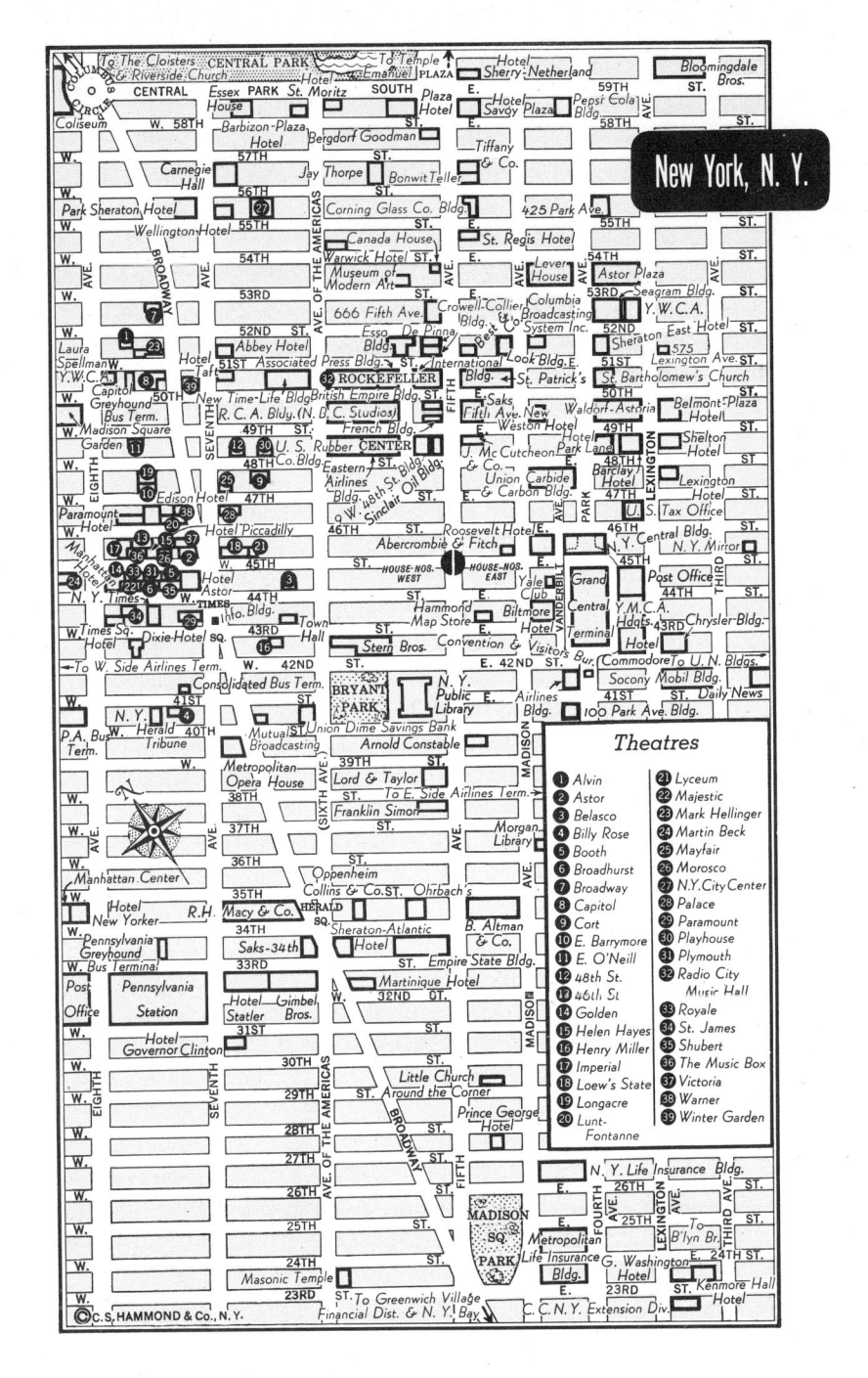

UNITED STATES

1. Jefferson Memorial, Washington, D. C.
2. Dunleith, Natchez, Miss.
3. Oldest House in the U. S., St. Augustine, Fla.
4. Bok Tower, Lake Wales, Fla.
5. State Capitol, Madison, Wis.

UNITED STATES

1. Ringling Museum of Art, Sarasota, Fla.
2. Independence Hall, Philadelphia, Pa.
3. Old Cathedral, St. Louis, Mo.
4. Lincoln's House, Springfield, Ill.

UNITED STATES

1. Mississippi River Boat, modern style, U.S.A.
2. Chief Massasoit's statue near Plymouth Rock, Plymouth, Mass., U.S.A.
3. Cable cars, San Francisco, California, U.S.A.
4. Lakefront Drive, Chicago, Ill., U.S.A.

UNITED STATES

1. Big Bend National Park is a remote, untamed wilderness
2. A typical hot pool—Yellowstone National Park
3. A "20-mule team" recalls prospecting days of the last century—Death Valley National Park
4. The spectacular Blue Ridge Parkway—Great Smoky Mountains National Park

any of the entertainment features of New York is a daily newspaper, *Cue* magazine or *New Yorker* magazine. Rockefeller Center fills the area between 48th and 51st Streets, Fifth and Sixth Avenues with the world's biggest and most striking group of business buildings. It houses offices for more than a thousand firms, a major radio and television network and one of the largest and most elaborate theaters, **Radio City Music Hall**. A walk through the floral displays on the Promenade leads to the outdoor skating rink on the Lower Plaza. Guided tours of the buildings and NBC studios are well worth while. Opposite Rockefeller Center on Fifth Avenue is St. Patricks Cathedral, seat of the Roman Catholic Archdiocese of New York. The graceful towers of the French Gothic church are patterned after the spires of Cologne Cathedral. For museums New York probably has no equal, there being museums for just about every interest. The more famous are: the **Museum of Natural History** on Central Park West, which includes the Hayden Planetarium; **Metropolitan Museum of Art** across the Park, one of the great art galleries of the world, and **Museum of Modern Art** on West 53rd Street off Fifth Avenue. **Central Park** is a resort in itself with a small zoo, lakes, skating rink, a carousel and some fine landscaped areas. . . . In northern Manhattan on the west side at Morningside Heights are found a group of buildings and institutions which are famous. They include Columbia University, Cathedral of St. John the Divine, Riverside Church and Grant's Tomb. Spanning the Hudson at 178th Street is the **George Washington Bridge**, second to the San Francisco Golden Gate Bridge in size. The impressive structure carries 25 million vehicles a year in eight lanes. **The Cloisters** in Fort Tryon Park to the north is one of New York's most unusual exhibits. It is a museum set on a wooded knoll above the river. The building incorporates within a modern structure parts of several medieval monasteries. The prize collection of medieval art and relics together with the superb setting overlooking the Hudson make the Cloisters a must for visitors. . . . **Coney Island**, at the southwestern tip of Long Island, about fifteen miles from Manhattan and easily reached by subway, is the city's popular ocean beach as well as a huge amusement park with every facility for beguilement and fun. On a hot Sunday afternoon the Coney Island Beach will draw a million or more visitors, which, while making the beach difficult for bathing, is a sight worth seeing in itself. **Bronx Zoo** also on the outskirts of the city can be reached by subway. The collection of animals is the world's largest with almost every known one represented. As many as possible are shown in their natural habitat.

New York offers unlimited events in the sports world with three major league baseball teams, a professional football team and numerous top-flight college athletic teams. Whatever sport one wishes, be it boxing, soccer, basketball, boccie or cricket, New York probably has it.

No city in the world has more good restaurants of varied type than New York. For international cuisine there is a long list of foreign restaurants in the Classified Telephone Directory. New York has few local specialties but many international dishes have become standard menu items in restaurants. Sea foods are popular and plentiful, for New York serves as a distribution point for the East.

LONG ISLAND is the maritime province of New York State, reaching 125 miles into the Atlantic. At the western end are the populated boroughs of Queens and Brooklyn. Further out on the island the congestion diminishes gradually, becoming suburban and eventually rural in eastern Suffolk County. The Atlantic side of the island is a series of long sandy beaches ideal for salt-water bathing. Atlantic Beach, Long Beach, Jones Beach, Fire Island, the Hamptons and Montauk are noted for their bathing facilities. **Jones Beach** has added to its fine facilities a huge Marine Theater for lavish spectaculars and water shows. Long Island Sound is a large yachting center. Pleasure craft and fishing boats sail from the many fine harbors. Salt water fishermen, whether they be the big-game variety, surf casters or patrons of the party boats, find plenty of opportunities to try their skill.

SAG HARBOR, once a whaling center, has an interesting whaling museum and one of the most beautiful churches in America, **Old Whalers Church**. Long Island has more 18th century windmills standing than any other section of the country. The **Hook Mill** at EASTHAMPTON is still able to grind flour with its old wooden machinery. . . . The island is famous for its sea food and also its farm products; Long Island ducklings are a specialty.

One of the great rivers of the world, the **Hudson** has been well-known to generations of travelers for the beauty of its scenery. This mighty river begins at a small lake in the Adirondacks and flows south, gathering strength and momentum to carve its way through the mountains. The southern terminus is below the rampartlike **Palisades**, beyond lower New York Bay, for it continues ninety miles on into the Atlantic as a great underwater canyon. Ever since white man came to these shores, the river has played an important role in the lives of the settlers. Dutch names of river towns recall the days when the Hudson was part of the Holland Empire. During the Revolution the defense of the Hudson Valley became a vital necessity if the new nation was to survive. The mansions and castles that line the valley are landmarks of more peaceful times. . . . At TARRYTOWN is Washington Irving's home Sunnyside, a curious mansion with crow-step gables and ornate cupolas giving a gingerbread appearance. NORTH TARRYTOWN has Philipse Castle, a restored 17th-century manor house, with heirloom furnishings and work buildings. . . . **Bear Mountain State Park** on the west side of the Hudson is a popular recreation area that can be reached by pleasant excursion steamer from New York. Further north the **Storm King Highway**, one of the most spectacular highways, follows the highlands above the river, the road in places perching on a narrow ledge cut in the mountains. **West Point** on the plateau overlooking the river is a colorful setting for the U.S. Military Academy, training ground for future generals. A visit to the Point on a Saturday in the fall is a memorable occasion with a stirring full-dress parade of the corps of cadets prior to an Army football game at Michie Stadium. . . . NEWBURGH and BEACON, across the river from each other are two historic sites. Washington had his headquarters at **Hasbrouck House** in Newburgh. Beacon on the east shore was named for the signal fires that warned Revolutionary troops of the movements of the British. An **inclined railway** climbs the steep slopes of **Mt. Beacon**. To the north is POUGHKEEPSIE, formerly the site of a classic in boat racing. Vassar College on the east side of the city is one of the foremost women's colleges of the country. . . . HYDE PARK, north of Poughkeepsie, was the ancestral home of President Franklin D. Roosevelt. The President's grave in the rose garden, the home and a special

NEW YORK CITY SKYLINE

TWA—Trans World Airline

library housing the many papers, books and other interesting belongings of the President are maintained as a national historic site. Nearby is the **Vanderbilt Mansion,** an impressive 19th-century estate now open to the public.

West of the Hudson beyond KINGSTON are the haze-shrouded **Catskill Mountains,** a rural vacationland for metropolitans. The popularity of this region has created hundreds of lavish hotels featuring entertainment from metropolitan theaters and night clubs. WOODSTOCK is noted for its art colony and summer theater. Throughout this land of legend are many old stone houses antedating the Revolution. Noteworthy are those at HURLEY and NEW PALTZ. . . . ALBANY, capital of the Empire State, was originally a Dutch trading post. Colonial buildings such as the **Schuyler Mansion** in Albany and **Fort Crailo** in RENSSELAER provide a glimpse of the nostalgic past of this region. Three prominent buildings in the Capitol Hill area of Albany are the chateaulike **State House,** the **State Education Building** and the **Alfred E. Smith State Office Building.** . . . West of Albany, near COBLESKILL, **Howe Caverns,** the caves of the northeast, give visitors an opportunity to sightsee underground. Nearby COOPERSTOWN is a village of museums. The **State Historical Association** is located here along with **Baseball's Hall of Fame,** commemorating the birthplace of America's national sport. A third attraction is the **Farmers Museum** with early agricultural tools and gadgets and a complete re-created rural town. . . . North of Albany the **Saratoga-Lake George region,** now a quiet scenic area, was the wilderness background for the bloody campaigns of upper New York State. The **Battleground of Saratoga,** now a National Historic Park, was the scene of the defeat of Burgoyne's British Army, a turning point in the Revolution. SARATOGA SPRINGS is famed for its mineral waters, its horse racing and its old hotels. On elm-shaded Union Avenue the outdated hotels with endless verandas recall the spacious grandeur of the post-Civil War period when Saratoga was the social and sporting center of the North.

The **Adirondack Mountains,** New York's rugged mountain area, is famous for its beautiful wild scenery — its clear lakes, tumbling streams and waterfalls, its trails and purple-tinted peaks. On the eastern fringe of this wilderness is **Lake Champlain** and **Lake George.** Between the two lakes lies the reconstructed **Fort Ticonderoga,** important during the French and Indians Wars and the Revolution. Near Lake Champlain is **Ausable Chasm,** an impressive gorge which may be viewed from the galleries cut in the rock walls or from boats sent through the "flume." For a thrilling view of the Adirondack area the peak of **Mt. Whiteface** can be reached by automobile from WILMINGTON. Lake Placid is just one of the many lake resorts. It has become prominent as a winter resort center, often is called the St. Moritz of America. . . . The Thousand Islands and St. Lawrence still retain the irresistible beauty that thrilled French explorers a few hundred years ago. Les Mille Isles, more than 1,700 gems set in azure-hued expanse of the St. Lawrence

NIAGARA FALLS

NYSPIX-Commerce

River, attract travelers from all parts of the world. Some of the islands are just points of rock; others are large enough for whole villages. Tour boats ply among the unspoiled islands and visit places like **Boldt Castle** in Alexandria Bay, a landmark from the time when island residents were limited to millionaires. The view from **International Bridge** is outstanding.

South of Lake Ontario are located the **Finger Lakes** of New York State. On the gentle slopes of the low-lying hills are grown the grapes for New York State wines. Every September the quiet countryside at **Lower Seneca Lake** is broken by the roar of sports-car motors in the Grand Prix of America, WATKINS GLEN sports-car race. . . . Niagara Falls, mighty cataract between Lakes Erie and Ontario, have been equalled and surpassed in height by many falls but none has ever matched the majesty of the thundering waters of Niagara. The constant roar of the falling water, the clouds of mist rising upward, the frantic fury of the **Whirlpool Rapids** make an awesome spectacle. From **Goat Island** elevators take visitors down to the **Cave of the Winds** at the base of the falls. The boat trip on the "**Maid of the Mist**" is another way to get a close view of the falls.

NEW JERSEY

Almost legendary is the fascination of the **New Jersey shore.** The 125-mile-long shore from Sandy Hook to Cape May is an inviting stretch of white, surf-washed sand. Surf bathing is the seashore number one activity but promenading and enjoying the attractions of the boardwalk is a close second. Amusement parks, big movie houses and steel piers featuring name bands and variety acts compete for the patronage of the vacationists. . . . The centers of this resort life are LONG BRANCH and ASBURY PARK in the north, ATLANTIC CITY further south and WILDWOOD on Cape May. ATLANTIC CITY is a big convention city; the Miss America contest held here is an annual September pageant. CAPE MAY on the south has a somewhat quieter atmosphere reminiscent of New England. At Cape May, on the undeveloped stretches of shore line, the sea-bird colonies of terns, heron and sandpipers have laid claim to the wind-swept beaches and dunes. Salt-water fishing is a big attraction along the whole coast. . . . New Jersey's important part in the Revolutionary War is marked by a number of historic sites. At MORRISTOWN Washington and his ragged army spent two winters. The stately **Ford Mansion** served as Washington's headquarters. Three miles from Morristown at **Jockey Hollow** the main army was encamped. Of interest here are the reconstructed barracks and hospital.

Southwest of the industrial lowland of New Jersey is the beautiful university town of PRINCETON. Points of interest are the **Princeton Battlefield,** old **Nassau Hall,** famed in song and story, and **Nassau Inn** which was originally built in 1756 and has been serving Princeton men for 200 years. At TRENTON 12 miles away Washington surprised Hessian troops after crossing the Delaware during a bitter snowstorm. The **Old Barracks** in Trenton which housed Hessian soldiers is one of the finest specimens of colonial barracks.

PENNSYLVANIA

PHILADELPHIA . . . . . , the birthplace of the nation, is an industrial giant that William Penn would never recognize as the "greene countrie towne" he laid out in 1681. Besides being one of the great ports of the world, the City of Brotherly Love has grown to become a center of insurance and banking. Curtis Publishing Company, one of the oldest publishing enterprises (Benjamin Franklin started it in 1730) has grown to be one of the largest in the magazine field. . . . Within the bustling modern metropolis is the old city of Penn and Franklin — the city where a new nation was founded. On **Independence Square** is the classic Georgian building **Independence Hall**, scene of the signing of the Declaration of Independence. In the same building eleven years later the Constitution was written. In the main corridor of Independence Hall stands the **Liberty Bell**, symbol of freedom for the new nation. A block from Independence Square stands **Carpenter Hall**, the meeting place for the first Continental Congress. Other historic buildings nearby are **Christ Church**, where leaders of the Revolution worshiped, and charming **Betsy Ross House** where, according to tradition, the Stars and Stripes were born. In the new city of Philadelphia the broad tree-shaded Benjamin Franklin Parkway leads from City Hall northwest to the **Philadelphia Museum of Art** containing a priceless collection. Behind the museum is Fairmount Park with a zoo, old mansions and some 3,500 acres of park. . . . The **University of Pennsylvania**, west of the Schuylkill, has a large campus with some notable buildings. The archaeological collection at the university is probably the world's best. . . . At Logan Circle on Benjamin Franklin Parkway there is a group of cultural buildings that includes the **Franklin Memorial Institute** and the **Free Library**. West of Philadelphia, beyond the "Main Line" residential area, lies one of America's great historic shrines, **Valley Forge**. A large state park encloses the breastworks and reconstructed huts where the ragged Continental Army encamped during the winters of 1777-8. The rural stone house where Washington conferred with his generals Lafayette, Pulaski and von Steuben has been preserved intact.

In rural eastern Pennsylvania lies the **Pennsylvania German** country. Often called Pennsylvania Dutch, these hardworking people who tend the rich lands around **ALLENTOWN, READING** and **LANCASTER** are widely known for their picturesque speech, well-kept farms with immense red barns painted with decorative hex symbols, their devotion to religion and avoidance of the evils of modern living. The Amish have come to typify the various religious groups of the Pennsylvania Dutch with their traditional garb of black. Others in the plain sects are the Mennonites, the Moravians and Dunkards. Traditional foods of the Pennsylvania Dutch make a long list of dishes as easy to eat as they are hard to pronounce. To name a few there are schnitz-und-knepp (dried apples, smoked ham, dumplings), lebkuchen, Schwenkfelden bread, Mennonite toast fried in deep fat, seven sweets and seven sours, and shoo-fly pie. . . . In northeast Pennsylvania are the **Poconos**, a resort country of hills, lakes and generally lots of outdoors. **Mt. Pocono** is the center of an increasingly popular ski region. Near **STROUDSBURG** the Delaware River cuts through the Kittatinny range to form the impressive **Delaware Water Gap**. . . . In central Pennsylvania are a series of parallel mountains that form a part of the great Appalachian chain. The great mountain-making forces produced Pennsylvania's great coal deposits. The anthracite fields around **WILKES-BARRE** while not exactly a tourist area are interesting to see especially if a tour is made of one of the huge colleries where the coal is processed. . . . The state capital of **HARRISBURG** is on the Susquehanna River in central Pennsylvania. The large impressive capitol building enjoys a prominent site overlooking the river. South of Harrisburg in the attractive farmland country of southern Pennsylvania is **GETTYSBURG**. Outside the limits of this crossroads town two great armies, Union and Confederate, clashed in a battle that was to continue for three bloody days. At the close of this terrible struggle with tremendous losses on both sides the Confederate Army withdrew, ending the invasion of the North and the hopes of victory for the South. The battlefield is now a National Military Park. . . . **PITTSBURGH** . . . . is Pennsylvania's second greatest city. The valleys of the bituminous coal region have become the world's greatest iron and steel center. The city is located at the triangle of land where two rivers join to form the mighty Ohio River. At the apex of this triangle Fort Pitt was located.. The **Blockhouse**, part of the original frontier fort, remains standing in the new Point Park development, a part of Pittsburgh's ambitious building program. Several modern buildings of the great face-lifting project have already been completed. Greater Pittsburgh Airport, included in the scheme, was created by slicing off the top of a mountain. The **Oakland Civic Center**, east of the triangle, contains a remarkable assortment of scientific and cultural buildings. Here is the University of Pittsburgh's **Cathedral of Learning**, a skyscraper college; Mellon and Carnegie Institutes and the **Stephen Foster Memorial**.

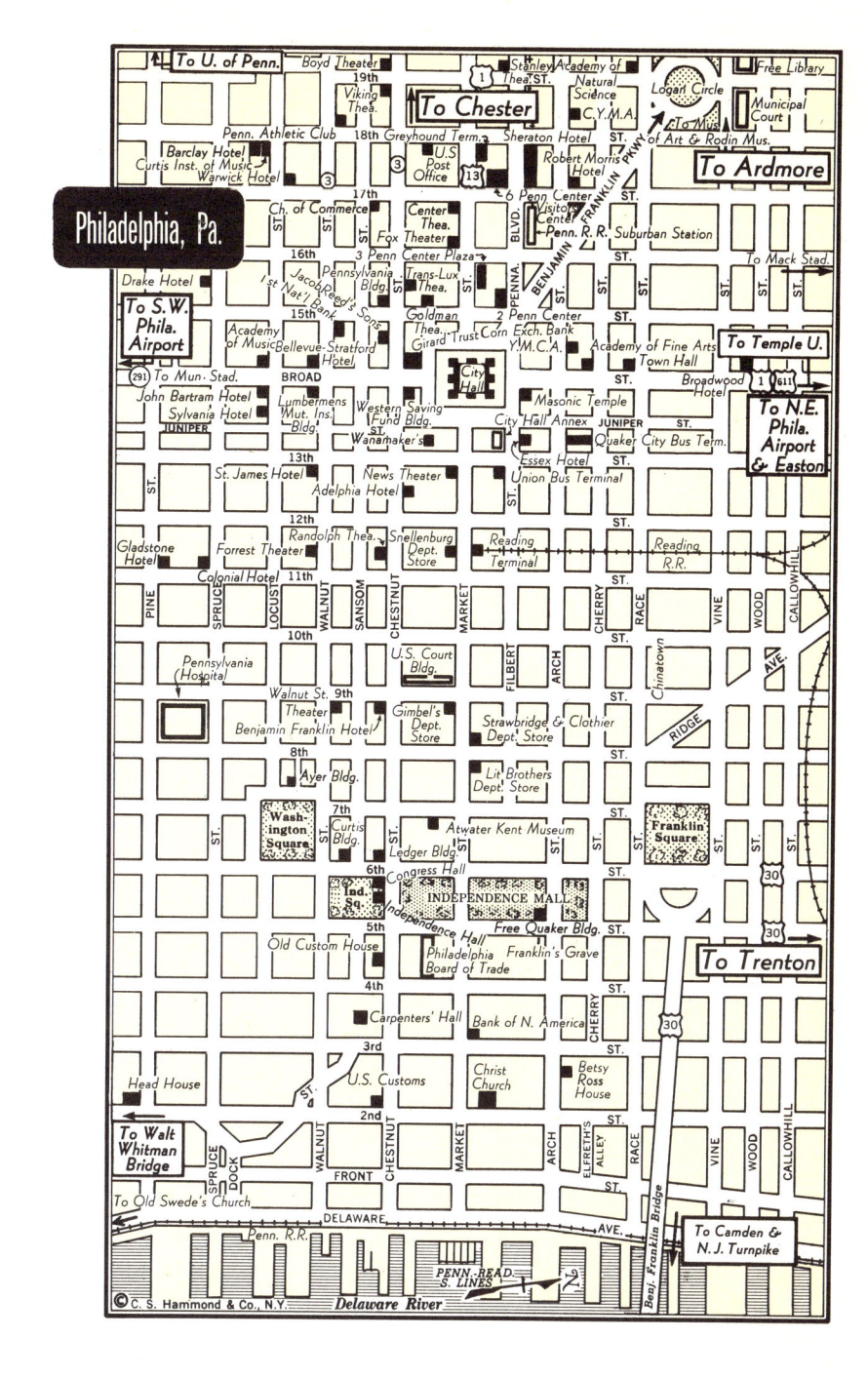

DELAWARE

Although Delaware is the second smallest state of the Union, there is much to see and do in this old colonial state. The beaches of **Rehoboth** and Bethany are well-known to vacationists from neighboring cities of Philadelphia, Washington and Baltimore. The warm waters of the coast and inland bays are not the only attraction, however. The early settlements which passed through successive Swedish, Dutch and English rule have preserved many pre-Revolutionary homes and administrative buildings. The Dutch settled at LEWES many years before the landing of the Pilgrims at Plymouth. The Zwaanendael Museum replica of the Dutch town hall at Hoorn, Holland, commemorates that first settlement. NEW CASTLE, state capital until 1777, has some excellent examples of Georgian architecture including Read House. At DOVER, Delaware State House is the nation's second oldest capitol building still in use. Both Dover and New Castle have birthday celebrations when historic old homes are open to public view. ... The industrial city of WILMINGTON, home of the DuPont firm, holds a colorful religious festival, the "Big Quarterly," on the last Sunday in August; feasting and religious service continuing for the greater part of the day.

MARYLAND

Maryland is divided by the broad waters of Chesapeake Bay to form two separate and distinct regions. Western Maryland is characterized by the mountains of the Appalachians. The southern boundary is marked by the Potomac River which winds its way through the hills, past HARPERS FERRY and CUMBERLAND. The river never achieved the great hopes of Washington and other investors who saw it as a commercial waterway for the interior. It was important, however, in the struggles of the Civil War. Only twice were the Confederates able to cross the river in force. The first ended in the bloody engagement at ANTIETAM and the second in the already mentioned Gettysburg. ... The eastern shore is a rich agricultural area with many estates and plenty of ocean beaches. OCEAN CITY is popular with Washingtonians escaping the summer heat of the capital. The whole bay area is a fisherman's paradise. Here is the watery home of the oysters, crabs and finfish that grace the dinner tables of the East. At the head of Chesapeake Bay is BALTIMORE . . . . . . , an "in-between" city since it is close to Philadelphia and Washington. But notwithstanding this geographical proximity Baltimore has a proud history and important facilities of its own. The principal sights are widely scattered. Johns Hopkins University, on the north side of town, is world-renowned for its medical school and hospital. Overlooking the busy harbor of the city is Fort McHenry. The defense of the fort during the British bombardment in the War of 1812 inspired Francis Scott Key to write the national anthem. The Transportation Museum has an interesting collection of locomotives from the most ancient vintage steam engines to the latest diesels. Baltimore has a tradition for fine foods, especially sea foods and pastries. Soft-shell crabs and pan-roasted oysters head the list of popular dishes. Diamondback terrapin stew and Maryland chicken fried in salt pork fat and served in hot cream are two regional favorites. ... Also on Chesapeake Bay, south of Baltimore, is ANNAPOLIS, state capital and home of the U.S. Naval Academy. In visiting the academy do not overlook the town itself, with the State House and several colonial homes of interest.

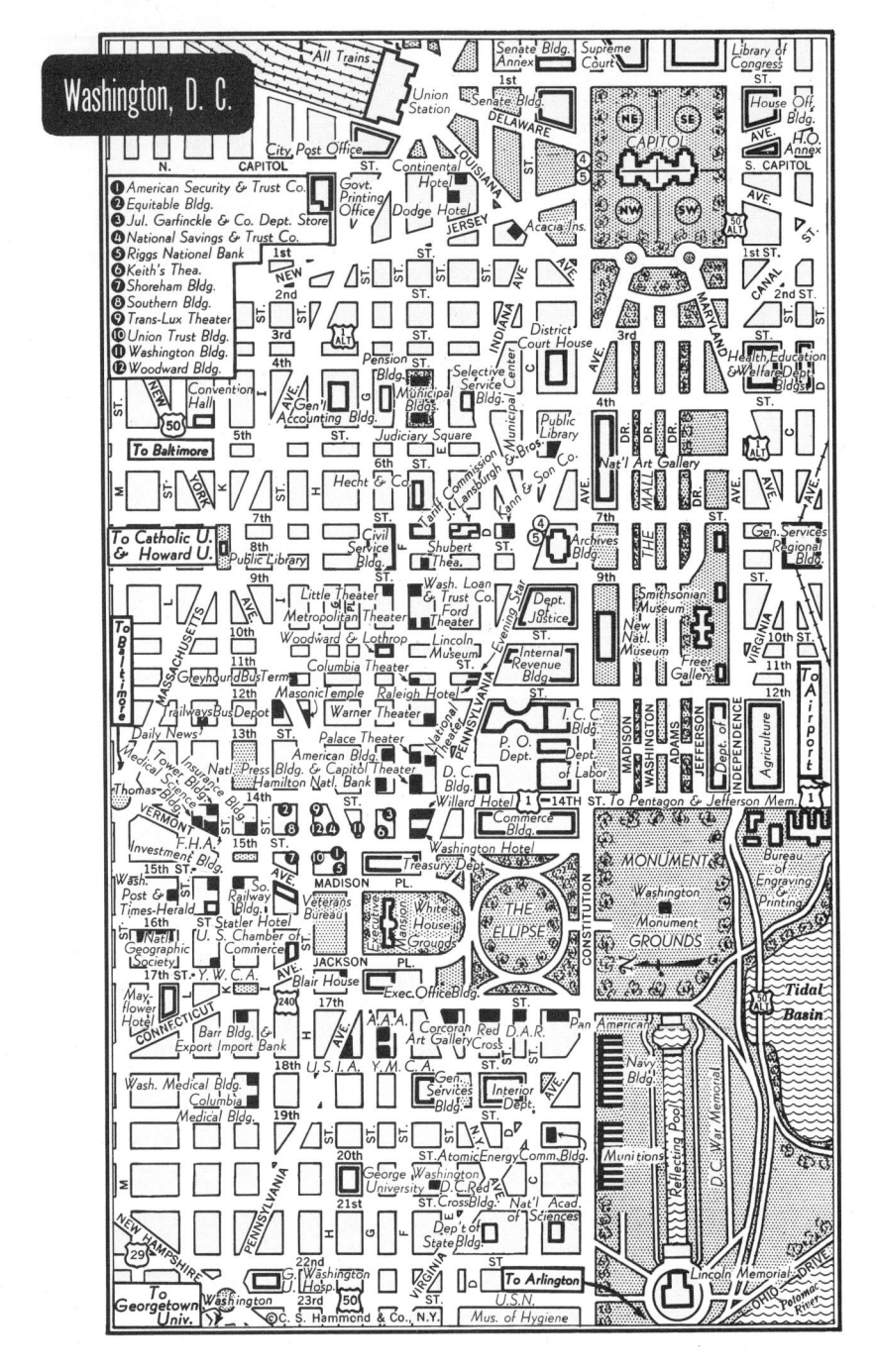

WASHINGTON, D. C.

WASHINGTON . . . . . capital of the nation, has been acclaimed one of the most beautiful and cosmopolitan cities in the world. Wide tree-lined avenues and green parks serve to set off the impressive government buildings. Since it is a city where government is the big business, there are no industries to mar the sky line or to laden the air with the soot that blights so many metropolitan cities. Washington is the first great world capital that was built from a carefully made master plan. Although the plans of engineer Pierre Charles L'Enfant have not always been followed, the city has come to fulfill the dreams of its creators. ... Most visitors wish to see first the Capitol, the home of the Legislative Branch of the Government. It stands in spacious grounds on the crest of a hill dominating the entire city. The great dome awash with lights at nighttime is an impressive sight. A visit to the galleries of the Senate and House of Representatives may prove somewhat disappointing in that much of the work of Congress is done not on the floor but in the committee rooms and in the nearby office buildings reached by miniature subway. ... To the east, the Library of Congress with its ornate architecture houses the world's greatest collection of books. It has some notable exhibits of rare books and presidential papers. Next to the library is the Supreme Court building. Relatively new, it is built of dazzling white marble with a stately columned portico; it is regarded by many as the finest building in Washington. The courtroom is open to the public when the court is in session. . . . On the mall west of the Capitol is the **National Gallery of Art,** rapidly becoming one of the world's great galleries. The building itself is a showpiece; the fountain and dark marble columns in the rotunda are especially striking. On the other side of the mall is the **Smithsonian Institution,** a scattered group of buildings housing Lindbergh's plane, the "Spirit of St. Louis," besides a thousand and one other relics, inventions and curiosities. North of the mall between Constitution and Pennsylvania Avenues is the **Federal Triangle.** It is the longest, most expensive and impressive collection of government buildings anywhere. They include the Departments of Commerce, Labor and Justice. At the Department of Justice, the FBI provides an unusual public tour every half hour through its crime detection labs and exhibits. The **Archives Building,** also in this group, has on display America's great historic documents including the Constitution, the Declaration of Independence and the Bill of Rights. . . . **The White House** on Pennsylvania Avenue is the home of the President. The dignified mansion set in beautifully kept grounds has recently been completely remodeled. A number of the stately rooms on the first floor are open to the public at specified hours. . . . At the western end of the mall is **Washington Monument,** a severe marble shaft rising 555 feet into the air. An elevator takes visitors to the observation windows at the top. Directly south of the Washington Monument, on the east shore of the Tidal Basin, setting for Washington's famed Japanese cherry trees, is the **Jefferson Memorial.** The monument is in circular pantheon form, a design favored by Jefferson in his home, Monticello, in Charlottesville, Virginia. Within the memorial is a towering statue of Jefferson with significant quotations of Jefferson carved on the walls. Completing the axis of the mall is the **Lincoln Memorial.** The stately building overlooks the Arlington Memorial Bridge spanning the Potomac River. Inside the memorial is the colossal seated statue of Lincoln by Daniel Chester French and on the walls are the noble words of Lincoln's Gettysburg Address and Second Inaugural Address. . . . The Arlington Memorial Bridge leads directly to the Arlington National Cemetery on the Virginia side of the Potomac. It is the largest and most famous of all national burying grounds, covering over 400 acres. Its most famous grave is the **Tomb of the Unknown Soldier,** guarded day and night by sentries. . . . Southeast of the cemetery is the **Pentagon,** the Defense Department's huge office building. . . . Northwest of the downtown area, across Rock Creek Park, is Georgetown, the fashionable residential quarter of the city. It has some fine colonial and Georgian mansions among which is Dumbarton Oaks, famous for its Byzantine art collection and many fine gardens.

Washington offers excellent park facilities. **Rock Creek Park** is a rugged, rambling park of unusual beauty. Its best known feature is the Washington Zoo. On the old **Chesapeake and Ohio Canal,** the National Park service provides a canal boat tour along the Maryland side of the Potomac River. **Embassy Row** on Massachusetts Avenue is another sightseeing attraction with many of the foreign embassies and legations. Also on Massachusetts Avenue may be found the new **Islamic Center** and **Washington Cathedral,** a large Gothic structure still under construction. . . . Washington has its share of Broadway shows, either prior to their New York run or afterwards.

New England

LAND OF AMERICAN FREEDOM

New England, birthplace of American freedom, offers a unique variety of attractions to the visitor. Proud possessor of some of the finest scenic wonders in the world, it can boast of picturesque towns, rugged sea coasts, rolling green hills, wide river valleys and granite mountains. Historic landmarks abound to remind the visitor of New England's heritage. Here the protests against the unjust rule of England broke out into open revolt. The old fishing ports retain their charm, and rural towns with village greens and white churches have not changed like their industrial neighbors. Summer theaters and art colonies seem to thrive in New England. Fishing and hunting facilities are excellent and sailing on the coastal waters is a popular pastime. Summer camps abound throughout the region. Although the six New England states share a com-

UNITED STATES CAPITOL BUILDING, WASHINGTON, D. C.

LINCOLN MEMORIAL, WASHINGTON, D. C.

mon history and are alike in many ways, they preserve separate local characteristics that mark their accents and ways of life. Everywhere, however, the visitor is welcome, for this land has long entertained summer and winter guests.

ABOUT FOOD

Regional dishes of New England make up a long list of tempting foods. Sea food is probably the most famous with Maine lobster, clam chowder, codfish cakes, and clams steamed on hot rocks in a traditional New England clambake. Other local dishes are: New England boiled dinner, baked beans and brown bread, hot cakes with maple syrup, pumpkin pie with Vermont cheese, New Hampshire deep-dish blueberry pie and real country cider.

BOSTON

Historic capital of the Commonwealth of Massachusetts, Boston . . . . . is a combination of the old and the new. Wide avenues leading into the city disappear into narrow crooked streets that follow the same winding path as the old colonial lanes. Modern buildings tower above graceful spires of colonial churches and quiet burial grounds are to be found in the shadows of office buildings. A walking tour of the historic sites of the downtown area is recommended. Start with the State House on Beacon Street; the gold-domed building, designed by Bulfinch, houses the Senate and Hall of Representatives. Of interest inside are the hall of flags and other historical souvenirs such as the Sacred Cod hanging in the Hall of Representatives. Below the State House is the **Boston Common**, the popular city park which began as a community cow pasture. At the Old Granary Burial Grounds on Tremont Street are the graves of such famous Americans as Paul Revere, Samuel Adams and John Hancock. Old South **Meeting House** at the corner of Milk and Washington Streets was once the meeting hall for fervent revolutionary patriots. Nearby, Paul Revere had his shop, and Benjamin Franklin learned the printing trade just around the corner. The Old State House, built in 1713 for representatives of the Crown, still retains the royal emblem of the Lion and the Unicorn. The building now houses an interesting historical and marine museum. Nearby **Faneuil Hall**, called the "Cradle of Liberty," was the scene of violent protests against the British. Paul Revere's House on North Square has been restored and furnished as it was in the days of Revere. North Church with its steeple rebuilt for the second time was the lookout from which the British approach was signalled to the patriots in Charlestown.

To return to the center of the city, the Public Gardens' ordered flower beds and popular **swan boats** provide a pleasant place to rest a while. North of the State House is the Beacon Hill area, long the home of many famous Boston families. Further north along the Charles River lies the **Esplanade**, a mile-long park where summer band concerts are held. In the Copley Square area can be found Trinity Church, a fine Romanesque building and the John Hancock Life Insurance Building, a landmark in the more modern style with an observation tower giving a fine view of the city and harbor. Also on the square is **Boston Public Library**, one of the world's best. Further west are the Christian Science Church and Publishing House. The Mother Church is a large edifice of Italian Renaissance architecture with a dome which rises 200 feet to mark the Boston skyline. The adjacent publishing house issues church publications including the *Christian Science Monitor* and can be visited during the summer. Symphony **Hall**, home of the Boston Symphony Orchestra and Boston "Pops" Orchestra, is on Huntington Avenue. On the same avenue may be found the Museum of Fine Arts which has an impressive collection of art and some exceptionally fine colonial rooms. The Boston area is a center of education; the number of institutions of higher learning is impressive. Most well-known, of course, are Harvard University and Massachusetts Institute of Technology. They are located across the Charles River in Cambridge. Harvard, the oldest university in the country, has a fine campus, combining the old in the historic "yard" and the new in the more recent houses fronting the Charles River. The Agassiz Museum at Harvard houses the world's finest collection of glass flowers. Massachusetts Institute of Technology, better known as MIT, is America's leading engineering school. Just east of Harvard, the MIT campus has some unusual exhibits plus some impressive new buildings of modern architecture. Further east in the Charlestown area is the Bunker Hill Monument, an austere obelisk marking the low hill (actually Breed's Hill) where British troops met the determined opposition of Americans in the famous Battle of Bunker

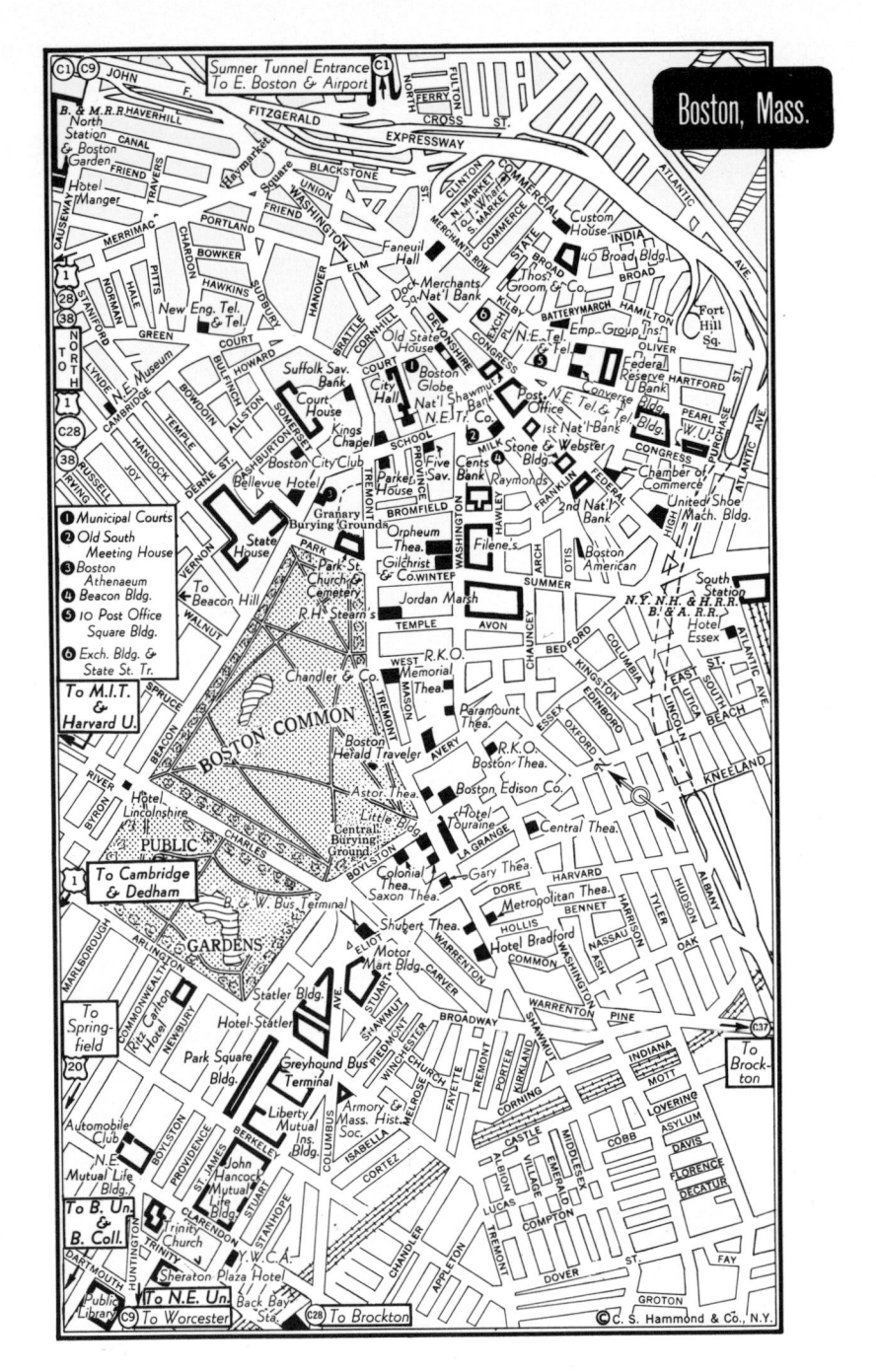

Hill. **Boston Navy Yard,** nearby at the junction of the Charles and Mystic Rivers, has been an active naval establishment for 150 years; on display is the naval **frigate Constitution,** immortalized as "Old Ironsides." Also in Cambridge, near Harvard, the **Longfellow House** on Brattle Street is just one of the many colonial buildings of interest. Built in 1759 this house served as Washington's headquarters early in the war and later as the home of the poet Longfellow.

Boston has a world-wide reputation for its fine foods, especially those New England dishes such as clam chowder, boiled dinners and sea food of all sorts. Of local origin are Boston cream pie, brown bread and baked beans and Parker House rolls; the latter originated by the chef of the Parker House Hotel.

Sporting events are constantly being held with both college and professional teams competing for national rankings in baseball, football, basketball and hockey.

For the theatergoer the area south of the Common boasts of many theaters where Broadway shows appear following their New York run.

MASSACHUSETTS' ATTRACTIONS

North of Boston is the city of **SALEM** where the witchcraft trials took place in 1692. The buildings that remain from these early dark days include the Court House, the Witch House and the reconstructed jail. From the more glorious days of the Clipper Ships when Salem was a famous shipping center there are the many old captains' homes on Chestnut Street. **Salem Maritime National Historic Site** preserves the old Custom House, Derby Wharf and Derby House. Also in Salem is Hawthorne's **House of the Seven Gables.** . . . On **CAPE ANN** is the old fishing port of **GLOUCESTER** with narrow streets and miles of colorful wharves where boats in from the Grand Banks unload tons of fish. . . . In a wide area around Boston are found the industrial cities of New England: Lawrence, Lowell, Worcester, Waltham and Manchester. These busy cities are interspaced with many small, New England towns complete with tidy village greens and white churches, towns like **LEXINGTON** and **CONCORD** where the first engagements occurred between British troops and American Minute Men. On the Lexington Green the first volleys of the war were fired as a small number of Minute Men under Capt. John Parker opposed the British marching on Concord. Dispersed by the British, the Americans fought a second battle that same day at the bridge at Concord, ending with the complete rout of seasoned British troops. **LEXINGTON** today is a quiet town whose main activity centers around the 7:15 commuter train to Boston. . . . **CONCORD** added to her colonial history by becoming an important literary center. Emerson, Thoreau and Hawthorne all lived here;

TIOGA TOWERS, MARBLEHEAD, MASS.

PLYMOUTH ROCK

the sleepy pond of Walden is only a short distance away.

On lovely **Buzzards Bay** in Massachusetts, **New Bedford** was once the most important whaling port in the world. The whaling days passed with the discovery of petroleum but their reminders are present in an interesting **whaling museum** on Johnny Cake Hill and the **seaman's chapel** made famous in Melville's *Moby Dick*. . . . A pleasant boat trip takes visitors from New Bedford to the islands of **Martha's Vineyard** and **Nantucket** and to **Woods Hole** on Cape Cod. **Nantucket** and **Martha's Vineyard,** once important as whaling centers, now attract visitors as summer resorts. Much of the old charm of the seafaring towns remains to be enjoyed along with the fine beaches and good fishing waters. . . . **CAPE COD,** long a summer playground, is marked by sand dunes and beaches whose dazzling whiteness is relieved by green marshlands and blue tidal inlets. Small resort towns dot the long arm of the cape. The larger summer colonies are at **HYANNIS** and **PROVINCETOWN.** At **DENNIS** there is the **Cape Playhouse,** one of the more successful summer theatres with big name stars. **SANDWICH** once produced the famous Sandwich colored glass. A collection of this now rare and valuable glass may be seen at the town's historical society. Summer theaters and artists' colonies abound, but despite the unavoidable commercialism there is still plenty of natural beauty to enjoy. . . . Across Cape Cod Bay from Provincetown is **PLYMOUTH,** site of the first permanent colony of the Pilgrims. **Plymouth Rock** where the Pilgrims first stepped ashore is now protected with a granite monument. Nearby has been built a full-size replica of a pilgrim house. A **Pilgrim Trail** directs the visitor to the places of historic interest throughout the town. During the month of August and at Thanksgiving time local citizens dressed in Pilgrim attire re-enact the scene of the Pilgrims' going to church.

NEW HAMPSHIRE AND MAINE

The coastline of New Hampshire has only one seaport, PORTSMOUTH. Here there are many reminders of its colonial past in fine old houses and narrow winding streets. A protective harbor shelters many pleasure craft as well as the ships of the U.S. Navy. . . . Just beyond the narrow bit of coast claimed by New Hampshire is MAINE, almost as large as the rest of the New England states combined. The famous rugged coastline of Maine has its southern beginnings in a subdued coastal strip of sandy beaches such as that of OLD ORCHARD. . . . At PORTLAND further north, the shore line becomes more dramatic, where unprotected headlands bear the attack of the seas while the long-fingered bays offer calm and safety. A steamboat from Portland takes visitors around Casco Bay, stopping at the many resort islands. A short way inland from Portland is Sebago Lake, popular resort area for children and adult camps. . . . Northeast from Portland the indented coast presents a succession of resort communities with summer theaters, art colonies and old sailing ship cruises. In all these coastal towns Maine lobster and other sea food fresh from the sea is at its best. . . . On one of the long peninsulas jutting out into the ocean is BOOTHBAY HARBOR, a pleasant old seaport with a quiet harbor. . . . At ACADIA NATIONAL PARK on Mt. Desert Island, there is an inspiring combination of ocean and mountain scenery. Here the granite cliffs have been undermined at the base by the pounding surf, leaving caves in some places. Mt. Cadillac, accessible by car, presents a fine view of the harbor and islands. Trails, roads and sea cruises have helped to make this magnificent region one of the finest vacation spots in the East. The center of the island's social life here is BAR HARBOR. . . . Inland, a journey up the Penobscot River leads to the lumber center of BANGOR and OLD TOWN, site of the Old Town canoe factory (open to visitors). . . . The many lakes of Maine are the last remains of the great ice sheet that once covered the area. Those lakes closer to the metropolitan areas are sites of popular summer camps, where movies and ice cream are only as far as a drive to a nearby town. . . . In the northern woods, however, lakes are set among the trackless forests and provide ample solitude and unblemished wilderness for nature lovers or sportsmen. From Moosehead Lake north to the Canadian border there are no roads; only the waterways of the Alagash, St. John and other rivers penetrate the endless forests. . . . Northeast of Moosehead is Mt. Katahdin in BAXTER STATE PARK, one of America's great fish and game preserves. Katahdin is Maine's highest peak and marks the beginning of the Appalachian Mountain Trail, over which hikers may go as far south as Georgia if ambitious enough. . . . In northeast Maine, along the Canadian boundary, is the large agricultural country of Aroostook, producer of Maine's great potato crop. Twenty communities take part each summer in a Potato Blossom Festival to celebrate the coming harvest. . . . In the Blue Mountains of western Maine are the sprawling Rangeley Lakes, long famous for their trout and landlocked salmon. Not only fishermen come here, however, for there are opportunities for the other outdoor sports of horseback riding, hiking, etc. In wintertime the Blue Mountains are a popular skiing region.

In northern NEW HAMPSHIRE the White Mountains rival Maine's scenic wonders. The beauty of New Hampshire lies in her granite peaks, rushing mountain streams, endless wooded hills, well-kept valley farms and neat villages. Each summer thousands visit the areas to view the mountain passes of Franconia Notch and Crawford Notch; the Flume, a 700-foot sluiceway through granite cliffs; Old Man of the Mountain, the stern profile of man, carved by nature, and Lost River Reservation, a series of caverns and giant potholes carved by an ancient glacial stream. Towering above this enticing country is Mt. Washington. The windy summit of New England's highest mountain is reached by a quaint cog railway, from near Bretton Woods on the west or by hairpin road from Pinkham Notch on the east side. With the arrival of the winter snow this whole area becomes a great winter sports land. The slopes around BERLIN and NORTH CONWAY offer excellent ski facilities for both novice and expert skier alike. . . . The area south of the White Mountains is not without its own attractions. The Connecticut and Merrimac Rivers, many small lakes and the giant Lake Winnipesaukee provide ample recreational facilities. Winnipesaukee with hundreds of islands, bays, and coves is one of New England's loveliest lakes. Boats make daily circuit of the lake during the summer. Water sports are a popular attraction at The Weirs. . . . At HANOVER, Dartmouth College breaks out from the academic world each February to put on a popular Winter Carnival, featuring skiing and skating exhibitions and ice sculptures.

COG RAILWAY, MT. WASHINGTON
Douglas B. Grundy

AROUND VERMONT

In VERMONT the Green Mountains reach from Canada to Massachusetts in a long never-ending chain of forested hills overlooking quiet towns and valley farms. The Long Trail which follows the ridges of the Green Mountains throughout their length provides hikers with a well-marked trail with numerous shelters and campsites. In the north the slopes of Mt. Mansfield have made STOWE a skiers' haven with deep snow, excellent trails, lifts and tows and pleasant inns and lodges. . . Nearby Smugglers Notch was once used by smugglers bringing goods from Canada. At BURLINGTON, on Lake Champlain, the University of Vermont is located. From the campus there is a fine view of the lake, with the Adirondacks as a backdrop. MONTPELIER, the state capital, is set in the narrow Winooski River Valley. The handsome granite State House is topped by a gold dome. There are a number of interesting historical items to be seen in the building proper as well as in the annex housing the Vermont Historical Society.

Nearby BARRE is the center of the granite industry. Visitors should take time to visit the quarries and interesting finishing shops here at the granite center of Barre or around RUTLAND, to the south, where marble is extracted from deep within the ground. At PROCTOR on exhibit are specimens of fine stone work. South of Rutland is MANCHESTER, a well-known winter and summer resort and golfing center. Further south is the historic area around BENNINGTON. This is the homeland of Ethan Allen and his followers, the "Green Mountain Boys," whose exploits against the British are famous. The plans for the capture of Fort Ticonderoga were laid in the Catamount Tavern in Bennington. The important Battle of Bennington is commemorated by a tall monument. In the town itself there are many colonial buildings including the **First Congregational Church**, one of New England's finest churches, and Walloomsac Inn, used continuously since 1764. . . . East of Bennington is the recently opened ski area of **WILMINGTON**.

THE BERKSHIRES

In western **MASSACHUSETTS**, the **Berkshire Hills** offer miles of scenic motor roads, hiking and skiing trails and dozens of lakes for summer sports. **TANGLEWOOD** in the pleasant town of Lenox, is the permanent home of the **Berkshire Music Festival** with the Boston Symphony performing under the foremost conductors. Nearby are two other cultural attractions, Berkshire Playhouse at **STOCKBRIDGE** and the **Jacob's Pillow Dance Festival** at **LEE**. . . . As the Connecticut River valley winds its way through southern New England, the quiet of the fertile valley of farms and tobacco sheds is interrupted by the activity of several large industrial cities. **SPRINGFIELD**, center of the firearms industry, has an interesting **armory** with displays of old and new weapons.

CONNECTICUT

In western **CONNECTICUT** the rolling Litchfield hills, a part of the Berkshire range, are a pleasant rural vacationland. Of the many charming small towns of the area, **LITCHFIELD** is outstanding for its street of 18th century mansions. . . . Hartford, to the east, has an impressive sky line of tall insurance buildings. Of interest besides the **State Capitol** are the **Mark Twain home** and the **Colt Museum** for firearms. . . . At Danbury, near New York State, the annual fair in October is a big attraction of the East. Close to New York City are the suburban communities of **GREENWICH**, **STAMFORD** and **DARIEN** with many fine old homes along with the new housing developments that have sprung up to meet the demand for pleasant country living. Further east along the Sound, **WESTPORT** has become a flourishing art colony with many top-notch artists and writers. The **Westport Summer Playhouse** draws upon New York talent for its shows. **BRIDGEPORT**, one of the larger industrial centers which occupy the deep tidal river inlets has a beautiful beach at **Seaside Park** and The **P. T. Barnum Museum** of circus life. . . . To the east, **STRATFORD** sponsors a Shakespeare drama festival. . . . In **NEW HAVEN** the **Yale University Campus** is interesting. The entire southern boundary on Long Island Sound is lined with pleasant summer resort towns, with excellent bathing and yachting facilities. The smaller bays swarm with dinghies and small-class sailboats while on open waters the prize sailing yachts prepare for ocean cruises. . . . Of the many pleasant Connecticut towns with their elm-arched streets and old homes, it is possible to name only a few. East of New Haven, **MADISON**'s village green is lined with early-American homes; the **Nathaniel Allis House** contains a museum of colonial period furnishings. **OLD SAYBROOK**, at the mouth of the Connecticut River, and **NIANTIC** are just two of the older seaports that have become popular summer resorts. **NEW LONDON**, once a home port for whaling ships, now shelters the gray hulls of U. S. Navy submarines. The **U.S. Coast Guard Academy** is located here as well as the Connecticut College for Women, noted for its **Summer School of Dance** which specializes in modern dance. . . . To the east of New London **MYSTIC**, a small trim maritime community, earned world renown for the first clipper ships built there. The **Marine Historical Museum** is a treasure house of ship models, figureheads and sailing gear. Among the outdoor exhibits are the whaling ship *Charles W. Morgan* and the square rigger *Joseph Conrad*.

RHODE ISLAND

The smallest state of the Union is highly industrialized but not without the charm of a colonial past and many fine recreational areas. Sailing and fishing are popular sports in the Narragansett Bay waters. The principal places of interest are on the shores of the bay. At **WICKFORD**, on the west side of the bay may be found St. Pauls Episcopal Church built in 1707. In nearby **EXETER** the **South County Museum** contains exhibits of colonial crafts and Americana. The resort island of **Jamestown**, to the south, boasts a colonial windmill. **NEWPORT** across the bay (reached by ferries from Jamestown) is perhaps unique in America for its varied history and activities. In early American times it was successively a colonial seaport, then a center for naval activities during the Revolution and the War of 1812. In the old port city may be seen colonial mansions and city buildings such as the **Old Colony House** and the **Old City Hall of 1761**. Along the shore drives outside of town are found the fabulous mansions that made Newport the resort center for the socially prominent families of New York at the turn of the 19th century; the palatial homes of the so-called "400" can best be seen on "Ocean Drive." **The Breakers**, the Vanderbilt mansion, is open to the public. Newport sport attractions are the tennis matches held in August and the June deep-water sailing classic to Bermuda and Annapolis in alternate years. The newest phenomenon to come to Newport is a summer **Jazz Festival** featuring the top names in Dixie-Land and modern jazz. . . . **PROVIDENCE**, the state capital, is particularly interesting around **Brown University**. The campus is attractive as well as the fine old residences of Providence's more wealthy citizens. The **First Baptist Church** organized by Roger Williams is one of the city's finer buildings; also the place of Brown commencements since 1775. **Roger Williams Park** has spacious grounds with rose gardens, drives and an outdoor amphitheater for special events. . . . Block Island, 25 miles south of Narragansett Bay, offers some outstanding tuna and swordfish fishing waters on the Atlantic. Ferry service is available from the mainland at **NARRAGANSETT** and New London.

PAUL REVERE STATUE WITH OLD NORTH CHURCH IN THE BACKGROUND, BOSTON _{Mass. Development and Industrial Comm.}

249

Alaska

FROM TOTEM TO TUNDRA

Comprising the northwest peninsula of North America, two geologically related archipelagos and numerous off-lying islands, Alaska covers an area of 586,400 square miles, indented by numerous coastal waterways, incised by several mountain ranges and crowned by the loftiest summit in North America, Mt. McKinley. Popularly known as America's last frontier, Alaska is quickly becoming, through the development of communications spurred by the defense necessities of World War II, America's first playground. Since it is richly endowed in face and fortune, the new state still intrigues, beckoning everyone from the scientist probing the secrets of the earth to the sightseer scanning the scapes of land and sea. From the native village of the Aleut on the southeast island chain, to the Eskimo igloo on the fringe of the Arctic Circle, Alaska is an avenue of adventure.

FLORA

Alaskan bean vines may not grow as high as a Jack's beanstalk, but cabbages do weigh as much as fifty pounds, cucumbers and carrots extend the length of a man's forearm and strawberries grow almost as large as our tomatoes. The long hours of sunshine, in this land where the summer nights never really become dark, and the fertile black soil account for the phenomenal size of the vegetables and flowers, some of which grow as high as nine feet. Alaska's official flower, the forget-me-not, and colorful alpine flowers, in many shades of bright red, burnt orange, blue and golden yellow, spread over the tundra. A soft, mushy, mossy terrain with strange, stunted trees, the tundra appears from a distance like a dark, reddish-brown carpet. A few feet under the tundra is the famous permafrost earth that normally never thaws because of the very few summer days staying above freezing. In Alaska's early days, many a minor disaster occurred when the heat from the sourdoughs' homes thawed the permafrost underneath them and the foundations buckled as the ground softened.

AND FAUNA

Alaska is notable for big-game hunting and sport fishing, since the game is still plentiful even near the settlements and the streams still bulge with fish. Biggest challenge of all is the rugged Kodiak bear, which sometimes weighs as much as 2,000 pounds, with a pelt thirteen feet six inches long, but the black bear, moose (the Kenai moose is the biggest in the world), caribou, elk, deer, smaller game and birds also offer exciting hunting. Alaska still abounds with shaggy white mountain goat and mountain sheep, although few hunters have the patience and agility required to stalk them. Greyling, Mackinaw, rainbow, steelhead, eastern brook, cutthroat, Dolly Varden trout all compete with the noted salmon for the fishermen's interest.

COAST OF SOUTHEASTERN ALASKA — Bradford Washburn

THE INDISPENSABLE MAN

Air transportation plays the leading role today in Alaska's economy, and Alaska is truly air-minded: it leads the world in per capita flying! The landing fields and float-plane bases in Anchorage and Fairbanks are busy terminals during the snow-free months, with planes constantly taking off as others land, with no lessening of activity during the winter months, when the wheels or pontoons are replaced by skis. Also for the hunter, fisherman and even the sightseer, the bush pilot is the man of the hour, because the very best locations are usually far from roads or railroads, and without him the Alaskan visit would be far less exciting or unusual. Only by air can the people in Alaska get completely off the beaten path, to see all of this Great Land.

LAST FRONTIER

KETCHIKAN is the first port of call for northbound steamers and a scheduled stop on the daily flights to and from Juneau. The "Salmon Capital of the World," the city is the home of a mighty fishing fleet. Situated on Revillagigedo Island, Ketchikan is in a setting of natural beauty, where the hunter, fisherman or camper can be guided to a choice of sites for his sport. During August and September salmon can be seen fighting their way up the falls of **Ketchikan Creek**. Nearby is **Saxman Indian Village** and the thirty-eight-acre **Old Kasaan National Monument**, with totem poles, grave houses, monuments and parts of the original framework of an abandoned Haida Indian village. . . . WRANGELL, north of Ketchikan, is the second oldest town in southeastern Alaska. Port of call for all steamship lines, its excellent land-locked harbor is practically ice-free the year round. Rich in tradition, picturesque Wrangell, founded in 1833 by Russians on an old Indian settlement, has become historically famous for its totem poles. Located near the mouth of the Stikine River, it was, at the turn of the century, the embarkation point of prospectors setting out for the Yukon gold fields and is now an outfitting point for hunting and fishing trips into popular Cassiar country. . . . Located on the north end of the Wrangell Narrows is PETERSBURG, "the peaceful city." Some of the world's most beautiful mink coats come from this section, where pelts raised on surrounding farms command the highest prices of any Alaskan section. Its most scenic attraction is nearby **LaConte Glacier**, from which thousands of icebergs fall annually into LaConte Bay, originally called **Hutli** (Thunder) by the Stikine Indians because of the crashing roar of falling icebergs. From here the **Baird** and **Patterson Glaciers** can also be seen. . . . Sprawling along placid Gastineau Channel is JUNEAU, capital of Alaska. Situated in a mountainous setting, crested by **Mount Juneau**, the capital resembles a typical American city. Its six-story **Capitol Building** houses the U. S. District Court, post office, Historical Museum and other governmental departments. It is an important sea and air port of entry, enjoying a continuous flow of trade. The first white settlement founded in Alaska under the American flag, dating back to 1880 when gold was discovered in nearby Silver Bow, Juneau gained financial strength and stability from mining, fishing and lumber industries. Urban though it may be, it is still a sportsman's paradise, since its mountains, valleys and waters are the habitat of big game, birds and fish, all adequately protected by governmental game laws. At

Hasselborg Lake, seventy miles away, is a hunting lodge maintained by the Forest Service, with many adjoining moderate-size lakes that are virtually virgin fishing grounds. Not far from the city is Douglas, "city of homes," and one of the oldest communities in southeastern Alaska.... Once called the "Paris of the New World," SITKA was the capital of Alaska during the days of Russian administration. Reminiscent of that era is the Greek Russian Orthodox Church, standing in the center of the city. The timbers of its central towers were salvaged from a Russian warship wrecked on Kruzof Island and among its treasures are priceless icons, rich carvings and religious art. Nearby is Castle Hill, historically significant because it was here that the United States and Russia signed the transfer title to Alaska. A 200-bed tuberculosis sanitorium and a large vocational school are among the city's most recent developments.... Situated on Kodiak Island, "Alaska's Sunshine Island," is the thriving city of KODIAK, apex of the world's largest fishing banks and home of the renowned Kodiak bear, the world's largest carnivore. A wealthy city, Kodiak is on its way to becoming the commercial center of the entire North Pacific. It is now the site of American Army and Navy bases. Opposite Kodiak Island is Katmai National Monument, site of 7,500-foot Mt. Katmai, which in 1912 staged one of the greatest volcanic eruptions of this century. Located here, too, is the Valley of Ten Thousand Smokes, where jets of steam rise from the earth's crevices....
ANCHORAGE, located on the shores of Cook Inlet and protected by the Chugach Range, Talkeetna Mountains and the Alaska Range, is the territory's largest and fastest growing city. It is the hub of an "aviation life line" stretching to the furthermost Aleutians, a main stop for Great Circle Flights to the Orient and a jumping-off point for flights to Nome and Bristol Bay. A major northern defense center, it is the site of Fort Richardson and Elmendorf Air Force Base. It is also the headquarters of the Alaska Railroad, to which the city owes its beginning in 1915 and its rich industrial life. On what has been described as one of the most scenic rail trips in the world, this railroad services farmers, fishermen and vacationists of the Kenai Peninsula, residents of the rich Matanuska Valley agricultural area, the Bristol Bay fishing region and the coal, gold and platinum districts of the north. Proud of its national and municipal achievements, Anchorage has a modern Federal Building, fireproof and earthquakeproof schools and fourteen churches, including Alaska's oldest Greek Russian Orthodox Church in the Russian village on Kuskokwim River. Approximately 150 miles from Anchorage is Mt. McKinley, the highest mountain in North America, and the scenic site of Mt. McKinley National Park. Within the park are 91 miles of road for saddle horses, pack trains and seasoned guides leaving from Camp Eielson and Wonder Lake. Thirty-four species of animals and 112 kinds of birds live within the park's confines. The second highest tides in the world — second only to those of the Bay of Fundy — occur in vividly named Turnagain Bay, near Anchorage, where the tide actually comes in as a massive wall of water. From Anchorage special summer flights are made to the colorful Pribilof Islands, in the Bering Sea, to observe the colonies of the famous Alaska seals.... The "Golden Heart of Alaska," FAIRBANKS is situated deep within the interior in the center of a vast gold-mining district, the Tanana Valley. At the back door of this modern town is a region of unlimited mineral resources, including the potentially wealthy Barrow Oil Fields, covering an estimated 70,000 square miles, and since it is the terminus of the Alaska Railroad and the Alaska Highway, Fairbanks is the logical shipping center for these fields. It is also a chief departure point for flights to Nome, Barrow, Wiseman and the vast interior regions and during the summer months, tourist flights to the Arctic Circle leave from here. It is a hunting region for caribou, moose, bear and other big game, as well as a fisherman's paradise. America's northernmost university, the University of Alaska, is just outside the town, and it also claims the northernmost golf and country club in the world.... NOME, the famed gold-rush town of 1900, is situated on the shores of the Bering Sea. Today it is a modern town with governmental offices, several churches, excellent schools and active civic organizations, although still the main supply center for a rich mining district. Eskimo ivory carving and needlecraft are growing industries, as is the reindeer industry supplying much food and clothing. From its romantic past can be seen a few of the old buildings erected during the gold-rush days and two huge gold dredges still operate within driving distance from the town.

JUNEAU'S FISHING FLEET — Alaska Development Board

VOLCANO, ALEUTIAN ISLANDS — Official Photo U.S. Navy

Hawaii

PACIFIC PARADISE

Eons ago a series of eruptions began in a 2000-mile cleft on the floor of the Pacific Ocean. Thus was born the chain of volcanic mountains which now form the enchanting HAWAIIAN ISLANDS. It took many centuries for the lava flows to build these mountains to a maximum height of 32,000 feet — Mauna Kea on the island of Hawaii is 14,000 feet above sea level and 18,000 feet below–the highest peak in the islands. It took more centuries for the bald peaks to become covered with soil and seeds brought by the sea from other lands; rain and sun helped these early plantings to develop into the luxuriant foliage of today. A visit to these beautiful islands is a traveler's delight — no passports, no language difficulties, the comforts of home in the tourist centers — all this in exotic settings differing in character on each island. You will be soothed by Hawaiian music (Polynesian chants, blended with hymns of the early missionaries, form the basis of modern Hawaiian music), and entranced by girls dancing the hula. The real hula is a very graceful dance — the hands tell the story and the hips and feet provide the rhythm. Many customs of the Polynesians have been carried down through the ages in spite of the Western way of life in modern Hawaii.

FOOD

One of the high spots of a visit to Hawaii is to attend a *luau* (feast). This typically Hawaiian entertainment has become famous. Pigs, roasted in a pit with potatoes and fish wrapped in ti leaves, are served with shellfish, fresh pineapple, cocoanut pudding and other South Sea side dishes, at ti-leaf covered tables decorated with brilliant flowers. During the feast you listen to Hawaiian music and watch the hula dancers. Another famous dish is *poi*, a starchy pudding made from taro root pounded into a paste and allowed to ferment. Chicken cooked with taro leaves in cocoanut milk is also popular.

SPORTS

For recreation, water sports lead the field; surfboard riding, the sport of Hawaiian kings, has been popular for centuries; a trip in an outrigger canoe is fun; deep-sea and spear fishing furnishes exhilarating sport. Baseball, basketball and football are seasonal sports.

AROUND THE ISLANDS

The island of HAWAII is the largest of the Hawaiian chain and, geologically, the youngest. Its two active volcanoes, Mauna Loa, nearly 14,000 feet high, and

DIAMOND HEAD AS SEEN FROM MAKIKI HEIGHTS — Hawaii Visitors Bureau

Kilauea, form the nucleus of the part of Hawaiian National Park located on Hawaii island, a wonderland of Nature's creation. You can drive through the Park over a good road, bordered with giant ferns — some rising to a height of 40 feet — to a plateau from which you may safely watch the boiling lava in Kilauea's main crater. The drama of the building of the Hawaiian Islands unfolds before you when watching an eruption. . . . HILO, on the east coast, is the orchid center of the island. These exquisite and fragrant flowers are everywhere — they border lawns, are woven into leis and are shipped all over the world. Large sugar plantations surround Hilo and a drive to visit them is interesting. . . . You might also want to see the black beach at Kalapana — the black "sand" is powdered lava. . . . Puna Warm Springs, ringed with ferns, has its waters warmed by volcanic heat. . . . A drive from Hilo to KONA on the west coast takes you through one of the fascinating scenic areas of the world. The first Christian church was established at Kona in 1820 by the first misisonaries who came from New England in clipper ships. The summer palace of Hawaiian royalty is open to visitors and a monument marks the spot where Captain Cook was killed. . . . HONAUNAU is an ancient "City of Refuge" for hunted men. The foundations of a temple believed to have been built in the 12th century to mark the site of ancient pagan rites, have been restored. Kona attracts vacationists because of its restful "Old Hawaiian" atmosphere. . . . MAUI, second largest of the Hawaiian Islands, has, in its part of Hawaiian National Park, a dormant volcano for its chief attraction — Haleakala, "House of the Sun." Legend says the god

HAWAIIAN CATTLE RANCH — Hawaii Visitors Bureau

Maui stood on the summit of the mountain, trapped the Sun and extracted his promise to slow his pace over the land. Afterward, the mountain exploded creating the world's largest crater, 21 miles around the rim and 3000 feet deep; most visitors plan to get there early enough to see the changing colors of dawn bursting over the crater's rim. You watch in awesome silence as the sun appears and the glorious spectacle makes you understand why the primitive people of the island called the mountain "The House of the Sun.". . . On Maui are many lovely valleys, but the loveliest is **Iao Valley**; its walls, rising to a height of 4000 feet, form an amphitheater around a 1200-feet spire of rock called "The Needle.". . . The HANA district is also a very scenic area — rushing mountain streams, cascades, waterfalls, exotic plants and trees, all under a clear, intensely blue sky, make a panorama to delight the eye. . . . You arrive on Maui near WAILUKU, on the western side of the island; from there a short plane trip, or a drive through ever-changing scenery, will bring you to HANA. The comfort of a fine hotel awaits you, while the unhurried life of old Hawaii is about you. . . . OAHU is the third largest of the Hawaiian Islands. Oahu means "Gathering Place" and the name is still appropriate. It is the chief center for all the islands and the "crossroads of the Pacific.". . . HONOLULU . . . . . largest city and capital is the gateway to all Hawaii; its airport is one of the busiest in the world. It is probably the only city in the world where steamer and plane arrivals and departures are, traditionally, colorful occasions. Symbolic of the warm friendliness of island people is the **aloha** greeting with the placing of a **lei** (wreath) around the shoulders of each passenger. Aloha means friendship, good fellowship, love, and people submit courteously to this expression of "hail" or "farewell.". . . There is much to see in beautiful Honolulu; the Bishop Museum has a wonderful collection of Polynesian relics; the **Academy of Art** has interesting displays; you may drive through the campus of the **University of Hawaii** and the throne room at **Iolani Palace**, a former royal residence, is open to visitors. An interesting drive from Honolulu takes you to **Pearl Harbor**, **Schofield Barracks** and **Hickam Field**, places where history was made on December 7, 1941. Beautifully laid out in the long-dormant crater of **Punchbowl** volcano is the **Pacific National Memorial Cemetery**, where rest the dead from the Pacific area of World War II. . . . South of Honolulu is famous **Waikiki Beach** and the equally famous Hawaiian landmark, **Diamond Head**, an extinct volcano, the legendary home of Pele, the goddess of fire. . . . Some seven miles from Honolulu is **Nuuanu Pali**, a pass at the head of **Nuuanu Valley**. The beauty of this valley is unequalled anywhere in the islands; the north face is a sheer rocky cliff, in places 2000 feet high. . . . KAUAI, fourth in size of the Hawaiian chain, is, geologically, the oldest of the group — the first to appear above sea level. Some clear traces of pre-historic people have been found on this island. An interesting place to visit is the first sugar plantation started in 1836 and still in operation. Kauai was the first island to be protected by cannon mounted on bastions. In **Hanalei Valley** rice paddies are cultivated as in ancient days; the luxuriant foliage on the slopes and a blue half-moon bay are a scenic delight. The eerie **Haena Caves** are interesting. . . . Along the southern shore of the island you can visit the **Spouting Horn**, a geyser-like spectacle caused by the surf shooting through cavernous rocks and making a weird noise at each "eruption.". . . **Waimea Canyon** is also one of the beauty spots of the islands; its huge cliffs, deep gorges and soft colors, change constantly in the sunshine — a truly inspiring sight. At Kalalau Lookout one sees the complete grandeur of the canyon with the view of **Kalalau** Valley. . . . MOLOKAI "The Friendly Isle," is fifth in size of the Hawaiian group. For the traveler who wishes to get away from the strenuous life of the modern cities, Molokai offers the ideal vacation land. The scenery is delightful and some place names fascinating, such as **Puu Peelua**, Hill of the Caterpillar God or **Puu Mano**, Hill of the Shark God. Some of the best game fishing in the Pacific is found in the waters off Molokai.

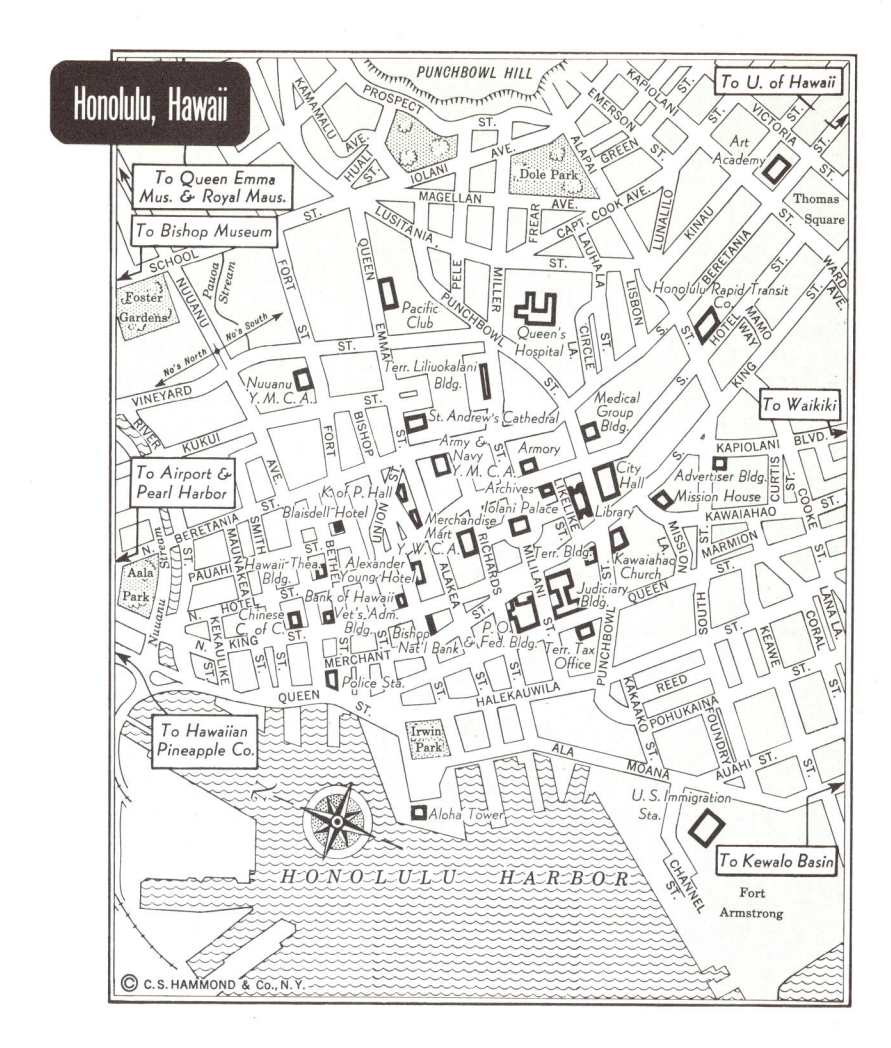

CONTOUR PINEAPPLE FIELDS

Index

Aachen, Germany 44
Aalborg, Denmark 53
Aarhus, Denmark 53
Abbottabad, Pakistan 122
Abbotsford, Scotland 19
Aberdeen, Scotland 20
Abergele, Wales 13
Aberyswyth, Wales 13
Abilene, Kansas 220
Abisko, Sweden 57
Acadia Nat'l. Park, Maine 248
Acajutla, El Salvador 181
Acapulco, Mexico 178
Adelaide, Australia 137
Adirondack Mountains, N.Y. 242
Admant, Austria 68
Agadir, Morocco 93
Agate Beach, Oregon 206
Agra, India 119
Aix-en-Provence, France 32
Aix-les-Bains, France 34
Ako (Acre), Israel 117
Akron, Ohio 228
Alabama, United States 237
Alajuela, Costa Rica 183
Alameda, California 204
Alamo, The, Texas 234
Alamogordo, N. Mexico 215
Alamosa, Colorado 210
Alaska, U.S. 250
Alassio, Italy 82
Albany, New York 242
Alberta Province, Canada 175
Albertville, Belgian Congo 102
Albi, France 31
Albuquerque, N. Mexico 214
Alcala de Henares, Spain 74
Alcobaca, Portugal 71
Aleppo, Syria 111
Alexandria, Egypt 97
Algiers, Algeria 94
Alice Springs, Australia 137
Allentown, Pennsylvania 243
Alloway, Scotland 19
Alta Gracia, Argentina 166
Altamira, Spain 74
Amalfi, Italy 81
Amana Villages, Iowa 224
Amarillo, Texas 234
Amazon River, Brazil 155
Ambato, Ecuador 149
Amboise, France 30
Amman, Jordan 115
Amsterdam, Netherlands 40
Anaconda, Montana 212
Anchorage, Alaska 251
Andalusia, Spain 75
Andes Mountains, Argentina 164
Andes Mountains, Peru 162
Andorra, France 31
Andros, Bahamas 186
Angel Falls, Venezuela 146
Angers, France 30
Angouleme, France 30
Ankara, Turkey 88
Ann Arbor, Michigan 229
Annapolis, Maryland 244
Annecy, France 34
Antibes, France 33
Antietam, Maryland 244
Antigua, Guatemala 179
Antigua Island 187
Antrim, N. Ireland 22
Antofagasta, Chile 161
Antwerp, Belgium 37
Anuradhapura, Ceylon 123
Aran, Spain 75
Arco, Idaho 212
Ardara, Ireland 23
Ardmore, Oklahoma 233
Arequipa, Peru 151
Arica, Chile 161
Argentina 164
Arizona, United States 216
Arkansas, United States 232
Arles, France 32
Armagh, N. Ireland 22
Arnhem, Neth. 41
Arnhem Land, Australia 138
Arta, Spain 76
Asbury Park, New Jersey 242
Ascona, Switzerland 63
Asheville, N. Carolina 236
Aspen, Colorado 210
Assen, Netherlands 40
Assisi, Italy 81
Astoria, Oregon 206
Asturias, Spain 74
Asuncion, Paraguay 158
Aswan, Egypt 101
Atacama Desert, Chile 161
Athens, Greece 86
Athlone, Ireland 21
Atlanta, Georgia 236
Atlantic City, New Jersey 242
Auckland, New Zealand 139
Augsburg, Germany 46
Auray, France 29
Austin, Texas 234
Australia 136
Austria 65
Auvergne, France 32
Auyerre, France 34
Avery Island, Louisiana 232
Avignon, France 31
Avila, Spain 74
Avranches, France 29
Ayllon, Spain 74
Ayr, Scotland 19
Aysen, Chile 163
Ayutthaya, Thailand 129
Azores Islands, Portugal 71
Babulsar, Iran 112
Babylon Ruins, Iraq 113
Bacolod, Phil. Is. 132
Bad Hofgastein, Austria 68
Baden-Baden, Germany 46
Badgastein, Austria 68
Badlands, N. Dakota 222
Badlands Nat'l Monument, S. Dakota 222
Baghdad, Iraq 113
Bagneres de Bigorre, France 31
Baguio, Phil. Is. 131
Bahama Islands 186
Bahia (Salvador) Brazil 154
Baie de Chaleur, Canada 171
Bakersfield, California 203
Balboa, Canal Zone 184
Balearic Isles, Spain 76
Balestrand, Norway 55
Ballybofey, Ireland 23
Ballybunion, Ireland 24
Ballycastle, N. Ireland 22
Ballyclare, N. Ireland 22
Ballycotton, Ireland 24
Ballyshannon, Ireland 23
Baltimore, Maryland 244
Banars, India 119
Banbridge, N. Ireland 22
Banbury, England 15
Bandung, Indonesia 130
Bangkok, Thailand 129
Bangor, Maine 248
Bannockburn, Scotland 19
Banylus, France 31
Bar Harbor, Maine 248
Baraboo, Wisconsin 230
Barada River, Syria 110
Barbados Island 187
Barbizon, France 27
Barbuda Island 187
Barcelona, Spain 75
Bareges, France 31
Banff National Park, Canada 175
Barquisimeto, Venezuela 146
Barranquilla, Colombia 147
Barre, Vermont 248
Barron Falls, Australia 138
Barrow, Alaska 251
Barstow, California 202
Basse-Terre, Guadeloupe 195
Bastad, Sweden 55
Bastogne, Belgium 37
Batalha, Portugal 71
Bath, England 12
Baton Rouge, Louisiana 231
Baxter State Park, Maine 248
Bayeaux, France 29
Bayfield, Wisconsin 230
Bayonne, France 31
Beacon, New York 241
Beatitudes, Mount of, Israel 117
Beaulieu, France 33
Beaune, France 34
Bedloes Island, New York 240
Beirut, Lebanon 111
Belem, Brazil 154
Belfast, N. Ireland 22
Belgium 35
Bell Island, Canada 171
Bella Vista, Arkansas 233
Bellagio, Italy 84
Belleek, N. Ireland 23
Bellingham, Washington 208
Belo Horizonte, Brazil 154
Bemidji, Minnesota 223
Benburb, N. Ireland 23
Beni, Belgian Congo 103
Bennington, Vermont 248
Berchtesgaden, Germany 47
Berkeley, California 205
Berkshire Mountains, Mass. 249
Bergen, Norway 54
Berlin, New Hampshire 248
Berlin, Germany 50
Bermuda 185
Bern, Switzerland 59
Bethlehem, Jordan 115
Biarritz, France 31
Bijapur, India 119
Bilbao, Spain 74
Biloxi, Mississippi 238
Bimini, Bahamas 186
Bingham Canyon, Utah 213
Birmingham, Alabama 238
Birmingham, England 13
Biscayne Bay, Florida 238
Biskra, Algiers 95
Bismarck, N. Dakota 222
Black Hills, S. Dakota 221
Block Island, Rhode Island 249
Blanding, Utah 213
Blanquefort, France 31
Blarney Castle, Ireland 24
Bloemfontein, Union of S. Africa 106
Blois, France 30
Blue Mountains, Maine 248
Blue Ridge Mountains, Va. 235
Boca Chica, Dominican Rep. 192
Bogota, Colombia 148
Bois-le-Duc (Hertogenbosch), Netherlands 41
Boise, Idaho 212
Bolivia 156
Bologna, Italy 85
Bombay, India 119
Bonn, Germany 44
Boothbay Harbor, Maine 248
Boppard, Germany 44
Boradel Rio, Mexico 178
Bordeaux, France 30
Bornholm, Denmark 54
Boston, Massachusetts 246
Braemar, Scotland 20
Brainerd, Minnesota 223
Brandon, Canada 175
Brandon, Oregon 206
Brasilia, Brazil 152
Bray, Ireland 21
Brazil 152
Brecon, Wales 12
Bregenz, Austria 65
Breitenbush Springs, Oregon 206
Bremen, Germany 50
Bremerton, Washington 208
Brest, France 29
Bridgend, Wales 13
Bridgeport, Connecticut 249
Bridgetown, Barbados 187
Brighton, England 12
Brisbane, Australia 138
British Columbia Province, Canada 176
British West Indies 187
Broadstairs, England 12
Broome, Australia 137
Browning, Montana 212
Brownsville, Texas 234
Bruges, Belgium 37
Bruhl, Germany 44
Brunnen, Switzerland 64
Brussel, Belgium 35
Bryce Canyon Nat'l Park, Utah 213
Bukavu, Belgian Congo 102
Bukidnon, Phil. Is. 132
Buenos Aires, Argentina 164
Bundoran, Ireland 23
Burbank, California 201
Burgundy, France 34
Burlington, Vermont 248
Bursa, Turkey 88
Bussaco, Portugal 71
Butiaba, Uganda 103
Butte, Montana 212
Buzzards Bay, Mass. 247
Cadillac, France 31
Cadillac, Michigan 229
Caen, France 29
Caernarvon, Wales 13
Caerleon, England 12
Caesarea, Israel 117
Cairns, Australia 138
Cairo, Egypt 99
Calcutta, India 119
Calgary, Canada 176
Cali, Colombia 148
California, United States 200
Cambridge, England 16
Canada 170
Canal Zone 184
Canberra, Australia 136
Cannes, France 33
Cannock, Eng. 14
Cannon Beach, Oregon 206
Canterbury, England 11
Canyon, Texas 234
Cap d'Antibes, France 33
Cap-Haitien, Haiti 191
Cape Ann, Massachusetts 247
Cape Breton Highland Nat'l Park, Canada 171
Cape Cod, Massachusetts 247
Cape Hatteras, N. Carolina 236
Cape May, New Jersey 242
Capetown, Union of S. Africa 105
Capiata, Paraguay 158
Capilla del Monte, Argentina 166
Capri, Italy 80
Caracas, Venezuela 145
Caraquet, Canada 171
Carcassone, France 31
Carlsbad Caverns, N. Mexico 215
Carmarthen, Wales 13
Carnac, France 29
Carrasco Beach, Uruguay 160
Carrickfergus, N. Ireland 22
Carrickmacross, Ireland 23
Carrick-on-Shannon, Ireland 24
Cartagena, Colombia 147
Cartago, Costa Rica 183
Carthage, Tunisia 96
Casablanca, Morocco 92
Casbah, Algiers 94
Cascais, Portugal 70
Casco Bay, Maine 248
Cashel, Ireland 24
Casper, Wyoming 211
Castile, Spain 74
Castleblayney, Ireland 23
Castries, St. Lucia 187
Catania, Italy 83
Catskill Mountains, New York 242
Caumbo River, Venezuela 146
Cauterets, France 31
Cavan, Ireland 23
Cayman Islands, Jamaica 190
Cebu, Phil. Is. 131
Cedar City, Utah 213
Cedar Rapids, Iowa 224
Celle, Germany 49
Central Africa 102
Central City, Colorado 210
Ceylon 123
Challis, Idaho 212
Chambord, France 30
Chantilly, France 27
Chapel Hill, N. Carolina 236
Charleston, S. Carolina 236
Charleston, W Virginia 239
Charlestown, W. Virginia 239
Charlotte Amalie, Virgin Islands 194
Charlottetown, Canada 171
Charlottesville, Virginia 235
Chartres, France 27
Chateauneuf-du- Pape, France 32
Chateau-Thierry, France 28
Chaumont, France 30
Chesapeake Bay, Maryland 244
Chester, England 17
Cheverny, France 30
Cheyenne, Wyoming 211
Chicago, Ilinois 226
Chichicastenango, Guat. 179
Chile 161
Chillicothe, Ohio 228
Chiriqui Islands, Panama 184
Chittagong Hill Tracts, Pakistan 122
Christchurch, New Zealand 140
Christiana, Jamaica 190
Christiansfeld, Denmark 53
Christiansted, Virgin Islands 194
Chuzenji Lake, Japan 124
Cienfuegos, Cuba 189
Ciudad Bolivar, Venezuela 146
Ciudad Real, Spain 74
Ciudad Trujillo, Dominican Republic 192
Claremore, Oklahoma 233
Clermont-Ferrand, France 33
Cleveland, Ohio 228
Clones, Ireland 23
Cluny, France 34
Coban, Guatemala 179
Cobleskill, New York 242
Cocagne, Canada 171
Cody, Wyoming 211
Cognac, France 30
Coimbra, Portugal 71
Colleraine, N. Ireland 22
Collioure, France 31
Colmar, France 28
Cologne, Germany 43
Coloma, California 205
Colombia 147
Colombo, Ceylon 123
Colon, Panama 184
Colorado, United States 209
Colorado Springs, Colorado 210
Columbia, Missouri 219
Columbus, Ohio 228
Colwyn Bay, Wales 13
Comayagua, Honduras 180
Como, Italy 84
Compeigne, France 28
Concarneau, France 29
Concord, Massachusetts 247
Connecticut, United States 249
Connecticut River, New Hampshire 248
Constance, Germany 46
Constantine, Algeria 95
Coober Pedy, Australia 137
Cookstown, N. Ireland 23
Cooperstown, New York 242
Coos Bay, Oregon 206
Copacabana, Bolivia 157
Copan, Honduras 180
Copenhagen, Denmark 52
Cordoba, Argentina 166
Cordoba, Spain 76
Cordoba Sierras, Argentina 164
Corinth, Greece 87
Corner Brook, Canada 171
Coronado, California 201
Cortina Ampezzo, Italy 84
Corvallis, Oregon 206
Costa Brava, Spain 75
Costa Rica 183
Cotabato, Philippine Islands 132
Cotopaxi Volcano, Ecuador 149
Coutances, France 29
Coventry, England 14
Crawford Notch, New Hamp. 248
Crescent City, Utah 213
Crete Island, Greece 87
Cristobal, Canal Zone 184
Crosshaven, Ireland 24
Crown Point, Oregon 206
Cuba 188
Culver City, California 201
Cumberland, Maryland 244
Cumberland Gap, Kentucky 239
Curacao 196
Cusco, Peru 151
Cyprus 111
Dacca, Pakistan 122
Dallas, Texas 234
Damascus, Syria 110
Danbury, Connecticut 249
Darien, Connecticut 249
Dartmouth, England 12
Darwin, Australia 137
Dauphine Region, France 34
Davao, Philippine Islands 132
Dayton, Ohio 228
Dead Sea, Israel 115
Deadwood, S. Dakota 222
Deal, England 12
Dearborn, Michigan 229
Death Valley Nat'l Monument, California 203
Deauville, France 29
Delaware, United States 243
Delft, Netherlands 39
Delhi, India 119
Delos, Greece 87
Den Helder, Netherlands 40
Denmark 52
Denver, Colorado 209
Derrynane, Ireland 24
Des Moines, Iowa 224
Detroit, Michigan 229
Dhahran, Saudi Arabia 114
Dhakuria Lakes, India 120
Diamantina, Brazil 154
Diamond Head Volcano, Hawaii 253
Digby, Canada 171
Dijon, France 34
Dinant-sur-Meuse, Belg. 37
Dinard, France 29
Dingle, Ireland 24
Djerba, Tunisia 96
Djokjakarta, Indonesia 130
Dodge City, Kansas 220
Dominica Island 187
Dominican Republic 192
Domremy, France 28
Donegal, Ireland 23
Dordogne, France 33
Dordrecht, Netherlands 39
Dover, Delaware 244
Dover, England 12
Dublin, Ireland 20
Duluth, Minnesota 223
Dumfries, Scotland 19
Dun Laoghaire, Ireland 21
Dunbar, Scotland 19
Dundalk, Ireland 21
Dundee, Scotland 20
Dunedin, New Zealand 140
Dungannon, N. Ireland 22
Durango, Colorado 210
Durban, Union of S. Africa 105
Durham, England 16
Durham, N. Carolina 236
Dusseldorf, Germany 43
East Lansing, Michigan 229
Eastbourne, England 12
Easthampton, New York 241
Echternach, Luxembourg 39
Ecuador 149
Edinburgh, Scotland 18
Edmonton, Canada 176
Egmont Nat'l Park, N. Zea. 140
Egypt 97
El Boqueron, El Salvador 181
El Paso, Texas 234
El Salvador 181
El Yunque Forest, Puerto Rico 193
Elburz Mountains, Iran 112
Eleuthera, Bahamas 186
Elisabethville, Belgian Congo 102
Elkins, West Virginia 239
Elko, Nevada 218
Ellensburg, Washington 209
Ely, England 16
Englishtown, Canada 171
Ennis, Ireland 24
Enniskillen, N. Ireland 23
Enriquillo Lake, Dom. Rep. 192
Enschede, Netherlands 41
Epernay, France 29
Ericeira, Portugal 71
Essen, Germany 43
Estes Park, Colorado 210
Estoril, Portugal 70
Eugene, Oregon 206
Euphrates River, Iraq 113
Eureka, California 205
Eureka Springs, Arkansas 233
Everglades Nat'l Park, Fla. 238
Evora, Portugal 71
Exeter, England 12
Exeter, Rhode Island 249
Exmouth, England 12
Fairbanks, Alaska 251
Falaise, France 29
Falmouth, Jamaica 190
Farellones, Chile 162
Fargo, Georgia 237
Fatima, Portugal 71
Feldkirch, Austria 65
Fez, Morocco 94
Fiesole, Italy 82
Figueira da Foz, Portugal 71
Finland 57
Fiordland Nat'l. Park, N. Z. 140
Fjallnas, Sweden 57
Flagstaff, Arizona 216
Flensburg, Germany 48
Flin Flon, Canada 175
Florence, Italy 81
Flores, Guatemala 179
Florida, United States 237
Foix, France 31
Folkestone, England 12
Font-Romeu, France 31
Fontainebleau, France 27
Fontevrault, France 30
Foret des Pins, Haiti 191
Fort Anne, Canada 171
Fort-de-France, Martinique 195
Fort Portal, Uganda 103
Fort Raleigh, N. Carolina 236
Fort Recovery, Ohio 228
Fort Smith, Arkansas 233
Fort William, Scotland 20
Fort Worth, Texas 234
Fort Yates, N. Dakota 222
Fortress of Louisbourg, Can. 171
France 25
Franconia Notch, N. Hamp. 248
Frankfurt, Germany 45
Fredericksburg, Virginia 235
Fredericton, Canada 170
Frederiksted, Virgin Islands 194
French West Indies 195
Friday Harbor, Washington 208

Frisian Islands, Germany 48
Fuji Mountain, Japan 124
Galena, Illinois 227
Galicia, Spain 74
Galilee Region, Israel 116
Gallup, New Mexico 215
Galveston, Texas 235
Galway, Ireland 23
Ganges River, India 119
Gardone Riviera, Italy 84
Garmisch-Partenkirchen, Ger. . 47
Garrison, N. Ireland 23
Garrison Dam, N. Dakota 222
Gary, Indiana 228
Gaspe Peninsula Canada 172
Gavarnie, France 31
Geiranger, Norway 55
Geneva, Switzerland 61
Genoa, Italy 82
Georgia, United States 236
Gerardmer, France 28
Geraldton, Australia 137
Germany 42
Gettysburg, Pennsylvania 243
Ghent, Belgium 37
Gibraltar 76
Giethoorn, Netherlands 40
Gifu, Japan 124
Girvan, Scotland 19
Glacier Nat'l. Park, Montana ..212
Glasgow, Scotland 17
Glendale, California 201
Glendalough, Ireland 21
Gloucester, Massachusetts 247
Gothenburg, Sweden 55
Gotland, Sweden 57
Granada, Nicaragua 182
Granada, Spain 76
Grand Canyon, Arizona 217
Grand Junction, Colorado 210
Grand Pre, Canada 171
Grand Rapids, Michigan 229
Grass Valley, California 205
Grasse, France 33
Graz, Austria 68
Great Barrier Reef, Australia ..138
Great Britain 8
Great Exuma, Bahamas 186
Great Lakes 225
Great Salt Lake, Utah 213
Great Smoky Mountains,
N. Carolina 236
Greece 86
Green Bay, Wisconsin 230
Green Mountains, Vermont 248
Greensboro, Alabama 238
Greenwich, Connecticut 249
Greenwich Village, New York .240
Grenada 187
Guadeloupe Island 195
Guatavita Lake, Colombia 147
Guatemala 179
Guatemala City, Guatemala 179
Guayaquil, Ecuador 149
Guerande, France 30
Guimaraes, Portugal 71
Gunnison, Colorado 210
Gwalior, India 119
Haarlem, Netherlands 40
Haifa, Israel 117
Haiti 191
Hakone, Japan 124
Halifax, Canada 171
Hallein, Austria 66
Hallstatt, Austria 68
Halmstad, Sweden 55
Halsingborg, Sweden 56
Hama, Syria 111
Hamadan, Iran 112
Hamburg, Germany 49
Hamilton, Bermuda 185
Hamilton, Canada 174
Hannibal, Missouri 219
Hanover, New Hampshire 248
Harappa, Pakistan 122
Harbour Island, Bahamas 186
Hardin, Montana 211
Harpers Ferry, Maryland 244
Harpers Ferry, W. Virginia 239
Harrington Sound, Bermuda 185
Harrisburg, Pennsylvania 243
Harrogate, England 16
Hartford, Connecticut 249
Hastings, England 12
Hatay (Antakya, Antioch),
Turkey 88
Hautes Alpes Region, France ...34
Havana, Cuba 188
Hawaii 252
Hawick, Scotland 19
Hebrides, Scotland 20
Heidelberg, Germany 46
Heiligenblut Austria 68
Helgoland, Island, Germany ... 48
Helsinki, Finland 57
Hendaye, France 31
Henley-on-Thames, England ... 11
Hennebont, France 29
Heredia, Costa Rica 183
Herne Bay, England 11
Hibbing, Minnesota 223
Hilo, Hawaii 252
Himalaya Mountains 118
Himeji, Japan 125
Hiroshima, Japan 125
Hobart, Australia 137
Hodgenville, Kentucky 239
Hofuf, Saudi Arabia 114
Hoggar Route, Algeria 96
Hohwald, France 28
Hokkaido, Japan 125
Holbrook, Arizona 217
Holland, Michigan 229
Honaunau, Hawaii 252
Honduras 180
Hong Kong 127
Honolulu, Hawaii 253
Honshu Island, Japan 125
Hood River, Oregon 206
Hoover Dam, Nevada 218
Hot Springs Nat'l Park,
Arkansas 232
Houston, Texas 234
Huancayo, Peru 151
Huntington, W. Virginia 239
Hurley, New York 242
Hyannis, Massachusetts 247
Hyde Park, New York 241
Idaho, United States 212
Iguassu Falls, Brazil 155
Iguazu Falls, Argentina 166
Inagua, Bahamas 186
Indiana, United States 227
Indianapolis, Indiana 227
Illinois, United States 226
Ilobasco, El Salvador 181
Iloilo, Philippine Islands 132
India 118
Indonesia 130
Innsbruck, Austria 65
Interlaken, Switzerland 62
Inverness, Scotland 20
Inyo-Mono, California 203
Iona, Scotland 20
Iowa, United States 224
Iquique, Chile 161
Iran (Persia) 112
Iraq 113
Irazu Volcano, Costa Rica 183
Ireland 20
Iron Mountain, Michigan 229
Isla de Lobos (Seal Island),
Uruguay 160
Isle of Pines, Cuba 189
Israel 116
Istanbul, Turkey 88
Italy 77
Itaugua, Paraguay 158
Izalco, El Salvador 181
Izmir, Turkey 88
Jaffa-Tel Aviv, Israel 117
Jamaica 190
Jamestown, Rhode Island 249
Jamestown, Virginia 235
Japan 124
Jasper Nat'l Park, Canada 175
Jefferson City, Missouri 219
Jerome, Idaho 212
Jerusalem (New City), Israel ..117
Jerusalem (Old City) Jordan ...115
Jesus Maria, Argentina 166
Jidda, Saudi Arabia 114
Jipijapa, Ecuador 149
Johannesburg, Union of
S. Africa 104
Johnsville, California 205
Jordan 115
Josselin, France 30
Juan-les-Pins, France 33
Juarez, Mexico 234
Jujuy, Argentina 166
Juneau, Alaska 250
Kairouan, Tunisia 96
Kalapana, Hawaii 252
Kalgoorlie, Australia 137
Kalmar, Sweden 56
Kamakura, Japan 124
Kampala, Uganda 103
Kansas, United States 220
Kansas City, Missouri 220
Kapti Island, New Zealand 139
Karachi, Pakistan 121
Karnak, Egypt 161
Kashmir 121
Katmai Mountain, Alaska 251
Kauai Island, Hawaii 253
Kefar Nahum (Capernaum),
Israel 117
Kegon Waterfall, Japan 124
Kellogg, Idaho 212
Ken Wood, England 11
Kenscoff, Haiti 191
Kent, England 11
Kentucky, United States 239
Kerkyra, Greece 87
Kericho, Kenya 103
Ketchikan, Alaska 250
Key West, Florida 238
Khyber Pass, Pakistan 122
Kidwelly, Wales 13
Kiel, Germany 48
Kilauea Volcano, Hawaii 252
Kilcar, Ireland 23
Kilkenny, Ireland 21
Killarney, Ireland 24
Kilpisjarvi, Finland 58
Kimberly, Union of S. Africa ..105
Kingston, Canada 174
Kingston, Jamaica 190
Kingston, New York 242
Kiruna, Sweden 57
Kitty Hawk, N. Carolina 236
Kitzbuhel, Austria 66
Kleve, Germany 43
Knokke-Le Zoute, Belgium 37
Knoxville, Tennessee 239
Koblenz, Germany 44
Kodiak, Alaska 251
Kona, Hawaii 252
Kongolo, Belgian Congo 102
Kruger National Park,
U. of S. Africa 106
Kut, Iraq 113
Kyoto, Japan 124
Kyrenia, Cyprus 111
Kyushu Island, Japan 125
La Catalina, Costa Rica 183
La Coruna, Spain 74
La Granja, Spain 74
La Guaira, Venezuela 144
La Jolla, California 201
La Paz, Bolivia 156
La Plata, Argentina 165
La Porte, California 205
La Rochelle, France 30
La Toma, El Salvador 181
Labouiche, France 31
Lacovia, Jamaica 190
Lagoa Santa, Brazil 154
Laguna de San Rafael, Chile ..163
Lahore, Pakistan 122
Lake Champlain, New York 241
Lake Charles, Louisiana 232
Lake Como, Italy 84
Lake District, England 17
Lake Garda, Italy 84
Lake George, New York 242
Lake Louise, Canada 175
Lake Maggiore, Italy 84
Lake Mead, Nevada 218
Lake Placid, New York 242
Lake Tahoe, California 205
Lake Wales, Florida 237
Lake Winnipesaukee,
New Hampshire 248
Lanao, Philippine Islands 132
Lancaster, Pennsylvania 243
Languedoc, France 31
Lannion, France 29
Laredo, Texas 234
Larne, N. Ireland 22
Las Pinas, Philippine Islands ..131
Las Vegas, Nevada 217
Latakia, Syria 111
Latour-de-Carol, France 31
Laurentian Mountains, Canada 173
Lausanne, Switzerland 62
Lawrence, Massachusetts 247
Le Puy, France 33
Lead, S. Dakota 222
Leamington, England 14
Leavenworth, Kansas 220
Lebanon 111
Lee, Massachusetts 249
Leeuwarden, Netherlands 40
Leeward Islands 187
Legaspi, Philippine Islands 131
Leghorn, Italy 82
Leiden, Netherlands 39
Leon, Nicaragua 182
Lenox, Massachusetts 249
Leopoldville, Belgian Congo ..102
Les Baux, France 32
Lewiston, Idaho 212
Lexington, Kentucky 239
Lexington, Massachusetts 247
Leyte Island, Phil. Is. 132
Liberty Island (Bedloe's I.),
New York 240
Lichfield, England 14
Liege, Belgium 37
Lienz, Austria 68
Lillehammer, Norway 55
Lima, Peru 150
Limerick, Ireland 24
Limoges, France 33
Lincoln, Nebraska 221
Lincoln City, Indiana 227
Linz, Austria 66
Lisbon, Portugal 70
Litchfield, Connecticut 249
Little Exuma, Bahamas 186
Little Rock, Arkansas 232
Liverpool,, England 15
Livingston, Guatemala 179
Llandudno, Wales 13
Locarno, Switzerland 63
Loch Ness, Scotland 20
Lofer, Austria 66
London, England 9
Londonderry, N. Ireland 22
Long Beach, California 201
Long Beach, Washington 208
Long Branch, New Jersey 242
Long Island, New York 241
Longford, Ireland 21
Los Angeles, California 200
Louisiana, United States 230
Louisville, Kentucky 239
Lourdes, France 31
Lowell, Massachusetts 247
Lubeck, Germany 48
Lucca, Italy 82
Lucerne, Switzerland 63
Lugano, Switzerland 63
Lund, Sweden 56
Luneburg, Germany 49
Lunenburg, Canada 171
Luso, Portugal 71
Luxembourg 37
Luxor, Egypt 101
Luzon, Philippine Islands 131
Lyon, France 34
Maastricht, Netherlands 41
Macon, France 34
Machu Pichu, Peru 151
Mackinac Island, Michigan 229
Madeira Islands, Portugal 71
Madison, Connecticut 249
Madison, Wisconsin 230
Madonna di Campiglio, Italy .. 84
Madras, India 120
Madrid, Spain 73
Madurai, India 121
Mafra, Portugal 71
Magdalena River, Colombia 147
Mahabalipuram, India 121
Maidenhead, England 11
Maine, United States 248
Mainz, Germany 44
Malaga, Spain 76
Malmaison, France 27
Malmo, Sweden 56
Mammoth Cave, Kentucky 239
Managua, Nicaragua 182
Manaus, Brazil 155
Manchester, Massachusetts 247
Manchester, Vermont 248
Mandan, N. Dakota 222
Mandeville, Jamaica 190
Manila, Philippine Islands 132
Manitoba Province, Canada 175
Manitou Springs, Colorado 210
Mapocho River, Chile 162
Mar del Plata, Argentina 165
Maracaibo, Venezuela 146
Maracay, Venezuela 145
Marajo Island, Brazil 154
Marathon, Texas 234
Margarita Island, Venezuela ..146
Margate, England 12
Marietta, Ohio 228
Marina, India 120
Marquette, Michigan 229
Marrakech, Morocco 94
Marseilles, France 32
Marstrand, Sweden 55
Martha's Vineyard Mass. 247
Martinique, Island 195
Maryland, United States 244
Massachusetts, United States 247
Matanzas, Cuba 189
Matsushima (Pine Islands),
Japan 125
Mauleon, France 31
Mauna Kea Mountain, Hawaii .252
Mauna Loa Volcano, Hawaii 252
Mayaguez, Puerto Rico 193
Mayrhofen, Austria 65
Mazagan, Morocco 93
Mecca, Saudi Arabia 114
Medellin, Venezuela 148
Medina, Saudi Arabia 114
Medora, S. Dakota 222
Meeks Bay, Nevada 219
Megiddo, Israel 117
Meknes, Morocco 94
Melbourne, Australia 137
Memphis, Tenn. 239
Mendoza, Argentina 166
Menton, France 33
Mercedes, Uruguay 160
Merrimac River, New Hamp. ..248
Metz, France 28
Mexican Hat, Utah 213
Mexico 177
Mexico City, Mexico 177
Miami, Florida 237
Miami Beach, Florida 237
Michigan, United States 228
Middelburg, Netherlands 41
Milan, Italy 83
Miles City, Montana 211
Milwaukee, Wisconsin 230
Mina Clavero, Argentina 166
Minas Gerais, Brazil 154
Mindanao Island, Phil. Is. 132
Mindoro Island, Phil. Is. 132
Mineral Point, Wisconsin 230
Minneapolis, Minnesota 224
Minnesota, United States 223
Mission Beach, California 201
Mississippi, United States 238
Missouri, United States 219
Mitla, Mexico 178
Moab, Utah 213
Mobile, Alabama 238
Moen Island, Denmark 54
Mogador, Morocco 93
Mohenjo-Daro, Pakistan 122
Mojave, California 202
Molde, Norway 55
Moline, Ill. 227
Molokai Island, Hawaii 253
Monaco 33
Monaghan, Ireland 23
Moncton, Canada 171
Mont Blanc Region, France 34
Montana, United States 211
Monte Carlo, Monaco 33
Montego Bay, Jamaica 190
Monterey, California 205
Montevideo, Uruguay 159
Montferrand, France 33
Montmorency Falls, Canada 173
Montpelier, Vermont 248
Montpellier, France 32
Montreal, Canada 173
Montreux, Switzerland 62
Montserrat Island 187
Moose, Wyoming 211
Moosehead Lake, Maine 248
Mora, Sweden 57
Morges, Switzerland 62
Morlaix, France 29
Morocco 92
Morrilton, Arkansas 232
Morristown, New Jersey 242
Morro Castle, Cuba 188
Moss Glen, Canada 171
Mount Aconcagua, Argentina ..166
Mount Cadillac, Maine 248
Mount Carmel, Israel 117
Mount Demavend, Iran 112
Mount Desert Island, Maine ...248
Mount Katahdin, Maine 248
Mt. McKinley, Alaska 251
Mt. McKinley Nat'l Park,
Alaska 251
Mount Mansfield, Vermont 248
Mount Rainier, Washington 208
Mount Rushmore Nat'l Memorial,
S. Dakota 221
Mt. Vernon, Virginia 235
Mount Washington,
New Hampshire 248
Mount Wellington, Australia 137
Mt. Whitney, California 203
Mull, Scotland 20
Mullingar, Ireland 21
Multan, Pakistan 122
Munich, Germany 47
Murano, Italy 85
Murfreesboro, Arkansas 232
Mykonos, Greece 87
Mystic, Connecticut 249
Nagasaki, Japan 125
Nagoya, Japan 124
Nairobi, Kenya 103
Nahuel Huapi Nat'l Peak,
Argentina 165
Nancy, France 28
Nantucket, Massachusetts 247
Naples, Italy 79
Nara, Japan 124
Narragansett, Rhode Island ...249
Nashville, Tennessee 239
Nassau, Bahamas 186
Natchez, Mississippi 238
Nazare, Portugal 71
Nazareth, Israel 117
Nebraska, United States 220
Negev Mountains, Israel 117
Negros, Philippine Islands 131
Netanya, Israel 117
Netherlands 39
Nevada, United States 217
Nevada City, California 205
Nevis Island 187
New Bedford, Mass. 247
New Brunswick Province,
Canada 170
New Castle, Delaware 244
New Delhi, India 119
New Glarus, Wisconsin 230
New Haven, Connecticut 249
New Hampshire, U.S. 248
New Harmony, Indiana 227
New Iberia, Louisiana 232
New Jersey, United States 242
New London, Connecticut 249
New Mexico, United States 214
New Orleans, Louisiana 230
New Paltz, New York 242
New Philadelphia, Ohio 228
New Providence, Bahamas 186
New Salem, Illinois 227
New York, New York 239
New York, United States 239
New Zealand 139
Newburgh, New York 241
Newcastle, England 17
Newcastle, N. Ireland 22
Newfoundland Province,
Canada 171
Newmarket, England 16
Newport, England 12
Newport, Oregon 206
Newport, Rhode Island 249
Niagara Falls, New York 242
Nicaragua 182
Nice, France 33
Nicosia, Cyprus 111
Nijmegen, Netherlands 41
Nikko Nat'l Park, Japan 124
Nimes, France 32
Nome, Alaska 251
Nordlingen, Germany 46
Norfolk, Virginia 236
North Africa 92
North Berwick, Scotland 19
North Carolina, United States 236
North Conway, New Hamp. 248
North Dakota, United States ..222
Northwest Territory, Canada ..176
Norway 54
Norwich, England 16
Nova Scotia Province, Canada 171
Oahu Island, Hawaii 253
Oak Ridge, Tennessee 239
Oakland, California 204
Oaxaca, Mexico 178
Oban, New Zealand 140
Oban, Scotland 19
Oberammergau, Germany 47
Obidos, Portugal 71
Ocean City, Maryland 244
Oceanside, California 202
Ochos Rios, Jamaica 190
Odense, Denmark 53
Ogden, Utah 213
Ohio, United States 228
Okefenokee Swamp, Georgia ..237
Oklahoma, United States 233
Oklahoma City, Oklahoma 233
Oland, Sweden 56
Old Orchard, Maine 248
Old Saybrook, Connecticut 249
Old Town, Maine 248
Olinda, Brazil 154
Omagh, N. Ireland 22
Omaha, Nebraska 221
Ontario Province, Canada 173
Oporto, Portugal 71
Oradour-sur-Glane, France 33
Orange, France 31
Orbey, France 28
Oregon, United States 205
Orinoco River, Venezuela 144
Orlando, Florida 237
Orleans, France 30
Orontes River, Syria 111
Orosi (Enchanted Valley)
Costa Rica 183
Oruro, Bolivia 157
Osaka, Japan 125
Oslo, Norway 54
Ottawa, Canada 170
Ouachita Mountains, Ark. 232
Ouro Prẹto, Brazil 154

Oxford, England 15
Ozark Mountains, Arkansas 233
Paimpol, France 29
Painted Desert, Arizona 217
Pakistan 121
Palawan Island, Phil. Is. 132
Palermo, Italy 81
Palm Beach, Florida 237
Palm Springs, California 202
Palma, Spain 76
Palo Alto, California 205
Panajachel, Guatemala 179
Panama 184
Panama City, Panama 184
Panay Island, Phil. Is. 132
Para, Brazil 154
Paraguay 158
Paris, France 25
Parknasilla, Ireland 24
Pasadena, California 201
Pascagoula, Mississippi 238
Pasco, Washington 209
Pass Christian, Mississippi 238
Paterson Inlet, New Zealand 140
Pau, France 31
Peebles, Scotland 19
Pendleton, Oregon 206
Pennsylvania, United States 242
Penobscot River, Maine 248
Penzance, England 12
Perigueux, France 33
Perpignan, France 31
Persia (Iran) 112
Perth, Australia 137
Perth, Scotland 20
Peru 149
Perugia, Italy 81
Peshawar, Pakistan 122
Petersburg, Alaska 250
Petersburg, W. Va. 239
Petionville, Haiti 191
Petrified Forest, Arizona 217
Petropolis, Brazil 154
Philadelphia, Pennsylvania 242
Philippines 131
Phoenix, Arizona 216
Pike's Peak, Colorado 210
Pilcomayo River, Paraguay 158
Pinar del Rio, Cuba 189
Pisa, Italy 82
Pismo Beach, California 202
Pittsburgh, Pennsylvania 243
Placerville, California 205
Platt Nat'l Park, Oklahoma 233
Playas, Ecuador 149
Plymouth, England 12
Plymouth, Massachusetts 247
Poblet, Spain 75
Pocitos Beach, Uruguay 160
Pocono Mountains, Pa. 243
Pocos de Caldas, Brazil 154
Pointe-a-Pitre, Guadeloupe 195
Poitiers, France 30
Pomeroy, N. Ireland 23
Pomona, California 201
Pompeii, Italy 81
Ponce, Puerto Rico 193
Pontevedra, Spain 74
Popayan, Colombia 148
Popocatepetl, (Smoking Mountain), Mexico 178
Port Angeles, Washington 208
Port Antonio, Jamaica 190
Port Arthur, Australia 137
Port-au-Prince, Haiti 191
Port of Spain, Trinidad 187
Port Royal, Canada 171
Port Royal, Honduras 180
Port William, New Zealand 140
Portillo, Chile 163
Portland, Maine 248
Portland, Oregon 206
Portobello, Canal Zone 184
Portofino, Italy 82
Portree, Scotland 20
Portsmouth, England 12
Portsmouth, New Hampshire 248
Portstewart, N. Ireland 22
Portugal 69
Posadas, Argentina 166
Potomac River, Maryland 244
Potosi, Bolivia 157
Poughkeepsie, New York 241
Prades, France 31
Prestatyn, Wales 13
Prestwick, Scotland 19
Pretoria, Union of S. Africa 106
Pribilof Islands Alaska 251
Prince Albert, Canada 175
Prince Edward Island, Canada 171
Princeton, New Jersey 242
Proctor, Vermont 248
Providence, Rhode Island 249
Provincetown, Massachusetts 247
Provo, Utah 213
Puebla, Mexico 178
Puenta del Inca, Argentina 166
Puerto Barrios, Guatemala 179
Puerto Cabello, Venezuela 146
Puerto Iguazu, Argentina 166
Puerto Montt, Chile 163
Puerto Rico 193
Puno, Peru 151
Punta Arenas ,Chile 163
Punta del Este, Uruguay 160
Pyramids, Egypt 100
Pyrenees Region, France 34
Quebec, Canada 172
Quebec Province, Canada 172
Queen Elizabeth Game Park, Uganda 103
Queenstown, New Zealand 140
Quezaltenango, Guatemala 179
Quezon City, Philippine Islands 131
Quimper, France 29
Quito, Ecuador 149
Rabat, Morocco 94
Racine, Wisconsin 230
Raleigh, N. Carolina 236
Ramsar, Iran 112
Ramsgate, England 12
Rangeley Lakes, Maine 248
Rapallo, Italy 82
Rapid City, S. Dakota 222
Rattvik, Sweden 57
Reading, Pennsylvania 243
Recife, Brazil 154
Regina, Canada 175
Reims, France 29
Rennes, France 30
Reno, Nevada 218
Rensselaer, New York 242
Rhinelander, Wisconsin 230
Rhode Island, United States 249
Rhodes Island, Greece 87
Ribe, Denmark 53
Ribeauville, France 28
Richibucto, Canada 171
Richmond, California 205
Richmond, England 11
Richmond, Virginia 235
Riksgransen, Sweden 57
Rimac River, Peru 151
Ringsted, Denmark 53
Rio de la Plata, Argentina 165
Rio Grande do Sul, Brazil 155
Rio Grande River, Texas 234
Rio de Janeiro, Brazil 152
Riobamba, Ecuador 149
Ripon, England 16
River Jordan, Jordan 115
Riviera Region, France 34
Riyadh, Saudi Arabia 114
Roanoke Island, N. Carolina 236
Roatan, Honduras 180
Rocamadour, France 33
Rocha, Uruguay 160
Rochester, England 11
Rochester, Minnesota 224
Rocky Mt. Nat'l Park, Colorado 210
Rogersville, Canada 171
Rome, Italy 78
Ronda, Spain 76
Rosario, Argentina 165
Rosario de la Frontera, Argentina 166
Roscommon, Ireland 24
Roskilde, Denmark 53
Rosses Point, Ireland 24
Rothenburg, Germany 46
Rotterdam,, Netherlands 39
Rouen, France 29
Running Springs, California 202
Rutland, Vermont 248
Sackville, Canada 171
Sacramento, California 205
Safed (Tsefat) Israel 117
Safi, Morocco 93
Sag Harbor, New York 241
Saguenay River, Canada 172
St. Andrews, Canada 171
St. Anton, Austria 65
St. Augustine, Florida 237
St. Briac, France 29
St. Cast, France 29
St. Christopher Island, (St. Kitts) 187
St. Croix, Virgin Islands 194
St. David's Island, Bermuda 185
Saint Denis, France 27
St. Francisville, Louisiana 231
St. Gallen, Switzerland 63
St. George, Bermuda 185
St. George's, Granada 187
St. Germain-en-Laye, France 27
St. Girons, France 31
St. Guilhelm-le-Desert 32
St. Jean de Luz, France 31
St.-Jean-Pied-de-Port, France 31
Saint John, Canada 170
St. John Island, Virgin Islands 194
St. John's, Canada 171
St. Joseph, Missouri 220
St.-Lo, France 29
St. Louis, Missouri 219
St. Louis de Kent, Canada 171
St. Lucia Island 187
St. Lunaire, France 29
St.-Malo, France 29
Saint Marc, Haiti 191
St. Martinville, Louisiana 232
St. Moritz, Switzerland 63
St. Paul, Minnesota 223
St. Raphael, France 33
St. Thomas Island, Virgin Islands 194
St. Tropez, France 33
St. Vincent Island 187
Sainte Anne de Beaupre, Canada 173
Ste. Maries de la Mer, France 32
Salem, Massachusetts 247
Salem, Oregon 206
Salina, Kansas 220
Salinas, Ecuador 149
Salisbury, England 12
Salt Lake City, Utah 213
Salt River, Virgin Islands 194
Salta, Argentina 166
Salto, Uruguay 160
Salzburg, Austria 66
Samar Island, Phil. Is. 132
San Antonio, Texas 234
San Bernardino, Paraguay 158
San Blas Islands, Panama 184
San Bruno, California 205
San Carlos de Bariloche, Argentina 165
San Diego, California 201
San Francisco, California 203
San Joaquin, California 203
San Jose, Costa Rica 183
San Juan, Puerto Rico 193
San Juan Teotihuacan, Mex. 178
San Juancito, Honduras 180
San Marino, Italy 85
San Martino di Castrozza, Italy 84
San Mateo, California 205
San Miguel de los Banos, Cuba 189
San Pedro Harbor, California 201
San Remo, Italy 82
San Salvador, El Salvador 181
San-Sebastian, France 31
San Sebastian, Spain 74
San Vicente, El Salvador 181
Sanchi, India 119
Sancti Spiritus, Cuba 189
Sandy's, Bermuda 185
Sandwich, Massachusetts 247
Santa Ana, El Salvador 181
Santa Barbara, California 202
Santa Claus, Indiana 227
Santa Cruz, Bolivia 157
Santa Cruz, California 205
Santa Elena Canyon, Texas 234
Santa Fe, Argentina 165
Santa Fe, New Mexico 214
Santa Rosa de Copan, Honduras 180
Santa Tecla (Nuevo San Salvador), El Salvador 181
Santa Teresa Nat'l Park, Uruguay 160
Santander, Spain 74
Sante Margherita Ligure, Italy 82
Santiago, Chile 161
Santiago de Compostela, Spain 74
Santiago de Cuba, Cuba 189
Santiago, Dominican, Repub. 192
Santo Domingo de los Colorados, Ecuador 150
Santorini (Thera) Island, Greece 87
Santos, Brazil 155
Santurce, Puerto Rico 193
Sao Paulo, Brazil 155
Saragossa, Spain 74
Sarasota, Florida 238
Saratoga Springs, New York 242
Sarnath, India 119
Saskatchewan Province, Canada 175
Saudi Arabia 114
Saulieu, France 34
Sault Ste. Marie, Canada 174
Sault Ste. Marie, Michigan 229
Saumur, France 30
Savannah, Georgia 236
Savoy Region, France 34
Scandinavia 52
Scarborough, England 16
Scarborough, Tobago 187
Sea of Galilee (Lake Tiberias), Israel 117
Seaford, England 12
Seaside, Oregon 206
Seattle, Washington 207
Sebago Lake, Maine 248
Segovia, Spain 74
Selva di Gardena, Italy 84
Sendai, Japan 125
Sens, France 34
Sequoia National Park, California 203
Sestriere, Italy 83
Setubal, Portugal 70
Seville, Spain 76
Sevres, France 27
Sfax, Tunisia 96
Shannon Airport, Ireland 24
Shasta Mountain, California 205
Shelburne, Canada 171
Shelton, Washington 208
Shikoku Island, Japan 125
Shikotsu-Toya Nat'l Park, Japan 125
Shippigan, Canada 171
Shreveport, Louisiana 232
Siam (Thailand) 129
Sicily, Italy 81
Sidi Bel Abbes, Algeria 94
Siena, Italy 81
Sierra Nevada, Spain 76
Sigiriya Mountains, Ceylon 123
Silkeborg, Denmark 53
Simla, India 119
Singapore 128
Sintra, Portugal 71
Sitges, Spain 75
Sitka, Alaska 251
Siwa, Egypt 101
Skye, Scotland 20
Slagelse, Denmark 53
Sligo, Ireland 24
Smugglers Notch, Vermont 248
Snow Valley, California 202
Soledad, Venezuela 146
Sonoma, California 205
Soo Junction, Michigan 229
Soria, Spain 74
Sorrento, Italy 81
Sosua, Dominican Repub. 192
Soulac, France 31
South Bend, Indiana 228
South Carolina, United States 236
South Dakota, United States 221
South Shore Region, Bermuda 185
Southampton, Bermuda 185
Southsea, England 12
Spain 72
Spearfish, S. Dakota 222
Sphinx, Egypt 100
Spittal, Austria 68
Spokane, Washington 209
Springfield, Illinois 227
Springfield, Massachusetts 249
Squaw Valley, California 219
Srinagar, Kashmir 121
Stanleyville, Belgian Congo 102
Staten Island, New York 240
Stamford, Connecticut 249
Stavanger, Norway 54
Steamboat Springs, Colo. 210
Stewart Island, New Zealand 140
Stirling, Scotland 19
Stockbridge, Massachusetts 249
Stockholm, Sweden 56
Stoke Poges, England 11
Storlien, Sweden 57
Stowe, Vermont 248
Strabane, N. Ireland 23
Strandhill, Ireland 23
Stranorlar, Ireland 23
Strasbourg, France 28
Stratford, Canada 174
Stratford, Connecticut 249
Stratford-upon-Avon, Eng. 15
Stresa Italy 84
Stroudsburg, Pennsylvania 243
Stuttgart, Arkansas 232
Sucre, Bolivia 157
Sugar Loaf Mountain, Brazil 153
Sulphur, Oklahoma 233
Summerside, Canada 171
Sun Valley, Idaho 212
Sundarbans Forest Region, Pakistan 122
Superior, Wisconsin 230
Superior Nat'l Forest, Minn. 223
Swansea, Wales 13
Sweden 55
Switzerland 59
Sydney, Australia 136
Syria 110
Taal Volcano, Phil. Is. 131
Taboga Island, Panama 184
Tacoma, Washington 208
Tagaytay City, Phil. Is. 131
Tahoe City, Nevada 219
Taj Mahal, India 119
Taluksangay, Phil. Is. 132
Tama, Iowa 224
Tandil, Argentina 165
Tanezrouft Route, Algeria 96
Tanglewood, Massachusetts 249
Taormina, Italy 81
Taos, New Mexico 214
Tara, Ireland 21
Tarpon Springs, Florida 238
Tarragona, Spain 75
Tarrytown, New York 241
Tasmania Island, Australia 137
Tatta, Pakistan 122
Tebessa, Algeria 95
Tegucigalpa, Honduras 180
Teheran, Iran 112
Tel Aviv-Jaffa, Israel 117
Tennessee, United States 239
Teresopolis, Brazil 154
Texas 233
Thailand (Siam) 129
The Dalles, Oregon 206
The Hague ('s-Gravenhage), Netherlands 39
The Pas, Canada 175
The Weirs, New Hampshire 248
Three Rivers, Canada 173
Tiahuanacu, Bolivia 157
Tiberias Lake (Sea of Galilee), Israel 117
Tigris River, Iraq 113
Tijuana, Mexico 201
Tijuca Forest, Brazil 153
Timaru, New Zealand 140
Tipitapa, Nicaragua 182
Tipperary, Ireland 24
Titicaca Lake, Bolivia 156
Titicaca Lake, Peru 151
Tlemcen, Algeria 94
Tobago 187
Tokyo, Japan 126
Toledo, Ohio 228
Toledo, Spain 74
Tombstone, Arizona 216
Topeka, Kansas 220
Tordesillas, Spain 74
Torquay, England 12
Toronto, Canada 174
Tortola Island, Virgin Islands 194
Toulouse, France 31
Tours, France 30
Tralee, Ireland 24
Transvaal, Union of S. Africa 106
Traverse City, Michigan 229
Trenton, New Jersey 242
Trier, Germany 44
Trinidad, Cuba 189
Trinidad, Paraguay 158
Trinidad Island 187
Tromso, Norway 55
Trondheim, Norway 55
Tucson, Arizona 216
Tucuman, Argentina 166
Tulsa, Oklahoma 233
Tunbridge Wells, England 11
Tunis, Tunisia 96
Tunisia 96
Turin, Italy 82
Turkey 88
Turku, Finland 58
Twin Falls, Idaho 212
Ulu Dag Mountain, Turkey 88
Union of South Africa 104
Unzen Nat'l Park, Japan 125
Uppsala, Sweden 57
Uruguay 159
Utah, United States 213
Utrecht, Netherlands 41
Valadalen, Sweden 57
Valencia, Spain 75
Valencia, Venezuela 146
Valley of Fire State Park 218
Valparaiso, Chile 162
Van Buren, Missouri 220
Vancouver, Canada 176
Vannes, France 29
Varadero Beach, Cuba 189
Vejle, Denmark 53
Vence, France 33
Venezuela 144
Venice, Italy 85
Veracruz, Mexico 178
Verdun, France 28
Vermont, United States 248
Versailles, France 27
Viana do Castelo, Portugal 71
Vianden, Luxembourg 39
Viareggio, Italy 82
Vicksburg, Mississippi 239
Victoria, Canada 176
Victoria Falls, Africa 103
Victorville, California 202
Vienna, Austria 66
Vigo, Spain 74
Villa Beach, Phil. Is. 132
Villa Nogues, Argentina 166
Villach, Austria 68
Villefranche, France 33
Vina del Mar, Chile 163
Vincennes, Indiana 227
Virgin Gorda Island, Virgin Islands 194
Virgin Islands 194
Virginia, Ireland 23
Virginia, United States 235
Virginia Beach, Virginia 236
Virginia City, Montana 212
Virginia City, Nevada 218
Visayas, Philippine Islands 131
Vitre, France 30
Vittel, France 28
Vouvray, France 30
Waikiki Beach, Hawaii 253
Wailuku, Hawaii 253
Waldport, Oregon 206
Wales 12
Waltham, Massachusetts 247
Warwick, England 14
Washington, D.C., U.S. 244
Washington, United States 207
Waterton Lakes Nat'l Park, Canada 176
Watford City, N. Dakota 222
Watkins Glen, New York 242
Wausau, Wisconsin 230
Waycross, Georgia 237
Wellington, New Zealand 139
Wenatchee, Washington 209
West Point, New York 241
West Virginia, United States 239
Westport, Connecticut 249
Westport, Ireland 24
Wexford Ireland 21
Whitby, England 16
White Mountains, New Hampshire 248
White Sulphur Springs, W. Virginia 239
Whitefish, Montana 212
Wickford, Rhode Island 249
Wiesbaden, Germany 45
Wildwood, New Jersey 242
Wilkes-Barre, Pennsylvania 243
Willemstad, Curacao 196
Williamsburg, Virginia 235
Wilmington, Delaware 244
Wilmington, New York 242
Wilmington, Vermont 249
Windward Islands 187
Winnipeg, Canada 175
Winston-Salem, N. Carolina 236
Winter Haven, Florida 237
Wisconsin, United States 230
Wolverhampton, England 14
Woods Hole, Massachusetts 247
Woodstock, New York 242
Worcester, Massachusetts 247
Worms, Germany 46
Wrangell, Alaska 250
Wuppertal, Germany 43
Wurzburg, Germany 46
Wyoming, United States 211
Xochimilco, Mexico 178
Yarmouth, Canada 171
Yellow Springs, Ohio 228
Yellowstone Nat'l Park, Wyo. 211
York, England 16
Yorktown, Virginia 236
Yosemite Nat'l Park, Calif. 203
Youghal, Ireland 24
Ypacaray Lake, Paraguay 158
Yukon Territory, Canada 176
Zao Mountain, Japan 125
Zamboanga, Philippine Isls. 132
Zell am See, Austria 66
Zermatt, Switzerland 63
Zimbabwe Ruins, So. Rhod. 103
Zion Nat'l Park, Utah 213
Zurich, Switzerland 64
Zutphen, Netherlands 41

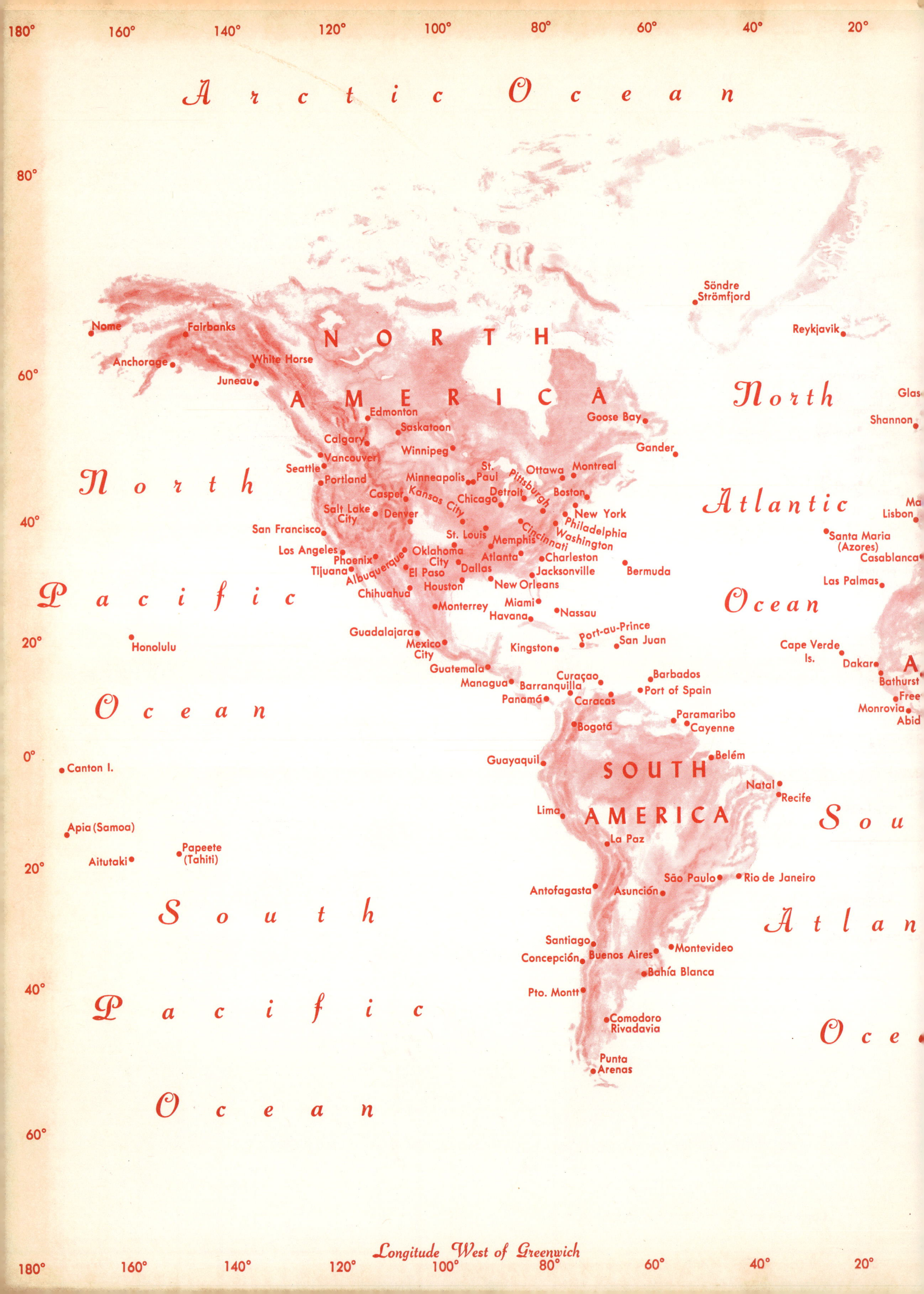

180°
160°
140°
120°
100°
80°
60°
40°
20°
Arctic Ocean
80°
Söndre Strömfjord
Reykjavik
Nome
Fairbanks
NORTH AMERICA
Anchorage
White Horse
Juneau
60°
North Atlantic Ocean
Glas
Shannon
Edmonton
Goose Bay
Saskatoon
Calgary
Winnipeg
Gander
Vancouver
Seattle
Portland
Minneapolis
St. Paul
Ottawa
Montreal
North Pacific Ocean
Pittsburgh
Detroit
Boston
Casper
Kansas City
Chicago
Salt Lake City
Denver
New York
Philadelphia
Washington
Ma
Lisbon
40°
San Francisco
St. Louis
Memphis
Cincinnati
Santa Maria (Azores)
Los Angeles
Oklahoma City
Atlanta
Charleston
Casablanca
Phoenix
Tijuana
Albuquerque
El Paso
Dallas
Jacksonville
Bermuda
Houston
New Orleans
Las Palmas
Chihuahua
Monterrey
Miami
Nassau
Havana
Guadalajara
Port-au-Prince
Honolulu
Mexico City
Kingston
San Juan
Cape Verde Is.
20°
Dakar
Guatemala
Curaçao
Barbados
Bathurst
Managua
Barranquilla
Port of Spain
Free
Panamá
Caracas
Monrovia
Abid
Paramaribo
Cayenne
Bogotá
0°
Canton I.
Guayaquil
Belém
SOUTH AMERICA
Natal
Recife
Lima
Apia (Samoa)
La Paz
South Atlantic Ocean
Papeete (Tahiti)
Aitutaki
São Paulo
Rio de Janeiro
20°
Antofagasta
Asunción
South Pacific Ocean
Santiago
Montevideo
Concepción
Buenos Aires
Bahía Blanca
40°
Pto. Montt
Comodoro Rivadavia
Punta Arenas
60°
Longitude West of Greenwich
180°
160°
140°
120°
100°
80°
60°
40°
20°